DISPOSITIF

DISPOSITIF

A CARTOGRAPHY

EDITED BY GREG BIRD AND GIOVANBATTISTA TUSA

THE MIT PRESS   CAMBRIDGE, MASSACHUSETTS   LONDON, ENGLAND

© 2023 Massachusetts Institute of Technology

All rights reserved. No part of this book may be reproduced in any form by any electronic or mechanical means (including photocopying, recording, or information storage and retrieval) without permission in writing from the publisher.

The MIT Press would like to thank the anonymous peer reviewers who provided comments on drafts of this book. The generous work of academic experts is essential for establishing the authority and quality of our publications. We acknowledge with gratitude the contributions of these otherwise uncredited readers.

This book was set in Stone Serif and Avenir Lt Std by Westchester Publishing Services. Printed and bound in the United States of America.

Library of Congress Cataloging-in-Publication Data
Names: Bird, Greg, 1978– editor. | Tusa, Giovanbattista, 1979– editor.
Title: Dispositif : a cartography / edited by Greg Bird and Giovanbattista Tusa.
Description: Cambridge, Massachusetts : The MIT Press, [2023] | Includes bibliographical references and index.
Identifiers: LCCN 2022057295 | ISBN 9780262544337
Subjects: LCSH: Disposition (Philosophy)
Classification: LCC B105.D56 D537 2023 | DDC 111—dc23/eng/20230509
LC record available at https://lccn.loc.gov/2022057295

10 9 8 7 6 5 4 3 2 1

CONTENTS

ACKNOWLEDGMENTS ix

    PROBLEMATIZING DISPOSITIFS 1
    Greg Bird

I ARCHITECTRONICS/MECHANISMS

    1   FRAGMENT ON MACHINES 23
        Karl Marx

    2   IN THE PENAL COLONY 35
        Franz Kafka

    3   MACHINE AND ORGANISM 59
        Georges Canguilhem

    4   GENESIS OF THE TECHNICAL OBJECT: THE PROCESS OF CONCRETIZATION 89
        Gilbert Simondon

    5   MACHINE FRAGMENTS 103
        Gerald Raunig

    6   IS A MUSEUM A FACTORY? 113
        Hito Steyerl

    7   OF STRUCTION 123
        Jean-Luc Nancy

    8   WE, MACHINIC SUBJECTS 133
        Michael Hardt and Antonio Negri

9 COGNITIVE ASSEMBLAGES: TECHNICAL AGENCY AND HUMAN INTERACTIONS 147
N. Katherine Hayles

II POSITIVITY/TACTICS

10 THE IDEA OF POSITIVITY 163
Jean Hyppolite

11 THE QUESTION CONCERNING TECHNOLOGY 171
Martin Heidegger

12 THE DISPOSITIF OF SEXUALITY 195
Michel Foucault

13 THE CONFESSION OF THE FLESH 205
Michel Foucault

14 LATENT AND MANIFEST ORIENTALISM 219
Edward Said

15 WHAT IS A DISPOSITIF? 231
Gilles Deleuze

16 GENDER TROUBLE 239
Judith Butler

17 WHAT IS AN APPARATUS? 251
Giorgio Agamben

18 BEFORE THE LAW: HUMANS AND OTHER ANIMALS IN A BIOPOLITICAL FRAME 263
Cary Wolfe

III PROSTHETICS/EMBODIMENTS

19 IDEOLOGY AND IDEOLOGICAL STATE APPARATUSES 277
Louis Althusser

20 THE TECHNOLOGY OF GENDER 289
Teresa de Lauretis

21 POSTSCRIPT ON THE SOCIETIES OF CONTROL 305
Gilles Deleuze

22 THE OTHER QUESTION: STEREOTYPE, DISCRIMINATION AND THE DISCOURSE OF COLONIALISM 311
Homi K. Bhabha

23 SYNTACTICS: THE GRAMMAR OF FEMINISM AND TECHNOSCIENCE 323
Donna J. Haraway

- 24 ONTOLOGY OF THE ACCIDENT: AN ESSAY ON DESTRUCTIVE PLASTICITY   333
  Catherine Malabou

- 25 THE DISPOSITIF OF THE PERSON   341
  Roberto Esposito

- 26 THE BIOPOLITICAL BIRTH OF GENDER: SOCIAL CONTROL, HERMAPHRODITISM, AND THE NEW SEXUAL APPARATUS   351
  Jemima Repo

- 27 SOMATECHNICS   363
  Nikki Sullivan

- 28 DISCIPLINE AND CONTROL   367
  Jasbir K. Puar

- 29 DISPOSITIFS OF PLEASURE   375
  Anita Chari

- 30 DISPOSITIF   383
  Franco Berardi (Bifo)

IV INOPERATIVITY/RESISTANCE

- 31 THE PARERGON   389
  Jacques Derrida

- 32 THE PRACTICE OF EVERYDAY LIFE   399
  Michel de Certeau

- 33 FROM BIOPOWER TO BIOPOLITICS   413
  Maurizio Lazzarato

- 34 "A CRITICAL METAPHYSICS COULD EMERGE AS A SCIENCE OF APPARATUSES . . ."   425
  Tiqqun

- 35 INDIGENOUS INTERRUPTIONS: MOHAWK NATIONHOOD, CITIZENSHIP AND THE STATE   435
  Audra Simpson

- 36 APPARATUS   453
  Eukariot

- 37 HUMAN STRIKE, REPRODUCTION, AND MAGIC MATERIALISM   465
  Claire Fontaine

  DISPOSITIFS: CARTOGRAPHIES OF DISORIENTATION   487
  Giovanbattista Tusa

ACKNOWLEDGMENTS

The editors and publisher gratefully acknowledge the permission granted to reproduce the copyrighted material in this book.

Bird, Greg. "Problematizing Dispositifs." Printed with permission of the author.

Raqs Media Collective. *Time Set Free*. Printed with permission of the artists.

PART I: ARCHITECTRONICS/MECHANISMS

Canguilhem, Georges. "Machine and Organism." In *Knowledge of Life*, translated by Stefanos Geroulanos and Daniela Ginsburg, 75–97. New York: Fordham University Press, 2008. Copyright 1965 Librairie Philosophique J. Vrin. Reprinted with permission by Librarie Philosophique J. Vrin and Fordham University Press.

Hardt, Michael, and Antonio Negri. Selections from "We, Machinic Subjects." In *Assembly*, 107–123. New York: Oxford University Press, 2017. © 2017 Oxford University Press. Reproduced with permission of the Licensor through PLSclear.

Hayles, N. Katherine. Selections from "Cognitive Assemblages: Technical Agency and Human Interactions." In *Unthought: The Power of the Cognitive Nonconscious*, 115–141. Chicago: University of Chicago Press, 2017. Reprinted with permission of the publisher.

Kafka, Franz. *In the Penal Colony*. Translated by Ian Johnstone, 2003. Public Domain. www.kafka.org.Marx, Karl. Selections from "Fragment on Machines (Notebooks VI & VII)." In *Grundrisse: Foundations of the Critique of Political Economy*. New York: Penguin Books, 1973. Reprinted with permission of the publisher.

Nancy, Jean-Luc. Selections from "Of Struction," translated by Travis Holloway and Flor Méchain. *Parrhesia: A Journal of Critical Philosophy* 17 (2013): 1–10. Reprinted courtesy of the author and editor of *Parrhesia*.

Raunig, Gerald. "Machine Fragments." In *A Thousand Machines: A Concise Philosophy of the Machine as Social Movement*, translated by Aileen Derieg, 18–34. Los Angeles: Semiotext(e), 2010. Reprinted with permission of the publisher.

Simondon, Gilbert. Selections from "Genesis of the Technical Object: The Process of Concretization." In *On the Mode of Existence of Technical Objects*, translated by Cécile Malaspina and John Rogove. Minneapolis, Minnesota: University of Minnesota Press, 2017. Originally published in *Du mode d'existence des objets techniques*. Copyright Aubier (department of Flammarion) Paris, 1958 and 2012. Reprinted courtesy of the estate, and by permission of both publishers.

Steyerl, Hito. "Is a Museum a Factory?" *e-flux Journal* 7 (2019). Reprinted courtesy of the author and editor of *e-flux Journal*.

Woodgate, Agustina. *National Times*. 2019. Reprinted by permission of the artist.

PART II: POSITIVITY/TACTICS

Agamben, Giorgio. "What is an Apparatus?" In *What is an apparatus? And Other Essays*, translated by David Kishik and Stefan Pedatella, 1–24. Stanford, CA: Stanford University Press, 2009. Reprinted with permission of the publisher.

Butler, Judith. Selections from *Gender Trouble: Feminism and the Subversion of Identity*. New York: Routledge, 1990. Reprinted with permission of the publisher.

Deleuze, Gilles. "What is a Dispositif?" In *Michel Foucault, Philosopher: Essays Translated from the French and German*, edited by Timothy J. Armstrong, 159–168. New York, NY: Routledge, 1992. Reprinted with permission of the publisher.

Foucault, Michel. Selections from "The Confession of the Flesh." In *Power/Knowledge: Selected Interviews and Other Writings*, edited by Colin Gordon, 194–228. New York, NY: Pantheon Books, 1980. Reprinted with permission of Penguin Random House LLC.

Foucault, Michel. "Domain." Chapter 3 of Part 4 "The Deployment of Sexuality." In *The History of Sexuality, Volume I: An Introduction*, translated by Robert Hurley, 103–114. New York: Vintage Books, 1990. Reprinted with permission of Penguin Random House LLC.

Heidegger, Martin. "The Question Concerning Technology." In *The Question Concerning Technology and Other Essays*, translated and with an Introduction by William Lovitt 3–35. New York: Harper & Row Publishers, 1977. Reprinted with permission of HarperCollins Publishers.

Hyppolite, Jean. "The Idea of Positivity." In *Introduction to Hegel's Philosophy of History*, translated by Bond Harris and Jacqueline Bouchard Spurlock, 20–25. Gainesville, Florida: University of Florida Press, 1996. Reprinted with permission of the publisher.

Lake, Suzy. *The Queen and I on a Broken Board* (2018/2019), from the *Game Theory: Global Gamesmanship* series. Reprinted by permission of the artist.

Said, Edward. Selections from "Latent and Manifest Orientalism." In *Orientalism*, 201–225. New York: Random House, 1994. Reprinted with permission of Penguin Random House LLC.

Wolfe, Cary. "I." In *Before the Law: Humans and Other Animals in a Biopolitical Frame*, 3–11. Chicago: University of Chicago Press, 2013. Reprinted with permission of the publisher.

PART III: PROSTHETICS/EMBODIMENTS

Althusser, Louis. Selections from "Ideology and Ideological State Apparatuses." In *Lenin and Philosophy and Other Essays*, translated by Ben Brewster, 127–187. New York: Monthly Review Press, 1971. Reprinted with permission from Monthly Review Press.

Berardi, Franco (Bifo). "Dispositif." Essay commissioned for this anthology. Printed with permission of the author.

Bhabha, Homi K. Selections from "The Other Question: Stereotype, Discrimination and the Discourse of Colonialism." In *The Location of Culture*, 94–120. New York: Routledge, 1994. Reprinted by permission of Taylor & Francis Books UK.

Chari, Anita. "Dispositifs of Pleasure." Essay commissioned for this anthology. Printed with permission of the author.

Deleuze, Gilles. "Postscript on the Societies of Control." *October* 59 (Winter 1992). MIT Press. Originally appeared in *L'Autre journal*, no. 1, May 1990. Reprinted by permission of Georges Borchardt, Inc., for Les Editions de Minuit.

Esposito, Roberto. Selections from "The Dispositif of the Person." Translated by Timothy Campbell. *Law, Culture and the Humanities* 8, no. 17 (2012): 17–30. Reprinted with permission of the author and SAGE Publications.

Haraway, Donna J. Selections from "Syntactics: The Grammar of Feminism and Technoscience." In *Modest_Witness@Second_Millennium. FemaleMan©_Meets_OncoMouse™: Feminism and Technoscience*, xiii–xiv & 1–16. New York: Routledge, 1997. Reprinted with permission of the publisher.

Jacob, Luis. *The Riddle*. Reprinted by permission of the artist.

Lauretis, Teresa de. Selections from "The Technology of Gender." In *Technologies of Gender: Essays on Theory, Film, and Fiction*, 1–30. Indianapolis: Indiana University Press, 1987. Reprinted with permission of the publisher.

Malabou, Catherine. *Ontology of the Accident: An Essay on Destructive Plasticity*, 7–18. Translated by Carolyn Shread. Cambridge: Polity Press, 2012. Reprinted with permission of the publisher.

Puar, Jasbir K. Selections from "Introduction: The Cost of Getting Better." In *The Right to Maim*, 1–31. Durham N.C.: Duke University Press, 2017. Reprinted with permission of the publisher.

Repo, Jemima. Selections from "The Biopolitical Birth of Gender: Social Control, Hermaphroditism, and the New Sexual Apparatus." *Alternatives: Global, Local, Political* 38 no. 3 (2013): 228–244. Reprinted with permission of the author and SAGE Publications.

Sullivan, Nikki. "Somatechnics." *TSQ: Transgender Studies Quarterly* 1 nos. 1–2 (2014): 187–190. Reprinted with permission of Duke University Press.

PART IV: INOPERATIVITY/RESISTANCE

Certeau, Michel de. Selections from *The Practices of Everyday Life*. Berkeley, California: University of California Press, 1984. Reprinted with permission of the publisher.

Derrida, Jacques. Selections from "The Parergon." Translated by Craig Owens. *October* 9 (1979): 3–41. Reprinted courtesy of the MIT Press.

Eukariot. "Apparatus." *Eukariot: Counter-propaganda Cell* 1, 2015. Available at https://www.eukariot.com/apparatus.html. Reprinted courtesy of the author.

Fontaine, Claire. "Human Strike, Reproduction, and Magic Materialism." Essay commissioned for this anthology. Printed with permission of the author.

Lazzarato, Maurizio. "From Biopower to Biopolitics." Translated by Ivan A. Ramirez. *Pli: Warwick Journal of Philosophy* 11 (2002): 99–110. Reprinted courtesy of the journal and the Graduate School of the Department of Philosophy at the University of Warwick.

Nazzal, Rehab. *Resistance Dance*. 2018. Reprinted by permission of the artist.

Simpson, Audra. Selections from "Indigenous Interruptions: Mohawk Nationhood, Citizenship and the State." In *Mohawk Interruptus: Political Life Across the Borders of Settler States*. Durham N.C.: Duke University Press, 2014. Reprinted with permission of the publisher.

Tiqqun. Selections from "A Critical Metaphysics Could Emerge as a Science of Apparatuses. . . ." In *This Is Not a Program*, translated by Joshua David Jordan, 135–204. Los Angeles: Semiotext(e), 2011. Reprinted with permission of the publisher.

Tusa, Giovannbattista. "Dispositifs. Cartographies of Disorientation." Printed with permission of the author.

PROBLEMATIZING DISPOSITIFS

Greg Bird

Foucault talked of lines of sedimentation but also of lines of "breakage" and of "fracture." Untangling these lines within a social apparatus [dispositif] is, in each case, like drawing up a map, doing cartography, surveying unknown landscapes, and this is what he calls "working on the ground."
—Gilles Deleuze, *What Is a Dispositif?*

Dispositif is one of the most prevalent yet allusive terms in contemporary thought. A wide range of words have been used to translate this French term or its Italian equivalent *dispositivo*. Three core texts have shaped the English reception of *dispositif*. The translators of these texts have each used different terms. First, Robert Hurly rendered Michel Foucault's *"le dispositif de sexualité"* as "the deployment of sexuality" in his translation of the first volume of *The History of Sexuality*.[1] An entire decade and a half later, Timothy J. Armstrong chose to Anglicize *dispositif* as "social apparatus" in his translation of Gilles Deleuze's *"Qu'est-ce qu'un dispositif?"*[2] Finally, a decade later still, David Kishik and Stefan Pedatella used "apparatus" in their translation of Giorgio Agamben's *"Che cos'è un dispositivo?"*[3]

Deployment is not entirely off the mark as a translation for *dispositif*. Like devices, tactics, or machines, *dispositifs* deploy the materials of which they engage. *Dispositifs* disassemble and reassemble things, unfolding them and taking them apart *in order to* reconfigure and redistribute them. Deployment is often used to describe a military operation. To deploy troops means spreading them out and increasing their numbers to form an extensive front line. This description covers certain aspects of Foucault's account of the *dispositif* of sexuality. It manufactures and codifies a new terrain of sexual desires and norms that radically alters sexual dispositions. New sexualized subjecthoods are established. The commanders range from scientific experts to officers of the law. Occupying a proper place and maintaining a correct disposition is essential. As a translation for *dispositif*, however, deployment is far too specific. It is also a nominalized verb that emphasizes the actions and operations but leaves little room for examining the composition of *dispositifs*. For various reasons, it proved impractical for scholars working in sexuality studies, and it was dropped as a possible translation for those working on *dispositifs*.

The translators of Deleuze, Agamben, and Foucault's interview established "apparatus" as the generally accepted term. Most of the English authors included in this anthology have used "apparatus." Nevertheless, this term also has its shortcomings. An apparatus consists of a collection of tools or utensils that make ready, prepare, produce, and make appear (*apparare*). In a sense, it is a device that represents things, makes them appear *as such*. An apparatus is also a means. Not a pure means such as the ever-evasive pure modality sought by ascetics—Agamben's notion of use—but a means that is always, already directed toward ends. Apparatuses are thus purposeful instruments that capture and modulate the matter they work with *in order to* transform it into something that can serve their ends. In this sense, apparatuses are operations that put to use. This term also covers some aspects of *dispositifs*, but it is a limited term like deployment. A *dispositif* is a much more complex set of operations, and a single *dispositif* is often composed of several apparatuses.

Dispositifs are positive operations that set out and put things forward, position them *as such*—shape, order, regulate, frame, *positivité, Gestell, ponere*. . . . *Dispositifs* do more than modify how we operate in the world; they reconfigure and modulate our ways of being in the world. They also modulate how things can be conceived and what things are conceivable. *Dispositifs* divide ("device"), prepare ("apparatus"), arrange ("tactic"), put in order ("syntactic"), enable ("machine"), and make that which they hold together (the content) appear as if it belongs within the same or similar order ("assemblages"). After being disposed of and held together (contained), the content is rendered available to be grasped, taken in, and appropriated, but only for those who have already been predisposed. The *dispositif* of sexuality, for example, modulates sexual desires precisely by rearranging the relationship between subjects and objects. *Dispositifs* do not just make sense; they make the world make sense. At the level of individuals, *dispositifs* position subjects: arrange, order, control, regulate, and distribute (*disponere*). *Dispositifs* shape subjective *dispositions*, including predominate inclinations, habits, ways of understanding, states of mind, and characteristics. In an overly simplified sentence, *dispositifs* are composed of discursive and material elements embedded in institutions, frame the world, and configure subjective positions.

In short, none of the alternative translations for *dispositif* captures the dynamism of this term. There is a philological angle at play here. *Dispositif* bears a rich and nuanced genealogy, embedded within a complex web of derivative relations scattered across different Latin vocabularies. Etymology is also at play here, but the point is not to uncover an *etymon*. What matters is how the term's formations and meanings have been developed historically. Many of the authors in this cartography are aware of these dynamics. We encourage the reader to pay close attention to how authors make full use of them in their texts, including Karl Marx.

Moreover, it does not make sense to refer to *dispositif* as a word. It is not even a concept. I am using "term" here due to the constraints of language. Nevertheless, this still does not address the initial problem: how to translate *dispositif*. There is another option in English. We could use a cognate albeit largely obsolete term. "Dispositive" appeared in the early seventeenth century. It had two primary meanings. First, it conveyed a sense of being preparatory, conducive, or contributory—to be disposed of, inclined, or to have a disposition. Second, a dispositive directs, controls, or disposes of things. This second sense was used primarily in terms of the law. For example, the "dispositive clause" in Scots Law addressed specificities of conveyance in a deed or will: what, where, and how to dispose of something and to whom this thing will be bestowed. After much discussion, we elected not to re-introduce this term into this literature. It was not our intention to generate even further scholastic debates in a field that is already stymied by the wide range of translations.

The point of this cartography is to draw loose connections between seemingly disparate texts. We want to draw the reader's attention to common themes, ways of thinking, and political concerns. For example, how many scholars have recognized that Judith Butler originally formulated gender as an apparatus? Moreover, Butler's formulation was inspired by Foucault's "dispositif of sexuality?" What impacts will such a finding have on how we conceptualize gender or sexuality? Jemima Repo first brought these insights to light in her series of close readings of both thinkers.[4] The key to her groundbreaking studies is the centrality of dispositifs. For these reasons, we have elected neither to coin a new term nor to re-introduce a largely obsolete yet cognate word such as "dispositive" with its particular history and meanings. Most English readers today are aware of the term *dispositif* (and *dispositivo*). It is time to stop searching for substitutions, cognate or figurative. None are adequate. We must move on from this issue and simply assimilate *dispositif* as a loanword: dispositif. Agamben and Deleuze, after all, were referring to Foucault (and others) not Althusser. It makes more sense to Anglicize the term with minimal violence by simply removing the italics.

Translation issues aside, two general problematics are raised in the formative and seminal texts on dispositifs: the problem of dispositifs and the dispositif problem. I address both in this introductory essay. In part I, I focus on the problem of defining dispositifs. Some of this work has already been done, but the definition I have thus far provided remains vague and incomplete. I turn to the three definitive texts by Foucault, Deleuze, and Agamben. For the remainder of this introductory essay, I focus on the dispositif problem. That is, the tasks, questions, and propositions that dispositifs posit. It would be egregious to claim that there is a single, central dispositif problem. That said, after working on this cartography for a few years with Giovanbattista Tusa, from deciding which texts to include and which to exclude to figuring out how to abridge those included, a problem emerged for me. At this point, I am unsure whether this problem has emerged from how we have drawn together and assembled the texts in a particular order or if the problem was already there. It is likely a mixture of the two—cartography is hardly a phenomenological vocation. The problem that emerged is the problem of engineering. It is clearly articulated at the start of our genealogy with Marx's "Fragment on Machines."[5] From this text onward, engineering becomes a problem. This is evident in texts that engage with mechanical, technological, or biological engineering. However, it is also present in texts focused on colonialism, gender, sex, sexuality, personhood, race, animals, biopolitics, and other issues. In this second part, I focus more on Marx. I will not summarize the content of this cartography, as the texts speak for themselves. Instead, I merely highlight a few problems in what can only be called "dispositif thinking."

I. THE PROBLEM OF DISPOSITIFS

When seeking to answer the question "What is a dispositif?" three seminal texts stand out. Before turning to Foucault's famous interview, we should start with the two texts that brought this problem to prominence. First, at a conference in Paris in January 1988 held in honor of Foucault, Deleuze delivered his short paper "What Is a Dispositif?" Deleuze argues that Foucault's dispositifs are composed of fractured and crisscrossing lines of force that determine what can and cannot be seen, what and how something can be said ("machines that make one see and speak"), and what forms of being are available to subjects.[6] That is, dispositifs are composed of curves of visibility and enunciation as well as lines of force and subjectification. Second, in "What Is an Apparatus?" Agamben likens a dispositif to an *oikonomia*: "a set of practices, bodies of knowledge, measures, and institutions that aim to manage, govern, control, and orient—in a way that purports to be useful—the behaviours, gestures, and thoughts of human beings."[7] A few pages later, he claims that a dispositif is "anything that has in some way the capacity to capture, orient, determine, intercept, model, control, or secure the gestures, behaviours, opinions, or discourses of living beings."[8]

In reference to *Discipline and Punish*, Michel de Certeau claims that Foucault employed a "variety of synonyms, words that dance about and successfully approach an impossible proper name: 'apparatuses' [*dispositifs*], 'instrumentalities,' 'techniques,' 'mechanisms,' 'machineries,' etc."[9] Agamben claims that Foucault "never offers a complete definition," but he "does come close to something like it."[10] This proximate definition is found in Foucault's threefold response to Alain Grosrichard's query about the "meaning" and "methodological function" of the "dispositif of sexuality" in "The Confession of the Flesh" interview.[11]

First, Foucault states that a dispositif is a "system" or "network of relations" [*réseau*] that is established in a "heterogeneous ensemble consisting of discourses, institutions, architectural forms, regulatory decisions, laws, administrative measures, scientific statements, philosophical, moral and philanthropic propositions—in short, the said as much as the unsaid." Second, there is an interplay between constantly shifting and modifying positions and functions, which describes the relations in this assemblage. Third, dispositifs arise in response to an emergency or crisis [*une urgence*]; that is, they have a "strategic function." In a follow-up response, he notes that a dispositif is always "inscribed in the play of power" and "linked to certain coordinates of knowledge." That is, a dispositif "consists in: strategies of relations of forces supporting, and supported by, types of knowledge." In summary, Foucault roughly describes a dispositif as *a strategic assemblage composed of an intricate web of relations of force and knowledge embedded in the discursive and material fields, which arises as a response to a crisis.*

Some of these elements are present in the French definition of *dispositif*. Agamben points out that in French, *dispositif* refers to "the section of a sentence that decides, or the enacting clause of a law [*la parte della sentenza (o di una legge) che decide e dispone*]," the arrangement/ordering [*disposizione*] of the parts of a machine and a mechanism itself, and the arrangement/ordering [*disposti*] of the means to conform to a plan.[12] That is, *dispositif* is used in juridical, technological, and militaristic terminologies. Foucault makes use of each sense, notes Agamben. However, dictionaries, especially those that ignore the "historical-etymological character" of words, fail to convey the "historical development and articulation of a unique original meaning" of *dispositif*. *Dispositif* refers "to a set of practices and mechanisms (both linguistic and nonlinguistic, juridical, technical, and military)," which are strategically deployed to address a matter of urgency and obtain an immediate effect. Dictionaries, in other words, do not account for the political and historical context—the "strategy of practices or of thought"— which not only define words but also determine how to put them to use.

Our process of selecting texts and then thematizing them for this cartography was guided primarily by intertextual references. Agamben's short essay played a significant role in helping us to make these decisions. For example, the passage I just discussed follows a section on the genealogy of *dispositif* in Foucault, which Agamben traces back to Foucault's former teacher's term *positivité*.[13] This short passage helped us arrange the second theme in this book: positivity/tactics. Tactics arrange, order, and dispose of things, understood in a specifically militaristic-political sense (*taktike technè*). Positivity connotes the legal procedure of laying down/positing the law. However, it has many other meanings. As a grid of intelligence, it reorders the world, establishes new frameworks for thinking and seeing, sets parameters, reshapes what belongs together, and creates new positive laws—no term covers this sense more clearly than Martin Heidegger's *Ge-stell*.[14] Positivity is also a fundamental aspect of this book's other three themes. It addresses the process of positioning subjects (subjectification). This aspect of dispositifs is best represented by texts found in the section covering prosthetics and embodiments. Positivity also signifies the positive, productive forces of dispositifs. Foucault was clear on this sense of positivity in *The Will to Knowledge*. He argues that the positive form of power emerged with the rise of *mécanismes positifs* and the *technologies positives de pouvoir*, that is, dispositifs.[15] Texts focused on these architectonic and mechanistic aspects of dispositifs were placed in the first section of this book. Finally, texts that dedicate more space to figuring out how to render the positive mechanisms of dispositifs inoperative were placed in our fourth section. In truth, many of the texts included in this book could have been easily placed under any of the four themes.

II. THE DISPOSITIF PROBLEM

THE DISPOSITIF OF ENGINEERING

[O]nce adopted into the production process of capital, the means of labour passes through different metamorphoses, whose culmination is the machine, or rather, an automatic system of machinery (system of machinery: the automatic one is merely its most complete, most

adequate form, and alone transforms machinery into a system), set in motion by an automaton, a moving power that moves itself; this automaton consisting of numerous mechanical and intellectual organs, so that the workers themselves are cast merely as its conscious linkages.
—Karl Marx, *Grundrisse*

The era of the dispositif is marked by an obsession with engineering. In the Occidental telling of this story, "man" the engineer emerged at the dawn of industrial capitalism. The steam engine gave rise to an entirely different world. Goods and resources could be propelled across the countryside, ocean, and later factories at astonishing speeds. Previously unimaginable wealth and human powers were produced and accumulated. Over the course of a relatively short period of history, minerals and spices, goods and products, and even humans were transformed into resources that would be put to use as the energy that would further propel its seemingly limitless drive. As the vast *assemblage of machinery* took hold of humanity, the drive toward progress and advancement radically reshaped much more than the production process. Human ways of thinking, seeing, desiring, doing, and being were radically reconfigured—epistemological and ontological dispositions.

During the industrial capitalist stage, two figures emerged as primary subjects of the assemblage of machinery: the engineer and the mechanic. The engineer is the ideal subject of the dispositif of engineering—the quintessential manifestation of *Homo faber*. In terms of knowledge, the engineer is an active contributor. The engineer does not simply contribute to scholarship alone because the engineer is also a craftsperson. Engineering is a practical science. It is a purposeful science that only makes sense when put to use. The science of engineering is applied to material things, radically reshaping and sometimes transforming them. Its method is the application, which is a form of joining or combining, we might even say assembling. It is a science disposed into things which are, in turn, disposed themselves—the engineer figures as a master of the assemblage of machinery. The engineer is a rare sort who can seamlessly transition from a scholar's cap into a mechanic's hard hat. Neither looks out of place on the engineer, but the engineer usually feels more comfortable wearing the latter. We might even say, drawing from Marx still, that the engineer works in their office on formulas in the morning, gets their hands dirty fixing machines in the factory during the afternoon, reads a newspaper in the evening, and criticizes after dinner. If an engineer masters their craft, they may even find time to fish or hunt. A modern engineer could even find extra time to cook some meals and clean the house. In short, the engineer has no exclusive sphere of activity because the entire society is their domain, their *oikos*. If we were to grant them a specialization, we could only conclude that engineers are assemblers.

In the metropoles, the two primary subject positions took hold. The vast majority were disposed of as mechanics with the simplified task of attending to the machinery. A smaller class of engineers also emerged, only they were tasked with designing the broader assemblage of machinery. This does not mean that early mechanics were not assemblers in their own right. Mechanics must put parts together, often based on the plans and instructions devised by the engineers and dictated by the machines they had designed. Whether their task was to use a machine to mix an already prepared composite material with a liquid material (mixing concrete, paint, or batter), ensure that two parts are securely connected (fastening a screw, tightening a connective coil, or welding metal parts), pulling threads of fabric together (spinning cotton, stitching leather, weaving wool), or even fabricating the parts of the machines and materials used in each of these tasks, assembling is an essential activity. Mechanics put the engineer's products to use. With the advent of the assembly line, this activity became even more central to the production process. The process of assembling was now rigidly organized according to the designs, rhythms, and pace of the assembly line. Ford radically dissected and further divided the process into even more minute elements. It also facilitated the growth of the managerial class of workers. Line managers, whether in actual factories, on construction sites, or even in fast food chain restaurants, were tasked with not only ensuring that the assembly line was functioning correctly but also with assembling the assemblers. I could continue, but this point need not be belabored here. Engineers and mechanics assemble. If a distinction is to be made, it can only be between putting in order and putting to use, generic and specified assembling.

This asymmetrical division between intellectual and physical labor was replicated in much more brutal and extreme forms in the colonies. With the powerful assemblage of machinery at hand, colonial powers plundered and decimated native populations with godlike forces and velocities. Those who survived were immediately dispossessed and targeted for redisposal by colonial machinery. Many were disposed of as slaves condemned to depraved lives on the plantations. Some would be uprooted and redeployed as mechanics serving the colonial machinery in the factories, fields, or armies, while a select few would be sent to the metropoles to be completely redisposed and then returned as a comprador class of engineers tasked with designing and managing the colonial machinery. Mechanical engineering made all of this not only possible but also plausible.

Once biological life was discovered, roughly at the start of the nineteenth century, engineering had a new subject. What started with tools and devices, appendages to the human, quickly turned back upon itself to search for improvements in capacities, physiologies, and eventually biologies. Society was also discovered and targeted by engineering projects. Malthusianism, social Darwinism, and eugenics are rooted in the broader dispositif of engineering. Human races, nationalities, ethnicities, genders, sexualities, abilities, classes, and so forth have been subjected to grand social engineering projects. Biologies, physiologies, and psychologies had to be disassembled and reassembled, de-engineered from their natural states and re-engineered to achieve optimal states. So-called undesirables, however, are not always subjected to positive eugenics. Many have been marked as either unfixable and thus pushed aside and abandoned or pathogenetic and thus targeted for elimination by negative eugenic technologies. Genocidal acts, from the most technologically sophisticated to those deploying cruder techniques, result from sociobiological engineering projects. Genocide is the *nomos* of the sociobiological engineering project that has gradually taken hold of humanity since the inception of the era of engineering. Targeted killing of a *genos* prevents it from regenerating. Genocide ranges from biological to cultural, from razed villages to erased cultural histories, from gas chambers to destroyed cultural institutions, and even from forced sex-reassignment surgery to restricting personal pronouns.

Engineers are fetishized in the era of the dispositif of engineering, from early pioneers such as Leonardo da Vinci, Blaise Pascal, James Watt, Thomas Edison, Nikola Tesla, and Henry Ford, up to more recent mythologized figures such as Steve Jobs, Bill Gates, Elon Musk, and Mark Zuckerberg. Each figure in this abridged list of engineers, all white men, is distinguished and celebrated as an inventor who has made a significant contribution to engineering. Subjects thoroughly predisposed to engineering derive great pleasure from hearing tales about these folk heroes. Nothing excites entrepreneurial-minded twenty-first-century university students more than a lecture covering one of these iconic engineers. Not the entire lecture, however. Eyes will glaze over whenever the lecture turns to the broader assemblage of factors that form the architectural support systems that have enabled their inventions. Developments in the engineering sciences, sociohistorical context, economic factors, or the broader social impacts of the inventions are not exciting discussion topics. For the majority, the only lecture materials that grab their undivided attention—speak directly to their inclinations and aspirations—are those covering the inventor's quirky personality traits, trials and tribulations, and drive to overcome all obstacles. Stereotypes and cliches of profit-driven entrepreneurial subjects must be mobilized to frame analyses of the inventions. Personal biographies of inventors are more significant than cartographies of inventions. Ted Talks are much more interesting than university lectures. The sad truth is that most of those bedazzled by these tales are predisposed and thus destined to become mechanics. To become a genuine engineer, one must be excited by and willing to study the entire assemblage. However, this does not make for an exciting talk. It certainly will not produce a popular nonfiction book that can be hyped up by the publishing industry and promoted on the shelves of large chain bookstores. What is lost in these distorted accounts is that the iconic figures are not just entrepreneurs but rather entrepreneurial engineers.

This was a banal and curt retelling of a central narrative repeated in various guises in the literature on dispositifs. When read genealogically, the story begins with the rise of mechanical engineering and its systematic attack on the natural world. However, it quickly morphs into a story about biological, social, cultural, and colonial engineering. The genealogical overview of the dispositif of engineering in this section is pertinent to understanding dispositif thinking, which is less a philosophy of science than a philosophy of scientific application—a philosophy of engineering. Engineering is the bridge that connects and defines the relationship between humanity and nature, culture and nature—the "and."

"FRAGMENT ON MACHINES"

The measure of wealth is then not any longer, in any way, labour time, but rather disposable time. *Labour time as the measure of value* posits wealth itself as founded on poverty, and disposable time as existing *in and because of the antithesis to surplus labour time*; or, the positing of an individual's entire time as labour time, and his degradation therefore to mere worker, subsumption under labour. *The most developed machinery thus forces the worker to work longer than the savage does, or than he himself did with the simplest, crudest tools.*
—Karl Marx, *Grundrisse*

In the genealogy of dispositif thinking, Marx's "Fragment on Machines" has been retroactively appointed as a prologue to this line of thought by multiple interlocutors. If there is a dispositif to be found in this text, it is a dispositif not of machinery but rather of engineering. The dispositif of engineering is manifested *in* the assemblage of machinery, which is a strategic assemblage composed of an intricate web of relations of forces and knowledge, embedded in a field of discursive and material relations, and produces new subjects.[16] After the industrial revolution, humanity had no choice but to embrace the assemblage of machinery. Any vision of communism that is not grounded in this fact is doomed to fail, whether a Luddite post-mechanical world without machines, mechanistic modes of living, and mechanics, or a high-tech futuristic world where automatons build and operate the machinery while humanity lives and plays freely in an engineered state of nature. Communism cannot simply dispose of the assemblage of machinery; rather, communism must be configured in accordance with this assemblage. Anything else will lead to disastrous outcomes. Capitalism has proven this truth. For Marx, the assemblage of machinery operates as a quasi-tangible object that must be collectively appropriated and utilized to correct our relationship to the dispositif of engineering. Socializing the assemblage of machinery represents a step, or stage, that opens the possibility of communalizing the dispositif of engineering. In the fragment, this entire problematic pivots around the question of *disposability*.

On the surface, the disposable is unnecessary—that which could be used as designed, used differently, or merely discarded as not useful; in short, that which may be done without. It is superfluous, excessive, frivolous, insignificant, dispensable, and redundant. In Marx's fragment, however, to be marked as disposable means that the item must have already been placed in a position to be put to use. The item is a product of the assemblage of machinery, which has already been predisposed—arranged and ordered—for the purposes of being put to use. It is evaluated on its capacity (ability) for use only on these grounds. Thus, when reading Marx's treatment of the disposable in the fragment, it should not be read as that which stands entirely outside of use valuation and something that cannot be put to use. Disposable items are, to state the obvious, not in-disposable. They may appear unfit or incapable of being put to use; yet, because they have been marked as disposable, they still retain the capacity to be put to use, even if their usefulness is of lower quality and thus devalued.

Marx's account of disposability in the fragment oscillates between statements about disposable labor power and disposable labor time. In the center stands the laborer as a disposable part of the assemblage of machinery. There is a real material dimension to this process and an ideological dimension. Ideologically, mechanization appears to render the labor power of workers superfluous.[17] The "production process appears as not subsumed under the direct skillfulness [*unmittelbare Geschicklichkeit*] of the worker, but rather as the technological application of science [*technologische Anwendung der Wissenschaft*]."[18] The worker becomes a "mere living accessory [*bloßes lebendiges Zubehör*]," whose task is increasingly "mechanical" with simple "supervisory and regulatory activity." Each becomes an easily replaceable "mechanism" in this assemblage.[19] It even appears as if a machine "possesses skill and strength in place of the worker," which has seemingly become "itself the virtuoso, with a soul of its own in the mechanical laws acting through it."[20] From this perspective, the workers' labor power becomes fully disposable.

In material reality, however, something else is occurring. A new division of labor between engineers and mechanics has emerged. Machines are the "product of human industry," "*organs of the human brain, created by the human hand*; the power of knowledge objectified."[21] Engineers are the creators of these machines. Their labor power becomes indispensable intellectually as active participants in the "general intellect" (collective knowledge of society) and physically because the products of their labor are put to use. On the other end, the labor power of the mechanics is treated *as if* it is disposable. This new assemblage renders their physical skills and intellectual powers disposable because they are only minimally put to use.[22]

There is no point rehashing these details here. We know how the division between intellectual and physical labor is classified in Marxism. What matters is how workers have been placed in a position to be put to use. In the assemblage of machinery, a worker "steps to the side of the production process instead of being its chief actor."[23] A traditional reading would lead us to conclude that a radical decentering occurs with the workers being replaced by the engineers via machines. This is not, however, how assemblages are configured. They are complicated and multilayered. Workers are not entirely tossed aside and disposed of as inessential rubbish. Workers are not Lumpen proletarians in Marx's vernacular. They continue to be positioned in the center, only in diminished positions as subsidiaries or accessories to the core operations. Rendering the workers' labor power disposable is indispensable to the assemblage. Drawing from Derrida, it makes more sense to say that their labor power is treated as a mere addition to the work (*para-ergon*) rather than the power or energy (*en-ergon*) that generates the work process. They are neither interior nor exterior, "summoned and assembled like a supplement because of the lack—a certain 'internal' indetermination—in the very thing it enframes."[24] In a manner, workers are assembled around the machinery framing it, but it is unnecessary to push this line further here. What can be said is that the parergonal positioning of the workers around the machinery provides them with a strategic opportunity.

Disposable time (an English phrase in the original German notebooks) is a by-product of the industrial assemblage of machinery. With the introduction of a mechanized labor process, the necessary labor time to produce the materials and goods decreases rapidly. As disposable, this is a time freed up and set apart from the labor process. It is an additional, superfluous time that is insignificant in producing goods, at least when organized according to real social needs. Marx raises the question of how this extra time is put to use. In capitalism, surplus labor time is increased "by all the means of art and science" and then immediately appropriated and used to generate profit for the capitalist. "The measure of wealth" in capitalism "is then not any longer, in any way, labour time, but rather disposable time."[25] The workers are therefore put to use in this formulation. They generate surplus value during this extra time for the bourgeoisie. Yet, this extra time is "antithetical" to their existence. It is not only an unnecessary additional or wasted time spent standing idly beside the machines; it is also a time of personal degradation, waste, and, ultimately, impoverishment. How disposable time is put to use in capitalism is a critical factor in disposing of the workers—rendering them intellectually and physically, in the long term, *indisponible* or indisposed for the purposes of work.

Disposable time also presents a strategic opening in the assemblage of machinery. "Not-labour time, free time" could be put to use for the benefit of humanity if socialized as "social disposable time" (also in English in the original).[26] Labor time could be reduced "for the whole society to a diminishing minimum, and thus to free everyone's time for their own development." Advancements of the assemblage of machinery have brought this contradiction to light, but to properly reconfigure this arrangement, the "mass of workers must themselves appropriate their own surplus labour." The needs of the social individual could become the new measure of necessary labor time, and "the power of production will grow so rapidly" that "*disposable time* will grow for all."[27] The "measure of wealth," as stated in the quote at the beginning of this section, "is then not any longer, in any way, labour time, but rather disposable time." The question is for what purpose should disposable labor time be put to use: to generate private profit (surplus labor time) or to serve the common good (social disposable time)?

If surplus labor time were put to use as social disposable time, workers would have more time to develop their intellectual skills. "The free development of individualities," he argues, "corresponds to the artistic, scientific etc. development of the individuals in the time set free, and with the means created, for all of them."[28] A few pages later, Marx states:

Free time—which is both idle time and time for higher activity—has naturally transformed its possessor into a different subject, and he then enters into the direct production process as this different subject [*als dies andre Subjekt*]. This process is then both discipline, as regards the human being in the process of becoming; and, at the same time, practice, experimental science, materially creative and objectifying science, as regards the human being who has become, in whose head exists the accumulated knowledge of society.[29]

Engineers emerge as active participants in the general intellect. They could become mechanical engineers, but nothing prevents them from taking up other forms of engineering. After all, with the advent of the assemblage of machinery, "general social knowledge has become a *direct force of production*, and . . . the conditions of the process of social life itself have come under control of the general intellect and been transformed in accordance with it."[30] Economics, society, and life are present in this formula—an almost biopolitical statement. Not only must mechanical engineering be socialized to assert collective control over the machines, but so too must the "general intellect." Social workers must replace mechanical workers.

At this point, I have pushed the reading past Marx. Marxism *could* be read as a philosophy of the science of engineering. This reading stems from a highly fetishized treatment of engineering. In this interpretation, social, economic, and political engineering projects are mere by-products of Marx's paradigmatic science of mechanical engineering. The factories are the laboratories where this science is put to use, tested, and developed before being redeployed into other spheres of society. Joseph Stalin's Five-Year Plans were, after all, heavily influenced by Taylorism and Fordism. Other interlocutors have taken Marx and Marxism beyond economism, even beyond social factories and productivism.

THE DISPOSITIF OF ENGINEERING AFTER MARX

The question of mechanical engineering figures prominently in the early texts on dispositifs. In his 1947 lecture "Machine and Organism," for example, George Canguilhem attempts to find a solution to this problem by examining how modern mechanistic epistemologies represent living beings as mechanical "devices" [*dispositifs*].[31] He traces this epistemological framework through several sources, ranging from seventeenth-century mechanistic philosophy, biology, political economy, even ethnography. Read closely, Canguilhem makes a series of scattered yet important references to the relationship between engines, engineering, and ingenuity on the one hand and dispositifs and dispositions on the other. Right up front, he remarks that philosophers and biologists who are wedded to this mechanistic epistemology view the "engineer" [*l'ingénieur*] as the central "scientist" or "scholar" [*savant*].[32] Canguilhem shares with Marx a concern regarding the mechanistic domination over organic elements. Writing some 100 years later, however, he is less optimistic about the prospect of managing the assemblage of machinery. Canguilhem is critical of any "technicist assimilation of the human organism to the machine," such as Taylor's "mechanization of the organism."[33] We must find ways to reverse the mechanistic and organic order. Tools and machines must be adapted to the organic, not the other way around. A new sense of "technique" must be developed as a "universal biological phenomenon and no longer only an intellectual operation of man," such as "bio-engineering."[34] In this way, the human could be embedded in "the continuity with life through technique."[35]

The nature/culture dichotomy traverses all the literature deploying dispositifs ranging well beyond anti-capitalist post-industrial theses and science and technology studies. It also appears in feminist texts addressing the sex/gender binary, anti-colonial scholarship seeking to disrupt the reduction of race to biology, and even trans theorists who question the notion that a trans person is born into the "wrong body." Most scholars representing these strands of dispositif thinking in this anthology are also concerned with rethinking the nature/culture division. At the heart of this issue rests the problem of engineering: human–machine, nature–culture, artifice–intelligence. The dispositif problem is addressed through a philosophy of engineering. This cannot be reduced simply to the relationship between nature and culture, the living versus technical object, or the domination of one over the other, but rather their combination. Nested in the unfolding and folding of this problem, its development and application, rests the issue of their concretization (of their growing together). We might even say—drawing from Gilbert Simondon—that the problem raised in the abstract texts is the relation between the *engine* and the *concrete*, between giving birth/begetting and growth, which is found in the fully concretized intertwinement of nature–culture.[36] *Generare* and *crescere*—to give birth, bring forth, produce, grow, thrive, and increase—are translated into a technical lexicon.

It should come as no surprise to readers of Simondon that the first concrete example in his chapter on concretization is the *engine*.[37] Without slipping into the trappings of the "sexual difference" thesis, romanticizing the "natural," it is notable that the genealogy of dispositif thinking starts with a series of cisgender men. The issues addressed in these texts are raised by men and formulated in masculine terms and as masculine concerns. The subject is, after all, mechanical engineering. These authors include one who notoriously described birth as being thrown into the world, one who scripts a short story with not a single speaking female character, while another who drags his readers through seemingly endless descriptions of the minutiae of various technical objects in the history of engines and engineering. "Man-the-engineer," in this philosophy of mechanical engineering, gradually replaces the "natural" process of begetting and nurturing. That said, this line should not be pushed too far because it leads in a direction that reifies sex differences according to the nature–culture dichotomy: a technical-masculine philosophy erases a more natural, feminine nature. In contemporary dispositif thinking, theorists such as Karen Barad and Donna Haraway have also addressed the nature–culture admixture in feminist technoscience studies. Each points in directions that do not reify the feminine as natural.[38] Besides, the dispositif of gender,[39] the technologies of gender,[40] or somatechniques[41] are intricately wrapped up in this problem.

Traces of mechanical engineering become more concrete as the dispositif problem unfolds. In its development, the natural is not replaced but supplemented. The abstract problem of mechanical engineering is rearticulated by biological, or biotechnical, engineering. The natural is wholly absorbed in the technical—no longer just mechanically so—as the biological. Again, staying with Simondon a little longer, abstract technical objects were gradually concretized as biological objects. Even if it occurs on a slightly altered temporal scale, this movement runs parallel to the transition from disciplinary to biopower, even in the transition from industrial capitalism to post-industrial capitalism. Life itself was first subjected to a technical dispositif that superficially engineered the body on top of the body. In Kafka's penal colony, for example, the "apparatus" [*Apparat*] was designed by the Commandant (a mechanical engineer) and operated by an officer who identified more as a mechanic. Justice was mechanically executed on the body of the prisoners.[42] With the advent of biopower, life itself is engineered, either directly by biotechnologies or indirectly by governmental techniques. Life is subjected to biological, or biotechnical, engineering. Life becomes the object, much more so than nature. It is no longer nature per se, the natural course of things, of being born (*natus*), that is an issue, but life and living. From the purview of the dispositif of engineering, life is without its own proper engine; instead, it is engineerable. It requires interventions. This point comes to the fore in most of the contemporary texts on dispositifs, ranging from feminist, queer, and trans dispositif theorists, to anti-colonial and anti-racist theorists, to those taking up these issues from the perspective of ecology, environmental studies, and animal studies, up to those falling under the broad heading of Italian anti-capitalist philosophy.

NOTES

1. Michel Foucault, *The History of Sexuality: Volume 1: The Will to Knowledge,* trans. Robert Hurley (London: Penguin Books, 1981).

2. Gilles Deleuze, "What Is a *Dispositif?*," in *Michel Foucault, Philosopher,* trans. Timothy J. Armstrong (New York: Routledge, 1992).

3. Giorgio Agamben, "What Is an Apparatus?" in *What Is an Apparatus? And Other Essays,* trans. David Kishik and Stefan Pedatella (Stanford, CA: Stanford University Press, 2009). Colin Gordon

et al. also translate *dispositif* as apparatus in Foucault's famous interview on *dispositifs*. See Foucault, "Confessions of the Flesh," in *Power/Knowledge: Selected Interviews & Other Writings, 1972–1977*, ed. Colin Gordon, trans. Colin Gordon et al. (New York: Pantheon Books, 1980).

4. Although this cartography draws from one article by Repo, the culmination of these studies is found in her important book *The Biopolitics of Gender* (New York: Oxford University Press, 2016).

5. Karl Marx, *Grundrisse. Foundations of the Critique of Political Economy*, trans. Martin Nicolaus (London: Penguin Books, 1973).

6. Deleuze, "What Is a Dispositif?" 159–161. Frank Kessler notes that Deleuze and Guattari preferred to use the term *rhizomes* and *agencement* (assemblage) as slightly more open, less totalizing, notions of bringing parts together in a manner that is simultaneously territorializing and deterritorializing. He contrasts assemblage with Agamben's more structural reading of dispositifs. See Frank Kessler, "Notes on Dispositif" (Unpublished, 2007).

7. Agamben, "What Is an Apparatus?" 12.

8. Ibid., 14.

9. Michel de Certeau, *The Practice of Everyday Life*, trans. Steven Rendall (Berkeley: University of California Press, 1984), 45.

10. Agamben, "What Is an Apparatus?" 1–2.

11. Foucault, "The Confession of the Flesh," 194–196.

12. Agamben, "What Is an Apparatus?" 7–8/*Che cos'è un dispositivo?* 13–15. Note that in the original Italian text, Agamben emphasizes the verb *disporre* (from *disponere* in Latin, "to dispose" in modern English).

13. Jean Hyppolite, "The Idea of Positivity," in *Introduction to Hegel's Philosophy of History*, trans. Bond Harris and Jacqueline Bouchard Spurlock (Gainesville: University of Florida Press, 1996), 20–25.

14. Martin Heidegger, "The Question Concerning Technology," in *The Question Concerning Technology and Other Essays*, trans. William Levitt (New York: Harper & Row, 1997), 3–35.

15. Foucault, *The History of Sexuality*, 73, 82 (French 98 and 108).

16. "The machine" in this fragment, notes Gerald Raunig, "is not at all limited to its technical aspects, but is instead a mechanical-intellectual, even social assemblage." Gerald Raunig, *A Thousand Machines: A Concise Philosophy of the Machine as Social Movement*, trans. Aileen Derieg (Los Angeles: Semiotext(e), 2010), 24.

17. Marx defines "labour-power" as both the physical and intellectual capacities. Karl Marx, *Capital, Vol. 1*, trans. Ben Fowkes (New York: Penguin Books, 1990), 270.

18. Marx, *Grundrisse*, 699. Note, there are no page numbers in the German edition I am using.

19. Ibid., 693, 709, 704.

20. Ibid., 692.

21. Ibid., 706.

22. It is hard not to think of Frederick Winslow Taylor's "intelligent gorillas" when reading the fragment. As Harry Braverman argues, Taylor established a clear division of labor between the conception and the execution of work, in the form of "task work." See Harry Braverman, *Labor and*

Monopoly Capital (New York: Monthly Review Press, 1974). We also should not overlook the fact that Taylor was a mechanical engineer who has posthumously been anointed as the founder of "industrial engineering"—a managerial science aimed at optimizing the assemblage of machinery in factories and other workplaces.

23. Marx, *Grundrisse*, 705.

24. Jacques Derrida, "The Parergon," trans. Craig Owens, *October* no. 9 (Summer 1979), 33.

25. Marx, *Grundrisse*, 708. I am intentionally skipping over many of the factors involved in calculating value here—this is not an essay on Marxist political economy.

26. Ibid.

27. Ibid.

28. Ibid., 706.

29. Ibid., 712.

30. Ibid., 706.

31. Georges Canguilhem, *Knowledge of Life*, trans. Stefanos Geroulanos and Daniela Ginsburg (New York: Fordham University Press, 2008), 75–97.

32. Ibid., 76.

33. Ibid., 96.

34. Ibid.

35. Ibid., 97.

36. Gilbert Simondon, *On the Mode of Existence of Technical Objects*, trans. Cécile Malaspina and John Rogove (Minneapolis, MN: Univocal, 2017).

37. Ibid., 25.

38. See Donna J. Haraway, *Modest_Witness@Second_Millennium. FemaleMan©_Meets_OncoMouse™: Feminism and Technoscience* (New York: Routledge, 1997), xii–xiii and 8–14, and Karen Barad, "Posthumanist Performativity: Toward an Understanding of How Matter Comes to Matter," *Signs: Journal of Women in Culture and Society* 28, no. 3 (2003): 801–831.

39. Judith Butler defines gender as an apparatus in *Gender Trouble: Feminism and the Subversion of Identity* (New York: Routledge, 1990), 11. Jemima Repo traces the genealogy of the gender apparatus in *The Biopolitics of Gender* (New York: Oxford University Press, 2016).

40. Teresa De Lauretis refers to the sex-gender system as a "semiotic apparatus" in *Technologies of Gender: Essays on Theory, Film, and Fiction* (Indianapolis: Indiana University Press, 1987), 5.

41. Nikki Sullivan, "Somatechnics," *Transgender Studies Quarterly* 1, no. 1–2 (May 2014): 187–190.

42. Franz Kafka, "In the Penal Colony," in *Franz Kafka: The Complete Stories*, trans. Will Muir and Edwin Muir (New York: Schocken Books, 1971), 140–167. The relationship between colonialism and mechanical engineering in this text is uncanny. Dispositif thinking is also present in other anti-colonial scholarship that uses dispositifs. Edward Said refers to orientalism as a "cultural apparatus" in *Orientalism* (New York: Random House, 1979), 204. Homi K. Bhabha defines colonial discourse as an apparatus in *The Location of Culture* (New York: Routledge, 1994), 100–101. More recently, two significant anti-colonial feminist scholars have used dispositifs (or apparatuses) to examine the nuanced and intricate ways settler colonial states subjugate and, in some cases, eliminate colonized

Indigenous populations. For an account of how Israeli settler colonial apparatuses are used against Indigenous Palestinians, see Jasbir K. Puar, *The Right to Maim: Debility, Capacity, Disability* (Durham, NC: Duke University Press, 2017). For an account of how settler colonial apparatuses continue to be used against Indigenous peoples on Turtle Island, specifically the Mohawks of the Haudenosaunee Confederacy, see Audra Simpson, *Mohawk Interruptus: Political Life Across the Borders of Settler States* (Durham, NC: Duke University Press, 2014).

BIBLIOGRAPHY

Agamben, Giorgio. "What Is an Apparatus?" In *What Is an Apparatus? And Other Essays*. Translated by David Kishik and Stefan Pedatella, 1–24. Stanford, CA: Stanford University Press, 2009. Originally published as *Che cos'è un dispositivo?* Roma: Nottetempo, 2006.

Barad, Karen. "Posthumanist Performativity: Toward an Understanding of How Matter Comes to Matter." *Signs: Journal of Women in Culture and Society* 28, no. 3 (2003): 801–831.

Bhabha, Homi K. *The Location of Culture*. New York: Routledge, 1994.

Braverman, Harry. *Labor and Monopoly Capital: The Degradation of Work in the Twentieth Century*. New York: Monthly Review Press, 1974.

Butler, Judith. *Gender Trouble: Feminism and the Subversion of Identity*. New York: Routledge, 1990.

Canguilhem, Georges. "Machine and Organism." In *Knowledge of Life*. Translated by Stefanos Geroulanos and Daniela Ginsburg, 75–97. New York: Fordham University Press, 2008.

Certeau, Michel de. *The Practice of Everyday Life*. Translated by Steven Rendall. Berkeley: University of California Press, 1984.

Deleuze, Gilles. "What Is a Dispositif?" In *Michel Foucault, Philosopher*. Translated by Timothy J. Armstrong, 159–168. New York: Routledge, 1992.

Derrida, Jacques. "The Parergon." Translated by Craig Owens. *October*, no. 9 (Summer 1979): 3–41.

Foucault, Michel. "Confessions of the Flesh." In *Power/Knowledge: Selected Interviews & Other Writings, 1972–1977*. Edited by Colin Gordon. Translated by Colin Gordon et al., 194–228. New York: Pantheon Books, 1980.

Foucault, Michel. *The History of Sexuality: Volume 1: The Will to Knowledge*. Translated by Robert Hurley. London: Penguin Books, 1981.

Haraway, Donna J. *Modest_Witness@Second_Millennium. FemaleMan©_Meets_OncoMouse™: Feminism and Technoscience*. New York: Routledge, 1997.

Heidegger, Martin. "The Question Concerning Technology." In *The Question Concerning Technology and Other Essays*. Translated by William Levitt, 3–35. New York: Harper & Row, 1997.

Hyppolite, Jean. "The Idea of Positivity." In *Introduction to Hegel's Philosophy of History*. Translated by Bond Harris and Jacqueline Bouchard Spurlock, 20–25. Gainesville: University of Florida Press, 1996.

Kafka, Franz. "In the Penal Colony." In *Franz Kafka: The Complete Stories*. Translated by Will Muir and Edwin Muir, 140–167. New York: Schocken Books, 1971.

Lauretis, Teresa de. *Technologies of Gender: Essays on Theory, Film, and Fiction*. Indianapolis: Indiana University Press, 1987.

Marx, Karl. *Capital, Vol. 1*. Translated by Ben Fowkes. New York: Penguin Books, 1990.

Marx, Karl. *Grundrisse: Foundations of the Critique of Political Economy*. Translated by Martin Nicolaus. New York: Penguin Books, 1973. Originally published as *Grundrisse der Kritik der Politischen Ökonomie*. In *Marx/Engels Werke*, 42. Berlin: Dietz Verlag, 1983.

Puar, Jasbir K. *The Right to Maim: Debility, Capacity, Disability*. Durham, NC: Duke University Press, 2017.

Raunig, Gerald. *A Thousand Machines: A Concise Philosophy of the Machine as Social Movement*. Translated by Aileen Derieg. Los Angeles: Semiotext(e), 2010.

Repo, Jemima. *The Biopolitics of Gender*. New York: Oxford University Press, 2016.

Said, Edward. *Orientalism*. New York: Random House, 1979.

Simondon, Gilbert. *On the Mode of Existence of Technical Objects*. Translated by Cécile Malaspina and John Rogove. Minneapolis, MN: Univocal, 2017.

Simpson, Audra. *Mohawk Interruptus: Political Life Across the Borders of Settler States*. Durham, NC: Duke University Press, 2014.

Sullivan, Nikki. "Somatechnics." *Transgender Studies Quarterly* 1, no. 1–2 (May 2014): 187–190.

I

ARCHITECHTRONICS/MECHANISMS

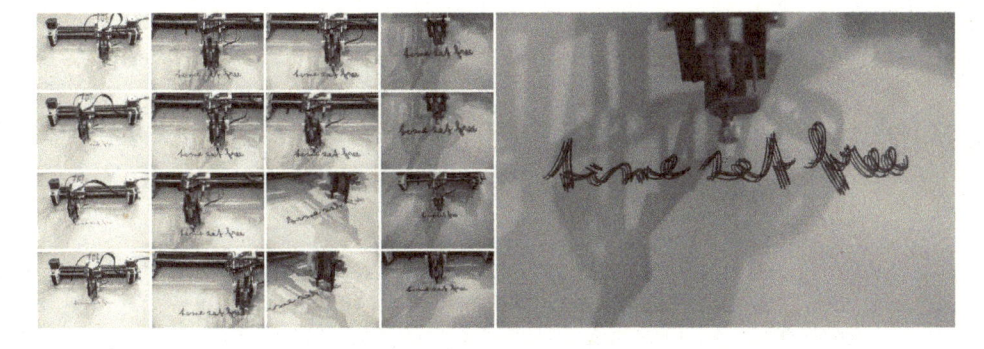

Raqs Media Collective, *Time Set Free*. Reprinted by permission of the artist.

1

FRAGMENT ON MACHINES

Karl Marx

Capital which consumes itself in the production process, or fixed capital, is the *means of production* in the strict sense. In a broader sense the entire production process and each of its moments, such as circulation—as regards its material side—is only a means of production for capital, for which value alone is the end in itself. Regarded as a physical substance, the raw material itself is a means of production for the product etc.

But the determination that the use value of fixed capital is that which eats itself up in the production process is identical to the proposition that it is used in this process only as a means, and itself exists merely as an agency for the transformation of the raw material into the product. As such a means of production, its use value can be that it is merely the technological condition for the occurrence of the process (the site where the production process proceeds), as with buildings etc., or that it is a direct condition of the action of the means of production proper, like all *matières instrumentales*. Both are in turn only the material presuppositions for the production process generally, or for the employment and maintenance of the means of labour. The latter, however, in the proper sense, serves only within production and for production, and has no other use value.

Originally, when we examined the development of value into capital, the labour process was simply included within capital, and, as regards its physical conditions, its material presence, capital appeared as the totality of the conditions of this process, and correspondingly sorted itself out into certain qualitatively different parts, *material of labour* (this, not raw material, is the correct expression of the concept), *means of labour* and *living labour*. On one side, capital was divided into these three elements in accordance with its material composition; on the other, the *labour process* (or the merging of these elements into each other within the process) was their moving unity, the product their static unity. In this form, the material elements—material of labour, means of labour and living labour—appeared merely as the essential moments of the labour process itself, which capital appropriates. But this material side—or, its character as use value and as real process—did not at all coincide with its formal side.

[. . .]

As long as the means of labour remains a means of labour in the proper sense of the term, such as it is directly, historically, adopted by capital and included in its realization process, it undergoes a merely formal modification, by appearing now as a means of labour not only in regard to its material side, but also at the same time as a particular mode of the presence of capital, determined by its total process—as *fixed capital*. But, once adopted into the production process of capital, the means of labour passes through different metamorphoses, whose culmination is the *machine* [*Maschine*], or rather, an *automatic system of machinery* (system of machinery: the *automatic* one is merely its most complete, most adequate form, and alone transforms machinery into a system), set in motion by an automaton, a moving power that moves itself; this automaton consisting of numerous mechanical and intellectual organs [*mechanischen und intellektuellen Organen*], so that the workers themselves are cast merely as its conscious linkages. In the machine, and even more in machinery as an automatic system, the use value, i.e. the material quality of the means of labour, is transformed into an existence adequate to fixed capital and to capital as such; and the form in which it was adopted into the production process of capital, the direct means of labour, is superseded by a form posited by capital itself and corresponding to it. In no way does the machine appear as the individual worker's means of labour. Its distinguishing characteristic is not in the least, as with the means of labour, to transmit the worker's activity to the object; this activity, rather, is posited in such a way that it merely transmits the machine's work, the machine's action, on to the raw material—supervises it and guards against interruptions. Not as with the instrument [*Instrument*], which the worker animates and makes into his organ with his skill and strength, and whose handling therefore depends on his virtuosity. Rather, it is the machine which possesses skill and strength in place of the worker, is itself the virtuoso, with a soul of its own in the mechanical laws acting through it; and it consumes coal, oil etc. (*matières instrumentales*), just as the worker consumes food, to keep up its perpetual motion. The worker's activity, reduced to a mere abstraction of activity, is determined and regulated on all sides by the movement of the machinery, and not the opposite. The science which compels the inanimate limbs of the machinery, by their construction, to act purposefully, as an automaton, does not exist in the worker's consciousness, but rather acts upon him through the machine as an alien power, as the power of the machine itself. The appropriation of living labour by objectified labour—of the power or activity which creates value by value existing for-itself—which lies in the concept of capital, is posited, in production resting on machinery, as the character of the production process itself, including its material elements and its material motion. The production process has ceased to be a labour process in the sense of a process dominated by labour as its governing unity. Labour appears, rather, merely as a conscious organ, scattered among the individual living workers at numerous points of the mechanical system [*mechanischen Systems*]; subsumed under the total process of the machinery itself, as itself only a link of the system, whose unity exists not in the living workers, but rather in the living (active) machinery, which confronts his individual, insignificant doings as a mighty organism. In machinery, objectified labour confronts living labour within the labour process itself as the power which rules it; a power which, as the appropriation of living labour, is the form of capital. The transformation of the means of labour into machinery, and of living labour into a mere living accessory of this machinery, as the means of its action, also posits the absorption of the labour process in its material character as a mere moment of the realization process of capital. The increase of the productive force of labour and the greatest possible negation of necessary labour is the necessary tendency of capital, as we have seen. The transformation of the means of labour into machinery is the realization of this tendency. In machinery, objectified labour materially confronts living labour as a ruling power and as an active subsumption of the latter under itself, not only by appropriating it, but in the real production process itself; the relation of capital as value which appropriates value-creating activity is, in fixed capital existing as machinery, posited at the same time as the relation of the use value of capital to the use value of labour capacity; further, the value objectified in machinery appears as a presupposition against which the value-creating power of the individual labour capacity is an infinitesimal, vanishing magnitude; the production in enormous mass quantities which is posited with machinery destroys every connection of the product with the direct need of the producer, and hence with direct use value; it is already posited in the form of the product's production and in the relations in which it is produced that it is produced only as a conveyor of value, and its use value only as condition to that end. In machinery, objectified labour itself appears not only in the form of product or of the product employed as means of labour, but in the form of the force of production itself. The development of the means of labour into machinery is not an accidental moment of capital, but is rather the historical reshaping of the traditional, inherited means of labour into a form adequate to capital. The accumulation of knowledge and of skill, of the general productive forces of the social brain [*der allgemeinen Produktivkräfte des gesellschaftlichen Hirns*], is thus absorbed into capital, as opposed to labour, and hence appears as an attribute of capital, and more specifically of *fixed capital*, in so far as it enters into the production process as a means of production proper. *Machinery* appears, then, as the most adequate form of *fixed capital*, and fixed capital, in so far as capital's relations with itself are concerned, appears as *the most adequate form of capital* as such. In another respect, however, in so far as fixed capital is condemned to an existence within the confines of a specific use value, it does not correspond to the concept of capital, which, as value, is indifferent to every specific form of use value, and can adopt or shed any of them as equivalent incarnations. In this respect, as regards capital's external relations, it is *circulating capital* which appears as the adequate form of capital, and not fixed capital.

Further, in so far as machinery develops with the accumulation of society's science [*der Akkumulation der gesellschaftlichen Wissenschaft*], of productive force generally, general social labour presents itself not in labour but in capital. The productive force of society is measured in *fixed capital*, exists there in its objective form; and, inversely, the productive force of capital grows with this general progress, which capital appropriates free of charge. This is not the place to go into the development of machinery in detail; rather only in its general aspect; in so far as the *means of labour*, as a physical thing, loses its direct form, becomes *fixed capital*, and confronts the worker physically as *capital*. In machinery, knowledge appears as alien, external to him; and living labour [as] subsumed under self-activating objectified labour. The worker appears as superfluous to the extent that his action is not determined by [capital's] requirements.

The full development of capital, therefore, takes place—or capital has posited the mode of production corresponding to it—only when the means of labour has not only taken the economic form of *fixed capital*, but has also been suspended in its immediate form, and when *fixed capital* appears as a machine within the production process, opposite labour; and the entire production process appears as not subsumed under the direct skillfulness of the worker, but rather as the technological application of science [*technologische Anwendung der Wissenschaft*]. [It is,] hence, the tendency of capital to give production a scientific character; direct labour [is] reduced to a mere moment of this process. As with the transformation of value into capital, so does it appear in the further development of capital, that it presupposes a certain given historical development of the productive forces on one side—science too [is] among these productive forces—and, on the other, drives and forces them further onwards.

Thus the quantitative extent and the effectiveness (intensity) to which capital is developed as fixed capital indicate the general degree to which capital is developed as capital, as power over living labour, and to which it has conquered the production process as such. Also, in the sense that it expresses the accumulation of objectified productive forces, and likewise of objectified labour. However, while capital gives itself its adequate form as use value within the production process only in the form of machinery and other material manifestations of fixed capital, such as railways etc. (to which we shall return later), this in no way means that this use value—machinery as such—is capital, or that its existence as machinery is identical with its existence as capital; any more than gold would cease to have use value as gold if it were no longer *money*. Machinery does not lose its use value as soon as it ceases to be capital. While machinery is the most appropriate form of the use value of fixed capital, it does not at all follow that therefore subsumption under the social relation of capital is the most appropriate and ultimate social relation of production for the application of machinery.

To the degree that labour time—the mere quantity of labour—is posited by capital as the sole determinant element, to that degree does direct labour and its quantity disappear as the determinant principle of production—of the creation of use values—and is reduced both quantitatively, to a smaller proportion, and qualitatively, as an, of course, indispensable but subordinate moment, compared to general scientific labour [*allgemeine wissenschaftliche Arbeit*], technological application of natural sciences, on one side, and to the general productive force arising from social combination [*gesellschaftlichen Gliederung*] in total production on the other side—a combination which appears as a natural fruit of social labour (although it is a historic product). Capital thus works towards its own dissolution as the form dominating production.

While, then, in one respect the transformation of the production process from the simple labour process into a scientific process, which subjugates the forces of nature and compels them to work in the service of human needs, appears as a quality of *fixed capital* in contrast to living labour; while individual labour as such has ceased altogether to appear as productive, is productive, rather, only in these common labours which subordinate the forces of nature to themselves, and while this elevation of direct labour into social labour appears as a reduction of individual labour to the level of helplessness in face of the communality [*Gemeinsamkeit*] represented by and concentrated in capital; so does it now appear, in another respect, as a quality of *circulating capital*, to maintain labour in one branch of production by means of *coexisting labour* in another. In small-scale circulation, capital advances the worker the wages which the latter exchanges for products necessary for his consumption. The money he obtains has this power only because others are working alongside him at the same time; and capital can give him claims on alien labour, in the form of money, only because it has appropriated his own labour. This exchange of one's own labour with alien labour appears here not as mediated and determined by the simultaneous existence of the labour of others, but rather by the advance which capital makes. The worker's ability to engage in the exchange of substances necessary for his consumption during production appears as due to an attribute of the part of *circulating capital* which is paid to the worker, and of circulating capital generally. It appears not as an exchange of substances between the simultaneous labour powers, but as the metabolism [*Stoffwechsel*] of capital; as the existence of circulating capital. Thus all powers of labour are transposed into powers of capital; the productive power of labour into fixed capital (posited as external to labour and as existing independently of it (as object [*sachlich*])); and, in circulating capital, the fact that the worker himself has created the conditions for the repetition of his labour, and that the exchange of this, his labour, is mediated by the co-existing labour of others, appears in such a way that capital gives him an advance and posits the simultaneity of the branches of labour. (These last two aspects actually belong to accumulation.) Capital in the form of circulating capital posits itself as mediator between the different workers.

Fixed capital, in its character as means of production, whose most adequate form [is] machinery, produces value, i.e. increases the value of the product, in only two respects: (1) in so far as it *has* value; i.e. is itself the product of labour, a certain quantity of labour in objectified form; (2) in so far as it increases the relation of surplus labour to necessary labour, by enabling labour, through an increase of its productive power, to create a greater mass of the products required for the maintenance of living labour capacity in a shorter time. It is therefore a highly absurd bourgeois assertion that the worker shares with the capitalist, because the latter, with fixed capital (which is, as far as that goes, itself a product of labour, and of *alien labour* merely appropriated by capital) makes labour easier [*erleichtert*] for him (rather, he robs it of all independence and attractive character, by means of the machine), or makes his labour shorter. Capital employs machinery, rather, only to the extent that it enables the worker to work a larger part of his time for capital, to relate to a larger part of his time as time which does not belong to him, to work longer for another. Through this process, the amount of labour necessary for the production of a given object is indeed reduced to a minimum, but only in order to realize a maximum of labour in the maximum number of such objects. The first aspect is important, because capital here—quite unintentionally—reduces human labour, expenditure of energy, to a minimum. This will redound to the benefit of emancipated labour, and is the condition of its emancipation. From what has been said, it is clear how absurd Lauderdale is when he wants to make fixed capital into an independent source of value, independent of labour time. It is such a source only in so far as it is itself objectified labour time, and in so far as it posits surplus labour time [*Surplusarbeitszeit*]. The employment of machinery itself historically presupposes—see above, Ravenstone—superfluous hands [*überflüssige Hände*]. Machinery inserts itself to replace labour only where there is an overflow of labour powers [*Überfluß an Arbeitskräften*]. Only in the imagination of economists does it leap to the aid of the individual worker. It can be effective only with masses of workers, whose concentration relative to capital is one of its historic presuppositions, as we have seen. It enters not in order to replace labour power where this is lacking, but rather in order to reduce massively available labour power to its necessary measure. Machinery enters only where labour capacity is on hand in masses. (Return to this.)

Lauderdale believes himself to have made the great discovery that machinery does not increase the productive power of labour, because it rather replaces the latter, or does what labour cannot do with its own power. It belongs to the concept of capital that the increased productive force of labour is posited rather as the increase of a force [*Kraft*] outside itself, and as labour's own debilitation [*Entkräftung*]. The hand tool makes the worker independent—posits him as proprietor. Machinery—as fixed capital—posits him as dependent, posits him as appropriated. This effect of machinery holds only in so far as it is cast into the role of fixed capital, and this it is only because the worker relates to it as wage-worker, and the active individual generally, as mere worker.

[. . .]

In machinery, the appropriation of living labour by capital achieves a direct reality in this respect as well: It is, firstly, the analysis and application of mechanical and chemical laws, arising directly out of science, which enables the machine to perform the same labour as that previously performed by the worker. However, the development of machinery along this path occurs only when large industry has already reached a higher stage, and all the sciences have been pressed into the service of capital; and when, secondly, the available machinery itself already provides great capabilities. Invention then becomes a business, and the application of science to direct production itself becomes a prospect which determines and solicits it. But this is not the road along which machinery, by and large, arose, and even less the road on which it progresses in detail. This road is, rather, dissection [*Analyse*]—through the division of labour, which gradually transforms the workers' operations into more and more mechanical ones, so that at a certain point a mechanism can step into their places. [. . .] Thus, the specific mode of working here appears directly as becoming transferred from the worker to capital in the form of the machine, and his own labour capacity devalued thereby. Hence the workers' struggle against machinery. What was the living worker's activity becomes the activity of the machine. Thus the appropriation of labour by capital confronts the worker in a coarsely sensuous form; capital absorbs labour into itself—"as though its body were by love possessed."[1]

The exchange of living labour for objectified labour—i.e. the positing of social labour in the form of the contradiction of capital and wage labour—is the ultimate development of the *value-relation* and of production resting on value. Its presupposition is—and remains—the mass of direct labour time, the quantity of labour employed, as the determinant factor in the production of wealth. But to the degree that large industry develops, the creation of real wealth comes to depend less on labour time and on the amount of labour employed than on the power of the agencies set in motion during labour time, whose 'powerful effectiveness' is itself in turn out of all proportion to the direct labour time spent on their production, but depends rather on the general state of science and on the progress of technology, or the application of this science to production. (The development of this science, especially natural science, and all others with the latter, is itself in turn related to the development of material production.) Agriculture, e.g., becomes merely the application of the science of material metabolism, its regulation for the greatest advantage of the entire body of society. Real wealth manifests itself, rather—and large industry reveals this—in the monstrous disproportion between the labour time applied, and its product, as well as in the qualitative imbalance between labour, reduced to a pure abstraction, and the power of the production process it superintends. Labour no longer appears so much to be included within the production process; rather, the human being comes to relate more as watchman and regulator to the production process itself. (What holds for machinery holds likewise for the combination of human activities and the development of human intercourse.) No longer does the worker insert a modified natural thing [*Naturgegenstand*] as middle link between the object [*Objekt*] and himself; rather, he inserts the process of nature, transformed into an industrial process, as a means between himself and inorganic nature, mastering it. He steps to the side of the production process instead of being its chief actor [*Hauptagent*]. In this transformation, it is neither the direct human labour he himself performs, nor the time during which he works, but rather the appropriation of his own general productive power, his understanding of nature and his mastery over it by virtue of his presence as a social body—it is, in a word, the development of the social individual which appears as the great foundation-stone of production and of wealth. The *theft of alien labour time, on which the present wealth is based*, appears a miserable foundation in face of this new one, created by large-scale industry itself. As soon as labour in the direct form has ceased to be the great well-spring of wealth, labour time ceases and must cease to be its measure, and hence exchange value [must cease to be the measure] of use value. The *surplus labour of the mass* has ceased to be the condition for the development of general wealth, just as the *non-labour of the few*, for the development of the general powers of the human mind [*allgemeinen Mächte des menschlichen Kopfes*]. With that, production based on exchange value breaks down, and the direct, material production process is stripped of the form of penury and antithesis. The free development of individualities, and hence not the reduction of necessary labour time so as to posit surplus labour, but rather the general reduction of the necessary labour of society to a minimum, which then corresponds to the artistic, scientific etc. development of the individuals in the time set free [*freigewordne Zeit*], and with the means created, for all of them. Capital itself is the moving contradiction, [in] that it presses to reduce labour time to a minimum, while it posits labour time, on the other side, as sole measure and source of wealth. Hence it diminishes labour time in the necessary form so as to increase it in the superfluous form; hence posits the superfluous in growing measure as a condition—question of life or death [*question de vie et de mort*]—for the necessary. On the one side, then, it calls to life all the powers of science and of nature, as of social combination and of social intercourse, in order to make the creation of wealth independent (relatively) of the labour time employed on it. On the other side, it wants to use labour time as the measuring rod for the giant social forces thereby created, and to confine them within the limits required to maintain the already created value as value. Forces of production and social relations—two different sides of the development of the social individual—appear to capital as mere means, and are merely means for it to produce on its limited foundation. In fact, however, they are the material conditions to blow this foundation sky-high. "Truly wealthy a nation, when the working day is 6 rather than 12 hours. *Wealth* is not command over surplus labour time [*Surplusarbeitszeit*]" (real wealth), "but rather, *disposable time* [*verfügbare Zeit*] outside that needed in direct production, for *every individual* and the whole society."[2]

Nature builds no machines, no locomotives, railways, electric telegraphs, self-acting mules etc. These are products of human industry; natural material transformed into organs of the human will over nature, or of human participation in nature. They are *organs of the human brain, created by the human hand*; the power of knowledge, objectified. The development of fixed capital indicates to what degree general social knowledge has become a *direct force of production*, and to what degree, hence, the conditions of the process of social life itself have come under the control of the general intellect and been transformed in accordance with it. To what degree the powers of social production have been produced, not only in the form of knowledge, but also as immediate organs of social practice, of the real life process.

[. . .]

The creation of a large quantity of disposable time apart from necessary labour time for society generally and each of its members (i.e. room for the development of the individuals' full productive forces, hence those of society also), this creation of not-labour time [*Nicht-Arbeitszeit*] appears in the stage of capital, as of all earlier ones, as not-labour time, free time, for a few. What capital adds is that it increases the surplus labour time of the mass by all the means of art and science, because its wealth consists directly in the appropriation of surplus labour time; since *value* [*is*] *directly its purpose*, not use value. It is thus, despite itself, instrumental in creating the means of social disposable time, in order to reduce labour time for the whole society to a diminishing minimum, and thus to free everyone's time for their own development. But its tendency always, on the one side, *to create disposable time, on the other, to convert it into surplus labour*. If it succeeds too well at the first, then it suffers from surplus production, and then necessary labour is interrupted, because *no surplus labour can be realized by capital*. The more this contradiction develops, the more does it become evident that the growth of the forces of production can no longer be bound up with the appropriation of alien labour, but that the mass of workers must themselves appropriate their own surplus labour. Once they have done so—and *disposable time* thereby ceases to have an *antithetical* existence—then, on one side, necessary labour time will be measured by the needs of the social individual, and, on the other, the development of the power of social production will grow so rapidly that, even though production is now calculated for the wealth of all, *disposable time* will grow for all. For real wealth is the developed productive power of all individuals. The measure of wealth is then not any longer, in any way, labour time, but rather disposable time. *Labour time as the measure of value* posits wealth itself as founded on poverty, and disposable time as existing *in and because of the antithesis to surplus labour time*; or, the positing of an individual's entire time as labour time, and his degradation therefore to mere worker, subsumption under labour. *The most developed machinery thus forces the worker to work longer than the savage does, or than he himself did with the simplest, crudest tools.*

[. . .]

In direct exchange, individual direct labour appears as realized in a particular product or part of the product, and its communal, social character—its character as objectification of general labour and satisfaction of the general need—as posited through exchange alone. In the production process of large-scale industry, by contrast, just as the conquest of the forces of nature by the social intellect is the precondition of the productive power of the means of labour as developed into the automatic process, on one side, so, on the other, is *the labour of the individual in its direct presence posited as suspended individual, i.e. as social, labour. Thus the other basis of this mode of production falls away.*

[. . .]

Real economy—saving—consists of the saving of labour time (minimum (and minimization) of production costs); but this saving [is] identical with development of the productive force. Hence in no way *abstinence from consumption*, but rather the development of power, of capabilities of production, and hence both of the capabilities as well as the means of consumption. The capability to consume is a condition of consumption, hence its primary means, and this capability is the development of an individual potential, a force of production. The saving of labour time [is] equal to an increase of free time, i.e. time for the full development of the individual, which in turn reacts back upon the productive power of labour as itself the greatest productive power. From the standpoint of the direct production process it can be regarded as the production of *fixed capital*, this fixed capital being man himself. It goes without saying, by the way, that direct labour time itself cannot remain in the abstract antithesis to free time in which it appears from the perspective of bourgeois economy. Labour cannot become play, as Fourier would like,[3] although it remains his great contribution to have expressed the suspension not of distribution, but of the mode of production itself, in a higher form, as the ultimate object. Free time—which is both idle time [or leisure time, *Mußezeit*] and time for higher activity—has naturally transformed its possessor into a different subject, and he then enters into the direct production process as this different subject. This process is then both discipline, as regards the human being in the process of becoming; and, at the same time, practice [*Ausübung*], experimental science, materially creative and objectifying science, as regards the human being who has become, in whose head exists the accumulated knowledge of society. For both, in so far as labour requires practical use of the hands and free bodily movement, as in agriculture, at the same time exercise.

As the system of bourgeois economy has developed for us only by degrees, so too its negation, which is its ultimate result. We are still concerned now with the direct production process. When we consider bourgeois society in the long view and as a whole, then the final result of the process of social production always appears as the society itself, i.e. the human being itself in its social relations. Everything that has a fixed form, such as the product etc., appears as merely a moment, a vanishing moment, in this movement. The direct production process itself here appears only as a moment. The conditions and objectifications of the process are themselves equally moments of it, and its only subjects are the individuals, but individuals in mutual relationships, which they equally reproduce and produce anew. The constant process of their own movement, in which they renew themselves even as they renew the world of wealth they create.

NOTES

1. Johann Wolfgang von Goethe, *Faust*, Pt I, Act 5, Auerbach's Cellar in Leipzig: *"als hätt es Lieb im Leibe."*
2. Charles Wentworth Dilke, "The Source and Remedy of the National Difficulties, Deduced from Principles of Political Economy," in *A Letter to Lord John Russell* (London, 1821), 6.
3. Charles Fourier, *Le Nouveau Monde industriel et sociétaire*, Vol. VI, 242–252.

2

IN THE PENAL COLONY

Franz Kafka

"It's a peculiar apparatus [*Apparat*]," said the Officer to the Traveler, gazing with a certain admiration at the device [*Apparat*], with which he was, of course, thoroughly familiar. It appeared that the Traveler had responded to the invitation of the Commandant only out of politeness, when he had been invited to attend the execution of a soldier condemned for disobeying and insulting his superior. Of course, interest in the execution was not very high, not even in the penal colony itself. At least, here in the small, deep, sandy valley, closed in on all sides by barren slopes, apart from the Officer and the Traveler there were present only the Condemned, a vacant-looking man with a broad mouth and dilapidated hair and face, and the Soldier, who held the heavy chain to which were connected the small chains which bound the Condemned Man by his feet and wrist bones, as well as by his neck, and which were also linked to each other by connecting chains. The Condemned Man had an expression of such dog-like resignation that it looked as if one could set him free to roam around the slopes and would only have to whistle at the start of the execution for him to return.

The Traveler had little interest in the apparatus and walked back and forth behind the Condemned Man, almost visibly indifferent, while the Officer took care of the final preparations. Sometimes he crawled under the apparatus, which was built deep into the earth, and sometimes he climbed up a ladder to inspect the upper parts. These were really jobs which could have been left to a mechanic, but the Officer carried them out with great enthusiasm, maybe because he was particularly fond of this apparatus or maybe because there was some other reason why one could not trust the work to anyone else. "It's all ready now!" he finally cried and climbed back down the ladder. He was unusually tired, breathing with his mouth wide open, and he had pushed two fine lady's handkerchiefs under the collar of his uniform.

"These uniforms are really too heavy for the tropics," the Traveler said, instead of asking some questions about the apparatus, as the Officer had expected. "That's true," said the Officer. He washed the oil and grease from his dirty hands in a bucket of water standing ready, "but they mean home, and we don't want to lose our homeland." "Now, have a look at this apparatus," he added immediately, drying his hands with a towel and pointing to the device. "Up to this point I had to do some work by hand, but from now on the apparatus should work entirely on its own." The Traveler nodded and followed the Officer. The latter tried to protect himself against all eventualities by saying, "Of course, breakdowns [*Störungen*] do happen. I really hope none will occur today, but we must be prepared for it. The apparatus is supposed to keep going for twelve hours without interruption. But if any breakdowns do occur, they'll only be very minor, and we'll deal with them right away."

"Don't you want to sit down?" he asked finally, as he pulled out a chair from a pile of cane chairs and offered it to the Traveler. The latter could not refuse. He sat on the edge of the pit, into which he cast a fleeting glance. It was not very deep. On one side of the hole the piled earth was heaped up into a wall; on the other side stood the apparatus. "I don't know," the Officer said, "whether the Commandant has already explained the apparatus to you." The Traveler made a vague gesture with his hand. That was good enough for the Officer, for now he could explain the apparatus himself.

"This apparatus," he said, grasping a connecting rod and leaning against it, "is our previous Commandant's invention. I also worked with him on the very first tests and took part in all the work right up to its completion. However, the credit for the invention belongs to him alone. Have you heard of our previous Commandant? No? Well, I'm not claiming too much when I say that the organization of the entire penal colony is his work. We, his friends, already knew at the time of his death that the administration of the colony was so self-contained that even if his successor had a thousand new plans in mind, he would not be able to alter anything of the old plan, at least not for several years. And our prediction has held. The New Commandant has had to recognize that. It's a shame that you didn't know the previous Commandant!"

"However," the Officer said, interrupting himself, "I'm chattering, and his apparatus stands here in front of us. As you see, it consists of three parts. With the passage of time certain popular names have been developed for each of these parts. The one underneath is called the bed, the upper one is called the inscriber, and here in the middle, this moving part is called the harrow." "The harrow?" the Traveler asked. He had not been listening with full attention. The sun was excessively strong, trapped in the shadowless valley, and one could hardly collect one's thoughts. So the Officer appeared to him all the more admirable in his tight tunic weighed down with epaulettes and festooned with braid, ready to go on parade, as he explained the matter so eagerly and, while he was talking, adjusted screws here and there with a screwdriver.

The Soldier appeared to be in a state similar to the Traveler. He had wound the Condemned Man's chain around both his wrists and was supporting himself with his hand on his weapon, letting his head hang backward, not bothering about anything. The Traveler was not surprised at that, for the Officer spoke French, and clearly neither the Soldier nor the Condemned Man understood the language. So it was all the more striking that the Condemned Man, in spite of that, did what he could to follow the Officer's explanation. With a sort of sleepy persistence he kept directing his gaze to the place where the Officer had just pointed, and when the question from the Traveler interrupted the Officer, the Condemned Man looked at the Traveler, too, just as the Officer was doing.

"Yes, the harrow," said the Officer. "The name fits. The needles are arranged as in a harrow, and the whole thing is driven like a harrow, although it stays in one place and is, in principle, much more artistic. You'll understand in a moment. The condemned is laid out here on the bed. First, I'll describe the apparatus and only then let the procedure go to work. That way you'll be able to follow it better. Also a sprocket in the inscriber is excessively worn. It really squeaks. When it's in motion one can hardly make oneself understood. Unfortunately replacement parts are difficult to come by in this place. So, here is the bed, as I said. The whole thing is completely covered with a layer of cotton wool, the purpose of which you'll find out in a moment. The condemned man is laid out on his stomach on the cotton wool—naked, of course. There are straps for the hands here, for the feet here, and for the throat here, to tie him in securely. At the head of the bed here, where the man, as I have mentioned, first lies face down, is this small protruding lump of felt, which can easily be adjusted so that it presses right into the man's mouth. Its purpose is to prevent him screaming and biting his tongue to pieces. Of course, the man has to let the felt in his mouth—otherwise the straps around his throat would break his neck." "That's cotton wool?" asked the Traveler and bent down. "Yes, it is," said the Officer smiling, "feel it for yourself."

He took the Traveler's hand and led him over to the bed. "It's a specially prepared cotton wool. That's why it looks so unrecognizable. I'll get around to mentioning its purpose in a moment." The Traveler was already being won over a little to the apparatus. With his hand over his eyes to protect them from the sun, he looked at the apparatus in the hole. It was a massive construction. The bed and the inscriber were the same size and looked like two dark chests. The inscriber was set about two metres above the bed, and the two were joined together at the corners by four brass rods, which almost reflected the sun. The harrow hung between the chests on a band of steel.

The Officer had hardly noticed the earlier indifference of the Traveler, but he did have a sense now of how the latter's interest was being aroused for the first time. So he paused in his explanation in order to allow the Traveler time to observe the apparatus undisturbed. The Condemned Man imitated the Traveler, but since he could not put his hand over his eyes, he blinked upward with his eyes uncovered.

"So now the man is lying down," said the Traveler. He leaned back in his chair and crossed his legs.

"Yes," said the Officer, pushing his cap back a little and running his hand over his hot face. "Now, listen. Both the bed and the inscriber have their own electric batteries. The bed needs them for itself, and the inscriber for the harrow. As soon as the man is strapped in securely, the bed is set in motion. It quivers with tiny, very rapid oscillations from side to side and up and down simultaneously. You will have seen similar devices in mental hospitals. Only with our bed all movements are precisely calibrated, for they must be meticulously coordinated with the movements of the harrow. But it's the harrow which has the job of actually carrying out the sentence."

"What is the sentence?" the Traveler asked. "You don't even know that?" asked the Officer in astonishment and bit his lip. "Forgive me if my explanations are perhaps confused. I really do beg your pardon. Previously it was the Commandant's habit to provide such explanations. But the New Commandant has excused himself from this honourable duty. The fact that with such an eminent visitor"—the Traveler tried to deflect the honour with both hands, but the Officer insisted on the expression—"that with such an eminent visitor he didn't even once make him aware of the form of our sentencing is yet again something new, which . . ." He had a curse on his lips, but controlled himself and said merely: "I was not informed about it. It's not my fault. In any case, I am certainly the person best able to explain our style of sentencing, for here I am carrying"—he patted his breast pocket—"the relevant diagrams drawn by the previous Commandant."

"Diagrams made by the Commandant himself?" asked the Traveler. "Then was he in his own person a combination of everything? Was he soldier, judge, engineer, chemist, and draftsman?"

"He was indeed," said the Officer, nodding his head with a fixed and thoughtful expression. Then he looked at his hands, examining them. They didn't seem to him clean enough to handle the diagrams. So he went to the bucket and washed them again. Then he pulled out a small leather folder and said, "Our sentence does not sound severe. The law which a condemned man has violated is inscribed on his body with the harrow. This Condemned Man, for example," and the Officer pointed to the man, "will have inscribed on his body, 'Honour your superiors.'"

The Traveler had a quick look at the man. When the Officer was pointing at him, the man kept his head down and appeared to be directing all his energy into listening in order to learn something. But the movements of his thick pouting lips showed clearly that he was incapable of understanding anything. The Traveler wanted to raise various questions, but after looking at the Condemned Man he merely asked, "Does he know his sentence?" "No," said the Officer. He wished to get on with his explanation right away, but the Traveler interrupted him: "He doesn't know his own sentence?" "No," said the Officer once more. He then paused for a moment, as if he was asking the Traveler for a more detailed reason for his question, and said, "It would be useless to give him that information. He experiences it on his own body." The Traveler really wanted to keep quiet at this point, but he felt how the Condemned Man was gazing at him—he seemed to be asking whether he could approve of the process the Officer had described. So the Traveler, who had up to this point been leaning back, bent forward again and kept up his questions, "But does he nonetheless have some general idea that he's been condemned?" "Not that either," said the Officer, and he smiled at the traveler, as if he was still waiting for some strange revelations from him. "No?" said the Traveler, wiping his forehead, "then does the man also not yet know how his defence was received?" "He has had no opportunity to defend himself," said the Officer and looked away, as if he was talking to himself and wished not to embarrass the Traveler with an explanation of matters so self-evident to him. "But he must have had a chance to defend himself," said the Traveler and stood up from his chair.

The Officer recognized that he was in danger of having his explanation of the apparatus held up for a long time. So he went to the Traveler, took him by the arm, pointed with his hand at the Condemned Man, who stood there stiffly now that the attention was so clearly directed at him—the Soldier was also pulling on his chain—and said, "The matter stands like this. Here in the penal colony I have been appointed judge. In spite of my youth. For I stood at the side of our Old Commandant in all matters of punishment, and I also know the most about the apparatus. The basic principle I use for my decisions is this: Guilt is always beyond a doubt. Other courts could not follow this principle, for they are made up of many heads and, in addition, have even higher courts above them. But that is not the case here, or at least it was not that way with the previous Commandant. It's true the New Commandant has already shown a desire to get mixed up in my court, but I've succeeded so far in fending him off. And I'll continue to be successful. You want this case explained. It's simple—just like all of them. This morning a captain laid a charge that this man, who is assigned to him as a servant and who sleeps before his door, had been sleeping on duty. For his task is to stand up every time the clock strikes the hour and salute in front of the captain's door. That's certainly not a difficult duty—and it's necessary, since he is supposed to remain fresh both for guarding and for service. Yesterday night the captain wanted to check whether his servant was fulfilling his duty. He opened the door on the stroke of two and found him curled up asleep. He got his horsewhip and hit him across the face. Now, instead of standing up and begging for forgiveness, the man grabbed his master by the legs, shook him, and cried out, 'Throw away that whip or I'll eat you up.' Those are the facts. The captain came to me an hour ago. I wrote up his statement and right after that the sentence. Then I had the man chained up. It was all very simple. If I had first summoned the man and interrogated him, the result would have been confusion. He would have lied, and if I had been successful in refuting his lies, he would have replaced them with new lies, and so forth. But now I have him, and I won't release him again. Now, does that clarify everything? But time is passing. We should be starting the execution, and I haven't finished explaining the apparatus yet."

He urged the Traveler to sit down in his chair, moved to the apparatus again, and started, "As you see, the shape of the harrow corresponds to the shape of a man. This is the harrow for the upper body, and here are the harrows for the legs. This small cutter is the only one designated for the head. Is that clear to you?" He leaned forward to the Traveler in a friendly way, ready to give the most comprehensive explanation.

The Traveler looked at the harrow with a wrinkled frown. The information about the judicial procedures had not satisfied him. However, he had to tell himself that here it was a matter of a penal colony, that in this place special regulations were necessary, and that one had to give precedence to military measures right down to the last detail. Beyond that, however, he had some hopes in the New Commandant, who obviously, although slowly, was intending to introduce a new procedure which the limited understanding of this Officer could not cope with.

Following this train of thought, the Traveler asked, "Will the Commandant be present at the execution?" "That is not certain," said the Officer, embarrassingly affected by the sudden question, and his friendly expression made a grimace. "That's why we need to hurry up. As much as I regret the fact, I'll have to make my explanation even shorter. But tomorrow, once the apparatus is clean again—the fact that it gets so very dirty is its only fault—I could add a detailed explanation. So now, only the most important things. When the man is lying on the bed and it starts quivering, the harrow sinks onto the body. It positions itself automatically in such a way that it touches the body only lightly with the needle tips. Once the machine is set in this position, this steel cable tightens up into a rod. And now the performance begins. Someone who is not an initiate sees no external difference among the punishments. The harrow seems to do its work uniformly. As it quivers, it sticks the tips of its needles into the body, which is also vibrating from the movement of the bed. Now, to enable someone to check on how the sentence is being carried out, the harrow is made of glass. That gave rise to certain technical difficulties with fastening the needles securely, but after several attempts we were successful. We didn't spare any efforts. And now, as the inscription is made on the body, everyone can see through the glass. Don't you want to come closer and see the needles for yourself?"

The Traveler stood slowly, moved up, and bent over the harrow. "You see," the Officer said, "two sorts of needles in a multiple arrangement. Each long needle has a short one next to it. The long one inscribes, and the short one squirts water out to wash away the blood and keep the inscription always clear. The bloody water is then channeled here in small grooves and finally flows into these main gutters, and the outlet pipe takes it to the pit." The Officer pointed with his finger to the exact path which the bloody water had to take. As he began to demonstrate with both hands at the mouth of the outlet pipe, in order to make his account as clear as possible, the Traveler raised his head and, feeling behind him with his hand, wanted to return to his chair. Then he saw to his horror that the Condemned Man had also, like him, accepted the Officer's invitation to inspect the arrangement of the harrow up close. He had pulled the sleeping Soldier holding the chain a little forward and was also bending over the glass. One could see how with a confused gaze he also was looking for what the two gentlemen had just observed, but how he didn't succeed because he lacked the explanation. He leaned forward this way and that. He kept running his eyes over the glass again and again. The Traveler wanted to push him back, for what he was doing was probably punishable. But the Officer held the Traveler firmly with one hand, and with the other he took a lump of earth from the wall and threw it at the Soldier. The latter opened his eyes with a start, saw what the Condemned Man had dared to do, let his weapon fall, braced his heels in the earth, and pulled the Condemned Man back, so that he immediately collapsed. The Soldier looked down at him, as he writhed around, making his chain clink. "Stand him up," cried the Officer. Then he noticed that the Condemned Man was distracting the Traveler too much. The latter was even leaning out away from the harrow, without paying any attention to it, wanting to find out what was happening to the Condemned Man. "Handle him carefully," the Officer yelled again. He ran around the apparatus, personally grabbed the Condemned Man under the armpits and, with the help of the Soldier, stood the man, whose feet kept slipping, upright.

"Now I know all about it," said the Traveler, as the Officer turned back to him again. "Except the most important thing," said the latter, grabbing the Traveler by the arm and pointing up high. "There in the inscriber is the mechanism which determines the movement of the harrow, and this mechanism is arranged according to the diagram on which the sentence is set down. I still use the diagrams of the previous Commandant. Here they are." He pulled some pages out of the leather folder. "Unfortunately I can't hand them to you. They are the most cherished thing I possess. Sit down, and I'll show you them from this distance. Then you'll be able to see it all well." He showed the first sheet. The Traveler would have been happy to say something appreciative, but all he saw was a labyrinthine series of lines, criss-crossing each other in all sort of ways. These covered the paper so thickly that only with difficulty could one make out the white spaces in between. "Read it," said the Officer. "I can't," said the Traveler. "But it's clear," said the Officer. "It's very elaborate," said the Traveler evasively, "but I can't decipher it."

"Yes," said the Officer, smiling and putting the folder back again, "it's not calligraphy for school children. One has to read it a long time. You too will finally understand it clearly. Of course, it has to be a script that isn't simple. You see, it's not supposed to kill right away, but on average over a period of twelve hours. The turning point is set for the sixth hour. There must also be many, many embellishments surrounding the basic script. The essential script moves around the body only in a narrow belt. The rest of the body is reserved for decoration. Can you now appreciate the work of the harrow and the whole apparatus? Just look at it!" He jumped up the ladder, turned a wheel, and called down, "Watch out—move to the side!" Everything started moving. If the wheel had not squeaked, it would have been marvelous. The Officer threatened the wheel with his fist, as if he was surprised by the disturbance it created. Then he spread his arms, apologizing to the Traveler, and quickly clambered down, in order to observe the operation of the apparatus from below.

Something was still not working properly, something only he noticed. He clambered up again and reached with both hands into the inside of the inscriber. Then, in order to descend more quickly, instead of using the ladder, he slid down on one of the poles and, to make himself understandable through the noise, strained his voice to the limit as he yelled in the Traveler's ear, "Do you understand the process? The harrow is starting to write. When it's finished with the first part of the script on the man's back, the layer of cotton wool rolls and turns the body slowly onto its side to give the harrow a new area. Meanwhile those parts lacerated by the inscription are lying on the cotton wool which, because it has been specially treated, immediately stops the bleeding and prepares the script for a further deepening. Here, as the body continues to rotate, prongs on the edge of the harrow then pull the cotton wool from the wounds, throw it into the pit, and the harrow goes to work again. In this way it keeps making the inscription deeper for twelve hours. For the first six hours the condemned man goes on living almost as before. He suffers nothing but pain. After two hours, the felt is removed, for at that point the man has no more energy for screaming. Here at the head of the bed warm rice pudding is put in this electrically heated bowl. From this the man, if he feels like it, can help himself to what he can lap up with his tongue. No one passes up this opportunity. I don't know of a single one, and I have had a lot of experience. He first loses his pleasure in eating around the sixth hour. I usually kneel down at this point and observe the phenomenon. The man rarely swallows the last bit. He turns it around in his mouth and spits it into the pit. When he does that, I have to lean aside or else he'll get me in the face. But how quiet the man becomes around the sixth hour! The most stupid of them begin to understand. It starts around the eyes and spreads out from there. A look that could tempt one to lie down under the harrow. Nothing else happens. The man simply begins to decipher the inscription. He purses his lips, as if he is listening. You've seen that it's not easy to figure out the inscription with your eyes, but our man deciphers it with his wounds. True, it takes a lot of work. It requires six hours to complete. But then the harrow spits him right out and throws him into the pit, where he splashes down into the bloody water and cotton wool. Then the judgment is over, and we, the Soldier and I, quickly bury him."

The Traveler had leaned his ear towards the Officer and, with his hands in his coat pockets, was observing the machine at work. The Condemned Man was also watching, but without understanding. He bent forward a little and followed the moving needles, as the Soldier, after a signal from the Officer, cut through his shirt and trousers with a knife from the back, so that they fell off the Condemned Man. He wanted to grab the falling garments to cover his bare flesh, but the Soldier held him up and shook the last rags from him. The Officer turned the machine off, and in the silence which then ensued the Condemned Man was laid out under the harrow. The chains were taken off and the straps fastened in their place. For the Condemned Man it seemed at first glance to signify almost a relief. And now the harrow sunk down a stage lower, for the Condemned was a thin man. As the needle tips touched him, a shudder went over his skin. While the Soldier was busy with the right hand, the Condemned Man stretched out his left, with no sense of its direction. But it was pointing to where the Traveler was standing. The Officer kept looking at the Traveler from the side, without taking his eyes off him, as if he was trying to read from his face the impression he was getting of the execution, which he had now explained to him, at least superficially.

The strap meant to hold the wrist ripped off. The Soldier probably had pulled on it too hard. The Soldier showed the Officer the torn-off piece of strap, wanting him to help. So the Officer went over to him and said, with his face turned towards the Traveler, "The machine is very complicated. Now and then something has to tear or break. One shouldn't let that detract from one's overall opinion. Anyway, we have an immediate replacement for the strap. I'll use a chain—even though that will affect the sensitivity of the movements for the right arm." And while he put the chain in place, he kept talking, "Our resources for maintaining the machine are very limited at the moment. Under the previous Commandant, I had free access to a cash box specially set aside for this purpose. There was a store room here in which all possible replacement parts were kept. I admit I made almost extravagant use of it. I mean earlier, not now, as the New Commandant claims. For him everything serves only as a pretext to fight against the old arrangements. Now he keeps the cash box for machinery under his own control, and if I ask him for a new strap, he demands the torn one as a piece of evidence, the new one doesn't arrive for ten days, and it's an inferior brand, of not much use to me. But how I am supposed to get the machine to work in the meantime without a strap—no one's concerned about that."

The Traveler was thinking: it's always questionable to intervene decisively in strange circumstances. He was neither a citizen of the penal colony nor a citizen of the state to which it belonged. If he wanted to condemn the execution or even hinder it, people could say to him: You're a foreigner—keep quiet. He would have nothing in response to that, but could only add that he did not understand what he was doing on this occasion, for the purpose of his traveling was merely to observe and not to alter other people's judicial systems in any way. True, at this point the way things were turning out it was very tempting. The injustice of the process and the inhumanity of the execution were beyond doubt. No one could assume that the Traveler was acting out of any sense of his own self-interest, for the Condemned Man was a stranger to him, not a countryman and not someone who invited sympathy in any way. The Traveler himself had letters of reference from high officials and had been welcomed here with great courtesy. The fact that he had been invited to this execution even seemed to indicate that people were asking for his judgment of this trial. This was all the more likely since the Commandant, as he had now heard only too clearly, was no supporter of this process and maintained an almost hostile relationship with the Officer.

Then the Traveler heard a cry of rage from the Officer. He had just shoved the stub of felt in the Condemned Man's mouth, not without difficulty, when the Condemned Man, overcome by an irresistible nausea, shut his eyes and threw up. The Officer quickly yanked him up off the stump and wanted to turn his head aside toward the pit. But it was too late. The vomit was already flowing down onto the machine. "This is all the Commandant's fault!" cried the Officer and mindlessly rattled the brass rods at the front. "My machine's as filthy as a pigsty." With trembling hands he showed the Traveler what had happened. "Haven't I spent hours trying to make the Commandant understand that a day before the execution there should be no more food served. But the new lenient administration has a different opinion. Before the man is led away, the Commandant's women cram sugary things down his throat. His whole life he's fed himself on stinking fish, and now he has to eat sweets! But that would be all right—I'd have no objections—but why don't they get a new felt, the way I've been asking him for three months now? How can anyone take this felt into his mouth without feeling disgusted—something that a hundred man have sucked and bitten on it as they were dying?"

The Condemned Man had laid his head down and appeared peaceful. The Soldier was busy cleaning up the machine with the Condemned Man's shirt. The Officer went up to the Traveler, who, feeling some premonition, took a step backwards. But the Officer grasped him by the hand and pulled him aside. "I want to speak a few words to you in confidence," he said. "May I do that?" "Of course," said the Traveler and listened with his eyes lowered.

"This process and execution, which you now have an opportunity to admire, have no more open supporters in our colony. I am its only defender, just as I am the single advocate for the legacy of the Old Commandant. I can no longer think about a more extensive organization of the process—I'm using all my powers to maintain what there is at present. When the Old Commandant was alive, the colony was full of his supporters. I have something of the Old Commandant's power of persuasion, but I completely lack his power, and as a result the supporters have gone into hiding. There are still a lot of them, but no one admits to it. If you go into a tea house today—that is to say, on a day of execution—and keep your ears open, perhaps you'll hear nothing but ambiguous remarks. They are all supporters, but under the present Commandant, considering his present views, they are totally useless to me. And now I'm asking you: Should such a life's work," he pointed to the machine, "come to nothing because of this Commandant and the women influencing him? Should people let that happen? Even if one is a foreigner and only on our island for a couple of days? But there's no time to lose. People are already preparing something against my judicial proceedings. Discussions are already taking place in the Commandant's headquarters, to which I am not invited. Even your visit today seems to me typical of the whole situation. People are cowards and send you out—a foreigner. You should have seen the executions in earlier days! The entire valley was overflowing with people, even a day before the execution. They all came merely to watch. Early in the morning the Commandant appeared with his women. Fanfares woke up the entire campsite. I delivered the news that everything was ready. The whole society—and every high official had to attend—arranged itself around the machine. This pile of cane chairs is a sorry left over from that time. The machine was freshly cleaned and glowed. For almost every execution I had new replacement parts. In front of hundreds of eyes—all the spectators stood on tip toe right up to the hills there—the condemned man was laid down under the harrow by the Commandant himself. What nowadays is done by a common soldier was then my work as the senior judge, and it was an honour for me. And then the execution began! No discordant note disturbed the work of the machine. Many people did not look any more at all, but lay down with closed eyes in the sand. They all knew: now justice was being carried out. In silence people listened to nothing but the groans of the condemned man, muffled by the felt. These days the machine no longer manages to squeeze a strong groan out of the condemned man—something the felt is not capable of smothering. But back then the needles which made the inscription dripped a caustic liquid which we are not permitted to use any more today. Well, then came the sixth hour. It was impossible to grant all the requests people made to be allowed to watch from up close. The Commandant, in his wisdom, arranged that the children should be taken care of before all the rest. Naturally, I was always allowed to stand close by, because of my official position. Often I crouched down there with two small children in my arms, on my right and left. How we all took in the expression of transfiguration on the martyred face! How we held our cheeks in the glow of this justice, finally attained and already passing away! What times we had, my friend!"

The Officer had obviously forgotten who was standing in front of him. He had put his arm around the Traveler and laid his head on his shoulder. The Traveler was extremely embarrassed. Impatiently he looked away over the Officer's head. The Soldier had ended his task of cleaning and had just shaken some rice pudding into the bowl from a tin. No sooner had the Condemned Man, who seemed to have fully recovered already, noticed this than his tongue began to lick at the pudding. The Soldier kept pushing him away, for the pudding was probably meant for a later time, but in any case it was not proper for the Soldier to reach in and grab some food with his dirty hands and eat it in front of the famished Condemned Man.

The Officer quickly collected himself. "I didn't want to upset you in any way," he said. "I know it is impossible to make someone understand those days now. Besides, the machine still works and operates on its own. It operates on its own even when it is standing alone in this valley. And at the end, the body still keeps falling in that incredibly soft flight into the pit, even if hundreds of people are not gathered like flies around the hole the way they used to be. Back then we had to erect a strong railing around the pit. It was pulled out long ago."

The Traveler wanted to turn his face away from the Officer and looked aimlessly around him. The Officer thought he was looking at the wasteland of the valley. So he grabbed his hands, turned him around in order to catch his gaze, and asked, "Do you see the shame of it?"

But the Traveler said nothing. The Officer left him alone for a while. With his legs apart and his hands on his hips, the Officer stood still and looked at the ground. Then he smiled at the Traveler cheerfully and said, "Yesterday I was nearby when the Commandant invited you. I heard the invitation. I know the Commandant. I understood right away what he intended with his invitation. Although his power might be sufficiently great to take action against me, he doesn't yet dare to. But my guess is that with you he is exposing me to the judgment of a respected foreigner. He calculates things with care. You are now in your second day on the island. You didn't know the Old Commandant and his way of thinking. You are trapped in a European way of seeing things. Perhaps you are fundamentally opposed to the death penalty in general and to this kind of mechanical style of execution in particular. Moreover, you see how the execution is a sad procedure, without any public participation, using a partially damaged machine. Now, if we take all this together (so the Commandant thinks) surely one could easily imagine that you would not consider my procedure proper? And if you didn't consider it right, you wouldn't keep quiet about it—I'm still speaking the mind of the Commandant—for you no doubt have faith that your tried-and-true convictions are correct. It's true that you have seen many peculiar things among many peoples and have learned to respect them. Thus, you will probably not speak out against the procedure with your full power, as you would perhaps in your own homeland. But the Commandant doesn't really need that. A casual word, merely a careless remark, is enough. It doesn't have to match your convictions at all, so long as it corresponds to his wishes. I'm certain he will use all his shrewdness to interrogate you. And his women will sit around in a circle and perk up their ears. You will say something like, 'Among us the judicial procedures are different,' or 'With us the accused is questioned before the verdict,' or 'We had torture only in the Middle Ages.' For you these observations appear as correct as they are self-evident—innocent remarks which do not impugn my procedure. But how will the Commandant take them? I see him, our excellent Commandant—the way he immediately pushes his stool aside and hurries out to the balcony—I see his women, how they stream after him. I hear his voice—the women call it a thunder voice. And now he's speaking: 'A great Western explorer who has been commissioned to inspect judicial procedures in all countries has just said that our process based on old customs is inhuman. After the verdict of such a personality it is, of course, no longer possible for me to tolerate this procedure. So from this day on I am ordering . . . and so forth.' You want to intervene—you didn't say what he is reporting—you didn't call my procedure inhuman; by contrast, in keeping with your deep insight, you consider it most humane and most worthy of human beings. You also admire this machinery. But it is too late. You don't even go onto the balcony, which is already filled with women. You want to attract attention. You want to cry out. But a lady's hand is covering your mouth, and I and the Old Commandant's work are lost."

The Traveler had to suppress a smile. So the work which he had considered so difficult was easy. He said evasively, "You're exaggerating my influence. The Commandant has read my letters of recommendation. He knows that I am no expert in judicial processes. If I were to express an opinion, it would be that of a lay person, no more significant than the opinion of anyone else, and in any case far less significant than the opinion of the Commandant, who, as I understand it, has very extensive powers in this penal colony. If his views of this procedure are as definite as you think they are, then I'm afraid the time has come for this procedure to end, without any need for my humble opinion."

Did the Officer understand by now? No, he did not yet get it. He shook his head vigorously, briefly looked back at the Condemned Man and the Soldier, who both flinched and stopped eating the rice, went up really close up to the Traveler, without looking into his face, but gazing at parts of his jacket, and said more gently than before: "You don't know the Commandant. Where he and all of us are concerned you are—forgive the expression—to a certain extent innocent. Your influence, believe me, cannot be overestimated. In fact, I was blissfully happy when I heard that you were to be present at the execution by yourself. This order of the Commandant was aimed at me, but now I'll turn it to my advantage. Without being distracted by false insinuations and disparaging looks—which could not have been avoided with a greater number of participants at the execution—you have listened to my explanation, looked at the machine, and are now about to view the execution. Your verdict is no doubt already fixed. If some small uncertainties remain, witnessing the execution will remove them. And now I'm asking you—help me with the Commandant!"

The Traveler did not let him go on talking. "How can I do that," he cried. "It's totally impossible. I can help you as little as I can harm you."

"You could do it," said the Officer. With some apprehension the Traveler observed that the Officer was clenching his fists. "You could do it," repeated the Officer, even more emphatically. "I have a plan which must succeed. You think your influence is insufficient. I know it will be enough. But assuming you're right, doesn't saving this whole procedure require one to try even those methods which may be inadequate? So listen to my plan. To carry it out, it's necessary, above all, for you to keep as quiet as possible today in the colony about your verdict on this procedure. Unless someone asks you directly, you should not express any view whatsoever. But what you do say must be short and vague. People should notice that it's difficult for you to speak about the subject, that you feel bitter, that, if you were to speak openly, you'd have to burst out cursing on the spot. I'm not asking you to lie, not at all. You should only give brief answers—something like, 'Yes, I've seen the execution' or 'Yes, I've heard the full explanation.' That's all—nothing further. For that will be enough of an indication for people to observe in you a certain bitterness, even if that's not what the Commandant will think. Naturally, he will completely misunderstand the issue and interpret it in his own way. My plan is based on that. Tomorrow a large meeting of all the higher administrative officials takes place at headquarters under the chairmanship of the Commandant. He, of course, understands how to turn such a meeting into a spectacle. A gallery has been built, which is always full of spectators. I'm compelled to take part in the discussions, though they fill me with disgust. In any case, you will certainly be invited to the meeting. If you follow my plan today and behave accordingly, the invitation will become an emphatic request. But should you for some inexplicable reason still not be invited, you must make sure you request an invitation. Then you'll receive one without question. Now, tomorrow you are sitting with the women in the Commandant's box. With frequent upward glances he reassures himself that you are there. After various trivial and ridiculous agenda items designed for the spectators—mostly harbour construction—always harbour construction—the judicial process comes up for discussion. If it's not raised by the Commandant himself or does not occur soon enough, I'll make sure that it comes up. I'll stand up and report on today's execution. Really briefly—just the report. Such a report is not really customary; however, I'll do it, nonetheless. The Commandant thanks me, as always, with a friendly smile. And now he cannot restrain himself. He seizes this excellent opportunity. 'The report of the execution,' he'll say, or something like that, 'has just been given. I would like to add to this report only the fact that this particular execution was attended by the great explorer whose visit confers such extraordinary honour on our colony, as you all know. Even the significance of our meeting today has been increased by his presence. Should we not now ask this great explorer for his appraisal of the execution based on old customs and of the process which preceded it?' Of course, there is the noise of applause everywhere, universal agreement. And I'm louder than anyone. The Commandant bows before you and says, 'Then in everyone's name, I'm putting the question to you.' And now you step up to the railing. Place your hands where everyone can see them. Otherwise the ladies will grab them and play with your fingers. And now finally come your remarks. I don't know how I'll bear the tension up to then. In your speech you mustn't hold back. Let truth resound. Lean over the railing and shout it out—yes, yes, roar your opinion at the Commandant, your unshakeable opinion. But perhaps you don't want to do that. It doesn't suit your character. Perhaps in your country people behave differently in such situations. That's all right. That's perfectly satisfactory. Don't stand up at all. Just say a couple of words. Whisper them so that only the officials underneath you can just hear them. That's enough. You don't even have to say anything at all about the lack of attendance at the execution or about the squeaky wheel, the torn strap, the disgusting felt. No. I'll take over all further details, and, believe me, if my speech doesn't chase him out of the room, it will force him to his knees, so he'll have to admit it: 'Old Commandant, I bow down before you.' That's my plan. Do you want to help me carry it out? But, of course, you want to. More than that—you have to."

And the Officer gripped the Traveler by both arms and looked at him, breathing heavily into his face. He had yelled the last sentences so loudly that even the Soldier and the Condemned Man were paying attention. Although they couldn't understand a thing, they stopped eating and looked over at the Traveler, still chewing.

From the start the Traveler had had no doubts about the answer he must give. He had experienced too much in his life to be able to waver here. Basically he was honest and unafraid. Still, with the Soldier and the Condemned Man looking at him, he hesitated a moment. But finally he said, as he had to, "No." The Officer's eyes blinked several times, but he did not take his eyes off the Traveler. "Would you like an explanation," asked the Traveler. The Officer nodded dumbly. "I am opposed to this procedure," said the Traveler. "Even before you took me into your confidence—and, of course, I will never abuse your confidence under any circumstances—I was already thinking about whether I was entitled to intervene against this procedure and whether my intervention could have the smallest chance of success. And if that was the case, it was clear to me whom I had to turn to first of all—naturally, to the Commandant. You clarified the issue for me even more, but without reinforcing my decision in any way—quite the reverse. I find your conviction genuinely moving, even if it cannot deter me."

The Officer remained quiet, turned toward the machine, grabbed one of the brass rods, and then, leaning back a little, looked up at the inscriber, as if he was checking that everything was in order. The Soldier and the Condemned Man seemed to have made friends with each other. The Condemned Man was making signs to the Soldier, although, given the tight straps on him, this was difficult for him to do. The Soldier was leaning into him. The Condemned Man whispered something to him, and the Soldier nodded. The Traveler went over to the Officer and said, "You don't yet know what I'll do. Yes, I will tell the Commandant my opinion of the procedure—not in a meeting, but in private. In addition, I won't stay here long enough to be able to get called in to some meeting or other. Early tomorrow morning I leave, or at least I go on board ship." It didn't look as if the Officer had been listening. "So the process has not convinced you," he said to himself, smiling the way an old man smiles over the silliness of a child, concealing his own true thoughts behind that smile.

"Well then, it's time," he said finally and suddenly looked at the Traveler with bright eyes which contained some sort of demand, some appeal for participation. "Time for what?" asked the Traveler uneasily. But there was no answer.

"You are free," the Officer told the Condemned Man in his own language. At first the man did not believe him. "You are free now," said the Officer. For the first time the face of the Condemned Man showed signs of real life. Was it the truth? Was it only the Officer's mood, which could change? Had the foreign Traveler brought him a reprieve? What was it? That's what the man's face seemed to be asking. But not for long. Whatever the case might be, if he could he wanted to be truly free, and he began to shake back and forth, as much as the harrow permitted.

"You're tearing my straps," cried the Officer. "Be still! We'll undo them right away." And, giving a signal to the Soldier, he set to work with him. The Condemned Man said nothing and smiled slightly to himself. He turned his face to the Officer and then to the Soldier and then back again, without ignoring the Traveler.

"Pull him out," the Officer ordered the Soldier. This process required a certain amount of care because of the harrow. The Condemned Man already had a few small wounds on his back, thanks to his own impatience.

From this point on, however, the Officer paid him hardly any attention. He went up to the Traveler, pulled out the small leather folder once more, leafed through it, finally found the sheet he was looking for, and showed it to the Traveler. "Read that," he said. "I can't," said the Traveler. "I've already told you I can't read these pages." "But take a close look at the page," said the Officer, and moved up right next to the Traveler in order to read with him. When that didn't help, he raised his little finger high up over the paper, as if the page must not be touched under any circumstances, so that using this he might make the task of reading easier for the Traveler. The Traveler also made an effort so that at least he could satisfy the Officer, but it was impossible for him. Then the Officer began to spell out the inscription and then read out once again the joined up letters. "'Be just!' it states," he said. "Now you can read it." The Traveler bent so low over the paper that the Officer, afraid that he might touch it, moved it further away. The Traveler didn't say anything more, but it was clear that he was still unable to read anything. "'Be just!' it says," the Officer remarked once again.

"That could be," said the Traveler. "I do believe that's written there." "Good," said the Officer, at least partially satisfied. He climbed up the ladder, holding the paper. With great care he set the page in the inscriber and appeared to rotate the gear mechanism completely around. This was very tiring work. It must have required him to deal with extremely small wheels. He had to inspect the gears so closely that sometimes his head disappeared completely into the inscriber.

The Traveler followed this work from below without looking away. His neck grew stiff, and his eyes found the sunlight pouring down from the sky painful. The Soldier and the Condemned Man were keeping each other busy. With the tip of his bayonet the Soldier pulled out the Condemned Man's shirt and trousers which were lying in the hole. The shirt was horribly dirty, and the Condemned Man washed it in the bucket of water. When he was putting on his shirt and trousers, the Soldier and the Condemned Man had to laugh out loud, for the pieces of clothing were cut in two up the back. Perhaps the Condemned Man thought that it was his duty to amuse the Soldier. In his ripped-up clothes he circled around the Soldier, who crouched down on the ground, laughed, and slapped his knees. But they restrained themselves out of consideration for the two gentlemen present.

When the Officer was finally finished up on the machine, with a smile he looked over the whole thing and all its parts one more time, and this time closed the cover of the inscriber, which had been open up to this point. He climbed down, looked into the hole and then at the Condemned Man, observed with satisfaction that he had pulled out his clothes, then went to the bucket of water to wash his hands, recognized too late that it was disgustingly dirty, and was upset that now he couldn't wash his hands. Finally he pushed them into the sand. This option didn't satisfy him, but he had to do what he could in the circumstances. Then he stood up and began to unbutton the coat of his uniform. As he did this, the two lady's handkerchiefs, which he had pushed into the back of his collar, fell into his hands. "Here you have your handkerchiefs," he said and threw them over to the Condemned Man. And to the Traveler he said by way of an explanation, "Presents from the ladies."

In spite of the obvious speed with which he took off the coat of his uniform and then undressed himself completely, he handled each piece of clothing very carefully, even running his fingers over the silver braids on his tunic with special care and shaking a tassel into place. But in great contrast to this care, as soon he was finished handling an article of clothing, he immediately flung it angrily into the hole. The last items he had left were his short sword and its harness. He pulled the sword out of its scabbard, broke it in pieces, gathered up everything—the pieces of the sword, the scabbard, and the harness—and threw them away so forcefully that they rattled against each other down in the pit.

Now he stood there naked. The Traveler bit his lip and said nothing. For he was aware what would happen, but he had no right to hinder the Officer in any way. If the judicial process to which the Officer clung was really so close to the point of being cancelled—perhaps as a result of the intervention of the Traveler, something to which he for his part felt duty-bound—then the Officer was now acting in a completely correct manner. In his place, the Traveler would not have acted any differently.

The Soldier and the Condemned Man at first didn't understand a thing. To begin with they didn't look, not even once. The Condemned Man was extremely happy to get the handkerchiefs back, but he couldn't enjoy them very long, for the Soldier snatched them from him with a quick grab, which he had not anticipated. The Condemned Man then tried to pull the handkerchiefs out from the Soldier's belt, where he had put them for safe keeping, but the Soldier was too wary. So they were fighting, half in jest. Only when the Officer was fully naked did they start to pay attention. The Condemned Man especially seemed to be struck by a premonition of some sort of significant transformation. What had happened to him was now taking place with the Officer. Perhaps this time the procedure would play itself out to its conclusion. The foreign Traveler had probably given the order. So that was revenge. Without having suffered all the way to the end himself, nonetheless he would be completely revenged. A wide, silent laugh now appeared on his face and did not go away.

The Officer, however, had turned towards the machine. If earlier on it had already become clear that he understood the machine thoroughly, one might well get alarmed now at the way he handled it and how it obeyed. He only had to bring his hand near the harrow for it to rise and sink several times, until it had reached the correct position to make room for him. He only had to grasp the bed by the edges, and it already began to quiver. The stump of felt moved up to his mouth. One could see how the Officer really didn't want to accept it, but his hesitation was only momentary—he immediately submitted and took it in. Everything was ready, except that the straps still hung down on the sides. But they were clearly unnecessary. The Officer did not have to be strapped down. When the Condemned Man saw the loose straps, he thought the execution would be incomplete unless they were fastened. He waved eagerly to the Soldier, and they ran over to strap in the Officer. The latter had already stuck out his foot to kick the crank designed to set the inscriber in motion. Then he saw the two men coming. So he pulled his foot back and let himself be strapped in. But now he could no longer reach the crank. Neither the Soldier nor the Condemned Man would find it, and the Traveler was determined not to touch it. But that was unnecessary. Hardly were the straps attached when the machine already started working. The bed quivered, the needles danced on his skin, and the harrow swung up and down. The Traveler had already been staring for some time before he remembered that a wheel in the inscriber was supposed to squeak. But everything was quiet, without the slightest audible hum.

Because of its silent working, the machine did not really attract attention. The Traveler looked over at the Soldier and the Condemned Man. The Condemned Man was the livelier of the two. Everything in the machine interested him. At times he bent down—at other times he stretched up, all the time pointing with his forefinger in order to show something to the Soldier. For the Traveler it was embarrassing. He was determined to remain here until the end, but he could no longer endure the sight of the two men. "Go home," he said. The Soldier might have been ready to do that, but the Condemned Man took the order as a direct punishment. With his hands folded he begged and pleaded to be allowed to stay there. And when the Traveler shook his head and was unwilling to give in, he even knelt down. Seeing that orders were of no help here, the Traveler wanted to go over and chase the two away.

Then he heard a noise from up in the inscriber. He looked up. So was the gear wheel going out of alignment? But it was something else. The lid on the inscriber was lifting up slowly. Then it fell completely open. The teeth of a cog wheel were exposed and lifted up. Soon the entire wheel appeared. It was as if some huge force was compressing the inscriber, so that there was no longer sufficient room for this wheel. The wheel rolled all the way to the edge of the inscriber, fell down, rolled upright a bit in the sand, and then fell over and lay still. But already up on the inscriber another gear wheel was moving upwards. Several others followed—large ones, small ones, ones hard to distinguish. With each of them the same thing happened. One kept thinking that now the inscriber must surely be empty, but then a new cluster with lots of parts would move up, fall down, roll in the sand, and lie still. With all this going on, the Condemned Man totally forgot the Traveler's order. The gear wheels completely delighted him. He kept wanting to grab one, and at the same time he was urging the Soldier to help him. But he kept pulling his hand back startled, for immediately another wheel followed, which, at least in its initial rolling, surprised him.

The Traveler, by contrast, was very upset. Obviously the machine was breaking up. Its quiet operation had been an illusion. He felt as if he had to look after the Officer, now that the latter could no longer look after himself. But while the falling gear wheels were claiming all his attention, he had neglected to look at the rest of the machine. However, when he now bent over the harrow, once the last gear wheel had left the inscriber, he had a new, even more unpleasant surprise. The harrow was not writing but only stabbing, and the bed was not rolling the body, but lifting it, quivering, up into the needles. The Traveler wanted to reach in to stop the whole thing, if possible. This was not the torture the Officer wished to attain. It was murder, pure and simple. He stretched out his hands. But at that point the harrow was already moving upwards and to the side, with the skewered body—just as it did in other cases, but only in the twelfth hour. Blood flowed out in hundreds of streams, not mixed with water—the water tubes had also failed to work this time. Then one last thing went wrong: the body would not come loose from the needles. Its blood streamed out, but it hung over the pit without falling. The harrow wanted to move back to its original position, but, as if it realized that it could not free itself of its load, it remained over the hole.

"Help," the Traveler yelled out to the Soldier and the Condemned Man and grabbed the Officer's feet. He wanted to push against the feet himself and have the two others grab the Officer's head from the other side, so he could be slowly taken off the needles. But now the two men could not make up their mind whether to come or not. The Condemned Man turned away at once. The Traveler had to go over to him and drag him to the Officer's head by force. At this point, almost against his will, he looked at the face of the corpse. It was as it had been in his life. He could discover no sign of the promised transfiguration. What all the others had found in the machine, the Officer had not. His lips were pressed firmly together, his eyes were open and looked as they had when he was alive, his gaze was calm and convinced. The tip of a large iron needle had gone through his forehead.

*

As the Traveler, with the Soldier and the Condemned Man behind him, came to the first houses in the colony, the Soldier pointed to one and said, "That's the tea house."

On the ground floor of one of the houses was a deep, low room, like a cave, with smoke-covered walls and ceiling. On the street side it was open along its full width. Although there was little difference between the tea house and the rest of the houses in the colony, which were all very dilapidated, except for the Commandant's palatial structure, the Traveler was struck by the impression of historical memory, and he felt the power of earlier times. Followed by his companions, he walked closer, going between the unoccupied tables, which stood in the street in front of the tea house, and took a breath of the cool, stuffy air which came from inside. "The old man is buried here," said the Soldier; "a place in the cemetery was denied him by the chaplain. For a long time people were undecided where they should bury him. Finally they buried him here. Of course, the Officer explained none of that to you, for naturally he was the one most ashamed about it. A few times he even tried to dig up the old man at night, but he was always chased off." "Where is the grave?" asked the Traveler, who could not believe the Soldier. Instantly both men, the Soldier and the Condemned Man, ran in front of him and with hands outstretched pointed to the place where the grave was located. They led the Traveler to the back wall, where guests were sitting at a few tables. They were presumably dock workers, strong men with short, shiny, black beards. None of them wore coats, and their shirts were torn. They were poor, oppressed people. As the Traveler came closer, a few got up, leaned against the wall, and looked at him. A whisper went up around the Traveler—"It's a foreigner. He wants to look at the grave." They pushed one of the tables aside, under which there was a real grave stone. It was a simple stone, low enough for it to remain hidden under a table. It bore an inscription in very small letters. In order to read it the Traveler had to kneel down. It read, "Here rests the Old Commandant. His followers, who are now not permitted to have a name, buried him in this grave and erected this stone. There exists a prophecy that the Commandant will rise again after a certain number of years and from this house will lead his followers to a re-conquest of the colony. Have faith and wait!"

When the Traveler had read it and got up, he saw the men standing around him and smiling, as if they had read the inscription with him, found it ridiculous, and were asking him to share their opinion. The Traveler acted as if he hadn't noticed, distributed some coins among them, waited until the table was pushed back over the grave, left the tea house, and went to the harbour.

In the tea house the Soldier and the Condemned Man had come across some people they knew who detained them. However, they must have broken free of them soon, because by the time the Traveler found himself in the middle of a long staircase which led to the boats, they were already running after him. They probably wanted to force the Traveler at the last minute to take them with him. While the Traveler was haggling at the bottom of the stairs with a sailor about his passage out to the steamer, the two men were racing down the steps in silence, for they didn't dare cry out. But as they reached the bottom, the Traveler was already in the boat, and the sailor at once cast off from shore. They could still have jumped into the boat, but the Traveler picked up a heavy knotted rope from the boat bottom, threatened them with it, and thus prevented them from jumping in.

3

MACHINE AND ORGANISM

Georges Canguilhem

The mechanical theory of the organism, after having long been accepted as dogma in biology, is today considered by biologists adhering to dialectical materialism to be a narrow and insufficient point of view. Dealing with this theory from a philosophical point of view could therefore seem to confirm the widespread notion that philosophy does not have its own domain, that it is but speculation's poor relation, obliged to dress in clothes worn out and abandoned by scientists. We would like to try to show that the subject is much more vast and complex, and that it is philosophically more important than its reduction to a matter of doctrine and method in biology presupposes.

We might even say that the science that would appropriate this problem is itself still a problem, for, though there are good works on technology, the very notion and methods of an "organology" remain vague. Thus, paradoxically, far from coming in belatedly to occupy an abandoned viewpoint, philosophy points science toward a position to take. Indeed, the problem of the relations between machine and organism has generally been studied only in one direction: almost always, the attempt has been to explain the structure and function of the organism on the basis of the structure and function of an already-constructed machine. Only rarely has anyone sought to understand the very construction of the machine on the basis of the structure and function of the organism.

Philosophers and mechanist biologists have taken the machine to be a given—or, when they have studied its construction, they have explained it by invoking human calculation. They have appealed to the engineer—that is, for them, to the scientist.

Deceived by the ambiguity of the term mechanical, they have seen machines as nothing but theorems solidified and displayed *in concreto* by a totally secondary operation of construction—the simple application of a knowledge conscious of its import and certain of its effects. However, we believe that it is not possible to address the biological problem of the organism-machine by separating it from a technological problem that it presumes resolved—that of the relationship between technique and science. This problem is usually explained by way of the logical and chronological anteriority of knowledge vis-a-vis its applications. But we will try to show that one cannot understand the phenomenon of the construction of machines by recourse to authentically biological notions without engaging at the same time the problem of the originality of the technical phenomenon in relation to the scientific phenomenon.

We will thus examine successively: the meaning of the comparison of the organism to a machine; the relationship between mechanism and finalism; the reversal of the traditional relationship between machine and organism; and the philosophical consequences of this reversal.

*

With the exception of vertebrates, living beings and their forms rarely display to the scrupulous observer devices [*dispositifs*] that could evoke the idea of a mechanism, in the sense given to this term by scientists. In *La pensée technique* [*Technical Thought*], for example, Julien Pacotte observes that the articulations of the limbs and the movements of the eyeball correspond, in the living organism, to what mathematicians call a mechanism.[1] We may define a machine as an artificial construct, a work of man, whose essential function depends on mechanisms. A mechanism is a configuration of solids in motion such that the motion does not abolish the configuration. The mechanism is thus an assemblage of deformable parts, with periodic restoration of the relations between them. The assemblage consists in a system of connections with a determined degree of freedom: for example, a pendulum and a cam valve each have one degree of freedom; a threaded screw has two. The material realization of these degrees of freedom consists in guides—that is, in limitations on the movements of solids in contact. In any machine, movement is thus a function of the assemblage, and mechanism is a function of configuration. The fundamental principles of a general theory of mechanisms thus understood can be found, for example, in Franz Reuleaux's well-known work on kinematics.[2]

The movements produced (but not created) by machines are geometrical, measurable displacements. The mechanism regulates and transforms a movement whose impulse is transmitted to it. A mechanism is not a motor. One of the simplest examples of such transformation of movements consists in gathering an initial translateral movement into rotational form via the intermediary of technical devices [*dispositifs techniques*] such as a wheel crank or an eccentric crank. Naturally, mechanisms can be combined, by superposition or by addition. One can construct mechanisms that modify the configuration of the original mechanism and render the machine alternately capable of several mechanisms. This is the case in modifications effected by release or engagement actions—for example, the freewheel [*le dispositif de roue libre*] on a bicycle.[3]

We have already stated that what is the rule in human industry is the exception in the structure of the organism and in nature, and we must add to this that, in the history of techniques, of human inventions, configurations by assemblage were not the earliest. The oldest known tools are made of one piece. The construction of axes or arrows by assembling a flint and a shaft, or the construction of nets or fabrics, was not primitive. Their appearance is generally dated to the end of the Quaternary.

This brief reminder of the elementary concepts of kinematics is useful in allowing us to pose in all its paradoxical significance the following problem: How do we explain the fact that a model for understanding the structure and functions of the organism has been sought in machines and in mechanisms, as defined above? It seems possible to answer that this is because the representation of the living being by a mechanical model does not involve only mechanisms of the kinematic type. A machine, as defined above, is not self-sufficient, since it must receive from elsewhere the movement it transforms. Therefore, one can only represent a machine in movement by associating it with a source of energy.[4]

For a very long time, kinematic mechanisms were set in motion by human or animal muscular effort. At that stage, it was obviously tautological to explain the movement of a living being by likening it to the movement of a machine dependent, for its own movement, on the muscular effort of a living thing. Thus, the mechanical explanation of the functions of life historically presupposes—as has often been shown—the construction of automatons, whose name signifies at once the miraculous character and the apparent self-sufficiency of a mechanism transforming an energy that is not—at least not immediately—the effect of a human or animal muscular effort.

This comes across in a well-known text:

Examine with some attention the physical economy of man: What do you find? The jaws armed with teeth: Are they anything but pliers? The stomach is but a retort; the veins, the arteries, the entire system of blood vessels are hydraulic tubes; the heart is a spring; the viscera are but filters, screens; the lungs are but bellows. And what are the muscles, if not cords? What is the ocular angle, if it is not a pulley? And so on. Let us leave it to the chemists with their grand words of "fusion," of "sublimation," of "precipitation" to want to explain nature and thus to establish a separate philosophy; it is nonetheless incontestable that all these phenomena must be related to the laws of equilibrium, of angles, of cords, of the spring, and of the other elements of mechanics.

This text is not from whom one might think, but from the *De praxi medica*,[5] published in 1696 and written by Giorgio Baglivi (1668–1706), an Italian doctor of the iatromechanic school. Founded by Giovanni Alfonso Borelli (1608–79), this school of iatromechanists clearly seems to have been influenced by Descartes, despite the fact that in Italy the school is more commonly linked to Galileo, for reasons of national prestige.[6] This text is of interest because it places angle, cord, and spring on the same level as principles of explanation. It is clear, nevertheless, that from a mechanical point of view there is a difference between these engines; whereas the cord is a mechanism of transmission and the angle a mechanism for the transformation of a given movement, the spring is a motor. No doubt, it is a motor that merely gives back what has been lent to it, but at the moment of its action it appears to be endowed with independence. In Baglivi's text, it is the heart—the *primum movens*—that is likened to a spring. In it resides the motor of the whole organism.

The formation of a mechanist explanation of organic phenomena thus requires that, in addition to machines in the sense of kinematic devices [*dispositifs cinématiques*], there exist machines as motors, drawing their energy, at the moment of its use, from a source other than animal muscle. This is why, although Baglivi's text should refer us to Descartes, we must actually trace back to Aristotle the likening of the organism to a machine. When considering the Cartesian theory of the animal-machine, it is difficult to establish whether Descartes had precursors in the matter. Those who look for Descartes' predecessors generally cite Gómez Pereira, a Spanish doctor of the second half of the sixteenth century. It is quite true that Pereira, before Descartes, thought he was able to demonstrate that animals are pure machines and that, in any case, they do not possess the sensory soul so often attributed to them.[7] But it is indisputable that Aristotle found in the construction of war machines such as catapults license to liken the movements of animals to mechanical, automatic movements. This has been established by Alfred Espinas in his article "L'organisme ou la machine vivante en Grèce au IVe siècle avant J.C." (The Organism or Living Machine in the Greece of the Fourth Century B.C.).[8] Espinas traces the kinship of the problems treated by Aristotle in his treatise *De motu animalium* and his collection *Quaestiones mechanicae*.[9] Aristotle indeed likens the organs of animal motion to *organa*, that is, to the parts of war machines (e.g., to the arm of a catapult, which launches a projectile), and he compares the course of their movement to that of machines capable of releasing, after being set off, a stored-up energy, automatic machines, of which catapults were the typical example in his period. In the same work, Aristotle likens the movement of limbs to mechanisms, in the sense given above—he is on this point faithful to Plato, who, in the *Timeaus*, defines the movement of vertebrates on the basis of pivots.[10]

It is true that Aristotle's theory of movement is very different from that of Descartes. According to Aristotle, the principle of all movement is the soul. All movement requires a first motor. Movement presupposes the immobile: what moves the body is desire, and what explains desire is the soul, just as what explains potentiality is actuality. Despite this difference in the explanation of motion, the fact remains that for Aristotle, as later for Descartes, the comparison of the organism to a machine presupposes man-made devices [*dispositifs*] in which an automatic mechanism is linked to a source of energy whose motor effects continue well after the human or animal effort they release has ceased. It is this interval between the storing up and the release of energy by the mechanism that allows one to forget the relationship of dependence between the mechanism's effects and the action of a living being. When Descartes turns to machines to find analogies in his explanation of the organism, he invokes automatons with springs and hydraulic automatons. He is thus a tributary, intellectually speaking, of the technical forms of his age: of the existence of clocks and watches, water mills, artificial fountains, pipe organs, etc. We may therefore say that, so long as a living human or animal "sticks" to the machine, the explanation of the organism by way of the machine cannot be born. This explanation can only be conceived once human ingenuity has constructed apparatuses [*appareils*] that imitate organic movements: for example, the launching of a projectile, the back and forth movement of a saw—apparatuses whose action (their construction and activation aside) takes place independently of man.

We have just said it twice: *can* be born. Is that to say that this explanation *must* be born? How do we account for the appearance, so clear and abrupt in Descartes' thought, of a mechanist interpretation of biological phenomena? This theory is evidently related to a change in the economic and political structure of Western societies, but the nature of this relationship remains obscure.

This question has been addressed by Pierre-Maxime Schuhl in *Machinisme et philosophie*.[11] Schuhl has shown that within ancient philosophy the opposition between science and technics overlies the oppositions between freedom and servitude, and, more profoundly, between nature and art. Schuhl refers to the Aristotelian opposition between natural and violent movement. The latter is engendered by mechanisms in order to counteract nature and has the following characteristics: it exhausts itself quickly, and it never engenders a habit—that is to say, a permanent, self-reproducing disposition [*disposition*].

Here we come across a rather difficult problem in the history of civilization and in the philosophy of history. In Aristotle, the hierarchy of freedom and servitude, theory and practice, nature and art parallels an economic and political hierarchy—the hierarchy, within the city, of free men and slaves.[12] A slave, says Aristotle in the *Politics*, is an animate machine.[13] From this emerges a question that Schuhl merely indicates. Does the Greek conception of the dignity of science engender contempt for technology and thereby a paucity of inventions, thus leading, in a certain sense, to a difficulty in transposing the results of technical activity to the explanation of nature?[14] Or, rather, does the concept of the eminent dignity of a purely speculative science, a contemplative and disinterested knowledge, translate the absence of technological inventions? Is a contempt for work the cause of slavery, or does an abundance of slaves, in connection with military supremacy, engender contempt for work? Must we here explain ideology by the economic structure of society or, rather, that structure by the orientation of ideas? Is it the ease with which man exploits man that leads to disdain for techniques of man's exploitation of nature—or is it the difficulty of man's exploitation of nature that necessitates justification of man's exploitation of man? Is there a causal relation here, and if so, in which direction? Or are we faced with a global structure of reciprocal relations and influences?

Father Lucien Laberthonnière poses an analogous problem in *Les études sur Descartes*, notably in the appendix to volume 2, "La physique de Descartes et la physique d'Aristote," which contrasts a physics of the artist and aesthete to a physics of the engineer and artisan.[15] Father Laberthonnière seems to think that here what is determinative is the idea, since the Cartesian revolution in the philosophy of technics presupposes the Christian revolution. For his right and duty to exploit matter, without any regard for it, to be affirmed, man first had to be conceived of as a being that transcends nature and matter. In other words, it was necessary that man be valorized for nature to be devalorized. It was then necessary that men be thought of as radically and originally equal so that, the political technique of the exploitation of man by man having been condemned, the possibility and duty of a technique for man's exploitation of nature could appear. This allows Father Laberthonnière to speak of the Christian origin of Cartesian physics. He himself then raises the following two objections. First, the physics and techniques made possible by Christianity came, with Descartes, well after the foundation of Christianity as a religion. Second, is there not an opposition between humanist philosophy, which sees man as master and possessor of nature, and Christianity, which was considered by the humanists to be a religion of salvation, of flight into the beyond, and thus responsible for a contempt for vital and technique-related values, for any technical arrangement of human life in this world below? Father Laberthonnière says: "Time plays no role in the matter." It is not certain that time plays no role in the matter. In any case, one cannot deny—and this has been shown in classic texts—that certain technical inventions, such as the horseshoe or the yoke, modifying the usage of animal motor force, did more for the emancipation of slaves than any preaching could.

We said earlier that one might look for a solution to the problem of the relationship between mechanist philosophy and the ensemble of economic and social conditions in which it arises in either of two directions: either in a causal relation or in a global structure. Franz Borkenau, in his book *Der Übergang vom feudalen zum bürgerlichen Weltbild* (*The Transition from a Feudal to a Bourgeois Worldview*), sees it as a causality.[16] This author affirms that, at the beginning of the seventeenth century, the mechanist conception eclipsed the qualitative philosophy of antiquity and of the Middle Ages. The success of this conception translates, within the ideological sphere, the economic fact of the organization and spread of factories. For Borkenau, the division of artisanal work into uniform and qualityless segmented acts of production imposed the conception of an abstract social work [*travail social abstrait*]. The breakdown of work into simple, identical, repeated movements demanded a comparison of labor hours, so that prices and salaries could be calculated, and thus led to the quantification of a process previously regarded as qualitative.[17] For him, the calculation of work as a pure, mathematically treatable quantity was the basis and the point of departure for a mechanist conception of the universe of life. It is thus through the reduction of all value to economic value, to a "callous cash payment," as Marx puts it in *The Communist Manifesto*, that the mechanist conception of the universe was a fundamentally bourgeois *Weltanschauung*.[18] Ultimately, says Borkenau, behind the theory of the animal-machine we should detect the norms of the nascent capitalist economy. Descartes, Galileo, and Hobbes would thus have been the unconscious harbingers of this economic revolution.

These ideas of Borkenau have been outlined and critiqued with great vigor in an article by Henryk Grossman.[19] According to Grossman, Borkenau does away with 150 years of economic and ideological history by making the mechanist conception contemporaneous with the appearance of manufacturing at the beginning of the seventeenth century. Borkenau writes as if Leonardo da Vinci had never existed. Referring to Pierre Duhem's work, in *Les origines de la statique*,[20] and to the 1904–1907 publication of Leonardo's manuscripts,[21] Grossman affirms, along with Gabriel Séailles, that the publication of Leonardo's manuscripts pushes the origins of modern science back by more than a century. The quantification of the notion of work is first of all mathematical, and this precedes its economic quantification. In addition, the norms for the capitalist assessment of production had been defined by Italian bankers beginning in the thirteenth century. Relying on Marx, Grossman reminds us that, as a general rule, there was, originally, no true division of labor in factories. Rather, the factory originally brought together in the same locale hitherto scattered artisans. It is thus not, according to him, the calculation of prices by labor hours but rather the development of mechanization that is the authentic cause of the mechanist conception of the universe. The development of mechanization has its origins in the Renaissance period. Descartes thus consciously rationalized a mechanist technique much more than he unconsciously translated the practices of a capitalist economy. Mechanics is, for Descartes, a *theory of machines*—it presupposes a spontaneous invention, which science must then consciously and explicitly promote.

Which machines modified man's relationship to nature before Descartes, giving birth to a hope unknown to the ancients and calling for the justification and the rationalization of this hope? They were, first and foremost, firearms, which interested Descartes scarcely at all, and only insofar as they related to the problem of projectiles.[22] By contrast, Descartes was greatly interested in watches and clocks, in hoisting machines, in water-powered machines, etc. Consequently, we say that Descartes integrated into his philosophy a human phenomenon—the construction of machines—much more than he transposed into ideology the social phenomenon of capitalist production.

What are, then, in Cartesian theory, the relations between mechanism and finalism contained within the comparison of organism to machine?

*

The theory of animal-machines is inseparable from *Cogito ergo sum*. The radical distinction between soul and body, thought and extension, entails affirming the substantial unity of all matter, regardless of its form, and of all thought, regardless of its function.[23] Given that the soul has but one function, that of judgment, it is impossible to admit the existence of animal souls, since we have no sign that animals judge, being incapable of language and invention.[24]

The refusal to grant a soul—that is to say, reason—to animals does not entail, according to Descartes, denying that they have life, which consists in no more than the warmth of the heart, or sensitivity, inasmuch as this depends on the arrangement of organs.[25]

In the same letter, there appears a moral foundation for the theory of the animal-machine. Descartes does to the animal what Aristotle did to the slave: he devalorizes it in order to justify its use by man as an instrument: "My opinion is not so much cruel toward animals as indulgent toward human beings—at least to those who are not given to the superstitions of Pythagoras—since it absolves them from the suspicion of crime when they eat or kill animals."[26] Remarkably, one finds this same argument reversed in a text by Leibniz:[27] if one is forced to see the animal as more than a machine, one must become a Pythagorean and give up dominating animals.[28] We find ourselves here in the presence of an attitude typical of Western man. The theoretical mechanization of life and the technical utilization of the animal are inseparable. Man can make himself master and possessor of nature only if he denies all natural purposes and can consider all of nature, including, apparently, animate nature—except for himself—to be a means.

This is what legitimates the construction of a mechanical model of the living body, including the human body—for already in Descartes the human body, if not man, is a machine. Descartes finds this mechanical model, as we have said, in automatons: that is to say, in moving machines.[29]

In order to give the full meaning of Descartes' theory, we now propose to read the beginning of his *Traité de l'homme* (*Treatise of Man*), first published in Leyden from a Latin version in 1662, and in French for the first time in 1664:

These men will be composed, as we are, of a soul and a body, and I must first separately describe for you the body; then, also separately, the soul; and finally I must show you how these two natures would have to be joined and united to constitute men resembling us. I assume their body to be but a statue, an earthen machine formed intentionally by God to be as much as possible like us. Thus not only does He give it externally the shapes and colors of all the parts of our bodies; He also places inside it all the pieces required to make it walk, eat, breathe, and imitate whichever of our own functions can be imagined to proceed from mere matter and to depend entirely on the arrangement of our organs. We see clocks, artificial fountains, mills, and similar machines which, though made entirely by man, lack not the power to move, of themselves, in various ways. And I think you will agree that the present machine could have even more sorts of movements than I have imagined and more ingenuity than I have assigned, for our supposition is that it was created by God.[30]

If one reads this text as naïvely as possible, it seems that the theory of the animal-machine depends for its meaning on the enunciation of two postulates, which are too often neglected. The first is that there exists a builder God, and the second is that the living is given as such, prior to the construction of machines. In other words, it is necessary, in order to understand the machine-animal, to see it as having been preceded, logically and chronologically, both by God as efficient cause and by a preexisting living being as formal and final cause to be imitated. In short, in the theory of the animal-machine, which has generally been seen as a rupture with the Aristotelian conception of causality, we propose that all the types of causality invoked by Aristotle are found, though not in the same place and not simultaneously.

The construction of the living machine implies, if one reads the text well, an obligation to imitate a prior organic given. The construction of a mechanical model presupposes a vital original, and, in the end, we may wonder whether Descartes is not closer here to Aristotle than to Plato. The Platonic demiurge copies the Ideas. The Idea is a model of which the natural object is a copy. The Cartesian God, the *Artifex Maximus*, works to equal the living itself. The model for the living machine is the living itself. The Idea of the living, which divine art imitates, is the living thing. And just as a regular polygon is inscribed within a circle, and in order to derive the circle from it, it is necessary to pass through infinity, so the mechanical artifice is inscribed within life, and to derive one from the other, it is necessary to pass through infinity—that is to say, God. It is this that seems to emerge at the end of the text: "And I think you will agree that the present machine could have even more sorts of movements than I have imagined and more ingenuity than I have assigned, for our supposition is that it was created by God."[31] The theory of the animal-machine would thus be to life what axiomatics is to geometry—that is to say, merely a rational reconstruction, which ignores only by means of a feint the existence of what it represents and the anteriority of production over rational legitimization.

This aspect of the Cartesian theory, moreover, was noticed by an anatomist of the time, the famous Nicolas Steno, in the *Discourse on the Anatomy of the Brain* [*Discours sur l'anatomie du cerveau*], delivered in Paris in 1665—that is, one year after the appearance of the *Treatise of Man*. Steno, while paying homage to Descartes (all the more remarkable given that anatomists have not always had much sympathy for Descartes' anatomy), observes that Descartes' man is man reconstructed by Descartes under the cover of God, but that this is not the man of the anatomist.[32] It may thus be said that, in substituting mechanism for the organism, Descartes effaces teleology from life, but he does so only in appearance, for he reassembles it, in its entirety, at his point of departure. Anatomical form substitutes for dynamic formation, but as this form is a technical product, all possible teleology is contained within the technique of production. In truth, one cannot, it seems, oppose mechanism and finalism, one cannot oppose mechanism and anthropomorphism, for if the functioning of a machine is *explained* by relations of pure causality, the construction of a machine can be *understood* neither without purpose nor without man. A machine is made by man and for man, with a view toward certain ends to be obtained, in the form of effects to be produced.[33] Thus, Descartes' project of explaining life mechanically eliminates purpose in its anthropomorphic form. Yet in realizing this project, one anthropomorphism substitutes for another. A technological anthropomorphism substitutes for a political anthropomorphism.

In *Description of the Human Body* [*La description du corps humain*], a short treatise written in 1648, Descartes undertakes to explain voluntary movement in man. He makes the case that the body obeys the soul only on the condition of first being mechanically predisposed [*mécaniquement disposé*] to do so—a claim that held sway over the entire theory of automatic and reflex movements until the nineteenth century. The soul's decision is not a sufficient condition for the movement of the body. Descartes says: "The soul cannot produce any movement without the appropriate disposition [*bien disposés*] of the bodily organs which are required for making the movement. On the contrary, when all the bodily organs are disposed [*disposés*] for some movement, the body has no need of the soul in order to produce that movement."[34] Descartes means that when the soul moves the body, it does not do so in the way that (as popular representation would have it) a king or a general commands his subjects or soldiers. Instead, by likening the body to a clock mechanism, he means to say that the movements of the organs direct one another like interlocked cogwheels. Thus, in Descartes, the technological image of "command" (a type of positive causality by a device [*de causalité positive par un dispositif*] or by the play of mechanical connections) substitutes for the political image of commandment (a kind of magical causality; causality by word or by sign).

Descartes' argument here is the opposite of Bernard's in his critique of vitalism in *Leçons sur les phénomènes de la vie communs aux animaux et aux végétaux* (1878–1879).[35] While refusing to accept the separate existence of a vital force, because such a force "could not possibly do anything," Bernard surprisingly admits that it could, however, direct "phenomena that it does not produce."[36] In other words, Bernard substitutes for the notion of a vital force conceived as a worker the notion of a vital force conceived as a legislator or a guide. This is to accept that it is possible to direct without acting; we might call this a magical conception of direction, because it implies that directing transcends execution. On the contrary, according to Descartes, a mechanical device that executes [*dispositif mécanique d'exécution*] replaces a power that directs and commands—but God has set the direction once and for all; the direction of the movement is included by the builder in the mechanical device that executes it.

In short, with the Cartesian explanation, in spite of appearances, it may seem that we have not taken a single step outside finalism. The reason is that mechanism can explain everything so long as we take machines as already granted, but it cannot account for the construction of machines. No machine builds machines—and one could even say that, in a certain sense, to explain organs or organisms through mechanical models is to explain the organ using the organ. It is a tautology, basically, because—and we shall try to justify this interpretation—machines can be considered organs of the human species.[37] A tool or a machine is an organ, and organs are tools or machines. Consequently, it is hard to see where the opposition between mechanism and finalism lies. No one doubts that a mechanism is needed to ensure the success of a given purpose, and inversely, every mechanism must have a sense, for a mechanism is not just an accidental series of interdependent movements. In reality, the opposition is between those mechanisms whose sense is manifest and those whose sense is latent. The sense of a lock or a clock is manifest; the sense of the pincers of a crab, so often invoked as marvels of adaptation, is latent. As a result, it does not seem possible to deny the purpose of certain biological mechanisms. Let us take an example that often serves as an argument for certain mechanist biologists. They deny the purpose of the enlargement of a woman's pelvis prior to giving birth; yet one need only turn the question around: given that the widest dimension of the fetus exceeds the widest dimension of the womb by 1 to 1.5 centimeters, if the womb were not to enlarge a bit, by a kind of loosening of the symphyses and a backward rocking motion of the sacrococcygien, then birth would be impossible. We are warranted in rejecting the suggestion that an act whose biological sense is so clear is possible only because a mechanism without any biological sense allows it. And we have to use the word *allow* here because the absence of this mechanism would forbid it. It is well known that, when confronted with an unfamiliar mechanism, in order to verify that it really is a mechanism—a necessary sequence of operations—we are obliged to try to find out what effect is expected from it, what end has been envisioned. We cannot determine its use from the form and structure of the apparatus [*appareil*] unless we already know the machine's use, or that of analogous machines. It is thus necessary first to see the machine functioning so as then to appear able to deduce the function from the structure.

*

We have come to the point where the Cartesian relationship between machine and organism is reversed.

In an organism—and this is too well known to need insisting—one observes phenomena of self-construction, self-conservation, self-regulation, and self-repair.

In a machine, its construction is foreign and presupposes the ingenuity of the mechanic [*l'ingéniosité du mécanicien*]; conservation demands the constant surveillance and vigilance of the machinist, and we know how irreparably certain complicated machines can be damaged through lack of attention or surveillance. As for regulation and repair, they also presuppose the periodic intervention of human action. There are doubtless devices [*dispositifs*] that regulate themselves, but these are machines superposed upon machines by man. The construction of servomechanisms or electronic automatons displaces the relationship of man to machine but does not alter its sense.

In the machine, the rules of a rational accounting are rigorously verified. The whole is strictly the sum of the parts. The effect is dependent on the order of causes. In addition, a machine displays a clear functional rigidity, a rigidity made increasingly pronounced by the practice of standardization. Standardization is the simplification of models and replacement parts, the rendering uniform of metric and qualitative characteristics, which allows for the interchangeability of parts. Any part is equivalent to any other with the same purpose-within, naturally, a margin of tolerance that defines manufacturing limits.

With the properties of a machine in comparison to those of the organism thus defined, is there more or less purpose in the machine than in the organism?

It can easily be said that there is more purpose in the machine than in the organism, because the purpose of the machine is rigid, univocal, univalent. A machine cannot replace another machine. The more limited the purpose, the more the margin of tolerance is reduced, and the more hardened and pronounced the purpose appears to be. In the organism, by contrast, one observes—and this again is too well known to be insisted upon—a vicariousness of functions, a polyvalence of organs. Doubtless, this vicariousness of functions and polyvalence of organs are not absolute, but they are so much greater than in the machine that there can really be no comparison.[38] As an example of the vicariousness of functions, one may cite a simple, well-known case: childhood aphasia. Hemiplegia on the right side is almost never accompanied by aphasia, because other regions of the brain ensure the language function. And when aphasia appears in a child under nine years old, it dissipates rapidly.[39] As for the matter of the polyvalence of organs, one may simply cite the fact that, although we believe that for most organs there is some defined function, in reality we are ignorant of other functions they may serve. In this manner, the stomach is said in principle to be the organ of digestion. Yet it is a fact that, following a gastrectomy to treat an ulcer, one observes problems of digestion less than problems of haematopoiesis. It was thus discovered that the stomach behaves like an internal secretion gland. We could also cite here—and not just as a display of wonders—the recent example of an experiment performed by Robert Courrier, professor of biology at the Collège de France. Courrier made an incision on a gravid rabbit's uterus, extracted one placenta, and placed it in the peritoneal cavity. The placenta grafted onto the intestine and nourished itself as normal. Once the graft was effected, the rabbit's ovaries were removed—that is to say, the pregnancy function of the *corpus luteum* was thereby suppressed. At this moment, all the placentas in the uterus aborted, and only the placenta placed in the peritoneal cavity came to term. Here is an example where the intestine behaves like a uterus, even, one could say, with more success than the uterus itself.

On this point, we are thus tempted to reverse a proposition of Aristotle's. He writes in the *Politics*: "For nature is not stingy, like the smith who fashions the Delphian knife for many uses; she makes each thing for a single use, and every instrument is best made when intended for one and not many things."[40] On the contrary, it seems that this definition of purpose is better suited to the machine than to the organism. We must at least admit that, in the organism, a plurality of functions can adapt to the singularity of an organ. An organism thus has greater latitude of action than a machine. It has less purpose and more potentialities.[41] The living organism acts in accordance with empiricism, whereas the machine, which is the product of calculation, verifies the norms of calculation, that is, the rational norms of identity, consistency, and predictability. Life, by contrast, is experience, that is to say, improvisation, the utilization of occurrences; it is an attempt in all directions. From this follows a massive and often neglected fact: life tolerates monstrosities. There is no machine monster. There is no mechanical pathology, as Bichat already observes in 1801 in *General Anatomy Applied to Physiology and Medicine* [*Anatomie générale appliquée à la physiologie et à la médecine*].[42] Whereas monsters are still living beings, there is no distinction between normal and pathological in physics and mechanics. The distinction between the normal and the pathological holds for living beings alone.

Above all, what led to the abandonment of mechanist representations in the interpretation of living phenomena was work in experimental embryology, which showed that the seed does not contain within it a sort of "specific machinery" (Cuénot[43]) destined, once set in motion, automatically to produce such and such an organ. That was undoubtedly Descartes' conception. In the "Description of the Human Body," he writes: "If one knew well all the parts of the seminal fluid of a species of particular animal—for example, man—one could deduce, from this alone and for sure and mathematical reasons, the entire figure and conformity of each of its members—just as, reciprocally, by knowing several particularities of this conformity, one could deduce the seminal fluid."[44] However, as Guillaume points out, it seems that the more one compares living beings to automatic machines, the better one understands their function but the less one understands their genesis.[45] If the Cartesian conception were true—that is to say, if there were both preformation in the seed and mechanism in development, an alteration at the outset would disturb or even entirely prevent the development of the egg.

In fact, this is far from being so—as, thanks to the works of Driesch, Hörstadius, Spemann, and Mangold, the study of the potentialities of the egg has made clear the difficulty of reducing embryological development to a mechanist model. Let us take as an example Hörstadius's experiments on the sea urchin egg. He cut sea urchin egg A at stage 16 along a horizontally symmetrical plane, and egg B along a vertically symmetrical plane. He then joined one-half of A to one-half of B, and the resulting egg developed normally. Driesch took a sea-urchin egg at stage 16 and compressed it between two strips, modifying the reciprocal position of the cells at the two poles; the egg developed normally. These two experiments allow us to conclude that the effect is indifferent to the way in which the causes are arranged. Another experiment is even more striking. It is also Driesch's, and it consists in extracting the blastomeres of the sea-urchin egg at stage 2. The blastomeres are dissociated either mechanically or chemically, in sea water depleted of calcium salts. The result is that each blastomere gives birth to a larva that is normal, apart from its dimensions. Here, consequently, the effect is indifferent to the quantity of the cause. The quantitative decrease in cause does not qualitatively alter the effect. And conversely, when one conjoins two sea-urchin eggs, one obtains a single larva, larger than normal. This is further confirmation of the effect's indifference to the quantity of the cause. The experiment by multiplication of the cause confirms the experiment by division of the cause.

It must be said that it is impossible to reduce the development of all eggs to this schema. It has long been asked whether we are dealing with two sorts of eggs—regulated eggs of the sea-urchin egg type and mosaic eggs of the frog-egg type, in which the cellular future of the first blastomeres, whether they are dissociated or stay together, is identical. Most biologists at present accept that there is simply a difference of precocity in the appearance of determination among "mosaic" eggs. For one thing, from a certain stage onward, regulation eggs behave like mosaic eggs; for another, the blastomere of a frog egg at stage 2 produces a complete embryo, as does a regulation egg if it is turned upside down.[46]

It seems to us, then, that it is an illusion to think that purpose can be expelled from the organism by comparing it to a composite of automatisms, no matter how complex. So long as the construction of the machine is not a function of the machine itself, so long as the totality of an organism is not equivalent to the sum of its parts (parts discovered by analysis once the organism has already been given), it seems legitimate to hold that biological organization must necessarily precede the existence and meaning of mechanical constructions. From the philosophical point of view, it is less important to explain the machine than to understand it. And to understand it is to inscribe it within human history by inscribing human history in life, without, however, neglecting the appearance, with man, of a culture irreducible to simple nature.

*

Thus we have come to see in the machine a *fact of culture* expressing itself in mechanisms that, for their part, are nothing but a *fact of nature to be explained*. In a famous text of the *Principles*, Descartes writes: "It is certain that all the rules of mechanics belong to physics, *to the extent that all artificial things are thereby natural*. Since, for example, when a watch counts the hours, by using the cogs from which it is made, this is no less natural for it than for a tree to produce fruit."[47] But, from our point of view, we can and we must invert the relationship between the watch and the tree, and say that the wheels a watch is made of, so as to show the hours, and, in general, all the pieces of mechanisms assembled so as to produce an effect—an effect at first only dreamed or desired—are the immediate or derived products of a technical activity as authentically organic as the bringing forth of fruit by trees, an activity, in the beginning, as little conscious of the rules and laws ensuring its efficacy as plant life is. The logical anteriority, at any given moment, of a knowledge of physics to the construction of machines cannot and must not allow us to forget the absolute chronological and biological anteriority of the construction of machines to the knowledge of physics.

Now, contrary to Descartes, one author has affirmed both the irreducibility of the organism to the machine and, symmetrically, the irreducibility of art to science. This is Kant, in the *Critique of Judgment*. It is true that in France we are not used to looking for a philosophy of techniques in Kant, but German writers who have been interested in these problems, especially from 1870 onward, have not failed to do so.

In paragraph 65 of the "Critique of the Teleological Power of Judgment," Kant uses the example of the watch, so dear to Descartes, to distinguish machine from organism. In a machine, he writes, each part exists for another, but not by another. No piece is produced by another piece; no piece is produced by the whole; nor is any whole produced by another whole of the same species. There is no watch-making watch. No part replaces itself by itself. No whole replaces a missing part. The machine thus possesses motor force, but not a formative energy capable of transmitting itself to external matter and propagating itself. In paragraph 75, Kant distinguishes man's intentional technique from life's unintentional technique. But in paragraph 43 (from the "Critique of the Aesthetic Power of Judgment"), Kant defines the originality of this intentional human technique relative to knowledge in an important text:

Art, as human skill, is distinguished also from *science* (as *ability* from *knowledge*), as a practical from a theoretical faculty, as technic from theory (as the art of surveying from geometry). For this reason, also, what one *can* do the moment one only *knows* what is to be done, hence without anything more than sufficient knowledge of the desired result, is not called art. To art that alone belongs for which the possession of the most complete knowledge does not involve one's having then and there the skill to do it. Camper describes very exactly how the best shoe must be made, but he, doubtless, was not able to turn one out himself.[48]

This text is cited by Paul Krannhals in *The Universal Meaning of Technique* [*Der Weltsinn der Technik*]; he sees in it, rightly, it would seem, a recognition of the fact that every technique essentially and positively includes a vital originality irreducible to rationalization.[49] Indeed, let us consider the fact that dexterity in making an adjustment, or synthesis in the process of production—what we customarily call ingenuity [*l'ingéniosité*], responsibility for which we sometimes delegate to an instinct—all this is as inexplicable in its formative movement as the production of a mammal egg outside of the ovary may be, even if we were to presume the physico-chemical composition of protoplasm and the sexual hormones to be completely known.

We therefore find that the works of ethnographers shed more (though still weak) light on the construction of machines than those of engineers [*ingénieurs*].[50] In France, it is ethnographers who are today closest to constituting a philosophy of technique, in which philosophers have lost interest, since they have been attentive, above all, to the philosophy of science. Ethnographers, by contrast, have been attentive to the relationship between the production of the first tools, the first devices [*dispositifs*] for acting on nature, and organic activity itself. The only philosopher in France who, to our knowledge, has asked questions of this order is Alfred Espinas, and we refer the reader to his classic 1897 work *Les origines de la technologie*.[51] This work includes an appendix, the outline of a course on Will given at the Faculté des Lettres in Bordeaux around 1890; in it, Espinas discusses human practical activity and, in particular, the invention of tools under the name of *will*. We know that Espinas borrowed his theory of organic projection, which he uses to explain the construction of the first tools, from a German author, Ernst Kapp (1808–96), who presented it for the first time in his 1877 work *Outlines of a Philosophy of Technique* [*Grundlinien einer Philosophie der Technik*].[52] This work, a classic in Germany, was so little known in France that certain psychologists who, on the basis of studies by Wolfgang Köhler and Paul Guillaume, have taken up the problems of animal intelligence and the use of tools by animals, attribute this theory of projection to Espinas himself, without noticing that Espinas explicitly declares at several points that he is borrowing from Kapp.[53] According to the theory of projection (whose philosophical foundations reach back, through Eduard von Hartmann and his *Philosophy of the Unconscious*,[54] to Schopenhauer), the first tools were no more than prolongations of human organs in motion. Flints, clubs, and levers prolong and extend the arm's organic movement of percussion. This theory, like all theories, has its limits and encounters notable obstacles in explaining inventions like fire or the wheel, which are so characteristic of human technique. One could search in vain, here, for the gestures and organs of which fire or the wheel would be the prolongation or extension, yet it is certain that this explanation is acceptable for instruments derived from the hammer or the lever, for all these families of instruments. In France, thus ethnographers have gathered not only the facts but also the hypotheses upon which a biological philosophy of technique could be constituted. Leroi-Gourhan, in his *Milieu et techniques*,[55] takes up what the Germans developed by way of philosophy[56]—for example, a theory of the development of inventions founded on Darwinian notions of variation and natural selection[57] or a theory of the construction of machines as a "tactic of life"[58]—without, so far as we know, any direct derivation. Leroi-Gourhan seeks to understand the phenomenon of the construction of the tool through a comparison with the movement of an amoeba, pushing out of its mass an extension that grasps and captures the external object of its desire in order to digest it. He writes: "If percussion has been proposed as the fundamental technical act, it is because there is, in almost all technical acts, the attempt to contact by touch, but while the expansion of the amoeba always pulls its prey toward the same digestive process, between the matter to be dealt with and the technical thought that envelops it are created, in each circumstance, specific organs of percussion."[59] The last chapters of this work constitute what is today the most striking example of a systematic and duly detailed attempt to bring biology and technology together. If one takes these views as a point of departure, the problem of the construction of machines receives a totally different solution from the traditional one, which was situated within a perspective that, for lack of a better term, we might call Cartesian, a perspective according to which technical invention consisted in the application of knowledge.

It is traditional to present the construction of the locomotive as a "marvel of science." And yet the construction of the steam engine is unintelligible if one does not understand that it is not an application of pre-existing theoretical knowledge but the solution to a millennial, truly technical problem—the problem of draining mines. To understand that the essential organ in a locomotive is a cylinder and piston, one must know the natural history of the forms of the pump; one must know of the existence of fire pumps, in which steam did not at first play the role of motor but served rather to create, by condensation under the piston of the pump, a vacuum that allowed the atmospheric pressure to act as a motor and to push down the piston.[60]

Leroi-Gourhan goes even further along these lines, and he looks for one of the locomotive's ancestors (in the biological sense of the word) in the spinning wheel. He writes: "Steam engines and actual motors developed from machines such as the spinning wheel. Around the circular movement is clustered all that the inventive spirit of our times has discovered that is highest among techniques: the crank, the pedal, the conveyor belt."[61] And later: "The reciprocal influence of inventions has not been sufficiently brought to light and we ignore that, without the spinning wheel, we would not have had the locomotive."[62] Further on: "The beginning of the nineteenth century did not know the forms that would become the materially utilizable embryos for the locomotive, the automobile, and the airplane. We discover the mechanical principles scattered in twenty applications known for several centuries. Therein lies the phenomenon that explains invention, but what is proper to invention is that it materializes, as it were, instantaneously."[63] One sees how, in light of these remarks, Science and Technique must be considered not as two types of activity, one of which is grafted onto the other, but as two types of activity, each of which borrows from the other sometimes its solutions, sometimes its problems. The rationalization of techniques makes one forget the irrational origin of machines. And it seems that in this area, as in any other, one must know how to cede a place to the irrational, even and especially when one wants to defend rationalism.[64]

To this we must add that the reversal of the relation between machine and organism that is brought about by a systematic understanding of technical inventions as behaviors of the living finds some confirmation in the attitude that the generalized use of machines has little by little imposed on men in contemporary industrialized societies. Georges Friedmann's important work *Problèmes humains du machinisme industriel* depicts the stages in the reaction that has restored the organism to first place in the relation between machine and human organism.[65] With Taylor and the first technicians of the rationalization of workers' movements, we see the human organism aligned, so to speak, with the functioning of the machine. Properly speaking, rationalization is a mechanization of the organism, inasmuch as it aims to eliminate movements that appear useless because they are seen solely from the viewpoint of output, considered as a mathematical function of certain factors. But the observation that technically superfluous movements are biologically necessary was the first stumbling block encountered by this exclusively technicist assimilation of the human organism to the machine. From here, the systematic examination of conditions physiological, psychotechnical, and even psychological, in the most general sense of the word (because by taking values into consideration one arrives at the most originary core of the personality), has led to a reversal: Friedmann sees the development of a technique for adapting machines to the human organism as an ineluctable revolution. This technique seems to him a scientific rediscovery of the empirical processes by which primitive peoples have always sought to adapt their tools to the organic norms of an efficient and biologically economical action—that is to say, an action that situates positive value in the evaluation of technical norms within the organism at work, which spontaneously defends itself against any exclusive subordination of the biological to the mechanical.[66] Friedmann can thus claim, without irony or paradox, that it is legitimate to consider the industrial development of the West from an ethnographic point of view.[67]

*

In summary, by considering technique to be a universal biological phenomenon and no longer only an intellectual operation of man,[68] one is led, first, to affirm the creative autonomy of arts and crafts from any knowledge capable of appropriating them so as to apply itself to them or informing them so as to multiply their effects. Second, in consequence, one is led to inscribe the mechanical within the organic. It is then naturally no longer a question of asking in what way the organism can or must be considered to be a machine, whether from the viewpoint of its structure or from the viewpoint of its functions. Rather, it is necessary to look for the reasons why the opposite, Cartesian opinion could have been born. We have tried to elucidate this problem. We have proposed that, in spite of initial appearances, a mechanist conception of the organism is no less anthropomorphic than a teleological conception of the physical world. The solution we have tried to defend has the advantage of showing man in continuity with life through technique prior to insisting on the rupture for which he assumes responsibility through science. This solution doubtless suffers from the inconvenience of appearing to reinforce the nostalgic indictments that, without much regard for the originality of their themes, too many writers address to technology and its progress. It is not our intention to come to their aid. It is quite clear that, if the human living has provided itself with a technique of the mechanical type, this massive phenomenon has a sense that is not gratuitous and that therefore cannot be revoked at will. But that is a question completely different from the one we have just examined.

NOTES

1. Julien Pacotte, *La pensée technique* (Paris: Alcan, 1931).
2. Franz Reuleaux, *The Kinematics of Machinery*, trans. Alexander Kennedy (London: Macmillan, 1876).
3. On matters of machines and mechanisms, see Pacotte, *La pensée technique*, chap. 3.
4. According to Marx, the tool is moved by human force and the machine, by a natural force. See Karl Marx, *Capital*, trans. Samuel Moore and Edward Aveling (New York: International Publishers, 1967), 1: 374–378.
5. [Georgio Baglivi, "De praxi medica," in *Opera omnia medico-practica et anatomica* (Venice, 1727), 2: 78.—Trans.]
6. On this point, see Charles Daremberg, *Histoire des sciences médicales*, 2 vols. (Paris: J. B. Bailliere, 1870), 879.
7. Gómez Pereira, *Antoniana Margarita, opus nempe physicis, medicis, ac theologis non minus utile, quam necessarium per Gometium Pereiram, medicum Methinae Duelli, quae Hispanorum lingua Medina de el Campo apellatur, nunc primum in lucem aeditum* (Methymme Campi, 1554).
8. Alfred Espinas, "L'organisme ou la machine vivante en Grèce au IVe siècle avant J.C.," *Revue de métaphysique et de morale* (1903): 702–715.
9. Aristotle, "Mechanical Problems," in *Minor Works*, trans. Walter Stanley Hett (Cambridge: Harvard University Press, 1980).
10. Plato, *Timaeus*, trans. Benjamin Jowett (New York: Macmillan, 1987), 74b6.
11. Pierre-Maxime Schuhl, *Machinisme et philosophie* (Paris: Alcan, 1938).
12. [Ibid., 34—Trans.]
13. Aristotle, *Politics* (Cambridge: Harvard University Press, 1932), 1253b23–1254b20, 14–19. [Schuhl, *Machinisme et philosophie*, 32.—Trans.]
14. [Schuhl, *Machinisme et philosophie*, 33. et al.—Trans.]
15. Lucien Laberthonnière, "La physique de Descartes et la physique d'Aristote," in Laberthonnière, *Les études sur Descartes* (Paris: Vrin, 1935), 2: 287–344.
16. Franz Borkenau, *Der Übergang vom feudalen zum bürgerlichen Weltbild: Studien zur Geschichte der Philosophie der Manufakturperiode* (Paris: Alcan, 1934).
17. La Fontaine's fable "The Cobbler and the Financier" illustrates very clearly the conflict between two conceptions of work and its remuneration [in *The Complete Fables of Jean de La Fontaine*, ed. Norman R. Shapiro (Urbana: University of Illinois Press, 2007), 189–190.—Trans.]
18. [Karl Marx and Friedrich Engels, *The Communist Manifesto* (New York: Penguin, 2002), 222.—Trans.]

19. Henryk Grossman, "Die gesellschaftlichen Grundlagen der mechanistischen Philosophie und die Manufaktur," *Zeitschrift für Sozialforschung*, no. 2 (1935): 161–231.

20. Pierre Duhem, *The Origins of Statics*, trans. Grant F. Leneux, Victor N. Vagliente, and Guy H. Wagener (Dordrecht: Kluwer Academic Publishers, 1991).

21. Marie Herzfeld, *Leonardo da Vinci, der Denker, Forscher, und Poet* (Leipzig: Diederichs, 1904); Gabriel Séailles, *Léonard de Vinci: L'artiste et le savant. Essai de biographie psychologique* (Paris: Perrin, 1906); Joséphin Péladan, *La philosophie de Léonard de Vinci d'après ses manuscripts* (Paris: Alcan, 1907).

22. In the *Principles of Philosophy* (IV, §109–113), several passages show that Descartes was equally interested in cannon powder, but he did not look for an explanatory principle analogous to the animal organism in the explosion of cannon powder as a source of energy. It was an English doctor, Thomas Willis (1621–1675), who constructed a theory of muscular movement explicitly based on an analogy with what takes place when powder explodes in an arquebus. Willis compared nerves to powder fuses, in a way that still remains valid according to some (we are thinking in particular of W. M. Bayliss). Nerves are a kind of Bickford fuse. They conduct a fire that sets off in muscles explosions that, according to Willis, can alone account for the phenomena of spasms and tetany observed by doctors.

23. René Descartes, "The Passions of the Soul," in *The Philosophical Writings of Descartes*, 3 vols., trans. John Cottingham, Robert Stoothoff, and Dugald Murdoch (Cambridge: Cambridge University Press, 1988), 1: 346: "For there is within us but one soul, and this soul has within it no diversity of parts: it is at once sensitive and rational too, and all its appetites are volitions."

24. René Descartes, "Fifth Discourse," in *Discourse on Method and Meditations on First Philosophy*, trans. Donald A. Cress (Indianapolis: Hackett Publishers, 1998), 25–34; René Descartes, "Letter to the Marquis of Newcastle," November 23, 1646, in *The Philosophical Writings of Descartes*, 3: 302.

25. René Descartes, "Letter to Henry More," February 5, 1649, in The *Philosophical Writings of Descartes*, 3: 366. To understand the relation between sensibility and the disposition of organs, one must know the Cartesian theory of degrees of sense; on this topic, see the René Descartes, "Responses to the Sixth Set of Objections," in *The Philosophical Writings of Descartes*, 2: 294–296.

26. René Descartes, "Letter to Henry More," 366.

27. Gottfried Wilhelm Leibniz, "Letter to Hermann Conring," March 19, 1678.

28. One finds this admirable text in Gottfried Wilhelm Leibniz, *Œuvres choisies*, ed. Lucy Prenant (Paris: Garnier, 1940), 52. One should bring together, in particular: the criteria that, according to Leibniz, distinguish the animal from an automaton, the analogous arguments invoked in the letter to Conring cited above, and also Edgar Allan Poe's profound reflections on the matter in "Maelzel's Chess-Player," [in Edgar Allan Poe, *The Complete Tales and Poems of Edgar Allan Poe* (New York: Random House, 1975), 421–439—Trans.]. On the Leibnizian distinction between machine and organism, see Gottfried Wilhelm Leibniz, "A New System of the Nature and Communication of Substances," in *Leibniz: Philosophical Papers*, ed. and trans. Leroy Loemker (Chicago: University of Chicago Press, 1956), and *Monadology and Other Philosophical Essays*, trans. Paul Schrecker and Anne Martin Schrecker (New York: Macmillan, 1985).

29. Leibniz was no less interested than Descartes in the invention and construction of machines, as well as the problem of automatons. See in particular his correspondence with Duke John of

Hanover (1676–1679), in *Sätmtliche Schriften und Briefe* (Darmstadt: Reichl, 1927), 1st series, vol. 2. In a 1671 text, *Bedenken von Aufrichtung einer Akademie oder Sozietät in Deutschland zu Aufnehmen der Künste und Wissenschaften*, 4th series (Darmstadt: Reichl, 1931), 1: 544, Leibniz exalts the superiority of German art, which had always applied itself to making moving works (watches, clocks, hydraulic machines, etc.) over Italian art, which had almost exclusively dedicated itself to making objects without life, immobile, and made to be contemplated from without.

30. René Descartes, *Treatise of Man*, trans. Thomas Steele Hall (Cambridge: Harvard University Press, 1972), 1–4.

31. Ibid., 4.

32. See Nicolas Steno, "Appendix 3: Extracts from the 'Discours sur l'anatomie du cerveau' ('Discourse on the Anatomy of the Brain'), delivered by Nicolas Steno in Paris in 1665 to the 'Messieurs de l'Assemblée de chez Monsieur Thivenot,'" in Georges Canguilhem, *Knowledge of Life*, trans. Stefanos Geroulanos and Daniela Ginsburg (New York: Fordham University Press, 2008), 153–154.

33. Moreover, Descartes can only formulate the meaning of God's construction of animal machines in terms of purpose. See *The Philosophical Writings of Descartes*, 2: 60.

34. René Descartes, "Description of the Human Body and All of Its Functions," in *The Philosophical Writings of Descartes*, 1: 315.

35. Claude Bernard, *Lectures on the Phenomena of Life Common to Animals and Plants*, trans. Hebbel E. Hoff, Roger Guillemin, and Lucienne Guillemin (Springfield, IL: Charles C. Thomas, 1974).

36. Ibid., 37.

37. Raymond Ruyer, *Éléments de psychobiologie* (Paris: Presses Universitaires de France, 1946), 46–47.

38. See Paul Valéry, *Cahier B* (Paris: Gallimard, 1910): "Artificial means: which tends towards a defined goal. And it thereby contrasts with *living*. Artificial, human, or anthropomorphic are distinct from what is only living or vital. Everything that comes to appear in the form of a clear and completed goal becomes artificial, and this is the tendency of an increasing consciousness. It is also the work of man when he imitates an object or a spontaneous phenomenon as closely as possible. Thought that is conscious of itself makes itself into an artificial system. If life had a goal, it would no longer be life."

39. Édouard Pichon, ed., *Le développement psychique de l'enfant et de l'adolescent* (Paris: Masson, 1936), 126; Paul Cossa, *Physiopathologie du système nerveux* (Paris: Masson, 1942), 845.

40. Aristotle, *Politics*, 1252b2–1252b5.

41. Max Scheler has remarked that the least specialized living beings are (contrary to what mechanists believe) the most difficult to explain in mechanist terms, because in them all functions are assumed by the entire organism. It is only with the increasing differentiation of functions and the complication of the nervous system that structures resembling a machine in some fashion appear; see Max Scheler, *Man's Place in Nature*, trans. Hans Meyerhoff (1928; Boston: Beacon Press, 1961), 75–81.

42. Xavier Bichat, *Anatomie générale appliquée à la physiologie et à la médecine* (Paris: Bureau de l'Encyclopédie, 1834).

43. Lucien Cuénot, *Invention et finalité en biologie* (Paris: Flammarion, 1941), 44.

44. René Descartes, "La description du corps humain," §66, in *Œuvres de Descartes*, ed. Charles Adam and Paul Tannery (Paris: Vrin, 1974), 11: 277.

45. Paul Guillaume, *La psychologie de la forme* (Paris: Flammarion, 1937), 131.

46. Max Aron and Pierre Grassé, *Précis de biologie animale* (Paris: Masson, 1935), 647ff.

47. René Descartes, "Principles of Philosophy," in *The Philosophical Works of Descartes*, 1: 288 [translation modified]. See our study "Descartes et la technique," *Travaux du 9ème Congrès international de philosophie* (Paris: Hermann, 1937), 2: 77ff.

48. Immanuel Kant, *Critique of Judgment*, trans. James Creed Meredith (New York: Oxford University Press, 2007), 133.

49. Paul Kranhalls, *Der Weltsinn der Technik* (Munich: Oldenbourg, 1932), 68.

50. The point of departure for these studies must be sought in Darwin's *The Descent of Man*. Marx understood well the importance of Darwin's ideas: see Marx, *Capital*, 406n2.

51. Alfred Espinas, *Les origines de la technologie* (Paris: Alcan, 1897).

52. Ernst Kapp, *Grundlinien einer Philosophie der Technik* (Braunschweig: Westermann, 1877).

53. We are alluding here to an excellent little book by Gaston Viaud, *Intelligence: Its Evolution and Forms*, trans. Arnold J. Pomerans (New York: Harper, 1960).

54. Eduard von Hartmann, *Philosophy of the Unconscious: Speculative Results According to the Inductive Method of Physical Science* (New York: Macmillan, 1884).

55. André Leroi-Gourhan, *Milieu et techniques* (Paris: Albin Michel, 1945).

56. See the work of Eberhard Zschimmer, *Deutsche Philosophen der Technik* (Stuttgart: Enke, 1937).

57. Alard Du Bois-Reymond, *Erfindung und Erfinder* (Berlin: Springer, 1906). Alain has sketched a Darwinian interpretation of technical constructions in a very good piece ("Prop d'Alain," *Nouvelle Revue Française*, no. 1 [1920]: 60), which is preceded and followed by several other pieces of interest for our problem. The same idea is gestured toward several times in the *Système des beaux-arts* (Paris: Gallimard, 1926), regarding the making of the violin (4:5), furniture (6:5), and rustic houses (6:3; 6:8).

58. Oswald Spengler, *Der Mensch und die Technik* (Munich: Beck, 1931).

59. Leroi-Gourhan, *Milieu et techniques*, 499.

60. James Watt perfected the double-acting steam engine in 1784. Sadi Carnot's 1824 work *Réflexions sur la puissance motrice du feu* (Paris: Bachelier, 1824) remained unknown until the middle of the nineteenth century. On this subject, see Pierre Ducassé, *Histoire des techniques* (Paris: Presses Universitaires de France, 1945), which emphasizes the anteriority of technique to theory. On the empirical sequence of the various organs and the various usages of the steam engine, see Arthur Vierendeel, *Esquisse d'une histoire de la technique* (Brussels: Vroment, 1921), which summarizes, in particular, a major work by Robert H. Thurston, *A History of the Growth of the Steam-Engine* (New York, 1878). On the history of Watt's work, see the chapter "James Watt ou Ariel ingénieur," in Pierre Devaux, *Les aventures de la science* (Paris: Gallimard, 1943).

61. Leroi-Gourhan, *Milieu et techniques*, 100.

62. Ibid., 104. One finds the same thing in an article by Arthur Haudricourt, "Les moteurs animés en agriculture," *Revue de botanique appliquée et d'agriculture tropicale*, no. 20 (1940): 762: "One must not forget that we owe inanimate motors to irrigation: the noria is at the origin of the hydraulic mill, as the pump is at the origin of the steam engine."

63. Leroi-Gourhan, *Milieu et techniques*, 406.

64. Henri Bergson, in *Two Sources of Morality and Religion*, trans. R. Ashley Audra and Cloudesley Brereton (New York: Holt, 1949), explicitly argues that the spirit of mechanical invention, although nourished by science, remains distinct and could even separate from the latter (329–330). Bergson is also one of the rare French philosophers, if not the only one, to have considered mechanical invention as a biological function, an aspect of the organization of matter by life. His *Creative Evolution*, trans. Arthur Mitchell (New York: Dover Publications, 1911), is, in a sense, a treatise of general organology. On the relations between explaining and doing, see also the two first texts in Paul Valéry, *Variété V* (Paris: Gallimard, 1945), "L'homme et la coquille" and "Discours aux Chirurgiens," also, in *Eupalinos*, the passage on the construction of boats. See Valéry, *Eupalinos; or, The Architect*, trans. William McCausland Stewart (London: Oxford University Press, 1932). Finally, see the admirable "In Praise of Hands," by Henri Focillon, in *The Life of Forms in Art*, trans. George Kubler (New York: Zone Books, 1989), 157–184.

65. Georges Friedmann, *Industrial Society: The Emergence of the Human Problems of Automation* (Glencoe, IL: Free Press, 1955), originally published as *Problèmes humains du machinisme industriel* (Paris: Gallimard, 1946).

66. Friedmann, *Problèmes humains du machinisme industriel*, 96.

67. Friedmann, *Problèmes humains du machinisme industriel*, 369.

68. This attitude is beginning to become familiar to biologists. See especially: Cuénot, *Invention et finalité en biologie*; Andrée Tétry, *Les outils chez les êtres vivants* (Paris: Gallimard, 1948); and Albert Vandel, *L'homme et l'évolution* (Paris: Gallimard, 1949). See especially, in the last of the above, the reflections on adaptation and invention, 12ff. One cannot ignore the fermenting role played in these matters by the ideas of Father Teilhard de Chardin. A recent discipline, called Bionics and born in the United States ten years ago, studies biological structures and systems that can be used by technology as models or analogues, in particular, in the construction of devices for detection, orientation, or equilibration to be used in airplane or missile equipment. Bionics is the art—very scientific—of information that draws knowledge from living nature. The frog, with its selective eye for instantly usable information; the pit viper, with its thermoception, which at night can sense the blood temperature of its prey; the common house fly, which equilibrates its flight with two cilia—these have supplied a new species of engineers with models. There exists in several universities in the United States a special discipline of Bio-engineering, which seems to have first found a home in the Massachusetts Institute of Technology. See Jean Dufrenoy, "Systèmes biologiques servant de modèles à la technologie," *Cahiers des ingénieurs agronomes* (June–July 1962): 21.

BIBLIOGRAPHY

Alain. "Les Propos d'Alain." *Nouvelle Revue Française*, no. 1 (1920).

Alain. *Système des beaux-arts*. Paris: Gallimard, 1926.

Aristotle. "Mechanical Problems." In *Minor Works*. Translated by Walter Stanley Hett. Cambridge: Harvard University Press, 1980.

Aristotle. *Politics*. Cambridge: Harvard University Press, 1932.

Aron, Max, and Pierre Grassé. *Précis de biologie animale*. Paris: Masson, 1935.

Baglivi, Georgio. "De praxi medica." In *Opera omnia medico-practica et anatomica*. Venice, 1727.

Bergson, Henri. *Creative Evolution*. Translated by Arthur Mitchell. New York: Dover Publications, 1911.

Bergson, Henri. *Two Sources of Morality and Religion*. Translated by R. Ashley Audra and Cloudesley Brereton. New York: Holt, 1949.

Bernard, Claude. *Lectures on the Phenomena of Life Common to Animals and Plants*. Translated by Hebbel E. Hoff, Roger Guillemin, and Lucienne Guillemin. Springfield, IL: Charles C. Thomas, 1974.

Bichat, Xavier. *Anatomie générale appliquée à la physiologie et à la médecine*. Paris: Bureau de l'Encyclopédie, 1834.

Borkenau, Franz. *Der Übergang vom feudalen zum bürgerlichen Weltbild: Studien zur Geschichte der Philosophie der Manufakturperiode*. Paris: Alcan, 1934.

Canguilhem, Georges. "Descartes et la technique." In vol. 2 of *Travaux du 9ème Congrès international de philosophie*. Paris: Hermann, 1937.

Carnot, Sadi. *Réflexions sur la puissance motrice du feu*. Paris: Bachelier, 1824.

Cossa, Paul. *Physiopathologie du système nerveux*. Paris: Masson, 1942.

Cuénot, Lucien. *Invention et finalité en biologie*. Paris: Flammarion, 1941.

Daremberg, Charles. *Histoire des sciences médicales*, vol. 2. Paris: J. B. Bailliere, 1870.

Descartes, René. "Fifth Discourse." In *Discourse on Method and Meditations on First Philosophy*. Translated by Donald A. Cress, 25–34. Indianapolis: Hackett Publishers, 1998.

Descartes, René "La description du corps humain." In vol. 11 of *Œuvres de Descartes*. Edited by Charles Adam and Paul Tannery. Paris: Vrin, 1974.

Descartes, René. *The Philosophical Writings of Descartes*. 3 vols. Translated by John Cottingham, Robert Stoothoff, and Dugald Murdoch. Cambridge: Cambridge University Press, 1988.

Descartes, René. "Description of the Human Body and All of Its Functions." In vol. 1 of *The Philosophical Writings of Descartes*, 314–324.

Descartes, René. "Letter to Henry More," February 5, 1649. In vol. 3 of *The Philosophical Writings of Descartes*, 360–367.

Descartes, René. "Letter to the Marquis of Newcastle," November 23, 1646. In vol. 3 of *The Philosophical Writings of Descartes*, 302–304.

Descartes, René. "Principles of Philosophy." In vol. 1 of *The Philosophical Works of Descartes*, 177–292.

Descartes, René. "Responses to the Sixth Set of Objections." In vol. 2 of *The Philosophical Writings of Descartes*, 285–301.

Descartes, René. "The Passions of the Soul." In vol. 1 of *The Philosophical Writings of Descartes*, 325–404.

Descartes, René. *Treatise of Man*. Translated by Thomas Steele Hall. Cambridge: Harvard University Press, 1972.

Devaux, Pierre. *Les aventures de la science*. Paris: Gallimard, 1943.

Du Bois-Reymond, Alard. *Erfindung und Erfinder*. Berlin: Springer, 1906.

Ducassé, Pierre. *Histoire des techniques*. Paris: Presses Universitaires de France, 1945.

Dufrenoy, Jean. "Systèmes biologiques servant de modèles à la technologie." *Cahiers des ingénieurs agronomes* (June–July 1962).

Duhem, Pierre. *The Origins of Statics*. Translated by Grant F. Leneux, Victor N. Vagliente, and Guy H. Wagener. Dordrecht: Kluwer Academic Publishers, 1991.

Espinas, Alfred. "L'organisme ou la machine vivante en Grèce au IVe siècle avant J.C." *Revue de métaphysique et de morale* (1903): 702–715.

Espinas, Alfred. *Les origines de la technologie*. Paris: Alcan, 1897.

Focillon, Henri. "In Praise of Hands." In *The Life of Forms in Art*. Translated by George Kubler, 157–184. New York: Zone Books, 1989.

Fontaine, Jean de la. *The Complete Fables of Jean de La Fontaine*. Edited by Norman R. Shapiro. Urbana: University of Illinois Press, 2007.

Friedmann, Georges. *Industrial Society: The Emergence of the Human Problems of Automation*. Glencoe, IL: Free Press, 1955. Originally published as *Problèmes humains du machinisme industriel*. Paris: Gallimard, 1946.

Guillaume, Paul. *La psychologie de la forme*. Paris: Flammarion, 1937.

Grossman, Henryk. "Die gesellschaftlichen Grundlagen der mechanistischen Philosophie und die Manufaktur." *Zeitschrift für Sozialforschung*, no. 2 (1935): 161–231.

Hartmann, Eduard von. *Philosophy of the Unconscious: Speculative Results According to the Inductive Method of Physical Science*. New York: Macmillan, 1884.

Haudricourt, Arthur. "Les moteurs animés en agriculture." *Revue de botanique appliquée et d'agriculture tropicale*, no. 20 (1940).

Herzfeld, Marie. *Leonardo da Vinci, der Denker, Forscher, und Poet*. Leipzig: Diederichs, 1904.

Kant, Immanuel. *Critique of Judgment*. Translated by James Creed Meredith. New York: Oxford University Press, 2007.

Kapp, Ernst. *Grundlinien einer Philosophie der Technik*. Braunschweig: Westermann, 1877.

Kranhalls, Paul. *Der Weltsinn der Technik*. Munich: Oldenbourg, 1932.

Laberthonnière, Lucien. "La physique de Descartes et la physique d'Aristote." In *Les études sur Descartes*. Paris: Vrin, 1935.

Leibniz, Gottfried Wilhelm. "A New System of the Nature and Communication of Substances." In *Leibniz: Philosophical Papers*. Edited and translated by Leroy Loemker. Chicago: University of Chicago Press, 1956.

Leibniz, Gottfried Wilhelm. *"Bedenken von Aufrichtung einer Akademie oder Sozietät in Deutschland zu Aufnehmen der Künste und Wissenschaften."* In 4th series, vol. 1 of *Sätmtliche Schriften und Briefe*. Darmstadt: Reichl, 1931.

Leibniz, Gottfried Wilhelm. "Correspondence with Duke John of Hanover (1676–1679)." In 1st series, vol. 2 of *Sätmtliche Schriften und Briefe*. Darmstadt: Reichl, 1927.

Leibniz, Gottfried Wilhelm. *Monadology and Other Philosophical Essays*. Translated by Paul Schrecker and Anne Martin Schrecker. New York: Macmillan, 1985.

Leibniz, Gottfried Wilhelm. *Œuvres choisies*. Edited by Lucy Prenant, 52. Paris: Garnier, 1940.

Leroi-Gourhan, André. *Milieu et techniques*. Paris: Albin Michel, 1945.

Marx, Karl. *Capital*, vol. 1. Translated by Samuel Moore and Edward Aveling. New York: International Publishers, 1967.

Marx, Karl, and Friedrich Engels. *The Communist Manifesto*. New York: Penguin, 2002.

Pacotte, Julien. *La pensée technique*. Paris: Alcan, 1931.

Péladan, Joséphin. *La philosophie de Léonard de Vinci d'après ses manuscripts*. Paris: Alcan, 1907.

Pereira, Gómez. *Antoniana Margarita, opus nempe physicis, medicis, ac theologis non minus utile, quam necessarium per Gometium Pereiram, medicum Methinae Duelli, quae Hispanorum lingua Medina de el Campo apellatur, nunc primum in lucem aeditum*. Methymme Campi, 1554.

Pichon, Édouard, ed. *Le développement psychique de l'enfant et de l'adolescent*. Paris: Masson, 1936.

Plato. *Timaeus*. Translated by Benjamin Jowett. New York: Macmillan, 1987.

Poe, Edgar Allan. "Maelzel's Chess-Player." In *The Complete Tales and Poems of Edgar Allan Poe*, 421–439. New York: Random House, 1975.

Reuleaux, Franz. *The Kinematics of Machinery*. Translated by Alexander Kennedy. London: Macmillan, 1876.

Ruyer, Raymond. *Éléments de psychobiologie*. Paris: Presses Universitaires de France, 1946.

Scheler, Max. *Man's Place in Nature*. Translated by Hans Meyerhoff. Boston: Beacon Press, 1961.

Schuhl, Pierre-Maxime. *Machinisme et philosophie*. Paris: Alcan, 1938.

Séailles, Gabriel. *Léonard de Vinci: L'artiste et le savant. Essai de biographie psychologique*. Paris: Perrin, 1906.

Spengler, Oswald. *Der Mensch und die Technik*. Munich: Beck, 1931.

Steno, Nicolas. "Appendix 3: Extracts from the 'Discours sur l'anatomie du cerveau' ('Discourse on the Anatomy of the Brain'), delivered by Nicolas Steno in Paris in 1665 to the 'Messieurs de l'Assemblée de chez Monsieur Thivenot.'" In Georges Canguilhem, *Knowledge of Life*. Translated by Stefanos Geroulanos and Daniela Ginsburg, 153–154. New York: Fordham University Press, 2008.

Tétry, Andrée. *Les outils chez les êtres vivants*. Paris: Gallimard, 1948.

Thurston, Robert H. *A History of the Growth of the Steam-Engine*. New York, 1878.

Valéry, Paul. *Cahier B*. Paris: Gallimard, 1910.

Valéry, Paul. *Eupalinos; or, The Architect*. Translated by William McCausland Stewart. London: Oxford University Press, 1932.

Valéry, Paul. *Variété V*. Paris: Gallimard, 1945.

Vandel, Albert. *L'homme et l'évolution*. Paris: Gallimard, 1949.

Viaud, Gaston. *Intelligence: Its Evolution and Forms*. Translated by Arnold. J. Pomerans. New York: Harper, 1960.

Vierendeel, Arthur. *Esquisse d'une histoire de la technique*. Brussels: Vroment, 1921.

Zschimmer, Eberhard. *Deutsche Philosophen der Technik*. Stuttgart: Enke, 1937.

4

GENESIS OF THE TECHNICAL OBJECT: THE PROCESS OF CONCRETIZATION

Gilbert Simondon

I. THE ABSTRACT TECHNICAL OBJECT AND THE CONCRETE TECHNICAL OBJECT

Although the technical object is subject to genesis, it is difficult to define the genesis of each technical object, since the individuality of technical objects is modified throughout the course of this genesis; technical objects are not easily defined by attribution to a technical kind; it is easy to summarily distinguish kinds according to practical usage, as long as one accepts grasping the technical object according to its practical end; however, this is an illusory specificity, because no fixed structure corresponds to a definite usage. The same result may be obtained from very different functionalities and structures: a steam engine, a gasoline engine, a turbine, and an engine powered by springs or weights are all equally engines, but there is a more genuine analogy between a spring engine and a bow or a cross-bow than between the spring engine and a steam engine; the engine of a pendulum clock is analogous to a winch, while an electric clock is analogous to a door bell or a buzzer. Usage unites these heterogeneous structures and operations under the banner of genera and species that draw their signification from the relation between this functioning and another functioning, which is that of the human being involved in the action. That to which one thereby gives a single name—for instance the engine—can thus be multiple in one instance and may vary in time by changing its individuality.

However, instead of starting out with the individuality of the technical object, or even with its specificity, which is very unstable, it is preferable to reverse the problem, if we want to try to define the laws of its genesis in light of its individuality or specificity: one can define the individuality and specificity of the technical object on the basis of the criteria of its genesis: the individual technical object is not this or that thing, given *hic et nunc*, but that of which there is genesis.[1] The unity of the technical object, its individuality, and its specificity are the characteristics of consistency and convergence in its genesis. The genesis of the technical object partakes in its being. The technical object is that which is not anterior to its coming-into-being, but is present at each stage of its coming-into-being; the technical object in its oneness is a unit of coming-into-being [*unité de devenir*]. The gasoline engine is not this or that engine given in time and space, but the fact that there is a succession, a continuity that runs through the first engines to those we currently know and which are still evolving. As such, as in a phylogenetic lineage, a definite stage of evolution contains dynamic structures and schemas within itself that partake in the principal stages of an evolution of forms. The technical being evolves through convergence and self-adaptation; it unifies itself internally according to a principle of inner resonance. Today's automobile engine is the descendent of the engine from 1910 not simply because the engine of 1910 was built by our ancestors. Nor is today's automobile engine its descendant simply because it has a greater degree of perfection in relation to use; in fact, for some uses the engine from 1910 remains superior to an engine from 1956. For instance, it can tolerate extensive heating without galling or rod bearing failure, having been built with more flexibility and without fragile alloys such as Babbitt metal; it is more autonomous, due to its having a magnetic ignition. Old engines function reliably on fishing boats after having been taken from a disused automobile. It is through internal examination of the regimes of causality and forms, insofar as they are adapted to these regimes of causality, that the contemporary automobile engine is defined as posterior to the engine from 1910. In a contemporary engine each important item is so well connected to the others via reciprocal exchanges of energy that it cannot be anything other than what it is. The shape of the combustion chamber, the shape and size of the valves, and the shape of the piston all belong to the same system within which a multitude of reciprocal causalities exist. To such a shape of these elements corresponds a certain compression ratio, which in turn requires a determinate ignition timing; the shape of the cylinder head, as well as the metal it is made of, produce a certain temperature in the spark plug electrodes in relation to all the other elements of the cycle; this temperature in turn causes a reaction leading to the characteristics of ignition and hence to the entire cycle. One could say that the contemporary engine is a concrete engine, whereas the old engine is an abstract engine. In the old engine each element intervenes at a certain moment in the cycle, and then is expected no longer to act upon the other elements; the pieces of the engine are like people who work together, each in their own turn, but who do not know one another.

Moreover, this is precisely how the functioning of thermal engines is explained to students in the classroom, each piece being isolated from the others like the lines that represent it on the blackboard in geometric space, *partes extra partes*. The old engine is a logical assemblage of elements defined by their complete and unique function. Each element can accomplish its own function best if it is, like a perfectly completed instrument, oriented entirely to accomplishing this function. A permanent exchange of energy between two elements appears as if it were an imperfection, unless this exchange itself belongs to the theoretical operation; furthermore there is a primitive form of the technical object, the abstract form, in which each theoretical and material unit is treated as an absolute, and is completed according to an intrinsic perfection that requires, in order for it to function, that it be constituted as a closed system; integration into an ensemble in this case raises a series of so-called technical problems that must be resolved and which are in fact problems of compatibility between already given ensembles.

These already given ensembles need to be maintained and preserved despite their reciprocal influences. What appears then are particular structures that one can call, for each constitutive unit, defense structures: the cylinder head of the thermal combustion engine bristles with cooling fins that are particularly well developed in the region of the valves, which is subject to intense thermal exchanges and high pressure. In the first engines these cooling fins are as if added from the outside to the theoretical cylinder and cylinder head, which are geometrically cylindrical; they serve only one function, that of cooling. In more recent engines, these cooling fins also play a mechanical role, as ribs that resist the deformation of the cylinder head under the pressure of the gasses; in these conditions one can no longer distinguish the volumetric unit (cylinder, cylinder head) from the thermal dissipation unit; if, in an engine that uses ambient air for cooling, one were to remove the cylinder heads fins by sawing or grinding, then the volumetric unit constituted by the cylinder head alone would no longer be viable, even as a volumetric unit: it would be deformed under the gaseous pressure; the volumetric and mechanical unit has become coextensive with the unit of thermal dissipation because the structure of the ensemble is bivalent: the fins constitute a cooling surface of thermal exchanges with the stream of external air; these same fins, insofar as they are a part of the cylinder head, limit the size of the combustion chamber through their un-deformable contour, using less metal than would be required by a shell without ribs; the development of this unique structure is not a compromise, but a concomitance and a convergence: a ribbed cylinder head can afford to be thinner than a smooth cylinder head with the same rigidity; a thin cylinder head, in turn, allows for more efficient thermal exchanges than a thick cylinder head would allow; the bivalent fin-rib structure improves the cooling not only by increasing the thermal exchange area (which is what characterizes the fin as a fin), but also by permitting a thinning of the cylinder head (which is what characterizes the fin as ribbing).

The technical problem is thus one of the convergence of functions into a structural unit, rather than one of seeking a compromise between conflicting requirements. If, in the case just considered, a conflict subsists between two aspects of a single structure, then this is only because the position of the ribbing that would correspond to maximum rigidity is not necessarily the same as that which corresponds best to their fastest cooling by way of air flowing between the fins when the vehicle is running. In this case the builder might have to retain a mixed, incomplete aspect: the fin-ribbing, if positioned for optimal cooling, will have to be thicker and more rigid than if it were for ribbing alone. If, on the contrary, they are positioned perfectly to resolve the problem of obtaining rigidity, then their area is larger, in order to compensate the reduction of the thermal exchange that had been diminished because of the slowed airstream, via the development of a larger area; the very structure of the fins may in the end also be a compromise between two forms, requiring a greater development than if a single function were taken as the sole purpose of the structure. This divergence of functional directions is like a residue of abstraction within the technical object and it is the progressive reduction of this margin between the functions of plurivalent structures that defines the progress of a technical object; it is this convergence that specifies the technical object, because in any given epoch there is no infinite plurality of possible functional systems; there are far fewer technical species than there are usages to which technical objects are destined; human necessity is infinitely diversifiable, but the directions of convergence of technical species are finite in number.

The technical object thus exists as a specific type obtained at the end of a convergent series. This series goes from the abstract to the concrete mode: it tends toward a state which would turn the technical being into a system that is entirely coherent within itself and entirely unified.

II. CONDITIONS OF TECHNICAL EVOLUTION

What are the *reasons* for this convergence that manifests itself in the evolution of technical structures? A certain number of extrinsic causes no doubt exist, in particular those which tend to produce the standardization of spare parts and organs. Nevertheless, these extrinsic causes are not more powerful than those that tend toward the multiplication of types, appropriated for an infinite variety of needs. If technical objects do evolve toward a small number of specific types then this is by virtue of an internal necessity and not as a consequence of economic influences or practical requirements; it is not the production-line that produces standardization, but rather intrinsic standardization that allows for the production-line to exist. An effort to discover the reason for the formation of specific types of technical objects within the transition from artisanal production to industrial production would mistake the consequence for its condition; the industrialization of production is rendered possible by the formation of stable types. Artisanal production corresponds to the primitive stage of the evolution of the technical object, i.e., to the abstract stage; industry corresponds to the concrete stage. The *made-to-measure* aspect one finds in the product of artisanal work is inessential; it is the result of this other, essential aspect of the abstract technical object: namely, that it is grounded in an analytical organization that always leaves the path open for new possibilities; these possibilities are the external manifestation of an internal contingency. In the confrontation between the coherence of technical work and the coherence of a system of the needs of utilization, it is the coherence of utilization that prevails, because the technical object that is made to measure is in fact an object without intrinsic measure; its norms are derived from the outside: it has not yet realized its internal coherence; it is not a system of the necessary; it corresponds to an open system of requirements.

Conversely, during the industrial stage, the object achieves its coherence and it is the system of needs that is now less coherent than the system of the object; needs mold themselves onto the industrial technical object, which in turn acquires the power to shape a civilization. It is utilization that becomes an ensemble chiseled to the measures of the technical object. When individual fancy calls for a customized automobile, the manufacturer can do no more than take a serial engine, a serial chassis, and externally modify some aspects, adding decorative details or externally adjusted accessories to the automobile, which is really the essential technical object: what can be made to measure are inessential aspects, because they are contingent.

The type of relation that exists between these inessential aspects and the nature proper to the technical type is a negative one: the more the car is required to answer to a large number of user demands, the more its essential characteristics are encumbered with external servitude; the bodywork burdens itself with accessories, shapes no longer correspond to the structures facilitating the best air flow. The made-to-measure aspect is not only inessential, it goes against the essence of the technical being, it is like a dead weight imposed from the outside. The car's center of gravity rises, its mass increases.

It is not enough, however, to claim that the evolution of the technical object occurs via a passage from an analytic order to a synthetic order, conditioning the passage from artisanal production to industrial production: even if this evolution is necessary, it is not automatic and one ought to seek the causes of this evolving movement. These causes essentially reside in the imperfection of the abstract technical object. Because of its analytic aspect, this object uses more material and requires more construction work; it is logically simpler, yet technically more complicated, because it is made up of a convergence of several complete systems. It is more fragile than the concrete technical object, because the relative isolation of each system that constitutes a functional sub-system threatens, in case of its malfunction, the preservation of the other systems.

[. . .]

Thus properly speaking, there is a convergence of economic constraints (a diminished quantity of raw material, of work and of energy consumption during use) and technical requirements: the object cannot be self-destructive, it must maintain itself in a stable state of functioning for as long as possible. As far as these two types of cause—the economic and the properly technical—are concerned, it would appear that it is the latter that predominates in technical evolution; economic causes indeed exist in all domains; yet it is mostly the domains where technical constraints prevail over economic constraints (aviation, military equipment) that become the most active sites for progress. Indeed, economic causes are not pure; they interfere with a diffuse network of motivations and preferences that attenuate or even reverse them (a taste for luxury, the users desire for very apparent novelty, commercial propaganda), to such an extent that in domains where the technical object is known through social myths or fads in public opinion, rather than being appreciated in itself, certain tendencies toward complication come to light; some car manufacturers thus present the use of overabundant automatism in accessories or the systematic recourse to servo-mechanisms as an increase in perfection, even where direct command does not in the least exceed the physical strength of the driver: some even go so far as to find a sales argument and proof of superiority in the suppression of direct means, as for instance that of the use of the crank as a back-up means of starting the engine, which in fact consists in making its operation more analytic in subordinating it to the use of available electric energy accumulated in batteries; technically this represents a complication, whereas the manufacturer presents this suppression as a simplification that would show how modern the car is, thereby making the unpleasant affective connotations of the stereotypical image of a car engine that is difficult to start a thing of the past. A nuance of ridicule is thus projected onto other cars—those that preserve the crank—which are somehow out of date, discarded into the past through an artifice of presentation. The automobile, a technical object charged with psychic and social inferences, is not suitable for technical progress: the automobile's progress comes from neighboring domains, such as aviation, shipping, and transportation trucks.

The specific evolution of technical objects occurs neither in an absolutely continuous nor completely discontinuous manner; it is made up of stages that are defined by the fact that they produce successive systems of coherence; between stages marking a structural re-organization there can be an evolution of a continuous kind; this is due to the progressive perfection of details resulting from experience and use, and from the production of better adapted raw materials or auxiliary devices; for thirty years the automobile engine improved through the use of metals that were better adapted to the conditions of utilization, through the increase of the compression ratio as a result of research into fuels, and through the study of the particular form of cylinder heads and piston heads in relation to the phenomenon of detonation. The problem that consists in producing combustion while avoiding detonation can be resolved only through work of a scientific kind on the propagation of the explosive wave at the heart of a carburized mix, at different pressure levels, at different temperatures, with diverse volumes and starting from determinate ignition points. This effort, however, does not itself lead directly to applications: the experimental work remains to be accomplished and there is a technicity proper to this path toward progressive perfection. What is essential in the coming-into-being of this object are the structural reforms that facilitate the technical object's self-specification; even if the sciences were to stop progressing for a time, the progress of the technical object toward specificity would continue; the principle of this progress is effectively the manner in which the object causes and conditions itself in its functioning and in the reactions of its functioning on its utilization; the technical object, issued forth from the abstract work of the organization of sub-systems, is the theater of a certain number of reciprocal causal relations.

It is due to these relations, given certain limits of the conditions of utilization, that the object encounters obstacles within its own operation: *the play of limits, whose overcoming constitutes progress, resides in the incompatibilities that arise from the progressive saturation of the system of sub-ensembles;*[2] yet because of its very nature, this overcoming can occur only as a leap, as a modification of the internal distribution of functions, a rearrangement of their system; what was once an obstacle must become the means of realization.

[. . .]

It seems contradictory, of course, to affirm that the evolution of the technical object obeys both a process of differentiation (the triode's command grid is divided into three grids within the pentode) and a process of concretization, where each structural element fulfills several functions rather than a single one; but these two processes are in fact tied to each other; differentiation is possible because, in a conscious and calculated manner and in view of a necessary result, it enables the integration of correlative effects of the global functioning into the functioning of the ensemble, effects which had until then been more or less corrected by palliatives that were separate from the principle function.

[. . .]

These two examples [evolution of the electronic tube and the Coolidge tube] tend to show that differentiation goes in the same direction as the condensation of multiple functions within the same structure, because the differentiation of structures within a system of reciprocal causalities allows one to suppress side-effects that were hitherto obstacles (by integrating them into the functioning). The specialization of each structure is a specialization of a synthetic positive functional unit [*une spécialisation d'unité fonctionnelle synthétique positive*], freed from undesired side-effects that affect functioning; the technical object progresses by way of an internal redistribution of functions into compatible units, replacing the contingency or antagonism of the primitive distribution; specialization does not occur *function after function*, but *synergy after synergy* [*synergie par synergie*], it is the synergetic group of functions and not the unique function that constitutes the true sub-system in the technical object. It is because of this search for synergies that the technical object's concretization can translate into an element of simplification; the concrete technical object is one that is no longer in conflict with itself, one in which no side-effect is detrimental to the functioning of the ensemble or left out of this functioning. In this manner and for this reason a function can be fulfilled by several synergistically associated structures in the technical object that has become concrete, whereas in the primitive and abstract technical object each structure is charged with the accomplishment of a definite function, and generally only one. The essence of the technical object's concretization is the organization of functional sub-ensembles within the total functioning; on the basis of this principle one can understand in what sense the redistribution of functions occurs in the network of different structures, both in the abstract technical object and in the concrete technical object: each structure fulfills several functions; but in the abstract technical object, it only fulfills one essential and positive function, integrated into the functioning of the ensemble; in the concrete technical object, all the functions fulfilled by the structure are positive, essential, and integrated into the functioning of the whole; the marginal consequences of the functioning, eliminated or attenuated in the abstract technical object by corrective measures, become stages or positive aspects in the concrete object; the schema of functioning incorporates marginal aspects; consequences that were irrelevant or harmful become chain-links in its functioning.

This progress presupposes that the engineer [*constructeur*] consciously endows each structure with characteristics that correspond to all the components of its functioning, as if there were no difference between the artificial object and a physical system studied from the point of view of all knowable aspects of exchanges of energy, as well as physical and chemical transformations; each piece, in the concrete object, is no longer simply that which essentially corresponds to the accomplishment of a function desired by the builder [*constructeur*], but part of a system where a multitude of forces act and produce effects that are independent of the fabricating intention. The concrete technical object is a physico-chemical system in which reciprocal actions take place according to all the laws of the sciences. The objective of the technical intention can attain perfection in the construction of an object only if it becomes identical to universal scientific knowledge. It should be emphasized that this latter knowledge must indeed be universal, because the fact that the technical object belongs to the class of fabricated objects, answering to this particular human need, does not in turn limit and in no way defines the type of physico-chemical actions that can occur in this object or between this object and the outside world. The difference between the technical object and the physico-chemical system studied as an object only resides within the imperfection of the sciences; the scientific knowledge that serves as a guide to predicting the universality of reciprocal actions exerted within the technical system is still affected by a certain imperfection; it doesn't allow for an absolute prediction with rigorous precision of all effects; this is why a certain distance remains between the system of technical intentions corresponding to a defined objective and the scientific system of knowledge of causal interactions that realize this objective; the technical object is never fully known; for this very reason, it is never completely concrete, unless it happens through a rare chance occurrence. The ultimate allocation of functions to structures and the exact calculation of structures could only be accomplished if the scientific knowledge of all phenomena likely to exist in the technical object were completely acquired; since this is not the case, a certain difference subsists between the technical scheme of the object (containing the representation of a human objective) and the scientific picture of phenomena for which it is the base (containing only schemas of reciprocal or recurrent efficient causality).

The concretization of technical objects is conditioned by way of narrowing the interval that separates the sciences and technology [*techniques*]; the primitive artisanal phase is characterized by a weak correlation between the sciences and technology, whereas the industrial phase is characterized by a strong correlation. The construction of a determinate technical object can only become industrial when this object has become concrete, which means that it is known in an almost identical manner according to the intention of construction [*l'intention constructive*] and according to the scientific view. This explains the fact that certain objects could be manufactured [*construits*] in an industrial manner well before others, a winch, a hoist, snatch blocks, and a hydraulic press are technical objects in which, for the most part, the phenomena of friction, electrical charging, electrodynamic induction, thermal and chemical exchanges can be neglected without leading to the destruction or malfunction of the object; rational classical mechanics [*la mécanique rationnelle classique*] are sufficient for a scientific knowledge of the principal phenomena that characterize the functioning of these objects we call simple machines [*machines simples*]: however, it would have been impossible to industrially manufacture a centrifugal gas pump or a thermal engine in the seventeenth century. The first industrially produced thermal engine, which was the Newcomen atmospheric engine, simply used the process of depression, because the phenomenon of the condensation of steam under the influence of cooling was scientifically known. Electrostatic machines also remained artisanal nearly to the present day, because the phenomena of the production and transport of charges via dielectrics and then flowing of charges via the Corona effect, which had been qualitatively known since at least the eighteenth century, had not yet been subjected to rigorous scientific study; after the Wimshurst machine, even the Van de Graaff generator retained something artisanal, despite its large size and greater power.

IV. ABSOLUTE ORIGINS OF THE TECHNICAL LINEAGE

[. . .]

A technical essence [*L'essence technique*] can be recognized by the fact that it remains stable across [*à travers*] the evolving lineage, and not only stable, but also productive of structures and functions through internal development and progressive saturation [. . .].

[. . .]

Concretization gives the technical object an intermediate place between the natural object and scientific representation. The abstract technical object, in other words the primitive technical object, is far from constituting a natural system; it is the translation into matter of a set of notions and scientific principles that are deeply separate from one another, which are attached only through their consequences and converge for the purpose of the production of a desired effect. This primitive technical object is not a natural, physical system, it is the physical translation [*traduction physique*] of an intellectual system. For this reason, it is an application or a bundle of applications; it comes after knowledge, and cannot teach anything; it cannot be examined inductively [*inductivement*] like a natural object, precisely because it is artificial.

On the contrary, the concrete technical object, which is to say the evolved technical object, comes closer to the mode of existence of natural objects, tending toward internal coherence, toward a closure of the system of causes and effects that exert themselves in a circular fashion within its bounds, and it moreover incorporates a part of the natural world that intervenes as a condition of functioning, and is thus part of the system of causes and effects. As it evolves, this object loses its artificial character: the essential artificiality of an object resides in the fact that man must intervene to maintain the existence of this object by protecting it against the natural world, giving it a status of existence that stands apart. Artificiality is not a characteristic denoting the fabricated origin of the object in opposition to spontaneous production in nature: artificiality is that which is internal to man's artificializing action, whether this action intervenes on a natural object or on an entirely fabricated one; a flower, grown in a greenhouse, which yields only petals (a double flower) without being able to engender fruit, is the flower of an artificialized plant: man diverted [*détourné*] the functions of this plant from their coherent fulfillment, to such an extent that it can no longer reproduce except through procedures such as grafting, requiring human intervention. Rendering a natural object artificial leads to the opposite results to that of technical concretization: the artificialized plant can only exist in a laboratory for plants, the greenhouse, with its complex system of thermal and hydraulic regulations. Its system of primitively coherent biological functions has opened up into functions that are independent of one another, and only become attached to one another through the gardener's care; its flowering has become a pure flowering, detached, anomic; the plant flowers until it is exhausted, without producing seeds. It loses its initial capacity of resistance against cold, drought, and sun; the regulations of the primitively natural object become the artificial regulations of the greenhouse. Artificialization is a process of abstraction within the artificialized object.

Conversely, technical concretization makes the primitively artificial object increasingly similar to a natural object. This object needed a regulative external milieu in the beginning, the laboratory, workshop, or sometimes the factory; it gradually increases its concretization, it becomes capable of doing without the artificial milieu, because its internal coherence increases, its functional systematicity closes as it organizes itself. The concretized object is comparable to the spontaneously produced object; the object frees itself from the originally associated laboratory and dynamically incorporates the laboratory into itself through the play of its functions; what enables the self-maintenance of the object's conditions of functioning is its relation to other technical and natural objects, and it is this relation that becomes regulative; this object is no longer isolated; it associates itself with other objects, or suffices unto itself, whereas at first it was isolated and heteronomous.

The consequences of this concretization are not only human and economical (allowing decentralization, for example), they are also intellectual: since the mode of existence of the concretized technical object is analogous to that of natural spontaneously produced objects, one can legitimately consider them as one would natural objects; in other words, one can submit them to inductive study. They are no longer mere applications of certain prior scientific principles. By existing, they prove the viability and stability of a certain structure that has the same status as a natural structure, even if it might be schematically different from all natural structures. The study of the functioning of concrete technical objects bears scientific value, since its objects are not deduced from a single principle; they are testimony to a certain mode of functioning and compatibility that exists in fact and has been built before having been planned: this compatibility was not contained in each of the separate scientific principles that served to build the object; it was discovered empirically; one can work backward from the acknowledgement of this compatibility to the separate sciences in order to pose the problem of the correlation of their principles and ground a science of correlations and transformations that would be a general technology or mechanology [*technologie générale ou méchanologie*].

However, for this general technology to make sense, one must avoid the improper identification of the technical object with the natural object and more specifically with the living being [*vivant*]. External analogies, or rather resemblances, must be rigorously banned: they have no signification and are only misleading. Dwelling on automata is dangerous because it risks limiting one to the study of external aspects and thereby to improper identifications. The only thing that counts is the exchange of energy and information within the technical object or between the technical object and its milieu; external behaviors as viewed by a spectator are not objects of scientific study. One needn't even found a separate science that would study the mechanisms of regulation and command in automata built to be automata: technology must deal with the universality of technical objects. In this sense, cybernetics is insufficient: it has the immense merit of being the first inductive study of technical objects, and of presenting itself as a study of the intermediate domain between the specialized sciences; but it has specialized its domain of investigation too narrowly, because it started from the study of a certain number of technical objects; it accepted as its point of departure that which technology must reject: a classification of technical objects according to criteria established according to genera and species. Automata are not a *species*; there are only technical objects, which in turn have a functional organization that results in various degrees of automatism.

What risks making the work of cybernetics partially inefficient as an inter-scientific study (which nevertheless is the objective Norbert Wiener attributes to his research) is the initial postulate concerning the identity between living beings and self-regulating technical objects. Yet the only thing we can say is that technical objects tend toward concretization, whereas natural objects, such as living beings, are concrete to begin with. One mustn't confuse the tendency toward concretization with the status of entirely concrete existence. To a certain extent, every technical object has residual aspects of abstraction; one mustn't go right to the limit and speak of technical objects as if they were natural objects. Technical objects must be studied in their evolution in order to discern the process of concretization as a tendency; but one mustn't isolate the last product of technical evolution in order to declare it entirely concrete; it is more concrete than the preceding ones, yet it is still artificial. Instead of considering one class of technical beings, automata, one must follow the lines of concretization throughout a temporal evolution of technical objects; it is only by following this path that the rapprochement between the living being and the technical object makes any true sense, beyond any mythology. In the absence of any end-point thought out and realized by living human beings on Earth, physical causality could not, in the majority of cases, have produced a positive and efficient concretization on its own, even though modulating structures exist in nature (relaxation oscillators, amplifiers)—wherever metastable states exist, and this is perhaps one of the aspects of the origins of life.

NOTES

1. According to determinate modalities that distinguish the genesis of the technical object from that of other types of objects: the aesthetic object, the living being. These specific modalities of genesis must be distinguished from a static specificity that one could establish after genesis by considering the characteristics of diverse types of objects; the point of using a genetic method is precisely to avoid using classification as a way of thinking that occurs after genesis only to distribute the totality of objects into genera and species suitable for discourse. The technical being retains the essence of its past evolution in the form of its technicity. According to the approach we shall call analectic, the technical being, as bearer of this technicity, can be the object of adequate knowledge only if the latter grasps the temporal sense of its evolution; this adequate knowledge is a culture of technics, distinct from technical knowledge, which is limited to the actuality of isolated schemas of operation. Considering that the relations that exist between one technical object and another at the level of technicity are horizontal as well as vertical, any form of knowledge that proceeds by genera and species becomes inadequate: we will attempt to point out the way in which the relation between technical objects is transductive.

2. They are the conditions of a system's individuation.

5

MACHINE FRAGMENTS

Gerald Raunig

But, once adopted into the production process of capital, the means of labour passes through different metamorphoses, whose culmination is the *machine*, or rather, an *automatic system of machinery* [. . .], set in motion by an automaton, a moving power that moves itself; this automaton consisting of numerous mechanical and intellectual organs, so that the workers themselves are cast merely as its conscious linkages.
—Karl Marx, "Fragment on Machines"

On the contrary, we think that the machine must be grasped in an immediate relation to a social body and not at all to a human biological organism. Given this, it is no longer appropriate to judge the machine as a new segment that, with its starting point in the abstract human being in keeping with this development, follows the tool. For human being and tool are already machine parts on the full body of the respective society. The machine is initially a social machine, constituted by the machine-generating instance of a full body and by human being and tools, which are, to the extent that they are distributed on this body, machinized.
—Gilles Deleuze, Félix Guattari, *Anti-Oedipus*

Is it about a machine? The question is not easy to answer, but correctly posed. The question should certainly not be: What is a machine? Or even: Who is a machine? It is not a question of the essence, but of the event, not about *is*, but about *and*, about concatenations and connections, compositions and movements that constitute a machine. Therefore, it is not a matter of saying "the bicycle *is* . . ."—a machine, for instance, but rather the bicycle *and* the person riding it, the bicycle and the person *and* the bicycle and the person mutually supporting one another, the bicycles *and* the bicycle thieves, etc.

The commonplace concept of the machine, however, refers to a technical object, which can be precisely determined in its physical demarcation and seclusion, as well as in its usability for a purpose. Regardless of how these characteristics may be verified today, the machine was once conceptualized quite differently, namely as a complex composition and as an assemblage that specifically could not be grasped and defined through its utilization. The meaning of the term machine gradually began to be limited to its technical, mechanistic and seemingly clearly-delimitable sense starting in the 13th century and has been developed since the 17th century as a radical disambiguation of the term. The term entered into the German and the English languages through the influence of the French *machine* as a purely technical term alongside the still existent Latin *machina* concept and its derivatives. The enormous leap in the development of technical apparatuses and equipment in the 17th and 18th centuries, their dissemination and the knowledge about them in every possible field of society, was followed in the 19th century by the development of an economic dispositif of technical apparatuses, in other words a dispositif of the economic functionality and the exploitation of these apparatuses to increase productivity.

The vehement restraint of the broader concept of *machina* as an assemblage of concepts that was previously not at all only technically connotated thus first began in the 17th century, and with it began the hierarchization of the various aspects of the machinic. The constriction of the terminological landscape also ushered in the increasing marginalization and metaphorization of all other meanings by the technical connotation. In this era there was a proliferation of metaphors of man as machine, of the state as machine, of the world as machine: with the introduction of a universal metaphor for a utilitarian and functional order on both the micro and the macro level, the functional and organizational mode of human organs, communal living, even the entire cosmos were to be explained with the constricted technical concept of the machine.

Yet deep in the 19th century there was already an indication of the de-/re-coding of the machine concept that was then to be completely actualized in the 20th century. Beyond the poles of increasingly exact calculations for the economic functionalization of technical machines on the one hand and social-romantic Luddism on the other, at the same time that the Industrial Revolution finally spread all over Europe there was an unmistakable movement in the direction that would lead to generalized machine thinking in the second half of the 20th century: in the "Fragment on Machines," a section of *Grundrisse der Kritik der politischen Ökonomie*, drafted in 1857–58, Karl Marx developed his ideas on the transformation of the means of labor from a simple tool into a form corresponding to fixed capital, in other words into technical machines and "machinery."

In general, Marx sees the machine succinctly as a "means for producing surplus-value," in other words certainly not intended to reduce the labor effort of the workers, but rather to optimize their exploitation. Marx describes this function of "machinery" in Chapter 13 of *Das Kapital* with the three aspects of enhancing the human being utilizable as labor power (especially women's and child labor), prolonging the working day and intensifying labor. In the "Fragment on Machines" Marx focuses especially on the historical development that he (and others) described, at the end of which the machine, unlike the tool, is not at all to be understood as a means of labor for the individual worker: instead it encloses the knowledge and skill of workers and scholars as objectified knowledge and skill, opposing the workers scattered in its plane of immanence as a dominant and central power. From this perspective the modes of subjectivation and socialization are certainly not to be regarded as the outside of the machine (and thus to be constructed as machine metaphors), but rather as enclosed in the technical machinery.

Marx describes the relationship between humans and machines primarily as *social subjection*, as the intervention of the machine as an alien force in the living labor of the scattered workers, who—"subsumed under the overall process of the machinery itself"—function as parts of a mechanical system, as living accessories to this machinery, as means of its action. Here Marx seems to follow the pair of metaphors depicting the machine as a gigantic organism and the human beings as its dependent, appropriated components. Capital develops in this as power over living labor that has "subjected itself to the production process as a whole."

The automatic system of machinery that seems to be set in motion by a "moving force that moves itself," this automaton, however, is not imagined even by Marx in the Machine Fragment as a purely technical apparatus, as a purely anorganic, non-living composition, but rather as "consisting of numerous mechanical and intellectual organs." The workers operating the apparatuses are just as much a part of the machine as the intellectual, cognitive labor of those who have developed the machine and make up its social environment: economists, managers, and engineers. Marx thus formulates on the one hand the separation of the workers from their means of work, their determination through the machines, the domination of living labor by objectified labor, and introduces the figure of the inverse relationship of humans and machines:

from the machine as a means for the human being to ease his or her working and living conditions to the human being as a means of the machine. From this perspective, human action on the machine, ultimately limited to preserving the machine from disruptions, is thoroughly subjected to the order of the machinery and not the other way around. Even the immaterial, intellectual, cognitive work that consisted in developing the machine, due to its enclosure in the technical apparatus, becomes an alien, extra-human power of the machine on the human components acting in the machine.

The reversal of the relationship of workers and means of labor in the direction of the domination of the machine over the human being is not only defined through the linear development from the tool to the composite technical apparatus and through the hierarchy in the labor process, but also as the inversion of power over knowledge. In the logic of social subjection, it seems that "all sciences are imprisoned in service to capital." Through the process of objectifying all forms of knowledge in the machine, the producers of this knowledge lose the undivided competency and the power over the labor process; living labor itself regards itself on the one hand as objectified, dead labor in the machine, on the other as scattered, divided among single living workers at many points in the machinery.

Yet even for Marx in the Machine Fragment, the enormous, self-active machine is more than a mechanism. The machine is not at all limited to its technical aspects, but is instead a mechanical-intellectual, even social assemblage: although technology and knowledge (as machine) have a one-sided impact on the workers, the machine is a concatenation not only of technology and knowledge, of the mechanical and the intellectual, but also and beyond this of social "organs," at least to the extent that it carries out the coordination of the scattered workers. What is evident in this, first of all, is an anticipation of the double relationship of *social subjection* and *machinic enslavement*: the machine not only forms its subjects, it structuralizes and striates not only the workers as an automaton, as an apparatus, as a structure, as a purely technical machine in the final stage of the development of the means of labor; it is also permeated by mechanical, intellectual and social "organs," which not only drive and operate it, but also successively develop, renew and even invent it.

The machine, however, also generates a flash of overcoming this double relationship of social subjection and machinic enslavement, hence the possible, if not the necessary collectivity of the human intellect. In a well-known passage of the Fragment, Marx opens up this potentiality with the concept of the *general intellect* which later became, especially for Italian Operaism and Postoperaism, the common point of reference for an emancipatory turn in machine theory: machines "are *organs of the human brain, created by the human hand*; the power of knowledge, objectified. The development of fixed capital indicates to what degree general social knowledge has become a *direct force of production*, and to what degree, hence, the conditions of the process of social life itself have come under the control of the general intellect and been transformed in accordance with it. To what degree the powers of social production have been produced, not only in the form of knowledge, but also as immediate organs of social practice, of the real life process."

The "Fragment on Machines" not only points to the fact that knowledge and skill are accumulated and absorbed in fixed capital as "general productive forces of the social brain" and that the process of turning production into knowledge is a tendency of capital, but also indicates the inversion of this tendency: the concatenation of knowledge and technology is not exhausted in fixed capital, but also refers beyond the technical machine and the knowledge objectified in it, to forms of social cooperation and communication, not only as machinic enslavement, but also as the capacity of immaterial labor—and this form of labor, as especially (post-) Operaist theory would later insist, can destroy the conditions under which accumulation develops. Marx at least writes in the "Fragment on Machines" that forces of production and social relations are the material conditions to blow the foundation of capital sky-high . . .

As early as the 19th century, a machinic thinking emerged which actualized the concatenation of technical apparatuses with social assemblages and with the intellect as a collective capacity, and recognizes revolutionary potentials in this. In multiple waves and in different fields and disciplines, now the process of narrowing and disambiguating the machine as a technical machine, which has predominated for over three hundred years, is turning around again. The long linear history of the expansion of the hand as a serving means of labor to the hand operating technical apparatuses (in which the hand itself becomes a prosthesis of the apparatus) to the complete autonomy of the machine and the subjection of the human being loses its significance. To the extent that it is not limited to the designation of technical apparatuses, the concept of the machine no longer refers only to a metaphor of the mechanic functioning of something other than technical machines. Although these kinds of ideas still remain dominant, they are being increasingly supplanted by a thinking that grasps the technical machine conversely as an indication of a more general notion of the machine behind it. From the excessive literary machine fantasies of Futurism, Constructivism and Surrealism through the cybernetics and socio-cybernetics of not only Norbert Wiener and the increasingly expanding research on the machine in the philosophy of science, for instance by Canguilhem and Simondon, there is an ongoing intensification of an extensive understanding of the machine reaching all the way to the cyborg theories of Donna Haraway and the Cyberfeminist International around the last turn of the century. However, this development is not to be regarded as a solely historical-linear one, from the pre-modern extension of the machine concept through modern demarcations to these boundaries finally becoming permeable (again and in a different way), but is instead also to be examined in the respective historical context of its movement.

In Félix Guattari's writings, especially what he wrote in the 1970s together with Gilles Deleuze, this movement is expanded and condensed: the technical machine is declared a subset of a more comprehensive machinic issue and terminology, which is opened up to the outside and to its machinic environment and maintains all kinds of relationships to social components and subjectivities.[1] It thus thwarts, first of all, the opposition of man and machine, of organism and mechanism developed over the course of centuries, on the basis of which one is explained by the other, the human from the machine or the machine from the human, in both anthropocentric and mechanistic world views. Both, although they seem to be in extreme opposition, see themselves in the conventional linear paradigms, even in the thwarting of their dichotomy as unbroken, without resistance, instrumental: mechanism and organism share the ideal notion of an endless, empty repetition without difference, of an overall functionality and of a rigorous subjection of the parts.

In contrast, for Deleuze and Guattari the (desiring) machine is only to be found in the simultaneity of flow and rupture. Human bodies collapse, technical apparatuses become dysfunctional or are brought to a halt with the wooden shoe of sabotage, states crumble in civil war or are evacuated in exodus. Yet the orgiastic paradigm of *Anti-Oedipus* does not foreground the human being, the technical apparatus, the state, but rather the relationship between the streams and ruptures of assemblages, in which organic, technical and social machines are concatenated.

In the "Appendix" to *Anti-Oedipus* Gilles Deleuze and Félix Guattari not only develop a "Balance Sheet Program for Desiring Machines," but also write their own machine concept, in undisguised, yet initially not explicit contrast to Marx's ideas on machinery. This involves an expansion or renewal of the concept, first of all against metaphorizing the machine. Deleuze and Guattari do not want to establish another "figurative sense" of the machine, but instead attempt to newly invent the term at a critical distance from both the everyday sense and Marxist scholars. Marx's machine theory (although not the machine theory from *Grundrisse* discussed above, but rather the less fragmentary, but theoretically smoother one from *Das Kapital*) is introduced here with the cipher "that classical scheme," but explicitly named only in the third and final part of the appendix. In the thirteenth chapter of *Das Kapital*, Marx addressed at some length the distinction between tool and machine, specifically under the aspect of how a means of labor is transformed from a tool (which Guattari calls a proto-machine) into a machine. With this he repeated the straight line from tools of the human organism to tools of a technical apparatus that he had already outlined in *The Misery of Philosophy*. This linear conception is criticized by Deleuze/Guattari as insufficient in many respects. They question less the immanent logic of the transformation of machines as described by Marx, but rather the framework that Marx presupposes as the basis of this logic: a dimension of man and nature common to all social forms. The linear development from tool (as an extension of the human being to relieve strain) toward an upheaval, in the course of which the machine ultimately becomes independent of the human being, so to speak, simultaneously determines the machine as one aspect in a mechanical series. This kind of schema, "stemming from the humanist spirit and abstract," especially isolates the productive forces from the social conditions of their application. Deleuze and Guattari hence shift the perspective from the question of the form in which the machine follows simpler tools, how humans and tools become machinized, to the question of which social machines make the occurrence of specific technical, affective, cognitive, semiotic machines and their concatenations possible and necessary.

Beyond evolutive schemes, the machine is no longer only a function in a series imagined as starting from the tool, which occurs at a certain point. Similar to the way the *technè* and *mechané* concepts of antiquity already meant both material object and practice, the machine is also not solely an instrument of work, in which social knowledge is absorbed and enclosed. Instead it opens up in respectively different social contexts to different concatenations, connections and couplings.

Instead of placing tool and machine in a series, Deleuze and Guattari seek a more fundamental differentiation of the two concepts. As in the following section of this text, this distinction can be described in the form of a different genealogy than the sequence from tool to machine, namely one that takes recourse to the pre-modern understanding of the *machina*. In *Anti-Oedipus*, however, this difference is treated conceptually/theoretically: the machine is a communication factor, the tool—at least in its non-machinic form—is, on the other hand, a communicationless extension or prosthesis. Conversely, the concrete tool in its use for exchange/connection with the human being is always more machine than the technical machine imagined in isolation. For Deleuze and Guattari, becoming a piece with something else means something fundamentally different from extending oneself, projecting oneself or being replaced by a technical apparatus.

By distinguishing the machine from something that simply extends or replaces the human being, Deleuze and Guattari not only refuse to affirm the simple cultural-pessimism figure of the machine's domination over the human being. They also posit a difference from an all too simplistic and optimistic celebration of a certain form of machine, which from Futurism to cyber-fans is in danger of overlooking the social aspect in ever new combinations of "man-machine." Technical prostheses as a sheer endless extension of the inadequate human being, fictions of artificial humans following Mary Shelley's Frankenstein, stories of machines increasingly penetrating into the human being usually prove to be reductionist complements to the paradigm of alienation. The narrative of man's becoming-machine as a purely technical alteration misses the machinic, both in its civilization-critical development and in its euphoric tendency. It is no longer a matter of confronting man and machine to estimate possible or impossible correspondences, extensions and substitutions of the one or the other, of ever new relationships of similarity and metaphorical relations between humans and machines, but rather of concatenations, of how man becomes a piece with the machine or with other things in order to constitute a machine. The "other things" may be animals, tools, other people, statements, signs or desires, but they only become machine in a process of exchange, not in the paradigm of substitution.

According to Guattari, the primary characteristic of the machine is the flowing of its components: every extension or substitution would be communicationlessness, and the quality of the machine is exactly the opposite, namely that of communication, of exchange. Contrary to the structure (and to the later conceptualized double of the structure, the state apparatus), which tends toward closure, the machinic corresponds to a tendentially permanent praxis of connection. From the text "Machine and Structure," written in 1969, to "Machinic heterogenesis," published in 1991, a year before his death, Guattari repeatedly pointed out the different quality of machine and structure, machine and state apparatus. The machine is not limited to managing and striating entities closed off to one another, but opens up to other machines and, together with them, moves machinic assemblages. It consists of machines and penetrates several structures simultaneously. It depends on external elements in order to be able to exist at all. It implies a complementarity not only with the human being that fabricates it, allows it to function or destroys it, but also exists in itself in a relationship of difference and exchange with other virtual or actual machines.

If we want to continue to approach a machine concept that is as extensive as it is ambivalent, then the historical context of Guattari's writings should also be included in our considerations. Which question does the concept of the machine answer here, which problem does it actualize? What is the reason for the intricate endeavor to tear the everyday machine concept from its commonplace connotation? Guattari had already started to develop his machine concept in the late 1960s, specifically against the background of micropolitical experiences and leftist experiments in organizing. These endeavors were initially directed against the hard segmentarity of Real-Socialist and Euro-Communist state left-wings, against the process of the structuralization of revolutionary movements also and particularly among the left; they were then further explored on the basis of the experiences of diverse subcultural and micropolitical practices, in Guattari's case especially on the basis of the anti-psychiatric practice of institutional analysis in the La Borde clinic. They ultimately flowed, even after 1968, into efforts to resist and reflect on the structuralization and closure of the 1968 generation in cadres, factions and circles.

The problem that Guattari deals with in his first machine text, written briefly after the experience of 1968, is the problem of a lasting revolutionary organization, an instituent machine that should guarantee that it does not close itself off in the various social structures, especially not in the state structure. From this perspective, Guattari's extensive machine concept is a strategy for opposing the machine to the danger of structuralization and state-apparatization, as well as against the identitary closing effects of concepts of community: the machine as a non-identitary concept for fleeing stratification and identification, for inventing new forms of the concatenation of singularities.

NOTE

1. At this point it should be noted that the way Guattari and Deleuze use the concept of the machine is thoroughly ambivalent. The shadow sides of machinization regularly appear, such as in the reflections on fascist and post-fascist forms of the war machine in *A Thousand Plateaus*, or in Guattari's 1980s concept of "machinic enslavement" in "worldwide integrated capitalism," as he called the phenomenon framed today as globalization. "Machinic enslavement" does not mean here simply the subordinated relationship of the human being to the social knowledge of objectifying technical machines, but rather a more general form of the collective administration of knowledge and the necessity of permanent, even if seemingly self-determined, participation. The machinic quality of postfordist capitalism appends to the traditional systems of direct oppression—and here Guattari is very close to the theories of neoliberal governmentality developed by Foucault—a range of control mechanisms requiring the complicity of individuals.

BIBLIOGRAPHY

Deleuze, Gilles, and Félix Guattari. *A Thousand Plateaus: Capitalism and Schizophrenia*. Translated by Brian Massumi. London: Continuum, 1987.

6

IS A MUSEUM A FACTORY?

Hito Steyerl

The film *La hora de los hornos* (*The Hour of the Furnaces*, 1968), a Third Cinema manifesto against neocolonialism, has a brilliant installation specification.[1] A banner was to be hung at every screening with text reading: "Every spectator is either a coward or a traitor."[2] It was intended to break down the distinctions between filmmaker and audience, author and producer, and thus create a sphere of political action. And where was this film shown? In factories, of course.

Now, political films are no longer shown in factories.[3] They are shown in the museum, or the gallery—the art space. That is, in any sort of white cube.[4]

How did this happen? First of all, the traditional Fordist factory is, for the most part, gone.[5] It's been emptied out, machines packed up and shipped off to China. Former workers have been retrained for further retraining, or become software programmers and started working from home. Secondly, the cinema has been transformed almost as dramatically as the factory. It's been multiplexed, digitized, and sequelized, as well as rapidly commercialized as neoliberalism became hegemonic in its reach and influence. Before cinema's recent demise, political films sought refuge elsewhere. Their return to cinematic space is rather recent, and the cinema was never the space for formally more experimental works. Now, political and experimental films alike are shown in black boxes set within white cubes—in fortresses, bunkers, docks, and former churches. The sound is almost always awful.

But terrible projections and dismal installation notwithstanding, these works catalyze surprising desire. Crowds of people can be seen bending and crouching in order to catch glimpses of political cinema and video art. Is this audience sick of media monopolies? Are they trying to find answers to the obvious crisis of everything? And why should they be looking for these answers in art spaces?

AFRAID OF THE REAL?

The conservative response to the exodus of political films (or video installations) to the museum is to assume that they are thus losing relevance. It deplores their internment in the bourgeois ivory tower of high culture. The works are thought to be isolated inside this elitist cordon sanitaire—sanitized, sequestered, cut off from "reality." Indeed, Jean-Luc Godard reportedly said that video installation artists shouldn't be "afraid of reality," assuming of course that they in fact were.[6]

Where is reality then? Out there, beyond the white cube and its display technologies? How about inverting this claim, somewhat polemically, to assert that the white cube is in fact the Real with a capital R: the blank horror and emptiness of the bourgeois interior.

On the other hand—and in a much more optimistic vein—there is no need to have recourse to Lacan in order to contest Godard's accusation. This is because the displacement from factory to museum never took place. In reality, political films are very often screened in the exact same place as they always were: in former factories, which are today, more often than not, museums. A gallery, an art space, a white cube with abysmal sound isolation. Which will certainly show political films. But which also has become a hotbed of contemporary production. Of images, jargon, lifestyles, and values. Of exhibition value, speculation value, and cult value. Of entertainment plus gravitas. Or of aura minus distance. A flagship store of Cultural Industries, staffed by eager interns who work for free.

A factory, so to speak, but a different one. It is still a space for production, still a space of exploitation and even of political screenings. It is a space of physical meeting and sometimes even common discussion. At the same time, it has changed almost beyond recognition. So what sort of factory is this?

PRODUCTIVE TURN

The typical setup of the museum-as-factory looks like this. Before: an industrial workplace. Now: people spending their leisure time in front of TV monitors. Before: people working in these factories. Now: people working at home in front of computer monitors.

Andy Warhol's Factory served as model for the new museum in its productive turn towards being a "social factory."[7] By now, descriptions of the social factory abound.[8] It exceeds its traditional boundaries and spills over into almost everything else. It pervades bedrooms and dreams alike, as well as perception, affection, and attention. It transforms everything it touches into culture, if not art. It is an a-factory, which produces affect as effect. It integrates intimacy, eccentricity, and other formally unofficial forms of creation. Private and public spheres get entangled in a blurred zone of hyper-production.

In the museum-as-factory, something continues to be produced. Installation, planning, carpentry, viewing, discussing, maintenance, betting on rising values, and networking alternate in cycles. An art space is a factory, which is simultaneously a supermarket—a casino and a place of worship whose reproductive work is performed by cleaning ladies and cellphone-video bloggers alike.

In this economy, even spectators are transformed into workers. As Jonathan Beller argues, cinema and its derivatives (television, Internet, and so on) are factories, in which spectators work. Now, "to look is to labor."[9] Cinema, which integrated the logic of Taylorist production and the conveyor belt, now spreads the factory wherever it travels. But this type of production is much more intensive than the industrial one. The senses are drafted into production, the media capitalize upon the aesthetic faculties and imaginary practices of viewers.[10] In that sense, any space that integrates cinema and its successors has now become a factory, and this obviously includes the museum. While in the history of political filmmaking the factory became a cinema, cinema now turns museum spaces back into factories.

WORKERS LEAVING THE FACTORY

It is quite curious that the first films ever made by Louis Lumière show workers leaving the factory. At the beginning of cinema, workers leave the industrial workplace. The invention of cinema thus symbolically marks the start of the exodus of workers from industrial modes of production. But even if they leave the factory building, it doesn't mean that they have left labor behind. Rather, they take it along with them and disperse it into every sector of life.

A brilliant installation by Harun Farocki makes clear where the workers leaving the factory are headed. Farocki collected and installed different cinematic versions of "Workers Leaving the Factory," from the original silent version(s) by Louis Lumière to contemporary surveillance footage.[11] Workers are streaming out of factories on several monitors simultaneously: from different eras and in different cinematic styles.[12] But where are these workers streaming to? Into the art space, where the work is installed.

Not only is Farocki's "Workers Leaving the Factory," on the level of content, a wonderful archaeology of the (non)representation of labor; on the level of form it points to the spilling over of the factory into the art space. Workers who left the factory have ended up inside another one: the museum.

It might even be the same factory. Because the former Lumière factory, whose gates are portrayed in the original *Workers Leaving the Lumière Factory* is today just that: a museum of cinema.[13] In 1995, the ruin of the former factory was declared a historical monument and developed into a site of culture. The Lumière factory, which used to produce photographic film, is today a cinema with a reception space to be rented by companies: "a location loaded with history and emotion for your brunches, cocktails and dinners."[14] The workers who left the factory in 1895 have today been recaptured on the screen of the cinema within the same space. They only left the factory to reemerge as a spectacle inside it.

As workers exit the factory, the space they enter is one of cinema and cultural industry, producing emotion and attention. How do *its* spectators look inside this new factory?

CINEMA AND FACTORY

At this point, a decisive difference emerges between classical cinema and the museum. While the classical space of cinema resembles the space of the industrial factory, the museum corresponds to the dispersed space of the social factory. Both cinema and Fordist factory are organized as locations of confinement, arrest, and temporal control. Imagine: Workers leaving the factory. Spectators leaving the cinema—a similar mass, disciplined and controlled in time, assembled and released at regular intervals. As the traditional factory arrests its workers, the cinema arrests the spectator. Both are disciplinary spaces and spaces of confinement.[15]

But now imagine: Workers leaving the factory. Spectators trickling out of the museum (or even queuing to get in). An entirely different constellation of time and space. This second crowd is not a mass, but a multitude.[16] The museum doesn't organize a coherent crowd of people. People are dispersed in time and space—a silent crowd, immersed and atomized, struggling between passivity and overstimulation.

This spatial transformation is reflected by the format of many newer cinematic works. Whereas traditional cinematic works are single-channel, focusing the gaze and organizing time, many of the newer works explode into space. While the traditional cinema setup works from a single central perspective, multi-screen projections create a multifocal space. While cinema is a mass medium, multi-screen installations address a multitude spread out in space, connected only by distraction, separation, and difference.[17]

The difference between mass and multitude arises on the line between confinement and dispersion, between homogeneity and multiplicity, between cinema space and museum installation space. This is a very important distinction, because it will also affect the question of the museum as public space.

PUBLIC SPACE

It is obvious that the space of the factory is traditionally more or less invisible in public. Its visibility is policed, and surveillance produces a one-way gaze. Paradoxically, a museum is not so different. In a lucid 1972 interview Godard pointed out that, because filming is prohibited in factories, museums, and airports, effectively 80% of productive activity in France is rendered invisible: "The exploiter doesn't show the exploitation to the exploited."[18] This still applies today, if for different reasons. Museums prohibit filming or charge exorbitant shooting fees.[19] Just as the work performed in the factory cannot be shown outside it, most of the works on display in a museum cannot be shown outside its walls. A paradoxical situation arises: a museum predicated on producing and marketing visibility can itself not be shown—the labor performed there is just as publicly invisible as that of any sausage factory.

This extreme control over visibility sits rather uncomfortably alongside the perception of the museum as a public space. What does this invisibility then say about the contemporary museum as a public space? And how does the inclusion of cinematic works complicate this picture?

The current discussion of cinema and the museum as public sphere is an animated one. Thomas Elsaesser, for example, asks whether cinema in the museum might constitute the last remaining bourgeois public sphere.[20] Jürgen Habermas outlined the conditions in this arena in which people speak in turn and others respond, all participating together in the same rational, equal, and transparent discourse surrounding public matters.[21] In actuality, the contemporary museum is more like a cacophony—installations blare simultaneously while nobody listens. To make matters worse, the time-based mode of many cinematic installation works precludes a truly shared discourse around them; if works are too long, spectators will simply desert them. What would be seen as an act of betrayal in a cinema—leaving the projection while it lasts—becomes standard behavior in any spatial installation situation. In the installation space of the museum, spectators indeed become traitors—traitors of cinematic duration itself. In circulating through the space, spectators are actively montaging, zapping, combining fragments—effectively co-curating the show. Rationally conversing about shared impressions then becomes next to impossible. A bourgeois public sphere? Instead of its ideal manifestation, the contemporary museum rather represents its unfulfilled reality.

SOVEREIGN SUBJECTS

In his choice of words, Elsaesser also addresses a less democratic dimension of this space. By, as he dramatically phrases it, arresting cinema—suspending it, suspending its license, or even holding it under a suspended sentence—cinema is preserved at its own expense when it is taken into "protective custody."[22] Protective custody is no simple arrest. It refers to a state of exception or (at least) a temporal suspension of legality that allows the suspension of the law itself. This state of exception is also addressed in Boris Groys's essay "Politics of Installation."[23] Harking back to Carl Schmitt, Groys assigns the role of sovereign to the artist who—in a state of exception—violently establishes his own law by "arresting" a space in the form of an installation. The artist then assumes a role as sovereign founder of the exhibition's public sphere.

At first glance, this repeats the old myth of artist as crazy genius, or more precisely, as petty-bourgeois dictator. But the point is: if this works well as an artistic mode of production, it becomes standard practice in any social factory. So then, how about the idea that inside the museum, almost everybody tries to behave like a sovereign (or petty-bourgeois dictator)? After all, the multitude inside museums is composed of competing sovereigns: curators, spectators, artists, critics.

Let's have a closer look at the spectator-as-sovereign. In judging an exhibition, many attempt to assume the compromised sovereignty of the traditional bourgeois subject, who aims to (re)master the show, to tame the unruly multiplicity of its meanings, to pronounce a verdict, and to assign value. But, unfortunately, cinematic duration makes this subject position unavailable. It reduces all parties involved to the role of workers—unable to gain an overview of the whole process of production. Many—primarily critics—are thus frustrated by archival shows and their abundance of cinematic time. Remember the vitriolic attacks on the length of films and video in Documenta 11? To multiply cinematic duration means to blow apart the vantage point of sovereign judgment. It also makes it impossible to reconfigure yourself as its subject. Cinema in the museum renders overview, review, and survey impossible. Partial impressions dominate the picture. The true labor of spectatorship can no longer be ignored by casting oneself as master of judgment. Under these circumstances, a transparent, informed, inclusive discourse becomes difficult, if not impossible.

The question of cinema makes clear that the museum is not a public sphere, but rather places its consistent *lack* on display—it makes this *lack* public, so to speak. Instead of filling this space, it conserves its absence. But it also simultaneously displays its potential and the *desire* for something to be realized in its place.

As a multitude, the public operates under the condition of partial invisibility, incomplete access, fragmented realities—of commodification within clandestinity. Transparency, overview, and the sovereign gaze cloud over to become opaque. Cinema itself explodes into multiplicity—into spatially dispersed multi-screen arrangements that cannot be contained by a single point of view. The full picture, so to speak, remains unavailable. There is always something missing—people miss parts of the screening, the sound doesn't work, the screen itself or any vantage point from which it could be seen are missing.

RUPTURE

Without notice, the question of political cinema has been inverted. What began as a discussion of political cinema in the museum has turned into a question of cinematic politics in a factory. Traditionally, political cinema was meant to educate—it was an instrumental effort at "representation" in order to achieve its effects in "reality." It was measured in terms of efficiency, of revolutionary revelation, of gains in consciousness, or as potential triggers of action.

Today, cinematic politics are post-representational. They do not educate the crowd, but produce it. They articulate the crowd in space and in time. They submerge it in partial invisibility and then orchestrate their dispersion, movement, and reconfiguration. They organize the crowd without preaching to it. They replace the gaze of the bourgeois sovereign spectator of the white cube with the incomplete, obscured, fractured, and overwhelmed vision of the spectator-as-laborer.

But there is one aspect that goes well beyond this. What else is missing from these cinematic installations?[24] Let's return to the liminal case of Documenta 11, which was said to contain more cinematic material than could be seen by a single person in the 100 days that the exhibition was open to the public. No single spectator could even claim to have even seen everything, much less to have exhausted the meanings in this volume of work. It is obvious what is missing from this arrangement: since no single spectator can possibly make sense of such a volume of work, it calls for a multiplicity of spectators. In fact, the exhibition could only be seen by a multiplicity of gazes and points of view, which then supplements the impressions of others. Only if the night guards and various spectators worked together in shifts could the cinematic material of d11 be viewed. But in order to understand what (and how) they are watching, they must meet to make sense of it. This shared activity is completely different from that of spectators narcissistically gazing at themselves and each other inside exhibitions—it does not simply ignore the artwork (or treat it as mere pretext), but takes it to another level.

Cinema inside the museum thus calls for a multiple gaze, which is no longer collective, but common, which is incomplete, but in process, which is distracted and singular, but can be edited into various sequences and combinations. This gaze is no longer the gaze of the individual sovereign master, nor, more precisely, of the self-deluded sovereign (even if "just for one day," as David Bowie sang). It isn't even a product of common labor, but focuses its point of rupture on the paradigm of productivity. The museum-as-factory and its cinematic politics interpellate this missing, multiple subject. But by displaying its absence and its lack, they simultaneously activate a desire for this subject.

CINEMATIC POLITICS

But does this now mean that all cinematic works have become political? Or, rather, is there still any difference between different forms of cinematic politics? The answer is simple. Any conventional cinematic work will try to reproduce the existing setup: a projection of a public, which is not public after all, and in which participation and exploitation become indistinguishable. But a political cinematic articulation might try to come up with something completely different.

What else is desperately missing from the museum-as-factory? An exit. If the factory is everywhere, then there is no longer a gate by which to leave it—there is no way to escape relentless productivity. Political cinema could then become the screen through which people could leave the museum-as-social-factory. But on which screen could this exit take place? On the one that is currently missing, of course.

NOTES

1. Grupo Cine Liberación (Fernando E. Solanas, Octavio Getino), Argentina, 1968. The work is one of the most important films of Third Cinema.

2. A quote from Frantz Fanon's *The Wretched of the Earth*. The film was of course banned and had to be shown clandestinely.

3. Or videos or video/film installations. To properly make the distinctions (which exist and are important) would require another text.

4. I am aware of the problem of treating all these spaces as similar.

5. At least in Western countries.

6. The context of Godard's comment is a conversation—a monologue, apparently—with young installation artists, whom he reprimands for their use of what he calls technological *dispositifs* in exhibitions. See "Debrief de conversations avec Jean-Luc Godard," the Sans casser des briques blog, March 10, 2009.

7. See Brian Holmes, "Warhol in the Rising Sun: Art, Subcultures and Semiotic Production," *16 Beaver ARTicles* (August 2004), http://16beavergroup.org/articles/2004/08/08/rene-brian-holmes-warhol-in-the-rising-sun/.

8. Sabeth Buchmann quotes Hardt and Negri: "The 'social factory' is a form of production which touches on and penetrates every sphere and aspect of public and private life, of knowledge production and communication," in "From Systems-Oriented Art to Biopolitical Art Practice," NODE.London.

9. Jonathan L. Beller, "Kino-I, Kino-World," in *The Visual Culture Reader*, ed. Nicholas Mirzoeff (New York: Routledge, 2002), 61.

10. Ibid., 67.

11. For a great essay about this work see Harun Farocki, "Workers Leaving the Factory," in *Nachdruck/Imprint: Texte/Writings*, trans. Laurent Faasch-Ibrahim (New York: Lukas & Sternberg, 2001), reprinted on the Senses of Cinema Website.

12. My description refers to the Generali Foundation show, "Kino wie noch nie" (2005).

13. "Aujourd'hui le décor du premier film est sauvé et abrite une salle de cinéma de 270 fauteuils. Là où sortirent les ouvriers et les ouvrières de l'usine, les spectateurs vont au cinéma, sur le lieu de son invention," Institut Lumière.

14. "La partie Hangar, spacieux hall de réception chargé d'histoire et d'émotion pour tous vos déjeuners, cocktail, dîners . . . [Formule assise 250 personnes ou formule debout jusqu'à 300 personnes]," Institut Lumière.

15. There is however one interesting difference between cinema and factory: in the rebuilt scenery of the Lumière museum, the opening of the former gate is now blocked by a transparent glass pane to indicate the framing of the early film. Leaving spectators have to go around this obstacle, and leave through the former location of the gate itself, which no longer exists. Thus, the current situation is like a negative of the former one: people are blocked by the former opening, which has now turned into a glass screen; they have to exit through the former walls of the factory, which have now partly vanished. See photographs at ibid.

16. For a more sober description of the generally quite idealized condition of multitude, see Paolo Virno, *A Grammar of the Multitude*, trans. Isabella Bertoletti, James Cascaito, and Andrea Casson (New York: Semiotext(e), 2004).

17. As do multiple single screen arrangements.

18. "Godard on *Tout va bien*" (1972).

19. "Photography and video filming are not normally allowed at Tate." However, filming there is welcomed on a commercial basis, with location fees starting at £200 an hour. Policy at the Centre Pompidou is more confusing: "You may film or photograph works from permanent collections (which you will find on levels 4 and 5 and in the Atelier Brancusi) for your own personal use. You may not, however, photograph or film works that have a red dot, and you may not use a flash or stand."

20. Thomas Elsaesser, "The Cinema in the Museum: Our Last Bourgeois Public Sphere?" (conference presented at the International Film Studies Conference, "Perspectives on the Public Sphere: Cinematic Configurations of 'I' and 'We,'" Berlin, Germany, April 23–25, 2009.)

21. Jürgen Habermas, *The Structural Transformation of the Public Sphere: An Inquiry into a Category of Bourgeois Society*, trans. Thomas Burger with the assistance of Frederick Lawrence (Cambridge, MA: MIT Press, 1991 [1962]).

22. Elsaesser, "The Cinema in the Museum."

23. Boris Groys, "Politics of Installation," *e-flux Journal*, no. 2 (January 2009), https://www.e-flux.com/journal/02/68504/politics-of-installation/.

24. A good example would be "Democracies" by Artur Żmijewski, an un-synchronized multi-screen installation with trillions of possibilities of screen-content combinations.

BIBLIOGRAPHY

Beller, Jonathan L. "Kino-I, Kino-World." In *The Visual Culture Reader*. Edited by Nicholas Mirzoeff. New York: Routledge, 2002.

Holmes, Brian. "Warhol in the Rising Sun: Art, Subcultures and Semiotic Production." *16 Beaver ARTicles*. August 2004. http://16beavergroup.org/articles/2004/08/08/rene-brian-holmes-warhol-in-the-rising-sun/.

Farocki, Harun. "Workers Leaving the Factory." In *Nachdruck/Imprint: Texte/Writings*. Translated by Laurent Faasch-Ibrahim. New York: Lukas & Sternberg, 2001.

Groys, Boris. "Politics of Installation." *e-flux Journal*, no. 2 (January 2009). https://www.e-flux.com/journal/02/68504/politics-of-installation/.

Habermas, Jürgen. *The Structural Transformation of the Public Sphere: An Inquiry into a Category of Bourgeois Society*. Translated by Thomas Burger with the assistance of Frederick Lawrence. Cambridge, MA: MIT Press, 1991 [1962].

Virno, Paolo. *A Grammar of the Multitude*. Translated by Isabella Bertoletti, James Cascaito, and Andrea Casson. New York: Semiotext(e), 2004.

7

OF STRUCTION

Jean-Luc Nancy

Technology supplants and supplements nature.[1] It comes to supplant or take the place of nature wherever nature does not provide certain ends (such as a house or a bed), and it comes to supplement nature when it adds itself onto nature's ends and means. This twofold value is what Derrida inscribes into the "logic of the supplement," and one could say that this logic itself has no other source or medium than precisely this relationship between technology and nature. The supplement and its twofold concept always fall under the category of technology, artifice, or art, three words which are nearly synonymous in this regard.

Two conditions are necessary for this to be the case: to begin with, nature must present a few characteristic lacks (it is able to offer shelters, but not houses); then, it must be possible for technology to be grafted onto nature (using its materials, its forces). This is indeed the case: on the one hand, the animals of the *homo* species or varieties at least express needs that nature does not satisfy (inhabiting, warming up), and on the other hand, the technologies invented by *homo* take their operating resources (sharp stones, fire) from nature. Fire represents, perhaps, the symbolic meeting point where supplanting and supplementing occurs: it can light up during a thunderstorm, a volcanic eruption, or a spontaneous combustion of gas, and it constitutes the major "invention" of the first human beings despite the fact that it is not combustion that they invent but rather the conservation and "technological" production of combustion. What applies to fire also applies to electricity, semiconductors, optical fibers, and the energy that is released by atomic fission and fusion.

Nature always contains and offers the prime matter for technology, whereas technology alters, transforms, and converts natural resources toward its own ends.

This very simple consideration has an important consequence: technology does not come from outside of nature. It has a place within nature, and furthermore, if nature is defined as what achieves its own ends by itself, then technology too must be defined as one of nature's ends, since it is from nature that the animal that is capable of—or in need of—technology is born.

Technology in turn undergoes its own development: it no longer simply responds to its own shortcomings; it generates its own expectations and tries to respond to the demands that come from itself. This is what happens as soon as the artificial selection of plants and livestock is invented. What follows from this is the construction of an order that is specific to technology, a relatively autonomous order that develops new expectations and demands from out of its own possibilities. It not only consists in the assemblage of materials and forces (what are called "simple machines": lever, mill, etc.), but also in the elaboration of logics that are structured by a given that is itself produced in view of a new end: good examples include the power of vapor, oil and gas, electricity, and the atom, and later cybernetics and numerical computation (immaterial givens which at once presuppose and bring about new treatments and assemblages of matter, such as with silicon or deuterium).

What profoundly instructs this development is not "the machine," as it is all too often thought. The machine does not suddenly emerge from out of nowhere. It is machined itself—that is to say, it is conceived, elaborated, and structured by the ends that one proposes oneself. A few anecdotes about inventions that are due to chance (the observation of vapor raising the lid of a boiling pot) cannot obscure the fact that the process of technological invention is a process which is specific to the unfolding of aims and investigations that are oriented by this aim. We attempt to go faster and further, to cross oceans, to produce in greater quantities, to reach the enemy from afar, etc. At one and the same time we attempt to transport more goods, make investments for this, and insure against the risks of it: financial technologies are on an equal footing with nautical technologies within a development that presupposes the existence of independent and competing entrepreneurs—that is, an entire sociopolitical and juridical technology that structures the whole space of our common way of life [*la vie commune*].

*

Thus "technology" itself is not only limited to the order of "technologies" in the sense that one speaks of them today. Technology is a structuration of ends—it is a thought, a culture, or a civilization, however one wants to word it—of the indefinite construction of complexes of ends that are always more ramified, intertwined, and combined, but above all of ends that are characterized by the constant redevelopment of their own constructions. The transmission of sound, image, and information without a tangible medium creates new assemblages [*nouveaux agencements*] of both apparatuses [*appareils*] and modes of life or ways of living. The possibility of acting on certain diseases or else on fertility or life spans through interventions and substances that are invented for these purposes or ends creates new social, sexual, and affective conditions.

At this stage or level, ends and means never stop changing roles with one another. Technology develops a general regime of inventing ends that are themselves thought through the perspective of means (How can sterility be overcome? How can an animated image be transmitted?), and by consequence, that are thought through the perspective of means that are taken as ends (it's good to live longer, it's good that money yields more money). This is also why the technologies of the arts—that is to say, technologies as "arts" or the enjoyment of ends in themselves, or forms that have value on their own—can become on the one hand the highest standard of every relationship to ends (everything must be put into image, sound, rhythm, everything must be hypostasized into a monstration: bodies, products, and places) and on the other hand the privileged domain for an interrogation into finality (Why art? What is it for?) that becomes suspicious of identity (What is art? What is it in the service of?).

Construction and deconstruction are closely interconnected with one another. What is constructed according to a logic of ends and means is deconstructed when it comes into contact with the outermost edge where ends reveal themselves to be endless and where means, for their part, reveal themselves to be temporary ends that generate new possibilities for construction. The automobile has given birth to the highway, which has given birth to new modes and norms of transport. It is also making the city have to reinvent both its means of transportation (streetcars, etc.) and over time the very aims or ends of a "city." Digital cameras and editing processes are deconstructing and reconstructing not only the formal landscape of cinema, but also the signification and the stakes of this art form (along with digital audio processing).

[. . .]

*

There has thus been something like an enlargement of construction: not so much the edification or erection of buildings, for which the temple, the palace, and the tomb formed the triple paradigm, but rather the montage, assemblage, and composition of forces [*composition de forces*] whereby the "engineering structure" [*ouvrage d'art*] almost gives it its concept (bridge, pier, fort, hall, etc.). The engineering structure requires an engineer [*ingénieur*] more than a builder [*bâtisseur*], a constructor more than a founder (and incidentally one also *constructs* roads, vessels, silos, chariots, and machines). Construction becomes dominant when edification, on the one hand, and making, on the other hand, become industrial and engineered [*s'industrialisent et s'ingéniérisent*], or in other words, when they bring into play the construction of operational, dynamic, and energy-producing schemata which serve ends that are themselves invented and constructed according to defined aims (production power, speed, durability, reproducibility, etc.).

The constructive paradigm that has been spread through urbanization, means of exploration and transportation, and the mobilization of non-manifest energies (coal, gas, oil, electricity, magnetism, digital computation, etc.)—a paradigm that has rendered ends and means more and more consubstantial—has led to a response of destruction. This does not concern ruining and demolishing so much as it concerns detaching oneself from what could be called "constructivism" (if one reappropriates a term whose invention in the beginning of the 20th century is nevertheless not insignificant). The Heideggerian *Destruktion* of ontology, which expressly distinguishes itself from demolition (*Zerstörung*), is "destruction" in this sense (Granel and Derrida translate it as "deconstruction"). In a way it gives a philosophical counterpart to the existential and aesthetic Destructions of Baudelaire and Mallarmé. Construction as such is brought into play (as well as "instruction," as what puts knowledge into an order: one could demonstrate it through the recent use of the term "instruction" in school contexts—the expression *"instruction publique"* [public education] dates back to the French Revolution and *"instruction religieuse"* [religious education] is not any older than this).

*

Onto what does destruction open? Perhaps onto the very movement of modern construction? What is of concern is not to "re-construct" (contrary to the incessantly repeated petition addressed to "deconstructionists": will you reconstruct already?). Nor is it to return to founding, building, constituting, or instituting gestures, even if it is to open and inaugurate, to allow for a birth of sense. What is at stake beyond construction and deconstruction is *struction* as such.[2]

Struo signifies "to amass," "to heap." It is truly not a question of order or organization that is implied by *con-* and in-struction. It is the heap, the non-assembled ensemble [*ensemble non assemblé*]. Surely it is contiguity and co-presence, but without a principle of coordination.

By speaking of "nature," we used to suppose or rather superimpose that there was a coordination that was proper and immanent to the profusion of beings (a spontaneous or rather divine construction). With "technology," we used to suppose that there was a coordination that was ruled or regulated by ends that were particular to "humankind" (their needs, capacities, and expectations). By acting retroactively, if one may say so, onto "nature" from where it comes out of or emerges (we cannot decide between these two concepts . . .), "technology" muddles the two possibilities for coordination. It invites the consideration of a struction: the uncoordinated simultaneity of things or beings, the contingency of their belonging together, the dispersion of profusions of aspects, species, forces, forms, tensions, and intentions (instincts, drives, inclinations, and momentums). In this profusion, no order is valued more than the others: they all—instincts, responses, irritabilities, connectivities, equilibriums, catalyses, metabolisms—seem destined to collide or dissolve into one another or to be confused with one another.

Whereas the paradigm had been architectural, and consequently architectonic in a more metaphysical way, it then became more structural—a composition, surely, an assembling, but without constructive finality—and finally structional, that is to say, relative to an assembling that is labile, disordered, aggregated, or amalgamated rather than conjoined, reunited, paired with, or associated.

In fact, it is the question of a "sociation" in general that is posed alongside struction. Can there be an association, a society—if the *socius* is the one who "goes with" or "accompanies" and if, as a result, she or he brings into play an active or positive value of the "with" or *cum* around which or through which something akin to a sharing [*partage*] plays out? What I am calling here "struction" would be the state of the "with" deprived of the value of sharing, bringing into play only simple contiguity and its contingency. It may be, to take back the terms that Heidegger wants to distinguish in his approach to the "with" (the *mit* in the *Mitdasein* as the ontological constitution of the existent), a "with" that is uniquely categorial and not existential: the pure and simple juxtaposition that does not make sense.

*

Perhaps struction is the lesson of technology—a construction-deconstruction of the ensemble of beings without any distinction between "nature" and "art"—insofar as it instructs us with this instruction (which indeed we do not comprehend and which appears badly constructed to us). Following this instruction, sense from now on will not let itself be constructed or instructed. What is given to us only consists in the juxtaposition and simultaneity of a copresence in which the *co-* does not bear any other particular value than that of contiguity or juxtaposition within the limits according to which the universe itself is given. At the same time, these limits themselves are only given with the caveat that it is impossible to properly assign them as delimitations of a world in relation to what is beyond or behind it. On the one hand, the universe is said to be expanding as the same time as it is finite; on the other hand, it cannot even be called a "universe" but only a "multiverse." And yet, in order to think beyond the "universe," it is no longer necessary of course to understand the multiple worlds as one (or several) other world(s). "They are not somewhere else but modes of relating to what is 'outside-of-itself.'"[3]

The idea of the universe contains a schema of construction or architecture: a basis, a foundation, and a substruction (a word that is also found in the work of Mallarmé!) that forms the base on which uni-totality is erected and assembled [*s'agence*]. Uni-totality is posited on the basis of its own supposition and refers essentially to itself; in short, it is in itself (and "Being" is Being "in itself" within the thought that is sustained by this schema). But copresence [*coprésence*] and coappearance [*comparution*] both turn away from the in-itself and construction: "Being" is no longer in itself, but rather contiguity, contact, tension, distortion, crossing, and assemblage. "Being," of course, shows traits of "construction" understood as mutual disposition and mutual distribution [*disposition et distribution mutuelles*] of the multiverses which belong to each other, but not as a (sup)position [*(sup)position*] of a Being or a fundamental real.[4] The real does not dissolve itself at all in unreality, but rather opens onto the reality of its nonsupposition [*insupposition*]. This is what is signified by the dissolution of the *technè/phusis* opposition or what we call "the reign of technology."

This is what has occurred in our history. We have come to a point in which architectonics and architecture—understood as the determinations of an essential construction or essence as construction—no longer have value. They have worn themselves out by themselves.

Still it has not only been a question of being worn out. It is not only a construction that has been destroyed by time. It is the very principle of construction that has been weakened.

The accumulation, noted above, of motifs of destruction at that time—around 1900, which is traditionally considered as "the" turn of the century *par excellence*, the time in which in fact something was inverted and overturned, where an edifice was weakened to the point that one could say, in every possible sense, that the edifying and the edified trembled—this accumulation bears witness to a sort of saturation point and a rupture in the model of "construction." This signifies that construction bore within itself the seed of deconstruction. What first presented itself as the extension of the assemblage and montage of *tools*—continuations of bodies and simple machines—and later as the expansion of a gesture of mastery or command—the administration and governance of energies (vapor, electricity, chemical reactions) in lieu of the mere use of forces (moving water, winds, gravity)—revealed another nature: one of combination, interaction, and, later, feedback.

In reality, an entire *organicity* or a quasi-organicity has been developed. In sum, the constructive paradigm is overcoming itself; it is overconstructing itself by tending towards an organic autonomy. Overconstruction is turning into struction.

*

Or rather, according to another, slightly different perspective, it is the organic autonomy of our own behavior that has been extended very far beyond not only our bodies but even our minds by asking the latter to export and expose itself under the form of highly self-referential "machines" whose laws and schemas of organization require certain operations from our behavior in return. We learn how to use a computer, on our desk as well as in our car, in the train, on a plane, on a boat, for archeological excavations and for recording data, and in the "creation" of sounds and images. This use does not only imply a new domain of expertise but also a different space-time that incidentally is nonhomogenous and non-unitary or "universal": we are, at each moment and all at once, in the extension of certain modules that are put into operation everywhere (a digital procedure, a use of signals or icons) and also in the renewal of unprecedented possibilities, which are without a doubt very repetitive (everyone takes the same photos of the same monuments, etc.) but whose very repetition lights up a new reality. We are no longer in the process of discovering a world that has remained in part unknown; we are in a spiraling, growing pile of pieces, parts, zones, fragments, slivers, particles, elements, outlines, seeds, kernels, clusters, points, meters, knots, arborescences, projections, proliferations, and dispersions according to which we are now more than ever taken hold of, interwoven into, absorbed into, and dislodged from a prodigious mass that is unstable, moving, plastic, and metamorphic, a mass which renders the distinction between "subject" and "object" or between "man" and "nature" or "world" less and less possible for us.

In fact, we are perhaps no longer within a world or "in the world" [*au monde*]. What is disappearing or being diluted is the more advanced sense of the *cosmos* or beautiful unity that is composed according to a superior order that directs it and which it also reflects. Our "world"—or our element—is instead composed of bits and pieces which, taken all together, are proliferated from the same source (humankind, the technological animal of nature, the constructive appendage of a great all that shows itself to be rarely constructed but incredibly rich in con-de-in-structive potentialities). Still the bits and pieces or "elements"—which are never elementary enough—of this great "element"—in the sense of a milieu or an ecosystem which is an *ecotechnology* [*écotechnie*]—constantly escape the grasp of every construction. Their assemblage does not refer to a first or final construction but rather to a kind of continuous creation where what is constantly rekindled and renewed is the very possibility of the world—or rather the multiplicity of worlds.

In this sense, struction opens less onto a past or future and more onto a present that is never really accomplished in presence. It opens onto a temporality that definitely cannot correspond to a linear diachrony. Within this temporality there is something synchronic, which is not so much a cut across diachrony as it is a mode of uniting the segments of traditional time, which is the very unity of the present as it is *presenting itself*, as it is arriving, taking place, or coming about. This *coming about* is the time of struction: an event whose significance is not only that of the unexpected or inaugural—not only the significance of rupture or regeneration in the timeline—but also the significance of the passage, of ephemerality intermixed with eternity.

There is something outside of time at the heart of time: surely nothing else than what was perceived in all of our chronic thought in how time flies or gets away from us, or in the present instant's perpetual flight. Still here "flight" does not signify a disappearance any more than the event signifies an appearance. As with (de)(con)struction, it is necessary to uncouple (dis)(ap)pearance. "Pearance" or appearance is the appearing—but not as the manifestation of a phenomenon or as the semblance of appearance. As it is suggested by the former use of the word, "appearing" is coming into presence, presenting itself or oneself. That is, coming near to or beside. It is always appearing with [*comparaître*].

Within this appearing with a displacement is revealed, a curve in the phenomenological apparatus [*dispositif phénoménologique*]. It does not so much concern the relationship between an aim and its fulfillment as it does the correlation of appearing between themselves [*corrélation des paraître entre eux*]. It is not so much about a subject and a world than it is about references that send the world back into itself and to itself, about the profusion of these referrals and the way that they thus create what could be called a sense, a sense of the world [*sens du monde*] that is nothing other than its appearing with: that there is a world, and all that is in the world, and not nothing.

*

This kind of brute obviousness might seem to bring us back to a nascent, infantile, and rudimentary state. We would have nothing else to receive, project, or express than the crudest of conditions. We could not account for the world or give any kind of justice to the fact of its existence. Technology would have both withdrawn any kind of final aim or end or supreme good and also rendered reason to be proliferating, exorbitant, and even delirious in its very self-sufficiency—growing like a cancer.

However, to have arrived at the state of struction does not necessarily signify having regressed or degenerated. There may be progress in the passage beyond the processes of construction, instruction, and destruction. Struction is liberation from the obsession that wants to think the real or Being under a schema of construction and that thus exhausts itself in the pointless quest for an architect or mechanic of the world.

Struction offers a dis-order that is neither the contrary nor the destruction or ruin of order: it is situated somewhere else in what we call contingency, fortuity, dispersion, or errancy, which could equally be called surprise, invention, chance, meeting, or passage. It is nothing but the copresence or better yet the appearing-together [*comparution*] of all that appears, that is, of all that is.

That which is, in effect, does not appear from out of a Being in itself. Being is itself appearing; it is appearing in an integral way. Nothing comes before or follows the "phenomenon" that is Being itself. Being itself is therefore not at all beings since it is the appearing of a being that "is" only appearing and appearing with. Thus in addition one must say that everything appears-through together: everything refers back to everything and thus everything shows itself through everything. Without end—and more precisely, without beginning or end.

[. . .]

*

To this, one must also add the following: we are not only living technicians perplexed by the development of their art or know-how. We are not only overwhelmed and disconcerted that all of the forms and aspects of sense have been brought into play and called into question. We are also ourselves already caught up in this transformation. We have been inserting ourselves into a technosphere, which is our development; what we call "technology" exceeds the entire order of tools, instruments, and machines. It does not concern what is possible through command or mastery (a means to an end), but rather the expansion of the brain (if one wants to call it this) within a network of "intelligence" that extrapolates a mastery that is significant by itself and for itself, a mastery that is an end and a means in itself indefinitely.

Since it is pointless to cast a veil over the errancy in struction—the veil of any preconceived "sense" that is taken from a model of "intelligence" which is supposedly "good"—then it is incumbent on us to reinvent everything beginning with "sense." Sense does not correspond anymore to a schema of construction or to one of destruction and reconstruction: it must correspond to a "destinerrance" [*destinerrance*] which signifies that even though we are not going towards any term or limit—as a result of providence, tragic destiny, or fabricated history—we are still not devoid of "going." We are not devoid of advancing, roaming, crossing, and also experiencing [*faire l'expérience*], a word that used to express "going to the very end, to the outermost limit."

Wisdom cries out from all sides: "This must stop at once! How far will it go?" This is because, in effect, it is limitlessness that is sprouting up on all sides. It is cropping up in genetic manipulations and in financial markets, in networks and poverties and social and technological pathologies. It cannot be a question of establishing limits for what, in itself, ignores the limit. Either this limitlessness will be self-destructive—a construction that goes up but only to fall down right at the end—or we will find a way to recognize "sense" in struction—at the place where there is neither end, nor means, nor assembly, nor disassembly, nor top, nor bottom, nor east, nor west. But merely an all together.

NOTES

1. [The polysemantic word *la technique*, which is translated as "technology" in this essay, could also be correctly translated as "technique" or "technics." While in French *la technique* may suggest, like Aristotle's *technè*, a kind of skill, know-how, or technique, *la technique* may also imply technology in the sense of Heidegger's *die Technik*, which has typically been translated into French as *la technique* and into English as "technology" or, more recently, as "technics." Still, whereas Heidegger generally does not translate *technè* with *die Technik* because he considers modern technology or *die Technik* as being very different from the Greek sense of *technè*, Nancy views modern technology as a one of many "maturations" of *technè* and has even offered *la technique* as a translation for *technè* in Jean-Luc Nancy, "The Technique of the Present: On On Kawara," in *Multiple Arts: The Muses II*, ed. Simon Sparks (Stanford: Stanford University Press, 2006).—Trans.]

2. It so happens that *struction* is also a concept in graph theory, which is not relevant here.

3. Aurélien Barrau, "Quelques éléments de physique et de philosophie des multivers," *Laboratoire de Physique Subatomique et de Cosmologie CNRS-IN2P3*, https://pdf4pro.com/amp/view/quelques-233-l-233-ments-de-physique-et-de-philosophie-des-multivers-54cbb4.html, 122.

4. On this topic see the use of the term "construction" in the work cited in the previous footnote.

8

WE, MACHINIC SUBJECTS

Michael Hardt and Antonio Negri

The passions of the common, beyond private property, demand a new conception of the subject or, better, they require an adequate process of subjectivation. We need to verify here, moreover, that a multitude is formed capable of ruling and leading itself, able [. . .] to conceive and carry out strategic goals. This potential emerges from below, from within the processes of cooperative social production and reproduction, but the value produced in these processes is constantly captured and extracted. This issue becomes all the more complex when we recognize that technologies, modes of production, and forms of life are increasingly woven together, and some of these technological developments are creating cataclysmic disasters for humanity and the earth. This is not a matter, however, merely of liberating ourselves from technology. Such a project makes little sense since our bodies and minds are (and always have been) mixed inextricably with various technologies. And just as labor is not passive with respect to capital, we have active relations to technology: we create technologies and suffer from them, renovate them and go beyond them. Instead of rejecting technology, then, we must start from within the technological and biopolitical fabric of our lives and chart from there a path of liberation.

THE RELATION OF HUMAN AND MACHINE

Before considering how new subjectivities of production and reproduction are being and can be configured, we need to dispel some prevalent illusions regarding the dehumanizing effects of machines and technology. Let us consider two influential philosophical propositions, which are really both sophisticated versions of assumptions about the opposition between humans and technology that too often function today as common sense.

Max Horkheimer and Theodor Adorno's *Dialectic of Enlightenment* (1947), written in the shadow of the crimes of the Nazi regime and with enormous influence in the second half of the twentieth century, is based on the claim that the Enlightenment quest for freedom and progress, along with its institutions and technologies, leads to an aporia: "the very concept of that [Enlightenment] thinking, no less than the concrete historical forms, the institutions of society with which it is intertwined, already contains the germ of the regression which is taking place everywhere today."[1] What can be done when all aspects of public life and even the masses themselves are constantly commodified and degraded, and thus when attempts at progress inevitably result in its opposite? Since the Odyssey of bourgeois civilization develops in secret (or open) complicity with domination, that question seems unanswerable. Indeed Horkheimer and Adorno's tragic assessment of modern humanity, its ideology, and its technologies can lead only to bitter resignation rather than to any active project.

Heidegger, in "The Question Concerning Technology," published just a few years later, agrees in effect with Horkheimer and Adorno on a central point: science and technology are not neutral. The essence of technology, he claims, is to reveal or "enframe" the truth, but today this relation to truth has been broken and instrumentalized. Whereas peasants working the earth made it reveal its truth, the enframing of modern technology does not reveal the truth but only an instrumental relation to resources. "The earth now reveals itself as a coal mining district," Heidegger writes, "the soil as a mineral deposit."[2] The primary threat to humanity, then, is not nuclear weapons or other lethal technologies. "The actual threat," he warns, "has already affected man in his essence. The rule of Enframing threatens man with the possibility that it could be denied to him to enter into a more original revealing and hence to experience the call of a more primal truth."[3] Heidegger thus responds to Horkheimer and Adorno from a metaphysical standpoint, upping the ante and radicalizing the catastrophe. This is no longer the product of a contradiction, the result of the lost hope for human liberation, and it is not a moment of a negative dialectics, but, on the contrary, it is a radical loss of the sense of being. Heidegger, as much as Horkheimer and Adorno, claims that theories of progress have reached the point of exhaustion, but now from a metaphysical rather than a historical perspective.[4]

Is modern technology, though, really responsible for this damage and this destiny of humanity? At first sight, there seems to be no denying it: technology's social and ecological disasters have not only created misery and disease but also have set human history and the ecosystems of the earth on a path to destruction. We should never forget this, but it is not really enough. We should not forget either that humanity and human civilization are incomprehensible without technology, mechanical and thinking machines that configure our world and our selves. It makes no sense to construct some sort of tribunal to pass judgment on technology as such or even modern technology. Instead we can only judge specific technologies and their social uses and control.

A first response to these verdicts on modern technology requires historicizing their arguments. The standpoint of Heidegger's analysis, as Günther Anders rightly noted, is preindustrial and even precapitalist.[5] Even Horkheimer and Adorno's analysis is limited to the phase of capitalist development dominated by large-scale industry, and in this regard their phenomenology does not really go much further than the fabulations of Ernst Jünger and his colleagues in the 1930s. The world of large-scale industry was effectively deposed from the pinnacle of the capitalist economy when forms of resistance, revolutionary movements, and class struggle made necessary the reorganization of the subjectivities at work. Today's reality is different, and the new conditions of production are continually transformed by "human machines" that are put to work.

A more profound response to these arguments requires that we recognize their mistake in posing an *ontological* division and even opposition between human life and machines. Human thought and action has always been interwoven with techniques and technologies. The human mind itself, as Spinoza explains, constructs intellectual tools, internal to its functioning, that allow it to increase its power of thought, and these are perfectly analogous to the material tools that humans develop to perform more complex tasks more efficiently.[6] Our intellectual and corporeal development are inseparable from the creation of machines internal and external to our minds and bodies. Machines constitute and are constituted by human reality.

This ontological fact does not change but is only revealed more clearly in the contemporary, postindustrial world. Many early theorists of cybernetics grasped the ontological relation between humans and machines but were confused about its implications: they conceived of the development of new technologies effectively in terms of *lowering* the human to the level of machines. At the historic Macy Conferences, which from 1943 to 1954 brought together prominent researchers such as Norbert Wiener, cybernetic theorists generally conceived human neural structures in terms of information processing and grasped subjectivity in disembodied form. Humans were thus seen primarily, Katherine Hayles explains, "as information-processing entities who are *essentially* similar to intelligent machines."[7] Later cybernetic theorists, however, such as Humberto Maturana and Francisco Varela, paved the way for recognizing machines and humans alike in terms of embodied and distributed cognition. The second and third waves of cybernetic theory, which emerged together with postindustrial production, no longer lowered the notion of the human but *elevated* machines to the ontological plane of the human, a common plane of embodied cognition. If our contemporary reality is posthuman, Hayles maintains, that signals not a coming apocalyptic rule of machines but instead the opening of new potentials for humans to cooperate intensively with machines and other living beings.[8]

Gilbert Simondon moves in the same direction when he criticizes the standard view that opposes human culture to technology. Like Spinoza, Simondon recognizes that humans and machines belong to the same ontological plane. "What resides in machines is human reality," he argues, "human actions [*du geste humain*] that are fixed and crystalized in machines."[9] Against those who celebrate human culture as a sort of barricade, then, a defensive barrier to protect us from the advance of supposedly inhuman technologies, Simondon calls for a technical culture, which recognizes, on the ontological plane, the fully human nature of machines. Deleuze and Guattari heed and build on Simondon's call: "The object is no longer to compare humans and the machine in order to evaluate the correspondences, the extensions, the possible or impossible substitutions of the ones for the other, but to bring them into communication in order to show how *humans are a component part* of the machine, or combine with something else to constitute a machine."[10] Humans and machines are part of a mutually constituted social reality.

The fact that machines are part of human reality and constituted by human intelligence does not mean, of course, that all machines are good or that technology solves all problems. They contain the potential for both servitude and liberation. The problem lies at not the ontological but the political level. We must recognize, specifically, how human actions, habits, and intelligence crystallized in technologies are separated from humans and controlled by those in power. *Fixed capital*, in Marx's terminology, is a kind of social repository in the banks of scientific knowledge and in machines, in software and hardware, of the accomplishments of living labor and living intelligence, that is, to use Marx's terms, of the social brain and general intellect. Think of your smartphone, just as much as the spinning jenny, a patented method to temper steel, or a pharmaceutical formula, as the concrete result of the intelligence of not only the corporate CEO or even just the paid employees but also and most important a wide social network of cooperating actors. Despite the fact that it is produced socially, however, fixed capital becomes a weapon that can be used antisocially, so to speak, for capitalist profit as well as for war and destruction. And through the successive periods of capitalist production, from manufacture to large-scale industry and now to the phase dominated by general intellect, the role of science and technology, the repositories of social intelligence, become ever more crucial. The curtain raises on the field of battle over the control of fixed capital.

Walter Benjamin, reflecting on the tragic experiences of the First World War, is rightly suspicious of those who use evidence of technological disasters to indict technology as a whole:

> This immense wooing of the cosmos was enacted for the first time on a planetary scale, that is, in the spirit of technology. But because the lust for profit of the ruling class sought satisfaction through it, technology betrayed man and turned the bridal bed into a bloodbath. The mastery of nature, so the imperialists teach, is the purpose of all technology. But who would trust a cane wielder who proclaimed the mastery of children by adults to be the purpose of education? Is not education above all the indispensable ordering of the relationship between generations and therefore mastery, if we are to use this term, of that relationship and not of children? And likewise technology is not the mastery of nature but of the relation between nature and man.[11]

Today we must immerse ourselves into the heart of technologies and attempt to make them our own against the forces of domination that deploy technologies against us.

THE CHANGING COMPOSITION OF CAPITAL

In the early 1970s, facing a cycle of struggles that had put in serious crisis the Fordist mode of industrial production in the dominant countries, capital struck back by using automation and robotics in the factories to replace rebellious workers, and using information networks to extend production socially, beyond the factory walls. Cybernetics and information technologies helped create a relation of force favorable to the owners against the workers and, at the same time, construct a society of obedient subjects, dedicated to the production of ever more abstract commodities in cooperative social networks. "Industrial *automation* and social *necromation*" is what we used to call this gigantic project to displace the industrial working class from its position as a central (and potentially revolutionary) actor in productive society and to impoverish almost everyone.

That project has become a reality. Over the course of a half century the spheres of capitalist production and society have been radically transformed, extending the primary site of production from the factory to society. Automation constituted the central point of transformation—not only from the political point of view (destroying the power of the working class and expelling workers from the factories in dominant parts of the world) but also from the technical point of view (intensifying the rhythms of production). In order to re-establish profits that could no longer be obtained in the factories, capital had to put the social terrain to work, and the mode of production had to be interwoven ever more tightly with forms of life. While the automated industrial processes produced more material goods, outside of the robotized factories grew productive and ever more complex and integrated "services," bringing together complex technologies and fundamental science, industrial services and human services. In this second phase, digitization became more important than automation: this, in fact, spreads throughout society a transformation of the technical composition of labor-power that has already taken place in the factory.

[. . .]

Although [the] "objective" arguments from *Capital* seem crucial to us, we are even more interested in his proposal in the *Grundrisse* that the changing composition of capital also contributes, subjectively, to strengthening the position of labor and that today the general intellect is becoming a protagonist of economic and social production. We should also recognize, perhaps now beyond Marx, as production is increasingly socialized, how fixed capital tends to be implanted into life itself, creating a machinic humanity. "Hence it is evident," Marx writes in a jagged sentence typical of the *Grundrisse*, "that the material productive power already present, already worked out, existing in the form of fixed capital, together with the population, etc., in short all conditions of wealth, i.e. the abundant development of the social individual—that the development of the productive forces brought about by the historical development of capital itself, when it reaches a certain point, suspends the self-realization of capital, instead of positing it."[12] Fixed capital, that is, the memory and storehouse of past physical and intellectual labor, is increasingly embedded in "the social individual," a fascinating concept in its own right. To the same degree that capital, as this process proceeds, loses the capacity for self-realization, the social individual gains autonomy.

Marx could only take this analysis so far, of course, given when he was writing. Today, in a "biopolitical" context, we can see more clearly how the transformations of the composition of capital and the fact that fixed capital is being incarnated in and by social production present new potentials for laboring subjects. "What comes to be called immaterial and intellectual capital," Carlo Vercellone argues, "is in reality essentially incorporated in humans and thus corresponds fundamentally to the intellectual and creative faculties of labor-power." This then poses a challenge or even a potential threat to capital because the primary role in the social organization of production tends to be played by the living knowledges embodied in and mobilized by labor rather than the dead knowledges deployed by management and management science.[13] Furthermore, Vercellone continues, this "mass intellectuality" or Marx's general intellect, which tends today to invest and configure the entire social field, derives from the appropriation of fixed capital and implies an anthropological transformation of working subjects, with capacities for production and valorization that are fundamentally collective and cooperative. The productive social cooperation of workers endowed with fixed capital, although it now yields the surplus it produces to capital, poses the potential for the autonomy of workers, inverting the relation for force between labor and capital.

[...]

MACHINIC SUBJECTIVITIES

Young people today, according to a cultural commonplace, enter almost spontaneously into digital worlds, which for previous generations were unknown and only engaged later, with difficulty. Today's youth grow up in these worlds and find joy and community there. Often they are drafted into forms of work that seem like games; sometimes they think they are merely consumers when they are also producers—"prosumers," as Christian Fuchs and others say.[14] Certainly the characterizations of the new freedom of digital life promoted by corporate advertisers, product marketers, and management gurus are mystifications, but they can also help us recognize the nature of the machinic subjectivities and machinic assemblages that are forming.

We conceive the "machinic" in contrast not only to the mechanical but also to the notion of a technological realm separate from and even opposed to human society. Félix Guattari argues that, whereas traditionally the problem of machines has been seen as secondary to the question of technè and technology, we should instead recognize that the problem of machines is primary and technology is merely a subset. We can see this, he continues, once we understand the machine's social nature: "Since 'the machine' is opened out towards its machinic environment and maintains all sorts of relationships with social constituents and individual subjectivities, the concept of technological machine should therefore be broadened to that of *machinic assemblages* [*agencements machiniques*]."[15] The *machinic*, then, never refers to an individual, isolated machine but always an assemblage. To understand this, start by thinking of mechanical systems, that is, machines connected to and integrated with other machines. Then add human subjectivities and imagine humans integrated into machine relations and machines integrated into human bodies and human society. Finally, Guattari (and together with Deleuze) conceives machinic assemblages as going even further and incorporating all kinds of human and nonhuman elements or singularities.

In the context of twentieth-century French thought the concepts of the machinic, machinic consistency, and machinic assemblage respond effectively to philosophers, such as Louis Althusser, who, to combat the spiritualist ontologies that plagued theories of the subject, pose "a process without a subject." Deleuze and Guattari certainly appreciate the political importance of this polemic. Althusser asserts that "the individual *is interpellated as a (free) subject in order that he shall submit freely to the commandments of the Subject, i.e. in order that he shall (freely) accept his subjection*, i.e. in order that he shall make the gestures and actions of his subjection 'all by himself.' *There are no subjects except by and for their subjection.*"[16] We seem to be caught, however, in a double bind: the "subject" functions as part of apparatuses of domination, but one cannot live or construct community on the basis of a pure and simple cancellation of the subject.[17] The concept of the machinic in Deleuze and Guattari—just as, in a different way, the concept of production in Foucault—addresses this need, adopting, without identity, subjectivities of knowledge and action, and demonstrating how their production emerges in material connections. These connections are also ontological connections. The machinic thus constitutes, stripping away every metaphysical illusion, a humanism of and in the present—a humanism after the critical adoption of the Nietzschean declaration of the "death of man."

A machinic assemblage, then, is a dynamic composition of heterogeneous elements that eschew identity but nonetheless function together, subjectively, socially, in cooperation. It thus shares characteristics with our concept of multitude, which attempts to pose political subjectivities as composed of heterogeneous singularities—one significant difference being that whereas we usually pose the multitude exclusively in terms of human singularities, a machinic assemblage is composed of a wider range of beings, human and nonhuman. Donna Haraway's conception of the cyborg and her various efforts to combat identity and essentialized subjects lead her further in this direction, recognizing the breach in our standard divisions between humans and machines and between humans and other animals.[18] But machinic assemblages extend the elements of subjective compositions even further to include all beings or elements that reside on the plane of immanence. All of this is based on the ontological claim that places humans, machines, and (now) other beings on the same ontological plane.

In economic terms, the machinic appears clearly in the subjectivities that emerge when fixed capital is reappropriated by labor-power, that is, when the material and immaterial machines and knowledges that crystallize past social production are reintegrated into the present cooperative and socially productive subjectivities. Machinic assemblages are thus grasped in part by the notion of "anthropogenetic production." Some of today's most intelligent Marxist economists, such as Robert Boyer and Christian Marazzi, characterize the novelty of contemporary economic production—and the passage from Fordism to post-Fordism—as centering on the production of humans by humans [*la production de l'homme par l'homme*] in contrast to the traditional notion of the production of commodities by means of commodities.[19] The production of subjectivity and forms of life are increasingly central to capitalist valorization, and this logic leads directly to notions of cognitive and biopolitical production. The machinic extends this anthropogenetic model further to incorporate various nonhuman singularities into the assemblies that produce and are produced. Specifically, when we say fixed capital is reappropriated by laboring subjects we do not mean simply that it becomes their possession but instead that it is integrated into the machinic assemblages, as a constituent of subjectivity.

The machinic is always an assemblage, we said, a dynamic composition of human and other beings, but the power of these new machinic subjectivities is only virtual so long as it is not actualized and articulated in social cooperation and in the common. If, in fact, the reappropriation of fixed capital were to take place individually, transferring private ownership from one individual to another, it would just be a matter of robbing Peter to pay Paul, and have no real significance. When, in contrast, the wealth and productive power of fixed capital is appropriated socially and thus when it is transformed from private property to the common, then the power of machinic subjectivities and their cooperative networks can be fully actualized. The machinic notion of assemblages, the productive forms of cooperation, and the ontological basis of the common are here woven together ever more tightly.

When we look at young people today who are absorbed in machinic assemblages, we should recognize that their very existence is resistance. Whether they are aware or not, they produce in resistance. Capital is forced to recognize a hard truth. It must consolidate the development of that common that is produced by subjectivities, from which it extracts value, but the common is only constructed through forms of resistance and processes that reappropriate fixed capital. The contradiction becomes ever more clear. Exploit yourself, capital tells productive subjectivities, and they respond, we want to valorize ourselves, governing the common that we produce. Any obstacle in the process—and even the suspicion of virtual obstacles—can determine a deepening of the clash. If capital can expropriate value only from the cooperation of subjectivities but they resist that exploitation, then capital must raise the levels of command and attempt increasingly arbitrary and violent operations of the extraction of value from the common.

NOTES

1. Max Horkheimer and Theodor Adorno, *The Dialectic of Enlightenment*, trans. John Cumming (New York: Continuum, 1972), xvi.

2. Martin Heidegger, "The Question concerning Technology," in *The Question Concerning Technology and Other Essays*, trans. William Lovitt (New York: Garland, 1977), 14.

3. Ibid., 28.

4. In some respects the pessimistic anthropology of Arnold Gehlen, another Nazi, is a variant on Heidegger's view of the relation of humans to technology. Gehlen maintains that technology, which has accompanied humanity from its origins, addresses a radical lack or insufficiency in humans, who are unable to exist on their own. See, for example, Arnold Gehlen, *Man in the Age of Technology*, trans. Patrice Lipscomb (New York: Columbia University Press, 1980). And even when other German anthropologists contest Gehlen's anthropological pessimism, they seldom go beyond a functionalism that refers human technology, just beyond lack and insufficiency, to some organic disposition. See, for instance, Heinrich Popitz in *Der Aufbruch Zur Artifiziellen Gesellschaft: Zur Anthropologie Der Technik* (Tübingen: Mohr Siebeck, 1995), who constructs an "optimistic" [sic!] perspective insisting on the fact that the relationship of humanity to the world is already in some sense naturally determined by material or physiological predispositions. For excellent interpretations of Gehlen and these developments in anthropology, see Ubaldo Fadini, *Configurazioni antropologiche* (Napoli: Liguori, 1991); and *Sviluppo tecnologico e identità personali* (Bari: Dedalo, 2000).

5. Günther Anders, *Die Antiquiertheit des Menschen* (Munich: C. H. Beck, 2009).

6. Baruch Spinoza, *The Collected Works of Spinoza*, ed. Edwin Curley, vol. 1, *The Emendation of the Intellect*, (Princeton, NJ: Princeton University Press, 1985), 17: "But just as men, in the beginning, were able to make the easiest things with the tools they were born with (however laboriously and imperfectly), and once these had been made, made other, more difficult things with less labor and more perfectly, and so, proceeding gradually from the simplest works to tools, and from tools to other works and tools, reached the point where they accomplished so many and so difficult things with little labor, in the same way the intellect, by its inborn power, makes intellectual tools for itself, by which it acquires other powers for other intellectual works, and from these works still other tools, or the power of searching further, and so proceeds by stages, until it reaches the pinnacle of wisdom."

7. Nancy Katherine Hayles, *How We Became Postmodern* (Chicago: University of Chicago Press, 1999), 7.

8. Ibid., 283–291.

9. Gilbert Simondon, *Du mode d'existence des objets techniques* (Paris: Aubier, 1958), 12. For a development along these lines, see also Bernard Stiegler, *Technics and Time 1: The Fault of Epimetheus*, trans. Richard Beardsworth and George Collins (Palo Alto, CA: Stanford University Press, 1998).

10. Gilles Deleuze and Félix Guattari, "Balance-Sheet for 'Desiring Machines,'" in Félix Guattari, *Chaosophy: Texts and Interviews, 1972–1977*, ed. Sylvère Lotringer, trans. David L. Sweet, Jarred Becker, and Taylor Adkins (Los Angeles: Semiotext(e), 2009), 91, originally published in Gilles Deleuze and Félix Guattari, *L'anti-oedipe. Capitalism et schyzophrénie I* (Paris: Éditions de Minuit, 1972).

11. Walter Benjamin, "One Way Street," in *One Way Street and Other Writings*, trans. Edmund Jeffcott and Kingsley Shorter (New York: New Left Books, 1979), 104.

12. Karl Marx, *Grundrisse. Foundations of the Critique of Political Economy*, trans. Matin Nicolaus (London: Penguin, 1973), 749.

13. Carlo Vercellone, "Composizione organica di capitale e composizione di classe," in *La crisi messa a valore* (CWPress and Sfumature edizioni, 2015), 114.

14. See, for example, Christian Fuchs, "Labor in Informational Capitalism and on the Internet," *Information Society* 26, no. 3 (2010): 179–196.

15. Félix Guattari, "On Machines," trans. Vivian Constantinopoulos, *Journal of Philosophy and Visual Arts*, no. 6 (1995): 8–12, originally published as "À propos des machines," in *Chimères*, no 19 (Spring 1993): 85–96. For an excellent analysis of the concept of machine in Guattari, see Gerald Raunig, "A Few Fragments on Machines," trans. Aileen Derieg, https://transversal.at/transversal/1106/raunig1/en; and *Tausend Maschinen. Eine kleine Philosophie der Maschine als sozialer Bewegung* (Berlin: Turia+Kant Verlag, 2008).

16. Louis Althusser, "Ideology and State Ideological Apparatuses," in *On Ideology*, trans. Ben Brewster (New York: Verso, 1971), 56.

17. This dilemma is not solved when followers such as Étienne Balibar amend Althusser's affirmation: "it is [only] *in the process without a subject* as a historical process that the 'constitution of the subject' can have meaning"; see Étienne Balibar, "L'objet d'Althusser," in *Politique et philosophie dans l'œuvre d'Althusser*, ed. Sylvain Lazarus (Paris: Presses Universitaire de France, 1993), 98.

18. See Donna Haraway, "A Cyborg Manifesto," in *Simians, Cyborgs, and Women. The Reinvention of Nature* (New York: Routledge, 1991), 149–182; and, more recently, "Anthropocene, Capitalocene, Plantationoscene, Chthulucene: Making Kin," *Environmental Humanities* 6, no. 1 (2015): 159–165.

19. On the anthropogenetic model, see Robert Boyer, *La croissance, début de siècle* (Paris: Albin Michel, 2002); and Christian Marazzi, "Capitalismo digitale e modello antropogenetico del lavoro," in *Reinventare il lavoro*, Christian Marazzi et al., eds. (Bari: Sapere 2000, 2005), 107–126.

BIBLIOGRAPHY

Althusser, Louis. "Ideology and State Ideological Apparatuses." In *On Ideology*. Translated by Ben Brewster, 1–60. New York: Verso, 1971.

Anders, Günther. *Die Antiquiertheit des Menschen*. Munich: C. H. Beck, 2009.

Balibar, Étienne. "L'objet d'Althusser." In *Politique et philosophie dans l'œuvre d'Althusser*. Edited by Sylvain Lazarus, 81–116. Paris: Presses Universitaire de France, 1993.

Benjamin, Walter. "One Way Street." In *One Way Street and Other Writings*. Translated by Edmund Jeffcott and Kingsley Shorter, 45–104. New York: New Left Books, 1979.

Boyer, Robert. *La croissance, début de siècle*. Paris: Albin Michel, 2002.

Deleuze, Gilles, and Félix Guattari. "Balance-Sheet for 'Desiring Machines.'" In Félix Guattari, *Chaosophy: Texts and Interviews, 1972–1977*. Edited by Sylvère Lotringer. Translated by David L. Sweet, Jarred Becker, and Taylor Adkins, 90–118. Los Angeles: Semiotext(e), 2009. Originally published in Gilles Deleuze and Félix Guattari, *L'anti-œdipe. Capitalisme et schyzophrénie I*. Paris: Éditions de Minuit, 1972.

Fadini, Ubaldo. *Configurazioni antropologiche*. Napoli: Liguori, 1991.

Fadini, Ubaldo. *Sviluppo tecnologico e identità personali*. Bari: Dedalo, 2000.

Fuchs, Christian. "Labor in Informational Capitalism and on the Internet." *Information Society* 26, no. 3 (2010): 179–196.

Gehlen, Arnold. *Man in the Age of Technology*. Translated by Patrice Lipscomb. New York: Columbia University Press, 1980.

Guattari, Félix. "On Machines." Translated by Vivian Constantinopoulos. *Journal of Philosophy and Visual Arts*, no. 6 (1995): 8–12. Originally published as "À propos des machines," in *Chimères*, no. 19 (Spring 1993): 85–96.

Haraway, Donna. "A Cyborg Manifesto." In *Simians, Cyborgs, and Women. The Reinvention of Nature*, 149–182. New York: Routledge, 1991.

Haraway, Donna. "Anthropocene, Capitalocene, Plantationoscene, Chthulucene: Making Kin." *Environmental Humanities* 6, no. 1 (2015): 159–165.

Hayles, Nancy Katherine. *How We Became Postmodern*. Chicago: University of Chicago Press, 1999.

Heidegger, Martin. "The Question concerning Technology." In *The Question Concerning Technology and Other Essays*. Translated by William Lovitt, 3–35. New York: Garland, 1977.

Horkheimer, Max, and Theodor Adorno. *The Dialectic of Enlightenment*. Translated by John Cumming. New York: Continuum, 1972.

Marazzi, Christian. "Capitalismo digitale e modello antropogenetico del lavoro." In *Reinventare il lavoro*. Edited by Christian Marazzi et al., 107–126. Bari: Sapere 2000, 2005.

Marx, Karl. *Grundrisse. Foundations of the Critique of Political Economy*. Translated by Matin Nicolaus. London: Penguin, 1973.

Popitz, Heinrich. *Der Aufbruch Zur Artifiziellen Gesellschaft: Zur Anthropologie Der Technik*. Tübingen: Mohr Siebeck, 1995.

Raunig, Gerald. "A Few Fragments on Machines." Translated by Aileen Derieg, 2005. https://transversal.at/transversal/1106/raunig1/en.

Raunig, Gerald. *Tausend Maschinen. Eine kleine Philosophie der Maschine als sozialer Bewegung.* Berlin: Turia+Kant Verlag, 2008.

Simondon, Gilbert. *Du mode d'existence des objets techniques.* Paris: Aubier, 1958.

Spinoza, Baruch. *The Emendation of the Intellect*, vol. 1 of *The Collected Works of Spinoza*. Edited by Edwin Curley. Princeton, NJ: Princeton University Press, 1985.

Stiegler, Bernard. *Technics and Time 1: The Fault of Epimetheus*. Translated by Richard Beardsworth and George Collins. Palo Alto, CA: Stanford University Press, 1998.

Vercellone, Carlo. "Composizione organica di capitale e composizione di classe." In *La crisi messa a valore*, 103–118. CWPress and Sfumature edizioni, 2015.

9

COGNITIVE ASSEMBLAGES: TECHNICAL AGENCY AND HUMAN INTERACTIONS

N. Katherine Hayles

In a passage from *Reassembling the Social: An Introduction to Actor-Network-Theory* (2007), Bruno Latour criticizes what he calls the "sociology of the social" for making an artificial distinction between humans and objects with this example. "Any human course of action might weave together in a manner of minutes, for instance, a shouted order to lay a brick, the chemical connection of cement with water, the force of a pulley unto a rope with a movement of the hand, the strike of a match to light a cigarette offered by a co-worker."[1] While I very much admire Latour's work and happily acknowledge the significant contributions of actor-network-theory (ANT) to science studies, this passage illustrates why a framework focusing on cognition adds an important dimension to existing approaches to complex human systems. Notice that the action begins with a "shouted order," and that material forces are then enlisted as a result of this decision. The cement could not by itself build a structure; for that matter, cement relies on human intervention to come into existence as a construction material. In short, cognitive processes play crucial roles in Latour's example, notwithstanding that he intends it to show the symmetry between human actions and material forces. The point, as I have emphasized, is not to glorify human choice but rather to expand the spectrum of decision makers to include all biological life-forms and many technical systems. Decision makers certainly can and do enlist material forces as their allies, but they are the ones who try to steer the ship in a particular direction.

The term I use to describe these complex interactions between human and nonhuman cognizers and their abilities to enlist material forces is "cognitive assemblage."

While Latour and Deleuze and Guattari also invoke "assemblage," a *cognitive* assemblage has distinctive properties not present in how they use the term. In particular, a cognitive assemblage emphasizes the flow of information through a system and the choices and decisions that create, modify, and interpret the flow. While a cognitive assemblage may include material agents and forces (and almost always does so), it is the cognizers within the assemblage that enlist these affordances and direct their powers to act in complex situations.

[. . .]

In Deleuze and Guattari's usage, "assemblage" [*agencement*] carries the connotations of connection, event, transformation, and becoming. They privilege desire, affect, and transversal energies over cognition, but the broader definition of "cognition" that I employ brings my argument somewhat closer to theirs, although significant differences remain. I want to convey the sense of a provisional collection of parts in constant flux as some are added and others lost. The parts are not so tightly bound that transformations are inhibited and not so loosely connected that information cannot flow between parts. An important connotation is the implication that arrangements can scale up, progressing from very low-level choices into higher levels of cognition and consequently decisions affecting larger areas of concern.

In focusing on cognition, which [. . .] I defined as "a process of interpreting information in contexts that connect it with meaning," I highlighted the activities of interpretation, choice, and decision and discussed the special properties that cognition bestows, namely flexibility, adaptability, and evolvability. A cognitive assemblage approach considers these properties from a systemic perspective as an arrangement of systems, subsystems, and individual actors through which information flows, effecting transformations through the interpretive activities of cognizers operating upon the flows. A cognitive assemblage operates at multiple levels and sites, transforming and mutating as conditions and contexts change.

Why choose assemblages rather than networks, the obvious alternative? The question is especially pertinent, since "network" is usually favored by Latour (witness ANT), although he tends at times to use "assemblage" as a synonym.[2] Networks are typically considered to consist of edges and nodes analyzed through graph theory, conveying a sense of sparse, clean materiality.[3] Assemblages, by contrast, allow for contiguity in a fleshly sense, touching, incorporating, repelling, mutating. When analyzed as dynamic systems, networks are like assemblages in that they function as sites of exchange, transformation, and dissemination, but they lack the sense of those interactions occurring across complex three-dimensional topologies, whereas assemblages include information transactions across convoluted and involuted surfaces, with multiple volumetric entities interacting with many conspecifics simultaneously.

Because humans and technical systems in a cognitive assemblage are interconnected, the cognitive decisions of each affect the others, with interactions occurring across the full range of human cognition, including consciousness/unconscious, the cognitive nonconscious, and the sensory/perceptual systems that send signals to the central nervous system. Moreover, human decisions and interpretations interact with the technical systems, sometimes decisively affecting the contexts in which they operate. As a whole, a cognitive assemblage performs the functions identified with cognition in general: flexibly responding to new situations, incorporating this knowledge into adaptive strategies, and evolving through experience to create new strategies and kinds of responses. Because the boundaries are fuzzy, where one draws the line often depends on the analytical perspective one uses and the purposes of the analysis. Nevertheless, for a given situation, it is possible to specify the kinds of cognitions involved and consequently to trace their effects through an evolutionary trajectory.

The most transformative technologies of the later twentieth century have been cognitive assemblages: the Internet is a prime example. While many modern technologies also had immense effects—the steam engine, railroads, antibiotics, nuclear weapons and energy—cognitive assemblages are distinct because their transformative potentials are enabled, extended, and supported by flows of information, and consequently cognitions between human and technical participants. Hybrid by nature, they raise questions about how agency is distributed among cognizers, how and in what ways actors contribute to systemic dynamics, and consequently how responsibilities—technical, social, legal, ethical—should be apportioned. They invite ethical inquiries that recognize the importance of technical mediations, adopting systemic and relational perspectives rather than an emphasis (I would say overemphasis) on individual responsibility.

[. . .]

DISTRIBUTED AGENCY AND TECHNICAL AUTONOMY

Cognitive technologies show a clear trajectory toward greater agency and autonomy. In some instances, this is because they are performing actions outside the realm of human possibility, as when high-frequency trading algorithms conduct trades in five milliseconds or less, something no human could do. In other cases, the intent is to lessen the load on the most limited resource, human attention, for example with self-driving cars. Perhaps the most controversial examples of technical autonomy are autonomous drones and robots with lethal capacity, now in development. In part because these technologies unsettle many traditional assumptions, they have been sites for intense debate, both within the military community and in general discussions. They can therefore serve as test cases for the implications of distributed agency and, more broadly, for the ways in which cognitive assemblages interact with complex human systems to create new kinds of possibilities, challenges, and dangers. To limit my inquiry, I will focus on autonomous drones, but many of the same problems attend the creation of robot warfighters, as well as nonmilitary technologies such as self-driving cars, and quasi-military technologies such as face-recognition systems.

The present moment is especially auspicious for analyzing technical autonomy, because the necessary technical advances are clearly possible, but the technical infrastructures are not so deeply embedded in everyday life that other paths are "locked out" and made much more difficult to pursue. In short, now is the time of decision. Debates entered into and choices made now will have extensive implications for the kinds of cognitive assemblages we develop or resist, and consequently for the kinds of future we fashion for ourselves and other cognitive entities with whom we share the planet.

[. . .]

I will focus on piloted and autonomous UAVs,[4] as well as multivehicle systems proceeding autonomously, with the swarm itself deciding which individual will play what role in an orchestrated attack. This range of examples, showing different levels of sensing abilities, cognitions, and decisional powers, illustrates why greater technical cognition might be enticing and the kinds of social, political, and ethical problems it poses.

With the massive shift after 9/11 from state-on-state violence to what Norman Friedman, a military analyst, calls expeditionary warfare, targets are not associated with a geographically defined entity but with highly mobile and flexible insurgents and "terrorists." Friedman points out that if surveillance can be carried out without the enemy's ability to perceive it, then the enemy is forced to devote resources to hiding and concealing its positions, which not only drains their ability to carry out offensives but also makes it more difficult for them to organize and extend their reach. These factors, he argues, combine to make UAVs superior to manned aircraft for expeditionary warfare. A fighter jet can typically stay aloft only for two hours before it needs to refuel and the pilot, fatigued from high altitudes, needs to rest. In contrast, the UAV Global Hawk can stay aloft literally for days, refueling in the air; with no pilot aboard, pilot fatigue is not a problem.[5] These factors have led to a significant redistribution of resources in the US Air force, with more UAV pilots currently being trained than pilots for all types of manned aircraft combined. Spending about $6 billion annually on drone development and purchase,[6] they currently deploy about 7,000 drones, compared to 10,000 manned aerial vehicles.[7]

The factors that have made UAVs the contemporary weapons of choice for the US Air Force required the coming together of many technological advances, including global satellite positioning, superior navigation tools, better aerodynamics for increased stability and fuel economy, increased computational power, and better sensors for visual reconnaissance, obstacle avoidance, and ground coordination. The weak link in this chain is the necessity to maintain communications between the UAV and the remote pilot. As long as the UAV's performance requires this link, it is subject to disruption either internally, as when the remote pilot banks too suddenly and the link is lost, or because the link has been hijacked and control wrested away by another party, as happened when a Lockheed Martin RQ170 Sentinel drone landed in Iranian territory in December 2007, likely because the UAV was fed false GPS coordinates by the Iranians. This implies that the next wave of development will be UAAVs, unmanned vehicles that fly autonomously, and UAAVS, multivehicle autonomous systems. Still at a nascent stage, UAAVs and UAAVS are nevertheless developing rapidly. The Navy, for example, is developing the experimental X-47B Stealth UAAV, which can perform missions autonomously and land on an aircraft carrier without a remote pilot steering it. Moreover, the technical components necessary to make UAAVs and UAAVS reliable and robust are coming together very quickly in transnational research projects, particularly in the United States and China.

A recent article written in English by Chinese researchers illustrates the growing awareness of UAAVS of their internal states as well as the environment.[8] The study discusses the development of software that allows a swarm to coordinate its individuals in cases where one or more vehicles are assigned to attack. The model uses an "auction" strategy, whereby each unit responds to a request for a bid by assessing what the authors call its "beliefs," "desires," and "intentions," which are calculated with weighted formulae resulting in a quantitative number for the bid. The software enables the swarm to balance competing priorities in rapidly changing conditions, taking into account their position, velocity, and proximity to one another ("beliefs"), their assigned mission priorities ("intentions"), and the intensity with which they will execute the mission ("desires"), with the latter parameters tailored for specific mission objectives. The anthropomorphic language is not merely an idiosyncratic choice, for it indicates that as the sensory knowledge of external and internal states, autonomous agency, and cognitive capabilities of the swarm increase, so too does their ability to make decisions traditionally reserved for humans.

With autonomous drones and other autonomous weapons on the horizon, there has been increased attention to the ethical implications of their use. Most of these discussions refer to the Geneva Conventions and similar protocols, which require that weapons must "distinguish between the civilian population and combatants."[9] In addition, international humanitarian law prohibits disproportionate attacks, defined as ones that "may be expected to cause incidental loss of civilian life, injury to civilians, damage to civilian objects, or a combination thereof, which would be excessive in relation to the concrete and direct military advantage anticipated."[10] Finally, additional requirements are the rather vague concept of "military necessity," defined by British scholar Armin Krishnan as dictating that "military force should only be used against the enemy to the extent necessary for winning the war,"[11] and the even vaguer "Martens Clause," intended to cover instances not explicit in the Geneva Conventions. It requires that weapons be consistent with the "principles of humanity" and the "dictates of public conscience."[12]

In assessing autonomous weapons in these terms, Human Rights Watch and the International Human Rights Clinic (IHRC) at the Harvard Law School argue that autonomous weapons, including autonomous drones, cannot possibly make the required distinctions between combatants and civilians, particularly in the context of insurgent tactics that deliberately seek cover within civilian populations. Peter Singer, for example, instances the case of a gunman who shot at a US Ranger with "an AK-47 that was propped between the legs of two kneeling women, while four children sat on the shooter's back."[13] They also argue that "proportionality" and "military necessity" are violated by drones, although "necessity" clearly is itself a moving target, given that what constitutes it is obviously context dependent and heavily influenced by the kinds of weaponry available.

The Geneva Conventions were, of course, forged in the aftermath of World War II, characterized by massive state-on-state violence, fire-bombings of cities, gratuitous destruction of cultural monuments, and the nuclear holocausts wreaked by the United States upon Nagasaki and Hiroshima. With the move to expeditionary warfare, rise of insurgent attacks, and continuing increases in US drone attacks, these protocols seem badly outdated, even inappropriate. Why keep coming back to them? On an even deeper level, why should we care about ethics in wars where the intent is precisely to kill and maim? Why, as Peter Singer puts it, try to determine what is right when so much is wrong, a question that drives straight to the oxymoron implicit in the phrase

"Laws of War."[14] His defense is that the Geneva Conventions, obsolete as they may be, are the only international accords on the conduct of warfare we have and that we are likely to have, short of another world war with even more devastating violence. He believes there is an important distinction between those who practice restraint in warfare and "barbarians"[15] who are willing to go to any extreme, however savage and brutal. To argue thus is to plunge into a definitional abyss, since what counts as "restraint" and "barbarism" are as contextually and culturally dependent as the distinctions they propose to clarify.

A better approach, I argue, is to evaluate the ethical questions surrounding piloted and autonomous drones from the relational and processual perspectives implicit in the idea of a cognitive assemblage. Mark Coeckelbergh, one of the few philosophers urging a relational perspective on robotics, observes that most ethical theories carry over to robotics the assumption characteristic of liberal individualism, taking "the main object of ethical concern [as] the individual robot."[16] In contrast, he argues that "both humans and robots must be understood as related to their larger techno-social environment."[17] Regarding ethical issues through the perspective of a cognitive assemblage foregrounds the interpretations, choices, and decisions that technical and human components make as information flows from the UAV's sensors, through choices performed by the UAV software, to interpretations that the sensor and vehicle pilots give to the transmitted data, on to the decision about whether to launch a missile, which involves the pilots, their tactical commander, and associated lawyers, on up to presidential advisors and staff. Autonomous drones and drone swarms would operate with different distributions of choices, interpretations, and decisions, but they too participate in a complex assemblage involving human and technical cognizers.

The choice, then, is not between human decision versus technical implementation, which is sometimes how the situation is parsed by commentators who prefer a simplistic picture to the more realistic complexities inherent in the situation. As Bruno Latour argues,[18] changing the means of technical affordances always already affects the terms in which the means are envisioned, so ends and means mutually coconstitute each other in cycles of continuous circular causality. That said, the human designer has a special role to play not easily assigned to technical systems, for she, much more than the technical cognitive systems in which she is enmeshed, is able to envision and evaluate ethical and moral consequences in the context of human sociality and world horizons that are the distinctive contributions of human conscious and nonconscious cognitions. Consequently, we need a framework in which human cognition is recognized for its uniquely valuable potential, without insisting that human cognition is the whole of cognition or that it is unaffected by the technical cognizers that interpenetrate it. Understanding the situation as a cognitive assemblage highlights this reality and foregrounds both the interplay between human and technical cognitions and the asymmetric distribution of ethical responsibility in whatever actions are finally taken.

Although the cognitive assemblage approach can provide useful perspectives on ethical issues, it does not by itself answer the urgent question of whether autonomous drones and drone swarms should be developed by the US military, and if developed, under what circumstances they should be deployed. Arguing in the affirmative, Ronald Arkin, a roboticist at Georgia Tech, envisions an "ethical governor"[19] that would be built into the weapon's software requiring the weapon first to determine whether the presumed target is a combatant, and then to assess whether the proportionality criteria are met. This proposal strikes me as naïve in the extreme, not only because of the ambiguities involved in these determinations, but more fundamentally, because of the presumption that the weapon's designers would agree to these criteria. Even if the US military decided to do so, when autonomous weapons designed by other states and nonstate entities fail to incorporate these restraints, would not "military necessity" dictate that the United States do likewise?

The issue, then, cannot be resolved through technical fixes but requires considered debate and reflection, an insight that highlights the importance of human cognizers as they act within cognitive assemblages. Ultimately the humans are the ones that decide how much autonomy should be given to the technical actors, always recognizing that these choices, like everything else within a cognitive assemblage, are interpenetrated by technical cognition. A chorus of voices argues that fully autonomous weapons should not be developed and certainly not deployed. Human Rights Watch and the IHRC, in their thoughtful white paper considering the issue, conclude, "The development of autonomous technology should be halted before it reaches the point where humans fall completely out of the loop."[20] The summary emerging from the Stockdale Center's year-long program on "Ethics and Emerging Military Technologies," which culminated in the Tenth Annual McCain Conference on Military Ethics and Leadership, reaches a similar conclusion: "extreme caution should govern the actual deployment of autonomous strike systems."[21] Even before deployment, however, they write, "We strongly advise against incorporating 'strong artificial intelligence' in such systems, which would render them capable of learning and even choosing ends, inasmuch as strong artificial intelligence is highly likely to introduce unpredictability and/or mitigate human responsibility."[22] Noel Sharkey of the University of Sheffield is more blunt; he is quoted by the website *Defense One* as saying, "Don't make them fully autonomous. That will proliferate just as quickly and then you are going to be sunk."[23] The risk of proliferation is real; already fifty-five countries have the capacity to manufacture or build arsenals of UAVs. Friedman's appendix listing UAVs larger than fifty kilograms in use around the world runs to a massive 220 pages.[24] Matthew Bolton of Pace University in New York City puts the issue of lethal force deployed autonomously through UAAVS eloquently. "Growing autonomy in weapons poses a grave threat to humanitarian and human rights law, as well as international peace and security.... Death by algorithm represents a violation of a person's inherent right to life, dignity, and due process."[25]

As these analyses recognize, the possibility of developing autonomous weapons signals a tectonic shift in how warfare is conducted. The masses of humans that required nations for mobilization, as in World Wars I and II, can potentially be replaced by masses of combat aerial vehicles, all operating autonomously and capable of delivering lethal force. UAVs can now be built for as little as $500–$1,000, making it possible to field a 2,000-vehicle swarm for as little as a million dollars, a sum that emphatically does not require the deep pockets of a national treasury. This enables an entirely different kind of warfare than that carried out by single UAVs, and it brings into view the possibility that UAAVS could be used to launch massive attacks almost anywhere by almost anyone.

[. . .]

Ironically, the threat of unlimited drone warfare may be the strongest motivation for the United States to reform its own drone policies first, in order to argue for international accords prohibiting further proliferation. The situation is analogous to the United States being the first to develop—and use—nuclear weapons, but then when other states acquired nuclear capability, being a leader in arguing for international controls. However cynically conceived, this strategy did rescue the world from all-out nuclear war. Nuclear weapons, of course, require massive resources to develop and build, which largely limits them to state enterprises. Autonomous drones are much cheaper. Whether the same strategy would work with them remains to be seen.

HUMAN EMOTION AND TECHNICAL COGNITION

So far my argument has emphasized the ways in which human and technical cognitions interact, but their cognitive capacities nevertheless have distinctive differences. On the technical side are speed, computational intensity, and rapid data processing; on the human side are emotion, an encompassing world horizon, and empathic abilities to understand other minds. Roboticist Arkin tends to present human emotion as a liability in a warfighter, clouding judgment and leading to poor decisions.[26] However, emotion and empathy also have positive sides; considered as part of a cognitive assemblage, they can make important contributions.

The French theorist Grégoire Chamayou refers to suicide bombers as "those who have nothing but their bodies."[27] Applied to groups such as Al-Qaeda and the Islamic State, this is obviously incorrect; they also have AK-47s, rocket grenades, suicide bombs, IEDs, and a host of other weaponry. There have, however, been instances of resistance by those who indeed have nothing but their bodies: the lone student confronting a tank in Tiananmen Square, the hundreds of satyagrahis (resistors) who followed Gandhi to the Dharasana Salt Works in India and were beaten by British soldiers. Intentionally making oneself vulnerable to harm for principled reasons has the capacity to evoke powerful emotions in those who witness it, as world outrage over the episode at the Dharasana Salt Works demonstrated. Vulnerability, whether intentional or not, can also evoke strong emotions in those who perpetrate violence, in some instances leading them to reject violence as a viable solution.

Such is the case of Brandon Bryant, who performed as a drone sensor pilot for the US Air Force for almost six years until he refused to go on, turning down a $109,000 bonus to reenlist. When he finally sought therapy, he was diagnosed with post-traumatic stress disorder. The diagnosis represents, as journalist Matthew Power notes, "a shift from a focusing on the violence that has been done to a person in wartime toward his feelings about what he has done to others—or what he's failed to do for them."[28] Chamayou sees this shift as a cynical tactic by the US military to claim that drone pilots suffer too, but this interpretation fails to do justice to Bryant's feeling that he has been through a "soul-crushing experience."[29] Granted that drone pilots suffer far less harm than those they kill or maim, the fact that some of them experience real "moral injury"[30] can be understood as one of the contributions human emotions make to cognitive assemblages—something unique to biological life-forms that has no real equivalence in technical systems.

Along with emotion, language, human sociality, and somatic responses, technological adaptations are crucial to the formations of modern humans. Whether warfare should be added to the list may be controversial, but the twentieth and twenty-first centuries suggest that it will persist, albeit in modified forms. As the informational networks and feedback loops connecting us and our devices proliferate and deepen, we can no longer afford the illusion that consciousness alone steers our ships. How should we reimagine contemporary cognitive ecologies so that they become life-enhancing rather than aimed toward dysfunctionality and death for humans and nonhumans alike? Recognizing the role played by nonconscious cognitions in human/technical hybrids and conceptualizing them as cognitive assemblages is of course not a complete answer, but it is a necessary component.

For the cultural critic, knowing precisely how the informational exchanges operate within a cognitive assemblage is a crucial starting point from which to launch analyses and arguments for modifications and transformations, deployments or abstentions, forward-moving trajectories or, as a contrary example, international accords banning autonomous weapon systems. Providing the conceptual scaffolding for such analyses is therefore a profoundly political act, self-evidently so in military contexts but also in many other everyday contexts in which technical nonconscious cognitions interpenetrate human systems, such as those instanced in this chapter.

We need to recognize that when we design, implement, and extend technical cognitive systems, we are partially designing ourselves as well as affecting the planetary cognitive ecology: we must take care accordingly. More accurate and encompassing views of how our cognitions enmesh with technical systems and those of other lifeforms will enable better designs, humbler perceptions of human roles in cognitive assemblages, and more life-affirming practices as we move toward a future in which we collectively decide to what extent technical autonomy should and will become increasingly intrinsic to human complex systems.

NOTES

1. Bruno Latour, *Reassembling the Social: An Introduction to Actor Network Theory* (London: Oxford University Press, 2007), 74.

2. Ibid.

3. See Alexander R. Galloway and Eugene Thacker, *The Exploit: A Theory of Networks* (Minneapolis: University of Minnesota Press, 2007).

4. Some nomenclature clarification is necessary. The technical term for drone is UAV: unmanned aerial vehicle, requiring two pilots, one to guide the craft and the other to monitor sensory data. If more than one aircraft is involved, it becomes UAVS, unmanned aerial vehicle *system*; if intended for combat, UCAVS, unmanned *combat* aerial vehicle system. Autonomous drones are also called UAVs, unmanned *autonomous* vehicles, "aerial" understood from context. To avoid confusion, I will call these UAAVs, unmanned autonomous aerial vehicles, and UAAVS, unmanned autonomous aerial multivehicle systems or swarms.

5. PBS, "Rise of the Drones." *Nova*, January 23, 2013, https://www.youtube.com/watch?v=HL4WjhSy5Kc.

6. Human Rights Watch, *Losing Humanity: The Case against Killer Robots* (Cambridge, MA: International Human Rights Clinic, Harvard Law School, 2012), 6.

7. Timothy Vasko, "Solemn Geographies of Human Limits: Drones and the Neocolonial Administration of Life and Death," *Affinities: A Journal of Radical Theory, Culture, and Action* 6, no. 1 (2013): 83–107, 84.

8. See Han, Jian, Changhong Wang, and Guoxing Yi, "Cooperative Control of UAV Based on Multi-Agent System," in *Proceedings of the 2013 IEEE 8th Conference on Industrial Electronics and Applications (ICIEA): 19–21 June 2013, Melbourne, Australia*. Piscataway (NJ: IEEE, 2013), https://ieeexplore.ieee.org/document/6566347 and "UAV Robust Strategy Control Based on MAS," *Abstract and Applied Analysis* (2014): Article ID 796859.

9. Article 48 of Additional Protocol 1 to the Geneva Conventions, cited in Human Rights Watch, *Losing Humanity*, 24.

10. From the *Customary International Humanitarian Law Database*, cited in Ibid.

11. Armin Krishnan, *Killer Robots: Legality and Ethicality of Autonomous Weapons* (Farnham, UK: Ashgate Publishing Limited, 2009), 91.

12. Human Rights Watch, *Losing Humanity*, 25.

13. Peter W. Singer, "The Ethics of Killer Applications: Why Is It So Hard to Talk about Morality When It Comes to New Military Technology?" *Journal of Military Ethics* 9, no. 4 (2010): 299–312, 303.

14. Ibid., 309.

15. Ibid.

16. Mark Coeckelbergh, "Is Ethics of Robotics about Robots? Philosophy of Robotics beyond Realism and Individualism," *Law, Innovation and Technology* 3, no. 2 (2011): 241–250, 245.

17. Ibid.

18. See Bruno Latour, "Morality and Technology: The End of the Means," trans. Couze Venn, *Theory, Culture and Society* 19 no. 5–6 (2002): 247–260.

19. Ronald C. Arkin, *Governing Lethal Behavior in Autonomous Robots* (Boca Raton, FL: CRC Press, 2009), 69.

20. Human Rights Watch, *Losing Humanity*, 36.

21. Stockdale Center for Ethical Leadership, US Naval Academy, McCain Conference. "Executive Summary and Command Brief," *Journal of Military Ethics* 9, no. 4 (2010): 424–431, 429.

22. Ibid., 429–430.

23. See Patrick Tucker, "Inside the Navy's Secret Swarm Robot Experiment," *Defense One*. October 5, 2014, http://www.defenseone.com/technology/2014/10/inside-navys-secret-swarm-robot-experiment/95813/.

24. See Norman Friedman, *Unmanned Combat Air Systems: A New Kind of Carrier Aviation* (Annapolis, MD: Naval Institute Press, 2010).

25. See Tucker, "Inside the Navy's Experiment."

26. See Ronald C. Arkin, "The Case for Ethical Autonomy in Unmanned Systems," *Journal of Military Ethics* 9, no. 4 (2010): 332–341.

27. Grégoire Chamayou, *A Theory of the Drone*, trans. Janet Lloyd (New York: New Press, 2015), 86.

28. Matthew Power, "Confessions of a Drone Warrior," *GQ*, October 23, 2013, http://www.gq.com/news-politics/big-issues/201311/drone-uav-pilot-assassination, 7.

29. Ibid.

30. Ibid.

BIBLIOGRAPHY

Arkin, Ronald C. *Governing Lethal Behavior in Autonomous Robots*. Boca Raton, FL: CRC Press, 2009.

Arkin, Ronald C. "The Case for Ethical Autonomy in Unmanned Systems." *Journal of Military Ethics* 9, no. 4 (2010): 332–341.

Chamayou, Grégoire. *A Theory of the Drone*. Translated by Janet Lloyd. New York: New Press, 2015.

Coeckelbergh, Mark. "Is Ethics of Robotics about Robots? Philosophy of Robotics beyond Realism and Individualism." *Law, Innovation and Technology* 3, no. 2 (2011): 241–250.

Friedman, Norman. *Unmanned Combat Air Systems: A New Kind of Carrier Aviation*. Annapolis, MD: Naval Institute Press, 2010.

Galloway, Alexander R., and Eugene Thacker. *The Exploit: A Theory of Networks*. Minneapolis: University of Minnesota Press, 2007.

Han, Jian, Changhong Wang, and Guoxing Yi. "Cooperative Control of UAV Based on Multi-Agent System." In *Proceedings of the 2013 IEEE 8th Conference on Industrial Electronics and Applications (ICIEA): 19–21 June 2013, Melbourne, Australia*. Piscataway. NJ: IEEE, 2013. https://ieeexplore.ieee.org/document/6566347.

Han, Jian, Changhong Wang, and Guoxing Yi. "UAV Robust Strategy Control Based on MAS." *Abstract and Applied Analysis* (2014): Article ID 796859.

Human Rights Watch. *Losing Humanity: The Case against Killer Robots*. Cambridge, MA: International Human Rights Clinic, Harvard Law School, 2012.

Krishnan, Armin. *Killer Robots: Legality and Ethicality of Autonomous Weapons*. Farnham, UK: Ashgate Publishing Limited, 2009.

Latour, Bruno. "Morality and Technology: The End of the Means." Translated by Couze Venn. *Theory, Culture and Society* 19, no. 5–6 (2002): 247–260.

Latour, Bruno. *Reassembling the Social: An Introduction to Actor Network Theory*. London: Oxford University Press, 2007.

PBS. "Rise of the Drones." *Nova*. January 23, 2013. https://www.youtube.com/watch?v=HL4WjhSy5Kc.

Power, Matthew. "Confessions of a Drone Warrior." *GQ*. October 23, 2013. http://www.gq.com/news-politics/big-issues/201311/drone-uav-pilot-assassination.

Singer, Peter W. "The Ethics of Killer Applications: Why Is It So Hard to Talk about Morality When It Comes to New Military Technology?" *Journal of Military Ethics* 9, no. 4 (2010): 299–312.

Stockdale Center for Ethical Leadership, US Naval Academy, McCain Conference. "Executive Summary and Command Brief." *Journal of Military Ethics* 9, no. 4 (2010): 424–431.

Tucker, Patrick. "Inside the Navy's Secret Swarm Robot Experiment." *Defense One*. October 5, 2014. http://www.defenseone.com/technology/2014/10/inside-navys-secret-swarm-robot-experiment/95813/.

Vasko, Timothy. "Solemn Geographies of Human Limits: Drones and the Neocolonial Administration of Life and Death." *Affinities: A Journal of Radical Theory, Culture, and Action* 6, no. 1 (2013): 83–107.

II
POSITIVITY/TACTICS

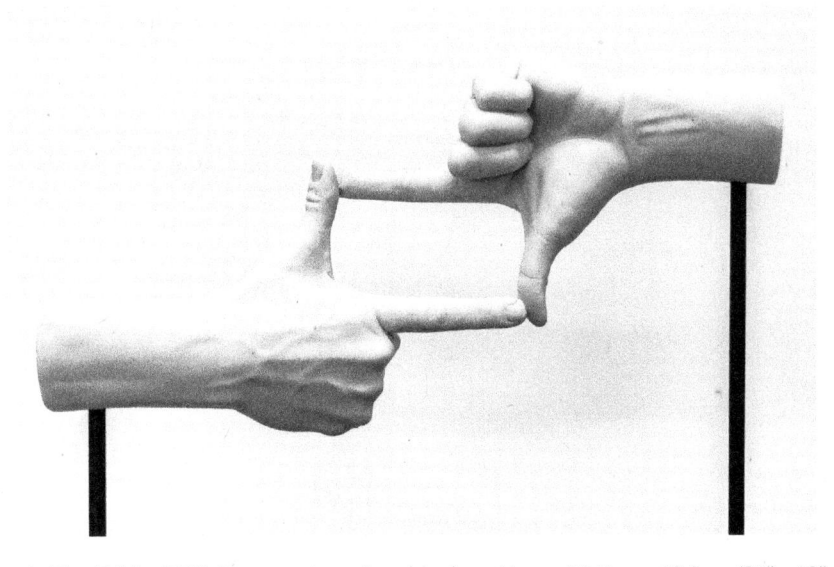

Luis Jacob, The Riddle, 2018. Epoxy resin and marble dust, 61 cm × 30.5 cm × 10.2 cm (24″ × 12″ × 4″). Image courtesy of the artist.

10

THE IDEA OF POSITIVITY

Jean Hyppolite

Hegel's philosophy consummates the philosophy of the eighteenth century and initiates the philosophy of the nineteenth; it is the hinge of two eras. This judgment is confirmed if we consider the position that Hegel takes toward History and Reason. Reason and History, we may say, are the two terms that he envisages to oppose or conciliate each other, as far back as his youthful writings, more particularly during the period of Berne and Frankfurt. The two fundamental studies of these periods are, in addition to a *Life of Jesus*, a writing on the *Positivity of the Christian Religion* and another on the *Spirit of Christianity and Its Destiny*.[1] Here the two key concepts to retain, around which all his meditations converge, are the concepts of positivity and destiny. Their meanings, at first trite, are progressively enriched. With these concepts, Hegel approaches the problem of the relationship of reason and history. At first he poses this problem with some subtle differences about man of the eighteenth century, but he resolves this problem in man of the nineteenth century. A historical reason is manifested at the end of these studies, a reason that is concretely enriched in history, as history is enlightened by reason.[2]

Let us consider first of all the term "positivity" and see what it means for Hegel. The opposition with *natural religion* is trivial in this era, and it is certainly relevant to religion that Hegel speaks of positivity. But the term has a larger application, and during the Jena period Hegel will be able to apply, *mutatis mutandis*, the result of his first works to the opposition: positive right—natural right.[3] In the eighteenth century positive religion was put in opposition to natural religion. "The concept of positivity of a religion has only taken birth and become important in contemporary times."[4] This opposition is presented because it is presupposed that there is a human nature and a natural religion corresponding to it, whereas we recognize in history a multitude of various religions that all diverge more or less by their institutions, ceremonies, and fundamental beliefs. Let us consider, for example, the position of a rationalist such as Voltaire in regard to religions. He reduces the beliefs that reason can admit to their simplest terms, namely, *the existence of God and the immortality of the soul*, and tends to consider as aberrations all religions that have been manifested in history and have added their superstitions to a rational foundation, a foundation Voltaire only appears to tolerate in matters of belief. A positive religion is therefore a historical religion. It adds to what human reason, reduced to itself alone, can give, beliefs that have appeared at a given moment in time, in certain places in space, and beliefs that could not be fully assimilated by reason, that come from other sources. We can therefore say with Hegel of positive religions that they are "either supernatural or antinatural." For example, a Christian acknowledges a particular revelation of God that constitutes a reality irreducible to pure thought, a sort of irrational that is both a given for reason and a historical phenomenon. If we master ever so little the problem of positivity, we discover the philosophic problem of realism and idealism. What is the positive, in fact, if it is not the given, or what appears to be imposed outside of reason? And that given being a historical given, the question raised here is that of the relations of reason and history like that of the irrational and the rational.

If we no longer consider this problem in its theoretical aspect but in its practical aspect, we will discover yet another opposition included in it, that of *constraint* and *freedom*, and it is this last opposition that we think is important to the reader of the *Critique of Practical Reason* and the *Religion within the Limits of Pure Reason*. "A positive religion," Hegel says, "implies feelings that are more or less impressed by constraint on the sensibilities; these are actions which are the effect of a commandment and the result of an obedience and are accompanied without direct interest."[5] In other words, in a positive religion there is an externality for practical reason. Man is not free but submits to a law that he has not given to himself. In the same way as for theoretical reason, the positive represents what is imposed outside of thought and what thought ought to receive passively. Likewise, the positive represents for practical reason an order and implies between God and Man a relation of master to slave. But Kant's great idea, which goes well beyond the dull rationalism of the *Aufklärung* but which nevertheless is the supreme expression of it, is that reason is practical by itself. The highest requirement of man is to be free, that is, to owe only to himself the rule of his action.

The idea of freedom and the idea of autonomy are the key concepts of the critique of practical reason. If, on the other hand, Kant speaks of having limited reason in order to make place for faith, it is not a question of understanding by this the acceptance of something irrational in the field of pure reason. The law that Kant admits is a moral law; it does not make any appeal to history or to a particular revelation. Pure freedom (autonomy) and the situation of man caught between this freedom and nature certainly lead us to postulates that can be admitted by reason without contradiction, but these postulates are only the existence of God and the immortality of the soul (derived from an indefinite progress possible in morality). There is nothing in this that goes beyond natural religion, if we mean by natural religion a religion that can be admitted by reason, always self-identical and thus nontemporal.[6] Kant wrote *Religion within the Limits of Pure Reason* and encountered even before Hegel the problem of positivity, but he discarded it. Christ appears there only as a model of morality, a scheme by which we can make ourselves sensitive to the moral ideal that reason offers us. Any other conception of Christianity would result in making freedom disappear, by transforming *morality* into *legalism*. This opposition, which Kant has insisted on so much and Hegel will later strive to transcend, is still useful to us to understand. the meaning that Hegel places on the problem of positivity. Legality is heteronomy; it is obedience by compulsion to a law that goes beyond us and that does not come from us. Morality is freedom itself or autonomy. We only follow a single law, one that we find in ourselves and that is our own. To be autonomous is to become greater and not to submit passively to a foreign order. For Hegel the most striking example of legalism is Judaism, the obedience to laws that divinity has imposed on man. Man only submits because he fears God, a God who is beyond him and whose slave he is. A positive religion is therefore, from the point of view of practical reason, a religion that is based on authority and that, by treating man as a child, imposes on him externally what is not contained in his reason. Positive religion makes God a master, but it makes man a slave and cultivates in him the feeling of slavery. The concepts of constraint and authority that appear here are antithetical to freedom, but that authority, not being based on human reason (in which case we could no longer speak of constraint), can be connected only with a temporal event, with a historical relation. That is why Hegel, summing up these various meanings of positivity, can say, "This historical element in general is called authority."[7]

Therefore, we see the complexity of the questions that are raised related to this concept of positivity, and Hegel's successive attempts to connect dialectically (a dialectic that is not yet conscious of itself) *pure reason* (theoretical and especially practical) and positivity, that is, the historical element. In a certain sense Hegel considered positivity as an obstacle to the freedom of man, and as such it is condemned. To investigate the positive elements of a religion, and we could add, of a social state, is to discover what is imposed by constraint on man, what blemishes the purity of reason, which in another sense ends up by involving positivity in the course of Hegel's development. Positivity ought to be reconciled with reason, which then loses its abstract character and becomes appropriate to the concrete richness of life. Therefore, we see why the concept of positivity is in the center of Hegelian perspectives.[8]

First of all, Hegel, by reviving Kant's study on *Religion within the Limits of Pure Reason*, tries to set Christ in opposition to Judaism, as the partisan of moral autonomy to a people who have known only legalism and separateness. But what a difference there already is between this life of Jesus and Kant's work! Jesus is no longer just a sensible scheme, a representation of the ideal of morality. He is an individual, and it is a real history that Hegel strives to retrace. It is a historical story; Jesus is certainly the moral ideal, but he is presented as a living being. However, it is the opposition of autonomy to heteronomy that characterizes Christ's teaching and life. "As you revere as your highest law the ordinances of the church and the laws of the State, you misunderstand the dignity and power in man to create for himself the concept of divinity."[9] Pure Kantian rationalism still seems to be the inspiration for this text: "Reason is what makes man know his destination, the unconditional purpose of his life. Certainly reason is often eclipsed, but reason can never be completely extinct. Even in the midst of darkness there always remains a feeble glimmer." The story finally ends with the death of Christ. It speaks neither of his miracles nor of his resurrection.[10]

In spite of this criticism of all positivity and of this life of Jesus, which is the first of the century that appears negative about every transcendence, we would be wrong to believe that Hegelian rationalism is of the same essence as Kantian rationalism. Many passages on love and life already indicate a distinct orientation in this work. For Hegel the essential opposition is not between pure reason and the empirical element, but rather the opposition between life and nonlife or between the living and the dead. In this sense the verdict concerning the positivity of a religion is no longer so simple. At the end of the Berne period Hegel contrasts the abstract concepts of human reason, those of the *Aufklärer*, and the modalities of life. In order to contrast positive religion and natural religion, it is necessary to be able to define once and for all the concept of human nature, that is, the requirements of human reason reduced to itself. But we have already seen in reference to a text on the transition from paganism to Christianity that the needs of practical reason were possibly not the same for people of antiquity as they are for us. Here Hegel writes: "But living nature is eternally something other than the concept of this nature and thus what for the concept was only modification, pure contingence and a superfluity, becomes the necessary, the living, perhaps the only natural and only beautiful thing."[11] In other words, these abstract ideas of human nature, these concepts of pure reason, are incapable of furnishing here the standard of measure that would show in a religion, as in a social world, what is positive and what is not. Measure is impossible: "The general concepts of human nature are too empty to be able to give a standard for the particular and necessarily diverse requirements of religiosity." No longer by reason does Hegel judge the positive but rather by relation to life, and in the development of his thought during the Frankfurt period this idea of life is going to become dominant in his reflection. The positive, in the pejorative sense of the word, will not be the concrete, historical element that is intimately connected to the development of a religion or a society, which makes contact with them and, therefore, is not imposed outside of them. It will be only the dead element, which has lost its living meaning and is no more than a residue of history. The figure of Christ in Hegel's studies becomes more and more concrete. What is positive in religion that has abandoned its prophesy is connected to what formerly was living and what depends strictly on its historical individuality. The very person of Christ furnishes the positive datum: he teaches and acts; he speaks on the basis of his own individuality and performs miracles; he is presented as one representative of the divine will. Finally, the attachment of the disciples to Christ's individuality, to his external presence in a here and now, is the very source of the transformation of Christianity into a positive religion. Therefore Hegel can say: "A religion was not originally positive, it could only became so. Then it remains only as a heritage of the past."[12]

But we still find an essential text that shows us at what point Hegel became conscious of the connection between historicity and of the life of man. "In a religion actions, persons, and recollections can pass as sacred. Reason demonstrates contingency in all that. It demands that what is sacred be eternal and imperishable. But by so doing it has not shown the positivity of these religious things, for man can relate to contingence and ought to relate the imperishable and the sacred to a contingent. In his thought of the eternal he relates the eternal to the contingency of his thought."[13] This last sentence in particular shows us the connection made by Hegel between reason and history. A new conception of freedom, not purely negative as in Kant, ought therefore to be made manifest. It is a question of a living freedom, of a reconciliation of man with his history. It is more possible that this history is presented to him as foreign, in which case we will speak of positivity, of an external relation between man and the absolute. Such is the destiny of the unfortunate peoples of history; but in the other cases there is no breach between man and his history. It is only an abstract and judgmental reason that speaks wrongly of positivity.

Therefore, the relation between this historical element and reason is the cause of it. By the very idea of life, by the idea of concrete man as opposed to the abstract concepts of the eighteenth century, Hegel is elevated to a more profound conception of freedom. But this conception, the key to his future system, can only receive all its meaning if one considers the other fundamental concept from Hegel's youthful works, that which reveals the tragic in his vision of the world, namely, the concept of Destiny.

NOTES

1. These various studies are contained in the volume by Herman Nohl, ed., *Hegels Theologische Jugendschriften* (Tübingen: J. C. B. Mohr, 1907), published in English as *On Christianity: Early Theological Writings*, trans. Thomas Malcom Knox (New York: Harper, 1948). A French translation of the Berne Life of Jesus exists, translated by Dumitru D. Rosca as *Vie de Jésus* (Paris: Gamber, 1928), and a more recent translation of *The Spirit of Christianity and Its Destiny* by Jacques Martin as *L'esprit du christianisme et son destin* (Paris: Vrin, 1948).

2. In a very obscure passage at the end of the *Phénoménologie*, Hegel will say that the modern task is to reconcile Spirit and Time as the eighteenth century wanted to reconcile Spirit and Extension.

3. We will interpret these works on Right later. In every case, the opposition that Hegel sees relevant to the notion of positivity has a very general application.

4. Nohl, *Hegels Theologische Jugendschriften*, 139; cf. David Hume, *Dialogues Concerning Natural Religion* (New York: Hafner, 1948).

5. Nohl, *Hegels Theologische Jugendschriften*, 139. It is relevant to this positivity that Hegel for the first time thinks about the relation of "master and slave." In a positive religion man is a slave before God. He obeys commandments that are for him foreign to his will and reason.

6. There is, however, a great difference between the natural religion of the eighteenth century and *postulated* religion in Kantianism. The first depends on theoretical reason whereas the second depends on the impotence of that reason and on the demands of practical reason. It is a faith connected to moral action.

7. Ibid., 145.

8. In other words, as is often the case with Hegelian concepts, there is a double meaning of positivity: one pejorative, the other laudatory. Positivity is like memory, living and organic. It is the past always present, inorganic and separate, and it is the past that no longer has any authentic presence.

9. Ibid., 89.

10. This Berne *Life of Jesus* already makes one think of the interpretations that the extreme left-wing Hegelians will later assign to the thought of the master.

11. Ibid., 141.

12. Positivity would result, therefore, from a necessary transformation of everything that is living.
13. Ibid., 143.

BIBLIOGRAPHY

Hume, David. *Dialogues Concerning Natural Religion*. New York: Hafner, 1948.

Hegel, Georg Wilhelm Friedrich. *L'esprit du christianisme et son destin*. Translated by Jacques Martin. Paris: Vrin, 1948.

Hegel, Georg Wilhelm Friedrich. *On Christianity: Early Theological Writings*. Translated by Thomas Malcom Knox. New York: Harper, 1948. Originally published as *Hegels Theologische Jugendschriften*. Edited by Herman Nohl. Tübingen: J. C. B. Mohr, 1907.

Hegel, Georg Wilhelm Friedrich. *Vie de Jésus*. Translated by Dumitru D. Rosca. Paris: Gamber, 1928.

11

THE QUESTION CONCERNING TECHNOLOGY

Martin Heidegger

In what follows we shall be *questioning* concerning technology. Questioning builds a way. We would be advised, therefore, above all to pay heed to the way, and not to fix our attention on isolated sentences and topics. The way is one of thinking. All ways of thinking, more or less perceptibly, lead through language in a manner that is extraordinary. We shall be questioning concerning *technology*, and in so doing we should like to prepare a free relationship to it. The relationship will be free if it opens our human existence to the essence of technology. When we can respond to this essence, we shall be able to experience the technological within its own bounds.

Technology is not equivalent to the essence of technology. When we are seeking the essence of "tree," we have to become aware that what pervades every tree, as tree, is not itself a tree that can be encountered among all the other trees.

Likewise, the essence of technology is by no means anything technological. Thus we shall never experience our relationship to the essence of technology so long as we merely represent and pursue the technological, put up with it, or evade it. Everywhere we remain unfree and chained to technology, whether we passionately affirm or deny it. But we are delivered over to it in the worst possible way when we regard it as something neutral; for this conception of it, to which today we particularly like to pay homage, makes us utterly blind to the essence of technology.

According to ancient doctrine, the essence of a thing is considered to be *what* the thing is. We ask the question concerning technology when we ask what it is. Everyone knows the two statements that answer our question. One says: Technology is a means to an end. The other says: Technology is a human activity. The two definitions of technology belong together. For to posit ends and procure and utilize the means to them is a human activity. The manufacture and utilization of equipment, tools, and machines, the manufactured and used things themselves, and the needs and ends that they serve, all belong to what technology is. The whole complex of these contrivances is technology. Technology itself is a contrivance—in Latin, an *instrumentum*.

The current conception of technology, according to which it is a means and a human activity, can therefore be called the instrumental and anthropological definition of technology.

Who would ever deny that it is correct? It is in obvious conformity with what we are envisaging when we talk about technology. The instrumental definition of technology is indeed so uncannily correct that it even holds for modern technology, of which, in other respects, we maintain with some justification that it is, in contrast to the older handicraft technology, something completely different and therefore new. Even the power plant with its turbines and generators is a man-made means to an end established by man. Even the jet aircraft and the high-frequency apparatus are means to ends. A radar station is of course less simple than a weather vane. To be sure, the construction of a high-frequency apparatus requires the interlocking of various processes of technical-industrial production. And certainly a sawmill in a secluded valley of the Black Forest is a primitive means compared with the hydroelectric plant on the Rhine River.

But this much remains correct: Modern technology too is a means to an end. This is why the instrumental conception of technology conditions every attempt to bring man into the right relation to technology. Everything depends on our manipulating technology in the proper manner as a means. We will, as we say, "get" technology "intelligently in hand." We will master it. The will to mastery becomes all the more urgent the more technology threatens to slip from human control.

But suppose now that technology were no mere means: how would it stand with the will to master it? Yet we said, did we not, that the instrumental definition of technology is correct? To be sure. The correct always fixes upon something pertinent in whatever is under consideration. However, in order to be correct, this fixing by no means needs to uncover the thing in question in its essence. Only at the point where such an uncovering happens does the true propriate. For that reason the merely correct is not yet the true. Only the true brings us into a free relationship with that which concerns us from its essence. Accordingly, the correct instrumental definition of technology still does not show us technology's essence. In order that we may arrive at this, or at least come close to it, we must seek the true by way of the correct. We must ask: What is the instrumental itself? Within what do such things as means and end belong? A means is that whereby something is effected and thus attained. Whatever has an effect as its consequence is called a cause. But not only that by means of which something else is effected is a cause. The end that determines the kind of means to be used may also be considered a cause. Wherever ends are pursued and means are employed, wherever instrumentality reigns, there reigns causality.

For centuries philosophy has taught that there are four causes: (1) the *causa materialis*, the material, the matter out of which, for example, a silver chalice is made; (2) the *causa formalis*, the form, the shape into which the material enters; (3) the *causa finalis*, the end, for example, the sacrificial rite in relation to which the required chalice is determined as to its form and matter; (4) the *causa efficiens*, which brings about the effect that is the finished, actual chalice, in this instance, the silversmith. What technology is, when represented as a means, discloses itself when we trace instrumentality back to fourfold causality.

But suppose that causality, for its part, is veiled in darkness with respect to what it is? Certainly for centuries we have acted as though the doctrine of the four causes had fallen from heaven as a truth as clear as daylight. But it might be that the time has come to ask: Why are there only four causes? In relation to the aforementioned four, what does "cause" really mean? From whence does it come that the causal character of the four causes is so unifiedly determined that they belong together?

So long as we do not allow ourselves to go into these questions, causality, and with it instrumentality, and with this the accepted definition of technology, remain obscure and groundless.

For a long time we have been accustomed to representing cause as that which brings something about. In this connection, to bring about means to obtain results, effects. The *causa efficiens*, but one among the four causes, sets the standard for all causality. This goes so far that we no longer even count the *causa finalis*, telic finality, as causality. *Causa, casus*, belongs to the verb *cadere*, to fall, and means that which brings it about that something turns out as a result in such and such a way. The doctrine of the four causes goes back to Aristotle. But everything that later ages seek in Greek thought under the conception and rubric "causality" in the realm of Greek thought and for Greek thought *per se* has simply nothing at all to do with bringing about and effecting. What we call cause [*Ursache*] and the Romans call *causa* is called *aition* by the Greeks, that to which something else is indebted [*das, was ein anderes verschuldet*]. The four causes are the ways, all belonging at once to each other, of being responsible for something else. An example can clarify this.

Silver is that out of which the silver chalice is made. As this matter (*hyle*), it is co-responsible for the chalice. The chalice is indebted to, i.e., owes thanks to, the silver for that of which it consists. But the sacrificial vessel is indebted not only to the silver. As a chalice, that which is indebted to the silver appears in the aspect of a chalice, and not in that of a brooch or a ring. Thus the sacred vessel is at the same time indebted to the aspect (*eidos*) of chaliceness. Both the silver into which the aspect is admitted as chalice and the aspect in which the silver appears are in their respective ways co-responsible for the sacrificial vessel.

But there remains yet a third something that is above all responsible for the sacrificial vessel. It is that which in advance confines the chalice within the realm of consecration and bestowal. Through this the chalice is circumscribed as sacrificial vessel. Circumscribing gives bounds to the thing. With the bounds the thing does not stop; rather, from within them it begins to be what after production it will be. That which gives bounds, that which completes, in this sense is called in Greek *telos*, which is all too often translated as "aim" and "purpose," and so misinterpreted. The *telos is* responsible for what as matter and what as aspect are together co-responsible for the sacrificial vessel.

Finally, there is a fourth participant in the responsibility for the finished sacrificial vessel's lying before us ready for use, i.e., the silversmith—but not at all because he, in working, brings about the finished sacrificial chalice as if it were the effect of a making; the silversmith is not a *causa efficiens*.

The Aristotelian doctrine neither knows the cause that is named by this term, nor uses a Greek word that would correspond to it.

The silversmith considers carefully and gathers together the three aforementioned ways of being responsible and indebted. To consider carefully [*überlegen*] is in Greek *legein, logos*. *Legein* is rooted in *apophainesthai*, to bring forward into appearance. The silversmith is co-responsible as that from which the sacred vessel's being brought forth and subsistence take and retain their first departure. The three previously mentioned ways of being responsible owe thanks to the pondering of the silversmith for the "that" and the "how" of their coming into appearance and into play for the production of the sacrificial vessel.

Thus four ways of owing hold sway in the sacrificial vessel that lies ready before us. They differ from one another, yet they belong together. What unites them from the beginning? In what does this playing in unison of the four ways of being responsible play? What is the source of the unity of the four causes? What, after all, does this owing and being responsible mean, thought as the Greeks thought it?

Today we are too easily inclined either to understand being responsible and being indebted moralistically as a lapse, or else to construe them in terms of effecting. In either case we bar from ourselves the way to the primal meaning of that which is later called causality. So long as this way is not opened up to us we shall also fail to see what instrumentality, which is based on causality, properly is.

In order to guard against such misinterpretations of being responsible and being indebted, let us clarify the four ways of being responsible in terms of that for which they are responsible. According to our example, they are responsible for the silver chalice's lying ready before us as a sacrificial vessel. Lying before and lying ready (*hypokeisthai*) characterize the presencing of something that is present. The four ways of being responsible bring something into appearance. They let it come forth into presencing [*Anwesen*]. They set it free to that place and so start it on its way, namely, into its complete arrival. The principal characteristic of being responsible is this starting something on its way into arrival. It is in the sense of such a starting something on its way into arrival that being responsible is an occasioning or an inducing to go forward [*Ver-an-lassen*]. On the basis of a look at what the Greeks experienced in being responsible, in *aitia*, we now give this verb "to occasion" a more inclusive meaning, so that it now is the name for the essence of causality thought as the Greeks thought it. The common and narrower meaning of "occasion," in contrast, is nothing more than a colliding and releasing; it means a kind of secondary cause within the whole of causality.

But in what, then, does the playing in unison of the four ways of occasioning play? These let what is not yet present arrive into presencing. Accordingly, they are unifiedly governed by a bringing that brings what presences into appearance. Plato tells us what this bringing is in a sentence from the *Symposium* (205b): *hē gar toi ek tou mē ontos eis to on ionti hotōioun aitia pasa esti poiēsis.* "Every occasion for whatever passes beyond the nonpresent and goes forward into presencing is *poiēsis*, bringing-forth [*Her-vor-bringen*]."

It is of utmost importance that we think bringing-forth in its full scope and at the same time in the sense in which the Greeks thought it. Not only handicraft manufacture, not only artistic and poetical bringing into appearance and concrete imagery, is a bringing-forth, *poiēsis*. *Physis*, also, the arising of something from out of itself, is a bringing-forth, *poiēsis*. *Physis* is indeed *poiēsis* in the highest sense. For what presences by means of *physis* has the irruption belonging to bringing-forth, e.g., the bursting of a blossom into bloom, in itself (*en heautōi*). In contrast, what is brought forth by the artisan or the artist, e.g., the silver chalice, has the irruption belonging to bringing-forth, not in itself, but in another (*en allōi*), in the craftsman or artist.

The modes of occasioning, the four causes, are at play, then, within bringing-forth. Through bringing-forth the growing things of nature as well as whatever is completed through the crafts and the arts come at any given time to their appearance.

But how does bringing-forth happen, be it in nature or in handicraft and art? What is the bringing-forth in which the fourfold way of occasioning plays? Occasioning has to do with the presencing [*Anwesen*] of that which at any given time comes to appearance in bringing-forth. Bringing-forth brings out of concealment into unconcealment. Bringing-forth propriates only insofar as something concealed comes into unconcealment. This coming rests and moves freely within what we call revealing [*das Entbergen*]. The Greeks have the word *alētheia* for revealing. The Romans translate this with *veritas*. We say "truth" and usually understand it as correctness of representation.

But where have we strayed to? We are questioning concerning technology, and we have arrived now at *alētheia*, at revealing. What has the essence of technology to do with revealing? The answer: everything. For every bringing-forth is grounded in revealing. Bringing-forth, indeed, gathers within itself the four modes of occasioning—causality—and rules them throughout. Within its domain belong end and means as well as instrumentality. Instrumentality is considered to be the fundamental characteristic of technology. If we inquire step by step into what technology, represented as means, actually is, then we shall arrive at revealing. The possibility of all productive manufacturing lies in revealing.

Technology is therefore no mere means. Technology is a way of revealing. If we give heed to this, then another whole realm for the essence of technology will open itself up to us. It is the realm of revealing, i.e., of truth.

This prospect strikes us as strange. Indeed, it should do so, as persistently as possible and with so much urgency that we will finally take seriously the simple question of what the name "technology" means. The word stems from the Greek. *Technikon* means that which belongs to *technè*. We must observe two things with respect to the meaning of this word. One is that *technè* is the name not only for the activities and skills of the craftsman but also for the arts of the mind and the fine arts. *Technè* belongs to bringing-forth, to *poiēsis*; it is something poetic.

The other thing that we should observe with regard to *technè* is even more important. From earliest times until Plato the word *technè* is linked with the word *epistēmē*. Both words are terms for knowing in the widest sense. They mean to be entirely at home in something, to understand and be expert in it. Such knowing provides an opening up. As an opening up it is a revealing. Aristotle, in a discussion of special importance (*Nicomachean Ethics*, Bk. VI, chaps. 3 and 4), distinguishes between *epistēmē* and *technè* and indeed with respect to what and how they reveal. *Technè* is a mode of *alētheuein*. It reveals whatever does not bring itself forth and does not yet lie here before us, whatever can look and turn out now one way and now another. Whoever builds a house or a ship or forges a sacrificial chalice reveals what is to be brought forth, according to the terms of the four modes of occasioning. This revealing gathers together in advance the aspect and the matter of ship or house, with a view to the finished thing envisaged as completed, and from this gathering determines the manner of its construction. Thus what is decisive in *technè* does not at all lie in making and manipulating, nor in the using of means, but rather in the revealing mentioned before. It is as revealing, and not as manufacturing, that *technè* is a bringing-forth.

Thus the clue to what the word *technè* means and to how the Greeks defined it leads us into the same context that opened itself to us when we pursued the question of what instrumentality as such in truth might be.

Technology is a mode of revealing. Technology comes to presence in the realm where revealing and unconcealment take place, where *alētheia*, truth, happens.

In opposition to this definition of the essential domain of technology, one can object that it indeed holds for Greek thought and that at best it might apply to the techniques of the handicraftsman, but that it simply does not fit modern machine-powered technology. And it is precisely the latter and it alone that is the disturbing thing, that moves us to ask the question concerning technology *per se*. It is said that modern technology is something incomparably different from all earlier technologies because it is based on modern physics as an exact science. Meanwhile, we have come to understand more clearly that the reverse holds true as well: modern physics, as experimental, is dependent upon technical apparatus and upon progress in the building of apparatus. The establishing of this mutual relationship between technology and physics is correct. But it remains a merely historiological establishing of facts and says nothing about that in which this mutual relationship is grounded. The decisive question still remains: Of what essence is modern technology that it thinks of putting exact science to use?

What is modern technology? It too is a revealing. Only when we allow our attention to rest on this fundamental characteristic does that which is new in modern technology show itself to us.

And yet, the revealing that holds sway throughout modern technology does not unfold into a bringing-forth in the sense of *poiēsis*. The revealing that rules in modern technology is a challenging [*Herausfordern*], which puts to nature the unreasonable demand that it supply energy which can be extracted and stored as such. But does this not hold true for the old windmill as well? No. Its sails do indeed turn in the wind; they are left entirely to the wind's blowing. But the windmill does not unlock energy from the air currents in order to store it.

In contrast, a tract of land is challenged in the hauling out of coal and ore. The earth now reveals itself as a coal mining district, the soil as a mineral deposit. The field that the peasant formerly cultivated and set in order appears differently than it did when to set in order still meant to take care of and maintain. The work of the peasant does not challenge the soil of the field. In sowing grain it places seed in the keeping of the forces of growth and watches over its increase. But meanwhile even the cultivation of the field has come under the grip of another kind of setting-in-order, which *sets upon* nature. It sets upon it in the sense of challenging it. Agriculture is now the mechanized food industry. Air is now set upon to yield nitrogen, the earth to yield ore, ore to yield uranium, for example; uranium is set upon to yield atomic energy, which can be unleashed either for destructive or for peaceful purposes.

This setting-upon that challenges the energies of nature is an expediting, and in two ways. It expedites in that it unlocks and exposes. Yet that expediting is always itself directed from the beginning toward furthering something else, i.e., toward driving on to the maximum yield at the minimum expense. The coal that has been hauled out in some mining district has not been produced in order that it may simply be at hand somewhere or other. It is being stored; that is, it is on call, ready to deliver the sun's warmth that is stored in it. The sun's warmth is challenged forth for heat, which in turn is ordered to deliver steam whose pressure turns the wheels that keep a factory running.

The hydroelectric plant is set into the current of the Rhine. It sets the Rhine to supplying its hydraulic pressure, which then sets the turbines turning. This turning sets those machines in motion whose thrust sets going the electric current for which the long-distance power station and its network of cables are set up to dispatch electricity. In the context of the interlocking processes pertaining to the orderly disposition of electrical energy, even the Rhine itself appears to be something at our command. The hydroelectric plant is not built into the Rhine River as was the old wooden bridge that joined bank with bank for hundreds of years. Rather, the river is dammed up into the power plant. What the river is now, namely, a water-power supplier, derives from the essence of the power station. In order that we may even remotely consider the monstrousness that reigns here, let us ponder for a moment the contrast that is spoken by the two titles: "The Rhine," as dammed up into the *power* works, and "The Rhine," as uttered by the *art*-work, in Hölderlin's hymn by that name. But, it will be replied, the Rhine is still a river in the landscape, is it not? Perhaps. But how? In no other way than as an object on call for inspection by a tour group ordered there by the vacation industry.

The revealing that rules throughout modern technology has the character of a setting-upon, in the sense of a challenging-forth. Such challenging happens in that the energy concealed in nature is unlocked, what is unlocked is transformed, what is transformed is stored up, what is stored up is in turn distributed, and what is distributed is switched about ever anew. Unlocking, transforming, storing, distributing, and switching about are ways of revealing. But the revealing never simply comes to an end. Neither does it run off into the indeterminate. The revealing reveals to itself its own manifoldly interlocking paths, through regulating their course. This regulating itself is, for its part, everywhere secured. Regulating and securing even become the chief characteristics of the revealing that challenges.

What kind of unconcealment is it, then, that is peculiar to that which results from this setting-upon that challenges? Everywhere everything is ordered to stand by, to be immediately on hand, indeed to stand there just so that it may be on call for a further ordering. Whatever is ordered about in this way has its own standing. We call it the standing-reserve [*Bestand*]. The word expresses here something more, and something more essential, than mere "stock." The word "standing-reserve" assumes the rank of an inclusive rubric. It designates nothing less than the way in which everything presences that is wrought upon by the revealing that challenges. Whatever stands by in the sense of standing-reserve no longer stands over against us as object.

Yet an airliner that stands on the runway is surely an object. Certainly. We can represent the machine so. But then it conceals itself as to what and how it is. Revealed, it stands on the taxi strip only as standing-reserve, inasmuch as it is ordered to insure the possibility of transportation. For this it must be in its whole structure and in every one of its constituent parts itself on call for duty, i.e., ready for takeoff. (Here it would be appropriate to discuss Hegel's definition of the machine as an autonomous tool. When applied to the tools of the craftsman, his characterization is correct. Characterized in this way, however, the machine is not thought at all from the essence of technology within which it belongs. Seen in terms of the standing-reserve, the machine is completely nonautonomous, for it has its standing only on the basis of the ordering of the orderable.)

The fact that now, wherever we try to point to modern technology as the revealing that challenges, the words "setting-upon," "ordering," "standing-reserve," obtrude and accumulate in a dry, monotonous, and therefore oppressive way—this fact has its basis in what is now coming to utterance.

Who accomplishes the challenging setting-upon through which what we call the actual is revealed as standing-reserve? Obviously, man. To what extent is man capable of such a revealing? Man can indeed conceive, fashion, and carry through this or that in one way or another. But man does not have control over unconcealment itself, in which at any given time the actual shows itself or withdraws. The fact that it has been showing itself in the light of Ideas ever since the time of Plato, Plato did not bring about. The thinker only responded to what addressed itself to him.

Only to the extent that man for his part is already challenged to exploit the energies of nature can this revealing that orders happen. If man is challenged, ordered, to do this, then does not man himself belong even more originally than nature within the standing-reserve? The current talk about human resources, about the supply of patients for a clinic, gives evidence of this. The forester who measures the felled timber in the woods and who to all appearances walks the forest path in the same way his grandfather did is today ordered by the industry that produces commercial woods, whether he knows it or not. He is made subordinate to the orderability of cellulose, which for its part is challenged forth by the need for paper, which is then delivered to newspapers and illustrated magazines. The latter, in their turn, set public opinion to swallowing what is printed, so that a set configuration of opinion becomes available on demand. Yet precisely because man is challenged more originally than are the energies of nature, i.e., into the process of ordering, he never is transformed into mere standing-reserve. Since man drives technology forward, he takes part in ordering as a way of revealing. But the unconcealment itself, within which ordering unfolds, is never a human handiwork, any more than is the realm man traverses every time he as a subject relates to an object.

Where and how does this revealing happen if it is no mere handiwork of man? We need not look far. We need only apprehend in an unbiased way that which has already claimed man so decisively that he can only be man at any given time as the one so claimed. Wherever man opens his eyes and ears, unlocks his heart, and gives himself over to meditating and striving, shaping and working, entreating and thanking, he finds himself everywhere already brought into the unconcealed. The unconcealment of the unconcealed has already propriated whenever it calls man forth into the modes of revealing allotted to him. When man, in his way, from within unconcealment reveals that which presences, he merely responds to the call of unconcealment, even when he contradicts it. Thus when man, investigating, observing, pursues nature as an area of his own conceiving, he has already been claimed by a way of revealing that challenges him to approach nature as an object of research, until even the object disappears into the objectlessness of standing-reserve.

Modern technology, as a revealing that orders, is thus no mere human doing. Therefore we must take the challenging that sets upon man to order the actual as standing-reserve in accordance with the way it shows itself. That challenging gathers man into ordering. This gathering concentrates man upon ordering the actual as standing-reserve.

That which primordially unfolds the mountains into mountain ranges and pervades them in their folded contiguity is the gathering that we call *Gebirg* [mountain chain].

That original gathering from which unfold the ways in which we have feelings of one kind or another we name *Gemüt* [disposition].

We now name the challenging claim that gathers man with a view to ordering the self-revealing as standing-reserve: *Ge-stell* [enframing].

We dare to use this word in a sense that has been thoroughly unfamiliar up to now.

According to ordinary usage, the word *Gestell* [frame] means some kind of apparatus, e.g., a bookrack. *Gestell* is also the name for a skeleton. And the employment of the word *Gestell* [enframing] that is now required of us seems equally eerie, not to speak of the arbitrariness with which, words of a mature language are so misused. Can anything be more strange? Surely not. Yet this strangeness is an old custom of thought. And indeed thinkers follow this custom precisely at the point where it is a matter of thinking that which is highest. We, late born, are no longer in a position to appreciate the significance of Plato's daring to use the word *eidos* for that which in everything and in each particular thing endures as present. For *eidos*, in the common speech, meant the outward aspect [*Ansicht*] that a visible thing offers to the physical eye. Plato exacts of this word, however, something utterly extraordinary: that it name what precisely is not and never will be perceivable with physical eyes. But even this is by no means the full extent of what is extraordinary here. For *idea* names not only the nonsensuous aspect of what is physically visible. Aspect (*idea*) names and also is that which constitutes the essence in the audible, the tasteable, the tactile, in everything that is in any way accessible. Compared with the demands that Plato makes on language and thought in this and in other instances, the use of the word *Gestell* as the name for the essence of modern technology, which we are venturing, is almost harmless. Even so, the usage now required remains something exacting and is open to misinterpretation.

Enframing means the gathering together of the setting-upon that sets upon man, i.e., challenges him forth, to reveal the actual, in the mode of ordering, as standing-reserve. Enframing means the way of revealing that holds sway in the essence of modern technology and that is itself nothing technological. On the other hand, all those things that are so familiar to us and are standard parts of assembly, such as rods, pistons, and chassis, belong to the technological. The assembly itself, however, together with the aforementioned stockparts, fall within the sphere of technological activity. Such activity always merely responds to the challenge of enframing, but it never comprises enframing itself or brings it about.

The word *stellen* [to set] in the name *Ge-stell* [enframing] does not only mean challenging. At the same time it should preserve the suggestion of another *Stellen* from which it stems, namely that producing and presenting [*Her-und Dar-stellen*], which, in the sense of *poiēsis*, lets what presences come forth into unconcealment. This producing that brings forth, e.g., erecting a statue in the temple precinct, and the ordering that challenges now under consideration are indeed fundamentally different, and yet they remain related in their essence. Both are ways of revealing, of *alētheia*. In enframing, the unconcealment propriates in conformity with which the work of modern technology reveals the actual as standing-reserve. This work is therefore neither only a human activity nor a mere means within such activity. The merely instrumental, merely anthropological definition of technology is therefore in principle untenable. And it may not be rounded out by being referred back to some metaphysical or religious explanation that undergirds it.

It remains true nonetheless that man in the technological age is, in a particularly striking way, challenged forth into revealing. Such revealing concerns nature, above all, as the chief storehouse of the standing energy reserve. Accordingly, man's ordering attitude and behavior display themselves first in the rise of modern physics as an exact science. Modern science's way of representing pursues and entraps nature as a calculable coherence of forces. Modern physics is not experimental physics because it applies apparatus to the questioning of nature. The reverse is true. Because physics, indeed already as pure theory, sets nature up to exhibit itself as a coherence of forces calculable in advance, it orders its experiments precisely for the purpose of asking whether and how nature reports itself when set up in this way.

But, after all, mathematical science arose almost two centuries before technology. How, then, could it have already been set upon by modern technology and placed in its service? The facts testify to the contrary. Surely technology got under way only when it could be supported by exact physical science. Reckoned chronologically, this is correct. Thought historically, it does not hit upon the truth.

The modern physical theory of nature prepares the way not simply for technology but for the essence of modern technology. For such gathering-together, which challenges man to reveal by way of ordering, already holds sway in physics. But in it that gathering does not yet come expressly to the fore. Modern physics is the herald of enframing, a herald whose provenance is still unknown. The essence of modern technology has for a long time been concealed, even where power machinery has been invented, where electrical technology is in full swing, and where atomic technology is well under way.

All coming to presence, not only modern technology, keeps itself everywhere concealed to the last. Nevertheless, it remains, with respect to its holding sway, that which precedes all: the earliest. The Greek thinkers already knew of this when they said: That which is earlier with regard to its rise into dominance becomes manifest to us men only later. That which is primally early shows itself only ultimately to men. Therefore, in the realm of thinking, a painstaking effort to think through still more primally what was primally thought is not the absurd wish to revive what is past, but rather the sober readiness to be astounded before the coming of the dawn.

Chronologically speaking, modern physical science begins in the seventeenth century. In contrast, machine-power technology develops only in the second half of the eighteenth century. But modern technology, which for chronological reckoning is the later, is, from the point of view of the essence holding sway within it, historically earlier.

If modern physics must resign itself ever increasingly to the fact that its realm of representation remains inscrutable and incapable of being visualized, this resignation is not dictated by any committee of researchers. It is challenged forth by the rule of enframing, which demands that nature be orderable as standing-reserve. Hence physics, in its retreat from the kind of representation that turns only to objects, which has been the sole standard until recently, will never be able to renounce this one thing: that nature report itself in some way or other that is identifiable through calculation and that it remain orderable as a system of information. This system is then determined by a causality that has changed once again. Causality now displays neither the character of the occasioning that brings forth nor the nature of the *causa efficiens*, let alone that of the *causa formalis*. It seems as though causality is shrinking into a reporting—a reporting challenged forth—of standing-reserves that must be guaranteed either simultaneously or in sequence. To this shrinking would correspond the process of growing resignation that Heisenberg's lecture depicts in so impressive a manner.[1]

Because the essence of modern technology lies in enframing, modern technology must employ exact physical science. Through its so doing the deceptive appearance arises that modern technology is applied physical science. This illusion can maintain itself precisely insofar as neither the essential provenance of modern science nor indeed the essence of modern technology is adequately sought in our questioning.

We are questioning concerning technology in order to bring to light our relationship to its essence. The essence of modern technology shows itself in what we call enframing. But simply to point to this is still in no way to answer the question concerning technology, if to answer means to respond, in the sense of correspond, to the essence of what is being asked about.

Where do we find ourselves if now we think one step further regarding what enframing itself actually is? It is nothing technological, nothing on the order of a machine. It is the way in which the actual reveals itself as standing-reserve. Again we ask: Does such revealing happen somewhere beyond all human doing? No. But neither does it happen exclusively *in* man, or definitively *through* man.

Enframing is the gathering together which belongs to that setting-upon which challenges man and puts him in position to reveal the actual, in the mode of ordering, as standing-reserve. As the one who is challenged forth in this way, man stands within the essential realm of enframing. He can never take up a relationship to it only subsequently. Thus the question as to how we are to arrive at a relationship to the essence of technology, asked in this way, always comes too late. But never too late comes the question as to whether we actually experience ourselves as the ones whose activities everywhere, public and private, are challenged forth by enframing. Above all, never too late comes the question as to whether and how we actually admit ourselves into that wherein enframing itself essentially unfolds.

The essence of modern technology starts man upon the way of that revealing through which the actual everywhere, more or less distinctly, becomes standing-reserve. "To start upon a way" means "to send" in our ordinary language. We shall call the sending that gathers [*versammelnde Schicken*], that first starts man upon a way of revealing, *destining* [*Geschick*]. It is from this destining that the essence of all history [*Geschichte*] is determined. History is neither simply the object of written chronicle nor merely the process of human activity. That activity first becomes history as something destined.[2] And it is only the destining into objectifying representation that makes the historical accessible as an object for historiography, i.e., for a science, and on this basis makes possible the current equating of the historical with that which is chronicled.

Enframing, as a challenging-forth into ordering, sends into a way of revealing. Enframing is an ordaining of destining, as is every way of revealing. Bringing-forth, *poiēsis*, is also a destining in this sense.

Always the unconcealment of that which is goes upon a way of revealing. Always the destining of revealing holds complete sway over men. But that destining is never a fate that compels. For man becomes truly free only insofar as he belongs to the realm of destining and so becomes one who listens, though not one who simply obeys.

The essence of freedom is *originally* not connected with the will or even with the causality of human willing.

Freedom governs the free space in the sense of the cleared, that is to say, the revealed. To the occurrence of revealing, i.e., of truth, freedom stands in the closest and most intimate kinship. All revealing belongs within a harboring and a concealing. But that which frees—the mystery—is concealed and always concealing itself. All revealing comes out of the free, goes into the free, and brings into the free. The freedom of the free consists neither in unfettered arbitrariness nor in the constraint of mere laws. Freedom is that which conceals in a way that opens to light, in whose clearing shimmers the veil that hides the essential occurrence of all truth and lets the veil appear as what veils. Freedom is the realm of the destining that at any given time starts a revealing on its way.

The essence of modern technology lies in enframing. Enframing belongs within the destining of revealing. These sentences express something different from the talk that we hear more frequently, to the effect that technology is the fate of our age, where "fate" means the inevitableness of an unalterable course.

But when we consider the essence of technology we experience enframing as a destining of revealing. In this way we are already sojourning within the free space of destining, a destining that in no way confines us to a stultified compulsion to push on blindly with technology or, what comes to the same, to rebel helplessly against it and curse it as the work of the devil. Quite to the contrary, when we once open ourselves expressly to the *essence* of technology we find ourselves unexpectedly taken into a freeing claim.

The essence of technology lies in enframing. Its holding sway belongs within destining. Since destining at any given time starts man on a way of revealing, man, thus under way, is continually approaching the brink of the possibility of pursuing and promulgating nothing but what is revealed in ordering, and of deriving all his standards on this basis. Through this the other possibility is blocked—that man might rather be admitted sooner and ever more primally to the essence of what is unconcealed and to its unconcealment, in order that he might experience as his essence the requisite belonging to revealing.

Placed between these possibilities, man is endangered by destining. The destining of revealing is as such, in every one of its modes, and therefore necessarily, *danger*.

In whatever way the destining of revealing may hold sway, the unconcealment in which everything that is shows itself at any given time harbors the danger that man may misconstrue the unconcealed and misinterpret it. Thus where everything that presences exhibits itself in the light of a cause-effect coherence, even God, for representational thinking, can lose all that is exalted and holy, the mysteriousness of his distance. In the light of causality, God can sink to the level of a cause, of *causa efficiens*. He then becomes even in theology the God of the philosophers, namely, of those who define the unconcealed and the concealed in terms of the causality of making, without ever considering the essential provenance of this causality.

In a similar way the unconcealment in accordance with which nature presents itself as a calculable complex of the effects of forces can indeed permit correct determinations; but precisely through these successes the danger may remain that in the midst of all that is correct the true will withdraw.

The destining of revealing is in itself not just any danger, but *the* danger.

Yet when destining reigns in the mode of enframing, it is the supreme danger. This danger attests itself to us in two ways. As soon as what is unconcealed no longer concerns man even as object, but exclusively as standing-reserve, and man in the midst of objectlessness is nothing but the orderer of the standing-reserve, then he comes to the very brink of a precipitous fall; that is, he comes to the point where he himself will have to be taken as standing-reserve. Meanwhile, man, precisely as the one so threatened, exalts himself and postures as lord of the earth. In this way the illusion comes to prevail that everything man encounters exists only insofar as it is his construct. This illusion gives rise in turn to one final delusion: it seems as though man everywhere and always encounters only himself. Heisenberg has with complete correctness pointed out that the actual must present itself to contemporary man in this way.[3] *In truth, however, precisely nowhere does man today any longer encounter himself, i.e., his essence*. Man stands so decisively in subservience to on the challenging-forth of enframing that he does not grasp enframing as a claim, that he fails to see himself as the one spoken to, and hence also fails in every way to hear in what respect he ek-sists, in terms of his essence, in a realm where he is addressed, so that he *can never* encounter only himself.

But enframing does not simply endanger man in his relationship to himself and to everything that is. As a destining, it banishes man into the kind of revealing that is an ordering. Where this ordering holds sway, it drives out every other possibility of revealing. Above all, enframing conceals that revealing which, in the sense of *poiēsis*, lets what presences come forth into appearance. As compared with that other revealing, the setting-upon that challenges forth thrusts man into a relation to whatever is that is at once antithetical and rigorously ordered. Where enframing holds sway, regulating and securing of the standing-reserve mark all revealing. They no longer even let their own fundamental characteristic appear, namely, this revealing as such.

Thus the challenging-enframing not only conceals a former way of revealing (bringing-forth) but also conceals revealing itself and with it that wherein unconcealment, i.e., truth, propriates.

Enframing blocks the shining-forth and holding sway of truth. The destining that sends into ordering is consequently the extreme danger. What is dangerous is not technology. Technology is not demonic; but its essence is mysterious. The essence of technology, as a destining of revealing, is the danger. The transformed meaning of the word "enframing" will perhaps become somewhat more familiar to us now if we think enframing in the sense of destining and danger.

The threat to man does not come in the first instance from the potentially lethal machines and apparatus of technology. The actual threat has already afflicted man in his essence. The rule of enframing threatens man with the possibility that it could be denied to him to enter into a more original revealing and hence to experience the call of a more primal truth.

Thus where enframing reigns, there is *danger* in the highest sense.
But where danger is, grows
The saving power also.

Let us think carefully about these words of Hölderlin.[4] What does it mean to "save"? Usually we think that it means only to seize hold of a thing threatened by ruin in order to secure it in its former continuance. But the verb "to save" says more. "To save" is to fetch something home into its essence, in order to bring the essence for the first time into its proper appearing. If the essence of technology, enframing, is the extreme danger, if there is truth in Hölderlin's words, then the rule of enframing cannot exhaust itself solely in blocking all lighting-up of every revealing, all appearing of truth. Rather, precisely the essence of technology must harbor in itself the growth of the saving power. But in that case, might not an adequate look into what enframing is, as a destining of revealing, bring the upsurgence of the saving power into appearance?

In what respect does the saving power grow also there where the danger is? Where something grows, there it takes root, from thence it thrives. Both happen concealedly and quietly and in their own time. But according to the words of the poet we have no right whatsoever to expect that there where the danger is we should be able to lay hold of the saving power immediately and without preparation. Therefore we must consider now, in advance, in what respect the saving power does most profoundly take root and thence thrive even where the extreme danger lies—in the holding sway of enframing. In order to consider this it is necessary, as a last step upon our way, to look with yet clearer eyes into the danger. Accordingly, we must once more question concerning technology. For we have said that in technology's essence roots and thrives the saving power.

But how shall we behold the saving power in the essence of technology so long as we do not consider in what sense of "essence" it is that enframing properly is the essence of technology?

Thus far we have understood "essence" in its current meaning. In the academic language of philosophy "essence" means *what* something is; in Latin, *quid*. *Quidditas*, whatness, provides the answer to the question concerning essence. For example, what pertains to all kinds of trees—oaks, beeches, birches, firs—is the same "treeness." Under this inclusive genus—the "universal"—fall all actual and possible trees. Is then the essence of technology, enframing, the common genus for everything technological? If this were the case then the steam turbine, the radio transmitter, and the cyclotron would each be an enframing. But the word "enframing" does not mean here a tool or any kind of apparatus. Still less does it mean the general concept of such resources. The machines and apparatus are no more cases and kinds of enframing than are the man at the switchboard and the engineer in the drafting room. Each of these in its own way indeed belongs as stockpart, available resource, or executor, within enframing; but enframing is never the essence of technology in the sense of a genus. Enframing is a way of revealing that is a destining, namely, the way that challenges forth. The revealing that brings forth (*poiēsis*) is also a way that has the character of destining. But these ways are not kinds that, arrayed beside one another, fall under the concept of revealing. Revealing is that destining which, ever suddenly and inexplicably to all thinking, apportions itself into the revealing that brings forth and the revealing that challenges, and which allots itself to man. The revealing that challenges has its origin as a destining in bringing-forth. But at the same time enframing, in a way characteristic of a destining, blocks *poiēsis*.

Thus enframing, as a destining of revealing, is indeed the essence of technology, but never in the sense of genus and *essentia*. If we pay heed to this, something astounding strikes us: it is technology itself that makes the demand on us to think in another way what is usually understood by "essence." But in what way?

If we speak of the "essence of a house" and the "essence of a state" we do not mean a generic type; rather we mean the ways in which house and state hold sway, administer themselves, develop, and decay—the way they "essentially unfold" [*wesen*]. Johann Peter Hebel in a poem, "Ghost on Kanderer Street," for which Goethe had a special fondness, uses the old word *die Weserei*. It means the city hall, inasmuch as there the life of the community gathers and village existence is constantly in play, i.e., essentially unfolds. It is from the verb *wesen* that the noun is derived. *Wesen* understood as a verb is the same as *währen* [to last or endure], not only in terms of meaning, but also in terms of the phonetic formation of the word. Socrates and Plato already think the essence of something as what it is that unfolds essentially, in the sense of what endures. But they think what endures is what remains permanently (*aei on*). And they find what endures permanently in what persists throughout all that happens, in what remains. That which remains they discover, in turn, in the aspect (*eidos, idea*), for example, the Idea "house."

The Idea "house" displays what anything is that is fashioned as a house. Particular, real, and possible houses, in contrast, are changing and transitory derivatives of the Idea and thus belong to what does not endure.

But it can never in any way be established that enduring is based solely on what Plato thinks as *idea* and Aristotle thinks as *to ti ēn einai* (that which any particular thing has always been), or what metaphysics in its most varied interpretations thinks as *essentia*.

All unfolding endures. But is enduring only permanent enduring? Does the essence of technology endure in the sense of the permanent enduring of an Idea that hovers over everything technological, thus making it seem that by technology we mean some mythological abstraction? The way in which technology unfolds lets itself be seen only on the basis of that permanent enduring in which enframing propriates as a destining of revealing. Goethe once uses the mysterious word *fortgewähren* [to grant continuously] in place of *fortwähren* [to endure continuously].[5] He hears *währen* [to endure] and *gewähren* [to grant] here in one unarticulated accord. And if we now ponder more carefully than we did before what it is that properly endures and perhaps alone endures, we may venture to say: *Only what is granted endures. What endures primally out of the earliest beginning is what grants.*

As the essencing of technology, enframing is what endures. Does enframing hold sway at all in the sense of granting? No doubt the question seems a horrendous blunder. For according to everything that has been said, enframing is rather a destining that gathers together into the revealing that challenges forth. Challenging is anything but a granting. So it seems, so long as we do not notice that the challenging-forth into the ordering of the actual as standing-reserve remains a destining that starts man upon a way of revealing. As this destining, the essential unfolding of technology gives man entry into something which, of himself, he can neither invent nor in any way make. For there is no such thing as a man who exists singly and solely on his own.

But if this destining, enframing, is the extreme danger, not only for man's essential unfolding, but for all revealing as such, should this destining still be called a granting? Yes, most emphatically, if in this destining the saving power is said to grow. Every destining of revealing propriates from a granting and as such a granting. For it is granting that first conveys to man that share in revealing that the propriative event of revealing needs. So needed and used, man is given to belong to the propriative event of truth. The granting that sends one way or another into revealing is as such the saving power. For the saving power lets man see and enter into the highest dignity of his essence. This dignity lies in keeping watch over the unconcealment—and with it, from the first, the concealment—of all essential unfolding on this earth. It is precisely in enframing, which threatens to sweep man away into ordering as the ostensibly sole way of revealing, and so thrusts man into the danger of the surrender of his free essence—it is precisely in this extreme danger that the innermost indestructible belongingness of man within granting may come to light, provided that we, for our part, begin to pay heed to the essence of technology.

Thus the essential unfolding of technology harbors in itself what we least suspect, the possible rise of the saving power.

Everything, then, depends upon this: that we ponder this rising and that, recollecting, we watch over it. How can this happen?

Above all through our catching sight of the essential unfolding in technology, instead of merely gaping at the technological. So long as we represent technology as an instrument, we remain transfixed in the will to master it. We press on past the essence of technology.

When, however, we ask how the instrumental unfolds essentially as a kind of causality, then we experience this essential unfolding as the destining of a revealing.

When we consider, finally, that the essential unfolding of the essence of technology propriates in the granting that needs and uses man so that he may share in revealing, then the following becomes clear:

The essence of technology is in a lofty sense ambiguous. Such ambiguity points to the mystery of all revealing, i.e., of truth.

On the one hand, enframing challenges forth into the frenziedness of ordering that blocks every view into the propriative event of revealing and so radically endangers the relation to the essence of truth.

On the other hand, enframing propriates for its part in the granting that lets man endure—as yet inexperienced, but perhaps more experienced in the future—that he may be the one who is needed and used for the safekeeping of the essence of truth. Thus the rising of the saving power appears.

The irresistibility of ordering and the restraint of the saving power draw past each other like the paths of two stars in the course of the heavens. But precisely this, their passing by, is the hidden side of their nearness.

When we look into the ambiguous essence of technology, we behold the constellation, the stellar course of the mystery.

The question concerning technology is the question concerning the constellation in which revealing and concealing, in which the essential unfolding of truth propriates.

But what help is it to us to look into the constellation of truth? We look into the danger and see the growth of the saving power.

Through this we are not yet saved. But we are thereupon summoned to hope in the growing light of the saving power. How can this happen? Here and now and in little things, that we may foster the saving power in its increase. This includes holding always before our eyes the extreme danger.

The essential unfolding of technology threatens revealing, threatens it with the possibility that all revealing will be consumed in ordering and that everything will present itself only in the unconcealment of standing-reserve. Human activity can never directly counter this danger. Human achievement alone can never banish it. But human reflection can ponder the fact that all saving power must be of a higher essence than what is endangered, though at the same time kindred to it.

But might there not perhaps be a more primally granted revealing that could bring the saving power into its first shining-forth in the midst of the danger that in the technological age rather conceals than shows itself?

There was a time when it was not technology alone that bore the name *technè*. Once the revealing that brings forth truth into the splendor of radiant appearance was also called *technè*.

There was a time when the bringing-forth of the true into the beautiful was called *technè*. The *poiēsis* of the fine arts was also called *technè*.

At the outset of the destining of the West, in Greece, the arts soared to the supreme height of the revealing granted them. They illuminated the presence [*Gegenwart*] of the gods and the dialogue of divine and human destinies. And art was called simply *technè*. It was a single, manifold revealing. It was pious, *promos*, i.e., yielding to the holding sway and the safekeeping of truth.

The arts were not derived from the artistic. Artworks were not enjoyed aesthetically. Art was not a sector of cultural activity.

What was art—perhaps only for that brief but magnificent age? Why did art bear the modest name *technè*? Because it was a revealing that brought forth and made present, and therefore belonged within *poiēsis*. It was finally that revealing which holds complete sway in all the fine arts, in poetry, and in everything poetical that obtained *poiēsis* as its proper name.

The same poet from whom we heard the words

But where danger is, grows
The saving power also . . .

says to us:

. . . poetically man dwells on this earth.

The poetical brings the true into the splendor of what Plato in the *Phaedrus* calls *to ekphanestaton*, that which shines forth most purely. The poetical thoroughly pervades every art, every revealing of essential unfolding into the beautiful.

Could it be that the fine arts are called to poetic revealing? Could it be that revealing lays claim to the arts most primally, so that they for their part may expressly foster the growth of the saving power, may awaken and found anew our vision of, and trust in, that which grants?

Whether art may be granted this highest possibility of its essence in the midst of the extreme danger, no one can tell. Yet we can be astounded. Before what? Before this other possibility: that the frenziedness of technology may entrench itself everywhere to such an extent that someday, throughout everything technological, the essence of technology may unfold essentially in the propriative event of truth.

Because the essence of technology is nothing technological, essential reflection upon technology and decisive confrontation with it must happen in a realm that is, on the one hand, akin to the essence of technology and, on the other, fundamentally different from it.

Such a realm is art. But certainly only if reflection upon art, for its part, does not shut its eyes to the constellation of truth, concerning which we are *questioning*.

Thus questioning, we bear witness to the crisis that in our sheer preoccupation with technology we do not yet experience the essential unfolding of technology, that in our sheer aesthetic-mindedness we no longer guard and preserve the essential unfolding of art. Yet the more questioningly we ponder the essence of technology, the more mysterious the essence of art becomes.

The closer we come to the danger, the more brightly do the ways into the saving power begin to shine and the more questioning we become. For questioning is the piety of thought.

NOTES

1. Werner Heisenberg, "Das Naturbild in der heutigen Physik," in *Die Künste im technischen Zeitalter* (Munich: Oldenbourg, 1954), 43ff. [See also Werner Heisenberg, *Physics and Philosophy: The Revolution in Modern Science* (New York: Harper & Row, 1958)].

2. See Martin Heidegger, "On the Essence of Truth," in *Basic Writings*, ed. David Farrell Krell (New York: HarperCollins, 1993), 126ff.

3. Heisenberg, "Das Naturbild," 60ff.

4. Friedrich Hölderlin, "Patmos," in *Poems and Fragments*, trans. Michael Hamburger (Ann Arbor: University of Michigan Press, 1966), 462–463.

5. Johann Wolfgang Goethe, *Die Wahlverwandtschaften*, pt. 2, chap. 10, in the novel *Die wunderlichen Nachbarskinder*.

BIBLIOGRAPHY

Heidegger, Martin. "On the Essence of Truth." In *Basic Writings*. Edited by David Farrell Krell, 111–138. New York: HarperCollins, 1993.

Heisenberg, Werner. "Das Naturbild in der heutigen Physik." In *Die Künste im technischen Zeitalter*, 43–69. Munich: Oldenbourg, 1954.

Heisenberg, Werner. *Physics and Philosophy: The Revolution in Modern Science*. New York: Harper & Row, 1958.

Hölderlin, Friedrich. "Patmos." In *Poems and Fragments*. Translated by Michael Hamburger, 462–463. Ann Arbor: University of Michigan Press, 1966.

12

THE DISPOSITIF OF SEXUALITY

Michel Foucault

Sexuality must not be described as a stubborn drive, by nature alien and of necessity disobedient to a power which exhausts itself trying to subdue it and often fails to control it entirely.[1] It appears rather as an especially dense transfer point for relations of power: between men and women, young people and old people, parents and offspring, teachers and students, priests and laity, an administration and a population. Sexuality is not the most intractable element in power relations, but rather one of those endowed with the greatest instrumentality: useful for the greatest number of maneuvers and capable of serving as a point of support, as a linchpin, for the most varied strategies.

There is no single, all-encompassing strategy, valid for all of society and uniformly bearing on all the manifestations of sex. For example, the idea that there have been repeated attempts, by various means, to reduce all of sex to its reproductive function, its heterosexual and adult form, and its matrimonial legitimacy fails to take into account the manifold objectives aimed for, the manifold means employed in the different sexual politics concerned with the two sexes, the different age groups and social classes.

In a first approach to the problem, it seems that we can distinguish four great strategic unities which, beginning in the eighteenth century, formed specific mechanisms [*dispositifs*] of knowledge and power centering on sex. These did not come into being fully developed at that time; but it was then that they took on a consistency and gained an effectiveness in the order of power, as well as a productivity in the order of knowledge, so that it is possible to describe them in their relative autonomy.

1. A hysterization of women's bodies: a threefold process whereby the feminine body was analyzed—qualified and disqualified—as being thoroughly saturated with sexuality; whereby it was integrated into the sphere of medical practices, by reason of a pathology intrinsic to it; whereby, finally, it was placed in organic communication with the social body (whose regulated fecundity it was supposed to ensure), the family space (of which it had to be a substantial and functional element), and the life of children (which it produced and had to guarantee, by virtue of a biologico-moral responsibility lasting through the entire period of the children's education): the Mother, with her negative image of "nervous woman," constituted the most visible form of this hysterization.
2. A pedagogization of children's sex: a double assertion that practically all children indulge or are prone to indulge in sexual activity; and that, being unwarranted, at the same time "natural" and "contrary to nature," this sexual activity posed physical and moral, individual and collective dangers; children were defined as "preliminary" sexual beings, on this side of sex, yet within it, astride a dangerous dividing line. Parents, families, educators, doctors, and eventually psychologists would have to take charge, in a continuous way, of this precious and perilous, dangerous and endangered sexual potential: this pedagogization was especially evident in the war against onanism, which in the West lasted nearly two centuries.
3. A socialization of procreative behavior: an economic socialization via all the incitements and restrictions, the "social" and fiscal measures brought to bear on the fertility of couples; a political socialization achieved through the "responsibilization" of couples with regard to the social body as a whole (which had to be limited or on the contrary reinvigorated), and a medical socialization carried out by attributing a pathogenic value—for the individual and the species—to birth-control practices.
4. A psychiatrization of perverse pleasure: the sexual instinct was isolated as a separate biological and psychical instinct; a clinical analysis was made of all the forms of anomalies by which it could be afflicted; it was assigned a role of normalization or pathologization with respect to all behavior; and finally, a corrective technology was sought for these anomalies.

Four figures emerged from this preoccupation with sex, which mounted throughout the nineteenth century—four privileged objects of knowledge, which were also targets and anchorage points for the ventures of knowledge: the hysterical woman, the masturbating child, the Malthusian couple, and the perverse adult. Each of them corresponded to one of these strategies which, each in its own way, invested and made use of the sex of women, children, and men.

What was at issue in these strategies? A struggle against sexuality? Or were they part of an effort to gain control of it? An attempt to regulate it more effectively and mask its more indiscreet, conspicuous, and intractable aspects? A way of formulating only that measure of knowledge about it that was acceptable or useful? In actual fact, what was involved, rather, was the very production of sexuality. Sexuality must not be thought of as a kind of natural given which power tries to hold in check, or as an obscure domain which knowledge tries gradually to uncover. It is the name that can be given to a historical construct [*dispositif historique*]: not a furtive reality that is difficult to grasp, but a great surface network in which the stimulation of bodies, the intensification of pleasures, the incitement to discourse, the formation of special knowledges, the strengthening of controls and resistances, are linked to one another, in accordance with a few major strategies of knowledge and power.

It will be granted no doubt that relations of sex gave rise, in every society, to a *dispositif of alliance* [*dispositif d'alliance*]: a system of marriage, of fixation and development of kinship ties, of transmission of names and possessions. This dispositif of alliance, with the mechanisms of constraint that ensured its existence and the complex knowledge it often required, lost some of its importance as economic processes and political structures could no longer rely on it as an adequate instrument or sufficient support. Particularly from the eighteenth century onward, Western societies created and deployed a new apparatus [*dispositif*] which was superimposed on the previous one, and which, without completely supplanting the latter, helped to reduce its importance. I am speaking of the *dispositif of sexuality* [*dispositif de sexualité*]: like the dispositif of alliance [*dispositif d'alliance*], it connects up with the circuit of sexual partners, but in a completely different way. The two systems can be contrasted term by term. The dispositif of alliance is built around a system of rules defining the permitted and the forbidden, the licit and the illicit, whereas the dispositif of sexuality operates according to mobile, polymorphous, and contingent techniques of power. The dispositif of alliance has as one of its chief objectives to reproduce the interplay of relations and maintain the law that governs them; the dispositif of sexuality, on the other hand, engenders a continual extension of areas and forms of control. For the first, what is pertinent is the link between partners and definite statutes; the second is concerned with the sensations of the body, the quality of pleasures, and the nature of impressions, however tenuous or imperceptible these may be. Lastly, if the dispositif of alliance is firmly tied to the economy due to the role it can play in the transmission or circulation of wealth, the dispositif of sexuality is linked to the economy through numerous and subtle relays, the main one of which, however, is the body—the body that produces and consumes. In a word, the dispositif of alliance is attuned to a homeostasis of the social body, which it has the function of maintaining; whence its privileged link with the law; whence too the fact that the important phase for it is "reproduction." The dispositif of sexuality has its reason for being, not in reproducing itself, but in proliferating, innovating, annexing, creating, and penetrating bodies in an increasingly detailed way, and in controlling populations in an increasingly comprehensive way. We are compelled, then, to accept three or four hypotheses which run counter to the one on which the theme of a sexuality repressed by the modern forms of society is based: sexuality is tied to recent devices of power [*dispositifs récents de pouvoir*]; it has been expanding at an increasing rate since the seventeenth century; the arrangement [*l'agencement*] that has sustained it is not governed by reproduction; it has been linked from the outset with an intensification of the body—with its exploitation as an object of knowledge and an element in relations of power.

It is not exact to say that the dispositif of sexuality supplanted the dispositif of alliance. One can imagine that one day it will have replaced it. But as things stand at present, while it does tend to cover up the dispositif of alliance, it has neither obliterated the latter nor rendered it useless. Moreover, historically it was around and on the basis of the dispositif of alliance that the dispositif of sexuality was constructed. First the practice of penance, then that of the examination of conscience and spiritual direction, was the formative nucleus: as we have seen, what was at issue to begin with at the tribunal of penance was sex insofar as it was the basis of relations; the questions posed had to do with the commerce allowed or forbidden (adultery, extramarital relations, relations with a person prohibited by blood or statute, the legitimate or illegitimate character of the act of sexual congress); then, coinciding with the new pastoral and its application in seminaries, secondary schools, and convents, there was a gradual progression away from the problematic of relations toward a problematic of the "flesh," that is, of the body, sensation, the nature of pleasure, the more secret forms of enjoyment or acquiescence. "Sexuality" was taking shape, born of a technology of power that was originally focused on alliance. Since then, it has not ceased to operate in conjunction with a system of alliance on which it has depended for support. The family cell, in the form in which it came to be valued in the course of the eighteenth century, made it possible for the main elements of the dispositif of sexuality (the feminine body, infantile precocity, the regulation of births, and to a lesser extent no doubt, the specification of the perverted) to develop along its two primary dimensions: the husband-wife axis and the parents-children axis. The family, in its contemporary form, must not be understood as a social, economic, and political structure of alliance that excludes or at least restrains sexuality, that diminishes it as much as possible, preserving only its useful functions. On the contrary, its role is to anchor sexuality and provide it with a permanent support. It ensures the production of a sexuality that is not homogeneous with the privileges of alliance, while making it possible for the systems of alliance to be imbued with a new tactic of power which they would otherwise be impervious to. The family is the interchange of sexuality and alliance: it conveys the law and the juridical dimension in the dispositif of sexuality; and it conveys the economy of pleasure and the intensity of sensations in the regime of alliance.

This interpenetration of the dispositif of alliance and that of sexuality in the form of the family allows us to understand a number of facts: that since the eighteenth century the family has become an obligatory locus of affects, feelings, love; that sexuality has its privileged point of development in the family; that for this reason sexuality is "incestuous" from the start. It may be that in societies where the mechanisms of alliance predominate, prohibition of incest is a functionally indispensable rule. But in a society such as ours, where the family is the most active site of sexuality, and where it is doubtless the exigencies of the latter which maintain and prolong its existence, incest—for different reasons altogether and in a completely different way—occupies a central place; it is constantly being solicited and refused; it is an object of obsession and attraction, a dreadful secret and an indispensable pivot. It is manifested as a thing that is strictly forbidden in the family insofar as the latter functions as a dispositif of alliance; but it is also a thing that is continuously demanded in order for the family to be a hotbed of constant sexual incitement. If for more than a century the West has displayed such a strong interest in the prohibition of incest, if more or less by common accord it has been seen as a social universal and one of the points through which every society is obliged to pass on the way to becoming a culture, perhaps this is because it was found to be a means of self-defense, not against an incestuous desire, but against the expansion and the implications of this dispositif of sexuality which had been set up, but which, among its many benefits, had the disadvantage of ignoring the laws and juridical forms of alliance. By asserting that all societies without exception, and consequently our own, were subject to this rule of rules, one guaranteed that this dispositif of sexuality, whose strange effects were beginning to be felt—among them, the affective intensification of the family space—would not be able to escape from the grand and ancient system of alliance. Thus the law would be secure, even in the new mechanics of power. For this is the paradox of a society which, from the eighteenth century to the present, has created so many technologies of power that are foreign to the concept of law: it fears the effects and proliferations of those technologies and attempts to recode them in forms of law. If one considers the threshold of all culture to be prohibited incest, then sexuality has been, from the dawn of time, under the sway of law and right. By devoting so much effort to an endless reworking of the transcultural theory of the incest taboo, anthropology has proved worthy of the whole modern dispositif of sexuality and the theoretical discourses it generates.

What has taken place since the seventeenth century can be interpreted in the following manner: the dispositif of sexuality which first developed on the fringes of familial institutions (in the direction of conscience and pedagogy, for example) gradually became focused on the family: the alien, irreducible, and even perilous effects it held in store for the dispositif of alliance (an awareness of this danger was evidenced in the criticism often directed at the indiscretion of the directors, and in the entire controversy, which occurred somewhat later, over the private or public, institutional or familial education of children[2]) were absorbed by the family, a family that was reorganized, restricted no doubt, and in any case intensified in comparison with the functions it formerly exercised in the dispositif of alliance. In the family, parents and relatives became the chief agents of a dispositif of sexuality which drew its outside support from doctors, educators, and later psychiatrists, and which began by competing with the relations of alliance but soon "psychologized" or "psychiatrized" the latter. Then these new personages made their appearance: the nervous woman, the frigid wife, the indifferent mother—or worse, the mother beset by murderous obsessions—the impotent, sadistic, perverse husband, the hysterical or neurasthenic girl, the precocious and already exhausted child, and the young homosexual who rejects marriage or neglects his wife. These were the combined figures of an alliance gone bad and an abnormal sexuality; they were the means by which the disturbing factors of the latter were brought into the former; and yet they also provided an opportunity for the alliance system to assert its prerogatives in the order of sexuality. Then a pressing demand emanated from the family: a plea for help in reconciling these unfortunate conflicts between sexuality and alliance; and, caught in the grip of this dispositif of sexuality which had invested it from without, contributing to its solidification into its modern form, the family broadcast the long complaint of its sexual suffering to doctors, educators, psychiatrists, priests, and pastors, to all the "experts" who would listen. It was as if it had suddenly discovered the dreadful secret of what had always been hinted at and inculcated in it: the family, the keystone of alliance, was the germ of all the misfortunes of sex. And lo and behold, from the mid-nineteenth century onward, the family engaged in searching out the slightest traces of sexuality in its midst, wrenching from itself the most difficult confessions, soliciting an audience with everyone who might know something about the matter, and opening itself unreservedly to endless examination. The family was the crystal in the dispositif of sexuality: it seemed to be the source of a sexuality which it actually only reflected and diffracted. By virtue of its permeability, and through that process of reflections to the outside, it became one of the most valuable tactical components of the dispositif.

But this development was not without its tensions and problems. Charcot doubtless constituted a central figure in this as well. For many years he was the most noteworthy of all those to whom families, burdened down as they were with this sexuality that saturated them, appealed for mediation and treatment. On receiving parents who brought him their children, husbands their wives, and wives their husbands, from the world over, his first concern was to separate the "patient" from his family, and the better to observe him, he would pay as little attention as possible to what the family had to say.[3] He sought to detach the sphere of sexuality from the system of alliance, in order to deal with it directly through a medical practice whose technicity and autonomy were guaranteed by the neurological model. Medicine thus assumed final responsibility, according to the rules of a specific knowledge, for a sexuality which it had in fact urged families to concern themselves with as an essential task and a major danger. Moreover, Charcot noted on several occasions how difficult it was for families to "yield" the patient whom they nonetheless had brought to the doctor, how they laid siege to the mental hospitals where the subject was being kept out of view, and the ways in which they were constantly interfering with the doctor's work. Their worry was unwarranted, however: the therapist only intervened in order to return to them individuals who were sexually compatible with the family system; and while this intervention manipulated the sexual body, it did not authorize the latter to define itself in explicit discourse. One must not speak of these "genital causes": so went the phrase—muttered in a muted voice—which the most famous ears of our time overheard one day in 1886, from the mouth of Charcot.

This was the context in which psychoanalysis set to work; but not without substantially modifying the pattern of anxieties and reassurances. In the beginning it must have given rise to distrust and hostility, for, pushing Charcot's lesson to the extreme, it undertook to examine the sexuality of individuals outside family control; it brought this sexuality to light without covering it over again with the neurological model; more serious still, it called family relations into question in the analysis it made of them. But despite everything, psychoanalysis, whose technical procedure seemed to place the confession of sexuality outside family jurisdiction, rediscovered the law of alliance, the involved workings of marriage and kinship, and incest at the heart of this sexuality, as the principle of its formation and the key to its intelligibility. The guarantee that one would find the parents-children relationship at the root of everyone's sexuality made it possible—even when everything seemed to point to the reverse process—to keep the dispositif of sexuality coupled to the system of alliance. There was no risk that sexuality would appear to be, by nature, alien to the law: it was constituted only through the law. Parents, do not be afraid to bring your children to analysis: it will teach them that in any case it is you whom they love. Children, you really shouldn't complain that you are not orphans, that you always rediscover in your innermost selves your Object-Mother or the sovereign sign of your Father: it is through them that you gain access to desire. Whence, after so many reticences, the enormous consumption of analysis in societies where the dispositif of alliance and the family system needed strengthening. For this is one of the most significant aspects of this entire history of the dispositif of sexuality: it had its beginnings in the technology of the "flesh" in classical Christianity, basing itself on the alliance system and the rules that governed the latter; but today it fills a reverse function in that it tends to prop up the old dispositif of alliance. From the direction of conscience to psychoanalysis, the dispositifs of alliance and sexuality were involved in a slow process that had them turning about one another until, more than three centuries later, their positions were reversed; in the Christian pastoral, the law of alliance codified the flesh which was just being discovered and fitted it into a framework that was still juridical in character; with psychoanalysis, sexuality gave body and life to the rules of alliance by saturating them with desire.

Hence the domain we must analyze in the different studies that will follow the present volume is that dispositif of sexuality: its formation on the basis of the Christian notion of the flesh, and its development through the four great strategies that were deployed in the nineteenth century: the sexualization of children, the hysterization of women, the specification of the perverted, and the regulation of populations—all strategies that went by way of a family which must be viewed, not as a powerful agency of prohibition, but as a major factor of sexualization.

The first phase corresponded to the need to form a "labor force" (hence to avoid any useless "expenditure," any wasted energy, so that all forces were reduced to labor capacity alone) and to ensure its reproduction (conjugality, the regulated fabrication of children). The second phase corresponded to that epoch of *Spätkapitalismus* in which the exploitation of wage labor does not demand the same violent and physical constraints as in the nineteenth century, and where the politics of the body does not require the elision of sex or its restriction solely to the reproductive function; it relies instead on a multiple channeling into the controlled circuits of the economy—on what has been called a hyper-repressive desublimation.

If the politics of sex makes little use of the law of the taboo but brings into play an entire technical machinery, if what is involved is the production of sexuality rather than the repression of sex, then our emphasis has to be placed elsewhere; we must shift our analysis away from the problem of "labor capacity" and doubtless abandon the diffuse energetics that underlies the theme of a sexuality repressed for economic reasons.

NOTES

1. [This chapter is called *Le dispositif de sexualité* in French, but it was translated as "The Deployment of Sexuality" in the English version. This selection comes from the subsection "Domain." Foucault examines how modern sexuality has been articulated through two distinct yet superimposed dispositifs of power: the *dispositif de sexualité* (translated as the "deployment of sexuality" in the original English) and the *dispositif d'alliance* (translated as "deployment of alliance" in the original English). Since this is a key text in dispositif thinking, we have re-translated "deployment" as "dispositif" throughout.—Eds.]

2. Molière's *Tartuffe* and Jakob Michael Lenz's *Tutor*, separated by more than a century, both depict the interference of the dispositif of sexuality in the family organization [*l'interférence du dispositif de sexualité sur le dispositif de famille*], apropos of spiritual direction in *Tartuffe* and education in *The Tutor*.

3. Jean-Martin Charcot, *Leçons de Mardi*, January 7, 1888: "In order to properly treat a hysterical girl, one must not leave her with her father and mother; she needs to be placed in a mental hospital.... Do you know how long well-behaved little girls cry for their mothers after they part company?... Let us take the average, if you will; it's not very long, a half-hour or thereabouts."

February 21, 1888: "In the case of hysteria of young boys, what one must do is to separate them from their mothers. So long as they are with their mothers, nothing is of any use.... The father is sometimes just as unbearable as the mother; it is best, then, to get rid of them both."

BIBLIOGRAPHY

Charcot, Jean-Martin, and Blin Emmery. *Leçons du mardi à la Salpêtrière, professeur Charcot : policlinique 1887–1888 / notes de cours de MM. Blin, Charcot et H. Colin*. Paris: Bureaux du "Progrès medical", 1892.

13

THE CONFESSION OF THE FLESH

Michel Foucault

A conversation with Alain Grosrichard, Gerard Wajeman, Jaques-Alain Miller, Guy Le Gaufey, Dominique Celas, Gerard Miller, Catherine Millot, Jocelyne Livi and Judith Miller.

GROSRICHARD: Let's begin with the general title of this new project of yours: the 'History of Sexuality.' What is the nature of this new historical object which you term 'sexuality'? Evidently it isn't sexuality in the sense that botanists or biologists speak or have spoken of it, something which is more a matter for historians of science. Nor is it a question of sexuality in the sense that traditional histories of ideas or customs might have understood the term, the point of view which you are now contesting with your doubts about the 'repressive hypothesis.' Nor even, finally, do you seem to be talking about sexual practices such as historians study today using new methods and techniques of analysis. You talk about a 'dispositif of sexuality.'[1] What is the meaning or the methodological function for you of this term, *dispositif*?

FOUCAULT: What I'm trying to pick out with this term is, firstly, a thoroughly heterogeneous ensemble consisting of discourses, institutions, architectural forms, regulatory decisions, laws, administrative measures, scientific statements, philosophical, moral and philanthropic propositions—in short, the said as much as the unsaid. Such are the elements of the dispositif. The dispositif itself is the system of relations [*réseau*] that can be established between these elements. Secondly, what I am trying to identify in this dispositif is precisely the nature of the connection that can exist between these heterogeneous elements. Thus, a particular discourse can figure at one time as the programme of an institution, and at another it can function as a means of justifying or masking a practice which itself remains silent, or as a secondary re-interpretation of this practice, opening out for it a new field of rationality. In short, between these elements, whether discursive or non-discursive, there is a sort of interplay of shifts of position and modifications of function which can also vary very widely. Thirdly, I understand by the term 'dispositif' a sort of—shall we say—formation which has as its major function at a given historical moment that of responding to an *urgent need*. The dispositif thus has a dominant strategic function. This may have been, for example, the assimilation of a floating population found to be burdensome for an essentially mercantilist economy: there was a strategic imperative acting here as the matrix for a dispositif which gradually undertook the control or subjection of madness, mental illness and neurosis.

WAJEMAN: So a dispositif is defined by a structure of heterogeneous elements, but also by a certain kind of genesis?

FOUCAULT: Yes. And I would consider that there are two important moments in this genesis. There is a first moment which is the prevalent influence of a strategic objective. Next, the dispositif as such is constituted and enabled to continue in existence insofar as it is the site of a double process. On the one hand, there is a process of *functional overdetermination*, because each effect—positive or negative, intentional or unintentional—enters into resonance or contradiction with the others and thereby calls for a readjustment or a re-working of the heterogeneous elements that surface at various points. On the other hand, there is a perpetual process of *strategic elaboration*. Take the example of imprisonment, that dispositif which had the effect of making measures of detention appear to be the most efficient and rational method that could be applied to the phenomenon of criminality. What did this dispositif produce? An entirely unforeseen effect which had nothing to do with any kind of strategic ruse on the part of some meta- or trans-historic subject conceiving and willing it. This effect was the constitution of a delinquent milieu very different from the kind of seedbed of illegalist practices and individuals found in eighteenth-century society. What happened? The prison operated as a process of filtering, concentrating, professionalising and circumscribing a criminal milieu. From about the 1830s onwards, one finds an immediate re-utilisation of this unintended, negative effect within a new strategy which came in some sense to occupy this empty space, or transform the negative into a positive. The delinquent milieu came to be re-utilised for diverse political and economic ends, such as the extraction of profit from pleasure through the organisation of prostitution. This is what I call the strategic completion [*remplissement*] of the dispositif.

GROSRICHARD: In *The Order of Things* and *The Archaeology of Knowledge*, you talked about the *episteme*, knowledge and discursive formations. Now you are more inclined to talk about 'dispositif' and 'disciplines.' Are these new concepts intended to replace the previous ones, which you would now want to abandon? Or do they rather reproduce them in a different register? Does this amount to a change in the way you would like your books to be used? Are you now selecting your objects of study, your way of approach and your conceptual instruments in terms of new objectives, namely the contemporary struggles that have to be fought, the world which has to be changed rather than interpreted? I am asking this now so that the questions we put to you afterwards won't be at cross purposes with what you are trying to do.

FOUCAULT: But bear in mind that it may be just as well if they're at cross purposes: that would show that my own undertaking is at cross purposes. But you are right to ask the question. With the notion of the dispositif, I find myself in a difficulty which I haven't yet been properly able to get out of. I said that the dispositif is essentially of a *strategic* nature, which means assuming that it is a matter of a certain manipulation of relations of forces, either developing them in a particular direction, blocking them, stabilising them, utilising them, etc. The dispositif is thus always inscribed in a play of power, but it is also always linked to certain coordinates of knowledge which issue from it but, to an equal degree, condition it. This is what the dispositif consists in: strategies of relations of forces supporting, and supported by, types of knowledge. In seeking in *The Order of Things* to write a history of the *episteme*, I was still caught in an impasse. What I should like to do now is to try and show that what I call a dispositif is a much more general case of the *episteme*; or rather, that the *episteme* is a specifically *discursive* dispositif, whereas the dispositif in its general form is both discursive and non-discursive, its elements being much more heterogeneous.

J.-A. MILLER: The complex which you are introducing under the term of dispositif is certainly conceived in a much more heterogeneous form than what you termed the *episteme*. You mingled together or distributed within your epistemes statements of very diverse kinds, those of philosophers, savants, obscure authors, practitioners theorising their practice: hence the effect of surprise your work produced, but it was still finally concerned with discursive utterances.

FOUCAULT: Certainly.

J.-A. MILLER: With the introduction of 'dispositifs,' you want to get beyond discourse. But these new ensembles, which articulate together so many different elements, remain nonetheless *signifying* ensembles. I can't quite see how you could be getting at a 'non-discursive' domain.

FOUCAULT: In trying to identify a dispositif, I look for the elements which participate in a rationality, a given form of co-ordination, except that. . . .

J.-A. MILLER: One shouldn't say rationality, or we would be back with the *episteme* again.

FOUCAULT: If you like, I would define the *episteme* retrospectively as the strategic dispositif which permits of separating out from among all the statements which are possible those that will be acceptable within, I won't say a scientific theory, but a field of scientificity, and, which it is possible to say are true or false. The *episteme* is the 'dispositif' which makes possible the separation, not of the true from the false, but of what may from what may not be characterised as scientific.

LE GAUFEY: But going back to this question of the 'non-discursive,' what is there in a dispositif, over and above the discursive utterances, except the 'institutions'?

FOUCAULT: The term 'institution' is generally applied to every kind of more-or-less constrained, learned behaviour. Everything which functions in a society as a system of constraint and which isn't an utterance, in short, all the field of the non-discursive social, is an institution.

J.-A. MILLER: But clearly the institution is itself discursive.

FOUCAULT: Yes, if you like, but it doesn't much matter for my notion of the dispositif to be able to say that this is discursive and that isn't. If you take Gabriel's architectural plan for the Military School together with the actual construction of the School, how is one to say what is discursive and what institutional? That would only interest me if the building didn't conform with the plan. But I don't think it's very important to be able to make that distinction, given that my problem isn't a linguistic one.

GROSRICHARD: In *The Will to Knowledge*, you study the constitution and the history of a dispositif: the dispositif of sexuality.[2] Very schematically, one can say that this dispositif is articulated, on the one hand, on to what you call power [*le pouvoir*], for which it serves as a means and expression, and that on the other hand it produces, as one might put it, an imaginary, historically datable object, namely sex. There follow from this two major series of questions about power, about sex, and about their relation to the dispositif of sexuality. Concerning power, you voice doubts about the conception of it that has been traditionally held. And what you are proposing is not so much a new theory of power as an *'analytic of power.'* How does this term, 'analytic' help you to throw light on what you refer to here as 'power' and its connection with the dispositif of sexuality?

FOUCAULT: Power in the substantive sense, *'le' pouvoir*, doesn't exist. What I mean is this. The idea that there is either located at—or emanating from—a given point something which is a 'power' seems to me to be based on a misguided analysis, one which at all events fails to account for a considerable number of phenomena. In reality power means relations, a more-or-less organised, hierarchical, coordinated cluster of relations. So the problem is not that of constituting a theory of power which would be a remake of Boulainvilliers on the one hand and Rousseau on the other. Both these authors start off from an original state in which all men are equal, and then, what happens? With one of them, a historical invasion, with the other a mythico-juridical event, but either way it turns out that from a given moment people no longer have rights, and power is constituted. If one tries to erect a theory of power one will always be obliged to view it as emerging at a given place and time and hence to deduce it, to reconstruct its genesis. But if power is in reality an open, more-or-less coordinated (in the event, no doubt, ill-coordinated) cluster of relations, then the only problem is to provide oneself with a grid of analysis which makes possible an analytic of relations of power.

[. . .]

MILLOT: Discussing what you call 'comprehensive dispositifs' [*'dispositifs d'ensemble'*] you write in *The Will to Knowledge* that "here the logic is perfectly clear, the aims decipherable, yet it turns out that no one can have conceived and very few formulated them: such is the implicit character of the great, anonymous, almost mute strategies which coordinate the voluble tactics [*tactiques*] whose 'inventors' or directors are often devoid of all hypocrisy. . . ."[3] You define here something like a strategy without a subject. How is this conceivable?

FOUCAULT: Let's take an example. From around 1825 to 1830 one finds the local and perfectly explicit appearance of definite strategies for fixing the workers in the first heavy industries at their work-places. At Mulhouse and in northern France various tactics [*techniques*] are elaborated: pressuring people to marry, providing housing, building *cités ouvrières*, practising that sly system of credit-slavery that Marx talks about, consisting in enforcing advance payment of rents while wages are paid only at the end of the month. Then there are the savings-bank systems, the truck-system with grocers and wine-merchants who act for the bosses, and so on. Around all this there is formed little by little a discourse, the discourse of philanthropy and the moralisation of the working class. Then the experiments become generalised by way of the institutions and societies consciously advocating programmes for the moralisation of the working class. Then on top of that there is superimposed the problem of women's work, the schooling of children and the relations between the two issues. Between the schooling of children, which is a centralised, Parliamentary measure, and this or that purely local initiative dealing with workers' housing, for example, one finds all sorts of support mechanisms (unions of employers, chambers of commerce, etc.) which invent, modify and re-adjust, according to the circumstances of the moment and the place—so that you get a coherent, rational strategy, but one for which it is no longer possible to identify a person who conceived it.

MILLOT: But then what role does the social class play?

FOUCAULT: Ah, here we are at the centre of the problem, and no doubt also of the obscurities of my own discourse. A dominant class isn't a mere abstraction, but neither is it a pre-given entity. For a class to become a dominant class, for it to ensure its domination and for that domination to reproduce itself is certainly the effect of a number of actual pre-meditated tactics operating within the grand strategies that ensure this domination. But between the strategy which fixes, reproduces, multiplies and accentuates existing relations of forces, and the class which thereby finds itself in a ruling position, there is a reciprocal relation of production. Thus one can say that the strategy of moralising the working class is that of the bourgeoisie. One can even say that it's the strategy which allows the bourgeois class to be the bourgeois class and to exercise its domination. But what I don't think one can say is that it's the bourgeois class on the level of its ideology or its economic project which, as a sort of at once real and fictive subject, invented and forcibly imposed this strategy on the working class.

J.-A. MILLER: So there is no subject, but there is an effect of finalisation.

FOUCAULT: An effect of finalisation relative to an objective—.

J.-A. MILLER: —An objective which is imposed, then.

FOUCAULT: Which turns out to be imposed. To reiterate: the moralisation of the working class wasn't imposed by Guizot, through his schools legislation, nor by Dupin through his books. It wasn't imposed by the employers' unions either. And yet it was accomplished, because it met the urgent need to master a vagabond, floating labour force. So the objective existed and the strategy was developed, with ever-growing coherence, but without it being necessary to attribute to it a subject which makes the law, pronouncing it in the form of 'Thou shalt' and 'Thou shalt not.'

J.-A. MILLER: But how is one to distinguish between the different subjects involved in this strategy? Mustn't one be able to distinguish, for instance, between those who produce it and those who only undergo it? Even if their respective initiatives often end by converging, are they all merged into one or do they singularise themselves? And if so, in what terms?

GROSRICHARD: Or to put it another way, is your model Mandeville's Fable of the Bees?

FOUCAULT: I wouldn't exactly say that, but I'll take another example: that of the constitution of a medico-legal dispositif, through which on the one hand psychiatry is utilised in the penal system while, conversely, penal types of controls and interventions are developed and multiplied to deal with the actions or behaviour of abnormal subjects. This led to that vast theoretical and legislative edifice constructed around the question of degeneracy and degenerates. What took place here? All sorts of subjects intervened, administrative personnel for example, for reasons of public order, but above all it was the doctors and magistrates. Can one talk of interests here? In the case of the doctors, why should they have wanted to intervene so directly in the penal domain, just when they had barely, and then only with difficulty, succeeded in detaching psychiatry from the sort of magma constituted by the practices of internment which occupied precisely the heart of the 'medico-legal' domain except for the fact that they were neither medical nor legal. Just when the alienists have barely isolated and marked out the theory and practice of mental alienation, here they are saying, 'There are crimes which are our business, these people belong to us!' Where is their interest as doctors in this? To say that there was a sort of imperialist dynamic of psychiatry aiming to annex crime and submit it to its rationality doesn't get us anywhere. I would be tempted to say that there was, in fact, a necessity here (which one doesn't have to call an interest) linked to the very existence of a psychiatry which had made itself autonomous but needed thereafter to secure a basis for its intervention by gaining recognition as a component of public hygiene. And it could establish this basis only through the fact that there was a disease (mental alienation) for it to mop up. There had also to be a danger for it to combat, comparable with that of an epidemic, a lack of hygiene, or suchlike. Now, how can it be proved that madness constitutes a danger except by showing that there exist extreme cases where madness, even though not apparent to the public gaze, without manifesting itself beforehand through any symptom except a few minute fissures, minuscule murmurings perceptible only to the highly trained observer, can suddenly explode into a monstrous crime. This was how the diagnosis of homicidal mania was constructed. Madness is a redoubtable danger precisely in that it is not foreseeable by any of those persons of good sense who claim to be able to recognise it. Only a doctor can spot it, and thus madness becomes exclusively an object for the doctor, whose right of intervention is grounded by the same token. In the case of the magistrates, one can say that it is a different necessity which leads them, despite their reluctance, to accept the intervention of the doctors. Along with the edifice of the Penal Code, the punitive machine of the prison which had been placed in their hands could function effectively only if it operated at the level of the individuality of the individual, the criminal and not the crime, so as to transform and reform him. But, once given that there were crimes whose reasons and motives could not be established, punishment became impossible. To punish a person whom one doesn't fully know is impossible for a penal system which no longer works through the *supplice* but through internment. (This is so much the case that the other day someone, an admirable person moreover, uttered this astounding sentence which ought to have left us all gaping: "You cannot execute Patrick Henry, you don't understand him." What does that mean? If they had understood him, would it have been all right to kill him?) The magistrates, therefore, so as to combine a penal code which was still based on punishment and expiation with a punitive practice which had become one of reform and imprisonment, were forced to make room for the psychiatrists. So here you have strategic necessities which are not exactly interests. . . .

J.-A. MILLER: You substitute for the notion of 'interest' those of 'problem' (for the doctors) and 'necessity' (for the magistrates). The gain appears very slight, and things remain still very imprecise.

LE GAUFEY: It seems to me that the metaphorical system governing your analysis is that of the organism, which makes possible the elimination of reference to a thinking, willing subject. A living organism tends always to persist in its being, and all means for its attaining that objective are good ones.

FOUCAULT: No, I don't agree with that at all. Firstly, I have never used the metaphor of the organism. Secondly, the problem isn't one of self-preservation. When I speak of strategy, I am taking the term seriously: in order for a certain relation of forces not only to maintain itself, but to accentuate, stabilise and broaden itself, a certain kind of manoeuvre is necessary. The psychiatrist had to manoeuvre in order to make himself recognised as part of the public hygiene system. This isn't an organism, any more than in the case of the magistrature, and I can't see how what I'm saying can imply that these are organisms.

GROSRICHARD: What is striking, however, is that it was during the nineteenth century that a theory of society conceived on the model of the organism was constituted—that of Auguste Comte for instance. But let's leave that. All the examples you have given us to show how you conceive this 'strategy without a subject' are drawn from the nineteenth century, a period where society and the State already possess a very centralised, technicised form. Are things equally clear for earlier periods?

J.-A. MILLER: In short, it's just at the moment when the strategy appears to have a subject that Foucault shows that it hasn't. . . .

FOUCAULT: In a sense, I would agree. I heard someone talking about power the other day—it's in fashion. He observed that the famous 'absolute' monarchy in reality had nothing absolute about it. In fact it consisted of a number of islands of dispersed power, some of them functioning as geographical spaces, others as pyramids, others as bodies, or through the influence of familial systems, kinship networks and so forth. One can see perfectly well why grand strategies couldn't emerge in such a system. The French monarchy was equipped with a very strong, but very rigid, administrative apparatus [*appareil administratif*]: one which let a tremendous amount slip through its grip. Certainly there was a King, the manifest representative of power, but in reality power wasn't centralised and didn't express itself through grand strategies, at once fine, supple and coherent. On the other hand, in the nineteenth century one finds all kinds of mechanisms and institutions—the parliamentary system, diffusion of information, publishing, the great exhibitions, the university, and so on: 'bourgeois power' was then able to elaborate its grand strategies, without one needing for all that to impute a subject to them.

J.-A. MILLER: As far as the space of 'theory' was concerned, after all, the old 'transcendental space without a subject' never really worried many people, whatever the reproaches that were made against you from the direction of *Les Temps Modernes* when you published *The Order of Things* complaints about the absence of any kind of causality from your shifts from one *episteme* to the next. But perhaps there is a problem when one is dealing not with the 'theoretical' but the 'practical' field. Given that there are relations of forces, and struggles, the question inevitably arises of who is doing the struggling and against whom? Here you can't escape the question of the subject, or rather the *subjects*.

FOUCAULT: Certainly, and this is what is preoccupying me. I'm not too sure what the answer is. But after all, if one considers that power has to be analysed in terms of relations of power, then it seems to me that one has a much better chance than in other theoretical procedures of grasping the relation that exists between power and struggles, and especially the class struggle. What I find striking in the majority—if not of Marx's texts then those of the Marxists (except perhaps Trotsky)—is the way they pass over in silence what is understood by *struggle* when one talks of class struggle. What does struggle mean here? Is it a dialectical confrontation? An economic battle? A war? Is civil society riven by class struggle to be seen as a war continued by other means?

CELAS: Perhaps one should take account here of the party, that other institution, which can't be assimilated to those others which don't have 'taking power' as their goal. . . .

GROSRICHARD: And then again, the Marxists do all the same ask the question, 'Who are our friends, who are our enemies?,' the question which serves to determine the real lines of confrontation within this field of struggles. . . .

J.-A. MILLER: So who ultimately, in your view, are the subjects who oppose each other?

FOUCAULT: This is just a hypothesis, but I would say it's all against all. There aren't immediately given subjects of the struggle, one the proletariat, the other the bourgeoisie. Who fights against whom? We all fight each other. And there is always within each of us something that fights something else.

J.-A. MILLER: Which would mean that there are only ever transitory coalitions, some of which immediately break up, but others of which persist, but that strictly speaking individuals would be the first and last components?

FOUCAULT: Yes, individuals, or even sub-individuals.

J.-A. MILLER: Sub-individuals?

FOUCAULT: Why not?
 [. . .]

GROSRICHARD: Now let's talk about sex. You treat it as a historical object, engendered in some sense by the dispositif of sexuality.

J.-A. MILLER: Your previous book dealt with criminality. Sexuality, apparently, is a different kind of object. Unless it were more interesting to show that it's the same? Which would you prefer?

FOUCAULT: I would say, let's try and see if it isn't the same. That's the stake in the game, and if I'm thinking of writing six volumes, it's precisely because it's a game!

This book is the only one I've written without knowing beforehand what I would call it, and right up to the last moment I couldn't think of a title. I use 'History of Sexuality' for want of anything better. The first projected title, which I subsequently dropped, was 'Sex and Truth.' All the same, that was my problem: what had to happen in the history of the West for the question of truth to be posed in regard to sexual pleasure? And this has been a problem that has exercised me ever since I wrote *Madness and Civilisation*. About that book historians say "Yes, that's fine, but why didn't you look at the different mental illnesses that are found in the seventeenth and eighteenth centuries? Why didn't you do the history of the epidemics of mental illnesses during that period?" I can't seem to be able to explain to them that indeed that is all extremely interesting, but that wasn't my problem. Regarding madness, my problem was to find out how the question of madness could have been made to operate in terms of discourses of truth, that is to say, discourses having the status and function of *true* discourses. In the West that means scientific discourse. That was also the angle from which I wanted to approach the question of sexuality.

GROSRICHARD: How would you define what you call 'sex' in relation to this dispositif of sexuality? Is it an imaginary object, a phenomenon, an illusion?

FOUCAULT: Well, I'll tell you what happened when I was writing the book. There were several successive drafts. To start with, sex was taken as a pre-given datum, and sexuality figured as a sort of simultaneously discursive and institutional formation which came to graft itself on to sex, to overlay it and perhaps finally to obscure it. That was the first line of approach. Then I showed some people the manuscript and came to realise that it wasn't very satisfactory. Then I turned the whole thing upside down. That was only a game, because I wasn't sure. . . . But I said to myself, basically, couldn't it be that sex—which seems to be an instance having its own laws and constraints, on the basis of which the masculine and feminine sexes are defined—be something which on the contrary is *produced* by the dispositif of sexuality? What the discourse of sexuality was initially applied to wasn't sex but the body, the sexual organs, pleasures, kinship relations, interpersonal relations, and so forth.

J.-A. MILLER: A heterogeneous ensemble.

FOUCAULT: Yes, a heterogeneous ensemble, one which was finally completely overlaid by the dispositif of sexuality, which in turn at a certain moment produced, as the keystone of its discourse and perhaps of its very functioning, the idea of sex.

G. MILLER: But isn't this idea of sex contemporaneous with the establishment of the dispositif of sexuality?

FOUCAULT: No, no! It seems to me that one sees sex emerging during the course of the nineteenth century.

G. MILLER: We have only sex since the nineteenth century?

FOUCAULT: We have sexuality [*sexualité*] since the eighteenth century, and sex [*sexe*] since the nineteenth. What we had before that was no doubt the flesh [*chair*]. The basic originator of it all was Tertullian.

[. . .]

J.-A. MILLER: Perhaps you could say a little about the women's and the homosexuals' liberation movements?

FOUCAULT: Well, regarding everything that is currently being said about the liberation of sexuality, what I want to make apparent is precisely that the object 'sexuality' is in reality an instrument formed a long while ago, and one which has constituted a centuries-long dispositif of subjection [*dispositif d'assujettissement*]. The real strength of the women's liberation movements is not that of having laid claim to the specificity of their sexuality and the rights pertaining to it, but that they have actually departed from the discourse conducted within the dispositif of sexuality. These movements do indeed emerge in the nineteenth century as demands for sexual specificity. What has their outcome been? Ultimately, a veritable movement of de-sexualisation, a displacement effected in relation to the sexual centering of the problem, formulating the demand for forms of culture, discourse, language, and so on, which are no longer part of that rigid assignation and pinning-down to their sex which they had initially in some sense been politically obliged to accept in order to make themselves heard. The creative and interesting element in the women's movements is precisely that.

J.-A. MILLER: The inventive element?

FOUCAULT: Yes, the inventive element. . . . The American homosexual movements make that challenge their starting-point. Like women, they begin to look for new forms of community, co-existence, pleasure. But, in contrast with the position of women, the fixing of homosexuals to their sexual specificity is much stronger, they reduce everything to the order of sex. The women don't.

LE GAUFEY: All the same it was these movements that succeeded in removing homosexuality from the nomenclature of mental illnesses. There is still a fantastic difference in the fact of saying, "You want us to be homosexuals, well, we are."

FOUCAULT: Yes, but the homosexual liberation movements remain very much caught at the level of demands for the right to their sexuality, the dimension of the sexological.

Anyway that's quite normal since homosexuality is a sexual practice which is attacked, barred and disqualified as such. Women on the other hand are able to have much wider economic, political and other kinds of objectives than homosexuals.

[. . .]

GROSRICHARD: In this idea of making the *supplice* serve a useful purpose, utilising this absolute power of execution for the profit of a better knowledge of life by in a sense forcing the condemned to confess a truth concerning life, there is a link with what you were saying about the confession, and the phenomena you analyse in the final section of your book. You write that there is a shift at a certain moment from a power exercised in the form of a right to put to death, to a 'power over life.' One might ask you this: is this power over life, this concern to master its excesses or defects, specific to modern Western societies? Take an example: Book XXIII of Montesquieu's *Esprit des Lois* is entitled, 'Of laws in their relation to the number of inhabitants.' He discusses as a grave problem the depopulation of Europe, and contrasts Louis XIV's edict of 1666 in favour of marriages with the different and much more effective measures practiced by the Romans. As though, under the Roman Empire, the question of a power over life—a discipline of sexuality from the standpoint of reproduction—had been posed and then forgotten, re-emerging finally in the middle of the eighteenth century. So is this shift from a power of death to a power over life really something unprecedented, or is it not rather periodic, linked for instance to ages and civilisations where urbanisation and the concentration of population, or conversely the depopulation caused by wars and epidemics seem to imperil the nation?

FOUCAULT: Certainly the problem of population in the form: "Aren't we getting too numerous?" or "Aren't we getting too few?" has long been posed, and there have long been different legislative solutions for it: taxes on bachelors, grants for numerous families, etc. But what is interesting in the eighteenth century is, firstly, the generalisation of these problems: account begins to be taken of all aspects of the phenomena of population (epidemics, conditions of habitats, hygiene . . .), and these aspects begin to be integrated into a central problem. Secondly, one finds all sorts of new types of knowledge being applied: the emergence of demography, observations regarding the spread of epidemics, enquiries into nurses and conditions of breastfeeding. Thirdly, the establishment of apparatuses of power [*appareils de pouvoir*] making possible not only observation but also direct intervention and manipulation in all these areas. I would say that at that moment, where hitherto there had only been vague improvisatory measures of promotion designed to alter a situation which was scarcely known, something begins to develop which can be called a power over life. In the eighteenth century, for instance, despite significant efforts made in statistics, people were convinced that the population was falling, whereas historians now know that on the contrary there was a massive growth in population.

[. . .]

NOTES

1. [Since this is a key text in dispositif thinking, we have fixed the translation of *"dispositif,"* which appears as "apparatus" in the original translation.—Eds.]

2. [We have corrected the English version of this interview, which refers to this book as *The Will to Know*.—Eds.]

3. [The term *"dispositifs d'ensemble"* was rendered "general apparatuses" in the English translation of this interview and "comprehensive system" in Michel Foucault, *The History of Sexuality: Volume 1: The Will to Knowledge*, trans. Robert Hurley (London: Penguin, 1981), 95.—Eds.]

BIBLIOGRAPHY

Foucault, Michel. *The History of Sexuality: Volume 1: The Will to Knowledge*. Translated by Robert Hurley. London: Penguin, 1981.

14

LATENT AND MANIFEST ORIENTALISM

Edward Said

In Chapter One [of *Orientalism*], I tried to indicate the scope of thought and action covered by the word *Orientalism*, using as privileged types the British and French experiences of and with the Near Orient, Islam, and the Arabs. In those experiences I discerned an intimate, perhaps even the most intimate, and rich relationship between Occident and Orient. Those experiences were part of a much wider European or Western relationship with the Orient, but what seems to have influenced Orientalism most was a fairly constant sense of confrontation felt by Westerners dealing with the East. The boundary notion of East and West, the varying degrees of projected inferiority and strength, the range of work done, the kinds of characteristic features ascribed to the Orient: all these testify to a willed imaginative and geographic division made between East and West, and lived through during many centuries. In Chapter Two my focus narrowed a good deal. I was interested in the earliest phases of what I call modern Orientalism, which began during the latter part of the eighteenth century and the early years of the nineteenth. Since I did not intend my study to become a narrative chronicle of the development of Oriental studies in the modern West, I proposed instead an account of the rise, development, and institutions of Orientalism as they were formed against a background of intellectual, cultural, and political history until about 1870 or 1880. Although my interest in Orientalism there included a decently ample variety of scholars and imaginative writers, I cannot claim by any means to have presented more than a portrait of the typical structures (and their ideological tendencies) constituting the field, its associations with other fields, and the work of some of its most influential scholars. My principal operating assumptions were—and continue to be—that fields of learning, as much as the works of even the most eccentric artist, are constrained and acted upon by society, by cultural traditions, by worldly circumstance, and by stabilizing influences like schools, libraries, and governments; moreover, that both learned and imaginative writing are never free, but are limited in their imagery, assumptions, and intentions; and finally, that the advances made by a "science" like Orientalism in its academic form are less objectively true than we often like to think. In short, my study hitherto has tried to describe the *economy* that makes Orientalism a coherent subject matter, even while allowing that as an idea, concept, or image the word *Orient* has a considerable and interesting cultural resonance in the West.

I realize that such assumptions are not without their controversial side. Most of us assume in a general way that learning and scholarship move forward; they get better, we feel, as time passes and as more information is accumulated, methods are refined, and later generations of scholars improve upon earlier ones. In addition, we entertain a mythology of creation, in which it is believed that artistic genius, an original talent, or a powerful intellect can leap beyond the confines of its own time and place in order to put before the world a new work. It would be pointless to deny that such ideas as these carry some truth. Nevertheless the possibilities for work present in the culture to a great and original mind are never unlimited, just as it is also true that a great talent has a very healthy respect for what others have done before it and for what the field already contains. The work of predecessors, the institutional life of a scholarly field, the collective nature of any learned enterprise: these, to say nothing of economic and social circumstances, tend to diminish the effects of the individual scholar's production. A field like Orientalism has a cumulative and corporate identity, one that is particularly strong given its associations with traditional learning (the classics, the Bible, philology), public institutions (governments, trading companies, geographical societies, universities), and generically determined writing (travel books, books of exploration, fantasy, exotic description). The result for Orientalism has been a sort of consensus: certain things, certain types of statement, certain types of work have seemed for the Orientalist correct. He has built his work and research upon them, and they in turn have pressed hard upon new writers and scholars. Orientalism can thus be regarded as a manner of regularized (or Orientalized) writing, vision, and study, dominated by imperatives, perspectives, and ideological biases ostensibly suited to the Orient. The Orient is taught, researched, administered, and pronounced upon in certain discrete ways.

The Orient that appears in Orientalism, then, is a system of representations framed by a whole set of forces that brought the Orient into Western learning, Western consciousness, and later, Western empire. If this definition of Orientalism seems more political than not, that is simply because I think Orientalism was itself a product of certain political forces and activities. Orientalism is a school of interpretation whose material happens to be the Orient, its civilizations, peoples, and localities. Its objective discoveries—the work of innumerable devoted scholars who edited texts and translated them, codified grammars, wrote dictionaries, reconstructed dead epochs, produced positivistically verifiable learning—are and always have been conditioned by the fact that its truths, like any truths delivered by language, are embodied in language, and what is the truth of language, Nietzsche once said, but a mobile army of metaphors, metonyms, and anthropomorphisms—in short, a sum of human relations, which have been enhanced, transposed, and embellished poetically and rhetorically, and which after long use seem firm, canonical, and obligatory to a people: truths are illusions about which one has forgotten that this is what they are.[1]

Perhaps such a view as Nietzsche's will strike us as too nihilistic, but at least it will draw attention to the fact that so far as it existed in the West's awareness, the Orient was a word which later accrued to it a wide field of meanings, associations, and connotations, and that these did not necessarily refer to the real Orient but to the field surrounding the word.

Thus Orientalism is not only a positive doctrine about the Orient that exists at any one time in the West; it is also an influential academic tradition (when one refers to an academic specialist who is called an Orientalist), as well as an area of concern defined by travelers, commercial enterprises, governments, military expeditions, readers of novels and accounts of exotic adventure, natural historians, and pilgrims to whom the Orient is a specific kind of knowledge about specific places, peoples, and civilizations. For the Orient idioms became frequent, and these idioms took firm hold in European discourse. Beneath the idioms there was a layer of doctrine about the Orient; this doctrine was fashioned out of the experiences of many Europeans, all of them converging upon such essential aspects of the Orient as the Oriental character, Oriental despotism, Oriental sensuality, and the like. For any European during the nineteenth century—and I think one can say this almost without qualification—Orientalism was such a system of truths, truths in Nietzsche's sense of the word. It is therefore correct that every European, in what he could say about the Orient, was consequently a racist, an imperialist, and almost totally ethnocentric. Some of the immediate sting will be taken out of these labels if we recall additionally that human societies, at least the more advanced cultures, have rarely offered the individual anything but imperialism, racism, and ethnocentrism for dealing with "other" cultures. So Orientalism aided and was aided by general cultural pressures that tended to make more rigid the sense of difference between the European and Asiatic parts of the world. My contention is that Orientalism is fundamentally a political doctrine willed over the Orient because the Orient was weaker than the West, which elided the Orient's difference with its weakness.

[...] The very presence of a "field" such as Orientalism, with no corresponding equivalent in the Orient itself, suggests the relative strength of Orient and Occident. A vast number of pages on the Orient exist, and they of course signify a degree and quantity of interaction with the Orient that are quite formidable; but the crucial index of Western strength is that there is no possibility of comparing the movement of Westerners eastwards (since the end of the eighteenth century) with the movement of Easterners westwards. Leaving aside the fact that Western armies, consular corps, merchants, and scientific and archaeological expeditions were always going East, the number of travelers from the Islamic East to Europe between 1800 and 1900 is minuscule when compared with the number in the other direction.[2] Moreover, the Eastern travelers in the West were there to learn from and to gape at an advanced culture; the purposes of the Western travelers in the Orient were, as we have seen, of quite a different order. In addition, it has been estimated that around 60,000 books dealing with the Near Orient were written between 1800 and 1950; there is no remotely comparable figure for Oriental books about the West. As a cultural apparatus Orientalism is all aggression, activity, judgment, will-to-truth, and knowledge. The Orient existed for the West, or so it seemed to countless Orientalists, whose attitude to what they worked on was either paternalistic or candidly condescending—unless, of course, they were antiquarians, in which case the "classical" Orient was a credit to *them* and not to the lamentable modern Orient. And then, beefing up the Western scholars' work, there wen numerous agencies and institutions with no parallels in Oriental society.

Such an imbalance between East and West is obviously a function of changing historical patterns. During its political and military heyday from the eighth century to the sixteenth, Islam dominated both East and West. Then the center of power shifted westwards, and now in the late twentieth century it seems to be directing itself back towards the East again. My account of nineteenth-century Orientalism in Chapter Two stopped at a particularly charged period in the latter part of the century, when the often dilatory, abstract, and projective aspects of Orientalism were about to take on a new sense of worldly mission in the service of formal colonialism. It is this project and this moment that I want now to describe, especially since it will furnish us with some important background for the twentieth-century crises of Orientalism and the resurgence of political and cultural strength in the East.

On several occasions I have alluded to the connections between Orientalism as a body of ideas, beliefs, clichés, or learning about the East, and other schools of thought at large in the culture. Now one of the important developments in nineteenth-century Orientalism was the distillation of essential ideas about the Orient—its sensuality, its tendency to despotism, its aberrant mentality, its habits of inaccuracy, its backwardness—into a separate and unchallenged coherence; thus for a writer to use the word *Oriental* was a reference for the reader sufficient to identify a specific body of information about the Orient. This information seemed to be morally neutral and objectively valid; it seemed to have an epistemological status equal to that of historical chronology or geographical location. In its most basic form, then, Oriental material could not really be violated by anyone's discoveries, nor did it seem ever to be revaluated completely. Instead, the work of various nineteenth-century scholars and of imaginative writers made this essential body of knowledge more clear, more detailed, more substantial—and more distinct from "Occidentalism." Yet Orientalist ideas could enter into alliance with general philosophical theories (such as those about the history of mankind and civilization) and diffuse world-hypotheses, as philosophers sometimes call them; and in many ways the professional contributors to Oriental knowledge were anxious to couch their formulations and ideas, their scholarly work, their considered contemporary observations, in language and terminology whose cultural validity derived from other sciences and systems of thought.

The distinction I am making is really between an almost unconscious (and certainly an untouchable) positivity, which I shall call *latent* Orientalism, and the various stated views about Oriental society, languages, literatures, history, sociology, and so forth, which I shall call *manifest* Orientalism. Whatever change occurs in knowledge of the Orient is found almost exclusively in manifest Orientalism; the unanimity, stability, and durability of latent Orientalism are more or less constant. In the nineteenth-century writers I analyzed in Chapter Two, the differences in their ideas about the Orient can be characterized as exclusively manifest differences, differences in form and personal style, rarely in basic content. Every one of them kept intact the separateness of the Orient, its eccentricity, its backwardness, its silent indifference, its feminine penetrability, its supine malleability; this is why every writer on the Orient, from Renan to Marx (ideologically speaking), or from the most rigorous scholars (Lane and Sacy) to the most powerful imaginations (Flaubert and Nerval), saw the

Orient as a locale requiring Western attention, reconstruction, even redemption. The Orient existed as a place isolated from the mainstream of European progress in the sciences, arts, and commerce. Thus whatever good or bad values were imputed to the Orient appeared to be functions of some highly specialized Western interest in the Orient. This was the situation from about the 1870s on through the early part of the twentieth century—but let me give some examples that illustrate what I mean.

Theses of Oriental backwardness, degeneracy, and inequality with the West most easily associated themselves early in the nineteenth century with ideas about the biological bases of racial inequality. Thus the racial classifications found in Cuvier's *Le règne animal*, Gobineau's *Essai sur l'inégalité des races humaines*, and Robert Knox's *The Dark Races of Man* found a willing partner in latent Orientalism. To these ideas was added second-order Darwinism, which seemed to accentuate the "scientific" validity of the division of races into advanced and backward, or European-Aryan and Oriental-African. Thus the whole question of imperialism, as it was debated in the late nineteenth century by pro-imperialists and anti-imperialists alike, carried forward the binary typology of advanced and backward (or subject) races, cultures, and societies. John Westlake's *Chapters on the Principles of International Law* (1894) argues, for example, that regions of the earth designated as "uncivilized" (a word carrying the freight of Orientalist assumptions, among others) ought to be annexed or occupied by advanced powers. Similarly, the ideas of such writers as Carl Peters, Leopold de Saussure, and Charles Temple draw on the advanced/backward binarism[3] so centrally advocated in late-nineteenth-century Orientalism.

Along with all other peoples variously designated as backward, degenerate, uncivilized, and retarded, the Orientals were viewed in a framework constructed out of biological determinism and moral-political admonishment. The Oriental was linked thus to elements in Western society (delinquents, the insane, women, the poor) having in common an identity best described as lamentably alien. Orientals were rarely seen or looked at; they were seen through, analyzed not as citizens, or even people, but as problems to be solved or confined or—as the colonial powers openly coveted their territory—taken over. The point is that the very designation of something as Oriental involved an already pronounced evaluative judgment, and in the case of the peoples inhabiting the decayed Ottoman Empire, an implicit program of action. Since the Oriental was a member of a subject race, he had to be subjected: it was that simple. The *locus classicus* for such judgment and action is to be found in Gustave Le Bon's *Les lois psychologiques de l'évolution des peuples* (1894).

But there were other uses for latent Orientalism. If that group of ideas allowed one to separate Orientals from advanced, civilizing powers, and if the "classical" Orient served to justify both the Orientalist and his disregard of modern Orientals, latent Orientalism also encouraged a peculiarly (not to say invidiously) male conception of the world. I have already referred to this in passing during my discussion of Renan. The Oriental male was considered in isolation from the total community in which he lived and which many Orientalists, following Lane, have viewed with something resembling contempt and fear. Orientalism itself, furthermore, was an exclusively male province; like so many professional guilds during the modern period, it viewed itself and its subject matter with sexist blinders. This is especially evident in the writing of travelers and novelists: women are usually the creatures of a male power-fantasy. They express unlimited sensuality, they are more or less stupid, and above all they are willing. Flaubert's Kuchuk Hanem is the prototype of such caricatures, which were common enough in pornographic novels (e.g., Pierre Louys's *Aphrodite*) whose novelty draws on the Orient for their interest. Moreover the male conception of the world, in its effect upon the practicing Orientalist, tends to be static, frozen, fixed eternally. The very possibility of development, transformation, human movement—in the deepest sense of the word—is denied the Orient and the Oriental. As a known and ultimately an immobilized or unproductive quality, they come to be identified with a bad sort of eternality: hence, when the Orient is being approved, such phrases as "the wisdom of the East."

[. . .]

What these widely diffused notions of the Orient depended on was the almost total absence in contemporary Western culture of the Orient as a genuinely felt and experienced force. For a number of evident reasons the Orient was always in the position both of outsider and of incorporated weak partner for the West. To the extent that Western scholars were aware of contemporary Orientals or Oriental movements of thought and culture, these were perceived either as silent shadows to be animated by the Orientalist, brought into reality by him, or as a kind of cultural and intellectual proletariat useful for the Orientalist's grander interpretative activity, necessary for his performance as superior judge, learned man, powerful cultural will. I mean to say that in discussions of the Orient, the Orient is all absence, whereas one feels the Orientalist and what he says as presence; yet we must not forget that the Orientalist's presence is enabled by the Orient's effective absence. This fact of substitution and displacement, as we must call it, clearly places on the Orientalist himself a certain pressure to reduce the Orient in his work, even after he has devoted a good deal of time to elucidating and exposing it.

[. . .]

I spoke earlier of incorporation and assimilation of the Orient, as these activities were practiced by writers as different from each other as Dante and d'Herbelot. Clearly there is a difference between those efforts and what, by the end of the nineteenth century, had become a truly formidable European cultural, political, and material enterprise. The nineteenth-century colonial "scramble for Africa" was by no means limited to Africa, of course. Neither was the penetration of the Orient entirely a sudden, dramatic after-thought following years of scholarly study of Asia. What we must reckon with is a long and slow process of appropriation by which Europe, or the European awareness of the Orient, transformed itself from being textual and contemplative into being administrative, economic, and even military. The fundamental change was a spatial and geographical one, or rather it was a change in the quality of geographical and spatial apprehension so far as the Orient was concerned. The centuries-old designation of geographical space to the east of Europe as "Oriental" was partly political, partly doctrinal, and partly imaginative; it implied no necessary connection between actual experience of the Orient and knowledge of what is Oriental, and certainly Dante and d'Herbelot made no claims about their Oriental ideas except that they were corroborated by a long *learned* (and not existential) tradition. But when Lane, Renan, Burton, and the many hundreds of nineteenth-century European travelers and scholars discuss the Orient, we can immediately note a far more intimate and even proprietary attitude towards the Orient and things Oriental. In the classical and often temporally remote form in which it was reconstructed by the Orientalist, in the precisely actual form in which the modern Orient was lived in, studied, or imagined, the *geographical space* of the Orient was penetrated, worked over, taken hold of. The cumulative effect of decades of so sovereign a Western handling turned the Orient from alien into colonial space. What was important in the latter nineteenth century was not *whether* the West had penetrated and possessed the Orient, but rather *how* the British and French felt that they had done it.

[. . .]

There were two principal methods by which Orientalism delivered the Orient to the West in the early twentieth century. One was by means of the disseminative capacities of modern learning, its diffusive apparatus in the learned professions, the universities, the professional societies, the explorational and geographical organizations, the publishing industry. All these, as we have seen, built upon the prestigious authority of the pioneering scholars, travelers, and poets, whose cumulative vision had shaped a quintessential Orient; the doctrinal—or doxological—manifestation of such an Orient is what I have been calling here latent Orientalism. So far as anyone wishing to make a statement of any consequence about the Orient was concerned, latent Orientalism supplied him with an enunciative capacity that could be used, or rather mobilized, and turned into sensible discourse for the concrete occasion at hand. Thus when Balfour spoke about the Oriental to the House of Commons in 1910, he must surely have had in mind those enunciative capacities in the current and acceptably rational language of his time, by which something called an "Oriental" could be named and talked about without danger of too much obscurity. But like all enunciative capacities and the discourses they enable, latent Orientalism was profoundly conservative—dedicated, that is, to its self-preservation. Transmitted from one generation to another, it was a part of the culture, as much a language about a part of reality as geometry or physics. Orientalism staked its existence, not upon its openness, its receptivity to the Orient, but rather on its internal, repetitious consistency about its constitutive will-to-power over the Orient. In such a way Orientalism was able to survive revolutions, world wars, and the literal dismemberment of empires.

The second method by which Orientalism delivered the Orient to the West was the result of an important convergence. For decades the Orientalists had spoken about the Orient, they had translated texts, they had explained civilizations, religions, dynasties, cultures, mentalities—as academic objects, screened off from Europe by virtue of their inimitable foreignness. The Orientalist was an expert, like Renan or Lane, whose job in society was to interpret the Orient for his compatriots. The relation between Orientalist and Orient was essentially hermeneutical: standing before a distant, barely intelligible civilization or cultural monument, the Orientalist scholar reduced the obscurity by translating, sympathetically portraying, inwardly grasping the hard-to-reach object. Yet the Orientalist remained outside the Orient, which, however much it was made to appear intelligible, remained beyond the Occident. This cultural, temporal, and geographical distance was expressed in metaphors of depth, secrecy, and sexual promise: phrases like "the veils of an Eastern bride" or "the inscrutable Orient" passed into the common language.

Yet the distance between Orient and Occident was, almost paradoxically, in the process of being reduced throughout the nineteenth century. As the commercial, political, and other existential encounters between East and West increased (in ways we have been discussing all along), a tension developed between the dogmas of latent Orientalism, with its support in studies of the "classical" Orient, and the descriptions of a present, modern, manifest Orient articulated by travelers, pilgrims, statesmen, and the like. At some moment impossible to determine precisely, the tension caused a convergence of the two types of Orientalism. Probably—and this is only a speculation—the convergence occurred when Orientalists, beginning with Sacy, undertook to advise governments on what the modern Orient was all about. Here the role of the specially trained and equipped expert took on an added dimension: the Orientalist could be regarded as the special agent of Western power as it attempted policy vis-à-vis the Orient. Every learned (and not so learned) European traveler in the Orient felt himself to be a representative Westerner who had gotten beneath the films of obscurity. This is obviously true of Burton, Lane, Doughty, Flaubert, and the other major figures I have been discussing.

The discoveries of Westerners about the manifest and modern Orient acquired a pressing urgency as Western territorial acquisition in the Orient increased. Thus what the scholarly Orientalist defined as the "essential" Orient was sometimes contradicted, but in many cases was confirmed, when the Orient became an actual administrative obligation. Certainly Cromer's theories about the Oriental—theories acquired from the traditional Orientalist archive—were vindicated plentifully as he ruled millions of Orientals in actual fact. This was no less true of the French experience in Syria, North Africa, and elsewhere in the French colonies, such as they were. But at no time did the convergence between latent Orientalist doctrine and manifest Orientalist experience occur more dramatically than when, as a result of World War I, Asiatic Turkey was being surveyed by Britain and France for its dismemberment. There, laid out on an operating table for surgery, was the Sick Man of Europe, revealed in all his weakness, characteristics, and topographical outline.

The Orientalist, with his special knowledge, played an inestimably important part in this surgery. Already there had been intimations of his crucial role as a kind of secret agent *inside* the Orient when the British scholar Edward Henry Palmer was sent to the Sinai in 1882 to gauge anti-British sentiment and its possible enlistment on behalf of the Arabi revolt. Palmer was killed in the process, but he was only the most unsuccessful of the many who performed similar services for the Empire, now a serious and exacting business entrusted in part to the regional "expert." Not for nothing was another Orientalist, D. G. Hogarth, author of the famous account of the exploration of Arabia aptly titled *The Penetration of Arabia* (1904),[4] made the head of the Arab Bureau in Cairo during World War I. And neither was it by accident that men and women like Gertrude Bell, T. E. Lawrence, and St. John Philby, Oriental experts all, posted to the Orient as agents of empire, friends of the Orient, formulators of policy alternatives because of their intimate and expert knowledge of the Orient and of Orientals. They formed a "band"—as Lawrence called it once—bound together by contradictory notions and personal similarities: great individuality, sympathy and intuitive identification with the Orient, a jealously preserved sense of personal mission in the Orient, cultivated eccentricity, a final disapproval of the Orient. For them all the Orient was their direct, peculiar experience of it. In them Orientalism and an effective praxis for handling the Orient received their final European form, before the Empire disappeared and passed its legacy to other candidates for the role of dominant power.

[...]

NOTES

1. Friedrich Nietzsche, "On Truth and Lie in an Extra-Moral Sense," in *The Portable Nietzsche*, ed. and trans. Walter Kaufmann (New York: Viking Press, 1954), 46–47.

2. The number of Arab travelers to the West is estimated and considered by Ibrahim Abu-Lughod in Ibrahim Abu-Lughod, *Arab Rediscovery of Europe: A Study in Cultural Encounters* (Princeton, NJ: Princeton University Press, 1963), 75–76 and passim.

3. See Philip D. Curtin, ed., *Imperialism: The Documentary History of Western Civilization* (New York: Walker & Co., 1972), 73–105.

4. David George Hogarth, *The Penetration of Arabia: A Record of the Development of Western Knowledge Concerning the Arabian Peninsula* (New York: Frederick A. Stokes, 1904). There is a good recent book on the same subject: Robin Bidwell, *Travelers in Arabia* (London: Paul Hamlyn, 1976).

BIBLIOGRAPHY

Abu-Lughod, Ibrahim. *Arab Rediscovery of Europe: A Study in Cultural Encounters.* Princeton, NJ: Princeton University Press, 1963.

Bidwell, Robin. *Travelers in Arabia.* London: Paul Hamlyn, 1976.

Curtin, Philip D., ed. *Imperialism: The Documentary History of Western.* New York: Walker & Co., 1972.

Hogarth, David George. *The Penetration of Arabia: A Record of the Development of Western Knowledge Concerning the Arabian Peninsula.* New York: Frederick A. Stokes, 1904.

Nietzsche, Friedrich. "On Truth and Lie in an Extra-Moral Sense." In *The Portable Nietzsche.* Edited and translated by Walter Kaufmann, 42–47. New York: Viking Press, 1954.

15

WHAT IS A DISPOSITIF?

Gilles Deleuze

Foucault's philosophy is often presented as an analysis of concrete social apparatuses [*dispositifs*]. But what is a dispositif? In the first instance it is a tangle, a multilinear ensemble. It is composed of lines, each having a different nature. And the lines in the apparatus do not outline or surround systems which are each homogeneous in their own right, object, subject, language, and so on, but follow directions, trace balances which are always off balance, now drawing together and then distancing themselves from one another. Each line is broken and subject to *changes in direction*, bifurcating and forked, and subject to *drifting*. Visible objects, affirmations which can be formulated, forces exercised and subjects in position are like vectors and tensors. Thus the three major aspects which Foucault successively distinguishes, Knowledge, Power and Subjectivity are by no means contours given once and for all, but series of variables which supplant one another. It is always in a crisis that Foucault discovers new dimensions, new lines. Great thinkers are somewhat seismic; they do not evolve but proceed by means of crisis, in fits and starts. Thinking in terms of moving lines was the process put forward by Herman Melville, and this involved fishing lines and lines of descent which could be dangerous, even fatal. Foucault talked of lines of sedimentation but also of lines of 'breakage' and of 'fracture.' Untangling these lines within a social apparatus is, in each case, like drawing up a map, doing cartography, surveying unknown landscapes, and this is what he calls 'working on the ground.' One has to position oneself on these lines themselves, these lines which do not just make up the social apparatus but run through it and pull at it, from North to South, from East to West, or diagonally.

The first two dimensions of a social apparatus—or those to which Foucault draws our attention in the first instance—are curves of visibility and curves of enunciation. The apparatuses are like Raymond Roussel's machines, such as Foucault analyses them; they are machines which make one see and speak. Visibility cannot be traced back to a general source of light which could be said to fall upon pre-existing objects: it is made of lines of light which form variable shapes inseparable from the apparatus in question. Each apparatus has its way of structuring light, the way in which it falls, blurs and disperses, distributing the visible and the invisible, giving birth to objects which are dependent on it for their existence, and causing them to disappear. This is the case not only for painting but also for architecture: like the 'prison apparatus' as an optical machine, used for seeing without being seen. If apparatuses have a historical nature, this is to be found in regimes of light, but also in regimes of enunciation. Affirmations [*énoncés*] in turn can be traced back to lines of enunciation over which the differential positions of their elements are distributed; and, if the curves are themselves affirmations [*énoncés*], this is because *énoncés* are curves which distribute variables and because a science, at a given moment, or a literary genre, or a state of law, or a social movement, can be defined precisely by the regimes of enunciations to which they give rise. They are neither subjects nor objects, but regimes which must be defined from the point of view of the visible and from the point of view of that which can be enunciated, with the drifting, transformations and mutations which this will imply. And in every apparatus the lines break through thresholds, according to which they might have been seen as aesthetic, scientific, political, and so on.

Thirdly, a social apparatus consists of lines of force. It could be said that they proceed from one unique point to another in the preceding lines; in a way they 'rectify' the preceding curves, they draw tangents, fill in the space between one line and another, acting as go-betweens between seeing and saying and vice versa, acting as arrows which continually cross between words and things, constantly waging battle between them. The line of force comes about 'in any relationship between one point and another,' and passes through every area in the apparatus. Though invisible and unsayable, it is closely knitted in with the others, yet separable. It is these lines that Foucault is interested in tracing, and he finds their trajectory in Roussel, Brisset, and in the painters Magritte and Rebeyrolle. This is the 'dimension of power,' and power is the third dimension of space, internal to the apparatus, variable to the apparatus. It is formed, like power, out of knowledge [*savoir*].

Finally, Foucault discovered lines of subjectification. This new dimension has already given rise to misunderstandings, the reasons for which are hard to see in precise terms.

More than anything else, the discovery of this new dimension arose out of a crisis in Foucault's thought, as if it had become necessary for him to redraw the map of social apparatuses, to find for them a new orientation in order to stop them from becoming locked into unbreakable lines of force which would impose definitive contours. Leibniz gave exemplary expression to this state of crisis which sets thought on the move again when one thinks a resolution has been found; we thought we were in port, but we were cast back out into the open sea. Foucault, for his part, was concerned that the social apparatuses which he was analyzing should not be circumscribed by an enveloping line, unless other vectors could be seen as passing above or below it. Maybe he is using the term 'breaking the line' in the sense of 'bypassing it.' This bypassing of the line of forces is what happens when it turns on itself, meanders, grows obscure and goes underground—or rather when the force, instead of entering into a linear relationship with another force, turns back on itself, works on itself or affects itself. This dimension of the Self is by no means a pre-existing determination which one finds ready-made. Here again, a line of subjectification is a process, a production of subjectivity in a social apparatus: it has to be made, inasmuch as the apparatus allows it to come into being or makes it possible. It is a line of escape. It escapes preceding lines and escapes *from* itself. The Self is neither knowledge nor power. It is a process of individuation which bears on groups and on people, and is subtracted from the power relations which are established as constituting forms of knowledge [*savoirs*]: a sort of surplus-value. It is not certain that all social apparatuses comprise these.

Foucault designates the Athenian city as the first place in which subjectification was invented: this is because it is, according to the original definition which he gives to it, the city which invented the line of forces which runs through the *rivalry of free men*. Now, from this line which makes it possible for one free man to command others, a very different one branches off which has it that a man who commands free men has to be seen as a master of himself. It is these optional rules of self-mastery which constitute subjectification, and this is autonomous, even if it is subsequently called upon to inspire new powers. One might wonder if these lines of subjectification do not form the extreme boundary of a social apparatus, and if perhaps they sketch the movement of one apparatus to another, in this sense preparing for 'lines of fracture.' And lines of subjectification have no general formula, any more than the other lines. Though cruelly interrupted, Foucault's research would have shown that processes of subjectification could take on quite different forms from the Greek mode: for example in Christian social apparatuses in modern societies, and so on. Can one not think of apparatuses where subjectification does not come about through aristocratic life or the aestheticised existence of the free man, but through the marginalised existence of the 'outsider'? Thus the Sinologist Tokeï explains how the liberated slave somehow lost his social status and found himself thrown back on an isolated, lamenting, *elegiac* existence, out of which he was to shape new forms of power and knowledge. The study of the variations in the process of subjectification seems to be one of the fundamental tasks which Foucault left to those who would follow him. I believe that there is great fecundity in this form of research, and that current projects concerning a history of private life only partially cover it. The creators of subjectivity can sometimes be the nobles, those who, according to Nietzsche, say 'we the good . . . ,' but in different conditions they are the excluded, the bad, the sinners, the hermits, or monastic communities, or heretics: a whole typology of subjective formations in a moving apparatus. And everywhere there are mix-ups to sort out: the productions of subjectivity escape from the powers and the forms of knowledge [*savoirs*] of one social apparatus in order to be reinserted in another, in forms which are yet to come into being.

These apparatuses, then, are composed of the following elements: lines of visibility and enunciation, lines of force, lines of subjectification, lines of splitting, breakage, fracture, all of which criss-cross and mingle together, some lines reproducing or giving rise to others, by means of variations or even changes in the way they are grouped. Two important consequences arise for a philosophy of social apparatuses. The first of these is the repudiation of universals. The universal, in fact, explains nothing; it is the universal which needs to be explained. All the lines are lines of variation, which do not even have constant co-ordinates. The One, the All, the True, the object, the subject are not universals, but singular processes—of unification, totalisation, verification, objectivation, subjectification—present in the given apparatus. Also each apparatus is a multiplicity in which operate processes of this nature still in formation, distinct from those operating in another. It is in this sense that Foucault's philosophy can be referred to as pragmatism, functionalism, positivism, pluralism. Perhaps it is Reason which poses the greatest problem because the processes of rationalisation can operate on segments or on regions of all lines under consideration. Foucault pays homage to Nietzsche regarding the historical nature of reason; and he suggests the importance of epistemological research on the different forms of rationality in knowledge [*savoir*] (Koyré, Bachelard, Canguilhem) and of sociopolitical research into modes of rationality in power (Max Weber). Perhaps he was reserving the third line for himself: the study of types of 'reasonableness' in subjects he was dealing with. But what he essentially refuses is the identification of this process with Reason *par excellence*. He challenges any attempt to restore universals in reflection, communication or consensus.

One might say in this respect that his relations with the Frankfurt School and the successors of this school were a series of misunderstandings for which he was not responsible. And, just as he does not admit of a universality in a founding subject or in Reason *par excellence* which would make it possible to judge social apparatuses he also does not admit of universals of catastrophe in which reason becomes alienated and collapses once and for all. As Foucault said to Gérard Raulet, there is not a bifurcation in reason, yet reason is forever bifurcating; there are as many bifurcations and branchings as there are foundations, as many collapses as there are constructions following the breaks brought about by the apparatus, and 'there is no sense in the propositions according to which reason is a long narrative which has now come to an end.' From this point of view, the question raised in objection to Foucault—the question as to how the relative value of a social apparatus can be assessed if one cannot evoke transcendental values by way of universal co-ordinates—is a question which leads us backwards and which, in itself, also risks meaninglessness. Does this mean that all social apparatuses are equally valid (nihilism)? It has been a long while since thinkers like Spinoza and Nietzsche first began to show that modes of existence have to be assessed according to immanent criteria, according to their content of 'possibilities,' liberty or creativity, without any appeal to transcendental values. Foucault even makes allusion to 'aesthetic' criteria, which are understood as criteria for life and replace on each occasion the claims of transcendental judgement with an immanent evaluation. When we read Foucault's last books, we have to do our best to understand the programme which he is placing in front of his readers. Could this be the intrinsic aesthetic of modes of existence as the ultimate dimension of social apparatuses?

The second consequence of a philosophy of social apparatuses is a change in orientation which turns one's interest away from the Eternal and towards the new. The new is not supposed to mean the same as the fashionable but, on the contrary, the variable creativity which arises out of social apparatuses. This fits in with the question which began to be asked in the twentieth century as to how the production of something new in the world might be possible. It is true that, throughout his theory of enunciation, Foucault explicitly impugns the 'originality' of an *énoncé* as being something which is of little relevance and interest. All he wishes to consider is the 'regularity' of *énoncés*. But what he understands by regularity is the sweep of the curve which passes through singular points or the differential values of the ensemble of enunciations (in the same way that he defines power relations by means of the distribution of singular elements in a social field). When he challenges the originality of an *énoncé*, he means that a contradiction which might arise between two *énoncés* is not enough to distinguish between them, or to mark the newness of one with regard to the other. What counts is the newness of the regime itself in which the enunciation is made, given that such a regime is capable of containing contradictory *énoncés*. One might, for example, ask what regime of *énoncés* appeared with the social apparatus of the French Revolution, or the Bolshevik Revolution: it is the newness of the regime that counts, not the newness of the *énoncé*. Each apparatus is thus defined in terms of its newness content and its creativity content, this marking at the same time its ability to transform itself, or indeed to break down in favour of a future apparatus, unless it concentrates its strength along its harder, more rigid, or more solid lines. Inasmuch as they escape the dimensions of power and knowledge, the lines of subjectification seem particularly capable of tracing paths of creation, which are continually aborting, but then restarting, in a modified way, until the former apparatus is broken. Foucault's as yet unpublished studies on various Christian processes probably open a number of different avenues in this respect. Yet it would not be right to think that the production of subjectivity is the territory only of religion: anti-religious struggles are also creative, just as regimes of light, enunciation and domination pass through different domains. Modern forms of subjectivation no longer resemble those of Greece any more than they do those of Christianity, and the same goes for their light, their enunciations and their forms of power.

We belong to social apparatuses and act within them. The newness of an apparatus in relation to those which have gone before is what we call its actuality, our actuality. The new is the current. The current is not what we are but rather what we are in the process of becoming—that is the Other, our becoming-other. In each apparatus it is necessary to distinguish what we are (what we are already no longer), and what we are in the process of becoming: *the historical part and the current part.* History is the archive, the drawing of what we are and what we are ceasing to be, whilst the current is the sketch of what we are becoming. In the same way, history or the archive is what still separates us from ourselves, whilst the current is the Other with which we are already coinciding. It is sometimes thought that Foucault paints a picture of modern societies in terms of disciplinary social apparatuses, in opposition to older social apparatuses in which sovereignty is the key concept. Yet this is by no means the case: the disciplines which Foucault describes are the history of what we gradually cease to be, and our present-day reality takes on the form of dispositions of overt and continuous *control* in a way which is very different from recent closed disciplines. Foucault agrees with Burroughs, who claims that our future will be controlled rather than disciplined. The question is not whether this is worse. For to ask this would be to make appeal to ways of producing subjectivity which would be capable of resisting this new form of domination, ways which would be very different from those which were formerly exercised against disciplines. Would this mean a new light, new enunciations, new power, new forms of subjectification? In each apparatus we have to untangle the lines of the recent past and those of the near future: that which belongs to the archive and that which belongs to the present; that which belongs to history and that which belongs to the process of becoming; *that which belongs to the analytic and that which belongs to the diagnostic*. If Foucault is a great philosopher, this is because he used history for the sake of something beyond it: as Nietzsche said: acting against time, and thus on time, for the sake of a time one hopes will come. For what appears to be the present-day or the new according to Foucault is what Nietzsche called the unseasonable, the uncontemporary, the becoming which bifurcates with history, the diagnostic which relays analysis with other roads. This is not to predict but to be attentive to the unknown which knocks at the door. Nothing shows this better than a fundamental passage in *L'Archéologie du savoir*, which is valid for the rest of Foucault's work:

As such the analysis of the archive comprises a privileged region which is at the same time close to us, but different from our present; it is the border of the time which surrounds our present, jutting over it and describing it by means of its otherness; it is that which is outside us and delimits us. To describe the archive is to set out its possibilities (and the mastery of its possibilities) on the basis of forms of discourse which have just recently ceased to be our own; the threshold of its existence is established by the break which separates us from what we can no longer say, and from that which falls outside our discursive practices; it begins with what is outside our own language [*langage*], its locus being its distance from our own discursive practices. In this sense it becomes valid as a diagnostic for us. This is not because it makes it possible for us to paint a picture of our distinctive traits and to sketch in advance what we will look like in the future. But it deprives us of our continuities; it dissolves this temporal identity in which we like to look at ourselves in order to conjure with breaks in history; it breaks the thread of transcendental teleologies; and at the point where anthropological thought questions the being of man or his subjectivity, it vividly draws attention to the other, to the outside. Understood in this way, the diagnostic does not establish the facts of our identity by means of the interplay of distinctions. It establishes that we are difference, that our reason is the difference of forms of discourse, our history is the difference of times, that our selves are the difference of masks.

The different lines of an apparatus divide into two groups: lines of stratification or sedimentation, and lines leading to the present day or creativity. The last consequence of this method concerns the whole of Foucault's work. In most of his books he specifies a precise archive, with extremely new historical methods, regarding the General Hospital of the seventeenth century, the clinic of the eighteenth century, the prison of the nineteenth century, the subjectivity of Ancient Greece, and then Christianity. But that is one half of his task. For, through a concern for rigorousness, through a desire not to mix things up and through confidence in his reader, he does not formulate the other half. He formulates this explicitly only in the interviews which take place contemporary with the writing of each of his major books: what can be said nowadays about insanity, prison, sexuality? What new modes of subjectification can be seen to appear today which, indeed, are neither Greek nor Christian? This last question, notably, haunts Foucault till the end (we who are no longer either Greeks or Christians . . .). Right till the end of his life Foucault attached a lot of importance to interviews, in France and even more so abroad, and this was not because he had a taste for them but because in them he was able to trace these lines leading to the present which required a different form of expression from the lines which were drawn together in his major books. These interviews are diagnostics. It is rather like the situation with Nietzsche, whose works are hard to read unless one sees them in the context of the *Nachlass* contemporary with each of them. The complete work of Foucault, such as Defert and Ewald conceive it to be, cannot separate off the books which have made such an impression on all of us from the interviews which lead us towards a future, towards a becoming: the underlying strata and the present day.

16

GENDER TROUBLE

Judith Butler

THE COMPULSORY ORDER OF SEX/GENDER/DESIRE

Although the unproblematic unity of "women" is often invoked to construct a solidarity of identity, a split is introduced in the feminist subject by the distinction between sex and gender. Originally intended to dispute the biology-is-destiny formulation, the distinction between sex and gender serves the argument that whatever biological intractability sex appears to have, gender is culturally constructed: hence, gender is neither the causal result of sex nor as seemingly fixed as sex. The unity of the subject is thus already potentially contested by the distinction that permits of gender as a multiple interpretation of sex.

If gender is the cultural meanings that the sexed body assumes, then a gender cannot be said to follow from a sex in any one way. Taken to its logical limit, the sex/gender distinction suggests a radical discontinuity between sexed bodies and culturally constructed genders. Assuming for the moment the stability of binary sex, it does not follow that the construction of "men" will accrue exclusively to the bodies of males or that "women" will interpret only female bodies. Further, even if the sexes appear to be unproblematically binary in their morphology and constitution (which will become a question), there is no reason to assume that genders ought also to remain as two.[1] The presumption of a binary gender system implicitly retains the belief in a mimetic relation of gender to sex whereby gender mirrors sex or is otherwise restricted by it. When the constructed status of gender is theorized as radically independent of sex, gender itself becomes a free-floating artifice, with the consequence that *man* and *masculine* might just as easily signify a female body as a male one, and *woman* and *feminine* a male body as easily as a female one.

This radical splitting of the gendered subject poses yet another set of problems. Can we refer to a "given" sex or a "given" gender without first inquiring into how sex and/or gender is given, through what means? And what is "sex" anyway? Is it natural, anatomical, chromosomal, or hormonal, and how is a feminist critic to assess the scientific discourses which purport to establish such "facts" for us?[2] Does sex have a history?[3] Does each sex have a different history, or histories? Is there a history of how the duality of sex was established, a genealogy that might expose the binary options as a variable construction? Are the ostensibly natural facts of sex discursively produced by various scientific discourses in the service of other political and social interests? If the immutable character of sex is contested, perhaps this construct called "sex" is as culturally constructed as gender; indeed, perhaps it was always already gender, with the consequence that the distinction between sex and gender turns out to be no distinction at all.[4]

It would make no sense, then, to define gender as the cultural interpretation of sex, if sex itself is a gendered category. Gender ought not to be conceived merely as the cultural inscription of meaning on a pregiven sex (a juridical conception); gender must also designate the very apparatus of production whereby the sexes themselves are established. As a result, gender is not to culture as sex is to nature; gender is also the discursive/cultural means by which "sexed nature" or "a natural sex" is produced and established as "prediscursive," prior to culture, a politically neutral surface *on which* culture acts. [. . .] At this juncture it is already clear that one way the internal stability and binary frame for sex is effectively secured is by casting the duality of sex in a prediscursive domain. This production of sex as the prediscursive ought to be understood as the effect of the apparatus of cultural construction designated by *gender*. How, then, does gender need to be reformulated to encompass the power relations that produce the effect of a prediscursive sex and so conceal that very operation of discursive production?

[. . .]

IDENTITY, SEX, AND THE METAPHYSICS OF SUBSTANCE

[. . .]

Gender can denote a *unity* of experience, of sex, gender, and desire, only when sex can be understood in some sense to necessitate gender—where gender is a psychic and/or cultural designation of the self—and desire—where desire is heterosexual and therefore differentiates itself through an oppositional relation to that other gender it desires. The internal coherence or unity of either gender, man or woman, thereby requires both a stable and oppositional heterosexuality. That institutional heterosexuality both requires and produces the univocity of each of the gendered terms that constitute the limit of gendered possibilities within an oppositional, binary gender system. This conception of gender presupposes not only a causal relation among sex, gender, and desire, but suggests as well that desire reflects or expresses gender and that gender reflects or expresses desire. The metaphysical unity of the three is assumed to be truly known and expressed in a differentiating desire for an oppositional gender—that is, in a form of oppositional heterosexuality. Whether as a naturalistic paradigm which establishes a causal continuity among sex, gender, and desire, or as an authentic-expressive paradigm in which some true self is said to be revealed simultaneously or successively in sex, gender, and desire, here "the old dream of symmetry," as Irigaray has called it, is presupposed, reified, and rationalized.

This rough sketch of gender gives us a clue to understanding the political reasons for the substantializing view of gender. The institution of a compulsory and naturalized heterosexuality requires and regulates gender as a binary relation in which the masculine term is differentiated from a feminine term, and this differentiation is accomplished through the practices of heterosexual desire. The act of differentiating the two oppositional moments of the binary results in a consolidation of each term, the respective internal coherence of sex, gender, and desire.

The strategic displacement of that binary relation and the metaphysics of substance on which it relies presuppose that the categories of female and male, woman and man, are similarly produced within the binary frame. Foucault implicitly subscribes to such an explanation. In the closing chapter of the first volume of *The History of Sexuality* and in his brief but significant introduction to *Herculine Barbin, Being the Recently Discovered Journals of a Nineteenth-Century Hermaphrodite*,[5] Foucault suggests that the category of sex, prior to any categorization of sexual difference, is itself constructed through a historically specific mode of *sexuality*. The tactical production of the discrete and binary categorization of sex conceals the strategic aims of that very apparatus of production by postulating "sex" as "a cause" of sexual experience, behavior, and desire. Foucault's genealogical inquiry exposes this ostensible "cause" as "an effect," the production of a given regime of sexuality that seeks to regulate sexual experience by instating the discrete categories of sex as foundational and causal functions within any discursive account of sexuality.

[. . .]

LANGUAGE, POWER AND THE STRATEGIES OF DISPLACEMENT

[. . .]

The differences between the materialist and Lacanian (and post-Lacanian) positions emerge in a normative quarrel over whether there is a retrievable sexuality either "before" or "outside" the law in the mode of the unconscious or "after" the law as a postgenital sexuality. Paradoxically, the normative trope of polymorphous perversity is understood to characterize both views of alternative sexuality. There is no agreement, however, on the manner of delimiting that "law" or set of "laws." The psychoanalytic critique succeeds in giving an account of the construction of "the subject"—and perhaps also the illusion of substance—within the matrix of normative gender relations. In her existential-materialist mode, Wittig presumes the subject, the person, to have a presocial and pregendered integrity. On the other hand, "the paternal Law" in Lacan, as well as the monologic mastery of phallogocentrism in Irigaray, bear the mark of a monotheistic singularity that is perhaps less unitary and culturally universal than the guiding structuralist assumptions of the account presume.[6]

But the quarrel seems also to turn on the articulation of a temporal trope of a subversive sexuality that flourishes *prior* to the imposition of a law, *after* its overthrow, or during its reign as a constant challenge to its authority. Here it seems wise to reinvoke Foucault who, in claiming that sexuality and power are coextensive, implicitly refutes the postulation of a subversive or emancipatory sexuality which could be free of the law. We can press the argument further by pointing out that "the before" of the law and "the after" are discursively and performatively instituted modes of temporality that are invoked within the terms of a normative framework which asserts that subversion, destabilization, or displacement requires a sexuality that somehow escapes the hegemonic prohibitions on sex. For Foucault, those prohibitions are invariably and inadvertently productive in the sense that "the subject" who is supposed to be founded and produced in and through those prohibitions does not have access to a sexuality that is in some sense "outside," "before," or "after" power itself. Power, rather than the law, encompasses both the juridical (prohibitive and regulatory) and the productive (inadvertently generative) functions of differential relations. Hence, the sexuality that emerges within the matrix of power relations is not a simple replication or copy of the law itself, a uniform repetition of a masculinist economy of identity. The productions swerve from their original purposes and inadvertently mobilize possibilities of "subjects" that do not merely exceed the bounds of cultural intelligibility, but effectively expand the boundaries of what is, in fact, culturally intelligible.

The feminist norm of a postgenital sexuality became the object of significant criticism from feminist theorists of sexuality, some of whom have sought a specifically feminist and/or lesbian appropriation of Foucault. This utopian notion of a sexuality freed from heterosexual constructs, a sexuality beyond "sex," failed to acknowledge the ways in which power relations continue to construct sexuality for women even within the terms of a "liberated" heterosexuality or lesbianism.[7] The same criticism is waged against the notion of a specifically feminine sexual pleasure that is radically differentiated from phallic sexuality. Irigaray's occasional efforts to derive a specific feminine sexuality from a specific female anatomy have been the focus of anti-essentialist arguments for some time.[8] The return to biology as the ground of a specific feminine sexuality or meaning seems to defeat the feminist premise that biology is not destiny. But whether feminine sexuality is articulated here through a discourse of biology for purely strategic reasons,[9] or whether it is, in fact, a feminist return to biological essentialism, the characterization of female sexuality as radically distinct from a phallic organization of sexuality remains problematic. Women who fail either to recognize that sexuality as their own or understand their sexuality as partially constructed within the terms of the phallic economy are potentially written off within the terms of that theory as "male-identified" or "unenlightened." Indeed, it is often unclear within Irigaray's text whether sexuality is culturally constructed, or whether it is only culturally constructed within the terms of the phallus. In other words, is specifically feminine pleasure "outside" of culture as its prehistory or as its utopian future? If so, of what use is such a notion for negotiating the contemporary struggles of sexuality within the terms of its construction?

The pro-sexuality movement within feminist theory and practice has effectively argued that sexuality is always constructed within the terms of discourse and power, where power is partially understood in terms of heterosexual and phallic cultural conventions. The emergence of a sexuality constructed (not determined) in these terms within lesbian, bisexual, and heterosexual contexts is, therefore, *not* a sign of a masculine identification in some reductive sense. It is not the failed project of criticizing phallogocentrism or heterosexual hegemony, as if a political critique could effectively undo the cultural construction of the feminist critic's sexuality. If sexuality is culturally constructed within existing power relations, then the postulation of a normative sexuality that is "before," "outside," or "beyond" power is a cultural impossibility and a politically impracticable dream, one that postpones the concrete and contemporary task of rethinking subversive possibilities for sexuality and identity within the terms of power itself. This critical task presumes, of course, that to operate within the matrix of power is not the same as to replicate uncritically relations of domination. It offers the possibility of a repetition of the law which is not its consolidation, but its displacement. In the place of a "male-identified" sexuality in which "male" serves as the cause and irreducible meaning of that sexuality, we might develop a notion of sexuality constructed in terms of phallic relations of power that replay and redistribute the possibilities of that phallicism precisely through the subversive operation of "identifications" that are, within the power field of sexuality, inevitable. If "identifications," following Jacqueline Rose, can be exposed as phantasmatic, then it must be possible to enact an identification that displays its phantasmatic structure. If there is no radical repudiation of a culturally constructed sexuality, what is left is the question of how to acknowledge and "do" the construction one is invariably in. Are there forms of repetition that do not constitute a simple imitation, reproduction, and, hence, consolidation of the law (the anachronistic notion of "male identification" that ought to be discarded from a feminist vocabulary)? What possibilities of gender configurations exist among the various emergent and occasionally convergent matrices of cultural intelligibility that govern gendered life?

Within the terms of feminist sexual theory, it is clear that the presence of power dynamics within sexuality is in no sense the same as the simple consolidation or augmentation of a heterosexist or phallogocentric power regime. The "presence" of so-called heterosexual conventions within homosexual contexts as well as the proliferation of specifically gay discourses of sexual difference, as in the case of "butch" and "femme" as historical identities of sexual style, cannot be explained as chimerical representations of originally heterosexual identities. And neither can they be understood as the pernicious insistence of heterosexist constructs within gay sexuality and identity. The repetition of heterosexual constructs within sexual cultures both gay and straight may well be the inevitable site of the denaturalization and mobilization of gender categories. The replication of heterosexual constructs in non-heterosexual frames brings into relief the utterly constructed status of the so-called heterosexual original. Thus, gay is to straight *not* as copy is to original, but, rather, as copy is to copy. The parodic repetition of "the original," [. . .] reveals the original to be nothing other than a parody of the *idea* of the natural and the original.[10] Even if heterosexist constructs circulate as the available sites of power/discourse from which to do gender at all, the question remains: What possibilities of recirculation exist? Which possibilities of doing gender repeat and displace through hyperbole, dissonance, internal confusion, and proliferation the very constructs by which they are mobilized?

Consider not only that the ambiguities and incoherences within and among heterosexual, homosexual, and bisexual practices are suppressed and redescribed within the reified framework of the disjunctive and asymmetrical binary of masculine/feminine, but that these cultural configurations of gender confusion operate as sites for intervention, exposure, and displacement of these reifications. In other words, the "unity" of gender is the effect of a regulatory practice that seeks to render gender identity uniform through a compulsory heterosexuality. The force of this practice is, through an exclusionary apparatus of production, to restrict the relative meanings of "heterosexuality," "homosexuality," and "bisexuality" as well as the subversive sites of their convergence and resignification. That the power regimes of heterosexism and phallogocentrism seek to augment themselves through a constant repetition of their logic, their metaphysic, and their naturalized ontologies does not imply that repetition itself ought to be stopped—as if it could be. If repetition is bound to persist as the mechanism of the cultural reproduction of identities, then the crucial question emerges: What kind of subversive repetition might call into question the regulatory practice of identity itself?

If there is no recourse to a "person," a "sex," or a "sexuality" that escapes the matrix of power and discursive relations that effectively produce and regulate the intelligibility of those concepts for us, what constitutes the possibility of effective inversion, subversion, or displacement within the terms of a constructed identity? What possibilities exist *by virtue of* the constructed character of sex and gender? Whereas Foucault is ambiguous about the precise character of the "regulatory practices" that produce the category of sex, and Wittig appears to invest the full responsibility of the construction to sexual reproduction and its instrument, compulsory heterosexuality, yet other discourses converge to produce this categorial fiction for reasons not always clear or consistent with one another. The power relations that infuse the biological sciences are not easily reduced, and the medico-legal alliance emerging in nineteenth-century Europe has spawned categorial fictions that could not be anticipated in advance. The very complexity of the discursive map that constructs gender appears to hold out the promise of an inadvertent and generative convergence of these discursive and regulatory structures. If the regulatory fictions of sex and gender are themselves multiply contested sites of meaning, then the very multiplicity of their construction holds out the possibility of a disruption of their univocal posturing.

Clearly this project does not propose to lay out within traditional philosophical terms an *ontology* of gender whereby the meaning of *being* a woman or a man is elucidated within the terms of phenomenology. The presumption here is that the "being" of gender is *an effect*, an object of a genealogical investigation that maps out the political parameters of its construction in the mode of ontology. To claim that gender is constructed is not to assert its illusoriness or artificiality, where those terms are understood to reside within a binary that counterposes the "real" and the "authentic" as oppositional. As a genealogy of gender ontology, this inquiry seeks to understand the discursive production of the plausibility of that binary relation and to suggest that certain cultural configurations of gender take the place of "the real" and consolidate and augment their hegemony through that felicitous self-naturalization.

If there is something right in Beauvoir's claim that one is not born, but rather *becomes* a woman, it follows that *woman* itself is a term in process, a becoming, a constructing that cannot rightfully be said to originate or to end. As an ongoing discursive practice, it is open to intervention and resignification. Even when gender seems to congeal into the most reified forms, the "congealing" is itself an insistent and insidious practice, sustained and regulated by various social means. It is, for Beauvoir, never possible finally to become a woman, as if there were a *telos* that governs the process of acculturation and construction. Gender is the repeated stylization of the body, a set of repeated acts within a highly rigid regulatory frame that congeal over time to produce the appearance of substance, of a natural sort of being. A political genealogy of gender ontologies, if it is successful, will deconstruct the substantive appearance of gender into its constitutive acts and locate and account for those acts within the compulsory frames set by the various forces that police the social appearance of gender. To expose the contingent acts that create the appearance of a naturalistic necessity, a move which has been a part of cultural critique at least since Marx, is a task that now takes on the added burden of showing how the very notion of the subject, intelligible only through its appearance as gendered, admits of possibilities that have been forcibly foreclosed by the various reifications of gender that have constituted its contingent ontologies.

[. . .]

This text continues, then, as an effort to think through the possibility of subverting and displacing those naturalized and reified notions of gender that support masculine hegemony and heterosexist power, to make gender trouble, not through the strategies that figure a utopian beyond, but through the mobilization, subversive confusion, and proliferation of precisely those constitutive categories that seek to keep gender in its place by posturing as the foundational illusions of identity.

NOTES

1. For an interesting study of the *berdache* and multiple-gender arrangements in Native American cultures, see Walter L. Williams, *The Spirit and the Flesh: Sexual Diversity in American Indian Culture* (Boston: Beacon Press, 1988). See also Sherry B. Ortner and Harriet Whitehead, eds., *Sexual Meanings: The Cultural Construction of Sexuality* (New York: Cambridge University Press, 1981). For a politically sensitive and provocative analysis of the *berdache*, transsexuals, and the contingency of gender dichotomies, see Suzanne J. Kessler and Wendy McKenna, *Gender: An Ethnomethodological Approach* (Chicago: University of Chicago Press, 1978).

2. A great deal of feminist research has been conducted within the fields of biology and the history of science that assess the political interests inherent in the various discriminatory procedures that establish the scientific basis for sex. See Ruth Hubbard and Marian Lowe, eds., *Genes and Gender*, 2 vols. (New York: Gordian Press, 1978–1979); the two issues on feminism and science of *Hypatia: A Journal of Feminist Philosophy* 2, no. 3 (Fall 1987), and 3, no. 1 (Spring 1988), and especially The Biology and Gender Study Group, "The Importance of Feminist Critique for Contemporary Cell Biology" in this last issue (Spring 1988): 61–76; Sandra Harding, *The Science Question in Feminism* (Ithaca: Cornell University Press, 1986); Evelyn Fox Keller, *Reflections on Gender and Science* (New Haven: Yale University Press, 1984); Donna Haraway, "In the Beginning was the Word: The Genesis of Biological Theory," *Signs: Journal of Women in Culture and Society* 6, no. 3 (Spring 1981): 469–481; Donna Haraway, *Primate Visions* (New York: Routledge, 1989); Sandra Harding and Jean F. O'Barr, *Sex and Scientific Inquiry* (Chicago: University of Chicago Press, 1987); Anne Fausto-Sterling, *Myths of Gender: Biological Theories About Women and Men* (New York: Norton, 1979).

3. Clearly Foucault's *History of Sexuality* offers one way to rethink the history of "sex" within a given modern Eurocentric context. For a more detailed consideration, see Thomas Lacqueur and Catherine Gallagher, eds., *The Making of the Modern Body: Sexuality and Society in the 19th Century* (Berkeley: University of California Press, 1987), originally published as an issue of *Representations*, no. 14 (Spring 1986).

4. See my "Variations on Sex and Gender: Beauvoir, Wittig, Foucault," in *Feminism as Critique*, ed. Seyla Benhabib and Drucilla Cornell (Minnesota: University of Minnesota Press, 1987), 128, 42.

5. Michel Foucault, ed., *Herculine Barbin, Being the Recently Discovered Memoirs of a Nineteenth-Century Hermaphrodite*, trans. Richard McDougall (New York: Colophon, 1980), originally published as *Herculine Barbin, dite Alexina B. presenté par Michel Foucault* (Paris: Gallimard, 1978). The French version lacks the introduction supplied by Foucault with the English translation.

6. It is, perhaps, no wonder that the singular structuralist notion of "the Law" clearly resonates with the prohibitive law of the Old Testament. The "paternal law" thus comes under a post-structuralist critique through the understandable route of a French reappropriation of Nietzsche. Nietzsche faults the Judeo-Christian "slave-morality" for conceiving the law in both singular and prohibitive terms. The will-to-power, on the other hand, designates both the productive and multiple possibilities of the law, effectively exposing the notion of "the Law" in its singularity as a fictive and repressive notion.

7. See Gayle Rubin, "Thinking Sex: Notes for a Radical Theory of the Politics of Sexuality," in *Pleasure and Danger*, ed. Carole S. Vance (Boston: Routledge and Kegan Paul, 1984), 267–319. Also see Carole S. Vance, "Pleasure and Danger: Towards a Politics of Sexuality," in *Pleasure and Danger*, 1–28; Alice Echols, "The Taming of the Id: Feminist Sexual Politics, 1968–1983," in *Pleasure and*

Danger, 50–72; Amber Hollibaugh, "Desire for the Future: Radical Hope in Pleasure and Passion," in *Pleasure and Danger*, 401–10. See Amber Hollibaugh and Cherríe Moraga, "What We're Rollin Around in Bed with: Sexual Silences in Feminism," in *Powers of Desire: The Politics of Sexuality*, ed. Ann Snitow, Christine Stansell, and Sharon Thompson (London: Virago, 1984), 394–405 and Alice Echols, "The New Feminism of Yin and Yang," in *Powers of Desire*, 439–59; *Heresies* 3, no. 4 (1981), the "sex issue"; Samois, ed., *Coming to Power* (Berkeley: Samois, 1981); Dierdre English, Amber Hollibaugh, and Gayle Rubin, "Talking Sex: A Conversation on Sexuality and Feminism," *Feminist Review*, no. 11 (1982): 40–52; Barbara T. Kerr and Mirtha N. Quintanales, "The Complexity of Desire: Conversations on Sexuality and Difference," *Conditions* 3, no. 2 (1982): 52–71.

8. Irigaray's perhaps most controversial claim has been that the structure of the vulva as "two lips touching" constitutes the nonunitary and autoerotic pleasure of women prior to the "separation" of this doubleness through the pleasure-depriving act of penetration by the penis. See Luce Irigaray, *Ce sexe qui n'en est pas un* (Paris: Les éditions de Minuit, 1977). Along with Monique Plaza and Christine Delphy, Wittig has argued that Irigaray's valorization of that anatomical specificity is itself an uncritical replication of a reproductive discourse that marks and carves up the female body into artificial "parts" like "vagina," "clitoris," and "vulva." At a lecture at Vassar College, Wittig was asked whether she had a vagina, and she replied that she did not.

9. See a compelling argument for precisely this interpretation by Diana J. Fuss, *Essentially Speaking* (New York: Routledge, 1989).

10. If we were to apply Fredric Jameson's distinction between parody and pastiche, gay identities would be better understood as pastiche. Whereas parody, Jameson argues, sustains some sympathy with the original of which it is a copy, pastiche disputes the possibility of an "original" or, in the case of gender, reveals the "original" as a failed effort to "copy" a phantasmatic ideal that cannot be copied without failure. See Fredric Jameson, "Postmodernism and Consumer Society," in *The Anti-Aesthetic: Essays on Postmodern Culture*, ed. Hal Foster (Port Townsend, WA: Bay Press, 1983), 127–141.

BIBLIOGRAPHY

Butler, Judith. "Variations on Sex and Gender: Beauvoir, Wittig, Foucault." In *Feminism as Critique*. Edited by Seyla Benhabib and Drucilla Cornell, 128–142. Minneapolis: University of Minnesota Press, 1987.

Echols, Alice. "The New Feminism of Yin and Yang." In *Powers of Desire: The Politics of Sexuality*. Edited by Ann Snitow, Christine Stansell, and Sharon Thompson, 439–459. London: Virago, 1984.

Echols, Alice. "The Taming of the Id: Feminist Sexual Politics, 1968–83." In *Pleasure and Danger: Exploring Female Sexuality*. Edited by Carol S. Vance, 50–72. Boston: Routledge and Kegan Paul, 1984.

English, Dierdre, Amber Hollibaugh, and Gayle Rubin. "Talking Sex: A Conversation on Sexuality and Feminism." *Feminist Review*, 11 (1982): 40–52.

Fausto-Sterling, Anne. *Myths of Gender: Biological Theories About Women and Men*. New York: Norton, 1979.

Foucault, Michel, ed., *Herculine Barbin, Being the Recently Discovered Memoirs of a Nineteenth-Century Hermaphrodite*. Translated by Richard McDougall. New York: Colophon, 1980. Originally published as *Herculine Barbin, dite Alexina B. presenté par Michel Foucault*. Paris: Gallimard, 1978.

Fox Keller, Evelyn. *Reflections on Gender and Science*. New Haven: Yale University Press, 1984.

Fuss, Diana J. *Essentially Speaking*. New York: Routledge, 1989.

Haraway, Donna. "In the Beginning was the Word: The Genesis of Biological Theory." *Signs: Journal of Women in Culture and Society* 6, no. 3 (Spring 1981): 469–481.

Haraway, Donna. *Primate Visions*. New York: Routledge, 1989.

Harding, Sandra. *The Science Question in Feminism*. Ithaca: Cornell University Press, 1986.

Harding, Sandra, and Jean F. O'Barr. *Sex and Scientific Inquiry*. Chicago: University of Chicago Press, 1987.

Hollibaugh, Amber. "Desire for the Future: Radical Hope in Pleasure and Passion." In *Pleasure and Danger: Exploring Female Sexuality*. Edited by Carol S. Vance, 401–410. Boston: Routledge and Kegan Paul, 1984.

Hollibaugh, Amber, and Cherríe Moraga. "What We're Rollin Around in Bed with: Sexual Silences in Feminism." In *Powers of Desire*. Edited by Ann Snitow, Christine Stansell, and Sharon Thompson, 394–405. London: Virago, 1984.

Hubbard, Ruth, and Marian Lowe, eds. *Genes and Gender*, 2 vols. New York: Gordian Press, 1978–79.

Irigaray, Luce. *Ce sexe qui n'en est pas un*. Paris: Les Éditions de Minuit, 1977.

Jameson, Fredric. "Postmodernism and Consumer Society." In *The Anti-Aesthetic: Essays on Postmodern Culture*. Edited by Hal Foster, 127–141. Port Townsend, WA: Bay Press, 1983.

Kerr, Barbara T., and Mirtha N. Quintanales. "The Complexity of Desire: Conversations on Sexuality and Difference." *Conditions* 3, no. 2 (1982): 52–71.

Kessler, Suzanne J., and Wendy McKenna. *Gender: An Ethnomethodological Approach*. Chicago: University of Chicago Press, 1978.

Lacqueur, Thomas, and Catherine Gallagher, eds. *The Making of the Modern Body: Sexuality and Society in the 19th Century*. Berkeley: University of California Press, 1987.

Ortner, Sherry B., and Harriet Whitehead, eds. *Sexual Meanings: The Cultural Construction of Sexuality*. New York: Cambridge University Press, 1981.

Rubin, Gayle. "Thinking Sex: Notes for a Radical Theory of the Politics of Sexuality." In *Pleasure and Danger: Exploring Female Sexuality*. Edited by Carol S. Vance, 267–319. Boston: Routledge and Kegan Paul, 1984.

Samois, ed. *Coming to Power*. Berkeley: Samois, 1981.

Snitow, Ann, Christine Stansell, and Sharon Thompson, eds. *Powers of Desire: The Politics of Sexuality*. London: Virago, 1984.

The Biology and Gender Study Group. "The Importance of Feminist Critique for Contemporary Cell Biology." *Hypatia* 3, no. 1 (Spring 1988): 61–76.

Vance, Carole S., ed. *Pleasure and Danger*. Boston: Routledge and Kegan Paul, 1984.

Vance, Carole S. "Pleasure and Danger: Towards a Politics of Sexuality." In *Pleasure and Danger: Exploring Female Sexuality*. Edited by Carol S. Vance, 1–28. Boston: Routledge and Kegan Paul, 1984.

Williams, Walter L. *The Spirit and the Flesh: Sexual Diversity in American Indian Culture*. Boston: Beacon Press, 1988.

17

WHAT IS AN APPARATUS?

Giorgio Agamben

1.

Terminological questions are important in philosophy. As a philosopher for whom I have the greatest respect once said, terminology is the poetic moment of thought. This is not to say that philosophers must always necessarily define their technical terms. Plato never defined *idea*, his most important term. Others, like Spinoza and Leibniz, preferred instead to define their terminology *more geometrico*.

The hypothesis that I wish to propose is that the word *dispositif* [*dispositivo*], or "apparatus" in English, is a decisive technical term in the strategy of Foucault's thought.[1] He uses it quite often, especially from the mid 1970s, when he begins to concern himself with what he calls "governmentality" or the "government of men." Though he never offers a complete definition, he comes close to something like it in an interview from 1977:

What I'm trying to single out with this term is, first and foremost, a thoroughly heterogeneous set consisting of discourses, institutions, architectural forms, regulatory decisions, laws, administrative measures, scientific statements, philosophical, moral, and philanthropic propositions—in short, the said as much as the unsaid. Such are the elements of the apparatus. The apparatus itself is the network that can be established between these elements . . .

. . . by the term "apparatus" I mean a kind of a formation, so to speak, that at a given historical moment has as its major function the response to an urgency. The apparatus therefore has a dominant strategic function . . .

. . . I said that the nature of an apparatus is essentially strategic, which means that we are speaking about a certain manipulation of relations of forces, of a rational and concrete intervention in the relations of forces, either so as to develop them in a particular direction, or to block them, to stabilize them, and to utilize them. The apparatus is thus always inscribed into a play of power, but it is also always linked to certain limits of knowledge that arise from it and, to an equal degree, condition it. The apparatus is precisely this: a set of strategies of the relations of forces supporting, and supported by, certain types of knowledge.[2]

Let me briefly summarize three points:

a. It is a heterogeneous set that includes virtually anything, linguistic and nonlinguistic, under the same heading: discourses, institutions, buildings, laws, police measures, philosophical propositions, and so on. The apparatus itself is the network that is established between these elements.
b. The apparatus always has a concrete strategic function and is always located in a power relation.
c. As such, it appears at the intersection of power relations and relations of knowledge.

2.

I would like now to try and trace a brief genealogy of this term, first in the work of Foucault, and then in a broader historical context.

At the end of the 1960s, more or less at the time when he was writing *The Archeology of Knowledge*, Foucault does not yet use the term "apparatus" in order to define the object of his research. Instead, he uses the term *positivité*, "positivity," an etymological neighbor of dispositif, again without offering us a definition.

I often asked myself where Foucault found this term, until the moment when, a few months ago, I reread a book by Jean Hyppolite entitled *Introduction à la philosophie de l'histoire de Hegel*. You probably know about the strong link that ties Foucault to Hyppolite, a person whom he referred to at times as "my master" (Hyppolite was in fact his teacher, first during the *khâgne* in the Lycée Henri-IV [the preparatory course for the École normale supérieure] and then in the École normale).

The third part of Hyppolite's book bears the title "Raison et histoire: Les idées de positivité et de destin" [Reason and History: The Ideas of Positivity and Destiny]. The focus here is on the analysis of two works that date from Hegel's years in Bern and Frankfurt (1795–96): The first is "The Spirit of Christianity and Its Destiny," and the second—where we find the term that interests us—"The Positivity of the Christian Religion" [*Die Positivität der christliche Religion*]. According to Hyppolite, "destiny" and "positivity" are two key concepts in Hegel's thought. In particular, the term "positivity" finds in Hegel its proper place in the opposition between "natural religion" and "positive religion." While natural religion is concerned with the immediate and general relation of human reason with the divine, positive or historical religion encompasses the set of beliefs, rules, and rites that in a certain society and at a certain historical moment are externally imposed on individuals. "A positive religion," Hegel writes in a passage cited by Hyppolite, "implies feelings that are more or less impressed through constraint on souls; these are actions that are the effect of command and the result of obedience and are accomplished without direct interest."[3]

Hyppolite shows how the opposition between nature and positivity corresponds, in this sense, to the dialectics of freedom and obligation, as well as of reason and history. In a passage that could not have failed to provoke Foucault's curiosity, because it in a way presages the notion of apparatus, Hyppolite writes:

> We see here the knot of questions implicit in the concept of positivity, as well as Hegel's successive attempts to bring together dialectically—a dialectics that is not yet conscious of itself—*pure reason* (theoretical and above all practical) and positivity, that is, *the historical element*. In a certain sense, Hegel considers positivity as an obstacle to the freedom of man, and as such it is condemned. To investigate the positive elements of a religion, and we might add, of a social state, means to discover in them that which is imposed through a constraint on man, that which obfuscates the purity of reason. But, in another sense—and this is the aspect that ends up having the upper hand in the course of Hegel's development—positivity must be reconciled with reason, which then loses its abstract character and adapts to the concrete richness of life. We see then why the concept of positivity is at the center of Hegelian perspectives.[4]

If "positivity" is the name that, according to Hyppolite, the young Hegel gives to the historical element—loaded as it is with rules, rites, and institutions that are imposed on the individual by an external power, but that become, so to speak, internalized in the systems of beliefs and feelings—then Foucault, by borrowing this term (later to become "apparatus"), takes a position with respect to a decisive problem, which is actually also his own problem: the relation between individuals as living beings and the historical element. By "the historical element," I mean the set of institutions, of processes of subjectification, and of rules in which power relations become concrete. Foucault's ultimate aim is not, then, as in Hegel, the reconciliation of the two elements; it is not even to emphasize their conflict. For Foucault, what is at stake is rather the investigation of concrete modes in which the positivities (or the apparatuses) act within the relations, mechanisms, and "plays" of power.

3.

It should now be clear in what sense I have advanced the hypothesis that "apparatus" is an essential technical term in Foucault's thought. What is at stake here is not a particular term that refers only to this or that technology of power. It is a general term that has the same breadth as the term "positivity" had, according to Hyppolite, for the young Hegel. Within Foucault's strategy, it comes to occupy the place of one of those terms that he defines, critically, as "the universals" [*les universaux*]. Foucault, as you know, always refused to deal with the general categories or mental constructs that he calls "the universals," such as the State, Sovereignty, Law, and Power. But this is not to say that there are no operative concepts with a general character in his thought. Apparatuses are, in point of fact, what take the place of the universals in the Foucauldian strategy: not simply this or that police measure, this or that technology of power, and not even the generality obtained by their abstraction. Instead, as he claims in the interview from 1977, an apparatus is "the network [*le réseau*] that can be established between these elements."

If we now try to examine the definition of "apparatus" that can be found in common French dictionaries, we see that they distinguish between three meanings of the term:

a. A strictly juridical sense: "Apparatus is the part of a judgment that contains the decision separate from the opinion." That is, the section of a sentence that decides [*che decide e dispone*], or the enacting clause of a law.
b. A technological meaning: "The way in which the parts of a machine or of a mechanism and, by extension, the mechanism itself are arranged [*sono dispositi*]."
c. A military use: "The set of means arranged [*dispositi*] in conformity with a plan."

To some extent, the three definitions are all present in Foucault. But dictionaries, in particular those that lack a historical-etymological character, divide and separate this term into a variety of meanings. This fragmentation, nevertheless, generally corresponds to the historical development and articulation of a unique original meaning that we should not lose sight of. What is this original meaning for the term "apparatus"? The term certainly refers, in its common Foucauldian use, to a set of practices and mechanisms (both linguistic and nonlinguistic, juridical, technical, and military) that aim to face an urgent need and to obtain an effect that is more or less immediate. But what is the strategy of practices or of thought, what is the historical context, from which the modern term originates?

4.

Over the past three years, I have found myself increasingly involved in an investigation that is only now beginning to come to its end, one that I can roughly define as a theological genealogy of economy. In the first centuries of Church history—let's say, between the second and sixth centuries C.E.—the Greek term *oikonomia* develops a decisive theological function. In Greek, *oikonomia* signifies the administration of the *oikos* (the home) and, more generally, management. We are dealing here, as Aristotle says (Politics 1255b21), not with an epistemic paradigm, but with a praxis, with a practical activity that must face a problem and a particular situation each and every time. Why, then, did the Fathers of the Church feel the need to introduce this term into theological discourse? How did they come to speak about a "divine economy"?

What is at issue here, to be precise, is an extremely delicate and vital problem, perhaps the decisive question in the history of Christian theology: the Trinity. When the Fathers of the Church began to argue during the second century about the threefold nature of the divine figure (the Father, the Son, and the Holy Spirit), there was, as one can imagine, a powerful resistance from reasonable-minded people in the Church who were horrified at the prospect of reintroducing polytheism and paganism to the Christian faith. In order to convince those stubborn adversaries (who were later called "monarchians," that is, promoters of the government of a single God), theologians such as Tertullian, Irenaeus, Hippolytus, and many others could not find a better term to serve their need than the Greek *oikonomia*. Their argument went something like this: "God, insofar as his being and substance is concerned, is certainly one; but as to his *oikonomia*—that is to say the way in which he administers his home, his life, and the world that he created—he is, rather, triple. Just as a good father can entrust to his son the execution of certain functions and duties without in so doing losing his power and his unity, so God entrusts to Christ the 'economy,' the administration and government of human history." *Oikonomia* therefore became a specialized term signifying in particular the incarnation of the Son, together with the economy of redemption and salvation (this is the reason why in Gnostic sects, Christ is called "the man of economy," *ho anthrōpos tēs oikonomias*). The theologians slowly got accustomed to distinguishing between a "discourse—or *logos*—of theology" and a "*logos* of economy." *Oikonomia* became thereafter an apparatus through which the Trinitarian dogma and the idea of a divine providential governance of the world were introduced into the Christian faith.

But, as often happens, the fracture that the theologians had sought to avoid by removing it from the plane of God's being, reappeared in the form of a caesura that separated in Him being and action, ontology and praxis. Action (economy, but also politics) has no foundation in being: this is the schizophrenia that the theological doctrine of *oikonomia* left as its legacy to Western culture.

5.

I think that even on the basis of this brief exposition, we can now account for the centrality and importance of the function that the notion of *oikonomia* performed in Christian theology. Already in Clement of Alexandria, *oikonomia* merges with the notion of Providence and begins to indicate the redemptive governance of the world and human history. Now, what is the translation of this fundamental Greek term in the writings of the Latin Fathers? *Dispositio*.

The Latin term *dispositio*, from which the French term *dispositif*, or apparatus, derives, comes therefore to take on the complex semantic sphere of the theological *oikonomia*. The "dispositifs" about which Foucault speaks are somehow linked to this theological legacy. They can be in some way traced back to the fracture that divides and, at the same time, articulates in God being and praxis, the nature or essence, on the one hand, and the operation through which He administers and governs the created world, on the other. The term "apparatus" [*dispositivo*] designates that in which, and through which, one realizes a pure activity of governance devoid of any foundation in being. This is the reason why apparatuses must always imply a process of subjectification, that is to say, they must produce their subject.

In light of this theological genealogy the Foucauldian apparatuses acquire an even more pregnant and decisive significance, since they intersect not only with the context of what the young Hegel called "positivity," but also with what the later Heidegger called *Gestell* (which is similar from an etymological point of view to *dis-positio, dis-ponere*, just as the German *stellen* corresponds to the Latin *ponere*). When Heidegger, in *Die Technik und die Kehre* (The Question Concerning Technology), writes that *Ge-stell* means in ordinary usage an apparatus [*Gerät*], but that he intends by this term "the gathering together of the (in)stallation [*Stellen*] that (in)stalls man, this is to say, challenges him to expose the real in the mode of ordering [*Bestellen*]," the proximity of this term to the theological *dispositio*, as well as to Foucault's apparatuses, is evident.[5] What is common to all these terms is that they refer back to this *oikonomia*, that is, to a set of practices, bodies of knowledge, measures, and institutions that aim to manage, govern, control, and orient—in a way that purports to be useful—the behaviors, gestures, and thoughts of human beings.

6.

One of the methodological principles that I constantly follow in my investigations is to identify in the texts and contexts on which I work what Feuerbach used to call the philosophical element, that is to say, the point of their *Entwicklungsfähigkeit* (literally, capacity to be developed), the locus and the moment wherein they are susceptible to a development. Nevertheless, whenever we interpret and develop the text of an author in this way, there comes a moment when we are aware of our inability to proceed any further without contravening the most elementary rules of hermeneutics. This means that the development of the text in question has reached a point of undecidability where it becomes impossible to distinguish between the author and the interpreter. Although this is a particularly happy moment for the interpreter, he knows that it is now time to abandon the text that he is analyzing and to proceed on his own.

I invite you therefore to abandon the context of Foucauldian philology in which we have moved up to now in order to situate apparatuses in a new context.

I wish to propose to you nothing less than a general and massive partitioning of beings into two large groups or classes: on the one hand, living beings (or substances), and on the other, apparatuses in which living beings are incessantly captured. On one side, then, to return to the terminology of the theologians, lies the ontology of creatures, and on the other side, the *oikonomia* of apparatuses that seek to govern and guide them toward the good.

Further expanding the already large class of Foucauldian apparatuses, I shall call an apparatus literally anything that has in some way the capacity to capture, orient, determine, intercept, model, control, or secure the gestures, behaviors, opinions, or discourses of living beings. Not only, therefore, prisons, madhouses, the panopticon, schools, confession, factories, disciplines, juridical measures, and so forth (whose connection with power is in a certain sense evident), but also the pen, writing, literature, philosophy, agriculture, cigarettes, navigation, computers, cellular telephones and—why not—language itself, which is perhaps the most ancient of apparatuses—one in which thousands and thousands of years ago a primate inadvertently let himself be captured, probably without realizing the consequences that he was about to face.

To recapitulate, we have then two great classes: living beings (or substances) and apparatuses. And, between these two, as a third class, subjects. I call a subject that which results from the relation and, so to speak, from the relentless fight between living beings and apparatuses. Naturally, the substances and the subjects, as in ancient metaphysics, seem to overlap, but not completely. In this sense, for example, the same individual, the same substance, can be the place of multiple processes of subjectification: the user of cellular phones, the web surfer, the writer of stories, the tango aficionado, the anti-globalization activist, and so on and so forth. The boundless growth of apparatuses in our time corresponds to the equally extreme proliferation in processes of subjectification. This may produce the impression that in our time, the category of subjectivity is wavering and losing its consistency; but what is at stake, to be precise, is not an erasure or an overcoming, but rather a dissemination that pushes to the extreme the masquerade that has always accompanied every personal identity.

7.

It would probably not be wrong to define the extreme phase of capitalist development in which we live as a massive accumulation and proliferation of apparatuses. It is clear that ever since Homo sapiens first appeared, there have been apparatuses; but we could say that today there is not even a single instant in which the life of individuals is not modeled, contaminated, or controlled by some apparatus. In what way, then, can we confront this situation, what strategy must we follow in our everyday hand-to-hand struggle with apparatuses? What we are looking for is neither simply to destroy them nor, as some naively suggest, to use them in the correct way.

For example, I live in Italy, a country where the gestures and behaviors of individuals have been reshaped from top to toe by the cellular telephone (which the Italians dub the *telefonino*). I have developed an implacable hatred for this apparatus, which has made the relationship between people all the more abstract. Although I found myself more than once wondering how to destroy or deactivate those *telefonini*, as well as how to eliminate or at least to punish and imprison those who do not stop using them, I do not believe that this is the right solution to the problem.

The fact is that according to all indications, apparatuses are not a mere accident in which humans are caught by chance, but rather are rooted in the very process of "humanization" that made "humans" out of the animals we classify under the rubric Homo sapiens. In fact, the event that has produced the human constitutes, for the living being, something like a division, which reproduces in some way the division that the *oikonomia* introduced in God between being and action. This division separates the living being from itself and from its immediate relationship with its environment—that is, with what Jakob von Uexküll and then Heidegger name the circle of receptors-disinhibitors. The break or interruption of this relationship produces in living beings both boredom—that is, the capacity to suspend this immediate relationship with their disinhibitors—and the Open, which is the possibility of knowing being as such, by constructing a world. But, along with these possibilities, we must also immediately consider the apparatuses that crowd the Open with instruments, objects, gadgets, odds and ends, and various technologies. Through these apparatuses, man attempts to nullify the animalistic behaviors that are now separated from him, and to enjoy the Open as such, to enjoy being insofar as it is being. At the root of each apparatus lies an all-too-human desire for happiness. The capture and subjectification of this desire in a separate sphere constitutes the specific power of the apparatus.

8.

All of this means that the strategy that we must adopt in our hand-to-hand combat with apparatuses cannot be a simple one. This is because what we are dealing with here is the liberation of that which remains captured and separated by means of apparatuses, in order to bring it back to a possible common use. It is from this perspective that I would like now to speak about a concept that I happen to have worked on recently. I am referring to a term that originates in the sphere of Roman law and religion (law and religion are closely connected, and not only in ancient Rome): profanation.

According to Roman law, objects that belonged in some way to the gods were considered sacred or religious. As such, these things were removed from free use and trade among humans: they could neither be sold nor given as security, neither relinquished for the enjoyment of others nor subjected to servitude. Sacrilegious were the acts that violated or transgressed the special unavailability of these objects, which were reserved either for celestial beings (and so they were properly called "sacred") or for the beings of the netherworld (in this case, they were simply called "religious"). While "to consecrate" (*sacrare*) was the term that designated the exit of things from the sphere of human law, "to profane" signified, on the contrary, to restore the thing to the free use of men. "Profane," the great jurist Trebatius was therefore able to write, "is, in the truest sense of the word, that which was sacred or religious, but was then restored to the use and property of human beings."

From this perspective, one can define religion as that which removes things, places, animals, or people from common use and transports them to a separate sphere. Not only is there no religion without separation, but every separation contains or conserves in itself a genuinely religious nucleus. The apparatus that activates and regulates separation is sacrifice. Through a series of minute rituals that vary from culture to culture (which Henri Hubert and Marcel Mauss have patiently inventoried), sacrifice always sanctions the passage of something from the profane to the sacred, from the human sphere to the divine. But what has been ritually separated can also be restored to the profane sphere. Profanation is the counter-apparatus that restores to common use what sacrifice had separated and divided.

9.

From this perspective, capitalism and other modern forms of power seem to generalize and push to the extreme the processes of separation that define religion. If we consider once again the theological genealogy of apparatuses that I have traced above (a genealogy that connects them to the Christian paradigm of *oikonomia*, that is to say, the divine governance of the world), we can then see that modern apparatuses differ from their traditional predecessors in a way that renders any attempt to profane them particularly problematic. Indeed, every apparatus implies a process of subjectification, without which it cannot function as an apparatus of governance, but is rather reduced to a mere exercise of violence. On this basis, Foucault has demonstrated how, in a disciplinary society, apparatuses aim to create—through a series of practices, discourses, and bodies of knowledge—docile, yet free, bodies that assume their identity and their "freedom" as subjects in the very process of their desubjectification. Apparatus, then, is first of all a machine that produces subjectifications, and only as such is it also a machine of governance. The example of confession may elucidate the matter at hand: the formation of Western subjectivity that both splits and, nonetheless, masters and secures the self, is inseparable from this centuries-old activity of the apparatus of penance—an apparatus in which a new I is constituted through the negation and, at the same time, the assumption of the old I. The split of the subject performed by the apparatus of penance resulted, therefore, in the production of a new subject, which found its real truth in the nontruth of the already repudiated sinning I. Analogous considerations can be made concerning the apparatus of the prison: here is an apparatus that produces, as a more or less unforeseen consequence, the constitution of a subject and of a milieu of delinquents, who then become the subject of new—and, this time, perfectly calculated—techniques of governance.

What defines the apparatuses that we have to deal with in the current phase of capitalism is that they no longer act as much through the production of a subject, as through the processes of what can be called desubjectification. A desubjectifying moment is certainly implicit in every process of subjectification. As we have seen, the penitential self is constituted only through its own negation. But what we are now witnessing is that processes of subjectification and processes of desubjectification seem to become reciprocally indifferent, and so they do not give rise to the recomposition of a new subject, except in larval or, as it were, spectral form. In the nontruth of the subject, its own truth is no longer at stake. He who lets himself be captured by the "cellular telephone" apparatus—whatever the intensity of the desire that has driven him—cannot acquire a new subjectivity, but only a number through which he can, eventually, be controlled. The spectator who spends his evenings in front of the television set only gets, in exchange for his desubjectification, the frustrated mask of the couch potato, or his inclusion in the calculation of viewership ratings.

Here lies the vanity of the well-meaning discourse on technology, which asserts that the problem with apparatuses can be reduced to the question of their correct use. Those who make such claims seem to ignore a simple fact: If a certain process of subjectification (or, in this case, desubjectification) corresponds to every apparatus, then it is impossible for the subject of an apparatus to use it "in the right way." Those who continue to promote similar arguments are, for their part, the product of the media apparatus in which they are captured.

10.

Contemporary societies therefore present themselves as inert bodies going through massive processes of desubjectification without acknowledging any real subjectification. Hence the eclipse of politics, which used to presuppose the existence of subjects and real identities (the workers' movement, the bourgeoisie, etc.), and the triumph of the *oikonomia*, that is to say, of a pure activity of government that aims at nothing other than its own replication. The Right and the Left, which today alternate in the management of power, have for this reason very little to do with the political sphere in which they originated. They are simply the names of two poles—the first pointing without scruple to desubjectification, the second wanting instead to hide behind the hypocritical mask of the good democratic citizen—of the same governmental machine.

This, above all, is the source of the peculiar uneasiness of power precisely during an era in which it confronts the most docile and cowardly social body that has ever existed in human history. It is only an apparent paradox that the harmless citizen of postindustrial democracies (the *Bloom*, as it has been effectively suggested he be called),[6] who readily does everything that he is asked to do, inasmuch as he leaves his everyday gestures and his health, his amusements and his occupations, his diet and his desires, to be commanded and controlled in the smallest detail by apparatuses, is also considered by power—perhaps precisely because of this—as a potential terrorist. While a new European norm imposes biometric apparatuses on all its citizens by developing and perfecting anthropometric technologies invented in the nineteenth century in order to identify recidivist criminals (from mug shots to fingerprinting), surveillance by means of video cameras transforms the public space of the city into the interior of an immense prison. In the eyes of authority—and maybe rightly so—nothing looks more like a terrorist than the ordinary man.

The more apparatuses pervade and disseminate their power in every field of life, the more government will find itself faced with an elusive element, which seems to escape its grasp the more it docilely submits to it. This is neither to say that this element constitutes a revolutionary subject in its own right, nor that it can halt or even threaten the governmental machine. Rather than the proclaimed end of history, we are, in fact, witnessing the incessant though aimless motion of this machine, which, in a sort of colossal parody of theological *oikonomia*, has assumed the legacy of the providential governance of the world; yet instead of redeeming our world, this machine (true to the original eschatological vocation of Providence) is leading us to catastrophe. The problem of the profanation of apparatuses—that is to say, the restitution to common use of what has been captured and separated in them—is, for this reason, all the more urgent. But this problem cannot be properly raised as long as those who are concerned with it are unable to intervene in their own processes of subjectification, any more than in their own apparatuses, in order to then bring to light the Ungovernable, which is the beginning and, at the same time, the vanishing point of every politics.

NOTES

1. [We follow here the common English translation of Foucault's term *dispositif* as "apparatus." In everyday use, the French word can designate any sort of device. Agamben points out that the torture machine from Kafka's *In the Penal Colony* is called an *Apparat*.—Trans.]

2. Michel Foucault, *Power/Knowledge: Selected Interviews and Other Writings*, 1972–1977, ed. Colin Gordon, trans. Colin Gordon et al. (New York: Pantheon Books, 1980), 194–196.

3. Jean Hyppolite, *Introduction to Hegel's Philosophy of History*, trans. Bond Harris and Jacqueline B. Spurlock (Gainesville: University Press of Florida, 1996), 21.

4. Ibid., 23.

5. Martin Heidegger, *Basic Writings*, ed. David Farrell Krell (New York: HarperCollins, 1993), 325.

6. [See *Théorie du Bloom* (Paris: Fabrique, 2000), by the French collective Tiqqun. The allusion is to Leopold Bloom, the main character in James Joyce's *Ulysses*.—Trans.]

BIBLIOGRAPHY

Foucault, Michel. *Power/Knowledge: Selected Interviews and Other Writings*, 1972–1977. Edited by Colin Gordon. Translated by Colin Gordon et al. New York: Pantheon Books, 1980.

Heidegger, Martin. *Basic Writings*. Edited by David Farrell Krell. New York: HarperCollins, 1993.

Hyppolite, Jean. *Introduction to Hegel's Philosophy of History*. Translated by Bond Harris and Jacqueline B. Spurlock. Gainesville: University Press of Florida, 1996.

Tiqqun. *Théorie du Bloom*. Paris: Fabrique, 2000.

18

BEFORE THE LAW: HUMANS AND OTHER ANIMALS IN A BIOPOLITICAL FRAME

Cary Wolfe

To begin at the beginning: I choose the word "frame" for my title (rather than adjacent terms such as, say, "context") for a few different reasons that interconnect some of the subterranean conceptual passageways of this long essay. First, I want to mark a lengthening genealogy of biopolitical thought that stretches back from current avatars such as Roberto Esposito, Judith Butler, and Giorgio Agamben, through the *locus classicus* of Michel Foucault's later work (a *locus* that is becoming more and more *classicus* by the day, thanks to the ongoing translation and publication of his lectures at the Collège de France), to what we are now in a position to see as biopolitical thought *avant la lettre*, as it were, in the work of Hannah Arendt and Martin Heidegger. Directly pertinent for my title is the sense of Heidegger's *Gestell* (or "enframing" or "framework," as it is often translated) from his well-known later essay, "The Question Concerning Technology."[1] There, Heidegger asserts that the essence of technology is not "anything technological" but rather how it discloses the world to us as mode of "bringing-forth" what is here for us, and how.[2] For Heidegger (and, as we shall see, for biopolitical thought generally), enframing is anything but a neutral concept; indeed, with the luxury of twenty-twenty hindsight, we can now see that it is deep background (as the journalists say) for what Foucault and others will call the dispositifs or apparatuses of biopolitics. *Gestell*, while neither natural nor human, frames the human's relation both to itself and to nature, and in ways that are far from sanguine in Heidegger's view.[3] "Where enframing reigns," Heidegger writes, "there is *danger* in the highest sense."[4] What we encounter here is a mode of revealing the world which sets it out before us in a mode of instrumentality and utility that Heidegger famously calls "standing-reserve" [*Bestand*]. As Heidegger puts it in a famous passage,

As soon as what is unconcealed no longer concerns man even as object, but does so, rather, exclusively as standing-reserve, and man in the midst of objectlessness is nothing but the orderer of the standing reserve, then he comes to the brink of a precipitous fall; that is, he comes to the point where he himself will have to be taken as standing-reserve. Meanwhile man, precisely as the one so threatened, exalts himself to the posture of lord of the earth. In this way the impression comes to prevail that everything man encounters exists only insofar as it is his construct. This illusion gives rise to one final delusion: It seems as though man everywhere and always encounters only himself.[5]

But the self he encounters is, as Heidegger notes, fallen, inauthentic: *"In truth, however,"* Heidegger continues, *"precisely nowhere does man today any longer encounter himself, i.e. his essence."*[6]

The effect of this enframing is thus two-fold: not only is the human being cut off from a more authentic relation to the natural world, it is also cut off from an authentic relationship to itself. Sounding notes that, as we'll see, both Michel Foucault and Peter Sloterdijk will amplify decades later, Heidegger asserts that humanity thus comes, in fact, to be seen as a kind of standing-reserve in and of itself—a fact reflected in the contemporary reframing of individuals as "human resources" and the like.[7] Over and against this work of *Gestell*, Heidegger sets what he calls the "saving power"[8] of a humanity (and a humanism) not wholly subordinated to calculation and utility, one that is able to engage artistically, poetically, and philosophically, in reflection and meditation, in questioning (hence Derrida's emphasis in the subtitle of his book on Heidegger, *Of Spirit*, on Heidegger and *"the question"*).[9]

We find here, then, not just one of the high water marks of humanism's familiar opposition of art and philosophy on the one hand to calculation and utility on the other, but also an even deeper and more decisive determination of the proper and improper relation of the human to technology, and hence to itself: "Technology is no mere means," Heidegger reminds us, and while it may operate improperly as calculation and resource management, it may also take on a more edifying role in "the arts of the mind and the fine arts," where it "belongs to bringing-forth, to *poiesis*."[10] In fact, as Heidegger's thought develops in both "The Question Concerning Technology" and the "Letter on Humanism," this difference between a proper and improper relationship to technology enables, in turn, a decisive ontological distinction between those who are fully human and those who are less than human, those others who have been so fundamentally distanced from Being by an improper relationship to technology that their very humanity is in question.[11] As Heidegger writes in the "Letter," "For this is humanism: meditating and caring, that man be human and not inhumane, 'inhuman,' that is, outside his essence."[12]

Now we know, as I have pointed out elsewhere (following well-known discussions by Derrida and others), that the primary means by which this "saving" takes place is above all through the capacity for language, which is, properly understood, not semiotic but phenomenological, and gives access to things "as such," as opposed to language understood as "communication," "information," and the like.[13] We thus find a fundamental distinction, as Timothy Campbell puts it, "between those, on one side who are mere subjects of communication; those who later will be enrolled among the ranks of *animalitas*; and others who, thanks to a proper writing, are seen as free, individual human beings, capable of 'care.'"[14] Precisely here, in this distinction between the proper and improper relation not just to technology, but more fundamentally of the human to itself, we may locate the hinge in Heidegger's work between the two main lines of contemporary biopolitical thought, one (associated with Foucault) focused on technology and dispositifs, and the other (associated with Agamben) focused on the subject's proper relation to its own singularity and uniqueness—its "ipseity" (to use the term Derrida will later unpack in relation to the question of sovereignty). By these lights, ipseity and sovereignty are taken to be in stark opposition to the "animal,"[15] and to the animality of the human when the human becomes something anonymous, either through massification (as in Foucault's studies of the mechanisms of biopolitics, such as population sciences and medicalization) or by being reduced to an equally anonymous condition of "bare life."[16] But what I want to emphasize here is Heidegger's opening up of a gap—a dangerous gap, as the history of biopolitics well shows, but also one jealously guarded by humanism—between humanity and animality as ontologically opposed zones. Indeed, the "humans *and other animals*" of my title is meant as a direct challenge to this distinction, so crucial to Heidegger's entire corpus—indeed, one of its central dogmas (to use Derrida's characterization[17]).

Heidegger's meditations on the frame and enframing will eventually be radicalized and pushed to their self-deconstructing conclusions in another famous discussion of the frame—namely, Derrida's analysis of the *parergon* (a term he borrows from Kant) as that "which simultaneously constitutes and destroys" what it frames, paradoxically supplementing that which is already complete.[18] It separates the inside from the outside, the intrinsic and the extrinsic, and yet also serves to bridge them, making them interdependent. Derrida's analysis of the *parergon* does to Heidegger's *Gestell* what his *pharmakon* will do to Heidegger's distinction between the proper and the improper—and in ways, as we will see, that connect directly to what Roberto Esposito and others have identified as the "immunitary" (and, with Derrida, "autoimmunitary") logic of the biopolitical.[19] To put it this way is to remind ourselves that the question of framing is not simply a logical or epistemological problem, but a social and material one, with consequences. Framing decides what we recognize and what we don't, what counts and what doesn't; and it also determines the consequences of falling outside the frame (in the case at hand in this book, outside the frame as "animal," as "*zoé*," as "bare life").

We are now in a better position to critically assess, however briefly, another towering figure in the prehistory of contemporary biopolitical thought, Hannah Arendt, to help clarify (against her own intentions, as it were) why talk about non-human animals *at all* in the context of biopolitics is not simply a category mistake. Arendt brilliantly argues in *The Origins of Totalitarianism* that the idea of "universal human rights" is dubious because it attempts to ground the standing of the subject of rights in the mere biological designation of the human being as *homo sapiens*, whereas rights themselves are always a product of membership in a political community. They are, as she puts it in *The Human Condition*, "artificial."[20] By contrast, a "human being in general—without a profession, without a citizenship, without an opinion"—belongs "to the human race in much the same way as animals belong to a specific animal species."[21] And more interesting still is Arendt's suggestion that groups founded to support universal human rights and the declarations they frame "showed an uncanny similarity in language and composition to that of societies for the prevention of cruelty to animals."[22]

Arendt is on to something here, but her humanist commitments prevent her from recognizing exactly what it is. Her resistance to what Jacques Derrida will later (and in agreement with Heidegger) reject as "biologistic continuism," and her recourse to what we might call a formal or conventional concept of rights is perfectly correct, as far as it goes, but it is immediately pressured and complicated by the historical fact that the very call of the Universal Declaration of Human Rights of 1948 arises on the basis of the massive presence of stateless persons—persons deprived of personhood in precisely her sense—during World War II and its wake. It arises, that is, with the increasingly undeniable presence of what biopolitical thought will canonically come to call "bare life."[23] And so the dilemma she faces is that her formal concept of rights, derived as they are from reciprocal membership in a political community, leaves her no immediately apparent way to recognize the claims of these newly stateless persons whose problem "is not that they are deprived of life, liberty, and the pursuit of happiness," but rather "that they no longer belong to any community whatsoever."[24] But when Arendt confronts the conundrum raised by this historical event—namely, how can the claim of these people be framed, what constitutes "a right to have rights"?—she falls back on a classically humanist argument that derives from Aristotle: for the "right to have rights" consists in the ability to enter into relations of reciprocal obligation (or what she calls, a little more lyrically, "a framework where one is judged by one's actions and opinions)."[25]

Here, then, we find the classic opposition, already familiar to us from Heidegger, of the authentically political as a realm of freedom, choice, "artifice" and so on versus the realm of necessity, utility, and mere "animal" or "natural" existence.[26] And, as in Aristotle, that opposition, like the right to have rights, in grounded in the human being's capacity for speech and language (and a rather naturalistically conceived idea of language at that).[27] As she puts it in *The Human Condition* (virtually paraphrasing Aristotle's famous passage from the *Politics*), "speech is what makes man a political being."[28] What Arendt is right about—and we will return to these issues in much more detail later—is that the designation of those who have standing, who have rights, is a matter of sheer convention outside of any naturalistic ground or biological designation. What she is wrong about is that the problem raised for humanism by "bare life"—how do we recognize the "right to have rights" for stateless persons but not for "savages" or "beasts" (her terms)[29]—can be solved by the gatekeeper function of "speech." Indeed, the most obvious symptom of this conundrum in Arendt's position is that "speech" appears to be both "natural" *and* "artificial."[30] On the one hand, speech provides the naturalistic basis, specific to humans, of the "right to have rights"; but on the other hand, speech alone is not enough to secure standing. It has to be "relevant" and recognized, as she puts it—has to hew, that is, to a set of artificial social conventions (indeed, that they *are* artificial and not "natural" is what makes them political).[31]

At this juncture, of course, we might question the relevance of speech for determining the rights-holding subject by means of Jeremy Bentham's famous observation (and Derrida's unpacking of it in *The Animal That Therefore I Am*) that that fundamental question here is not, "can they reason?," or "can they talk?," but "can they suffer?"[32] Here, the issue would be not the paradoxical nature of a speech that is both artificial and natural, redoubled in the difference between "rights" and "the right to have rights" (a right that is, paradoxically, not one), but rather the sheer irrelevance of speech itself to the question of standing (a question we will return to shortly). But what I want to underscore here instead is a logic implicit in Arendt's writings, particularly in *The Origins of Totalitarianism*—a logic that she doesn't quite tease out but one that will be central to biopolitical thought in the decades that follow: the fact, as Esposito puts it, that "the category of those who enjoy a certain right is defined only by contrast with those who, not falling within it, are excluded from it."[33]

And here—to move to the main part of my title—we can begin to glimpse the many senses of what it means to be "before the law": "before" in the sense of that which is ontologically and/or logically antecedent to the law, which exists prior to the moment when the law, in all its contingency and immanence, enacts its originary violence, installs its frame for who's in and who's out. This is the sense of "before" that is marked by Arendt's speculations on the "right to have rights," and it is against such a "before" that the immanence of the law and its exclusions is judged. And thus, "before" in another sense as well, in the sense of standing before the judgment of a law that is inscrutable not just because it establishes by fiat who falls inside and outside the frame, but also because it disavows its own contingency through violence: namely, the violence of sacrifice for which the distinction between human and animal has historically been bedrock, providing for the law the "foundation" for its exclusions that the law cannot provide for itself. As Derrida, Agamben, and others have reminded us, those who fall outside the frame, because they are marked by differences of race, or species, or gender, or religion, or nationality, are always threatened with "a non-criminal putting to death." As Derrida puts it in the interview "Eating Well," "Thou shalt not kill" turns out not to be a universalizable maxim, but one that only concerns those for whom it is a "proper" imperative, those who fall inside the frame.[34]

In this light, it is all the more instructive to recall, as Derrida points out in his essay "Before the Law," that when Freud addresses the problem of the origin of law (what is its basis? on what moral foundations does it rest?) he resorts to what amounts to a sacrifice of the animal, and more broadly of animality, as the means by which both the human and the basis of the law are secured.[35] Here and elsewhere, Freud's concept of "organic repression" marks the point at which the properly human breaks free of and rises above its animal origins, and it is on that basis that moral behavior is founded.[36] But this is not just a "schema of elevation," as Derrida puts it; it is also a "schema of purification"—purification of the animal in "man."[37] Since "man" has to *already* exist to find that which is repugnant in need of repression and thus rise above it, Freud's search for the origin of law simultaneously marks its own impossibility. Instead, the law is "an absolutely emergent order, absolute and detached from any origin."[38]

But if Derrida is right that this sacrificial structure is fundamental to the entire canonical discourse of "Western metaphysics or religions," the work that it accomplishes is anything but academic, since it is also of "the order of the political, the State, right, or morality," never far from the mundane violence of everyday life.[39] One of the most powerful insights of biopolitical thought is thus to raise this uncomfortable question: if the frame is about rules and laws, about what is proper, and not simply a matter of a line that is given by nature between those inside and those outside, then to live under biopolitics is to live in a situation in which we are all always already (potential) "animals" before the law—not just non-human animals according to zoological classification, but any group of living beings that is so framed. Here, the distinction "human/animal"—as the history of slavery, colonialism, and imperialism well shows—is a discursive resource, not a zoological designation; it is, as we will discuss in more detail, a kind of dispositif or apparatus. It is all the more ironic, then, that the main line of biopolitical thought has had little or nothing to say about how this logic effects non-human beings—a cruel irony indeed, given how "animalization" has been one of its main resources.

NOTES

1. Martin Heidegger, "The Question Concerning Technology," trans. William Lovitt, in *Basic Writings*, ed. and intro. David Farrell Krell (New York: Harper & Row, 1977), 302.

2. Ibid., 287, 294.

3. As David Wills aptly summarizes it, *Gestell* "is coined in the context of two other words, namely *Gebirge*, the gathering of mountains that produces the mountain 'range,' and *Gemüt*, the gathering of emotions that produces a 'disposition.' In comparison with a natural gathering on the one hand and human gathering on the other, *Gestell* will be the frameworking of what is set out, produced by and in the same movement ordered into instrumental service." David Wills, *Dorsality: Thinking Back Through Technology and Politics* (Minneapolis: University of Minnesota Press, 2008), 30.

4. Heidegger, "The Question Concerning Technology," 309.

5. Ibid., 308.

6. Ibid.

7. Ibid., 299.

8. Ibid., 310.

9. Ibid., 300.

10. Ibid., 294.

11. For as Timothy Campbell points out, the decisive question here is this: "What kind of man masters technology? The change in the species of man that attempts to extend his domination over technology . . . is in fact what is most dangerous about technology." Timothy Campbell, *Improper Life: Technology and Biopolitics from Heidegger to Agamben* (Minneapolis: University of Minnesota Press, 2011), 7.

12. Martin Heidegger, "Letter on Humanism," trans. Frank A. Capuzzi and J. Glenn Gray, in *Basic Writings*, 200.

13. See Cary Wolfe, *Animal Rites: American Culture, the Discourse of Species, and Posthumanist Theory*, foreword W. J. T. Mitchell (Chicago: University of Chicago Press, 2008), chapter two. As Heidegger puts it in the "Letter," "man is not only a living creature who possesses language along with other capacities. Rather, language is the house of Being in which man ek-sists by dwelling, in that he belongs to the truth of Being, guarding it." Heidegger, "Letter on Humanism," 213.

14. Campbell, *Improper Life*, 28.

15. Throughout this essay, I roughly alternate between the more technically correct term "non-human animal" and the more concise and felicitous term "animal," it being obvious that *homo sapiens* is but one member of the animal kingdom—and a member who has often sought to maintain that the "human" is not.

16. For Derrida's discussion of "ipseity," see the following: *Rogues: Two Essays on Reason*, trans. Pascale-Anne Brault and Michael Naas (Stanford: Stanford University Press, 2005), 143 and *The Beast and the Sovereign*, vol. 1, trans. Geoffrey Bennington, eds. Michel Lisse, Marie-Louise Mallet, and Ginette Michaud (Chicago: University of Chicago Press, 2009), 71. The canonical locus for the discussion of "bare life" in Agamben is *Homo Sacer: Sovereign Power and Bare Life*, trans. Daniel Heller-Roazen (Stanford: Stanford University Press, 1998).

17. See Jacques Derrida, "*Geschlecht II: Heidegger's Hand*," trans. John P. Leavey, Jr., in *Deconstruction and Philosophy*, ed. John Sallis (Chicago: University of Chicago Press, 1986), 173.

18. Jacques Derrida, "The Parergon," trans. Craig Owens, *October*, no. 9 (Summer 1979): 33. As Wills notes, *Gestell* is a kind of technology through which the human paradoxically reveals its essential, pre-technological, ontological nature to itself only on the basis of its prosthetic dependence on something external, technical, inorganic (Wills, *Dorsality*, 34).

19. See Roberto Esposito, *Immunitas: The Protection and Negations of Life*, trans. Zakiya Hanafi (London: Polity Press, 2011), 7.

20. Hannah Arendt, *The Human Condition*, intro. Margaret Conovan (Chicago: University of Chicago Press, 1998), 2.

21. Hannah Arendt, *The Origins of Totalitarianism* (New York: Harcourt, 1976), 302.

22. Arendt, *Origins of Totalitarianism*, 292. For an incisive discussion of this moment in Arendt, see Alistair Hunt, "The Rights of the Infinite," *Qui Parle* 19, no. 2 (Spring/Summer 2011): 223–251.

23. Jacques Derrida, *The Animal That Therefore I Am*, trans. David Wills, ed. Marie-Louise Mallet (New York: Fordham University Press, 2008), 30. See also Jacques Derrida, *Of Spirit: Heidegger and The Question*, trans. Geoffrey Bennington and Rachel Bowlby (Chicago: University of Chicago Press, 1989), 56. On "bare life," see Agamben, *Homo Sacer*.

24. Arendt, *Origins of Totalitarianism*, 295–296.

25. Ibid., 296–297.

26. As Arendt writes in her overview of the idea of politics inherited from the Greeks, in a passage whose direct lines of descent to Heidegger's humanism are clear enough, and in one of the great articulations of the biopolitical distinction between *bios* and *zoé* before Foucault, "The distinction between man and animal runs right through the human species itself: only the best (*aristoi*), who constantly prove themselves to be the best (*aristeuein*, a verb for which there is no equivalent in any other language) and who 'prefer immortal fame to mortal things,' are really human; the

others, content with whatever pleasures nature will yield them, live and die like animals" (*The Human Condition*, 19). See also 13, 24, 37.

27. See in particular her discussion of what she calls, in quotation marks, the "'language' of mathematical symbols" versus language proper, which partakes of the *topos* we have already discussed in Heidegger of the improper versus proper use relation to language as mere communication, information, in contrast to authentic expression and comprehension (*The Human Condition*, 3–4). See also *Origins of Totalitarianism*, 297.

28. Arendt, *The Human Condition*, 3; see also 27.

29. Arendt, *Origins of Totalitarianism*, 300.

30. See Jacques Derrida, "Structure, Sign, and Play in the Discourse of the Human Sciences," in *Margins of Philosophy*, trans. Alan Bass (Chicago: University of Chicago Press, 1978), 278–294.

31. As she writes in the "Prologue" to *The Human Condition*, "wherever the *relevance* of speech is at stake, matters become political by definition, for speech is what makes man a political being" (Arendt, *The Human Condition*, 4, emphasis mine). So speech is "natural" but, regarding its function as a foundation for rights, it may be *either* relevant or irrelevant. Indeed, as she notes in discussing Aristotle's political writings, "according to this opinion, everybody outside the *polis*—slaves and barbarians—was *aneu logou*, deprived, of course, not of the faculty of speech, but of *a way of life* in which speech and only speech made sense and where the central concern of all citizens was to talk with each other." (27, emphasis mine). All of the foregoing clarifies why Hunt is not quite right when he says of Arendt that "Insofar as the right to have rights is claimed by those reduced to a condition of rightlessness, perhaps the author of *The Human Condition*, one of the most magnificent humanist treatises of the twentieth century, is in her own way also an advocate of animal rights" ("The Rights of the Infinite," 225). The right to have rights would be barred to non-human animals because it rests upon the foundation of the capacity for speech.

32. Derrida, *The Animal That Therefore I Am*, 27–29.

33. "If it belonged to everyone," he continues, "like a biological characteristic, language or the ability to walk, for example, a right would not be a right, but simply a fact with no need for specific juridical denomination. In the same way, if the category of person coincided with that of human being, there would have been no need for it. Ever since its original juridical performance, personhood is valuable exactly to the extent to which it is not applicable to all, and finds its meaning precisely in the principled difference between those to whom it is, from time to time, attributed and those to whom it is not, or from whom, at a certain point, it is subtracted. Only if there are men (and women) who are not completely, or not at all, considered persons, can others be or become such." Roberto Esposito, "The Person and Human Life," trans. Diana Garvin and Thomas Kelso, in *Theory After "Theory"*, ed. Jane Elliott and Derek Attridge (London: Routledge, 2011), 209.

34. Jacques Derrida, "Eating Well, or the Calculation of the Subject: An Interview with Jacques Derrida," trans. Peter Connor and Avital Ronnell, in *Who Comes After the Subject?* ed. Eduardo Cadava, Peter Connor, and Jean-Luc Nancy (New York: Routledge, 1991), 112. It is worth voicing a clarification here with regard to "sacrifice." Sacrifice in Agamben would appear to be *opposed* to, not a part of, Derrida's "sacrificial symbolic economy" when Agamben asserts that *homo sacer* "is a human victim who may be killed but not sacrificed" (*Homo Sacer*, 83). But what "sacrificed" references here for Agamben is, additionally, an earlier religious order out of which the properly political emerges, which is assimilated in Derrida's reading to the same essential logic. "The political sphere of sovereignty . . .

takes the form of a zone of indistinction between sacrifice and homicide," Agamben writes (*Homo Sacer*, 83). In other words, *homo sacer* as he who may be "killed but not sacrificed" means, as it does in Derrida, "killable but not murderable" but retains in Agamben the earlier religious sense as well.

35. Derrida's title is taken, it should be noted (while speaking of frames), from the short story by Kafka of the same title, which itself appears as part of Kafka's longer text *The Trial*—and, moreover, as a text centrally engaged by Agamben in *Homo Sacer*, 49–57. Jacques Derrida, "Before the Law," trans. Avital Ronnell, in *Act of Literature*, ed. Derek Attridge (New York: Routledge, 1992), 193–194, 197–198.

36. It is, Derrida observes, "linked with the upright position, that is, to a certain *elevation*. The passage to the upright position raises man, thus distancing his nose from the sexual zones, anal or genital. This distance enables his height and leaves its traces by delaying his action. Delay, difference, ennobling elevation, diversion of the olfactory sense from the sexual stench, repression—here are the origins of morality" (Derrida, "Before the Law," 193). For a fuller discussion, see Wolfe, *Animal Rites*, chapter three.

37. Derrida, "Before the Law," 193.

38. Ibid., 194.

39. Derrida, "Eating Well," 112, 114.

BIBLIOGRAPHY

Agamben, Giorgio. *Homo Sacer: Sovereign Power and Bare Life*. Translated by Daniel Heller-Roazen. Stanford: Stanford University Press, 1998.

Arendt, Hannah. *The Human Condition*. Introduced by Margaret Conovan. Chicago: University of Chicago Press, 1998.

Arendt, Hannah. *The Origins of Totalitarianism*. New York: Harcourt, 1976.

Campbell, Timothy. *Improper Life: Technology and Biopolitics from Heidegger to Agamben*. Minneapolis: University of Minnesota Press, 2011.

Derrida, Jacques. "Before the Law." Translated by Avital Ronnell. In *Act of Literature*. Edited by Derek Attridge. New York: Routledge, 1992.

Derrida, Jacques. "Eating Well, or the Calculation of the Subject: An Interview with Jacques Derrida." Translated by Peter Connor and Avital Ronnell. In *Who Comes After the Subject?* Edited by Eduardo Cadava, Peter Connor, and Jean-Luc Nancy, 96–119. New York: Routledge, 1991.

Derrida, Jacques. "*Geschlecht II: Heidegger's Hand*." Translated by John P. Leavey, Jr. In *Deconstruction and Philosophy*. Edited by John Sallis, 161–196. Chicago: University of Chicago Press, 1986.

Derrida, Jacques. *Of Spirit: Heidegger and The Question*. Translated by Geoffrey Bennington and Rachel Bowlby. Chicago: University of Chicago Press, 1989.

Derrida, Jacques. *Rogues: Two Essays on Reason*. Translated by Pascale-Anne Brault and Michael Naas. Stanford: Stanford University Press, 2005.

Derrida, Jacques. "Structure, Sign, and Play in the Discourse of the Human Sciences." In *Margins of Philosophy*. Translated by Alan Bass, 278–294. Chicago: University of Chicago Press, 1978.

Derrida, Jacques. *The Animal That Therefore I Am*. Translated by David Wills. Edited by Marie-Louise Mallet. New York: Fordham University Press, 2008.

Derrida, Jacques. *The Beast and the Sovereign*, vol. 1. Translated by Geoffrey Bennington. Edited by Michel Lisse, Marie-Louise Mallet, and Ginette Michaud. Chicago: University of Chicago Press, 2009.

Derrida, Jacques. "The Parergon." Translated by Craig Owens. *October*, no. 9 (Summer 1979).

Esposito, Roberto. *Immunitas: The Protection and Negations of Life*. Translated by Zakiya Hanafi. London: Polity Press, 2011.

Esposito, Roberto. "The Person and Human Life." Translated by Diana Garvin and Thomas Kelso. In *Theory After "Theory."* Edited by Jane Elliott and Derek Attridge, 205–219. London: Routledge, 2011.

Heidegger, Martin. "Letter on Humanism." Translated by Frank A. Capuzzi and J. Glenn Gray. In *Basic Writings*. Edited and introduced by David Farrell Krell, 213–265. New York: Harper & Row, 1977.

Heidegger, Martin. "The Question Concerning Technology." Translated by William Lovitt. In *Basic Writings*. Edited and introduced by David Farrell Krell, 307–341. New York: Harper & Row, 1977.

Hunt, Alistair. "The Rights of the Infinite." *Qui Parle* 19, no. 2 (Spring/Summer 2011): 223–251.

Wills, David. *Dorsality: Thinking Back Through Technology and Politics*. Minneapolis: University of Minnesota Press, 2008.

Wolfe, Cary. *Animal Rites: American Culture, the Discourse of Species, and Posthumanist Theory*. Foreword by W. J. T. Mitchell. Chicago: University of Chicago Press, 2008.

III

PROSTHETICS/EMBODIMENTS

Suzy Lake, *The Queen and I on a Broken Board* (2018/2019), from the *Game Theory: Global Gamesmanship* series. Reprinted by permission of the artist.

19

IDEOLOGY AND IDEOLOGICAL STATE APPARATUSES

Louis Althusser

ON THE REPRODUCTION OF THE CONDITIONS OF PRODUCTION

I must now expose more fully something which was briefly glimpsed in my analysis when I spoke of the necessity to renew the means of production if production is to be possible. That was a passing hint. Now I shall consider it for itself.

As Marx said, every child knows that a social formation which did not reproduce the conditions of production at the same time as it produced would not last a year.[1] The ultimate condition of production is therefore the reproduction of the conditions of production. This may be 'simple' (reproducing exactly the previous conditions of production) or 'on an extended scale' (expanding them). Let us ignore this last distinction for the moment.

What, then, is *the reproduction of the conditions of production*?

Here we are entering a domain which is both very familiar (since *Capital* Volume Two) and uniquely ignored. The tenacious obviousnesses (ideological obviousnesses of an empiricist type) of the point of view of production alone, or even of that of mere productive practice (itself abstract in relation to the process of production) are so integrated into our everyday 'consciousness' that it is extremely hard, not to say almost impossible, to raise oneself to the *point of view of reproduction*. Nevertheless, everything outside this point of view remains abstract (worse than one-sided: distorted)—even at the level of production, and, *a fortiori*, at that of mere practice.

Let us try and examine the matter methodically.

To simplify my exposition, and assuming that every social formation arises from a dominant mode of production, I can say that the process of production sets to work the existing productive forces in and under definite relations of production.

It follows that, in order to exist, every social formation must reproduce the conditions of its production at the same time as it produces, and in order to be able to produce. It must therefore reproduce:

1. the productive forces,
2. the existing relations of production.

[. . .]

INFRASTRUCTURE AND SUPERSTRUCTURE

On a number of occasions[2] I have insisted on the revolutionary character of the Marxist conception of the 'social whole' insofar as it is distinct from the Hegelian 'totality.' I said (and this thesis only repeats famous propositions of historical materialism) that Marx conceived the structure of every society as constituted by 'levels' or 'instances' articulated by a specific determination: the *infrastructure*, or economic base (the 'unity' of the productive forces and the relations of production) and the *superstructure*, which itself contains two 'levels' or 'instances': the politico-legal (law and the State) and ideology (the different ideologies, religious, ethical, legal, political, etc.).

Besides its theoretico-didactic interest (it reveals the difference between Marx and Hegel), this representation has the following crucial theoretical advantage: it makes it possible to inscribe in the theoretical apparatus [*dispositif théorique*] of its essential concepts what I have called their *respective indices of effectivity*. What does this mean?

It is easy to see that this representation of the structure of every society as an edifice containing a base (infrastructure) on which are erected the two 'floors' of the superstructure, is a metaphor, to be quite precise, a spatial metaphor: the metaphor of a topography [*topique*].[3] Like every metaphor, this metaphor suggests something, makes something visible. What? Precisely this: that the upper floors could not 'stay up' (in the air) alone, if they did not rest precisely on their base.

Thus the object of the metaphor of the edifice is to represent above all the 'determination in the last instance' by the economic base. The effect of this spatial metaphor is to endow the base with an index of effectivity known by the famous terms: the determination in the last instance of what happens in the upper 'floors' (of the superstructure) by what happens in the economic base.

Given this index of effectivity 'in the last instance,' the 'floors' of the superstructure are clearly endowed with different indices of effectivity. What kind of indices?

It is possible to say that the floors of the superstructure are not determinant in the last instance, but that they are determined by the effectivity of the base; that if they are determinant in their own (as yet undefined) ways, this is true only insofar as they are determined by the base.

Their index of effectivity (or determination), as determined by the determination in the last instance of the base, is thought by the Marxist tradition in two ways: (1) there is a 'relative autonomy' of the superstructure with respect to the base; (2) there is a 'reciprocal action' of the superstructure on the base.

We can therefore say that the great theoretical advantage of the Marxist topography, i.e. of the spatial metaphor of the edifice (base and superstructure) is simultaneously that it reveals that questions of determination (or of index of effectivity) are crucial; that it reveals that it is the base which in the last instance determines the whole edifice; and that, as a consequence, it obliges us to pose the theoretical problem of the types of 'derivatory' effectivity peculiar to the superstructure, i.e. it obliges us to think what the Marxist tradition calls conjointly the relative autonomy of the superstructure and the reciprocal action of the superstructure on the base.

The greatest disadvantage of this representation of the structure of every society by the spatial metaphor of an edifice, is obviously the fact that it is metaphorical: i.e. it remains *descriptive*.

It now seems to me that it is possible and desirable to represent things differently. NB, I do not mean by this that I want to reject the classical metaphor, for that metaphor itself requires that we go beyond it. And I am not going beyond it in order to reject it as outworn. I simply want to attempt to think what it gives us in the form of a description.

I believe that it is possible and necessary to think what characterizes the essential of the existence and nature of the superstructure *on the basis of reproduction*. Once one takes the point of view of reproduction, many of the questions whose existence was indicated by the spatial metaphor of the edifice, but to which it could not give a conceptual answer, are immediately illuminated.

My basic thesis is that it is not possible to pose these questions (and therefore to answer them) *except from the point of view of reproduction*.

[. . .]

THE STATE

The Marxist tradition is strict, here: in the *Communist Manifesto* and the *Eighteenth Brumaire* (and in all the later classical texts, above all in Marx's writings on the Paris Commune and Lenin's on *State and Revolution*), the State is explicitly conceived as a repressive apparatus [*appareil répressif*]. The State is a 'machine' of repression, which enables the ruling classes (in the nineteenth century the bourgeois class and the 'class' of big landowners) to ensure their domination over the working class, thus enabling the former to subject the latter to the process of surplus-value extortion (i.e. to capitalist exploitation).

The State is thus first of all what the Marxist classics have called *the State apparatus* [*appareil d'État*]. This term means: not only the specialized apparatus [*appareil spécialisé*] (in the narrow sense) whose existence and necessity I have recognized in relation to the requirements of legal practice, i.e. the police, the courts, the prisons; but also the army, which (the proletariat has paid for this experience with its blood) intervenes directly as a supplementary repressive force in the last instance, when the police and its specialized auxiliary corps are 'outrun by events'; and above this ensemble, the head of State, the government and the administration.

Presented in this form, the Marxist-Leninist 'theory' of the State has its finger on the essential point, and not for one moment can there be any question of rejecting the fact that this really is the essential point. The State apparatus, which defines the State as a force of repressive execution and intervention 'in the interests of the ruling classes' in the class struggle conducted by the bourgeoisie and its allies against the proletariat, is quite certainly the State, and quite certainly defines its basic 'function.'

[. . .]

Even after a social revolution like that of 1917, a large part of the State apparatus survived after the seizure of State power by the alliance of the proletariat and the small peasantry: Lenin repeated the fact again and again.

It is possible to describe the distinction between State power and State apparatus as part of the 'Marxist theory' of the State, explicitly present since Marx's *Eighteenth Brumaire* and *Class Struggles in France*.

To summarize the 'Marxist theory of the State' on this point, it can be said that the Marxist classics have always claimed that (1) the State is the repressive State apparatus, (2) State power and State apparatus must be distinguished, (3) the objective of the class struggle concerns State power, and in consequence the use of the State apparatus by the classes (or alliance of classes or of fractions of classes) holding State power as a function of their class objectives, and (4) the proletariat must seize State power in order to destroy the existing bourgeois State apparatus and, in a first phase, replace it with a quite different, proletarian, State apparatus, then in later phases set in motion a radical process, that of the destruction of the State (the end of State power, the end of every State apparatus).

[. . .]

In order to advance the theory of the State it is indispensable to take into account not only the distinction between *State power* and *State apparatus*, but also another reality which is clearly on the side of the (repressive) State apparatus, but must not be confused with it. I shall call this reality by its concept: *the ideological State apparatuses*.

What are the ideological State apparatuses (ISAs)?

They must not be confused with the (repressive) State apparatus. Remember that in Marxist theory, the State Apparatus (SA) contains: the Government, the Administration, the Army, the Police, the Courts, the Prisons, etc., which constitute what I shall in future call the Repressive State Apparatus. Repressive suggests that the State Apparatus in question 'functions by violence'—at least ultimately (since repression, e.g. administrative repression, may take non-physical forms).

[. . .]

But now for what is essential. What distinguishes the ISAs from the (Repressive) State Apparatus is the following basic difference: the Repressive State Apparatus functions 'by violence,' whereas the Ideological State Apparatuses *function 'by ideology.'*

I can clarify matters by correcting this distinction. I shall say rather that every State Apparatus, whether Repressive or Ideological, 'functions' both by violence and by ideology, but with one very important distinction which makes it imperative not to confuse the Ideological State Apparatuses with the (Repressive) State Apparatus.

This is the fact that the (Repressive) State Apparatus functions massively and predominantly *by repression* (including physical repression), while functioning secondarily by ideology. (There is no such thing as a purely repressive apparatus.) For example, the Army and the Police also function by ideology both to ensure their own cohesion and reproduction, and in the 'values' they propound externally.

In the same way, but inversely, it is essential to say that for their part the Ideological State Apparatuses function massively and predominantly *by ideology*, but they also function secondarily by repression, even if ultimately, but only ultimately, this is very attenuated and concealed, even symbolic. (There is no such thing as a purely ideological apparatus.) Thus Schools and Churches use suitable methods of punishment, expulsion, selection, etc., to 'discipline' not only their shepherds, but also their flocks. The same is true of the Family. . . . The same is true of the cultural IS Apparatus (censorship, among other things), etc.

[. . .]

To my knowledge, *no class can hold State power over a long period without at the same time exercising its hegemony over and in the State Ideological Apparatuses*. I only need one example and proof of this: Lenin's anguished concern to revolutionize the educational Ideological State Apparatus (among others), simply to make it possible for the Soviet proletariat, who had seized State power, to secure the future of the dictatorship of the proletariat and the transition to socialism.[4]

[. . .]

IDEOLOGY IS A 'REPRESENTATION' OF THE IMAGINARY RELATIONSHIP OF INDIVIDUALS TO THEIR REAL CONDITIONS OF EXISTENCE

In order to approach my central thesis on the structure and functioning of ideology, I shall first present two theses, one negative, the other positive. The first concerns the object which is 'represented' in the imaginary form of ideology, the second concerns the materiality of ideology.

Thesis 1: Ideology represents the imaginary relationship of individuals to their real conditions of existence.

We commonly call religious ideology, ethical ideology, legal ideology, political ideology, etc., so many 'world outlooks.' Of course, assuming that we do not live one of these ideologies as the truth (e.g. 'believe' in God, Duty, Justice, etc. . . .), we admit that the ideology we are discussing from a critical point of view, examining it as the ethnologist examines the myths of a 'primitive society,' that these 'world outlooks' are largely imaginary, i.e. do not 'correspond to reality.'

However, while admitting that they do not correspond to reality, i.e. that they constitute an illusion, we admit that they do make allusion to reality, and that they need only be 'interpreted' to discover the reality of the world behind their imaginary representation of that world (ideology = *illusion/allusion*).

[. . .]

Thesis 2: Ideology has a material existence.

[. . .]

While discussing the ideological State apparatuses and their practices, I said that each of them was the realization of an ideology (the unity of these different regional ideologies—religious, ethical, legal, political, aesthetic, etc.—being assured by their subjection to the ruling ideology). I now return to this thesis: an ideology always exists in an apparatus, and its practice, or practices. This existence is material.

Of course, the material existence of the ideology in an apparatus and its practices does not have the same modality as the material existence of a paving-stone or a rifle. But, at the risk of being taken for a Neo-Aristotelian (NB Marx had a very high regard for Aristotle), I shall say that 'matter is discussed in many senses,' or rather that it exists in different modalities, all rooted in the last instance in 'physical' matter.

Having said this, let me move straight on and see what happens to the 'individuals' who live in ideology, i.e. in a determinate (religious, ethical, etc.) representation of the world whose imaginary distortion depends on their imaginary relation to their conditions of existence, in other words, in the last instance, to the relations of production and to class relations (ideology = an imaginary relation to real relations). I shall say that this imaginary relation is itself endowed with a material existence.

Now I observe the following.

An individual believes in God, or Duty, or Justice, etc. This belief derives (for everyone, i.e. for all those who live in an ideological representation of ideology, which reduces ideology to ideas endowed by definition with a spiritual existence) from the ideas of the individual concerned, i.e. from him as a subject with a consciousness which contains the ideas of his belief. In this way, i.e. by means of the absolutely ideological 'conceptual' device [*dispositif*] thus set up (a subject endowed with a consciousness in which he freely forms or freely recognizes ideas in which he believes), the (material) attitude of the subject concerned naturally follows.

The individual in question behaves in such and such a way, adopts such and such a practical attitude, and, what is more, participates in certain regular practices which are those of the ideological apparatus on which 'depend' the ideas which he has in all consciousness freely chosen as a subject. If he believes in God, he goes to Church to attend Mass, kneels, prays, confesses, does penance (once it was material in the ordinary sense of the term) and naturally repents and so on. If he believes in Duty, he will have the corresponding attitudes, inscribed in ritual practices 'according to the correct principles.' If he believes in Justice, he will submit unconditionally to the rules of the Law, and may even protest when they are violated, sign petitions, take part in a demonstration, etc.

Throughout this schema we observe that the ideological representation of ideology is itself forced to recognize that every 'subject' endowed with a 'consciousness' and believing in the 'ideas' that his 'consciousness' inspires in him and freely accepts, must '*act* according to his ideas,' must therefore inscribe his own ideas as a free subject in the actions of his material practice. If he does not do so, 'that is wicked.'

Indeed, if he does not do what he ought to do as a function of what he believes, it is because he does something else, which, still as a function of the same idealist scheme, implies that he has other ideas in his head as well as those he proclaims, and that he acts according to these other ideas, as a man who is either 'inconsistent' ('no one is willingly evil') or cynical, or perverse.

In every case, the ideology of ideology thus recognizes, despite its imaginary distortion, that the 'ideas' of a human subject exist in his actions, or ought to exist in his actions, and if that is not the case, it lends him other ideas corresponding to the actions (however perverse) that he does perform. This ideology talks of actions: I shall talk of actions inserted into *practices*. And I shall point out that these practices are governed by the *rituals* in which these practices are inscribed, within the *material existence of an ideological apparatus*, be it only a small part of that apparatus: a small mass in a small church, a funeral, a minor match at a sports' club, a school day, a political party meeting, etc.

[. . .]

But this very presentation reveals that we have retained the following notions: subject, consciousness, belief, actions. From this series I shall immediately extract the decisive central term on which everything else depends: the notion of the *subject*.

And I shall immediately set down two conjoint theses:

1. there is no practice except by and in an ideology;
2. there is no ideology except by the subject and for subjects.

I can now come to my central thesis.

IDEOLOGY INTERPELLATES INDIVIDUALS AS SUBJECTS

This thesis is simply a matter of making my last proposition explicit: there is no ideology except by the subject and for subjects. Meaning, there is no ideology except for concrete subjects, and this destination for ideology is only made possible by the subject: meaning, *by the category of the subject* and its functioning.

By this I mean that, even if it only appears under this name (the subject) with the rise of bourgeois ideology, above all with the rise of legal ideology,[5] the category of the subject (which may function under other names: e.g., as the soul in Plato, as God, etc.) is the constitutive category of all ideology, whatever its determination (regional or class) and whatever its historical date—since ideology has no history.

I say: the category of the subject is constitutive of all ideology, but at the same time and immediately I add that *the category of the subject is only constitutive of all ideology insofar as all ideology has the function (which defines it) of 'constituting' concrete individuals as subjects*. In the interaction of this double constitution exists the functioning of all ideology, ideology being nothing but its functioning in the material forms of existence of that functioning.

In order to grasp what follows, it is essential to realize that both he who is writing these lines and the reader who reads them are themselves subjects, and therefore ideological subjects (a tautological proposition), i.e. that the author and the reader of these lines both live 'spontaneously' or 'naturally' in ideology in the sense in which I have said that 'man is an ideological animal by nature.'

[. . .]

Thus in order to represent why the category of the 'subject' is constitutive of ideology, which only exists by constituting concrete subjects as subjects, I shall employ a special mode of exposition: 'concrete' enough to be recognized, but abstract enough to be thinkable and thought, giving rise to a knowledge.

As a first formulation I shall say: *all ideology hails or interpellates concrete individuals as concrete subjects*, by the functioning of the category of the subject.

This is a proposition which entails that we distinguish for the moment between concrete individuals on the one hand and concrete subjects on the other, although at this level concrete subjects only exist insofar as they are supported by a concrete individual.

I shall then suggest that ideology 'acts' or 'functions' in such a way that it 'recruits' subjects among the individuals (it recruits them all), or 'transforms' the individuals into subjects (it transforms them all) by that very precise operation which I have called *interpellation* or hailing, and which can be imagined along the lines of the most commonplace everyday police (or other) hailing: 'Hey, you there!'[6]

Assuming that the theoretical scene I have imagined takes place in the street, the hailed individual will turn round. By this mere one-hundred-and-eighty-degree physical conversion, he becomes a *subject*. Why? Because he has recognized that the hail was 'really' addressed to him, and that 'it was *really him* who was hailed' (and not someone else). Experience shows that the practical telecommunication of hailings is such that they hardly ever miss their man: verbal call or whistle, the one hailed always recognizes that it is really him who is being hailed. And yet it is a strange phenomenon, and one which cannot be explained solely by 'guilt feelings,' despite the large numbers who 'have something on their consciences.'

Naturally for the convenience and clarity of my little theoretical theatre I have had to present things in the form of a sequence, with a before and an after, and thus in the form of a temporal succession. There are individuals walking along. Somewhere (usually behind them) the hail rings out: 'Hey, you there!' One individual (nine times out of ten it is the right one) turns round, believing/suspecting/knowing that it is for him, i.e. recognizing that 'it really is he' who is meant by the hailing. But in reality these things happen without any succession. The existence of ideology and the hailing or interpellation of individuals as subjects are one and the same thing.

I might add: what thus seems to take place outside ideology (to be precise, in the street), in reality takes place in ideology. What really takes place in ideology seems therefore to take place outside it. That is why those who are in ideology believe themselves by definition outside ideology: one of the effects of ideology is the practical *denegation* of the ideological character of ideology by ideology: ideology never says, 'I am ideological.' It is necessary to be outside ideology, i.e. in scientific knowledge, to be able to say: I am in ideology (a quite exceptional case) or (the general case): I was in ideology. As is well known, the accusation of being in ideology only applies to others, never to oneself (unless one is really a Spinozist or a Marxist, which, in this matter, is to be exactly the same thing). Which amounts to saying that ideology *has no outside* (for itself), but at the same time *that it is nothing but outside* (for science and reality).

[. . .]

Thus ideology hails or interpellates individuals as subjects. As ideology is eternal, I must now suppress the temporal form in which I have presented the functioning of ideology, and say: ideology has always-already interpellated individuals as subjects, which amounts to making it clear that individuals are always-already interpellated by ideology as subjects, which necessarily leads us to one last proposition: *individuals are always-already subjects*. Hence individuals are 'abstract' with respect to the subjects which they always already are. This proposition might seem paradoxical. That an individual is always-already a subject, even before he is born, is nevertheless the plain reality, accessible to everyone and not a paradox at all. Freud shows that individuals are always 'abstract' with respect to the subjects they always-already are, simply by noting the ideological ritual that surrounds the expectation of a 'birth,' that 'happy event.' Everyone knows how much and in what way an unborn child is expected. Which amounts to saying, very prosaically, if we agree to drop the 'sentiments,' i.e. the forms of family ideology (paternal/maternal/conjugal/fraternal) in which the unborn child is expected: it is certain in advance that it will bear its Father's Name, and will therefore have an identity and be irreplaceable. Before its birth, the child is therefore

always-already a subject, appointed as a subject in and by the specific familial ideological configuration in which it is 'expected' once it has been conceived. I hardly need add that this familial ideological configuration is, in its uniqueness, highly structured, and that it is in this implacable and more or less 'pathological' (presupposing that any meaning can be assigned to that term) structure that the former subject-to-be will have to 'find' 'its' place, i.e. 'become' the sexual subject (boy or girl) which it already is in advance. It is clear that this ideological constraint and pre-appointment, and all the rituals of rearing and then education in the family, have some relationship with what Freud studied in the forms of the pre-genital and genital 'stages' of sexuality, i.e. in the 'grip' of what Freud registered by its effects as being the unconscious. But let us leave this point, too, on one side.
[. . .]

AN EXAMPLE: THE CHRISTIAN RELIGIOUS IDEOLOGY
[. . .]

Let me summarize what we have discovered about ideology in general.

The duplicate mirror-structure of ideology ensures simultaneously:

1. the interpellation of 'individuals' as subjects;
2. their subjection to the Subject;
3. the mutual recognition of subjects and Subject, the subjects' recognition of each other, and finally the subject's recognition of himself;[7]
4. the absolute guarantee that everything really is so, and that on condition that the subjects recognize what they are and behave accordingly, everything will be all right: Amen—'*So be it.*'

Result: caught in this quadruple system of interpellation as subjects, of subjection to the Subject, of universal recognition and of absolute guarantee, the subjects 'work,' they 'work by themselves' in the vast majority of cases, with the exception of the 'bad subjects' who on occasion provoke the intervention of one of the detachments of the (repressive) State apparatus. But the vast majority of (good) subjects work all right 'all by themselves,' i.e. by ideology (whose concrete forms are realized in the Ideological State Apparatuses). They are inserted into practices governed by the rituals of the ISAs. They 'recognize' the existing state of affairs [*das Bestehende*], that 'it really is true that it is so and not otherwise,' and that they must be obedient to God, to their conscience, to the priest, to de Gaulle, to the boss, to the engineer, that thou shalt 'love thy neighbour as thyself,' etc. Their concrete, material behaviour is simply the inscription in life of the admirable words of the prayer: '*Amen—So be it.*'

Yes, the subjects 'work by themselves.' The whole mystery of this effect lies in the first two moments of the quadruple system I have just discussed, or, if you prefer, in the ambiguity of the term *subject*. In the ordinary use of the term, subject in fact means: (1) a free subjectivity, a centre of initiatives, author of and responsible for its actions; (2) a subjected being, who submits to a higher authority, and is therefore stripped of all freedom except that of freely accepting his submission. This last note gives us the meaning of this ambiguity, which is merely a reflection of the effect which produces it: the individual *is interpellated as a (free) subject in order that he shall submit freely to the commandments of the Subject, i.e. in order that he shall (freely) accept his subjection*, i.e. in order that he shall make the gestures and actions of his subjection 'all by himself.' *There are no subjects except by and for their subjection*. That is why they 'work all by themselves.'

[. . .]

NOTES

1. Marx to Kugelmann, 11 July 1868, *Selected Correspondence* (Moscow: Progress Publishers, 1955), 209.

2. In *For Marx*, trans. Ben Brewster (New York: Verso Books, 2006) and *Reading Capital*, trans. Ben Brewster (New York: Verso Books, 2016).

3. *Topography* from the Greek *topos*: place. A topography represents in a definite space the respective *sites* occupied by several realities: thus the economic is *at the bottom* (the base), the superstructure *above it*.

4. In a pathetic text written in 1937, Krupskaya relates the history of Lenin's desperate efforts and what she regards as his failure.

5. Which borrowed the legal category of 'subject in law' to make an ideological notion: man is by nature a subject.

6. Hailing as an everyday practice subject to a precise ritual takes a quite 'special' form in the policeman's practice of 'hailing' which concerns the hailing of 'suspects.'

7. Hegel is (unknowingly) an admirable 'theoretician' of ideology insofar as he is a 'theoretician' of Universal Recognition who unfortunately ends up in the ideology of Absolute Knowledge. Feuerbach is an astonishing 'theoretician' of the mirror connexion, who unfortunately ends up in the ideology of the Human Essence. To find the material with which to construct a theory of the guarantee, we must turn to Spinoza.

BIBLIOGRAPHY

Althusser, Louis. *For Marx*. Translated by Ben Brewster. New York: Verso Books, 2006.

Althusser, Louis. *Reading Capital*. Translated by Ben Brewster. New York: Verso Books, 2016.

Marx, Karl. *Selected Correspondence*. Moscow: Progress Publishers, 1955.

20

THE TECHNOLOGY OF GENDER

Teresa de Lauretis

In the feminist writings and cultural practices of the 1960s and 1970s, the notion of gender as sexual difference was central to the critique of representation, the rereading of cultural images and narratives, the questioning of theories of subjectivity and textuality, of reading, writing, and spectatorship. The notion of gender *as* sexual difference has grounded and sustained feminist interventions in the arena of formal and abstract knowledge, in the epistemologies and cognitive fields defined by the social and physical sciences as well as the human sciences or humanities. Concurrent and interdependent with those interventions were the elaboration of specific practices and discourses, and the creation of social spaces (gendered spaces, in the sense of the "women's room," such as CR groups, women's caucuses within the disciplines, Women's Studies, feminist journal or media collectives, and so on) in which sexual difference itself could be affirmed, addressed, analyzed, specified, or verified. But that notion of gender as sexual difference and its derivative notions—women's culture, mothering, feminine writing, femininity, etc.—have now become a limitation, something of a liability to feminist thought.

With its emphasis on the sexual, "sexual difference" is in the first and last instance a difference of women from men, female from male; and even the more abstract notion of "sexual differences" resulting not from biology or socialization but from signification and discursive effects (the emphasis here being less on the sexual than on differences as *différance*), ends up being in the last instance a difference (of woman) from man—or better, the very instance of difference *in* man. To continue to pose the question of gender in either of these terms, once the critique of patriarchy has been fully outlined, keeps feminist thinking bound to the terms of Western patriarchy itself, contained within the frame of a conceptual opposition that is "always already" inscribed in what Fredric Jameson would call "the political unconscious" of dominant cultural discourses and their underlying "master narratives"—be they biological, medical, legal, philosophical, or literary—and so will tend to reproduce itself, to retextualize itself, as we shall see, even in feminist rewritings of cultural narratives.

The first limit of "sexual difference(s)," then, is that it constrains feminist critical thought within the conceptual frame of a universal sex opposition (woman as the difference from man, both universalized; or woman as difference *tout court*, and hence equally universalized), which makes it very difficult, if not impossible, to articulate the differences of women from Woman, that is to say, the differences among women or, perhaps more exactly, the differences *within women*. For example, the differences among women who wear the veil, women who "wear the mask" (in the words of Paul Laurence Dunbar often quoted by black American women writers), and women who "masquerade" (the word is Joan Riviere's) cannot be understood as sexual differences.[1] From that point of view, they would not be differences at all, and all women would but render either different embodiments of some archetypal essence of woman, or more or less sophisticated impersonations of a metaphysical-discursive femininity.

A second limitation of the notion of sexual difference(s) is that it tends to recontain or recuperate the radical epistemological potential of feminist thought inside the walls of the master's to borrow Audre Lorde's metaphor rather than Nietzsche's "prison-house of language," for reasons that will presently become apparent. By radical epistemological potential I mean the possibility, already emergent in feminist writings of the 1980s, to conceive of the social subject and of the relations of subjectivity to sociality in another way: a subject constituted in gender, to be sure, though not by sexual difference alone, but rather across languages and cultural representations; a subject engendered in the experiencing of race and class, as well as sexual, relations; a subject, therefore, not unified but rather multiple, and not so much divided as contradicted.

In order to begin to specify this other kind of subject and to articulate its relations to a heterogeneous social field, we need a notion of gender that is not so bound up with sexual difference as to be virtually coterminous with it and such that, on the one hand, gender is assumed to derive unproblematically from sexual difference while, on the other, gender can be subsumed in sexual differences as an effect of language, or as pure imaginary—nothing to do with the real. This bind, this mutual containment of gender and sexual difference(s), needs to be unraveled and deconstructed. A starting point may be to think of gender along the lines of Michel Foucault's theory of sexuality as a "technology of sex" and to propose that gender, too, both as representation and as self-representation, is the product of various social technologies, such as cinema, and of institutionalized discourses, epistemologies, and critical practices, as well as practices of daily life.

Like sexuality, we might then say, gender is not a property of bodies or something originally existent in human beings, but "the set of effects produced in bodies, behaviors, and social relations," in Foucault's words, by the deployment of "a complex political technology."[2] But it must be said first off, and hence the title of this essay, that to think of gender as the product and the process of a number of social technologies, of techno-social or bio-medical apparati, is to have already gone beyond Foucault, for his critical understanding of the technology of sex did not take into account its differential solicitation of male and female subjects, and by ignoring the conflicting investments of men and women in the discourses and practices of sexuality, Foucault's theory, in fact, excludes, though it does not preclude, the consideration of gender.

I will proceed by stating a series of four propositions in decreasing order of self-evidence and subsequently will go back to elaborate on each in more detail.

(1) Gender is (a) representation—which is not to say that it does not have concrete or real implications, both social and subjective, for the material life of individuals. On the contrary.

(2) The representation of gender *is* its construction—and in the simplest sense it can be said that all of Western Art and high culture is the engraving of the history of that construction.

(3) The construction of gender goes on as busily today as it did in earlier times, say the Victorian era. And it goes on not only where one might expect it to—in the media, the private and public schools, the courts, the family, nuclear or extended or single-parented—in short, in what Louis Althusser has called the "ideological state apparati." The construction of gender also goes on, if less obviously, in the academy, in the intellectual community, in avant-garde artistic practices and radical theories, even, and indeed especially, in feminism.

(4) Paradoxically, therefore, the construction of gender is also effected by its deconstruction; that is to say, by any discourse, feminist or otherwise, that would discard it as ideological misrepresentation. For gender, like the real, is not only the effect of representation but also its excess, what remains outside discourse as a potential trauma which can rupture or destabilize, if not contained, any representation.

[. . .]

When Althusser wrote that ideology represents "not the system of the real relations which govern the existence of individuals, but the imaginary relation of those individuals to the real relations in which they live" and which govern their existence, he was also describing, to my mind exactly, the functioning of gender.[3] But, it will be objected, it is reductive or overly simplistic to equate gender with ideology. Certainly Althusser does not do that, nor does traditional Marxist thought, where gender is a somewhat marginal issue, one limited to "the woman question."[4] For, like sexuality and subjectivity, gender is located in the private sphere of reproduction, procreation, and the family, rather than in the public, properly social, sphere of the superstructural, where ideology belongs and is determined by the economic forces and relations of production.

And yet, reading on in Althusser, one finds the emphatic statement *"All ideology has the function (which defines it) of 'constituting' concrete individuals as subjects."*[5] If I substitute *gender* for *ideology*, the statement still works, but with a slight shift of the terms: Gender has the function (which defines it) of constituting concrete individuals as men and women. That shift is precisely where the relation of gender to ideology can be seen, and seen to be an effect of the ideology of gender. The shift from "subjects" to "men and women" marks the conceptual distance between two orders of discourse, the discourse of philosophy or political theory and the discourse of "reality." Gender is granted (and taken for granted) in the latter but excluded from the former.

Although the Althusserian subject of ideology derives more from Lacan's subject (which is an effect of signification, founded on misrecognition) than from the unified class subject of Marxist humanism, it too is ungendered, as neither of these systems considers the possibility—let alone the process of constitution—of a female subject.[6] Thus, by Althusser's own definition, we are entitled to ask, If gender exists in "reality," if it exists in "the real relations which govern the existence of individuals," but not in philosophy or political theory, what do the latter in fact represent if not "the imaginary relation of individuals to the real relations in which they live"? In other words, Althusser's theory of ideology is itself caught and blind to its own complicity in the ideology of gender. But that is not all: more important, and more to the immediate point of my argument, Althusser's theory, to the extent that a theory can be validated by institutional discourses and acquire power or control over the field of social meaning, can itself function as a technology of gender.

[. . .]

For if the sex–gender system (which I prefer to call gender *tout court* in order to retain the ambiguity of the term, which makes it eminently susceptible to the grasp of ideology, as well as deconstruction) is a set of social relations obtaining throughout social existence, then gender is indeed a primary instance of ideology, and obviously not only for women. Furthermore, that is so regardless of whether particular individuals see themselves primarily defined (and oppressed) by gender, as white cultural feminists do, or primarily defined (and oppressed) by race and class relations, as women of color do.[7] The importance of Althusser's formulation of the subjective working of ideology—again, briefly, that ideology needs a subject, a concrete individual or person to work on—appears more clearly now, and more central to the feminist project of theorizing gender as a personal-political force both negative and positive as I will propose.

To assert that the social representation of gender affects its subjective construction and that, vice versa, the subjective representation of gender—or self-representation—affects its social construction, leaves open a possibility of agency and self-determination at the subjective and even individual level of micropolitical and everyday practices which Althusser himself would clearly disclaim. I, nevertheless, will claim that possibility [. . .]. For the moment, going back to proposition 2, which was revised as "The construction of gender is both the product and the process of its representation," I can rewrite it: *The construction of gender is the product and the process of both representation and self-representation.*

But now I must discuss a further problem with Althusser, insofar as a theory of gender is concerned, and that is that in his view, "ideology has no outside." It is a foolproof system whose effect is to erase its own traces completely, so that anyone who is "in ideology," caught in its web, believes "himself" to be outside and free of it. Nevertheless, there is an outside, a place from where ideology can be seen for what it is—mystification, imaginary relation, wool over one's eyes; and that place is, for Althusser, science, or scientific knowledge. Such is simply not the case for feminism and for what I propose to call, avoiding further equivocations, the subject of feminism.

By the phrase "the subject of feminism" I mean a conception or an understanding of the (female) subject as not only distinct from Woman with the capital letter, the *representation* of an essence inherent in all women (which has been seen as Nature, Mother, Mystery, Evil Incarnate, Object of [Masculine] Desire and Knowledge, Proper Womanhood, Femininity, et cetera), but also distinct from women, the real, historical beings and social subjects who are defined by the technology of gender and actually engendered in social relations. The subject of feminism I have in mind is one *not* so defined, one whose definition or conception is in progress, in this and other feminist critical texts; and, to insist on this point one more time, the subject of feminism, much like Althusser's subject, is a theoretical construct (a way of conceptualizing, of understanding, of accounting for certain *processes*, not women). However, unlike Althusser's subject, who, being completely "in" ideology, believes himself to be outside and free of it, the subject that I see emerging from current writings and debates within feminism is one that is at the same time inside *and* outside the ideology of gender, and conscious of being so, conscious of that twofold pull, of that division, that doubled vision.

[. . .]

It is obvious that feminism and a full adherence to the ideology of gender, in male-centered societies, are mutually exclusive. And I would add, further, that the consciousness of our complicity with gender ideology, and the divisions and contradictions attendant upon that, are what must characterize all feminisms today in the United States, no longer just white and middle-class women, who were the first to be forced to examine our relation to institutions, political practice, cultural apparati, and then to racism, anti-Semitism, hetero-sexism, classism, and so forth; for the consciousness of complicity with the gender ideologies of their particular cultures and subcultures is also emerging in the more recent writings of black women and Latinas, and of those lesbians, of whatever color, who identify themselves as feminists.[8] To what extent this newer or emerging consciousness of complicity acts with or against the consciousness of oppression, is a question central to the understanding of ideology in these postmodern and postcolonial times.

That is why, in spite of the divergences, the political and personal differences, and the pain that surround feminist debates within and across racial, ethnic, and sexual lines, we may be encouraged in the hope that feminism will continue to develop a radical theory and a practice of sociocultural transformation. For that to be, however, the ambiguity of gender must be retained—and that is only seemingly a paradox. We cannot resolve or dispel the uncomfortable condition of being at once inside and outside gender either by desexualizing it (making gender merely a metaphor, a question of *différance*, of purely discursive effects) or by androgynizing it (claiming the same experience of material conditions for both genders in a given class, race, or culture).

[. . .]

Most of us—those of us who are women; to those who are men this will not apply—probably check the *F* box rather than the *M* box when filling out an application form.

It would hardly occur to us to mark *M*. It would be like cheating or, worse, not existing, like erasing ourselves from the world. (For men to check the *F* box, were they ever tempted to do so, would have quite another set of implications.) For since the very first time we put a check mark on the little square next to the *F* on the form, we have officially entered the sex–gender system, the social relations of gender, and have become engendered as women; that is to say, not only do other people consider us females, but from that moment on *we* have been representing ourselves as women. Now, I ask, isn't that the same as saying that the *F* next to the little box, which we marked in filling out the form, has stuck to us like a wet silk dress? Or that while we thought that we were marking the *F* on the form, in fact the *F* was marking itself on us?

This is, of course, the process described by Althusser with the word *interpellation*, the process whereby a social representation is accepted and absorbed by an individual as her (or his) own representation, and so becomes, for that individual, real, even though it is in fact imaginary. However, my example is all too simple. It does not explain how the representation is constructed and how it is then accepted and absorbed. For that purpose we turn, first, to Michel Foucault.

The first volume of Foucault's *History of Sexuality* has become highly influential, especially his bold thesis that sexuality, commonly thought to be a natural as well as a private, intimate matter, is in fact completely constructed in culture according to the political aims of the society's dominant class. Foucault's analysis begins from a paradox: the prohibitions and regulations pertaining to sexual behaviors, whether spoken by religious, legal, or scientific authorities, far from constraining or repressing sexuality, have on the contrary produced it, and continue to produce it, in the sense in which industrial machinery produces goods or commodities, and in so doing also produces social relations.

Hence the notion of a "technology of sex," which he defines as "a set of techniques for maximizing life" that have been developed and deployed by the bourgeoisie since the end of the eighteenth century in order to ensure its class survival and continued hegemony. Those techniques involved the elaboration of discourses (classification, measurements, evaluation, etc.) about four privileged "figures" or objects of knowledge: the sexualization of children and of the female body, the control of procreation, and the psychiatrization of anomalous sexual behavior as perversion. These discourses, which were implemented through pedagogy, medicine, demography, and economics, were anchored or supported by the institutions of the state, and became especially focused on the family; they served to disseminate and to "implant," in Foucault's suggestive term, those figures and modes of knowledge into each individual, family, and institution. This technology, he remarked, "made sex not only a secular concern but a concern of the state as well; to be more exact, sex became a matter that required the social body as a whole, and virtually all of its individuals, to place themselves under surveillance."[9]

The sexualization of the female body has indeed been a favorite figure or object of knowledge in the discourses of medical science, religion, art, literature, popular culture, and so on. Since Foucault, several studies have appeared that address the topic, more or less explicitly, in his historical methodological framework;[10] but the connection between woman and sexuality, and the identification of the sexual with the female body, so pervasive in Western culture, had long been a major concern of feminist criticism and of the women's movement quite independently of Foucault, of course. In particular, feminist film criticism had been addressing itself to that issue in a conceptual framework which, though not derived from Foucault, yet was not altogether dissimilar.

For some time before the publication of volume I of *The History of Sexuality* in France (*La volonté de savoir*, 1976), feminist film theorists had been writing on the sexualization of the female star in narrative cinema and analyzing the cinematic techniques (lighting, framing, editing, etc.) and the specific cinematic codes (e.g., the system of the look) that construct woman as image, as the object of the spectator's voyeurist gaze; and they had been developing both an account and a critique of the psycho-social, aesthetic, and philosophical discourses that underlie the representation of the female body as the primary site of sexuality and visual pleasure.[11] The understanding of cinema as a social technology, as a "cinematic apparatus," was developed in film theory contemporaneously with Foucault's work but independently of it; rather, as the word *apparatus* suggests, it was directly influenced by the work of Althusser and Lacan.[12] There is little doubt, at any rate, that cinema—the cinematic apparatus—is a technology of gender, as I have argued throughout *Alice Doesn't*, if not in these very words, I hope convincingly.

The theory of the cinematic apparatus is more concerned than Foucault's with answering both parts of the question I started from: not only how the representation of gender is constructed by the given technology, but also how it becomes absorbed subjectively by each individual whom that technology addresses. For the second part of the question, the crucial notion is the concept of spectatorship, which feminist film theory has established as a gendered concept; that is to say, the ways in which each individual spectator is addressed by the film, the ways in which his/her identification is solicited and structured in the single film,[13] are intimately and intentionally, if not usually explicitly, connected to the spectators' gender. Both in the critical writings and in the practices of women's cinema, the exploration of female spectatorship is giving us a more subtly articulated analysis of the modalities of film viewing for women and increasingly sophisticated forms of address in filmmaking.

This critical work is producing a knowledge of cinema *and* of the technology of sex which Foucault's theory could not lead to, on its own terms; for there, sexuality is not understood as gendered, as having a male form and a female form, but is taken to be one and the same for all—and consequently male. I am not speaking of the libido, which Freud said to be only one, and I think he may have been right about that. I am speaking here of sexuality as a construct and a (self-) representation; and that does have both a male form and a female form, although in the patriarchal or male-centered frame of mind, the female form is a projection of the male's, its complementary opposite, its extrapolation—Adam's rib, so to speak. So that, even when it is located *in* the woman's body (seen, Foucault wrote, "as being thoroughly saturated with sexuality"[14]), sexuality is perceived as an attribute or a property of the male.

[. . .]

Hence the paradox that mars Foucault's theory, as it does other contemporary, radical but male-centered, theories: in order to combat the social technology that produces sexuality and sexual oppression, these theories (and their respective politics) will deny gender. But to deny gender, first of all, is to deny the social relations of gender that constitute and validate the sexual oppression of women; and second, to deny gender is to remain "in ideology," an ideology which (not coincidentally if, of course, not intentionally) is manifestly self-serving to the male-gendered subject.

[. . .]

I will then rewrite my third proposition: *The construction of gender goes on today through the various technologies of gender (e.g., cinema) and institutional discourses (e.g., theory) with power to control the field of social meaning and thus produce, promote, and "implant" representations of gender. But the terms of a different construction of gender also exist, in the margins of hegemonic discourses. Posed from outside the heterosexual social contract, and inscribed in micropolitical practices, these terms can also have a part in the construction of gender, and their effects are rather at the "local" level of resistances, in subjectivity and self-representation.*

[. . .]

So it is that, by displacing the question of gender onto an ahistorical, purely textual figure of femininity (Derrida); or by shifting the sexual basis of gender quite beyond sexual difference, onto a body of diffuse pleasures (Foucault) and libidinally invested surfaces (Lyotard), or a body-site of undifferentiated affectivity, and hence a subject freed from (self) representation and the constraints of identity (Deleuze); and finally by displacing the ideology, but also the reality—the historicity—of gender onto this diffuse, decentered, or deconstructed (but certainly not female) subject—so it is that, paradoxically again, these theories make their appeal to women, naming the process of such displacing with the term *becoming woman (devenir-femme)*.

In other words, only by denying sexual difference (and gender) as components of subjectivity in real women, and hence by denying the history of women's political oppression and resistance, as well as the epistemological contribution of feminism to the redefinition of subjectivity and sociality, can the philosophers see in "women" the privileged repository of "the future of mankind." That, Braidotti observes, "is nothing but the old mental habit [of philosophers] of thinking the masculine as synonymous with universal, the mental habit of translating women into metaphor."[15] That this habit is older, and so harder to break than the Cartesian subject, may account for the predominant disregard, when it is not outright contempt, that male intellectuals have for feminist theorizing, in spite of occasional gestures in the direction of "women's struggles" or the granting of political status to the women's movement. That should not, and does not, prevent feminist theorists from reading, rereading and rewriting their works.

On the contrary, the need for feminist theory to continue its radical critique of dominant discourses on gender, such as these are, even as they attempt to do away with sexual difference altogether, is all the more pressing since the word *postfeminism* has been spoken, and not in vain. This kind of deconstruction of the subject is effectively a way to recontain women in femininity (Woman) and to reposition female subjectivity *in* the male subject, however that will be defined. Furthermore, it closes the door in the face of the emergent social subject which these discourses are purportedly seeking to address, a subject constituted across a multiplicity of differences in discursive and material heterogeneity. Again, then, I rewrite: *If the deconstruction of gender inevitably effects its (re)construction, the question is, in which terms and in whose interest is the de-re-construction being effected?*

[. . .] The difficulty we find in theorizing the construction of subjectivity in textuality is greatly increased, and the task proportionately more urgent, when the subjectivity in question is en-gendered in a relation to sexuality that is altogether unrepresentable in the terms of hegemonic discourses on sexuality and gender. The problem, which is a problem for all feminist scholars and teachers, is one we face almost daily in our work, namely, that most of the available theories of reading, writing, sexuality, ideology, or any other cultural production are built on male narratives of gender, whether oedipal or anti-oedipal, bound by the heterosexual contract; narratives which persistently tend to re-produce themselves in feminist theories. They *tend to*, and will do so unless one constantly resists, suspicious of their drift. Which is why the critique of all discourses concerning gender, including those produced or promoted as feminist, continues to be as vital a part of feminism as is the ongoing effort to create new spaces of discourse, to rewrite cultural narratives, and to define the terms of another perspective—a view from "elsewhere."

For, if that view is nowhere to be seen, not given in a single text, not recognizable as a representation, it is not that we—feminists, women—have not yet succeeded in producing it. It is, rather, that what we have produced is not recognizable, precisely, as a representation. For that "elsewhere" is not some mythic distant past or some utopian future history: it is the elsewhere of discourse here and now, the blind spots, or the space-off, of its representations. I think of it as spaces in the margins of hegemonic discourses, social spaces carved in the interstices of institutions and in the chinks and cracks of the power-knowledge apparati. And it is there that the terms of a different construction of gender can be posed—terms that do have effect and take hold at the level of subjectivity and self-representation: in the micropolitical practices of daily life and daily resistances that afford both agency and sources of power or empowering investments; and in the cultural productions of women, feminists, which inscribe that movement in and out of ideology, that crossing back and forth of the boundaries—and of the limits—of sexual difference(s).

I want to be very clear about this movement back and forth across the boundaries of sexual difference. I do *not* mean a movement from one space to another beyond it, or outside: say, from the space of a representation, the image produced by representation in a discursive or visual field, to the space outside the representation, the space outside discourse, which would then be thought of as "real"; or, as Althusser would say, from the space of ideology to the space of scientific and real knowledge; or again, from the symbolic space constructed by the sex–gender system to a "reality" external to it. For, clearly, no social reality exists for a given society outside of its particular sex–gender system (the mutually exclusive and exhaustive categories of male and female). What I mean, instead, is a movement from the space represented by/in a representation, by/in a discourse, by/in a sex–gender system, to the space not represented yet implied (unseen) in them.

A while ago I used the expression "space-off," borrowed from film theory: the space not visible in the frame but inferable from what the frame makes visible. In classical and commercial cinema, the space-off is, in fact, erased, or, better, recontained and sealed into the image by the cinematic rules of narrativization (first among them, the shot/reverse-shot system). But avant-garde cinema has shown the space-off to exist concurrently and alongside the represented space, has made it visible by remarking its absence in the frame or in the succession of frames, and has shown it to include not only the camera (the point of articulation and perspective from which the image is constructed) but also the spectator (the point where the image is received, re-constructed, and re-produced in/as subjectivity).

Now, the movement in and out of gender as ideological representation, which I propose characterizes the subject of feminism, is a movement back and forth between the representation of gender (in its male-centered frame of reference) and what that representation leaves out or, more pointedly, makes unrepresentable. It is a movement between the (represented) discursive space of the positions made available by hegemonic discourses and the space-off, the elsewhere, of those discourses: those other spaces both discursive and social that exist, since feminist practices have (re)constructed them, in the margins (or "between the lines," or "against the grain") of hegemonic discourses and in the interstices of institutions, in counter-practices and new forms of community. These two kinds of spaces are neither in opposition to one another nor strung along a chain of signification, but they coexist concurrently and in contradiction. The movement between them, therefore, is not that of a dialectic, of integration, of a combinatory, or of *différance*, but is the tension of contradiction, multiplicity, and heteronomy.

If in the master narratives, cinematic and otherwise, the two kinds of spaces are reconciled and integrated, as man recontains woman in his (man)kind, his hom(m)osexuality, nevertheless the cultural productions and micropolitical practices of feminism have shown them to be separate and heteronomous spaces. Thus, to inhabit both kinds of spaces at once is to live the contradiction which, I have suggested, is the condition of feminism here and now: the tension of a twofold pull in contrary directions—the critical negativity of its theory, and the affirmative positivity of its politics—is both the historical condition of existence of feminism and its theoretical condition of possibility. The subject of feminism is en-gendered there. That is to say, elsewhere.

I wish to thank my students in the History of Consciousness seminar in "Topics in Feminist Theory: Technologies of Gender" for their comments and observations. and my colleague Hayden White for his careful reading of this essay, all of which helped me formulate more clearly some of the issues discussed here.

NOTES

1. For further discussion of these terms, see Teresa de Lauretis, ed., *Feminist Studies/Critical Studies* (Bloomington: Indiana University Press, 1986), especially the essays by Sondra O'Neale and Mary Russo.

2. Michel Foucault, *The History of Sexuality, vol. 1: An Introduction*, trans. Robert Hurley (New York: Vintage Books, 1980), 127.

3. Louis Althusser, "Ideology and Ideological State Apparatuses (Notes Towards an Investigation)," in *Lenin and Philosophy* (New York: Monthly Review Press, 1971), 165.

4. Cf. *The Woman Question: Selections from the Writings of Karl Marx, Frederick Engels, V. I. Lenin, Joseph Stalin* (New York: International Publishers, 1951).

5. Althusser, "Ideology," 171.

6. A clear exposition of the theoretical context of Althusser's subject in ideology can be found in Catherine Belsey, *Critical Practice* (London: Methuen, 1980), 56–65. In Lacan's theory of the subject, 'the woman' is, of course, a fundamental category, but precisely as 'fantasy' or 'symptom' for the man, as Jacqueline Rose explains: "Woman is constructed as an absolute category (excluded and elevated at one and the same time), a category which seems to guarantee that unity on the side of the man. The problem is that once the notion of 'woman' has been so relentlessly exposed as a fantasy, then any such question [the question of her own *Jouissance*] becomes an almost impossible one to pose" (Jacques Lacan, *Feminine Sexuality*, ed. Juliet Mitchell and Jacqueline Rose [New York: W. W. Norton, 1982], 47–51). On both Lacan's and Althusser's subjects together, see Stephen Heath, "The Turn of the Subject," *Cine-Tracts*, no. 8 (Summer-Fall 1979): 32–48.

7. See, for example, Patricia Hill Collins, "The Emerging Theory and Pedagogy of Black Women's Studies," *Feminist Issues* 6, no. 1 (Spring 1986): 3–17; Angela Davis, *Women, Race, and Class* (New York: Random House, 1981); and bell hooks, *Ain't I a Woman: Black Women and Feminism* (Boston: Long Haul Press, 1981).

8. See, for example, Cheryl Clark, "Lesbianism: An Act of Resistance," and Mirtha Quintanales, "I Paid Very Hard for My Immigrant Ignorance," both in *This Bridge Called My Back* (Albany: State University of New York Press, 2015); Cherrie Moraga, "From a Long Line of Vendidas," and Sheila Radford-Hill, "Considering Feminism as a Model for Social Change," both in de Lauretis, *Feminist Studies/Critical Studies*; and Elly Bulkin, Minnie Bruce Prall, and Barbara Smith, *Yours in Struggle: Three Feminist Perspectives on Anti-Semitism and Racism* (Brooklyn, NY: Long Haul Press, 1984).

9. Foucault, *The History of Sexuality*, 116. The preceding paragraph also appears in another essay in this volume, "The Violence of Rhetoric," written prior to this essay, where I first considered the applicability of Foucault's notion of a technology of sex to the construction of gender. I wrote: "Illuminating as his work is to our understanding of the mechanics of power in social relations, its critical value is limited by his unconcern for what, after him, we might call the 'technology of gender'—the techniques and discursive strategies by which gender is constructed."

10. For example, Mary Poovey, "'Scenes of an Indelicate Character': The Medical 'Treatment' of Victorian Women," *Representations*, no. 14 (Spring 1986): 137–168; and Mary Ann Doane, "Clinical Eyes: The Medical Discourse," a chapter in her book *The Desire to Desire: The "Woman's Film" of the 1940s* (Bloomington: Indiana University Press, 1987).

11. Although more detailed references to feminist work in film may be found in *Alice Doesn't*, I want to mention two fundamental critical texts, both published in 1975 (the year in which Foucault's *Surveiller et Punir* [Discipline and Punish] first appeared in France): Laura Mulvey, "Visual Pleasure and Narrative Cinema," *Screen* 16, no. 3 (August 1975): 6–18; and Stephen Heath, "Narrative Space," now in *Questions of Cinema* (Bloomington: Indiana University Press, 1981), 19–75.

12. Teresa de Lauretis and Stephen Heath, eds., *The Cinematic Apparatus* (London: Macmillan, 1980). [The term "cinematic apparatus" was first used in film theory in the early 1970s. French film theorist Jean-Louis Baudry wrote a series of essays on *"le dispositif cinématographique,"* which became a popular concept in the field and translated as "apparatus" in English.—Eds.]

13. In the single film text, but always by way of the entire apparatus, including cinematic genres, the "film industry," and the whole "history of the cinema-machine," as Stephen Heath has defined it ("The Cinematic Apparatus: Technology as Historical and Cultural Form," in de Lauretis and Heath, *The Cinematic Apparatus*, 7).

14. Foucault, *The History of Sexuality*, 104.

15. Rosi Braidotti, "Modelli di dissonanza: donne e/in filosofia," in *Le donne e i segni*, ed. Patrizia Magli (Urbino: Il Lavoro Editoriale, 1985), 34–35.

BIBLIOGRAPHY

Althusser, Louis. "Ideology and Ideological State Apparatuses (Notes Towards an Investigation)." In *Lenin and Philosophy*. Translated by Ben Brewster, 127–193. New York: Monthly Review Press, 1971.

Belsey, Catherine. *Critical Practice*. London: Methuen, 1980.

Braidotti, Rosi. "Modelli di dissonanza: donne e/in filosofia." In *Le donne e i segni*. Edited by Patrizia Magli, 23–36. Urbino: Il Lavoro Editoriale, 1985.

Bulkin, Elly, Minnie Bruce Prall, and Barbara Smith. *Yours in Struggle: Three Feminist Perspectives on Anti-Semitism and Racism*. Brooklyn, NY: Long Haul Press, 1984.

Clark, Cheryl. "Lesbianism: An Act of Resistance." In *This Bridge Called My Back*, 126–135. Albany: State University of New York Press, 2015.

Davis, Angela. *Women, Race, and Class*. New York: Random House, 1981.

Doane, Mary Ann. *The Desire to Desire: The "Woman's Film" of the 1940s*. Bloomington: Indiana University Press, 1987.

Foucault, Michel. *The History of Sexuality, vol. 1: An Introduction*. Translated by Robert Hurley. New York: Vintage Books, 1980.

Heath, Stephen. "Narrative Space." *Questions of Cinema*, 19–75. Bloomington: Indiana University Press, 1981.

Heath, Stephen. "The Turn of the Subject," *Cine-Tracts*, no. 8 (Summer–Fall 1979): 32–48.

Hill Collins, Patricia. "The Emerging Theory and Pedagogy of Black Women's Studies." *Feminist Issues* 6, no. 1 (Spring 1986): 3–17.

hooks, bell. *Ain't I a Woman: Black Women and Feminism.* Boston: Long Haul Press, 1981.

Lacan, Jacques. *Feminine Sexuality.* Edited by Juliet Mitchell and Jacqueline Rose. New York: W. W. Norton, 1982.

Lauretis, Teresa de, ed. *Feminist Studies/Critical Studies.* Bloomington: Indiana University Press, 1986.

Lauretis, Teresa de, and Stephen Heath, eds. *The Cinematic Apparatus.* London: Macmillan, 1980.

Moraga, Cherrie. "From a Long Line of Vendidas." In *Feminist Studies/Critical Studies*, 173–190. Bloomington: Indiana University Press, 1986.

Mulvey, Laura. "Visual Pleasure and Narrative Cinema." *Screen* 16, no. 3 (August 1975): 6–18.

Poovey, Mary. "'Scenes of an Indelicate Character': The Medical 'Treatment' of Victorian Women." *Representations*, no. 14 (Spring 1986): 137–168.

Quintanales, Mirtha. "I Paid Very Hard for My Immigrant Ignorance." In *This Bridge Called My Back*, 148–154. Albany: State University of New York Press, 2015.

Radford-Hill, Sheila. "Considering Feminism as a Model for Social Change." In *Feminist Studies/Critical Studies*, 157–172. Bloomington: Indiana University Press, 1986.

The Woman Question: Selections from the Writings of Karl Marx, Frederick Engels, V. I. Lenin, Joseph Stalin. New York: International Publishers, 1951.

21

POSTSCRIPT ON THE SOCIETIES OF CONTROL

Gilles Deleuze

1. HISTORICAL

Foucault located the *disciplinary societies* in the eighteenth and nineteenth centuries; they reach their height at the outset of the twentieth. They initiate the organization of vast spaces of enclosure. The individual never ceases passing from one closed environment to another, each having its own laws: first, the family; then the school ("you are no longer in your family"); then the barracks ("you are no longer at school"); then the factory; from time to time the hospital; possibly the prison, the preeminent instance of the enclosed environment. It's the prison that serves as the analogical model: at the sight of some laborers, the heroine of Rossellini's *Europa '51* could exclaim, "I thought I was seeing convicts."

Foucault has brilliantly analyzed the ideal project of these environments of enclosure, particularly visible within the factory: to concentrate; to distribute in space; to order in time; to compose a productive force within the dimension of space-time whose effect will be greater than the sum of its component forces. But what Foucault recognized as well was the transience of this model: it succeeded that of the *societies of sovereignty*, the goal and functions of which were something quite different (to tax rather than to organize production, to rule on death rather than to administer life); the transition took place over time, and Napoleon seemed to effect the large-scale conversion from one society to the other. But in their turn the disciplines underwent a crisis to the benefit of new forces that were gradually instituted and which accelerated after

World War II: a disciplinary society was what we already no longer were, what we had ceased to be.

We are in a generalized crisis in relation to all the environments of enclosure—prison, hospital, factory, school, family. The family is an "interior," in crisis like all other interiors—scholarly, professional, etc. The administrations in charge never cease announcing supposedly necessary reforms: to reform schools, to reform industries, hospitals, the armed forces, prisons. But everyone knows that these institutions are finished, whatever the length of their expiration periods. It's only a matter of administering their last rites and of keeping people employed until the installation of the new forces knocking at the door. These are the *societies of control*, which are in the process of replacing the disciplinary societies. "Control" is the name Burroughs proposes as a term for the new monster, one that Foucault recognizes as our immediate future. Paul Virilio also is continually analyzing the ultrarapid forms of free-floating control that replaced the old disciplines operating in the time frame of a closed system. There is no need here to invoke the extraordinary pharmaceutical productions, the molecular engineering, the genetic manipulations, although these are slated to enter into the new process. There is no need to ask which is the toughest or most tolerable regime, for it's within each of them that liberating and enslaving forces confront one another. For example, in the crisis of the hospital as environment of enclosure, neighborhood clinics, hospices, and day care could at first express new freedom, but they could participate as well in mechanisms of control that are equal to the harshest of confinements. There is no need to fear or hope, but only to look for new weapons.

2. LOGIC

The different internments or spaces of enclosure through which the individual passes are independent variables: each time one is supposed to start from zero, and although a common language for all these places exists, it is *analogical*. On the other hand, the different control mechanisms are inseparable variations, forming a system of variable geometry the language of which is *numerical* (which doesn't necessarily mean binary). Enclosures are *molds*, distinct castings, but controls are a *modulation*, like a self-deforming cast that will continuously change from one moment to the other, or like a sieve whose mesh will transmute from point to point.

This is obvious in the matter of salaries: the factory was a body that contained its internal forces at a level of equilibrium, the highest possible in terms of production, the lowest possible in terms of wages; but in a society of control, the corporation has replaced the factory, and the corporation is a spirit, a gas. Of course the factory was already familiar with the system of bonuses, but the corporation works more deeply to impose a modulation of each salary, in states of perpetual metastability that operate through challenges, contests, and highly comic group sessions. If the most idiotic television game shows are so successful, it's because they express the corporate situation with great precision. The factory constituted individuals as a single body to the double advantage of the boss who surveyed each element within the mass and the unions who mobilized a mass resistance; but the corporation constantly presents the brashest rivalry as a healthy form of emulation, an excellent motivational force that opposes individuals against one another and runs through each, dividing each within. The modulating principle of "salary according to merit" has not failed to tempt national education itself. Indeed, just as the corporation replaces the factory, *perpetual training* tends to replace the *school*, and continuous control to replace the examination. Which is the surest way of delivering the school over to the corporation.

In the disciplinary societies one was always starting again (from school to the barracks, from the barracks to the factory), while in the societies of control one is never finished with anything—the corporation, the educational system, the armed services being metastable states coexisting in one and the same modulation, like a universal system of deformation. In *The Trial*, Kafka, who had already placed himself at the pivotal point between two types of social formation, described the most fearsome of juridical forms. The *apparent acquittal* of the disciplinary societies (between two incarcerations); and the *limitless postponements* of the societies of control (in continuous variation) are two very different modes of juridical life, and if our law is hesitant, itself in crisis, it's because we are leaving one in order to enter into the other. The disciplinary societies have two poles: the signature that designates the *individual*, and the number or administrative numeration that indicates his or her position within a *mass*. This is because the disciplines never saw any incompatibility between these two, and because at the same time power individualizes and masses together, that is, constitutes those over whom it exercises power into a body and molds the individuality of each member of that body. (Foucault saw the origin of this double charge in the pastoral power of the priest—the flock and each of its animals—but civil power moves in turn and by other means to make itself lay "priest.") In the societies of control, on the other hand, what is important is no longer either a signature or a number, but a code: the code is a *password*, while on the other hand the disciplinary societies are regulated by *watchwords* (as much from the point of view of integration as from that of resistance). The numerical language of control is made of codes that mark access to information, or reject it. We no longer find ourselves dealing with the mass/individual pair. Individuals have become *"dividuals,"* and masses, samples, data, markets, or *"banks."* Perhaps it is money that expresses the distinction between the two societies best, since discipline always referred back to minted money that locks gold in as numerical standard, while control relates to floating rates of exchange, modulated according to a rate established by a set of standard currencies. The old monetary mole is the animal of the spaces of enclosure, but the serpent is that of the societies of control. We have passed from one animal to the other, from the mole to the serpent, in the system under which we live, but also in our manner of living and in our relations with others. The disciplinary man was a discontinuous producer of energy, but the man of control is undulatory, in orbit, in a continuous network. Everywhere *surfing* has already replaced the older *sports*.

Types of machines are easily matched with each type of society—not that machines are determining, but because they express those social forms capable of generating them and using them. The old societies of sovereignty made use of simple machines—levers, pulleys, clocks; but the recent disciplinary societies equipped themselves with machines involving energy, with the passive danger of entropy and the active danger of sabotage; the societies of control operate with machines of a third type, computers, whose passive danger is jamming and whose active one is piracy and the introduction of viruses. This technological evolution must be, even more profoundly, a mutation of capitalism, an already well-known or familiar mutation that can be summed up as follows: nineteenth-century capitalism is a capitalism of concentration, for production and for property. It therefore erects the factory as a space of enclosure, the capitalist being the owner of the means of production but also, progressively, the owner of other spaces conceived through analogy (the worker's familial house, the school). As for markets, they are conquered sometimes by specialization, sometimes by colonization, sometimes by lowering the costs of production. But, in the present situation, capitalism is no longer involved in production, which it often relegates to the Third World, even for the complex forms of textiles, metallurgy, or oil production. It's a capitalism of higher-order production. It no longer buys raw materials and no longer sells the finished products: it buys the finished products or assembles parts. What it wants to sell is services and what it wants to buy is stocks. This is no longer a capitalism for production but for the product, which is to say, for being sold or marketed. Thus it is essentially dispersive, and the factory has given way to the corporation. The family, the school, the army, the factory are no longer the distinct analogical spaces that converge towards an owner—state or private power—but coded figures—deformable and transformable—of a single corporation that now has only stockholders. Even art has left the spaces of enclosure in order to enter into the open circuits of the bank. The conquests of the market are made by grabbing control and no longer by disciplinary training, by fixing the exchange rate much more than by lowering costs, by transformation of the product more than by specialization of production. Corruption thereby gains a new power. Marketing has become the center or the "soul" of the corporation. We are taught that corporations have a soul, which is the most terrifying news in the world. The operation of markets is now the instrument of social control and forms the impudent breed of our masters. Control is short-term and of rapid rates of turnover, but also continuous and without limit, while discipline was of long duration, infinite and discontinuous. Man is no longer man enclosed, but man in debt. It is true that capitalism has retained as a constant the extreme poverty of three quarters of humanity, too poor for debt, too numerous for confinement: control will not only have to deal with erosions of frontiers but with the explosions within shanty towns or ghettos.

3. PROGRAM

The conception of a control mechanism, giving the position of any element within an open environment at any given instant (whether animal in a reserve or human in a corporation, as with an electronic collar), is not necessarily one of science fiction. Félix Guattari has imagined a city where one would be able to leave one's apartment, one's street, one's neighborhood, thanks to one's (dividual) electronic card that raises a given barrier; but the card could just as easily be rejected on a given day or between certain hours; what counts is not the barrier but the computer that tracks each person's position—licit or illicit—and effects a universal modulation.

The socio-technological study of the mechanisms of control, grasped at their inception, would have to be categorical and to describe what is already in the process of substitution for the disciplinary sites of enclosure, whose crisis is everywhere proclaimed. It may be that older methods, borrowed from the former societies of sovereignty, will return to the fore, but with the necessary modifications. What counts is that we are at the beginning of something. In the *prison system*: the attempt to find penalties of "substitution," at least for petty crimes, and the use of electronic collars that force the convicted person to stay at home during certain hours. For the *school system*: continuous forms of control, and the effect on the school of perpetual training, the corresponding abandonment of all university research, the introduction of the "corporation" at all levels of schooling. For the *hospital system*: the new medicine "without doctor or patient" that singles out potential sick people and subjects at risk, which in no way attests to individuation—as they say—but substitutes for the individual or numerical body the code of a "dividual" material to be controlled. In the *corporate system*: new ways of handling money, profits, and humans that no longer pass through the old factory form. These are very small examples, but ones that will allow for better understanding of what is meant by the crisis of the institutions, which is to say, the progressive and dispersed installation of a new system of domination. One of the most important questions will concern the ineptitude of the unions: tied to the whole of their history of struggle against the disciplines or within the spaces of enclosure, will they be able to adapt themselves or will they give way to new forms of resistance against the societies of control? Can we already grasp the rough outlines of these coming forms, capable of threatening the joys of marketing? Many young people strangely boast of being "motivated"; they re-request apprenticeships and permanent training. It's up to them to discover what they're being made to serve, just as their elders discovered, not without difficulty, the telos of the disciplines. The coils of a serpent are even more complex than the burrows of a molehill.

22

THE OTHER QUESTION: STEREOTYPE, DISCRIMINATION AND THE DISCOURSE OF COLONIALISM

Homi K. Bhabha

To concern oneself with the founding concepts of the entire history of philosophy, to deconstitute them, is not to undertake the work of the philologist or of the classic historian of philosophy. Despite appearances, it is probably the most daring way of making the beginnings of a step outside of philosophy.
—Jacques Derrida, "Structure, Sign and Play"

An important feature of colonial discourse is its dependence on the concept of 'fixity' in the ideological construction of otherness. Fixity, as the sign of cultural/historical/racial difference in the discourse of colonialism, is a paradoxical mode of representation: it connotes rigidity and an unchanging order as well as disorder, degeneracy and daemonic repetition. Likewise the stereotype, which is its major discursive strategy, is a form of knowledge and identification that vacillates between what is always 'in place,' already known, and something that must be anxiously repeated . . . as if the essential duplicity of the Asiatic or the bestial sexual licence of the African that needs no proof, can never really, in discourse, be proved. It is this process of *ambivalence*, central to the stereotype, that this chapter explores as it constructs a theory of colonial discourse. For it is the force of ambivalence that gives the colonial stereotype its currency: ensures its repeatability in changing historical and discursive conjunctures; informs its strategies of individuation and marginalization; produces that effect of probabilistic truth and predictability which, for the stereotype, must always be in excess of what can be empirically proved or logically construed. Yet the function of ambivalence as one of the most significant discursive and psychical strategies of discriminatory power—whether racist or sexist, peripheral or metropolitan—remains to be charted.

The absence of such a perspective has its own history of political expediency. To recognize the stereotype as an ambivalent mode of knowledge and power demands a theoretical and political response that challenges deterministic or functionalist modes of conceiving of the relationship between discourse and politics. The analytic of ambivalence questions dogmatic and moralistic positions on the meaning of oppression and discrimination. My reading of colonial discourse suggests that the point of intervention should shift from the ready recognition of images as positive or negative, to an understanding of the *processes of subjectification* made possible (and plausible) through stereotypical discourse. To judge the stereotyped image on the basis of a prior political normativity is to dismiss it, not to displace it, which is only possible by engaging with its *effectivity*; with the repertoire of positions of power and resistance, domination and dependence that constructs colonial identification subject (both colonizer and colonized). I do not intend to deconstruct the colonial discourse to reveal its ideological misconceptions or repressions, to exult in its self-reflexivity, or to indulge its liberatory 'excess.' In order to understand the productivity of colonial power it is crucial to construct its regime of truth, not to subject its representations to a normalizing judgement. Only then does it become possible to understand the *productive* ambivalence of the object of colonial discourse—that 'otherness' which is at once an object of desire and derision, an articulation of difference contained within the fantasy of origin and identity. What such a reading reveals are the boundaries of colonial discourse and it enables a transgression of these limits from the space of that otherness.

The construction of the colonial subject in discourse, and the exercise of colonial power through discourse, demands an articulation of forms of difference—racial and sexual. Such an articulation becomes crucial if it is held that the body is always simultaneously (if conflictually) inscribed in both the economy of pleasure and desire and the economy of discourse, domination and power. I do not wish to conflate, unproblematically, two forms of the marking—and splitting—of the subject nor to globalize two forms of representation. I want to suggest, however, that there is a theoretical space and a political place for such an *articulation*—in the sense in which that word itself denies an 'original' identity or a 'singularity' to objects of difference—sexual or racial. If such a view is taken, as Feuchtwang argues in a different context,[1] it follows that the epithets racial or sexual come to be seen as modes of differentiation, realized as multiple, cross-cutting determinations, polymorphous and perverse, always demanding a specific and strategic calculation of their effects. Such is, I believe, the moment of colonial discourse. It is a form of discourse crucial to the binding of a range of differences and discriminations that inform the discursive and political practices of racial and cultural hierarchization.

[. . .]

The difference of colonial discourse as an apparatus of power will emerge more fully as this chapter develops. At this stage, however, I shall provide what I take to be the minimum conditions and specifications of such a discourse. It is an apparatus that turns on the recognition and disavowal of racial/cultural/historical differences. Its predominant strategic function is the creation of a space for a 'subject peoples' through the production of knowledges in terms of which surveillance is exercised and a complex form of pleasure/unpleasure is incited. It seeks authorization for its strategies by the production of knowledges of colonizer and colonized which are stereotypical but antithetically evaluated. The objective of colonial discourse is to construe the colonized as a population of degenerate types on the basis of racial origin, in order to justify conquest and to establish systems of administration and instruction. Despite the play of power within colonial discourse and the shifting positionalities of its subjects (for example, effects of class, gender, ideology, different social formations, varied systems of colonization and so on), I am referring to a form of governmentality that in marking out a 'subject nation,' appropriates, directs and dominates its various spheres of activity. Therefore, despite the 'play' in the colonial system which is crucial to its exercise of power, colonial discourse produces the colonized as a social reality which is at once an 'other' and yet entirely knowable and visible. It resembles a form of narrative whereby the productivity and circulation of subjects and signs are bound in a reformed and recognizable totality. It employs a system of representation, a regime of truth, that is structurally similar to realism. And it is in order to intervene within that system of representation that Edward Said proposes a semiotic of 'Orientalist' power, examining the varied European discourses which constitute 'the Orient' as a unified racial, geographical, political and cultural zone of the world. Said's analysis is revealing of, and relevant to, colonial discourse:

Philosophically, then, the kind of language, thought, and vision that I have been calling orientalism very generally is a form or *radical realism*; anyone employing orientalism, which is the habit for dealing with questions, objects, qualities and regions deemed Oriental, will designate, name, point to, fix, what he is talking or thinking about with a word or phrase, which then is considered either to have acquired, or more simply to be, reality. . . . The tense they employ is the timeless eternal; they convey an impression of repetition and strength. . . . For all these functions it is frequently enough to use the simple copula is.[2]

For Said, the copula seems to be the point at which western rationalism preserves the boundaries of sense for itself. Of this, too, Said is aware when he hints continually at a polarity or division at the very centre of Orientalism.[3] It is, on the one hand, a topic of learning, discovery, practice; on the other, it is the site of dreams, images, fantasies, myths, obsessions and requirements. It is a static system of "synchronic essentialism," a knowledge of "signifiers of stability" such as the lexicographic and the encyclopaedic. However, this site is continually under threat from diachronic forms of history and narrative, signs of instability. And, finally, this line of thinking is given a shape analogical to the dreamwork, when Said refers explicitly to a distinction between "an unconscious positivity" which he terms *latent* Orientalism, and the stated knowledges and views about the Orient which he calls *manifest* Orientalism.

The originality of this pioneering theory could be extended to engage with the alterity and ambivalence of Orientalist discourse. Said contains this threat by introducing a binarism within the argument which, in initially setting up an opposition between these two discursive scenes, finally allows them to be correlated as a congruent system of representation that is unified through a political-ideological *intention* which, in his words, enables Europe to advance securely and *unmetaphorically* upon the Orient. Said identifies the *content* of Orientalism as the unconscious repository of fantasy, imaginative writings and essential ideas; and the *form* of manifest Orientalism as the historically and discursively determined, diachronic aspect. This division/correlation structure of manifest and latent Orientalism leads to the effectivity of the concept of discourse being undermined by what could be called the polarities of intentionality.

This produces a problem with Said's use of Foucault's concepts of power and discourse. The productivity of Foucault's concept of power/knowledge lies in its refusal of an epistemology which opposes essence/appearance, ideology/science. '*Pouvoir/ Savoir*' places subjects in a relation of power and recognition that is not part of a symmetrical or dialectical relation—self/other, master/slave—which can then be subverted by being inverted. Subjects are always disproportionately placed in opposition or domination through the symbolic decentring of multiple power relations which play the role of support as well as target or adversary. It becomes difficult, then, to conceive of the *historical* enunciations of colonial discourse without them being either functionally overdetermined or strategically elaborated or displaced by the *unconscious* scene of latent Orientalism. Equally, it is difficult to conceive of the process of subjectification as a placing *within* Orientalist or colonial discourse for the dominated subject without the dominant being strategically placed within it too.

The terms in which Said's Orientalism is unified—the intentionality and unidirectionality of colonial power—also unify the subject of colonial enunciation.

This results in Said's inadequate attention to representation as a concept that articulates the historical and fantasy (as the scene of desire) in the production of the 'political' effects of discourse. He rightly rejects a notion of Orientalism as the misrepresentation of an Oriental essence. However, having introduced the concept of 'discourse' he does not face up to the problems it creates for an instrumentalist notion of power/knowledge that he seems to require. This problem is summed up by his ready acceptance of the view that, "Representations are formations, or as Roland Barthes has said of all the operations of language, they are deformations."[4]

This brings me to my second point. The closure and coherence attributed to the unconscious pole of colonial discourse and the unproblematized notion of the subject, restrict the effectivity of both power and knowledge. It is not possible to see how power functions productively as incitement and interdiction. Nor would it be possible, without the attribution of ambivalence to relations of power/knowledge, to calculate the traumatic impact of the return of the oppressed—those terrifying stereotypes of savagery, cannibalism, lust and anarchy which are the signal points of identification and alienation, scenes of fear and desire, in colonial texts. It is precisely this function of the stereotype as phobia and fetish that, according to Fanon, threatens the closure of the racial/epidermal schema for the colonial subject and opens the royal road to colonial fantasy.

There is an underdeveloped passage in *Orientalism* which, in cutting across the body of the text, articulates the question of power and desire that I now want to take up. It is this:

Altogether an internally structured archive is built up from the literature that belongs to these experiences. Out of this comes a restricted number of typical encapsulations: the journey, the history, the fable, the stereotype, the polemical confrontation. These are the lenses through which the Orient is experienced, and they shape the language, perception, and form of the encounter between East and West. What gives the immense number of encounters some unity, however, is the vacillation I was speaking about earlier. Something patently foreign and distant acquires, for one reason or another, a status more rather than less familiar. One tends to stop judging things either as completely novel or as completely well-known; a new median category emerges, a category that allows one to see new things, things seen for the first time, as versions of a previously known thing. In essence such a category is not so much a way of receiving new information as it is a method of controlling what seems to be a threat to some established view of things. . . . The threat is muted, familiar values impose themselves, and in the end the mind reduces the pressure upon it by accommodating things to itself as either 'original' or 'repetitious'. . . . The orient at large, therefore, vacillates between the West's contempt for what is familiar and its shivers of delight in—or fear of—novelty.[5]

What is this other scene of colonial discourse played out around the 'median category'? What is this theory of encapsulation or fixation which moves between the recognition of cultural and racial difference and its disavowal, by affixing the unfamiliar to something established, in a form that is repetitious and vacillates between delight and fear? Does the Freudian fable of fetishism (and disavowal) circulate within the discourse of colonial power requiring the articulation of modes of differentiation—sexual and racial—as well as different modes of theoretical discourse—psychoanalytic and historical?

The strategic articulation of 'coordinates of knowledge'—racial and sexual—and their inscription in the play of colonial power as modes of differentiation, defence, fixation, hierarchization, is a way of specifying colonial discourse which would be illuminated by reference to Foucault's poststructuralist concept of the dispositif or apparatus. Foucault insists that the relation of knowledge and power within the apparatus are always a strategic response to an *urgent need* at a given historical moment. The force of colonial and postcolonial discourse as a theoretical and cultural intervention in our contemporary moment represents the urgent need to contest singularities of difference and to articulate diverse 'subjects' of differentiation. Foucault writes:

the apparatus is essentially of a strategic nature, which means assuming that it is a matter of a certain manipulation of relations of forces, either developing them in a particular direction, blocking them, stabilising them, utilising them, etc. The apparatus is thus always inscribed in a play of power, but it is also always linked to certain coordinates of knowledge which issue from it but, to an equal degree, condition it. This is what the apparatus consists in: strategies of relations of forces supporting and supported by, types of knowledge.[6]

In this spirit I argue for the reading of the stereotype in terms of fetishism. The myth of historical origination—racial purity, cultural priority—produced in relation to the colonial stereotype functions to 'normalize' the multiple beliefs and split subjects that constitute colonial discourse as a consequence of its process of disavowal. The scene of fetishism functions similarly as, at once, a reactivation of the material of original fantasy—the anxiety of castration and sexual difference—as well as a normalization of that difference and disturbance in terms of the fetish object as the substitute for the mother's penis. Within the apparatus of colonial power, the discourses of sexuality and race relate in a process of *functional overdetermination*, "because each effect . . . enters into resonance or contradiction with the others and thereby calls for a readjustment or a reworking of the heterogeneous elements that surface at various points."[7]

There is both a structural and functional justification for reading the racial stereotype of colonial discourse in terms of fetishism.[8] My rereading of Said establishes the *structural* link. Fetishism, as the disavowal of difference, is that repetitious scene around the problem of castration. The recognition of sexual difference—as the precondition for the circulation of the chain of absence and presence in the realm of the Symbolic—is disavowed by the fixation on an object that masks that difference and restores an original presence. The *functional* link between the fixation of the fetish and the stereotype (or the stereotype as fetish) is even more relevant. For fetishism is always a 'play' or vacillation between the archaic affirmation of wholeness/similarity—in Freud's terms: "All men have penises"; in ours: "All men have the same skin/race/culture"—and the anxiety associated with lack and difference—again, for Freud "Some do not have penises"; for us "Some do not have the same skin/race/culture." Within discourse, the fetish represents the simultaneous play between metaphor as substitution (masking absence and difference) and metonymy (which contiguously registers the perceived lack). The fetish or stereotype gives access to an 'identity' which is predicated as much on mastery and pleasure as it is on anxiety and defence, for it is a form of multiple and contradictory belief in its recognition of difference and disavowal of it. This conflict of pleasure/unpleasure, mastery/defence, knowledge/disavowal, absence/presence, has a fundamental significance for colonial discourse. For the scene of fetishism is also the scene of the reactivation and repetition of primal fantasy—the subject's desire for a pure origin that is always threatened by its division, for the subject must be gendered to be engendered, to be spoken.

The stereotype, then, as the primary point of subjectification in colonial discourse, for both colonizer and colonized, is the scene of a similar fantasy and defence—the desire for an originality which is again threatened by the differences of race, colour and culture. My contention is splendidly caught in Fanon's title *Black Skin, White Masks* where the disavowal of difference turns the colonial subject into a misfit—a grotesque mimicry or 'doubling' that threatens to split the soul and whole, undifferentiated skin of the ego. The stereotype is not a simplification because it is a false representation of a given reality. It is a simplification because it is an arrested, fixated form of representation that, in denying the play of difference (which the negation through the Other permits), constitutes a problem for the *representation* of the subject in significations of psychic and social relations.

When Fanon talks of the positioning of the subject in the stereotyped discourse of colonialism, he gives further credence to my point. The legends, stories, histories and anecdotes of a colonial culture offer the subject a primordial Either/Or.[9] *Either* he is fixed in a consciousness of the body as a solely negating activity *or* as a new kind of man, a new genus. What is denied the colonial subject, both as colonizer and colonized, is that form of negation which gives access to the recognition of difference. It is that possibility of difference and circulation which would liberate the signifier of *skin/culture* from the fixations of racial typology, the analytics of blood, ideologies of racial and cultural dominance or degeneration. "Wherever he goes," Fanon despairs, "the Negro remains a Negro"[10]—his race becomes the ineradicable sign of *negative difference* in colonial discourses. For the stereotype impedes the circulation and articulation of the signifier of 'race' as anything other than its *fixity* as racism. We always already know that blacks are licentious, Asiatics duplicitous . . .

[. . .]

In any specific colonial discourse the metaphoric/narcissistic and the metonymic/aggressive positions will function simultaneously, strategically poised in relation to each other; similar to the moment of alienation which stands as a threat to Imaginary plenitude, and 'multiple belief' which threatens fetishistic disavowal. The subjects of the discourse are constructed within an apparatus of power which *contains*, in both senses of the word, an 'other' knowledge—a knowledge that is arrested and fetishistic and circulates through colonial discourse as that limited form of otherness that I have called the stereotype. Fanon poignantly describes the effects of this process for a colonized culture:

a continued agony rather than a total disappearance of the preexisting culture. The culture once living and open to the future, becomes closed, fixed in the colonial status, caught in the yolk of oppression. Both present and mummified, it testifies against its members. . . . The cultural mummification leads to a mummification of individual thinking. . . . As though it were possible for a man to evolve otherwise than within the framework of a culture that recognises him and that he decides to assume.[11]

[. . .]

My concept of stereotype-as-suture is a recognition of the *ambivalence* of that authority and those orders of identification. The role of fetishistic identification, in the construction of discriminatory knowledges that depend on the 'presence of difference,' is to provide a process of splitting and multiple/contradictory belief at the point of enunciation and subjectification. It is this crucial splitting of the ego which is represented in Fanon's description of the construction of the colonized subject as effect of stereotypical discourse: the subject primordially fixed and yet triply split between the incongruent knowledges of body, race, ancestors. Assailed by the stereotype, "the corporeal schema crumbled, its place taken by a racial epidermal schema.... It was no longer a question of being aware of my body in the third person but in a triple person.... I was not given one, but two, three places."[12]

The stereotype is in that sense an 'impossible' object. For that very reason, the exertions of the 'official knowledges' of colonialism—pseudo-scientific, typological, legal-administrative, eugenicist—are imbricated at the point of their production of meaning and power with the fantasy that dramatizes the impossible desire for a pure, undifferentiated origin. Not itself the object of desire but its setting, not an ascription of prior identities but their production in the syntax of the scenario of racist discourse, colonial fantasy plays a crucial part in those everyday scenes of subjectification in a colonial society which Fanon refers to repeatedly. Like fantasies of the origins of sexuality, the productions of "colonial desire" mark the discourse as "a favoured spot for the most primitive defensive reactions such as turning against oneself, into an opposite, projection, negation."[13]

[...]

Racist stereotypical discourse, in its colonial moment, inscribes a form of governmentality that is informed by a productive splitting in its constitution of knowledge and exercise of power. Some of its practices recognize the difference of race, culture and history as elaborated by stereotypical knowledges, racial theories, administrative colonial experience, and on that basis institutionalize a range of political and cultural ideologies that are prejudicial, discriminatory, vestigial, archaic, 'mythical,' and, crucially, are recognized as being so. By 'knowing' the native population in these terms, discriminatory and authoritarian forms of political control are considered appropriate. The colonized population is then deemed to be both the cause and effect of the system, imprisoned in the circle of interpretation. What is visible is the *necessity* of such rule which is justified by those moralistic and normative ideologies of amelioration recognized as the Civilizing Mission or the White Man's Burden. However, there coexist within the same apparatus of colonial power, modern systems and sciences of government, progressive 'Western' forms of social and economic organization which provide the manifest justification for the project of colonialism—an argument which, in part, impressed Karl Marx. It is on the site of this coexistence that strategies of hierarchization and marginalization are employed in the management of colonial societies. And if my deduction from Fanon about the peculiar visibility of colonial power is justified, then I would extend that to say that it is a form of governmentality in which the 'ideological' space functions in more openly collaborative ways with political and economic exigencies. The barracks stands by the church which stands by the schoolroom; the cantonment stands hard by the 'civil lines.' Such visibility of the institutions and apparatuses of power is possible because the exercise of colonial power makes their *relationship* obscure, produces them as fetishes, spectacles of a 'natural'/racial preeminence. Only the seat of government is always elsewhere—alien and separate by that distance upon which surveillance depends for its strategies of objectification, normalization and discipline.

The last word belongs to Fanon:

this behaviour [of the colonizer] betrays a determination to objectify, to confine, to imprison, to harden. Phrases such as 'I know them,' 'that's the way they are,' show this maximum objectification successfully achieved. . . . There is on the one hand a culture in which qualities of dynamism, of growth, of depth can be recognised. As against this, [in colonial cultures] we find characteristics, curiosities, things, never a structure.[14]

NOTES

1. Stephan Feuchtwang, "Socialist, feminist and anti-racist struggles," *m/f* no. 4 (1980): 41.

2. Edward Said, *Orientalism* (London: Routledge & Kegan Paul, 1978), 72; emphasis added.

3. Ibid., 206.

4. Ibid., 273.

5. Ibid., 58–59.

6. Michel Foucault, "The Confession of the Flesh," in *Power/Knowledge*, ed. Colin Gordon (Brighton: Harvester Press, 1980), 196.

7. Ibid., 195.

8. See Sigmund Freud, "Fetishism," in *On Sexuality*, vol. 7, Penguin Freud Library (Harmondsworth: Penguin Books, 1981), 345ff; Christian Metz, *Psychoanalysis and Cinema: The Imaginary Signifier*, trans. Celia Britton (London: Macmillan, 1982), 67–78. See also Steve Neale, "The Same Old Story: Stereotypes and Differences," *Screen Education*, nos. 32/33 (Autumn–Winter 1979–80): 33–37.

9. Frantz Fanon, "The Fact of Blackness," in *Black Skin, White Masks*, trans. Charles Lam Markmann (London: Pluto Press, 1991), 109–140.

10. Ibid., 117, 127.

11. Frantz Fanon, "Racism and Culture," in *Toward the African Revolution*, trans. Haakon Chevalier (London: Pelican, 1970), 44.

12. Fanon, "The Fact of Blackness," 112.

13. Jean Laplanche and Jean-Bertrand Pontalis, "Phantasy (or fantasy)," in *The Language of Psychoanalysis*, trans. Donald Nicholson-Smith (London: Hogarth Press, 1980), 318.

14. Fanon, "Racism and Culture," 44.

BIBLIOGRAPHY

Derrida, Jacques. "Structure, Sign and Play in the Discourse of the Human Sciences." In *Writing and Difference*. Translated by Alan Bass, 351–370. Chicago: Chicago University Press, 1978.

Fanon, Frantz. "Racism and Culture." In *Toward the African Revolution*. Translated by Haakon Chevalier, 29–44. London: Pelican, 1970.

Fanon, Frantz. "The Fact of Blackness." In *Black Skin, White Masks*. Translated by Charles Lam Markmann, 109–140. London: Pluto Press, 1991.

Feuchtwang, Stephan. "Socialist, Feminist and Anti-Racist Struggles." *m/f* no. 4 (1980): 41–56.

Foucault, Michel. "The Confession of the Flesh." In *Power/Knowledge*. Edited by Colin Gordon, 194–228. Brighton: Harvester Press, 1980.

Freud, Sigmund. "Fetishism." In *On Sexuality*, vol. 7, Penguin Freud Library, 345–358. Harmondsworth: Penguin Books, 1981.

Laplanche, Jean, and Jean-Bertrand Pontalis. "Phantasy (or fantasy)." In *The Language of Psychoanalysis*. Translated by Donald Nicholson-Smith, 314–319. London: Karnac Books, 1988.

Metz, Christian. *Psychoanalysis and Cinema: The Imaginary Signifier*. Translated by Celia Britton. London: Macmillan, 1982.

Neale, Steve. "The Same Old Story: Stereotypes and Differences." *Screen Education*, nos. 32/33 (Autumn–Winter 1979–80): 33–37.

Said, Edward. *Orientalism*. London: Routledge & Kegan Paul, 1978.

23

SYNTACTICS: THE GRAMMAR OF FEMINISM AND TECHNOSCIENCE

Donna J. Haraway

Immeasurable Results is patterned after an advertisement for Hitachi's Magnetic Resonance Imaging (MRI) medical device.[1] The diagnostic film framed above the recumbent body of the draped woman records the assemblage of objects and dreams that fill family albums, clinical records, national imaginaries, and personal journals in technoscientific cultures at the end of the Second Christian Millennium. The material-semiotic event, for which the Hitachi machine is tool and trope, is an articulation of high-technology capital, diverse skills, interdisciplinary negotiations, bodily organic structures, marketing strategies, personal and public symbolic codes, medical doctrines, transnational economies, scientific industry's labor systems, and patient-consumer hopes and fears. The woman with her head in the imaging apparatus is the artist, Lynn M. Randolph. This is a self-portrait of interior psychic and diagnostic spaces and of exterior human and mechanical bodily postures. The painting shows a measuring device; its computer-mediated scanning image; and, on the same film with calibration cues in the righthand margin, the projected dreams and nightmares that remain immeasurable within the machine's information calculus. *Immeasurable Results* is a screen projection of conscious and unconscious layers proper to a biomedical world. Joining Randolph's metaphorical realism and cyborg surrealism, *Immeasurable Results* is the recursive screen-within-a-screen record of a material-semiotic apparatus of bodily production and reproduction in the regime of technobiopower. *Immeasurable Results* records a slice of what feminists call the "lived experience" of that apparatus.

A fantasy mermaid with an open fish mouth; a parallel floating penis and testes of the same piscine shape as the doll's; a pocketwatch without clock hands, armed instead with crab claws, whose nightmare timekeeping is outside mechanical chronology; a red demon hammering at the skull, echoing the pounding heard by the woman inside the MRI machine, punctuating the staccato bits of information emitted from the brain-machine interface; a day-of-the-dead Mexican skeleton poised with a spear to announce the impending death lurking in the traitorous flesh; an alligator-predator; and, in the center of this ring of surrealist beings, the technical, medical frontal section, cut without knives, through the brain, sinus cavities, and throat: These images are produced by the semiosis of the machine, body, and psyche in hybrid communication. All of these images—certainly including the bloodless optical slice of the woman's head and neck—are intensely personal. Technoscientific subjects and objects are gestating in the matrices of the MRI scan. The moment of reading and scanning, of being read and being scanned, is the moment of vulnerability through which new articulations are made. In Joseph Dumit's provocative terms, the brain-imaging device is part of an apparatus of "objective self fashioning."[2]

The specificity of the painting cannot be missed—its particular race- and gender-marked patient, her individual dreams and possible pathologies, the identifiable corporation selling computerized medical imaging devices, the web of beliefs and practices pertaining to health and disease, the economic configurations tying flesh and diagnostic film together. These signs make sense in the fiercely physical, semiotic world of technoscience, which is the real and imaginary field for *Modest_Witness@Second_Millennium*. We read these signs by the syntactical rules of technoscience. We are inside its material grammar; we both embody and contest its rules. But we are also in a world of immeasurable results, a world that exceeds its representations and blasts syntax. This excessive world defies both denunciation and celebration while exacting care and accountability. We are in the family saga, where FemaleMan© meets her sibling species called OncoMouse™ in the nodes of the Net. That encounter is my self-portrait in the durable traditions of Western self-fashioning.

[. . .]

FIGURES

Signs and wonders brings us to the next contaminated practice suffusing my book and built into the title *Modest_Witness@Second_Millennium.FemaleMan©_Meets_OncoMouse™*: that is, figuration. In my book, entities such as the modest witness of the

Scientific Revolution, the FemaleMan© of commodified transnational feminism, and OncoMouse™ of the biotechnical war on cancer are all figures in secular technoscientific salvation stories full of promise. The promises are cheek-by-jowl with ultimate threats as well. Apocalypse, in the sense of the final destruction of man's home world, and comedy, in the sense both of the humorous and of the ultimate harmonious resolution of all conflict through progress, are bedfellows in the soap opera of technoscience. Figuration in technoscientific texts and artifacts is often simultaneously apocalyptic and comedic. As we will examine in detail later, figuration in technoscience seems to operate according to the corporate slogan for the patented transgenic rodent, OncoMouse™, "available only from Du Pont, where better things for better living come to life."

[. . .]

Figuration is a complex practice with deep roots in the semiotics of Western Christian realism. I am especially interested in a specific sense of time built into Christian figuration. I think this kind of time is characteristic of the promises and threats of technoscience in the United States, with its ebullient, secular, disavowed, Christian national stories and practices. Despite the extraordinary multicultural, multiethnic, multireligious populations in the United States, with quite various traditions of signifying time and community, U.S. scientific culture is replete with figures and stories that can only be called Christian. Figural realism infuses Christian discourse in all of that religious tradition's contested and polyvocal variety, and this kind of figuration shapes much of the technoscientific sense of history and progress. That is why I locate my modest witness in the less than universal—to put it mildly—time zone of the end of the Second (Christian) Millennium. In the United States, at least, technoscience is a millenniarian discourse about beginnings and ends, first and last things, suffering and progress, figure and fulfillment. And the Onco-Mouse™ on the back cover of *Modest_Witness@Second_Millennium* doesn't have a crown of thorns on her head for no reason.

As Erich Auerbach explained in his great study of mimetic practice in Western literature, "Figural interpretation establishes a connection between two events or persons in such a way that the first signifies not only itself but also the second, while the second involves or fulfills the first. . . . They are both contained in the flowing stream which is historical life."[3] The heart of figural realism is the Christian practice of reading the story of Christ into Jewish scripture. Although in Christian figuration both figure and fulfillment are materially real, history is fully contained in the eternal plan of Divine Providence, which alone can supply the key to historical meaning. Containing and fulfilling the whole, (Christian) salvation history *is* history. Auerbach insists that his kind of temporality is utterly alien to the conceptions of classical antiquity, both Jewish and Greek.

Auerbach examines Dante's development of figural realism in *The Divine Comedy*. Dante's innovation was to draw the end of man with such extraordinary vividness and variety "that the listener is all too occupied by the figure in the fulfillment.... The fullness of life which Dante incorporates into that interpretation is so rich and so strong that its manifestations force their way into the listener's soul independently of any interpretation. The image of man eclipses the image of God."[4] The sense of history as a totality remains in this humanist order, and the overwhelming power of the images that promise fulfillment (or damnation) on earth infuses secular histories of progress and apocalypse. Secular salvation history depends on the power of images and the temporality of ultimate threats and promises to contain the heteroglossia and flux of events. This is the sense of time and of representation that I think informs technoscience in the United States. The discourses of genetics and information sciences are especially replete with instances of barely secularized Christian figural realism at work.

The legacy of figural realism is what puts my title's modest witness in the sacred secular time zones of the end of the Second Millennium and the New World Order. Second Millennium is the time machine that has to be reprogrammed by Nili's heretics, infidels, and Jews, who, it is crucial to remember, "have always considered getting knowledge part of being human." Challenging the material-semiotic practices of technoscience is in the interests of a deeper, broader, and more open scientific literacy, which this book will call situated knowledges.

Figuration has many meanings besides, or intersecting with, those proper to the legacy of Christian realism.[5] Aristotelian "figures of discourse" are about the spatial arrangements in rhetoric. A figure is geometrical and rhetorical; topics and tropes are both spatial concepts. The "figure" is the French term for the face, a meaning kept in English in the notion of the lineaments of a story. "To figure" means to count or calculate and also to be in a story, to have a role. A figure is also a drawing. Figures pertain to graphic representation and visual forms in general, a matter of no small importance in visually saturated technoscientific culture. Figures do not have to be representational and mimetic, but they do have to be tropic; that is, they cannot be literal and self-identical. Figures must involve at least some kind of displacement that can trouble identifications and certainties.

Figurations are performative images that can be inhabited. Verbal or visual, figurations can be condensed maps of contestable worlds. All language, including mathematics, is figurative, that is, made of tropes, constituted by bumps that make us swerve from literal-mindedness. I emphasize figuration to make explicit and inescapable the tropic quality of all material-semiotic processes, especially in technoscience. For example, think of a small set of objects into which lives and worlds are built—chip, gene, seed, fetus, database, bomb, race, brain, ecosystem. This mantra-like list is made up of imploded atoms or dense nodes that explode into entire worlds of practice. The chip, seed, or gene is simultaneously literal and figurative. We inhabit and are inhabited by such figures that map universes of knowledge, practice and power. To read such maps with mixed and differential literacies and without the totality, appropriations, apocalyptic disasters, comedic resolutions, and salvation histories of secularized Christian realism is the task of the mutated modest witness.

TIME AND SPACE

Figures always bring with them some temporal modality that organizes interpretive practice. I understand Foucault's concept of biopower[6] to refer to the practices of administration, therapeutics, and surveillance of bodies that discursively constitute, increase, and manage the forces of living organisms. He gives shape to his theoretical concept through delineating the nineteenth-century figures of the masturbating child, reproducing Malthusian couple, hysterical woman, and homosexual pervert. The temporality of these biopolitical figures is developmental.[7] They are all involved in dramas of health, degeneration, and the organic efficiencies and pathologies of production and reproduction. Developmental time is a legitimate descendant of the temporality of salvation history proper to the figures of Christian realism and technoscientific humanism.

Similarly, my cyborg figures inhabit a mutated time-space regime that I call technobiopower. Intersecting with—and sometimes displacing—the development, fulfillment, and containment proper to figural realism, the temporal modality pertaining to cyborgs is condensation, fusion, and implosion. This is more the temporality of the science-fictional wormhole, a spatial anomaly that casts travelers into unexpected regions of space, than of the birth passages of the biopolitical body. The implosion of the technical, organic, political, economic, oneiric, and textual that is evident in the material-semiotic practices and entities in late-twentieth-century technoscience informs my practice of figuration. Cyborg figures—such as the end-of-the-millennium seed, chip, gene, database, bomb, fetus, race, brain, and ecosystem—are the offspring of implosions of subjects and objects and of the natural and artificial. Perhaps cyborgs inhabit less the domains of "life," with its developmental and organic temporalities, than of "life itself"[8] with its temporalities embedded in communications enhancement and system redesign. Life itself is life enterprised up, where, in the dyspeptic version of the technoscientific soap opera, the species becomes the brand name and the figure becomes the price. Ironically, the millennarian fulfillment of development is the excessive condensation of implosion.

Temporalities intertwine with particular spatial modalities, and cyborg spatialization seems to be less about "the universal" than "the global." The globalization of the world, of "planet Earth," is a semiotic-material production of some forms of life rather than others. Technoscience is the story of such globalization; it is the travelogue of distributed, heterogeneous, linked, sociotechnical circulations that craft the world as a net called the global. The cyborg life forms that inhabit the recently congealed planet Earth—the "whole earth" of eco-activists and green commodity catalogs—gestated in a historically specific technoscientific womb. Consider, for example, only four horns of this multilobed reproductive wormhole:

1. The apparatuses of twentieth-century military conflicts, embedded in repeated world wars; decades of cold war; nuclear weapons and their institutional matrix in strategic planning, endless scenario production, and simulations in think tanks such as RAND; the immune system-like networking strategies for postcolonial global control inscribed in low-intensity-conflict doctrines; and post-Cold War, simultaneous-multiple-war-fighting strategics depending on rapid massive deployment, concentrated control of information and communications, and high-intensity, subnuclear precision weapons.[9]
2. The apparatuses of hyper capitalist market traffic and flexible accumulation strategies, all relying on stunning speeds and powers of manipulation of scale, especially miniaturization, which characterize the paradigmatic "high-technology" transnational corporations.[10]
3. The apparatuses of production of that technoscientific planetary habitat space called the ecosystem, with its constitutive birth pangs in resource management practices in such institutions as national fisheries in the 1920s and 1930s; in post-World War II theoretical fascination with all things cybernetic; in the Atomic Energy Commission-mediated research projects in the 1950s for tracing radioisotopes through food chains in the Pacific ocean; in 1970s global modeling practices indebted to the Club of Rome and to international projects such as the United Nations Educational, Scientific, and Cultural Organization's (UNESCO) Man and the Biosphere program; and in the early salvos of widespread "green war" as a

dominant New World Order security concern, with its diplomatic forms played out in 1992 at the Earth Summit in Rio de Janeiro.[11]

4. The apparatuses of production of globalized, extraterrestrial, everyday consciousness in the planetary pandemic of multisite, multimedia, multispecies, multicultural, cyborgian entertainment events such as *StarTrek, Blade Runner, Terminator, Alien*, and their proliferating sequelae in the daily information stream, embedded in transnational, U.S.-dominated, broad-spectrum media conglomerates, such as those forged by the mergers of Time-Warner with CNN and of the Disney universe with Capital Cities, owner of CBS.[12]

The offspring of these technoscientific wombs are cyborgs—imploded germinal entities, densely packed condensations of worlds, shocked into being from the force of the implosion of the natural and the artificial, nature and culture, subject and object, machine and organic body, money and lives, narrative and reality. Cyborgs are the stem cells in the marrow of the technoscientific body; they differentiate into the subjects and objects at stake in the contested zones of technoscientific culture. Cyborg figures must be read, too, with the mixed, unfinished literacies Nili is ready to teach.

So, what kinds of kin are allied in the proprietary forms of life in these days near the end of the Second Christian Millennium? How do we, who inhabit such stories, make psychic and commercial investments in forms of life, where the lines among human, machine, and organic nature are highly permeable and eminently revisable? How useful is my abiding suspicion that "biology"—the historically specific, congealed embodiments in the world as well as the technoscientific discourse positing such bodies—is an accumulation strategy? The point is less disreputable if I write that "biotechnology"—both the discourse and the body constituted as a biotechnics—is an accumulation strategy. But much of what is accumulated is more strange than capital, more kind than alien, more alluring than gold. It is time to move from grammar to content, from syntactics to semantics, from logic to body.

[. . .]

NOTES

1. *Immeasurable Results*. Lynn Randolph, oil on masonite, 9–1/2" × 10", 1994.

2. Joseph Dumit, "Mindful Images: PET Scans and Personhood in Biomedical America" (Ph.D. diss., History of Consciousness Board, University of California at Santa Cruz, 1995), 56–86.

3. Erich Auerbach, *Mimesis: The Representation of Reality in Western Literature* (Princeton: Princeton University Press, 1953), 64.

4. Ibid., 176.

5. I am in conversation with Rosi Braidotti's *Nomadic Subjects: Embodiment and Subjectivity in Contemporary Feminist Theory* (New York: Columbia University Press, 1994) in this discussion.

6. See Michel Foucault, *The History of Sexuality. Vol. 1: An Introduction*, trans. Robert Hurley (New York: Pantheon, 1978).

7. Or, as Claudia Castañeda put it, the child is the chronotope that organizes developmental time; see Claudia Castañeda, "Worlds in the Making: Childhood, Culture, and Globalization" (Ph.D. diss., History of Consciousness Board, University of California at Santa Cruz, 1996).

8. I owe "life itself" to Sarah Franklin, "Life Itself," paper delivered at the Center for Cultural Values, Lancaster University, June 9, 1993.

9. See Sharon Helsel, "The Comic Reason of Herman Kahn: Conceiving the Limits to Uncertainty in 1960" (Ph.D. diss., History of Consciousness Board, University of California at Santa Cruz, 1993); Chris Hables Gray, "Computers as Weapons and Metaphors: The U S. Military 1940–90 and Postmodern War" (Ph.D. diss., History of Consciousness Board, University of California at Santa Cruz, 1991); and Paul Edwards, *The Closed World: Computers and the Politics of Discourse in Cold War America* (Cambridge: MIT Press, 1996).

10. See David Harvey, *The Condition of Postmodernity: An Enquiry into the Origins of Cultural Change* (Oxford: Basil Blackwell, 1989); Paul Virilio and Sylvère Lotringer, *Pure War* (New York: Semiotext(e), 1983); and Emily Martin, "The End of the Body?" *American Ethnologist* 19, no. 1 (1992): 121–140.

11. See Arturo Escobar, "Welcome to Cyberia: Notes on the Anthropology of Cyberculture," *Current Anthropology* 35, no. 3 (1994): 211–231 and Peter Taylor and Frederick Buttel, "How Do We Know We Have Global Environmental Problems? Science and the Globalization of Environmental Discourse," *Geoforum* 23 (1992): 405–416.

The Maxis computer game *SimEarth* is one practical training exercise for learning to inhabit the systematically globalized "whole earth." Seldom has subject constitution been so literal, visible, and explicit. The game's promotional material on the box urges *SimEarth* players to "take charge of an entire planet from its birth to its death—10 billion years later. Guide life from its inception as single-celled microbes to a civilization that can reach for the stars." Players can "promote life, create and destroy continents, terraform hostile worlds." Finally, players are urged to "guide your intelligent species through trials of war, pollution, famine, disease, global warming, and the greenhouse effect." Nothing in *SimEarth* is abstract; the subjects and objects are materialized in located, particular practices. It is as if the chapter "Centers of Calculation" in Bruno Latour's *Science in Action: How to Follow Scientists and Engineers Through Society* (Cambridge: Harvard University Press, 1987) had been outlined by the software writers at Maxis: "View the entire world as either a flat projection or a spinning globe.... Close up views, for inspecting and modifying planets, display climate, life, and data layers."

12. See Joseba Gabilondo, "Cinematic Hyperspace, New Hollywood Cinema and Science Fiction Film: Image Commodification in Late Capitalism" (Ph.D. diss., Literature Department. University of California at San Diego, 1991); and Zoë Sofia, "Virtual Corporeality: A Feminist View." *Australian Feminist Studies* 15, Autumn (1992): 11–24.

Meanwhile, the Wells Fargo Bank is the biggest institutional shareholder of General Electric, which owns NBC. Notions of totalization come so naturally. Mixed and differential literacies for interpreting "global culture," and recognizing worlds outside the Net, must be deliberately cultivated.

BIBLIOGRAPHY

Auerbach, Erich. *Mimesis: The Representation of Reality in Western Literature*. Princeton: Princeton University Press, 1953.

Braidotti, Rosi. *Nomadic Subjects: Embodiment and Subjectivity in Contemporary Feminist Theory*. New York: Columbia University Press, 1994.

Castañeda, Claudia. "Worlds in the Making: Childhood, Culture, and Globalization." Ph.D. diss., History of Consciousness Board, University of California at Santa Cruz, 1996.

Dumit, Joseph. "Mindful Images: PET Scans and Personhood in Biomedical America." Ph.D. diss., History of Consciousness Board, University of California at Santa Cruz, 1995.

Edwards, Paul. *The Closed World: Computers and the Politics of Discourse in Cold War America*. Cambridge: MIT Press, 1996.

Escobar, Arturo. "Welcome to Cyberia: Notes on the Anthropology of Cyberculture." *Current Anthropology* 35, no. 3 (1994): 211–231.

Foucault, Michel. *The History of Sexuality. Vol. 1: An Introduction*. Translated by Robert Hurley. New York: Pantheon, 1978.

Franklin, Sarah. "Life Itself." Paper delivered at the Center for Cultural Values, Lancaster University, June 9, 1993.

Gabilondo, Joseba. "Cinematic Hyperspace, New Hollywood Cinema and Science Fiction Film: Image Commodification in Late Capitalism." Ph.D. diss., Literature Department. University of California at San Diego, 1991.

Gray, Chris Hables. "Computers as Weapons and Metaphors: The U.S. Military 1940–90 and Postmodern War." Ph.D. diss., History of Consciousness Board, University of California at Santa Cruz, 1991.

Harvey, David. *The Condition of Postmodernity: An Enquiry into the Origins of Cultural Change*. Oxford: Basil Blackwell, 1989.

Helsel, Sharon. 1993. "The Comic Reason of Herman Kahn: Conceiving the Limits to Uncertainty in 1960." Ph.D. diss., History of Consciousness Board, University of California at Santa Cruz.

Latour, Bruno. *Science in Action: How to Follow Scientists and Engineers Through Society*. Cambridge: Harvard University Press, 1987.

Martin, Emily. "The End of the Body?" *American Ethnologist* 19, no. 1 (1992): 121–140.

Sofia, Zoë. "Virtual Corporeality: A Feminist View." *Australian Feminist Studies* 15, Autumn (1992): 11–24.

Taylor, Peter, and Frederick Buttel. "How Do We Know We Have Global Environmental Problems? Science and the Globalization of Environmental Discourse." *Geoforum* 23 (1992): 405–416.

Virilio, Paul, and Sylvère Lotringer. *Pure War*. Translated by Mark Polizzotti. New York: Semiotext(e), 1983.

24

ONTOLOGY OF THE ACCIDENT: AN ESSAY ON DESTRUCTIVE PLASTICITY

Catherine Malabou

Let's start with the fact that rarely in the Western imaginary is metamorphosis presented as a real and total deviation of being. Perhaps never once has it been seen in this way. However bizarre the metamorphoses may be—the most striking are found in Ovid—the forms they create, the result of the transmutations of the poor wretches who are its victims, remain, so to speak, very much in the order of things. After all, it is only the external form of the being that changes, never its nature. Within change, being remains itself. The substantialist assumption is thus the travel companion of Western metamorphosis. Form transforms; substance remains.

In Greek mythology Metis, the goddess of cunning intelligence, "changed herself into all kinds of forms": "a lion, a bull, a fly, a fish, a bird, a flame or flowing water."[1] But still, her polymorphism is not infinite. It comprises a vast but finite palette of identities. When Metis runs dry, she must quite simply restart the cycle of her transformations, with no possibility of further innovation. Back to the start for the ruse. The returns of Metis cease with the drying up of the register of animal forms and this is why the other gods are able to triumph over her. If her metamorphic power were not limited, she would be invincible.

But this limit is hardly the failing of Metis alone. All the metamorphic gods systematically meet the same fate. All forms of transvestitism are included within a "range of possibilities" that can be catalogued and for which it is always possible to propose a typological schema, a panoply or sample.[2] Thus, for example:

When the god is taken by surprise, in order to escape he assumes the most baffling of forms, those which are most at variance with each other and most terrible; in quick succession he becomes flowing water, a burning flame, the wind, a tree, a bird, a tiger or a snake. But the series of transformations cannot continue indefinitely. They constitute a cycle of shapes which, once exhausted, returns to its point of departure. If the monster's enemy has been able not to lose his grip, at the end of the cycle the polymorphic god must resume his normal appearance and his original shape and retain them thereafter. So Chiron warns Peleus that whether Thetis turns herself into fire, water or a savage beast, the hero must not lose his hold until he sees her resume her first form.[3]

Likewise, Eidothee warns Menelaus against the ruses of Proteus:

Hold him fast no matter what he may try in his burning desire to free himself; he will assume every kind of form, will transform himself into whatever crawls upon the earth, into water and into divine fire; but you must hold on to him without flinching and grasp him even more tightly; and when in the end he will reach the point of agreeing to speak he will reassume the features you saw him to have when he was sleeping.[4]

Metamorphoses circulate in a cycle that links them, surrounds them, arrests them. Again, this is so because metamorphoses never carry off the true nature of being. If this nature, this identity were able to change deeply, substantively, then there would be no necessary return to prior forms, the circle would be broken, since what came before would suddenly be lacking in the ontological tangent it pursued. Transformation would no longer be a trick, a strategy or a mask always ready to be lifted to reveal the authentic features of the face. Transformation would betray an existential underground, which, beyond the round of metamorphoses, would enable the subject to become unrecognizable. Unrecognizable less because of a change in appearance than on account of a change in nature, a molting of the inner sculpture. Only death can end this plastic potential, a plasticity whose tricks are exhausted by nothing and that never reaches "the end of its tether" by itself. In principle we are capable of every mutation, unpredictable mutations irreducible to a range or typology. Our plastic possibilities are actually never-ending.

In the usual order of things, in classical metamorphoses, transformation intervenes in place of flight. For example, when Daphne, chased by Phoebus, is unable to run fast enough, she turns into a tree. But metamorphosis by destruction is not the same as flight; it is rather the form of the impossibility of fleeing. The impossibility of flight where flight presents the only possible solution. We must allow for the impossibility of flight in situations in which an extreme tension, a pain or malaise push a person towards an outside that does not exist.

What is a way out, what can a way out be, when there is no outside, no elsewhere? These are precisely the terms used by Freud to describe the drive, that strange excitation that cannot find its release outside the psyche and that, as he writes in *Instincts and their Vicissitudes*, determines that "no actions of flight avail against them."[5] The question is how to "eliminate" the constant force of the drive. Freud writes, "what follows is an attempt at flight."[6] The verb in "what follows" [*es kommt zu Bildung*], literally, "what comes to be formed," must be taken seriously here, for the verb not only announces the attempt to flee, it actually constitutes the attempt. Indeed, the only possible way out from the impossibility of flight appears to be the formation of a *form* of flight. In other words, both the formation of a type or ersatz of flight and the formation of an identity that flees itself, that flees the impossibility of fleeing itself. Identity abandoned, dissociated again, identity that does not reflect itself, does not live its own transformation, does not subjectivize its change.

Destructive plasticity enables the appearance or formation of alterity where the other is absolutely lacking. Plasticity is the form of alterity when no transcendence, flight or escape is left. The only other that exists in this circumstance is being other to the self.

It is all too true that Daphne can only escape Phoebus by transforming herself. In a sense, flight is impossible for her too. For her too, the moment of transformation is the moment of destruction: the granting and suppression of form are contemporaneous: "Her prayer was scarcely finished, when a heavy numbness seized on her limbs. Her soft breast was enveloped in a thin bark, her hair grew into foliage and her arms into branches; her foot that was just now so quick was stuck in sluggish roots, a tree top covered her face; only her radiance remained in her."[7] Nothing left of the former body other than a heart that for a time beats under the bark, a few tears. The formation of a new individual is precisely this explosion of form that frees up a way out and allows the resurgence of an alterity that the pursuer cannot assimilate. In the case of Daphne, paradoxically, the being-tree nonetheless conserves, preserves, and saves the being-woman. Transformation is a form of redemption, a strange salvation, but salvation all the same. By contrast, the flight identity forged by destructive plasticity flees itself first and foremost; it knows no salvation or redemption and is there for no one, especially not for the self. It has no body of bark, no armor, no branches. In retaining the same skin, it is forever unrecognizable.

In *Le Théorème d'Almodovar*, Antoni Casas Ros describes the car accident that disfigured him: a hart appeared on the road, the writer lost control of the car, his companion died on the spot, his face was completely destroyed. "At the beginning I believed the doctors, but in the end my reconstructive surgery was unable to rid my face of its Cubism. Picasso would have hated me, for I am the negation of his invention. To think that he too would have met me at the Perpignan train station Dali called the center of the universe. I am a blurred photograph, one that might remind you of a face."[8]

I have witnessed these types of transformation, even if they did not deform faces, even if they resulted less directly from recognizable accidents. Even if they were less spectacular, less brutal, they still had the power to start an end, to displace the meaning of a life. The couple unable to recover from an infidelity. The well-off woman whose son suddenly and inexplicably abandoned his family for a squat in the North of France. The colleague who upped and left for Texas believing he would be happy there. And in Central France, where I lived for years, all those people who at the age of 50 lost their job in the economic crisis of the mid-1980s. Teachers in underprivileged areas. People with Alzheimer's disease. In all these cases what was striking was that once the metamorphosis took place, however explicable its causes (unemployment, relational difficulties, illness), its effects were absolutely unexpected, and it became incomprehensible, displacing its cause, breaking all etiological links. All of a sudden these people became strangers to themselves because they could not flee. It was not, or not just, that they were broken, wracked with sorrow or misfortune; it was the fact that they became new people, others, re-engendered, belonging to a different species. Exactly as if they had had an accident. "An autobiography appears to be the tale of a full life. A succession of acts. The displacements of a body in space-time. Adventures, misdeeds, joys, unending suffering. My true life starts with an end."[9]

The crisis of the mid-1980s in France was a crisis of connection, a crisis that gave social exclusion its full meaning. It revolutionized the concepts of unhappiness and trauma and provoked a social upheaval whose extent we are only beginning to measure today. The jobless, the homeless, the sufferers of post-traumatic stress syndrome, the deeply depressed, the victims of natural catastrophes, all began to resemble one another as the new international whose physiognomy I tried to describe in *The New Wounded*.[10] Forms of post-traumatic subjectivity, as Zizek calls it; new figures of the void or of identitarian abandonment who elude most therapies, especially psychoanalysis.

Existing, in these cases—but, in the end, isn't it always the case?—amounts to experiencing a lack of exteriority, which is as much an absence of interiority, hence the impossible flight, the on the spot transformation. There is neither an inside nor an outside world. Consequently, the modification is all the more radical and violent; it fragments all the more readily. The worst dissensions of the subject with the self, the most serious conflicts, do not even look tragic. Paradoxically, they are signaled by indifference and coldness.

Kafka's *The Metamorphosis* is the most successful, beautiful, and relevant attempt to approach this kind of accident. Blanchot puts it well:

The state in which Gregor finds himself is the same state as that of a being unable to quit existence, one for whom to exist is to be condemned to always fall back into existence. Becoming vermin, he continues to live in the mode of degeneration, he digs deeper into animal solitude, he moves closer still to absurdity and the impossibility of living. But what happens? He just keeps on living.[11]

Metamorphosis is existence itself, untying identity instead of reassembling it. Gregor's awakening at the beginning of the story is the perfect expression of destructive plasticity. The inexplicable nature of his transformation into an insect continues to fascinate us as a possible danger, a threat for each of us. Who knows if tomorrow . . .

But the monster does manage to weave a cocoon. A cocoon which slowly becomes a text. The text is *The Metamorphosis*, and this metamorphosis is completed by us, the readers. The circle of plastic possibilities in some senses closes here again. The narrative voice is not entirely that of an insect. This invisible butterfly has a non-bestial voice, the voice of a man, the voice of a writer. What is a metamorphosis that can still speak itself, write itself, that does not remain entirely unique even when it experiences itself as such? As Kafka writes in his letters, art is no salvation. Yet it can preserve. After all, one can't help recognizing Daphne's bark in Gregor.

If Deleuze's reading of *The Metamorphosis* is unfair when it concludes that Kafka "fails," it is not entirely wrong. On the one hand, Deleuze recognizes the effectiveness of the "becoming-animal of Gregor, his becoming beetle, junebug, dungbeetle, cockroach, which traces an intense line of flight in relation to the familial triangle but especially in relation to the bureaucratic and commercial triangle."[12] The result of the metamorphosis is precisely a being in flight, one who constitutes a way out in the self, forming "a single process, a unique method that replaces subjectivity."[13] On the other hand, Deleuze also sees "the exemplary story of a re-Oedipalization"[14] in this metamorphosis, a trajectory that remains trapped in the family triangle: father-mother-sister. "Given over to his becoming-animal, Gregor finds himself re-Oedipalized by his family and goes to his death."[15] Gregor's death returns the metamorphosis to the order of things, in some senses annulling it. The family will not have been metamorphosed and Gregor will not have stopped recognizing the family, calling, naming his father, his mother, his sister.

But Deleuze attributes the "failure" of the metamorphosis to the fact that it concerns an adventure in form, the adventure of an identifiable animal. Gregor becomes a beetle. For Deleuze, a true metamorphosis would be a metamorphosis that, despite its name, would have nothing to do with a becoming-form. According to him, "as long as there is form, there is still reterritorialization."[16] This is why the "becoming-animal" is not "becoming *an* animal": the first is an arrangement; the second is a form, which can do nothing but freeze becoming.[17]

I do not believe that the problem of the limit of metamorphoses as traditionally conceived derives from the fact that they present themselves as the journey from one form to another. It is not form that is the problem; it's the fact that form can be thought separately from the nature of the being that transforms itself. The fact that form is presented as skin, vestment or finery, and that one can always leave without an alteration in what is essential. The critique of metaphysics does not want to recognize that in fact, despite what it claims loud and clear, metaphysics constantly instigates the dissociation of essence and form, or form and the formal, as if one could always rid oneself of form, as if, in the evening, form could be left hanging like a garment on the chair of being or essence. In metaphysics, form can always change, but the nature of being persists. It is this that is debatable—not the concept of form itself, which it is absurd to pretend to do without.

We must find a way to think a mutation that engages both form and being, a new form that is literally a form of being. Again, the radical metamorphosis I am trying to think here is well and truly the fabrication of a new person, a novel form of life, without anything in common with a preceding form. Gregor changes form; we will never know what he looked like before but in some ways he remains the same, awaiting meaning. He pursues his inner monologue and does not appear to be transformed in substance, which is precisely why he suffers, since he is no longer recognized as what he never ceases to be. But imagine a Gregor perfectly indifferent to his transformation, unconcerned by it. Now that's an entirely different story!

What destructive plasticity invites us to consider is the suffering caused by an absence of suffering, in the emergence of a new form of being, a stranger to the one before. Pain that manifests as indifference to pain, impassivity, forgetting, the loss of symbolic reference points. Yet the synthesis of another soul and body in that abandonment is still a form, a whole, a system, a life. In this case the term "form" does not describe the intensity of a presence or an idea, nor that of a sculptural contour.

A very specific plastic art is at work here, one that looks a lot like the death drive. Freud knew that the death drive creates forms, which he also called "examples." However, apart from sadism and masochism, he couldn't give any examples or refer to any types. How does one render the death drive *visible*?[18]

NOTES

1. Marcel Detienne and Jean-Pierre Vernant, *Cunning Intelligence in Greek Culture and Society*, trans. Janet Lloyd (Atlantic Highlands, NJ: Harvester Press, 1978).

2. See Jean-Pierre Vernant, *L'individu, la mort, l'amour: soi-même et l'autre en Grèce ancienne* (Paris: Gallimard, 1989, 29).

3. Detienne and Vernant, *Cunning Intelligence*, 112–113.

4. Ibid., 113.

5. Sigmund Freud, "Instincts and their Vicissitudes" (1915), in *Standard Edition of the Complete Psychological Works of Sigmund Freud*, vol. 14, ed. and trans. James Strachey (London: Hogarth Press, 1954), 119.

6. Sigmund Freud, "Repression," in ibid, 141–158, 155.

7. Ovid, *Metamorphoses I—IV*, Book 1, lines 549–552, trans. D. E. Hill (Wauconda, IL: Bolchazy-Carducci, 1985).

8. Antoni Casas Ros, *Le Théorème d'Almodovar* (Paris: Gallimard, 2008, 13). [—Author's translation.]

9. Ibid.

10. Catherine Malabou, *The New Wounded: From Neurosis to Brain Damage*, trans. Steven Miller (New York: Fordham, 2012) originally published as *Les Nouveaux Blessés, de Freud à la neurologie: Penser les traumatismes contemporains* (Paris: Bayard, 2007).

11. Maurice Blanchot, *De Kafka à Kafka* (Paris: Gallimard, 1981), 73. [—Author's translation.]

12. Gilles Deleuze and Félix Guattari, *Kafka: Toward a Minor Literature*, trans. Dana Polan (Minneapolis: University of Minnesota Press, 1986), 14.

13. Ibid., 36.

14. Ibid., 14.

15. Ibid., 39.

16. Ibid., 6.

17. See Gilles Deleuze and Félix Guattari, *A Thousand Plateaus: Capitalism and Schizophrenia*, trans. Brian Massumi (London: Continuum, 1987), 291–310.

18. For more on Freudian "examples" of the death drive, see *The New Wounded*, Chapter 10.

BIBLIOGRAPHY

Blanchot, Maurice. *De Kafka à Kafka*. Paris: Gallimard, 1981.

Casas Ros, Antoni. *Le Théorème d'Almodovar*. Paris: Gallimard, 2008.

Deleuze, Gilles, and Félix Guattari. *A Thousand Plateaus: Capitalism and Schizophrenia*. Translated by Brian Massumi. London: Continuum, 1987.

Deleuze, Gilles, and Félix Guattari. *Kafka: Toward a Minor Literature*. Translated by Dana Polan. Minneapolis: University of Minnesota Press, 1986.

Detienne, Marcel, and Jean-Pierre Vernant. *Cunning Intelligence in Greek Culture and Society*. Translated by Janet Lloyd. Atlantic Highlands, NJ: Harvester Press, 1978.

Freud, Sigmund. *Standard Edition of the Complete Psychological Works of Sigmund Freud*, vol. 14. Edited and translated by James Strachey, 109–140. London: Hogarth Press, 1954.

Freud, Sigmund. "Instincts and their Vicissitudes." In *Standard Edition of the Complete Psychological Works of Sigmund Freud*, vol. 14. Edited by James Strachey, 109–140. London: Hogarth Press, 1954.

Freud, Sigmund. "Repression." In *Standard Edition of the Complete Works of Sigmund Freud*, vol. 14. Edited by James Strachey, 141–158. London: Hogarth Press, 1954.

Malabou, Catherine. *The New Wounded: From Neurosis to Brain Damage*. Translated by Steven Miller. New York: Fordham, 2012. Originally published as *Les Nouveaux Blessés, de Freud à la neurologie: Penser les traumatismes contemporains*. Paris: Bayard, 2007.

Ovid. *Metamorphoses I—IV*. Translated by D. E. Hill. Wauconda, IL: Bolchazy-Carducci, 1985.

Vernant, Jean-Pierre. *L'individu, la mort, l'amour: soi-même et l'autre en Grèce ancienne*. Paris: Gallimard, 1989.

25

THE DISPOSITIF OF THE PERSON

Roberto Esposito

If the point of philosophical reflection is to critically dismantle contemporary opinion, to radically interrogate what is presented as immediately clear to all, there are few concepts so in need of dismantling as that of "person." No term in the Western tradition enjoys the wide-ranging success that the term person does today. I'm talking not only about those areas directly related to it that run from philosophy to law to anthropology, to finally theology, but also about those ideological perspectives that seem opposed to each other, like catholic and secularist bioethics. While for Catholics a living being is to be considered a person since the moment of conception, for secularists it is much later. But however both agree on the value that is to be attributed to the title of person. For both the personalisation is the crucial passage through which a biological material that lacks meaning becomes something intangible. Only a life that has crossed beforehand through the symbolic door of the person is believed to be sacred or is valued in terms of its qualities.

No doubt there are very good reasons for the extraordinary success of the category of person—a success that seems able to break down even the walls separating analytical and continental philosophy. Very few concepts outside of person exhibit such a degree of lexical richness, semantic flexibility, and power to evoke. Constituted in the intersection and productive tension between theatrical language, juridical weight and theological dogma, the concept of person seems to incorporate a potentiality of meaning so dense and varied as to appear to be something we cannot do without. But another no less important reason should be added. I'm speaking of its historical features, which explains the singular growth that the term person undergoes from the middle of the last century onward. It concerns the obvious need, after the end of the Second World War, to reconstitute that link between reason and body that Nazism had tried to rip apart in its catastrophic attempt to reduce human life to mere biology. This is the intention of the supporters of the 1948 Declaration of Human Rights. And this is the intention which, focusing on the value and dignity of the human person, continue to characterize contemporary philosophy: from post-Kantian transcendentalism to Husserlian phenomenology, leaving aside for now the frayed line that runs from Jacques Maritain and Emmanuel Mounier to Paul Ricœur, which urges forward precisely the category of person.

More difficult to understand, however, is what effect this increase of personalism has had. Was the category of person able to re-establish that connection, which 20th century totalitarianisms broke, between rights and life in a form that makes possible and effective something like "human rights"? It's difficult not to answer with a resounding no. A mere glance at today's statistics, read both in absolute and relative terms, of those who die every day because of famine, sickness, and war, seemingly gives the lie to the very pronouncement of a right to life. Of course one could easily respond by linking the impracticability of human rights to a question of contingency, to the lack of a power strong enough to impose these rights. One could speak as well of a forceful presence of civilization that has been impervious historically to universal juridical models. In that case, the problem appears to be that the paradigm of person hasn't been extended far enough or has been extended, but only partially. As reassuring as these interpretations might well be, it's useful to set out another point of view that puts into play a more problematic perspective. I think that the notion of person isn't able to join together the epochal hiatus between life and right, between *nomos* and *bios*, since it is the notion of person itself that produces it. In spite of all the self-congratulatory rhetoric of our political rituals we find that the original efficacy of the paradigm of person is joined to this production of a hiatus between life and right.

There is another preliminary consideration to be made before we take up the question at hand. When we allude to the effect of a concept, which in the case of the category of person gestates for very long periods, we find ourselves moving well beyond the strictly categorical definition of the term. Not all concepts produce effects. In very few instances, however, are those effects more numerous than in the case of person. It means that we are dealing with something quite different from a simple conceptual category. For these reasons, in the title of my paper, I refer to person in terms of dispositif. As is well known, when we speak of dispositif [*dispositivo*], we are dealing with a concept that Michel Foucault used in the 1960s and which Gilles Deleuze, on the one hand, and Giorgio Agamben more recently on the other, turn to again in two essays (both, curiously, have the same title, "What Is a Dispositif?"). It is Agamben who thinks that the root of dispositif can be found in the Christian idea of *oikonomia*, which the Church Fathers translated with *dispositio*. It's from them that the term dispositif derives, understood as the administration and the government which God exercises over man in the second person of the Holy Trinity, namely Christ. We can see here the possibility of uncovering a first relation between the functioning of the dispositif and the doubling that is implicit in the idea of person, in this case divine. Dispositif isn't only what separates being and praxis, ontology and the act of government in God. It is what also allows us to articulate a plurality in the divine unity, which in this specific case has the features of a trinity.

Another key figure, deeply associated with that of the Holy Trinity in Christian dogma, is the mystery of the Incarnation. It offers the same structure and indeed the same logic as the Holy Trinity. Here too what is at stake is a unity constituted by a separation and here too the dispositif allows us to formulate it as such, despite the inversion of roles. If three persons in God are constituted by a single substance, Christ unites within his person, without mixing them, two states or two natures that are substantially different. No less important with respect to the future developments of the paradigm is the fact that these two distinct states or natures that co-habitate in one person are not qualitatively the same, since one is divine and the other human. When we move from the doubled nature of Christ to what makes man a totality composed of soul and body, the qualitative difference between the two elements becomes decisive. Rather than being equal, these elements are actualized in an ordering that layers or superimposes one under the other. Such an hierarchic effect, which is quite clear in Saint Augustine, extends to all Christian doctrine so that there cannot be the least doubt: although the body isn't in itself something evil (because it too is a divine creation), nevertheless it constitutes the animal part of man. Here too the Christian idea of person is tied to a unity that isn't only constructed from a doubleness, but is put together in such a way that one of its elements is subordinated to another. This explains how Saint Augustine can describe the necessity of meeting man's bodily needs as an "illness,"[1] in the sense that it is the part not properly human in man, the impersonal part of the person. Keeping this perspective of an intricate web of humanization and dehumanization uppermost in mind, we can see how the dominant role that Foucault bestows on dispositif comes again into play, particularly in its capacity to subjectivize. We know that Foucault never separates this meaning of subjectivity from that of subjection: only by being subjected to others or to oneself do we become subjects. We also know that for an extremely long period that only concludes with Leibniz at the beginning of the 18th century, what philosophical language understands by "subject" is what we today call "object." It's here, in the essential indistinction between the two figures of subject and object, of subjectivization and subjection, that we find the particular role and function of the dispositif of the person [*dispositivo della persona*].

The paradigmatic role of this dispositif is precisely to divide a living being into two natures made up of different qualities—the one subjugated to the mastery of the other—and thus to create subjectivity through a process of subjection or objectivization. The dispositif of person makes a part of a body subject to another part, to the degree in which the latter part is the subject of the former. As the Catholic and personalist philosopher Jacques Maritain argues, the human person is "a totality that is lord over himself and his actions," adding that "if a healthy conception of politics depends above all on the proper consideration given the human person, it is important to remember that such a person is that of an animal that has the gift of reason and that the animal part is immense in that measure of reason."[2] Man is a person if, and only if, he masters the more properly animal part of his nature. Of course not everyone has this tendency or disposition to de-animalize himself. The degree of humanity present in all will derive from the greater or lesser intensity of this de-animalization and so too the underlying difference between he who enjoys the full title of person and he who can enjoy it only if certain conditions have previously been met. Also for Heidegger "we are still thinking of *homo animalis*—even when *anima* (soul) is posited as *animus sive mens* (spirit or mind), and this in turn is posited as subject, person, or spirit [*Geist*]."[3]

It is the Roman juridical codification that systematized in incredibly powerful fashion the metaphysics of person. The Roman codification shares with the Christian conception the constitutive nexus of unity and separation, leading the dispositif to its perfect, formal completion. Gaius's famous phrase, regarding the *summa divisio de iure personarum*, provides the strongest testimony. It prescribes a procedure of separation, not only between *servi* [slaves] and *liberi* [free men] but, within the latter, between *ingenui* [freemen born free] and *liberti* [those manumitted from legal slavery] and so on, in an unbroken chain of successive doublings. Person is, on the one hand, the more general category since it encompasses the entire human species. On the other hand, it is the prism through which the human species is separated in the hierarchical division between types defined precisely by their constitutive difference. It is thanks to the category of person that human beings are unified in the form of their separation. Two elements—unity and separation—are held together and cannot be separated. It's this absolutely obligatory binding that makes possible all the other juridical figures that descend from it. The exceptional force of Roman law, understood here in its totality, regardless of how much it changed over time, lies precisely in having founded this dialectic systematically in a fashion that is unparalleled. At its centre is the notion of person, pushed to its limits, so as to encompass even what is otherwise declared to be a thing (as in the case of the slave). So that mankind is subdivided into an infinite series of typologies, each of which is awarded different statutes, like *filii in potestate* [children under the power of the father], *uxores in matrimonio* [wives taken in marriage], *mulieres in manu* [subjected women] and so on, along an itinerary that gives form to newer and newer divisions.

Yet, the terrible legacy of the Roman dispositif of person doesn't lie only in the production of differential thresholds within mankind, but also in the continual movement between them. The constant presence of exception within the norm (and not outside it) responds to this demand. For Rome the norm constitutes the natural area in which the exception is used, just as the exception expresses not so much the excess or the break, as the mechanism by which the norm is recharged [*ricarica*]. For example, the archaic power of death that the *pater* enjoys with respect to the *filius* did not hold if the male child was younger than three years of age and was a first-born. But this exception was in turn superseded through another exception if the child in question was deformed or illegitimate. In such a case the second exception restored to the norm what was lost to the first, creating a circuit in which the exception derived from the norm and the norm from the exception. We know how this mechanism culminates today in modern juridical statutes, not only in the sphere of civil law, but also in that of public and even international law. To it is added another mechanism. I'm referring to the movement also implicit in the dispositif of the person between the various *status* [states]; not only those contiguous, in the case of family relations for instance, but also those more distant, such as the state of servitude and that of the free man, the latter in its various and multiple gradations.

In such a perspective the two complementary figures of *manumissio* [freeing of a slave] and *mancipatio* [enslaving for future emancipation] are shifts in the relation of dependence and domination that some individuals have vis-à-vis others. Therefore they regulate the mobile thresholds of depersonalization sanctioned most explicitly in the different degrees of the *dimunutio capitis* [loss of status] of *minima*, *media*, and *maxima*. Thus, no one in Rome was a full-fledged person from the beginning of life nor did one remain a person forever. Some became persons, as *filii* became *patres*;

others were excluded because they were prisoners of war or were debtors. Still others spent their entire lives caught between two poles, as was the case with children who were sold and then made subject to the buyer as well as to the natural father. What is striking here, even more than the absolute clarity of these distinctions, are the zones of indistinction and transition which the first distinctions give rise to their continual movement. If the servile *res* are in some way contained within the most generalised form of person, this means that the category of person encompasses all the intermediate stages of the person over time, of the potential person as well as the semi-person up to and including the non-person. It also indicates that the person not only includes within it its own proper negative, but constantly reproduces it.[4] Seen from this perspective, the mechanism of depersonalization is the reverse of personalization and vice-versa. It isn't possible to personalize someone without depersonalizing or reifying others, without pushing someone into the indefinite space that opens below the person. Silhouetted against the moving backdrop of the person looms the inert figure of the thing.

It's difficult to resist the temptation to connect this dialectic to the modern process of subjectivization and desubjectivization that Foucault connects to how the dispositif functions. No doubt between the two experiences one finds that profound middle ground constituted by the very same notion of subject, outside of and irreducible to the Roman juridical conception. Nevertheless, the conceptual and lexical distance need not cancel out a deeper paradigmatic continuity that belongs to its logical structure, which is embedded in juridical language from the outset. The decisive point of conjunction with modern conception of subjectivity is the separation, found first in the Christian formulation and even more in Roman law, between the category of person and the living being on which it is grafted. The person doesn't coincide with the body in which it inheres, just as the mask is never completely one with the actor's face. In this case as well the element that most strongly characterizes the "machine" of the person is to be traced in the subtle interval that always differentiates it from the character that acts, regardless of the qualities of the actor.

The same subjective right, which cannot be assimilated to Roman juridical objectivism, carries within it an element that refers precisely to the dispositif of the person. It's in this sense that from the end of the 18th century on, men are declared equal (at least in principle) as subjects of law. The formal separation of different typologies of individuals, driven out from the domain of species, is transposed, so to speak, within the single individual, which is doubled across two different and layered spheres: one capable of reason and will and therefore fully human and the other reduced to biology, practically assimilated to animal nature. While the first, called person, is considered to be the centre of juridical imputation, the second, coinciding with the body, constitutes a piece of property akin to an internal slave. If in Descartes the distinction between *res cogitans* and *res extensa* establishes an unbreakable line of separation between the subject and the body proper, the liberal tradition, from Locke to Mill, will want to award the mastery of the body to its legitimate owner; to him that inhabits it. Inevitably they will force the body to cross over it into the domain of the thing: man *is* not, but *has*, and possesses his own body and obviously he can do with it what he will.

More striking still is the hierarchical and exclusionary effect that the semantics of the person sets in motion within liberalism itself. I am speaking of authors like Peter Singer and Hugo Engelhardt, who, referring explicitly to Roman law and in particular to Gaius's formulation, make the distinction between two different categories of man, the first who can be ascribed fully to the category of person, and the second who is instead defined only as "members of the species of *homo sapiens*."[5] Between the two extremes, just as in the *ius personarum*, we find a series of intermediate steps, characterized by a presence of personality, which increases or decreases according to the point of view adopted. At its apex one finds the healthy adult, to whom can be awarded the title of being truly and properly a person; next there is the infant, who is considered to be a potential person; and then the elderly invalid, who has been reduced to a semi-person; to the terminally ill, to whom the status of non-person is given; to finally the madman who receives the role of anti-person. The consequence of this classification is subjugating "defective" persons to whole persons, who are free to dispose of them as they will on the basis of medical or even economic considerations. As Engelhardt citing Gaius argues: "Just as when we capture a wild animal, a bird or a fish, what we capture becomes ours and is held to belong to us as long as we take care of it," in the same way, when we speak of deformed children or the terminally ill, so too are these subject to the power of those persons who are free to decide whether to keep them alive or to ease them on their way towards death.[6]

Without wanting to make events and concepts equivalent that are both distant in their origin and their aims, such as that of ancient Rome and those periods closer to us, the unavoidable impression is that today we find ourselves facing something that goes well beyond a simple analogy, and which suggests a kind of repetition; a remnant [*resto*] that isn't subject to historical transformations that are reproduced again and again even if the context is completely different. The hypothesis implicit in what I've said to this point is that the past, or at least some of its most important figures (such as that of 'person') return thanks to their untimeliness [*inattualità*], that is thanks to their anachronistic features. Simone Weil is really the author who more than any other and with more force and originality attempted to locate the archaic in the present [*attuale*] or the present in the archaic. Reading her essays on the origins of Hitlerism that focus on parallels with ancient Rome, provides us with the most stunning kind of proof. According to Weil, the bridge between Roman law and violence is constituted by property: owning things and men transformed into things through the institution of slavery constitutes not only the context of the juridical order, but its form. Here, at the centre of an analysis of Nazism, the reifying effect of that logical-juridical dispositif re-emerges, which having divided human beings into free men and slaves, places between them a zone of indistinction that winds up superimposing them, making the free man the equivalent of a slave.

Yet the more pertinent element here, one that Weil also draws our attention to, is how the dispositif that functions via exclusion is joined to the category of the person: "The notion of rights, by its very mediocrity, leads on very naturally to that of the person, for rights are related to personal things. They are on that level."[7] Weil addresses this attack not only at the primacy of rights over duties, which is to say a subjectivist and individual [*particolaristica*] conception of justice, but at the division that such a category presupposes or produces within the unity of the living being. The same idea—which today has spread to the four corners of the globe—of the sacredness of the human person functions precisely by leaving behind or expelling what in man is not judged to be personal and what therefore can be violated without worry: "I see a passer-by in the street. He has long arms, blue eyes, and a mind whose thoughts I do not know, but perhaps they are commonplace. [. . .] If it were the human personality in him that was sacred to me, I could easily put out his eyes. As a blind man he would be exactly as much a human personality as before. [. . .] I should have destroyed nothing but his eyes."[8] More than anyone else Weil sets out with remarkable clarity the dehumanizing function of the mask of the person; once the mask is made safe [*salvaguardata*], it doesn't matter what happens to the face on which it rests and even less to the faces that do not own masks; to those who still aren't persons, or who no longer are persons, or to those who were never declared to be persons. It is the absolute lucidity of this point of view, one ignored by all the personalisms of yesterday and today (precisely because it challenges a platitude), that pushes Weil towards the impersonal. When soon after she writes that "[S]o far from its being his person, what is sacred in a human being is the impersonal in him. Everything which is impersonal in man is sacred, and nothing else," she inaugurates a path, no doubt difficult and complex, whose importance we are only able to discern today.[9] Even more, it suggests the possibility, one again largely ignored today, of profoundly changing our philosophical, juridical, and political lexicon.

NOTES

1. Augustine, *On the Trinity. Books 8–15*, ed. Gareth B. Matthews, trans. Stephen McKenna (New York: Cambridge University Press, 2002), XI, 1,1, 62. [—Translation modified.]
2. Jacques Maritain, *Humanisme intégral: Problèmes temporels et spirituels d'une nouvelle chrétienté* (Paris: Aubier, 1936), 17.
3. Martin Heidegger, "Letter on Humanism," in *Basic Writings*, ed. David Farell Krell, trans. Frank A. Capuzzi and J. Glenn Gray (San Francisco: HarperSanFrancisco, 1993), 227.
4. [Given Esposito's emphasis throughout the section on the servile *res* with reference to the thing, I have chosen to refer here to person by it and not he or she—Trans.]
5. Peter Singer, *Writings on an Ethical Life* (New York: Harper Perennial, 2001), 255.
6. Hugo Tristam Engelhardt, *The Foundations of Christian Bioethics* (New York: M and M Scrivener, 2000), 157.
7. Simone Weil, "Human Personality," in *Simone Weil: An Anthology*, ed. Siân Miles, trans. Richard Rees (London: Penguin Classics, 2005), 84.
8. Ibid., 70–71.
9. Ibid., 74.

BIBLIOGRAPHY

Engelhardt, Hugo Tristam. *The Foundations of Christian Bioethics*. New York: M and M Scrivener, 2000.

Heidegger, Martin. "Letter on Humanism." In *Basic Writings*. Edited by David Farell Krell. Translated by Frank A. Capuzzi and J. Glenn Gray, 213–266. San Francisco: HarperSanFrancisco, 1993.

Maritain, Jacques. *Humanisme intégral: problèmes temporels et spirituels d'une nouvelle chrétienté*. Paris: Aubier, 1936.

Singer, Peter. *Writings on an Ethical Life*. New York: Harper Perennial, 2001.

Weil, Simone. "Human Personality." In *Simone Weil: An Anthology*. Edited by Siân Miles. Translated by Richard Rees, 69–98. London: Penguin Classics, 2005.

26

THE BIOPOLITICAL BIRTH OF GENDER: SOCIAL CONTROL, HERMAPHRODITISM, AND THE NEW SEXUAL APPARATUS

Jemima Repo

In 1955, John Money (1921–2006), professor of medical psychology and paediatrics at Johns Hopkins University, published a series of articles with his colleagues introducing a radical idea that a person's psychological sex was learned and did not necessarily arise from biological factors. This idea was encapsulated in a new concept: gender. In this article, I argue that this moment marked the birth of a new apparatus of sexuality that would not challenge the old monarchy of sex as such, but address its newfound biological complexities that were epitomized in the problematic body and mind of the hermaphrodite.[1] I show how gender was introduced into the sexual order through a highly psychologized and medicalized field of knowledge production centred on the problem of gaining access to human life by controlling the behavioural system that upheld it. It produced individuals who possessed not only a sex but also learned a gender, expanding and multiplying the access points of power to the body, rendering it more elastic and malleable and hence, more governable.

In *Will to Knowledge*, Michel Foucault argues that sexuality was deployed in the nineteenth century as the hinge between the anatomopolitics of the body and the biopolitics of population. Sexuality was the point of access that connected the biopolitical strategy to manage and regulate the life of the population to the discipline of individual bodies and their organic functions. Sexuality was ushered in as "the index of a society's strength, revealing both its political energy and its biopolitical vigour."[2] Its regulation, Foucault writes, "was motivated by one basic concern: to ensure population, to reproduce labour capacity, to perpetuate the form of social relations."[3] Since

Foucault, however, few have continued his biopolitical genealogy of sexuality to examine how this access to life through sex has been guaranteed after the Victorian era. Feminist applications of Foucault's analysis, including the concept of the gender apparatus, have produced rich theories of the historical contingency and power-laden relations of gender constructs,[4] but not genealogical analyses of the apparatus of gender itself.

Gender is often treated as a universally applicable concept to describe, for instance, the socially constructed aspects of sex, or the system of power through which sexual difference and its norms are produced and upheld in different times and places. Sociology, Simone de Beauvoir, or other feminists are often credited as the inventors of the contemporary concept of gender, even though the idea actually originates from intersex case management in 1950s US psychiatry. It is only from this period that we can really conduct a genealogy of gender, understood as an apparatus. Moreover, to examine it as an apparatus, it is not enough to merely ask how the idea was formed in science. It is necessary to ask what were the rationalities underpinning its formation and at what kinds of social, political, and economic projects they were targeted. For Foucault, sexuality was not just a discourse of power, but an apparatus, which according to him is a "formation which has as its major function at a given historical moment that of responding to an *urgent need.*"[5] The task of genealogy is to examine "the history of the way in which things become a problem."[6] Foucault did not leave his analysis of sexuality at the level of the discipline of subjectivity but tied it to the broader socioeconomic changes of the day such as industrialization, urbanization, population, and marketization. Sexuality became regarded as a problem that affected each of these areas of biopolitical governmentality and hence was deployed as an instrument with which to regulate them. The strategic model of inquiry into gender therefore asks what force relationship made its deployment necessary, and what functions and effects of power and knowledge it ensures. How did gender order and link together various elements supporting and supported by types of knowledge that, through the manipulation of forces, were developed in a *particular direction*? How was gender deployed to enact the life-administering function of power through the urgent question of sex and life?

Postwar society of the 1950s differed greatly from the Victorian context analysed by Foucault in *Will to Knowledge*. Victorians had not suffered the economic destitution of the Great Depression, which also had a demographic cost: Western fertility rates slumped in the 1930s and did not begin to recover until the 1940s. Moreover, as Agamben and Esposito have argued,[7] the interwar period and the Second World War were distinctly thanatopolitical in character; the eugenic battles to make the life of the species flourish operated on logics defined by racial exclusion. After the wars, however, we can witness a shift from the Western preoccupation with social hygiene to a discourse of social control, in which the emergence of the apparatus of gender is located.

Structural functionalism, a theoretical framework that dominated sociology in the 1940s and 1950s, assumed social order was maintained through the socialisation of individuals into normative behaviours. The schema, adopted by numerous social science disciplines relied heavily on the family's role in ensuring that children were socialised into healthy, productive and reproductive citizens. For Talcott Parsons,[8] known as one of the founding fathers of structural functionalism, processes of socialisation and social control were crucial to ensure that individuals conformed to given roles and continued to reproduce the system in question. Parsons coined the term of the "nuclear family" to describe the ideal family model that he felt was essential for successful socialisation processes. The family's crucial function was to socialise children into what he termed "sex roles," ensuring the reproduction of adult sexual personalities in the population. This, Parsons argued, was a prerequisite for normal psychological development and ultimately, the maintenance of social order. What begins to emerge to the Foucauldian eye are changes to the Victorian rationalities that governed sexuality and life. The family was still at the heart of biopolitical control, but a new kind of attention was being paid to the psychological processes through which individuals conformed or deviated from norms. As Nikolas Rose observes,[9] Parsons' work in particular rendered psychiatry, clinical psychology and other forms of expert guidance significant to the maintenance of social order, extending the reach of government action into the family.

Ideas of behavioural conditioning, socialisation, and social order were central to the biomedical invention of gender. Below I detail how in the 1950s, gender emerged as an apparatus of biopower embedded in these logics of social control that reconfigured the sexual order of things.

GENDER: A NEW SEXUAL DISCOURSE OF BIOPOLITICAL CONTROL

In 1955, Money published four of articles in the *Bulletin of the Johns Hopkins Hospital*, three of which were co-authored with his colleagues Joan Hampson and John Hampson.[10] Reporting on the findings of four years of research, the first article in 1955 by Money and the Hampsons made a novel intervention into the medical practices of sex assignment arguing against using a single criterion of sex in the assignment of sex to hermaphrodites. Instrumental to their argument was the introduction of a new category of sex that challenged previous theories of psychosexual differentiation: gender role. Money borrowed the idea of "role" directly from Parsons, who was one of his teachers when he was studying for his PhD at Harvard University. Money combined Parson's role concept with "gender," which came from philology where it was used to denote the masculine, feminine, or neutral status of nouns and pronouns. John Money's work distinguished itself quickly in the sexology, psychiatry, paediatrics, and beyond.

The premise of the articles was a scathing critique of existing biological variables of sex. For many doctors in the 1950s the gonads still held the answer to a person's true sex, and in 1954 Canadian doctors had also found a means of determining chromosomal sex through skin biopsy. In addition to gonadal and chromosomal sex, other variables of sex included external genital morphology, hormonal sex and secondary sexual characteristics, internal accessory reproductive structures, and assigned sex.

The idea of "psychological sex" emerged not long before Money and the Hampsons made their contribution to the field. As Meyerowitz has shown,[11] it came into use by scientists and medical practitioners interested in transsexualism in the 1940s to distinguish biological sex from the sense of being a man or being a woman. Eminent doctors such as Michael Dillon, Christian Hamburger and Harry Benjamin still believed that psychological sex emanated from genetic or endocrine factors. The work of Money and the Hampsons challenged this view and in doing so they radically changed the location of the truth of sex from the genitals to being an outcome of *a behavioural control system*. They cross-examined the quantified sex variables of 76 hermaphrodites to argue that there was no "convincing evidence of a direct causal relationship"[12] between psychological sex and any of the biological categories of gonadal sex, chromosomal sex, external genital morphology, and internal accessory structures. Gender role, as they called it, was something learned postnatally and was not dependent on biological variables of sex.

Aiming to develop a "psychologic theory of sexuality,"[13] Money and the Hampsons showed how all seven variables of sex, that is, assigned sex, gonadal sex, chromosomal sex, hormonal sex, external genital morphology, and internal accessory reproductive structures and gender role took various combinations among the research subjects. The sex variables of the hermaphrodite subjects were organised into tables to reveal the extent to which these variables corresponded and contradicted each other. Addressing one variable at a time, the doctors showed how none of the biological variables could be used reliably to predict a person's gender role. Only assigned sex was consistently found to be in close conformity with gender role.

The central finding of these studies was that "gender role and orientation may be fully concordant with the sex of assignment and rearing, despite extreme contradiction of the other five variables of sex."[14] This enabled Money and the Hampsons to propose a new theory of sexuality that rejected a biologically deterministic account of the formation of psychological sex. They argued that their studies provided no evidence that any of the biological variables of sex were causal agents in the establishment of gender role. Because a person's gender role could be opposed to all other variables of sex, they concluded that the sexual mental make-up of a person did not "stem from something innate, instinctive" but rather it was the result of "postnatal experience and learning."[15] Money and the Hampsons therefore strongly refuted the idea that a person's sense of sexual self was predetermnied by genetic or other biological factors.

Gender was more than just the old idea of psychological sex taken to an extreme: it covered a host of material manifestations such as behaviour, mannerisms, speech, unconscious desires and personal preferences. Money and the Hampsons defined gender role as:

all those things that a person says or does to disclose himself or herself as having the status of a boy or man, girl or woman, respectively ... appraised in relation to the following: general mannerism, deportment and demeanour; play preferences and recreational interests; spontaneous topics of talk in unprompted conversation and casual comment; content of dreams, daydreams and fantasies; replies to oblique inquiries and projective tests; evidence of erotic pleasures and finally, the person's own replies to direct inquiry.[16]

Gender role therefore compassed a broad range of behavioural signs and subconscious indications through which people make themselves known to belong to a given sex. Money's gender role innovation marked a turn to a more behaviourist understanding of sex where psychosexual differentiation was not an innate biological occurrence, but rather an active postnatal process initiated through "the stimulus of interaction with a behavioural environment" that "can override the influence of the psychological variables of sex."[17] Cognition, stimuli and the behavioural environment therefore became new tactical fields of gender that did not so much contest as reinforce the apparatus of sex by multiplying the terrains of biopower through the innovations of behaviourism.

Indeed, this new idea of gender role was accompanied by a behaviourist theory of how this active process of psychosexual differentiation occurred. Money suggested that gender role was acquired through a process of imprinting, a phase-sensitive learning process that operates by inciting behavioural responses to perceptual stimuli. Gender imprinting, they argued, began in infancy reaching a critical period at the age of eighteen months and well established at two and a half years. Money's use of imprinting was modelled on the work of Konrad Lorenz, an Austrian zoologist who famously brought the concept of imprinting into dominance in the mid-twentieth century through his studies on wild mallard ducklings. Lorenz discovered right that after hatching, ducklings could be induced to regard him as if he were their mother by imitating the sounds and gestures of a mother mallard duck.

Lorenz's work made a strong impression on Money, who believed Lorenz's findings in animal psychology were also pertinent for humans.[18] To him, Lorenz's experiments suggested that gender role imprinting was like learning a native language, which was seen a human equivalent to imprinting behaviour in animals. Gender imprinting, he wrote, takes place during the first two and a half years of a child's life as an "active process of editing and assimilating experiences that are gender-specific," for example through the use of personal pronouns as well as "clothing style, haircut, and a thousand other gender-specific expectancies and attitudes."[19] Like a native language, once gender role was established, it could "fall into disuse and be supplanted by another, but never entirely eradicated."[20] For most people, he argued, gender role became "so indelibly engraved that not even flagrant contradictions of body functioning and morphology may displace it."[21] Gender as an imprinted psychological state therefore provided an explanation for how a person's sense of self as male or female could contradict the signs of sex in the physical body: Gender had little to do with the physical body—it was learned after birth.

The belief that gender role was permanent for the rest of a person's life once it was established had major implications for the subjects of Money's research. The invention of gender facilitated new standardised medical, surgical, and psychological sex reassignment protocols for the control of biological sex, sexual traits, and behaviours. Already before Money, doctors in the 1930s up to the 1950s would strive to "correct" ambiguous genitalia. In adults, they usually were altered to correspond to the person's psychological sex. Sex reassignments according to genetic sex were considered risky and unsuccessful as past attempts strongly indicated that they lead to mental health difficulties. The genitalia of infants, however, were commonly surgically altered to correspond to their genetic sex.[22] It was in this area that Money's work left its mark. If child sexuality was a crucial point of normalisation in the Victorian sexual discourse,[23] it only became more so through gender.

According to Money's infant sex reassignment protocols, which are more or less still followed today, any "corrective" surgery must consider into what gender role the child could be *best socialised* in order to produce a more mentally stable sexed subject. Because he believed that children were socialised into gender roles through responses to perceptual stimuli (i.e. the perception of their genital sex), he recommended that the appearance of the external genitalia be given primary consideration when contemplating corrective surgery. As Money and the Hampsons wrote, a person "becomes acquainted with and deciphers a continuous multiplicity of signs that point in the direction of his being a boy, or her being a girl . . . The most emphatic sign of all is, of course, the appearance of the genital organs. Presumably, it is the very ambiguity of the external genitals that makes hermaphrodites so adaptable to assignment in their sex."[24]

If a hermaphrodite's genitalia was ambiguous, they reasoned, there was a danger of "misprinting" an ambiguous gender role, a sign of misprinting. In gender misprinting "a more or less normal response, that of identifying with and impersonating a specific human being, becomes associated with the wrong perceptual stimulus."[25] To prevent misprinting, endocrinologists and surgeons could "correct" errors of body by altering the "wrong perceptual stimulus"—the sexed body and organs—to match the "right" imprinted gender. Changing bodily sex was a "mere" surgical procedure, versus the long and psychologically strenuous if not altogether impossible task of changing the permanently gender-imprinted mind.

If the infant's genitals were predominantly male or female, the question was easily settled: the infant should be assigned by the genitals alone and "all further surgical or hormonal endeavour should be directed toward maintaining the person in that sex,"[26] in other words, by removing possibly hidden opposite-sex organs, performing plastic surgery to make minor corrections such as repositioning the urethra, constructing vaginas, or administering cortisone doses or hormones when appropriate. If the external genitalia was ambiguous, however, Money and the Hampsons instructed an examination of gonadal and hormonal sex in combination with the external genitalia. More often than not, however, the morphology of the external genitalia was enough for the doctors to make a decision in either direction, whether the child was to be made to look male or female. To make the decision and implement it, a whole host of specialists had to be recruited into the effort to control sex: not just psychologists and psychiatrists, but also endocrinologists, urologists, plastic surgeons, and gynaecologists.

The aim of both sex reassignment surgery and localised hormone treatment was to fashion a "normal" appearance to the child's genitalia. The primary recommendation was that infants with ambiguous external morphology be reassigned as female, largely because it was easier for surgeons to construct a vaginal canal adequate for sexual intercourse and even orgasm. If subject could be provided through vaginoplasty with a "normal" sex and family life (aside from possible infertility, which could be compensated through adoption), this was usually enough for Money to advocate female reassignment.

Much like with the masturbating child, the discourse of the hermaphroditic child functioned to normalise child sexuality and sex, and ultimately, the reproduction of life. As Foucault explains, normalisation is not about intelligibility as such, nor is it about exclusion or rejection. Rather, he writes, "it is always linked to a positive technique of intervention and transformation, to a sort of normative project."[27] The logic behind Money's sex reassignment schema was the more "normal" the genitalia looked, the more likely the subject was to successfully develop the corresponding gender role. The constructed vagina could then be used for penile-vaginal penetration and pleasure, which was assumed to be the only kind of sexual activity that enabled a truly healthy adult sex life. Thus, the hermaphroditic subject was a subject of biopolitical potentiality: a subject who, through the surgical alteration of the genitals, could be psychologically managed into a different-sex desiring subject and hence become a subject useful for the reproduction of social order, and ultimately, life by either reproducing the normative order or procreation, if possible.

The deployment of gender quite literally acted on the child's as "a machinery of power that explore[d] it, br[oke] it down and rearrange[d] it."[28] It was made possible through behaviourist theories of conditioning that warned sexologists against the dangers of allowing deviant genital stimuli to rest, and by engaging with functionalist theories of social order, whereby incorrectly socialised gender roles threatened to destabilise the biopolitical order of things. As in the past, "the psychiatric hospital literally invented a new medical crisis,"[29] which now functioned to discipline bodies in order to discipline sexual behaviour and ultimately life itself.

GENDER AS A BIOPOLITICAL APPARATUS

The medical interest in intersexuality that gave birth to the notion of gender occurred at a time the West was rebuilding and re-establishing social, political and economic order after a ravaging Second World War. The postwar scientific control of ambiguous sex coincided with a conservative backlash against the socio-economic and political gains of equality between women and men. Also, the science of sex itself had become problematic: with five categories of biological sex, establishing a person's sex was increasingly difficult. Politically, socially, and medically the discourse of gender, by all means, responded to a specific biopolitical urgency, that is, the difficulty of controlling sex and life in the postwar period.

Money's theory of gender instigated a new order of truth about sex that radically reconfigured the sexual apparatus. It leaned on the disciplinary apparatuses of behaviourism and functionalism, providing the sexual apparatus with new rationalities for the governance of life through the control of the socialisation processes of individuals. Gender was born from these logics of social control and bound to the sexual apparatus thereafter. The truth of sex was no longer simply revealed by the body and confessed by the subject;[30] it was *learned* through imprinting and *constructed* through surgery. Gender worked by strategically interfering in the contingent cognitive processes of the behavioural control system of the mind, and by cutting up and reordering ambiguous genitals into normative and normalising stimuli. By providing new explanations for the misalignment of psychological sex and physiological sex, gender provided physicians with a framework with which to diagnose potential cognitive and structural sexual threats to the management of the life of the species.

I argue that gender emerged specifically as a new *apparatus* for the regulation of the life of the species. Indeed, Money's work alone rendered gender as a domain of power-knowledge not just for psychiatrists and surgeons, but also endocrinologists, urologists, obstetricians, and gynaecologists. It relied on theories of social order from sociology, psychology, biology, and social philosophy. Parents, friends, schools, and neighbours were incorporated into the disciplinary project of gender socialisation. Those who resisted it were delegated to the negative realm of the pathological. Gender came to dominate sexology just as sexuality did before it, and like sexuality it drastically transformed, multiplied and intensified the means of producing sexually different subjects, thus regulating social order and ultimately, life.

It is difficult to exaggerate the importance of Money's work. Not only was his theory of gender a radical new idea in the sexological field, but helping to disseminate it were a number of students that rose to prominent positions in the medical community, further and establishing gender as the foremost theory of psychosexual development. Such was the authoritative position to which Money rose that his protocols for intersex case management still endure in medical practice today.

The biopolitical development of the gender apparatus did not end with Money and has socio-political import beyond the medical field. There is no denying that gender has become a major discourse in the past decades. Universities have gender studies departments, governments are promoting gender equality, and in general gender has become a synonym for sex. The aim of this article has merely been to demonstrate the conditions of emergence of the gender discourse. It therefore sheds only light on the strategies of power that mobilised the apparatus in the first place. The history of the internal rationality, strategic function, and mechanisms of this new apparatus of biopower thereafter are a necessary area of further study to understand what gender means for the government of life in the present.

NOTES

1. I use the term *hermaphrodite*, rather than intersex, to reflect accurately the specific terminology used by Money and the Hampsons in the 1950s.

2. Michel Foucault, *The History of Sexuality: Volume 1: The Will to Knowledge*, trans. Robert Hurley (London: Penguin, 1981), 46.

3. Ibid., 37–38.

4. See Judith Butler, *Gender Trouble: Feminism and the Subversion of Identity* (London: Routledge, 1999), Teresa Lauretis, *Technologies of Gender: Essays on Theory, Film, and Fiction* (Bloomington and Indianapolis: Indiana University Press, 1987), and Joan W. Scott, *Gender and the Politics of History* (New York: Columbia University Press, 1999).

5. Foucault, "Confessions of the Flesh," in *Power/Knowledge: Selected Interviews & Other Writings, 1972–1977*, ed. Colin Gordon, trans. Colin Gordon et al. (New York: Pantheon Books, 1980), 195.

6. Foucault, "What Our Present Is," in *The Politics of Truth*, ed. Sylvère Lotringer, trans. Lysa Hochroth and Catherine Porter (Los Angeles: Semiotext(e), 2007), 141.

7. See Giorgio Agamben, *Homo Sacer: Soverign Power and Bare Life*, trans. Daniel Heller-Roazen (Stanford: Stanford University Press, 1998) and Roberto Esposito, *Bíos: Biopolitics and Philosophy*, trans. Timothy Campbell (Minneapolis: University of Minnesota Press, 2008).

8. See Talcott Parsons and Robert F. Bales, *Family, Socialization and Interaction Processes* (London: Routledge and Kegal Paul, 1956).

9. Nikolas Rose, *Governing the Soul: The Shaping of the Private Self* (London: Free Association Books, 1999), 175.

10. See John Money, Joan G. Hampson, and John L. Hampson, "Hermaphroditism: Recommendations Concerning Assignment of Sex, Change of Sex and Psychological Management," *Bulletin of the Johns Hopkins Hospital* 97, no. 4 (1955): 284–300; "An Examination of Some Basic Sexual Concepts: The Evidence of Human Hermaphroditism," *Bulletin of the Johns Hopkins Hospital* 97, no. 4 (1955): 301–319; and "Sexual Incongruities and Psychopathology: The Evidence of Human Hermaphroditism," *Bulletin of the Johns Hopkins Hospital* 98, no. 1 (1956): 43–57.

11. See Joanne Meyerowitz, *How Sex Changed: A History of Transsexuality in the United States* (Boston: Harvard University Press, 2002), 112–113.

12. John Money, "Hermaphroditism, Gender and Precocity in Hyperadrenocroticism: Psychological Findings," *Bulletin of the Johns Hopkins Hospital* 96, no. 6 (1955): 257.

13. Money et al., "An Examination": 301.

14. Ibid., 319.

15. John Money, "Psychosexual Differentiation," in Money, ed., *Sex Research: New Developments.* New York: Holt, Rinehart and Winston, 1965, 12.

16. Money et al., "An Examination": 302.

17. Money, "Psychosexual Differentiation," 20.

18. See Money et al., "Imprinting and the Establishment of Gender Role," *Archives of Neurology and Psychiatry*, no. 77 (1957): 335; and John Money and Anke A. Ehrhardt, *Man & Woman, Boy & Girl: Differentiation and Dimorphism of Gender Identity from Conception to Maturity* (Baltimore: Johns Hopkins University Press, 1972), 177.

19. Money, "Psychosexual Differentiation," 12.

20. Money et al., "An Examination": 310.

21. Ibid.

22. See Meyerowitz, *How Sex Changed*, 112.

23. Michel Foucault, *Abnormal: Lectures at the Collège de France, 1974–1975*, trans. Graham Burchell, New York: Picador, 2003, 59.

24. Money et al., "Imprinting": 335.

25. Richard A. B. Green and John Money, "Incongruous Gender Role: Nongenital Manifestations in Prepubertal Boys," *Journal of Nervous & Mental Disease* 131, no. 2 (1960): 167.

26. Money et al., "Hermaphroditism": 288.

27. Foucault, *Abnormal*, 50.

28. Michel Foucault, *Discipline and Punish: The Birth of the Prison*, trans. Alan Sheridan (London: Penguin, 1991), 138.

29. Michel Foucault, *Psychiatric Power: Lectures at the Collège de France: 1973–1974*, trans. Graham Burchell (New York: Picador, 2003), 252.

30. See Foucault, *History of Sexuality 1*.

BIBLIOGRAPHY

Agamben, Giorgio. *Homo Sacer: Soverign Power and Bare Life*. Translated by Daniel Heller-Roazen. Stanford: Stanford University Press, 1998.

Butler, Judith. *Gender Trouble: Feminism and the Subversion of Identity*. London: Routledge, 1999.

Esposito, Roberto. *Bíos: Biopolitics and Philosophy*. Translated by Timothy Campbell. Minneapolis: University of Minnesota Press, 2008.

Foucault, Michel. "Confessions of the Flesh." In *Power/Knowledge: Selected Interviews & Other Writings, 1972–1977*. Edited by Colin Gordon. Translated by Colin Gordon et al., 194–228. New York: Pantheon Books, 1980.

Foucault, Michel. *The History of Sexuality: Volume 1: The Will to Knowledge*. Translated by Robert Hurley. London: Penguin, 1981.

Foucault, Michel. *Discipline and Punish: The Birth of the Prison*. Translated by Alan Sheridan. London: Penguin, 1991.

Foucault, Michel. *Abnormal: Lectures at the Collège de France, 1974–1975*. Translated by Graham Burchell. New York: Picador, 2003.

Foucault, Michel. *Psychiatric Power: Lectures at the Collège de France: 1973–1974*. Translated by Graham Burchell. New York: Picador, 2003.

Foucault, Michel. "What Our Present Is." In *The Politics of Truth*. Edited by Sylvère Lotringer. Translated by Lysa Hochroth and Catherine Porter, 129–144. Los Angeles: Semiotext(e), 2007.

Green, Richard A. B., and John Money. "Incongruous Gender Role: Nongenital Manifestations in Prepubertal Boys." *Journal of Nervous & Mental Disease* 131, no. 2 (1960): 160–168.

Lauretis, Teresa de. *Technologies of Gender: Essays on Theory, Film, and Fiction*. Bloomington and Indianapolis: Indiana University Press, 1987.

Meyerowitz, Joanne. *How Sex Changed: A History of Transsexuality in the United States*. Boston: Harvard University Press, 2002.

Money, John. "Hermaphroditism, Gender and Precocity in Hyperadrenocroticism: Psychological Findings." *Bulletin of the Johns Hopkins Hospital* 96, no. 6 (1955): 253–164.

Money, John. "Psychosexual Differentiation." In *Sex Research: New Developments*. Edited by John Money, 3–23. New York: Holt, Rinehart and Winston, 1965.

Money, John, and Anke A. Ehrhardt. *Man & Woman, Boy & Girl: Differentiation and Dimorphism of Gender Identity from Conception to Maturity*. Baltimore: Johns Hopkins University Press, 1972.

Money, John, Joan G. Hampson, and John L. Hampson. "Hermaphroditism: Recommendations Concerning Assignment of Sex, Change of Sex and Psychological Management." *Bulletin of the Johns Hopkins Hospital* 97, no. 4 (1955): 284–300.

Money, John, Joan G. Hampson, and John L. Hampson. "An Examination of Some Basic Sexual Concepts: The Evidence of Human Hermaphroditism." *Bulletin of the Johns Hopkins Hospital* 97, no. 4 (1955): 301–319.

Money, John, Joan G. Hampson, and John L. Hampson. "Sexual Incongruities and Psychopathology: The Evidence of Human Hermaphroditism." *Bulletin of the Johns Hopkins Hospital* 98, no. 1 (1956): 43–57.

Money, John, Joan G. Hampson, and John L. Hampson. "Imprinting and the Establishment of Gender Role." *Archives of Neurology and Psychiatry*, no. 77 (1957): 333–336.

Parsons, Talcott, and Robert F. Bales. *Family, Socialization and Interaction Processes*. London: Routledge and Kegal Paul, 1956.

Rose, Nikolas. *Governing the Soul: The Shaping of the Private Self*. London: Free Association Books, 1999.

Scott, Joan W. *Gender and the Politics of History*. New York: Columbia University Press, 1999.

27

SOMATECHNICS

Nikki Sullivan

In 2003 a group of academics at Macquarie University organized a conference on body modification. The aim of the event was to articulate the diverse ways in which all bodies—not simply those that are tattooed or those that have undergone some sort of transformative surgical procedure—are always already modified. One of the keynote speakers at the conference was Susan Stryker, whose work in the field of transgender studies problematized the "common-sense" understanding of technology, which, at the time, underpinned the dominant model of the transsexual body as either requiring or having undergone technological intervention. Following the conference, Stryker and her colleagues at Macquarie coined the term *somatechnics* in an attempt to highlight what they saw as the inextricability of *soma* and *technè*, of the body (as a culturally intelligible construct) and the techniques (dispositifs and hard technologies) in and through which corporealities are formed and transformed. From the outset, then, somatechnics has addressed and been shaped by transgender issues, and this connection was explicitly articulated at the Transsomatechnics conference held at Simon Fraser University in 2008.

The term *somatechnics*, derived from the Greek *soma* (body) and *technè* (craftsmanship), supplants the logic of the "and," indicating that *technè* is not something we add or apply to the already constituted body (as object), nor is it a tool that the embodied self employs to its own ends. Rather, *technès* are the dynamic means in and through which corporealities are crafted: that is, continuously engendered in relation to others and to a world. What we see here, then, is a chiasmatic interdependence of *soma* and *technè*: of bodily being (or corporealities) as always already technologized and technologies (which are never simply "machinic") as always already enfleshed. Anna Munster nicely articulates this vision when she writes that technologies are "always in a dynamic relation to the matter which gives [them their] substance and to the other machines—aesthetic, social, economic—which substantiate [them] as . . . ensemble[s]."[1] To put it slightly differently, the categories of being that are integral to our (un)becoming-with, and the orientation(s) that shape them, are somatechnological (rather than simply natural or cultural, internal or external to us, enabling or oppressive). For example, transgender, like forms of bodily being commonly presumed *not* to be technologically produced, is a heterogeneous somatechnological construct that comes to matter in contextually specific ways and in relation to other discursive formations. In making this claim, I am not suggesting that modes and practices of embodiment (such as those we call transgender) are not "real." Indeed, they are the matter(ialization) of being, but this materialization takes place through certain highly regulated (situated) somatechnologies. Given this, the primary aim of somatechnics as a critical orientation is—at least as I understand it—to queer orderability by bringing to light the operations of power, the soma-techno-logic, that constitute(s) (un)becoming-with in situated ways. I will return to this point in due course.

The history of Western thought is, as Elizabeth Grosz and others have argued, subtended by "a profound somatophobia."[2] From the ancient Greeks, to Enlightenment thinkers (Descartes, Rousseau, Kant, Hobbes), to the common-sense fictions that shape contemporary life, the body has been conceived (and thus constituted) as a natural, biological entity, the fleshly shell of a soul, a self, and/or a mind that is superior to it. Given its status as both prison and property, the brute matter of the body (as object) is constituted in and through this particular imaginary as that which the subject must transcend, transform, master, and/or shape, and nowhere is this more apparent than in autobiographical transsexual narratives published in the west in the twentieth century. There have, of course, been various challenges posed, particularly from the mid-twentieth century on, to the kind of determinism associated with this model of the body, the self, and the relation between them, but all too often such attempts reiterate—albeit inadvertently—a sort of naive materialism in which the body appears as a fleshly substrate that simply *is* prior to its regulation. This ontological tendency is apparent, for example, in accounts of selfhood (often found in discussions of transgender) that rely on a presumed distinction between sex and gender—the idea that the sexed body is a natural biological substrate onto which contextually specific (that is, culturally determined) attributes, roles, and capacities are imposed—as well as in dominant conceptions of, and debates about, technology.

Technology, claimed Martin Heidegger in his influential essay, "The Question Concerning Technology," is commonly conceived both as a human activity and as a means to an end. The effect of this instrumentalist conception is that debates about technology tend to revolve around "our manipulating technology in the proper manner as a means."[3] In other words, the primary focus of discussions of particular technologies tends to be on whether, how, and to what extent they might be used to enhance life, to achieve integrity, to enable one to realize one's true self. Little has changed, it seems, in the sixty years since Heidegger first made these claims, and this is clear if one looks at accounts of so-called gender reassignment surgeries. In brief, such practices are framed by some as medical treatments that will enhance the lives of those who undergo them, while others have argued that such practices are (for a variety of reasons) unethical and/or immoral; that they constitute a misuse of technology. Some argue that individuals have a right to bodily self-determination, and others argue (variously) that such a right, if it exists, is never absolute and that therefore the use of technologies that (re)shape the body requires strict regulation. Despite the differences of opinion expressed in these claims, what they share is an instrumentalist view of technology, one in which technology is (constituted as) an object external to and manipulable by the subject(s) who deploy it to their own ends (whether those ends be a sense of bodily integrity, the fulfilment of a religious obligation, the construction of the self as altruistic, appropriately professional, morally responsible, or whatever). Indeed, each is subtended by a will to mastery which, Heidegger and Foucault would argue, is itself technological. Technology, suggests Heidegger in his critique of instrumentalist logic, is less a thing that is external to the self than an orientation, a way of thinking/knowing/seeing that brings forth (or engenders, shapes, and "orders") being, or, more accurately, (un)becoming. Technology, then, is at once the (contextually specific) means by which we order the world and the ways of thinking/knowing/seeing that precede us and make us be(come). Given this, the problem with instrumentalism as an orientation, and thus with the instrumentalist view of technology as separate from the self who deploys it as a means to an identifiable and achievable end, is that it veils over the coindebtedness, coresponsibility, coarticulation, and movement of (un)becoming-with.[4] Critiques of this view of technology and the ethicopolitical effects that such a way of thinking produces have been articulated at length by theorists as diverse as Donna Haraway, Jean-Luc

Nancy, Maurice Merleau-Ponty, Luce Irigaray, Gilles Deleuze, and Félix Guattari, to name but a few. Somatechnics adds another (heterogeneous) voice to these attempts to think otherwise, but it does so from the possibly unique position of having always already been shaped by trans*.

NOTES

1. Anna Munster, "Is There Postlife after Postfeminism? Tropes of Technics and Life in Cyberfeminism," *Australian Feminist Studies* 14, no. 29 (1999): 119–129, 121.

2. Elizabeth Grosz, *Volatile Bodies* (Bloomington: Indiana University Press, 1994), 1.

3. Martin Heidegger, "The Question Concerning Technology," in *The Question Concerning Technology and Other Essays*, trans. William Lovitt (New York: Harper Perennial, 1977), 5.

4. Elsewhere I speak of the movement of (un)becoming-with as "transing," see Nikki Sullivan, "Transsomatechnics and the Matter of 'Genital Modifications,'" *Australian Feminist Studies* 24, no. 60 (2009): 275–286.

BIBLIOGRAPHY

Grosz, Elizabeth. *Volatile Bodies*. Bloomington: Indiana University Press, 1994.

Heidegger, Martin. "The Question Concerning Technology." In *The Question Concerning Technology and Other Essays*. Translated by William Lovitt, 3–35. New York: Harper Perennial, 1977.

Munster, Anna. "Is There Postlife after Postfeminism? Tropes of Technics and Life in Cyberfeminism." *Australian Feminist Studies* 14, no. 29 (1999): 119–129.

Sullivan, Nikki. "Transsomatechnics and the Matter of 'Genital Modifications.'" *Australian Feminist Studies* 24, no. 60 (2009): 275–286.

28

DISCIPLINE AND CONTROL

Jasbir K. Puar

Capacity and debility entail theorizing not only specific disciplinary sites but also broader techniques of social control, marking a shift in terms from the regulation of normativity (the internalization of self/other subject formation) to what Foucault calls the regularization of bodies, or what has been hailed "the age of biological control."[1] This is akin to what Giorgio Agamben perceives as the difference between regulating to produce order (discipline) and regulating disorder (security).[2] While Deleuze's techno-optimism leads him to proclaim rapid and complete transitions from discipline to control, Foucault is very clear about their braided and enmeshed historical and spatial modalities.[3] The oscillation between disciplinary societies and control societies, following Foucault's "apparatuses of security," both refracts and projects numerous tensions.[4] In control societies, Patricia Clough argues, bodies will not be captured or set free by re/presentation, but rather through affect and attention.[5] There is thus an affective differential, whereby the body is curated not only through disciplinary drilling but also through a composite of statistics, from normal/abnormal to variegation, fluctuation, modulation, and tweaking. Discrete and discontinuous sites of punishment—the prison, the mental hospital, the school—are extended spatially and temporally through continuous regimes of securitization driven by calculated risks and averages. While disciplinary power works to distinguish those who should be included from those who must be excluded or eliminated, security apparatuses have the "constant tendency to expand . . . new elements are constantly being integrated . . . allowing the development of ever-wider circuits" through the management of circulation determining not whether to include, but how.[6] Discipline is centripetal while apparatuses of security are centrifugal. Intense oscillation occurs between the following: subject/object construction and microstates of differentiation; difference between and difference within; the policing of profile and the patrolling of affect; will and capacity; agency and affect; subject and body. And finally and, I believe, most important, between Althusserian interpellation (hey, you!) and an array of diverse switchpoints of the activation of the body, where bodies are positioned through openings and closings in order to ground practices of exploitation, extraction, dispossession, and expulsion commensurate with flexible modes of work and sociality.

How does disability function in control societies? Because there are gradations of capacity and debility in control societies—rather than the self-other production of being/not being—the distinction between disabled and non-disabled becomes fuzzier and blurrier. Disciplinary normalization, otherwise termed "normation" by Foucault, "goes from the norm to the final division between the normal and the abnormal" through "positing a model, an optimal model that is constructed in terms of a certain result"—the power of normalization versus normalization of power.[7] In security apparatuses, instead of distinguishing the normal from the abnormal, there are "different curves of normality . . . establishing an interplay between these different distributions of normality . . . acting to bring the most unfavorable in line with the more favorable. . . . The norm is an interplay of differential normalities."[8] Biopolitical apparatuses of control are invested in modulating a prolific range of affective bodily capacities and debilities—"differential normalities"—that invariably render rights-based interventions unable to fully apprehend the scenes of power. Disability identity is already part and parcel of a system of governing inclusion and exclusion, creating forms of what Robert McRuer calls "disability nationalism in crip times": liberal state and national recognition of people with disabilities that solicits the incorporation of certain disabilities into neoliberal economic circuits.[9] This conditional invitation latches onto and propagates celebratory claims of successful integration in order to continue to deplete resources from other, less acceptable bodies with disabilities. That is to say, the promoting and lauding of certain people with disabilities as markers of acceptance and progress ultimately serves to further marginalize and exclude most people with disabilities and serves also to sustain and create networks of debilitation in relation to these privileged disabled bodies. This is also what David Mitchell and Sharon Snyder analyze in *The Biopolitics of Disability*, in which they refer to the paradoxical means by which some disabled people gain entrance into late capitalist culture as "ablenationalism."[10]

This biopolitics of disability, I would further argue, is most efficient not just in the way it deploys some identities against others.[11] Rather, biopolitical control operates most perniciously and efficiently through reifying intersectional identity frames—these are frames that still hinge on discrete notions of inclusion and exclusion—as the most pertinent ones for political intervention, thus obfuscating forms of control that insidiously include in order to exclude, and exclude in order to include. Mitchell and Snyder state: "Control of the coordinates of bare biological life among citizens in market capitalism has been fashioned on the basis of systems of total oversight specific to disability and others occupying peripheral embodiments. . . . Disability is foundational to the development of cultural strategies in neoliberalism to 'seize hold of life in order to suppress it.' These strategies of seizure are the essence of bio-politics."[12]

The extraction and exploitation of body capacities and habituations pivot not only on the individual but more insidiously on the dividual. Foucault states that "discipline is a mode of individualization of multiplicities rather than something that constructs an edifice of multiple elements on the basis of individuals who are worked on as, first of all, individuals."[13] The individual is less a collection of multiplicities that form a whole than a stripping down or segregating of multiplicities, of "organizing a multiplicity, of fixing its points of implantation." Writing on vectors of control, Deleuze says of the hospital: "The new medicine 'without doctor or patient' . . . singles out potential sick people and subjects at risk, which in no way attests to individuation—as they say—but substitutes . . . the code of a dividual material to be controlled."[14] The code of dividual material, says Foucault, is generated by "security mechanisms [that] have to be installed around the random element inherent in a population of living beings so as to optimize a state of life."[15] Foucault explains that while discipline and control both work to maximize bodily extraction, unlike discipline, control does not work at "the level of the body itself: It is therefore not a matter of taking the individual at the level of individuality but, on the contrary, of using overall mechanisms and acting in such a way as to achieve overall states of equilibrium or regularity . . . a matter of taking control of life and the biological processes of man-as-species and of enduring that they are not disciplined, but regularized."[16]

The debate about discipline and control marks a shift in terms from the regulation of normativity (the internalization of self/other subject formation) to the regularization of bodies. Many relations between discipline (exclusion and inclusion) and control (modulation, tweaking) have been proffered. As various overlapping yet progressive stages of market capitalism and governmentality, the telos of discipline to control might function as a recasting of neoliberal modernity. Certain bodies are more subject to persisting disciplinary institutions (prisons, mental hospitals, military service, torture, factory work), relegating disciplinary sites as part of the primitive in a modernist telos.[17] Deleuze as well proclaims that hacking is replacing strikes, but are strikes being relegated to the "global south"?[18] Two suppositions can be inferred here: one, the distinction between bodies subjected to discipline and those "incorporated" into control economies is in itself a racializing technology; two, the intersections between discipline and control, and their techniques of power, on various bodies is precisely the mechanism that funnels populations into being. Helpfully, Foucault's own formulations are more porous: as coexisting models and exercises of power; control as the epitome of a disciplinary society par excellence, in that disciplinary forms of power exceed their sites to reproduce everywhere; and finally, discipline as a form of control and as a response to the proliferation of control. Ilana Feldman, in her work on governmentality in Gaza, argues that what Foucault seeks to "identify is a shift in emphasis, where different epochs display greater reliance on certain of these technologies."[19] These shifts themselves, I would argue, suggest the supplementary and entwined configurations of power that are adaptable across spatial and temporal variations.

And, in fact, control societies operate covertly by deploying disciplinary power to keep or deflect our attention around the subjection of the subject, thus allowing control to manifest unhindered. I suggest therefore that disciplinary apparatuses function in part as foils for control mechanisms and not in teleological or developmentalist progressions. Here I am following the lead of Seb Franklin's theorization of control as episteme with operational logics, rather than a system of power wedded solely to specific periodizations and geographies. Franklin's analysis demonstrates that the *logic* of control—as a partitioning, measuring, computational technology—permeates pre-digital schemas of power as well as non-computer-based realms of the social.[20]

Modulation of affect is a critical technology of control. One prominent example of the medicalization of affect may well be that of depression. Nikolas Rose maintains that depression will become the number one disability in the United States and the United Kingdom by 2020.[21] While it may well be the case, as Allan V. Horwitz and Jerome C. Wakefield have argued in *The Loss of Sadness*, that the third and fourth editions of the *Diagnostic and Statistical Manual of Mental Disorders* (*DSM-III* and *DSM-IV*) have caused major depressive disorder to be overdiagnosed because of "insufficiently restrictive definitions,"[22] this expansion of depressed populations, or depressives, will not occur only through a widespread increase of depression, or an increase of its dispensation as a diagnosis, but also through the finessing of gradation of populations. In other words, it will not occur through the hailing and interpellation of depressed subjects—and a distinction between who is depressed and who is not—but rather through the evaluation and accommodation of degrees: To what degree is one depressed?[23] One is already instructed by television advertisements for psychotropic drugs such as Abilify, claiming that "two out of three people on anti-depressants still have symptoms" and offering a top-off medication to add to a daily med regime. Through this form of medical administration bodies are (1) drawn into a modulation of subindividual capacities (this would be the diverse switchpoints); (2) surveilled not on identity positions alone (though the recent work of Dorothy Roberts and Jonathan Metzl elaborates how this remains a trenchant issue) but through affective tendencies, informational body-as-data, and statistical probabilities—through populations, risk, and prognosis; and (3) further stratified across registers of the medical-industrial complex: medical debt, health insurance, state benefits, among other feedback loops into the profitability of debility.[24] How the disaggregation of depressed subjects into various states, intensities, and tendencies will change the dimensionality of disability remains an open prospect, but at the very least, it forces recognition of the limits of disability as a category. The disability at stake is an affective tendency of sorts as well as a mental state, and as such challenges the basis upon which disability rights frames have routed their representational (visibility) politics.

NOTES

1. Michel Foucault, *"Society Must Be Defended": Lectures at the College de France, 1975–1976*, trans. David Macey (New York: Picador, 2003); Ian Wilmut, Keith Campbell, and Colin Tudge, *The Second Creation: Dolly and the Age of Biological Control* (Cambridge, MA: Harvard University Press, 2001).

2. Giorgio Agamben, "On Security and Terror," trans. Carolin Emcke, *Theory and Event* 5, no. 4 (2001): 30–53.

3. Gilles Deleuze, "Postscript on Control Societies," in *Negotiations 1972–1990*, trans. Martin Joughin (New York: Columbia University Press, 1995).

4. See the work of Michael Hardt, "The Withering of Civil Society," *Social Text* 14, no. 45 (1995): 27–44; Patricia Clough, "Future Matters: Technoscience, Global Politics, and Cultural Criticism," *Social Text* 22, no. 3 (2004): 1–23; Michael Hardt and Antonio Negri, *Empire* (Cambridge, MA: Harvard University Press, 2001); Michel Foucault, *Security, Territory, Population: Lectures at the Collège de France 1977–1978*, trans. Graham Burchell (New York: Picador, 2009); Deleuze, "Post-script on Control Societies."

5. Some important texts comprising the so-called affective turn include Patricia Clough, ed., *The Affective Turn: Theorizing the Social* (Durham, NC: Duke University Press, 2007); Melissa Gregg and Gregory J. Seigworth, eds., *The Affect Theory Reader* (Durham, NC: Duke University Press, 2010); Brian Massumi, *Parables for the Virtual: Movement, Affect, Sensation* (Durham, NC: Duke University Press, 2002); Teresa Brennan, *The Transmission of Affect* (Ithaca, NY: Cornell University

Press, 2004); Eve Kosofsky Sedgwick, *Touching Feeling: Affect, Pedagogy, Performativity* (Durham, NC: Duke University Press, 2003); Kathleen Stewart, *Ordinary Affects* (Durham, NC: Duke University Press, 2007), among others.

6. Foucault, *Security, Territory, Population*, 45.

7. Ibid., 57.

8. Ibid., 63.

9. Robert McRuer, "Disability Nationalism in Crip Times," *Journal of Literary and Cultural Disability Studies* 4, no. 2 (2010): 163–178.

10. David Mitchell and Sharon Snyder, *The Biopolitics of Disability: Neoliberalism, Ablenationalism, and Peripheral Embodiment* (Ann Arbor: University of Michigan Press, 2015).

11. See also an important collection of essays edited by Shelley Tremain, first published in 2005 and enlarged and revised for a 2015 edition, on the usefulness of Foucauldian theory to the study of disability. In the 2005 edition, Tremain writes: "A Foucauldian analysis of disability would show that the juridical conception of disability that is assumed within the terms of the social model and most existing disability theory obscures the productive constraints of modern (bio-)power. A Foucauldian approach to disability would show that the governmental practices into which the subject is inducted or divided from others produce the illusion that they have a prediscursive, or natural, antecedent (impairment), which in turn provides the justification for the multiplication and expansion of the regulatory effects of these practices." I am interested in both building off these analyses and also challenging the manner in which they deploy the category of disability or people with disabilities as a discrete, definable group or population, named and/or identified as such, instead of thinking of biopolitics as a variegated process of slow death. Shelley Tremain, "Foucault, Governmentality, and Critical Disability Theory: An Introduction," in *Foucault and the Government of Disability*, ed. Shelley Tremain (Ann Arbor: University of Michigan Press, 2005), 1–24.

12. Mitchell and Snyder, *The Biopolitics of Disability*.

13. Foucault, *Security, Territory, Population*, 12.

14. Deleuze, "Postscript on Control Societies."

15. Foucault, *"Society Must Be Defended,"* 246.

16. Foucault, *"Society Must Be Defended,"* 246–247.

17. Hardt, "The Withering of Civil Society."

18. Deleuze, "Postscript on Control Societies."

19. Illana Feldman, *Police Encounters: Security and Surveillance in Gaza under Egyptian Rule* (Stanford, CA: Stanford University Press, 2015), 13.

20. Seb Franklin, *Control: Digitality as Cultural Logic* (Cambridge, MA: MIT Press, 2015).

21. Nikolas Rose, "Neurochemical Selves," *Society* 3 (2003): 53, quoting the 2001 World Health Organization report.

22. Allan V. Horwitz and Jerome C. Wakefield, *The Loss of Sadness: How Psychiatry Transformed Normal Sorrow into Depressive Disorder* (Oxford: Oxford University Press, 2007).

23. Nikolas Rose, "Biopolitics in an Age of Biological Control," lecture presented at New York University, October 15, 2009.

24. Dorothy Roberts, *Fatal Invention: How Science, Politics, and Big Business Re-create Race in the Twenty-First Century* (New York: New Press, 2011); Jonathan Metzl, *The Protest Psychosis: How Schizophrenia Became a Black Disease* (Boston: Beacon, 2009). Rose also elaborates at length on the culture and industry of diagnostic testing, which is another important element of the debility of debt. Diagnostic testing has ironically become part of, if not substituted for, a "preventative care" regime that is even more profitable than responsive care.

BIBLIOGRAPHY

Agamben, Giorgio. "On Security and Terror." Translated by Carolin Emcke. *Theory and Event* 5, no. 4 (2001): 30–53.

Brennan, Teresa. *The Transmission of Affect*. Ithaca, NY: Cornell University Press, 2004.

Clough, Patricia. "Future Matters: Technoscience, Global Politics, and Cultural Criticism." *Social Text* 22, no. 3 (2004): 1–23.

Clough, Patricia, ed. *The Affective Turn: Theorizing the Social*. Durham, NC: Duke University Press, 2007.

Deleuze, Gilles. "Postscript on Control Societies." In *Negotiations 1972–1990*. Translated by Martin Joughin, 177–182. New York: Columbia University Press, 1995.

Feldman, Illana. *Police Encounters: Security and Surveillance in Gaza under Egyptian Rule*. Stanford, CA: Stanford University Press, 2015.

Foucault, Michel. *Security, Territory, Population: Lectures at the Collège de France 1977–1978*. Translated by Graham Burchell. New York: Picador, 2009.

Foucault, Michel. *"Society Must Be Defended": Lectures at the College de France, 1975–1976*. Translated by David Macey. New York: Picador, 2003.

Franklin, Seb. *Control: Digitality as Cultural Logic*. Cambridge, MA: MIT Press, 2015.

Gregg, Melissa, and Gregory J. Seigworth, eds. *The Affect Theory Reader*. Durham, NC: Duke University Press, 2010.

Hardt, Michael. "The Withering of Civil Society." *Social Text* 14, no. 45 (1995): 27–44.

Hardt, Michael, and Antonio Negri. *Empire*. Cambridge, MA: Harvard University Press, 2001.

Horwitz, Allan V., and Jerome C. Wakefield. *The Loss of Sadness: How Psychiatry Transformed Normal Sorrow into Depressive Disorder*. Oxford: Oxford University Press, 2007.

Massumi, Brian. *Parables for the Virtual: Movement, Affect, Sensation*. Durham, NC: Duke University Press, 2002.

McRuer, Robert. "Disability Nationalism in Crip Times." *Journal of Literary and Cultural Disability Studies* 4, no. 2 (2010): 163–178.

Metzl, Jonathan. *The Protest Psychosis: How Schizophrenia Became a Black Disease*. Boston: Beacon, 2009.

Mitchell, David, and Sharon Snyder. *The Biopolitics of Disability: Neoliberalism, Ablenationalism, and Peripheral Embodiment.* Ann Arbor: University of Michigan Press, 2015.

Roberts, Dorothy. *Fatal Invention: How Science, Politics, and Big Business Re-create Race in the Twenty-First Century.* New York: New Press, 2011.

Rose, Nikolas. "Neurochemical Selves." *Society* 3 (2003).

Sedgwick, Eve Kosofsky. *Touching Feeling: Affect, Pedagogy, Performativity.* Durham, NC: Duke University Press, 2003.

Stewart, Kathleen. *Ordinary Affects.* Durham, NC: Duke University Press, 2007.

Tremain, Shelley. "Foucault, Governmentality, and Critical Disability Theory: An Introduction." In *Foucault and the Government of Disability.* Edited by Shelley Tremain, 1–24. Ann Arbor: University of Michigan Press, 2005.

Wilmut, Ian, Keith Campbell, and Colin Tudge. *The Second Creation: Dolly and the Age of Biological Control.* Cambridge, MA: Harvard University Press, 2001.

29

DISPOSITIFS OF PLEASURE

Anita Chari

UN AMORE IDEALE

Leaving aside any notions of the authenticity of flesh, there is something provocative about the secret lives of humans who fall in love with a piece of silicon shaped into human form. Such is the complex and perverse exploration of the work *Still Lovers*, a set of photographs by the artist Elena Dorfman exploring the relationships between people and dolls.[1] The dolls, which in Dorfman's pictures take the shape of adult female bodies, could be seen as a kind of dispositif of love.

Still Lovers peers into the intimate lives of men who have romantic relationships with life-sized silicon dolls. That these female silicon bodies tend to have proportions that mainstream culture would call ideal—5'7", 36-24-36—and with racial and physical characteristics that can be selected by the person who buys the doll is, on the face of it, unsurprising and yet disturbing. The female doll, which contains a pliant orifice, completes a sexual fantasy that many might view as damaging to alive, female-sexed bodies who seldom conform to the dimensions that animate this ideal love object. Yet, Dorfman's images complicate the notion of the surrogate as simply a fetish object. In these photos, she is, rather, primarily an object of emotional intimacy. The photographs show scenes in which the dolls participate in the domestic and romantic lives of their owners in ways that extend beyond their status as sexual objects. A man sits in the park writing on his laptop as his beloved lays beside him with a book in her hands, her gaze drifting off from her immersion in the novel. Another doll sits at dinner with the family, which includes a husband, wife, and kids who chat and eat alongside her, oblivious to her inanimacy. As Dorfman notes, there is something touching about these situations, which depict surrogates as participants in the intimate lives of subjects.[2] The surrogate becomes a placeholder for an affective absence, which leads to a new form of solitude. Her status as a material object animates a utopia of presence.

Rather than an aberration of some more purportedly real form of contact that might occur among humans, the surrogate–human relationship expresses a more widespread patterning of enjoyment and desire. The surrogate allows for desire to correspond to an object. The relationship with the surrogate is specifically pleasurable because she does not push beyond the parameters of desire through her embodied singularity, her history, her dissatisfaction, or her incapacity. She mirrors the logic of contemporary hypercommodification. You receive what you expect to receive, no more and no less. This is what comes to be understood as value. This is what comes to be experienced as love. The correspondence of expectation (as a concretization of fantasy) to outcome.

The ideal love object in capitalist society is, in this sense, algorithmic.

ALGORITHMIC

We should probably be suspicious of almost anything that we enjoy. But beyond this, we have to think about why we enjoy one thing rather than another. What is enjoyable about being in love with a doll? There are myriad pleasures in this form of relationship. But among them is that the doll fulfills expectations, remains a receptacle of the projections that induce pleasure without resistance, without a singularity that disturbs us. This is an increasingly common format of pleasure. We feel pleasure when the internet sequences the information that conforms precisely to our preconceived notions of right and wrong, outrage and humor. We feel pleasure when the headlines are written in such a way as to communicate exactly what we will receive by reading the news and why we need to read it through the marketing logic of so-called deliverables. *Three things you need to know about society's inescapable decline into a fascist inferno. Seven surprising facts about the impending planetary apocalypse.* Surplus value, yes. But surplus affect, decidedly no.

We might term this form of enjoyment "algorithmic pleasure." Algorithmic pleasure occurs when we enjoy because our expectations are fulfilled without this surplus. The surplus would be the supplement of discomfort, disintegration, loss of control, disappointment that accompanies all non-narcissistically or economically fulfilled pleasures.

PLEASURE ZONES

The idea of the pleasure zone advances a specific notion of enjoyment. There are several types of pleasure zones, as Robert Venturi identifies in his book *Learning from Las Vegas*.[3] One type of pleasure zone occurs in places of environmental adversity, such as a desert. The city of Las Vegas is a quintessential example of this kind of pleasure zone. Pleasure there is experienced as a relief from the discomfort of the environment, which in this case is dry, hot, and unforgiving. The air-conditioned nightmare of Las Vegas is rendered enjoyable amid these circumstances. Then there is the self-created cycle of comfort and discomfort embedded in the pleasure style of Las Vegas. Gambling and drinking all night are exhausting. In the morning, you can find relief through an intravenous hangover drip or at one of the bizarrely abundant oxygen bars at the hotel. The flashing lights and putrid air of the casino are overstimulating and toxifying to the body. Cleanse your system with a massage or a trip to the spa. Slot machines are alienating in their monomaniacal abstraction of risk. Relieve the unbearable isolation of hypercapitalism by paying for sex.

The drinks in a market on the corner are marked with three labels: "Hydrate, Celebrate, Calibrate." Conforming to the addictive logic of dosing even in activities as fundamental as drinking a glass of water, one searches for the crevice between monotony and the overdose. There is very little on the Strip that does not conform to the dopamine cycle between gratification and its absence. The intensification of discomfort, by this logic, only increases your subsequent pleasure. It creates a situation in which the regulation of the nervous system and of bodily homeostasis becomes a constant preoccupation. The ensuing obsession with comfort, a naïve translation of the instinct to survive, commodifies all needs and renders the fulfillment of brute need into pleasure.

But let's not act as if Las Vegas exists outside of ourselves. It is merely a hyperbolic rendering of one of the basic logics of pleasure at play in hypercapitalism: the rendering into value a type of pleasure experienced as the reduction of pain. We will call this form of pleasure "anaesthetic pleasure."

I'M LOOKING THROUGH YOU

There are now devices in existence that can measure the minute indicators of one's affective and physical state—heart rate and skin temperature, certainly. More alarmingly, these devices operate in a way that is similar to the unconscious processes of the mind, recognizing and measuring social signals and interactions between individuals, including bodily movements, proximity to other people, and even the intensity of social interactions. One such device, the sociometer, predicts with great accuracy the behavioral implications of the information it measures. Rather than the externally and visually oriented kinds of surveillance we are accustomed to, Katherine Hayles calls this form of monitoring "somatic surveillance."[4]

The existence of the sociometer suggests that we face a present and future in which the state will use its knowledge of our fear, anxiety, and happiness to control and manage our behavior. Beyond this, we also confront the possibility that the sensing of the internal state of another person will become completely identified with these surveillance capacities, instead of with the capacities for emotional and somatic attunement that were formerly known as empathy. Being able to feel another person will become bound up with the process of somatic surveillance, a form of violation rather than a form of contact.

SECOND CHILDHOOD

The problem, however, is not only one of surveillance, sinister though this is. We know what happens when we outsource certain functions from our own brains to those of our devices. Smartphone map technology has created a situation in which large swaths of the population drive around in a state of constant disorientation, gazing anxiously every moment at a screen for directional guidance. We caress the phones as if they were our lovers. The device becomes looped into our system of bodily and mental regulation.

What will happen when we orient to an external device from moment to moment in order to sense somatic and social intensity? The sociometer has been used to provide guidance to individuals in group meetings to alert them as to when they are following conformist "groupthink" rather than listening to their own somatic signals and intuitions. The idea would be that the sociometer enhances our ability to act and think independently, thus fueling innovation and reinforcing the autonomy and creativity of the individual. But externalizing the capacity to sense oneself in relation to the other presupposes an alienation from one's most basic sensory impulses.

This externalization also assumes that creativity is asocial, rather than a set of impulses that we might feel together in attunement. The feral body, instinctual and unconscious, is detached and delegated to an agent outside of us. The sociometric dispositif then acts as a mirror of one's sensations. In childhood, this is the function of the mother, who mirrors back to us our primal impressions so we can begin to make sense of them as emotion, pain, and information about our mental and physical state.

The sociometer becomes a machinic mother. We do not yet know what the consequences of this second childhood will be.

BODY SUPERFLUOUS

In a sociometric world, the body itself would be superfluous. Our sociality would no longer rely on embodiment but on a literacy of the dispositif. We have seen an acceleration toward such a world in the context of the 2020 global pandemic—a rupture that paradoxically seems to confirm a technological continuity. Our bodies are quarantined within two-dimensional boxes and screens, while the third dimension exists within the hidden abode of hospitals, prisons, and nursing homes, where embodiment equates with illness and contagion. If sensation was already elusive, now it is splintered.

As we gaze at faces on the screen, we watch ourselves as much as we watch the other. The flow of relationship from feeling oneself to feeling the other and then back again has a detour. I watch my image. I watch/feel you. I feel myself. But the part about feeling my own bodily sensation in the midst of these exchanges sometimes falls out of the equation when I'm on the screen too long. I watch my image. I watch your image.

The dynamics of presence, sensation, and intimacy shift with these technological possibilities and constraints. Have we arrived at a point in time where sociometric sociality is necessary, even pleasurable?

HYPERMODULATION

From the perspective of the biopolitical state, in a state of quarantine, agency is grasped as immobilization. Movement happens only in perception, in virtual worlds that are becoming more and more identified with reality, even for those who have resisted for decades. There has been a rapid shift in the dimensionality of life, suddenly experienced with more vibrance in two dimensions than three. The cultural theorist Dominic Pettman's analysis of the virtual landscape with the concept of hypermodulation seems to be amplified in this context.[5] Hypermodulation refers to the rapid oscillation of our affective states that happens in the context of whatever algorithm it is that we are creating and following. At this moment, I am outraged about the abuse of workers on the frontlines. The next moment, I rejoice that the tigers are taking over the roads and the air is cleaner than it's been in a century. The next moment, I am devastated by isolation. And so on. I oscillate wildly. But every single other person is on their own stream. They modulate at a different rhythm than I do. They were happy about the tigers five minutes ago, but now they're devastated about fascism. We can't synch up, and this makes it difficult to feel collectivity through these hypermodulating technologies, according to Pettman.

On the other hand, although there is emotional dispersion, there is also a homogeneity that emerges from the media technologies themselves with their algorithms and our submission to them as the price of connection. A certain type of shared experience arises through the pandemic lens because it is all we can think about, feel, talk about, and hope to end. Imagine if everyone in the world were wishing for capitalism to end at the same time. It's an amazing and perverse thought. But this pandemic collectivization is deceptive. It too is highly mediated. We must question how we perceive collectivity within the frame of the hypermodulating technologies within which we are bound to experience these times.

In the midst of disaster, there is little point in criticizing technology. It is all we have, as touch with others outside of our households eludes us. A kiss, a shake of the hand, a gaze into receptive eyes. Such contact is stimulating in an entirely different way than the virtual. Physical contact gives us a different gauge for collective affect than technological contact. It raises the question of how we know what we know about society as we are gaining all of our information from it through our screens. We also gain information through walks in the neighborhood; panicked flights in emergency situations; waiting in line at the grocery store; avoiding oncoming passersby on the street; working on buses, hospitals, and grocery stores in the midst of danger.

It all depends on who you are.

HAPPINESS

As Giorgio Agamben writes, "At the root of each apparatus [*dispositivo*] lies an all-too-human desire for happiness. The capture and subjectification of this desire in a separate sphere constitutes the specific power of the apparatus [*dispositivo*]."[6] Agamben sees the dispositif as a crystallization of a potential for happiness that then becomes relegated to a sphere outside of us, henceforth only accessible by means of the dispositif. The dispositif captures the capacity for eudaemonic pleasure and binds it to a specific technology. The social concentration of pleasure within the field of the dispositif reveals the contours of society's disintegration.

But if we were to destroy the dispositifs, would happiness arise from their ashes?

UNKNOWN PLEASURES

There is another form of pleasure that comes through a destruction of the self, through its undoing. Freud alluded to this form of pleasure through his notion of the death drive.[7] At a certain moment, he could no longer conceive of pleasure solely in terms of the affirmative logic of Eros or of its negation. He needed to grasp the undeniable pleasure of annihilation. But this was not a new kind of pleasure. Nietzsche saw it already in the Bacchanals. And the Greeks certainly weren't the first to bow to these dark goddesses of destruction. The pleasure is not in death but in undoing, dissolving, expanding, and contracting beyond individuating form.

There are no dispositifs for achieving this kind of pleasure, for the pleasure of being undone is not an achievement. It is beyond knowing because it dissolves the one who knows. The subject and the dispositif merge. Sensations are separated from meaning. Feeling is liberated from preference. Pleasure emerges in the sensing of something new, in the movement of no longer owning the self. Nonlocal, nonbinary. It receives its cues from beyond the individualized body. And this annihilation is death only insofar as the self that is fortressed by skin, hair, and the law is submerged in a vast field of becoming.

There are no dispositifs for it, but there may be counter-dispositifs for deprivatizing the body. A certain gradient of vibration. Sound. Voice. Orders of sense that expand the mind beyond apperception. Agamben describes this process as one of profanation. Profanation brings back to the commons forms of life that have been sequestered, shaped, and privatized by technological dispositifs. The senses themselves must become profane, communal, subtle.

The question is how.

BALI

There is an apocryphal story that Deleuze, like many other European philosophers, learned about pleasure from the East.[8] Specifically, it was the concept of the plateau that he understood after he heard about the child-rearing practices of the Balinese, who, rather than encouraging their babies' cathartic fits of emotion, taught them to sit with the intensities that racked their tiny bodies, instilling in them a capacity for pleasure not bound to the dichotomy between concentration and discharge. Rather than going through life as a manic hunt for orgasm, every moment unfolds on the continuum of sensation, unhinged from a truth that is external to life. Pleasure is experienced as flow, not emission. This gestures toward a condition that I have often sensed, which is that orgasm would not have become colonial had it remained, as it might have, a provincial and minor form of access to sensation rather than a quasi-universal dispositif of pleasure—an aspiration, an orgy of feeling, that dampens life's intensity rather than deepens it.

But it remains to be understood whether this kind of theoretical knowledge of the folk practices of the plateau was a sufficient instruction in pleasure for Deleuze or for *us*.

Does it, yet again, convert a form of life into a dispositif?

NOTES

1. Elena Dorfman, *Still Lovers, 2001–2004. Un amore ideale*, exhibition at the Prada Foundation, Milano (February 21–July 23, 2019).

2. Claudia Ferri, *Surrogati. Un Amore Ideale: Exhibition Video*, http://www.fondazioneprada.org/project/surrogati-un-amore-ideale/?lang=en.

3. Robert Venturi, Steven Izenour, and Denise Scott Brown, *Learning from Las Vegas: The Forgotten Symbolism of Architectural Form* (Cambridge, MA: MIT Press, 1977).

4. Nancy Katherine Hayles, *Unthought: The Power of the Cognitive Nonconscious* (Chicago: University of Chicago Press, 2017), 126.

5. Dominic Pettman, *Infinite Distraction* (Malden, MA: Polity Press, 2015), 31–48.

6. Giorgio Agamben, *"What Is an Apparatus?" and Other Essays*, trans. David Kishik and Stefan Pedatella (Stanford, CA: Stanford University Press, 2009), 17.

7. Sigmund Freud, *Civilization and Its Discontents*, trans. James Strachey (New York: W. W. Norton, 2010), 110–111.

8. Annamarie Jagose, *Orgasmology* (Durham, NC: Duke University Press, 2013), 5.

BIBLIOGRAPHY

Agamben, Giorgio. *"What Is an Apparatus?" and Other Essays*. Translated by David Kishik and Stefan Pedatella. Stanford, CA: Stanford University Press, 2009.

Freud, Sigmund. *Civilization and Its Discontents*. Translated by James Strachey. New York: W. W. Norton, 2010.

Hayles, Nancy Katherine. *Unthought: The Power of the Cognitive Nonconscious*. Chicago: University of Chicago Press, 2017.

Jagose, Annamarie. *Orgasmology*. Durham, NC: Duke University Press, 2013.

Pettman, Dominic. *Infinite Distraction*. Malden, MA: Polity Press, 2015.

Venturi, Robert, Steven Izenour, and Denise Scott Brown. *Learning from Las Vegas: The Forgotten Symbolism of Architectural Form*. Cambridge, MA: MIT Press, 1977.

30

DISPOSITIF

Franco Berardi (Bifo)

From a phenomenological point of view, the concept of truth has no place, as truth implies a correspondence, an isomorphism between reality and words. The problem that is relevant, in my view, is the relation between *Lebenswelt* (living world), concept (synthetic comprehension of phenomena, the grasping together of many phenomena in a single act of mental comprehension), and dispositif, the epistemic tool that makes it possible to project the concept onto the world-making practice. From a phenomenological perspective, the world is the psychodynamic convergence of countless (infinite) projections mediated by dispositifs, tools that arrange. In fact, the French word *disposer* means to arrange, to organize, to structure.

In an article devoted to the concept of dispositif in Foucault, Gilles Deleuze writes:

A social apparatus [*dispositif*] consists of lines of force. It could be said that they proceed from one unique point to another in the preceding lines; in a way they "rectify" the preceding curves, they draw tangents, fill in the space between one line and another, acting as go-betweens between seeing and saying and vice versa, acting as arrows which continually cross between words and things, constantly waging battle between them. The line of force comes about "in any relationship between one point and another," and passes through every area in the apparatus. . . . These apparatuses, then, are composed of the following elements: lines of visibility and enunciation, lines of force, lines of subjectification, lines of splitting, breakage, fracture, all of which criss-cross and mingle together, some lines reproducing or giving rise to others, by means of variations or even changes in the way they are grouped. Two important consequences arise for a philosophy of social apparatuses [*dispositifs*]. The first of these is the repudiation of universals. The universal, in fact, explains nothing; it is the universal which needs to be explained. All the lines are lines of variation, which do not even have constant co-ordinates. The One, the All, the True, the object, the subject are not universals, but singular processes—of unification, totalisation, verification, objectivation, subjectification—present in the given apparatus. Also each apparatus is a multiplicity in which operate processes of this nature still in formation, distinct from those operating in another.[1]

The process of subjectivation, here, is meeting and intersecting with the process of world projection, in a sort of ever-expanding concatenation: from the self-perception of a living and conscious organism to the comprehension of the lines of connection between the organism and the surrounding phenomena to the arrangement of the environment, in a continuous process of becoming.

The dispositif therefore has to be seen as having an essentially projective character—the projection of a concept that makes it possible to arrange the environment according to the curves and lines of rupture and conjunction that are contained in a conceptual act of comprehension. We may define the dispositif as an object, a tool, also as an event, inasmuch as it is able to reframe the entire pattern of relations in the environment. This reframing is irresistible, and for the most part it is not linked to a conscious intention but rather is the effect of a concatenation of disarrangements. Disarrangements precede and prepare the establishment of a dispositif.

The dispositif is not the effect of a subjectivity; it is not the instrument of a project. It is a sort of readjustment in the order of signs, of machines and of desires.

I tried to write this text on the concept of dispositif—a word hardly to be found in the dictionary—during the period of sanitary confinement. But defining this concept is so difficult that I was on the brink of giving up at one point. Then, the long period of lockdown was officially lifted (or was it just suspended?), and as cautiously as possible, I dared to go outside, in the streets of the city. The urban landscape was transformed: no more crowds like three months before, people looked somehow dazed, slow. A sense of sadness, the consciousness that we, humans, have been defeated. This time it is not a provisional defeat but rather the beginning of the process of extinction, and we know it, although it is forbidden to speak out this intimate persuasion.

I took a cab and spoke with the cabdriver: "How are things? How is business?" He told me something that I was not aware of:

Since the beginning of lockdown, work was reduced to almost nothing. So, we decided to cut work hours by half. When the lockdown ended, we did not go back to our previous schedule; we are still working four hours instead of eight. This is the only way to give everybody the possibility of earning something. Not what they earned before, not even half of it, but still something. And what is more, dead time between rides has doubled. In other words, now, after the end of the lockdown, when things appear to be back to normal, we are still working 50 percent less than before.

Where is the dispositif in this story? Nowhere. However, as you might be aware, the sanitary masks and all the paraphernalia that became so fashionable in the days of coronavirus are sometimes called "sanitary dispositifs."

Now, little by little, despite the pretense of a return to normalcy, we are realizing that normalcy has been broken and disrupted and will never be restored because the dispositifs that held the social together until six months ago have been broken or simply disarranged. Social life has been derailed from the hinges that once enabled the crazy machine to function, amidst suffering, devastation, and despair. The hinge of employment, the hinge of debt, and the hinge of salary no longer hold the social together. Money, desperately thrown here and there in an attempt to fill the hole, has lost its charm and even its ability, apparently, to mobilize human energies.

From the malicious purple land of strange nightmares, a crooked shape is emerging. An invisible concretion of matter proliferates, corroding the hinges.

It is naïve to believe that the virus—a biological agent that passed from the depth of an invisible magma to the infosphere, to transmigrate then into the human psyche—is the original cause of the unhinging. For a long time now, the hinges were on the verge of collapsing. They creaked.

What I call hinges are actually to be considered as dispositions. A dispositif is the hinge that makes possible the concatenation of a living world with a frame of conceptualization, with a tool (material, perceptual, intellectual, technical) for the manipulation and organization of the surrounding magma of phenomena.

Now, under the effect of the viral storm, what seemed eternal is suddenly over, and what seemed impossible is suddenly necessary. That old Thatcherian slogan, "there is no alternative," has been reversed, and a sort of state socialism based on public investments is enforced. Yet, it does not seem to be up to the task: economic recovery is nowhere in sight, and the power of money seems weakened, unable to give back the required energy to a collective body that is exhausted, distanced, fearful of movement and contact. For a long time, the techno-financial acceleration and the overall precariousness have enfeebled the mental energies of humankind, ushering the world in a permanent state of debilitation. Debilitation and frenzy: frantic debilitation.

This is incompatible with the dispositifs of the past, with the ordered system of monetary exchange and neurotic pathologies. This is why we are in a sort of suspended time, and we need to create new dispositions in order to concatenate our living world (less and less living, in fact) and the concepts we are formulating during the process of mutation.

The biological substance released in the abstract cycle of techno-capital has broken the cycle of social reproduction. The bio-virus turned into info-virus, and now tends to saturate the collective mind with fear, suspicion, distancing. Furthermore, it will ultimately stabilize as a psycho-virus, a phobic pathology of epidemic contact, probably resulting in widespread depression and latent aggressive psychosis prone to erupt in daily life and in the unhinged geopolitical map.

The bio–info–psycho circuitry of the contagion makes useless the political will, reduced to the military implementation of a sanitary program.

The hinges of the unconscious are also slowly breaking down. Sensibility is at stake. Desire is at stake. The limits between conscious and unconscious have shifted during the modern century; now, we are on the brink of a new shift.

Permanent mobilization of nervous energy, stress, psychotic wave. Silence forbidden, slowing down impossible. Now, we are on the threshold. What is going to emerge in the age that comes after the current ambiguous psycho-deflation? What is going to be the long-term effect of the virus invading the sensual-affective environment?

The trauma is not evident now, in the wake of the viral invasion. Despite the martial declarations of bombastic politicians, we are not going through a war. The enemy is not visible. The wounds are not perceived immediately. Death is not exposed in the streets: death is concealed, funerals are undercover, hidden from public sight. So, the trauma will act slowly, under the cover of psycho-deflation.

We dwell in the threshold and feel calm in the distanced relation with the world, with the public sphere of social life. What is beyond this threshold? Trauma is going to reframe the expectations, and the living world, and the concepts. Then, we will be obliged or allowed to deal with new tools for shaping the environment: dispositions.

NOTES

1. Gilles Deleuze, "What Is a Dispositif?" in *Michel Foucault, Philosopher*, trans. Timothy J. Armstrong (New York: Routledge, 1992), 160, 162.

BIBLIOGRAPHY

Deleuze, Gilles. "What Is a Dispositif?" In *Michel Foucault, Philosopher*. Translated by Timothy J. Armstrong, 159–168. New York: Routledge, 1992.

IV
INOPERATIVITY/RESISTANCE

Rehab Nazzal, *Resistance Dance*, life-size vinyl prints (2018). Reprinted by permission of the artist.

31

THE PARERGON

Jacques Derrida

═══

I

[...]

"All form of objects of sense (both of external and also, mediately, of internal sense) is either *figure* or *play*. In the latter case it is either play of figures (in space: mimic and dance), or mere play of sensations (in time). The *charm* of colours, or of the agreeable tones of instruments, may be added: but the *design* in the former and the *composition* in the latter constitute the proper object of the pure judgement of taste. To say that the purity alike of colours and of tones, of their variety and contrast seem to contribute to beauty, is by no means to imply that, because in themselves agreeable, they therefore yield an addition [*supplement*] to the delight in the form [*Wohlgefallen an der Form*] and one on a par with it. The real meaning rather is that they make this form more clearly, definitely, and completely intuitable, and besides stimulate the representation by their charm, as they excite and sustain the attention directed to the object itself.

"Even what is called *ornamentation* [*Zierathen*: decoration, ornamentation, adornment] (*parerga*), i.e. what is only an adjunct, and not an intrinsic constituent in the complete representation of an object, in augmenting the delight of taste does so solely by means of its form. Thus it is with the frames [*Einfassungen*] of pictures or the drapery on statues, or the colonnades of palaces. But if the ornamentation does not itself enter into the composition of a beautiful form—if it is introduced [*simplement appliqué*] like a gold frame [*goldene Rahmen*] merely to win approval for the picture by means of its charm—it is then called finery [*parure*; *Schmuck*] and takes away from the genuine beauty."[1]

⌊
   the theory moves along smoothly⌉

⌊
   thus the drapery on statues—for example—would be ornamentation: *parerga*.⌉

Elsewhere Kant explains the necessity of his recourse to archaic, scholarly languages. Here Greek confers something approximating conceptual dignity on the notion of the hors d'oeuvre which does not remain simply outside of the work, acting from the sidelines, next to the work (*ergon*). Dictionaries most often give "hors d'oeuvre," which is the most literal translation, but also "accessory, foreign, or secondary object," "supplement," "aside," "remainder." It is that which *should not* become, by distinguishing itself, the principal subject: the legal education of children (*Laws*, 766a), or the definition of science (*Theatetus*, 184a) should not be treated as *parerga*. In the investigation of causes or the knowledge of principles, *parerga* should not be allowed to take precedence over the essential (*Nicomachean Ethics*, 1098–30). Philosophical discourse is always against the *parergon*. But what is it *against*.

A *parergon* is against, beside, and above and beyond the *ergon*, the work accomplished, the accomplishment of the work. But it is not incidental; it is connected to and cooperates in its operation from the outside.

[. . .]

If the *parergon*, this supplementary hors d'oeuvre, has something like the status of a philosophical concept, then it must designate a general formal predicative structure which may be carried over, either *intact* or *consistently* deformed, reformed, to other fields, where new contents may be submitted to it. Kant uses the word *parergon* elsewhere: the context is very different, but the structure is analogous and equally problematic. We find it in a lengthy note appended to the second and subsequent editions of *Religion within the Limits of Reason Alone*. The form in which it occurs is extremely important.

To what is the Note appended? To a "General Observation" which concludes Part Two.

What is the *parergon*? It is the concept of the observation, of this "General Observation," insofar as it defines what augments *Religion within the Limits of Reason Alone* while being neither part of it nor absolutely extrinsic to it. Each Part includes a

"General Observation" (*Allgemeine Anmerkung*), *parergon* on a *parergon*. Since there are four Parts, these four Observations on *parerga*, hors d'oeuvres, "adjuncts" which are neither internal nor external, effectively frame the work, but also square it.

At the beginning of the Note appended in the second edition to the first "General Observation," the status of the Observation is defined as *parergon*: "This General Observation is the first of four which are appended, one to each Book of this work, and which might bear the titles, (1) Works of Grace, (2) Miracles, (3) Mysteries, and (4) Means of Grace. These matters are, as it were, *parerga* to religion within the limits of pure reason; they do not belong within it, but border upon it [*aber stossen doch an sie an*: they touch upon it, put pressure on it, press against it, seek contact, exert pressure at the boundary]. Reason, conscious of her inability to satisfy her moral need, extends herself to high-flown ideas capable of supplying this lack [*Mangel*], without, however, appropriating these ideas as an extension of her domain [*Besitz*: possession]. Reason does not dispute the possibility or the reality of the objects of these ideas; she simply cannot adopt them into her maxims of thought and action. She even holds that, if in the inscrutable realm of the supernatural there is something more than she can explain to herself, which may yet be necessary as a complement to her moral insufficiency, this will be, even though unknown, available to her good will. Reason believes this with a faith which (with respect to the possibility of this supernatural complement) might be called *reflective*; for *dogmatic* faith which proclaims itself as a form of knowledge appears to her dishonest or presumptuous. To remove the difficulties, then, in the way of that which (for moral practice) stands firm in and for itself, is merely a by-work (*parergon*), when those difficulties have reference to transcendent questions."[2]

"By-work" is the translation of *Nebengeschäfte*: secondary business or busyness, activity or operation from the sidelines or nearby. The *parergon* inscribes something extra, *exterior* to the specific field (here, of pure reason and *Religion within the Limits of Reason Alone*), but whose transcendent exteriority touches, plays with, brushes, rubs, or presses against the limit and intervenes internally only insofar as the inside is missing. Missing something and is itself missing. Since reason is "conscious of her inability to satisfy her moral need," she has recourse to the *parergon*, to grace, mysteries, miracles. She requires a supplementary "by-work." Certainly the adjunct is a threat. Its function is critical. It entails a risk and enjoys itself at the expense of transforming the theory. A damage, an injury [*prejudice*; *Nachteil*] corresponds to each *parergon* in *Religion*, and the four classes of prejudice correspond to the four kinds of *parerga*: 1. to supposed internal experience (effects of grace), fanaticism, 2. to supposed external experience (miracles), superstition, 3. to supposed light of understanding of the supernatural order, illuminism, 4. to supposed supernatural actions (through grace), thaumaturgy. Nevertheless, these four deviations or seductions of reason are also aimed at a particular pleasure: pleasure-unto-God [*gottgefälliger Absicht*].

Thus, the drapery on statues, a privileged example, would function as *parergon*, as ornamentation. This means (*das heisst*) precisely what is not interior or intrinsic (*innerlich*), in the sense of an integral component (*als Bestandstück*), to the complete representation of the object (*in die ganze Vorstellung des Gegenstandes*), but which belongs to it only in an extrinsic fashion (*nur äusserlich*), as a surplus, an addition, an adjunct (*als Zuthat*).

The drapery on statues, which simultaneously adorns and veils their nudity, is hors d'oeuvre clinging to the work's edges as to the body represented, but—so the argument goes—not a part of the representative whole. What is represented by the representation is the nude body, *au naturel*; the representational essence of the statue tallies with it; and only in it may the representation be beautiful—essentially, purely, and intrinsically beautiful, "the proper object of a pure judgement of taste."

This definition of the center and of the integrity of the representation, of its inside and outside, may already appear peculiar. We may ask as well where the drapery begins. Where a *parergon* begins, and where it ends. Whether all drapery is *parergon*—G-strings and the like. What to do with absolutely transparent veils. And how to transpose the statement to painting. For example, Cranach's Lucretia holds nothing but a flimsy transparent veil over her sex: where is the *parergon*? Must we also consider a *parergon*—not part of her nude body, *au naturel*—the dagger which she points at herself and which touches her skin (only the point of the *parergon* touches her body, in the middle of a triangle formed by her two breasts and her navel)? Is her necklace also a *parergon*? It concerns the objectifying, representational essence, its inside and outside, the criteria used in this definition, the value attributed to the natural, and, either secondarily or principally, the privileged position of the human body. If every *parergon* is added, as proved in *Religion*, only because of a lack within the system it augments, then what deficiency in the representation of the body does drapery supplement? And what has art to do with it?

Our surprise at this paragraph has only begun. (*Parergon* also signifies the exceptional, the peculiar, the extraordinary.) I have somewhat too hastily torn "drapery" from the context of three examples, three *parerga* which are no less strange—first in themselves, and in relation to one another. The example which follows immediately is that of the colonnades of palaces (*Säulengänge um Prachtbäude*). These columns are also supplementary *parerga*. After drapery, the column. Why should the column be external to the edifice? According to what criterion, what critical organ, what *orga-non* of discernment? It is no less obscure than in the preceding case and presents yet another difficulty: in this case the *parergon* augments a work which *represents nothing* and which itself augments nature. We believe we know what is part and what is not part of the human body, what may be detached from it and what may not—even if the *parergon* is precisely a detachment which is not easily detached. But in an architectural work, the *Vorstellung*, the representation, is not structurally representational—or it is, but according to a detour so complicated that it would undoubtedly disconcert anyone who wanted to distinguish, in a critical manner, the inside from the outside, the integral from the detachable. So as not to complicate this even further, I set aside, provisionally, columns in the form of the human body supporting or representing the support of a window (and the window itself—is it part of the edifice? And a window in a painting of a building?), and which may be nude or draped and may represent either a man or a woman—a distinction to which Kant does not allude.

With the example of the colonnade, we encounter the entire problematic of inscription in a milieu, of distinguishing the work from a ground. It is always difficult to determine whether the ground is natural or artificial and, in the latter case, whether it is *parergon* or *ergon*. The ground, even if it is contiguous with the work, does not constitute a *parergon* in the Kantian sense. The natural site chosen for the erection of a temple is obviously not a *parergon*. Nor is an artificial site: neither the square, nor the church, nor the museum, nor the other surrounding works. But drapery or the column, yes. Why? Not because they are easily detached; on the contrary, they are very difficult to detach. Without them, without their quasidetachment, the lack within the work would appear or, what amounts to the same, would not appear. It is not simply their exteriority that constitutes them as *parerga*, but the internal structural link by which they are inseparable from a lack within the *ergon*. And this lack makes for the very unity of the *ergon*. Without it, the *ergon* would have no need of a *parergon*. The lack of the *ergon* is the lack of a *parergon*, of drapery or columns which nevertheless remain exterior to it. How do we determine the role of *energeia*?

May we attach the third example to this series of examples, to the question which they raise? The third is in fact the first—I have proceeded in reverse. It is, at least apparently, difficult to associate with the other two. It is the frames of paintings (*Einfassungen der Gemälde*). The frame: *parergon* like the others. This series may be surprising. How do we assimilate the function of the frame to that of drapery on (in, around, or against) sculpture, and to that of columns surrounding an edifice? And what about a frame which frames a painting representing a building surrounded by columns in the form of draped human figures? The incomprehensibility of the border, at the border, appears not only at the inner limit, between the frame and the painting, the drapery and the body, the column and the building, but also at its outer limit. *Parerga* have a thickness, a surface which separates them not only, as Kant would have it, from the body of the *ergon* itself, but also from the outside, from the wall on which the painting is hung, the space in which the statue or column stands, as well as from the entire historic, economic, and political field of inscription in which the drive of the signature arises (an analogous problem, as we will see later). No "theory," no "practice," no "theoretical practice" can be effective here if it does not rest on the frame, the invisible limit of (between) the interiority of meaning (protected by the entire hermeneutic, semiotic, phenomenological, and formalist tradition) *and* (of) all the extrinsic empiricals which, blind and illiterate, dodge the question.

The *parergon* is distinguished from both the *ergon* (the work) and the milieu; it is distinguished as a figure against a ground. But it is not distinguished in the same way as the work, which is also distinguished from a ground. The parergonal frame is distinguished from two grounds, but in relation to each of these, it disappears into the other. In relation to the work, which may function as its ground, it disappears into the wall and then, by degrees, into the general context. In relation to the general context, it disappears into the work. Always a form on a ground, the *parergon* is nevertheless a form which has traditionally been determined not by distinguishing itself, but by disappearing, sinking in, obliterating itself, dissolving just as it expends its greatest energy. The frame is never a ground in the way the context or the work may be, but neither does its marginal thickness form a figure. At least, it is a figure which arises of its own accord.

[. . .]

I may appear to be taking unfair advantage by persisting with two or three possibly fortuitous examples from a secondary subchapter; it might be better to deal with parts less marginal to the work, closer to its center and its depth. Of course. But the objection presupposes that we already know what the center and the depth of the third *Critique* are, that we have already located its frame and delimited its field. Yet nothing is more difficult to determine. The *Critique* is a work (*ergon*) in several ways; as such, it must center and frame itself, delimit its ground by distinguishing itself, by means of a frame, from a general background. However this frame is problematic. I do not know what is essential and what is secondary to a work. Above all I do not know what this thing is which is neither essential nor secondary, neither proper nor improper, which Kant calls *parergon*, for example, the frame. What is the place of the frame. Does it have a place. Where does it begin. Where does it end. What is its inner limit. Outer.

And the surface between the two limits. I do not know if the passage in the *Critique* which defines *parergon* is itself a *parergon*. Before deciding what is *parergonal* in a text which poses the question of the *parergon*, we must know what a *parergon* is, at least if one occurs in the text.

[. . .]

⌉

⌊

[. . .]

Not to force the point, but to describe a certain forcing on Kant's part, we will say that the entire frame of the analytic of the beautiful functions, with respect to that which determines content or internal structure, like a *parergon*; it has all the right characteristics: neither simply interior not simply exterior; not falling to one side of the work, as we might say of an exergue; indispensable to *energeia* to liberate surplus value because it confines the work (all contracts and first of all the contract of painting presuppose a process of framing; and to be effective here the work of deconstruction cannot dispense with a theory of the frame); summoned and assembled like a supplement because of the lack—a certain "internal" indetermination—in the very thing it enframes. This lack, which cannot be determined, localized, situated, *halted* inside or outside *before the framing* is, to borrow concepts belonging precisely to the classical logic of the frame, and to Kantian discourse, both *produced by* and *production of* the frame. If we apply to it the rule defined in "Exemplification," and if it becomes in its turn an example of what it allows us to consider as an example (frame described in the frame), we can take the content of the analytic of judgment as a work of art, a tableau whose frame, imported from the other *Critique*, plays the role of a *parergon* because of its formal beauty. If it were only a charming, seductive, amusing exergue which did not cooperate with the work itself, a pure depreciation of value and squandering of surplus value, then it would be mere finery. But it happens that this very analytic of judgment, in its frame, is what allows us to define the procedure of formality, the opposition of the formal and the material, the pure and the impure, the proper and the improper, the inside and the outside. The analytic *determines* the frame as *parergon*, that which simultaneously constitutes and destroys it, makes it hold (as in *hold together*, it constitutes, mounts, enshrines, sets, borders, assembles, protects—so many operations assembled by the *Einfassung*) and fall at the same time. A frame is in essence constructed and therefore fragile, this is the essence or the truth of the frame. If such a thing exists. But this "truth" can no longer be a "truth," it defines neither the transcendent nor the contingent character of the frame, only its character as *parergon*.

Philosophy wants to examine this "truth," but never succeeds. That which produces and manipulates the frame sets everything in motion to efface its effect, most often by naturalizing it to infinity, in God's keeping (to be confirmed in Kant). Deconstruction must neither reframe nor fantasize the pure and simple absence of the frame. These two apparently contradictory actions are precisely the systematically indissociable ones of that which is presently deconstructed.

If the procedures initiated, if the criteria proposed by the analytic of the beautiful depend upon this parergonality; if all the oppositions which dominate the philosophy of art (before and after Kant) depend upon it for their pertinence, their rigor, their purity, their propriety, then they will be affected by this logic of the *parergon* which is more powerful than the logic of the analytic. We could pursue the consequences of this infectious affection in detail. They cannot be local. The reflective procedure written on the frame (this is—written about the frame): a general law which is no longer a mechanical or teleological law of nature, of the accord or harmony of the faculties (etc.), but a certain repeated dislocation, an irrepressible, regulated deterioration, which splits the frame in general, embeds it in the corners of its angles and articulations, renders its internal limit external, takes its thickness into account, makes us see the painting from the side of the canvas or the wood, etc.

[. . .]

Quality (disinterest) is the very thing that determines the formality of the beautiful object: it must be free of all charm, all power to seduce, it must not provoke any emotion, allow any enjoyment. Thus the *opposition* between the formal and the material, between line and color (as nonform), between composition and sound (as nonform), the formal *parergon* and the material *parergon*, the opposition between the good and the bad *parergon* (which in itself is neither good nor bad) depends upon the framing of this quality, this framing-effect which we call quality, aspect of aspects, according to which, violently, everything appears to begin. Position: opposition: frame.

In "Exemplification" the discourse on sound and color develops, in similar fashion, within the angle of the two mathematical categories (quality and quantity), while the entire analytic of the beautiful undoes—incessantly and as if unwittingly—the work of the frame.

Actually, the frame warps as it works. As a locus of work, an origin structurally bordered with surplus value, that is, exceeded on both sides by that which it exceeds, in effect it warps. Like wood. It splits, breaks down, breaks up, at the same time that it cooperates in the production of the product, it exceeds it and deducts itself. It never simply exposes itself.

[. . .]

⌉

⌊

the *parergon*—give it up for lost (*faire son deuil*). Like the wholly other of heteroaffection, in pleasure without *jouissance* and without concept, it elicits *and* delimits the work of mourning, work *in general as* the work of mourning

⌉

⌊

Self-protection/self-adornment

⌉

⌊

reserve, economy, parsimony, preserve—self-protection of the work (*ergon*), contained restrained energy (the "binding" [*Verbindung*] of energy, condition of the "mastery" [*Herrschaft*] of the pleasure principle: the result "is not simple"—to be continued)

⌉

⌊

the self-protection of the work, of the *energeia* which only becomes *ergon* (because of) the *parergon*: not opposed to free, full, pure, unchained energy (the pure act and total presence of *energeia*, the Aristotelian prime mover), but opposed to what it *lacks*; not opposed to the lack as a posable or opposable negativity, substantial void, or determinable and contained absence (still verifiable essence and presence), but against the impossibility of fixing *différance* in its contour, of halting heterogeneity (*différance*) in place, of localizing, even in a metaempirical way, what metaphysics calls (we have just seen it) *lack*, to make it return, equal or similar to itself (*adaequatio-homoiosis*), to its proper place, following its own trajectory, preferably a circular one (castration as truth). Apparently opposed—or because opposed—these two *bordering* determinations of that against which the *parergon* works (the operation of free energy and pure productivity or the operation of the essential lack) are *the same* (metaphysics).

⌉

⌊

beyond the frame (the lethargy of the frame, its absolute value): naturalization of the frame. There is no natural frame. There *is* framing, but the frame *does not exist*.

The *parergon*—apotrope (allure, display) *of* the primary processes, of free energy, that is, of the "theoretical fiction." (*Ein psychischer Apparat, der nur den Primärvorgang besäße, existiert zwar unseres Wissens nicht und ist insoferne eine theoretische Fiktion.*) Thus only a particular application of the theoretical fiction can warp and work (against) the frame, (make or allow) it to play (against) itself. But we must not forget that the *content, the object* of this theoretical fiction (free energy of the originary process, pure productivity) is metaphysics, onto-theology itself. The *application* of the fiction always runs the risk of believing it, or in creating belief in it. The *application* of the fiction must therefore be careful not to palm off metaphysical truth once again under the label of fiction. There is fiction and fiction. Here, where there is play and work, we need an angle—diagonality—and to disclose the angularity of round frames (some do exist). Hegel: mind is linked to the apparition of the round form

⌉

⌊

everything will blossom beside a deconsecrated tomb: the free or vague (*pulchritudo vaga*) and nondependent (*pulchritudo adhearens*) beauty of the flower. This will be, an arbitrary example, a colorless, odorless tulip (even more securely than color, scent is lost for art and for the beautiful [paragraph 53]—try to frame a scent) which Kant undoubtedly did not pick in Holland but from a book by one Saussure, which he read frequently at that time. "A flower, on the other hand, *zum Beispiel eine Tulpe*, is regarded as beautiful, because we meet with a certain finality in its perception, which, in our estimate of it, is not referred to any end whatever"[3]

⌉

⌊

indeed

⌉

NOTES

1. Immanuel Kant, *The Critique of Judgement*, trans. James C. Meredith (Oxford: Oxford University Press, 1952), 65–68.

2. Immanuel Kant, *Religion within the Limits of Reason Alone*, trans. Theodore M. Greene and Hoyt H. Hudson (New York, Harper & Row, 1960), 47–49.

3. Kant, *Critique*, 80.

BIBLIOGRAPHY

Kant, Immanuel. *The Critique of Judgement*. Translated by James C. Meredith. Oxford: Oxford University Press, 1952.

Kant, Immanuel. *Religion within the Limits of Reason Alone*. Translated by Theodore M. Greene and Hoyt H. Hudson. New York: Harper & Row, 1960.

32

THE PRACTICE OF EVERYDAY LIFE

Michel de Certeau

In spite of measures taken to repress or conceal it, *la perruque* (or its equivalent) is infiltrating itself everywhere and becoming more and more common. It is only one case among all the practices which introduce *artistic* tricks and competitions of *accomplices* into a system that reproduces and partitions through work or leisure. Sly as a fox and twice as quick: there are countless ways of "making do."

From this point of view, the dividing line no longer falls between work and leisure. These two areas of activity flow together. They repeat and reinforce each other. Cultural techniques that camouflage economic reproduction with fictions of surprise ("the event"), of truth ("information") or communication ("promotion") spread through the workplace. Reciprocally, cultural production offers an area of expansion for rational operations that permit work to be managed by dividing it (analysis), tabulating it (synthesis) and aggregating it (generalization). A distinction is required other than the one that distributes behaviors according to their *place* (of work or leisure) and qualifies them thus by the fact that they are located on one or another square of the social checkerboard—in the office, in the workshop, or at the movies. There are differences of another type. They refer to the *modalities* of action, to the *formalities* of practices. They traverse the frontiers dividing time, place, and type of action into one part assigned for work and another for leisure. For example, *la perruque* grafts itself onto the system of the industrial assembly line (its counterpoint, in the same place), as a variant of the activity which, outside the factory (in another place), takes the form of *bricolage*.

Although they remain dependent upon the possibilities offered by circumstances, these transverse *tactics* do not obey the law of the place, for they are not defined or identified by it. In this respect, they are not any more localizable than the technocratic (and scriptural) *strategies* that seek to create places in conformity with abstract models. But what distinguishes them at the same time concerns the *types of operations* and the role of spaces: strategies are able to produce, tabulate, and impose these spaces, when those operations take place, whereas tactics can only use, manipulate, and divert these spaces.

We must therefore specify the operational schemas. Just as in literature one differentiates "styles" or ways of writing, one can distinguish "ways of operating"—ways of walking, reading, producing, speaking, etc. These styles of action intervene in a field which regulates them at a first level (for example, at the level of the factory system), but they introduce into it a way of turning it to their advantage that obeys other rules and constitutes something like a second level interwoven into the first (for instance, *la perruque*). These "ways of operating" are similar to "instructions for use," and they create a certain play in the machine through a stratification of different and interfering kinds of functioning. Thus a North African living in Paris or Roubaix (France) insinuates *into* the system imposed on him by the construction of a low-income housing development or of the French language the ways of "dwelling" (in a house or a language) peculiar to his native Kabylia. He superimposes them and, by that combination, creates for himself a space in which he can find *ways of using* the constraining order of the place or of the language. Without leaving the place where he has no choice but to live and which lays down its law for him, he establishes within it a degree of *plurality* and creativity. By an art of being in between, he draws unexpected results from his situation.

These modes of use—or rather re-use—multiply with the extension of acculturation phenomena, that is, with the displacements that substitute manners or "methods" of transiting toward an identification of a person by the place in which he lives or works. That does not prevent them from corresponding to a very ancient art of "making do." I give them the name of uses, even though the word most often designates stereotyped procedures accepted and reproduced by a group, its "ways and customs." The problem lies in the ambiguity of the word, since it is precisely a matter of recognizing in these "uses" "actions" (in the military sense of the word) that have their own formality and inventiveness and that discreetly organize the multiform labor of consumption.

[. . .]

STRATEGIES AND TACTICS

Unrecognized producers, poets of their own affairs, trailblazers in the jungles of functionalist rationality, consumers produce something resembling the *"lignes d'erre"* described by Deligny.[1] They trace "indeterminate trajectories" that are apparently meaningless, since they do not cohere with the constructed, written, and prefabricated space through which they move. They are sentences that remain unpredictable within the space ordered by the organizing techniques of systems. Although they use as their *material* the *vocabularies* of established languages (those of television, newspapers, the supermarket or city planning), although they remain within the framework of prescribed *syntaxes* (the temporal modes of schedules, paradigmatic organizations of places, etc.), these "traverses" remain heterogeneous to the systems they infiltrate and in which they sketch out the guileful ruses of *different* interests and desires. They circulate, come and go, overflow and drift over an imposed terrain, like the snowy waves of the sea slipping in among the rocks and defiles of an established order.

Statistics can tell us virtually nothing about the currents in this sea theoretically governed by the institutional frameworks that it in fact gradually erodes and displaces. Indeed, it is less a matter of a liquid circulating in the interstices of a solid than of different *movements* making use of the elements of the terrain. Statistical study is satisfied with classifying, calculating and tabulating these elements—"lexical" units, advertising words, television images, manufactured products, constructed places, etc.—and they do it with categories and taxonomies that conform to those of industrial or administrative production. Hence such study can grasp only the material used by consumer practices—a material which is obviously that imposed on everyone by production—and not the *formality* proper to these practices, their surreptitious and guileful "movement," that is, the very activity of "making do." The strength of these computations lies in their ability to divide, but this analytical ability eliminates the possibility of representing the tactical trajectories which, according to their own criteria, select fragments taken from the vast ensembles of production in order to compose new stories with them.

What is counted is *what* is used, not the *ways* of using. Paradoxically, the latter become invisible in the universe of codification and generalized transparency. Only the effects (the quantity and locus of the consumed products) of these waves that flow in everywhere remain perceptible. They circulate without being seen, discernible only through the objects that they move about and erode. The practices of consumption are the ghosts of the society that carries their name. Like the "spirits" of former times, they constitute the multiform and occult postulate of productive activity.

In order to give an account of these practices, I have resorted to the category of "trajectory." It was intended to suggest a temporal movement through space, that is, the unity of a diachronic *succession* of points through which it passes, and not the *figure* that these points form on a space that is supposed to be synchronic or achronic. Indeed, this "representation" is insufficient, precisely because a trajectory is drawn, and time and movement are thus reduced to a line that can be seized as a whole by the eye and read in a single moment, as one projects onto a map the path taken by someone walking through a city. However useful this "flattening out" may be, it transforms the *temporal* articulation of places into a *spatial* sequence of points. A graph takes the place of an operation. A reversible sign (one that can be read in both directions, once it is projected onto a map) is substituted for a practice indissociable from particular moments and "opportunities," and thus irreversible (one cannot go backward in time, or have another chance at missed opportunities). It is thus a mark *in place of* acts, a relic in place of performances: it is only their remainder, the sign of their erasure. Such a projection postulates that it is possible to take the one (the mark) for the other (operations articulated on occasions). This is a *quid pro quo* typical of the reductions which a functionalist administration of space must make in order to be effective.

A distinction between *strategies* and *tactics* appears to provide a more adequate initial schema. I call a *strategy* the calculation (or manipulation) of power relationships that becomes possible as soon as a subject with will and power (a business, an army, a city, a scientific institution) can be isolated. It postulates a *place* that can be delimited as its own and serve as the base from which relations with an *exteriority* composed of targets or threats (customers or competitors, enemies, the country surrounding the city, objectives and objects of research, etc.) can be managed. As in management, every "strategic" rationalization seeks first of all to distinguish its "own" place, that is, the place of its own power and will, from an "environment." A Cartesian attitude, if you wish: it is an effort to delimit one's own place in a world bewitched by the invisible powers of the Other. It is also the typical attitude of modern science, politics, and military strategy.

The establishment of a break between a place appropriated as one's own and its other is accompanied by important effects, some of which we must immediately note:

(1) The "proper" is a *triumph of place over time*. It allows one to capitalize acquired advantages, to prepare future expansions, and thus to give oneself a certain independence

with respect to the variability of circumstances. It is a mastery of time through the foundation of an autonomous place.

(2) It is also a mastery of places through sight. The division of space makes possible a *panoptic practice* proceeding from a place whence the eye can transform foreign forces into objects that can be observed and measured, and thus control and "include" them within its scope of vision.[2] To be able to see (far into the distance) is also to be able to predict, to run ahead of time by reading a space.

(3) It would be legitimate to define the *power of knowledge* by this ability to transform the uncertainties of history into readable spaces. But it would be more correct to recognize in these "strategies" a specific type of knowledge, one sustained and determined by the power to provide oneself with one's own place. Thus military or scientific strategies have always been inaugurated through the constitution of their "own" areas (autonomous cities, "neutral" or "independent" institutions, laboratories pursuing "disinterested" research, etc.). In other words, *a certain power is the precondition of this knowledge* and not merely its effect or its attribute. It makes this knowledge possible and at the same time determines its characteristics. It produces itself in and through this knowledge.

By contrast with a strategy (whose successive shapes introduce a certain play into this formal schema and whose link with a particular historical configuration of rationality should also be clarified), a *tactic* is a calculated action determined by the absence of a proper locus. No delimitation of an exteriority, then, provides it with the condition necessary for autonomy. The space of a tactic is the space of the other. Thus it must play on and with a terrain imposed on it and organized by the law of a foreign power. It does not have the means to *keep to itself*, at a distance, in a position of withdrawal, foresight, and self-collection: it is a maneuver "within the enemy's field of vision," as von Bülow put it,[3] and within enemy territory. It does not, therefore, have the options of planning general strategy and viewing the adversary as a whole within a district, visible, and objectifiable space. It operates in isolated actions, blow by blow. It takes advantage of "opportunities" and depends on them, being without any base where it could stockpile its winnings, build up its own position, and plan raids. What it wins it cannot keep. This nowhere gives a tactic mobility, to be sure, but a mobility that must accept the chance offerings of the moment, and seize on the wing the possibilities that offer themselves at any given moment. It must vigilantly make use of the cracks that particular conjunctions open in the surveillance of the proprietary powers. It poaches in them. It creates surprises in them. It can be where it is least expected. It is a guileful ruse.

In short, a tactic is an art of the weak. Clausewitz noted this fact in discussing deception in his treatise *On War*. The more a power grows, the less it can allow itself to mobilize part of its means in the service of deception: it is dangerous to deploy large forces for the sake of appearances; this sort of "demonstration" is generally useless and "the gravity of bitter necessity makes direct action so urgent that it leaves no room for this sort of game." One deploys his forces, one does not take chances with feints. Power is bound by its very visibility. In contrast, trickery is possible for the weak, and often it is his only possibility, as a "last resort": "The weaker the forces at the disposition of the strategist, the more the strategist will be able to use deception."[4] I translate: the more the strategy is transformed into tactics.

Clausewitz also compares trickery to wit: "Just as wit involves a certain legerdemain relative to ideas and concepts, trickery is a sort of legerdemain relative to acts."[5] This indicates the mode in which a tactic, which is indeed a form of legerdemain, takes an order by surprise. The art of "pulling tricks" involves a sense of the opportunities afforded by a particular occasion. Through procedures that Freud makes explicit with reference to wit,[6] a tactic boldly juxtaposes diverse elements in order suddenly to produce a flash shedding a different light on the language of a place and to strike the hearer. Cross-cuts, fragments, cracks and lucky hits in the framework of a system, consumers' ways of operating are the practical equivalents of wit.

Lacking its own place, lacking a view of the whole, limited by the blindness (which may lead to perspicacity) resulting from combat at close quarters, limited by the possibilities of the moment, a tactic is determined by the *absence of power* just as a strategy is organized by the postulation of power. From this point of view, the dialectic of a tactic may be illuminated by the ancient art of sophistic. As the author of a great "strategic" system, Aristotle was already very interested in the procedures of this enemy which perverted, as he saw it, the order of truth. He quotes a formula of this protean, quick, and surprising adversary that, by making explicit the basis of sophistic, can also serve finally to define a tactic as I understand the term here: it is a matter, Corax said, of "making the worse argument seem the better."[7] In its paradoxical concision, this formula delineates the relationship of forces that is the starting point for an intellectual creativity as persistent as it is subtle, tireless, ready for every opportunity, scattered over the terrain of the dominant order and foreign to the rules laid down and imposed by a rationality founded on established rights and property.

In sum, strategies are actions which, thanks to the establishment of a place of power (the property of a proper), elaborate theoretical places (systems and totalizing discourses) capable of articulating an ensemble of physical places in which forces are distributed. They combine these three types of places and seek to master each by means of the others. They thus privilege spatial relationships. At the very least they attempt to reduce temporal relations to spatial ones through the analytical attribution of a proper place to each particular element and through the combinatory organization of the movements specific to units or groups of units. The model was military before it became "scientific." Tactics are procedures that gain validity in relation to the pertinence they lend to time—to the circumstances which the precise instant of an intervention transforms into a favorable situation, to the rapidity of the movements that change the organization of a space, to the relations among successive moments in an action, to the possible intersections of durations and heterogeneous rhythms, etc. In this respect, the difference corresponds to two historical options regarding action and security (options that moreover have more to do with constraints than with possibilities): strategies pin their hopes on the resistance that the *establishment of a place* offers to the erosion of time; tactics on a clever *utilization of time*, of the opportunities it presents and also of the play that it introduces into the foundations of power. Even if the methods practiced by the everyday art of war never present themselves in such a clear form, it nevertheless remains the case that the two ways of acting can be distinguished according to whether they bet on place or on time.

[. . .]

SCATTERED TECHNOLOGIES: FOUCAULT

From the outset we face the problem of the relation of these procedures to discourse. Procedures lack the repetitive fixity of rites, customs or reflexes, kinds of knowledge which are no longer (or not yet) articulated in discourse. Their mobility constantly adjusts them to a diversity of objectives and "coups," without their being dependent on a verbal elucidation. Are they, however, completely autonomous with respect to the latter? Tactics in discourse can, as we have seen, be the formal indicator of tactics that have no discourse. Moreover, the ways of thinking embedded in ways of operating constitute a strange—and massive—case of the relations between practices and theories.

In *Discipline and Punish*, his study of the organization of the "procedures" of penitential, educational, and medical control at the beginning of the nineteenth century, Foucault offers a variety of synonyms, words that dance about and successively approach an impossible proper name: "apparatuses" ["*dispositifs*"], "instrumentalities," "techniques," "mechanisms," "machineries," etc.[8] The uncertainty and the mobility of the thing in language are already significant. But the very history he narrates, that of an enormous substitution, postulates and puts in position a dichotomy between "ideologies" and "procedures" in the process of tracing their distinct evolutions and their intersections. He analyzes the process of a chiasm: the place occupied by the reformist projects of the late eighteenth century has been "colonized," "vampirized," by the disciplinary procedures that subsequently organize the social space. This detective story about a substituted body would have pleased Freud.

In Foucault's work, the drama pits against each other two forces whose relationship is reversed by the tricks of time. On the one hand, the ideology of the Enlightenment, revolutionary with regard to penal justice. For the "torture" of the Ancien Régime, a violent corporal ritual dramatizing the triumph of royal order over felons chosen for their symbolic value, the reformist projects of the eighteenth century seek to substitute punishments applicable to all, in proportion to the crimes, useful to society, edifying for the condemned. In fact, disciplinary procedures gradually perfected in the army and in schools quickly won out over the vast and complex judicial apparatus constructed by the Enlightenment. These techniques are refined and extended without recourse to an ideology. Through a cellular space of the same type for everyone (schoolboys, soldiers, workers, criminals or the ill), the techniques perfected the visibility and the gridwork of this space in order to make of it a tool capable of disciplining under control and "treating" any human group whatever. The development is a matter of technological details, miniscule and decisive procedures. The details overcome theory: through these procedures the universalization of a uniform penalty—imprisonment—is imposed, which inverts revolutionary institutions from within and establishes everywhere the "penitentiary" in the place of penal justice.

Foucault thus distinguishes two heterogeneous systems. He outlines the advantages won by a political technology of the body over the elaboration of a body of doctrine. But he is not content merely to separate two forms of power. By following the establishment and victorious multiplication of this "minor instrumentality," he tries to bring to light the springs of this opaque power that has no possessor, no privileged place, no superiors or inferiors, no repressive activity or dogmatism, that is almost autonomously effective through its technological ability to distribute, classify, analyze and spatially individualize the object dealt with. (All the while, ideology babbles on!) In a series of clinical tableaux (also marvelously "panoptic"), he tries to name and classify in turn the "general rules," "conditions of functioning," "techniques" and "procedures," distinct "operations," "mechanisms," "principles," and "elements" that compose a "microphysics of power."[9] This gallery of diagrams has the twin functions of delimiting a social stratum of practices that have no discourse and of founding a discourse on these practices.

In what then does this level of decisive practices isolated by analysis consist? By a detour that characterizes the strategy of his inquiries, Foucault discerns at this level *the move [le geste] which has organized the discursive space*. This move is not, as in his earlier book, *The History of Madness*, the epistemological and social move of isolating excluded people from normal social intercourse in order to create the space that makes possible a rational order; rather it is the miniscule and ubiquitously reproduced move of "gridding" [*quadriller*] a visible space in such a way as to make its occupants available for observation and "information." The procedures that repeat, amplify, and perfect this move organize the discourse that has taken the form of the "human sciences." In that way a *non-discursive move* is identified which, being privileged for social and historical reasons that remain to be explained, is articulated in contemporary scientific knowledge.

To the extremely novel perspectives opened up by this analysis[10]—which would, moreover, allow the development of another theory of "style" (style, a way of walking through a terrain, a non-textual move or attitude, organizes the text of a thought)— we may add a few questions relevant to our inquiry:

1. In undertaking to produce an archeology of the human sciences (his explicit goal since *The Order of Things/Les mots et les choses*) and in seeking a "common matrix," viz., a "technology of power," which would be at the origin of both criminal law (the punishment of human beings) and the human sciences (the knowledge of human beings), Foucault is led to make a *selection* from the ensemble of procedures that form the fabric of social activity in the eighteenth and nineteenth centuries. This surgical operation consists in starting out from a proliferating contemporary system—a judicial and scientific technology—and *tracing it back through history, isolating* from the whole body the cancerous growth that has invaded it, and *explaining* its current functioning *by its genesis* over the two preceding centuries. From an immense body of historical material (penal, military, educational, medical), the operation extracts the optical and panoptical procedures which increasingly multiply within it and discerns in them the at first scattered indexes of an apparatus whose elements become better defined, combine with each other, and reproduce themselves little by little throughout all the strata of society.

This remarkable historiographical "operation" raises simultaneously two questions which must nevertheless not be confused: on the one hand, the decisive role of technological procedures and apparatuses in the organization of a society; on the other, the exceptional development of a particular category of these apparatuses. It is thus still necessary to ask ourselves:

(a) How can we explain the *privileged development* of the particular series constituted by panoptic apparatuses?
(b) What is the status of so many other series which, pursuing their silent itineraries, have not given rise to a discursive configuration or to a technological systematization? They could be considered as an *immense* reserve constituting either the beginnings or traces of *different developments*.

It is in any case impossible to reduce the functioning of a society to a dominant type of procedures. Recent studies have pointed to other technological apparatuses and their interplay with ideology; these studies which have also underlined the dominant character of these apparatuses, though from different points of view—thus, for example, the work of Serge Moscovici, especially on urban organization,[11] or that of Pierre Legendre, on the apparatus of medieval law.[12] These apparatuses seem to prevail over a more or less lengthy period of time, then fall back into the stratified mass of procedures, while others replace them in the role of "informing" a system.

A society is thus composed of certain foregrounded practices organizing its normative institutions *and* of innumerable other practices that remain "minor," always there but not organizing discourses and preserving the beginnings or remains of different (institutional, scientific) hypotheses for that society or for others. It is in this multifarious and silent "reserve" of procedures that we should look for "consumer" practices having the double characteristic, pointed out by Foucault, of being able to organize both spaces and languages, whether on a minute or a vast scale.

2. The final formation (the contemporary technologies of observation and discipline) which serves as the point of departure for the regressive history practiced by Foucault explains the impressive coherence of the practices he selects and examines. But can it be assumed that the ensemble of procedures exhibits the same coherence? A priori, no. The exceptional, indeed cancerous, development of panoptic procedures seems to be indissociable from the historical role to which they have been assigned, that of being a weapon to be used in combatting and controlling heterogeneous practices. The coherence in question is the result of a particular success, and will not be characteristic of all technological practices. Beneath what one might call the "monotheistic" privilege that panoptic apparatuses have won for themselves, a *"polytheism"* of *scattered practices* survives, dominated but not erased by the triumphal success of one of their number.

3. What is the status of a particular apparatus when it is transformed into the organizing principle of a technology of power? What effect does foregrounding have on it? What new relationships within the dispersed ensemble of procedures are established when one of them is institutionalized as a penitentiary-scientific system? The apparatus thus privileged might well lose the effectiveness that it owed, according to Foucault, to its miniscule and silent technical advances. By leaving the obscure stratum in which Foucault locates the determining mechanisms of a society, it would be in the position of institutions slowly "colonized" by still silent procedures. Perhaps in fact (this is, at least, one of the hypotheses of this essay), the system of discipline and control which took shape in the nineteenth century on the basis of earlier procedures, is today itself "vampirized" by other procedures.

4. Can one go even further? Is not the very fact that, as a result of their expansion, the apparatuses of control become an object of clarification and thus part of the language of the Enlightenment, proof that they ceased to determine discursive institutions? When the discourse can deal with some effects of the organizing apparatuses that means that they no longer play this determining role. One must ask what type of apparatus articulates the discourse in such a way that the discourse cannot make it its object. Unless it is the case that one discourse (that of *Discipline and Punish*), by analyzing the practices on which it itself depends, overcomes in this way the division, posited by Foucault, between "ideologies" and "procedures."

These questions, to which one could at the moment give only premature answers, indicate at least the transformations that Foucault has introduced into his analysis of procedures and the perspectives that have opened up since his study. By showing, in one case, the heterogeneity and equivocal relations of apparatuses and ideologies, he constituted as a treatable historical object this zone in which technological procedures have specific *effects of power*, obey their own *logical modes of functioning*, and can produce a fundamental *diversion* within the institutions of order and knowledge. It remains to be asked how we should consider other, equally infinitesimal, procedures, which have not been "privileged" by history but are nevertheless active in innumerable ways in the openings of established technological networks. This is particularly the case of procedures that do not enjoy the precondition, associated with all those studied by Foucault, of having *their own place* [*un lieu propre*] on which the panoptic machinery can operate. These techniques, which are also operational, but initially deprived of what gives the others their force, are the "tactics" which I have suggested might furnish a formal index of the ordinary practices of consumption.

NOTES

1. Fernand Deligny, *Les vagabonds efficaces* (Paris: Maspero, 1970), uses this word to describe the trajectories of young autistic people with whom he lives, writings that move through forests, wanderings that can no longer make a path through the space of language.

2. According to John von Neumann and Oskar Morgenstern, *Theory of Games and Economic Behaviour* (New York: John Wiley, 1964), "there is only strategy when the other's strategy is included."

3. "Strategy is the science of military movements outside of the enemy's field of vision; tactics, within it" (von Bülow).

4. Karl von Clausewitz, *Vom Kriege*; see *De la guerre* (Paris: Minuit, 1955), 212–213; *On War*, trans. Michael Howard and Peter Paret (Princeton: Princeton University Press, 1976). This analysis can be found moreover in many other theoreticians, ever since Machiavelli. See Yves Delahaye, "Simulation et dissimulation," in *La Ruse (Cause Commune 1977/1)* (Paris: UGE 10/18, 1977).

5. Clausewitz, *De la guerre*, 212.

6. Sigmund Freud, *Jokes and Their Relation to the Unconscious*, trans. James Strachey (London: The Hogarth Press and the Institute of Psychoanalysis, 1960).

7. Aristotle, *Rhetoric*, II, 24, 1402a: "by making the worse argument seem the better"; trans. William Rhys Roberts (New York: The Modern Library, 1954). The same "discovery" is attributed to Tisias by Plato (Phaedrus, 273b–c). See also W. K. C. Guthrie, *The Sophists* (Cambridge: Cambridge University Press, 1971), 178–179. On Corax's *technè* mentioned by Aristotle in relation to the "loci of apparent enthymemes," see Chaïm Perelman and Lucie Olbrechts-Tyteca, *Traité de l'argumentation* (Bruxelles: Université Libre, 1970), 607–609.

8. Michel Foucault, *Surveiller et punir* (Paris: Gallimard, 1975); *Discipline and Punish*, trans. Alan Sheridan (New York: Pantheon, 1977). On Foucault's earlier work, see Michel de Certeau, *L'Absent de l'histoire* (Paris: Marne, 1974), 115–132.

9. Foucault, *Surveiller et punir*, 28, 96–102, 106–116, 143–151, 159–161, 185, 189–194, 211–217, 238–251, 274–275, 276, etc.: a series of theoretical "tableaux" marks the development of the book; it isolates an historical object and invents a discourse adequate to it.

10. See especially Gilles Deleuze, "Écrivain, non: un nouveau cartographe," *Critique*, no. 343 (December 1975): 1207–1227.

11. Serge Moscovici, *Essai sur l'histoire humaine de la nature* (Paris: Flammarion, 1968).

12. Pierre Legendre, *L'Amour du censeur. Essai sur l'ordre dogmatique* (Paris: Seuil, 1974).

BIBLIOGRAPHY

Aristotle. *Rhetoric*. Translated by William Rhys Roberts. New York: The Modern Library, 1954.

Certeau, Michel de. *L'Absent de l'histoire*. Paris: Marne, 1974.

Clausewitz, Karl von. *De la guerre*. Paris: Minuit, 1955. Published in English as *On War*. Translated by Michael Howard and Peter Paret. Princeton: Princeton University Press, 1976.

Delahaye, Yves. "Simulation et dissimulation." In *La Ruse (Cause Commune 1977/1)*, 55–74. Paris: UGE 10/18, 1977.

Deleuze, Gilles. "Écrivain, non: un nouveau cartographe." *Critique*, no. 343 (December 1975): 1207–1227.

Deligny, Fernand. *Les vagabonds efficaces*. Paris: Maspero, 1970.

Foucault, Michel. *Surveiller et punir*. Paris: Gallimard, 1975. Published in English as *Discipline and Punish*. Translated by Alan Sheridan. New York: Pantheon, 1977.

Freud, Sigmund. *Jokes and their Relation to the Unconscious*. Translated by James Strachey. London: The Hogarth Press and the Institute of Psychoanalysis, 1960.

Guthrie, W. K. C. *The Sophists*. Cambridge: Cambridge University Press, 1971.

Legendre, Pierre. *L'Amour du censeur. Essai sur l'ordre dogmatique*. Paris: Seuil, 1974.

Moscovici, Serge. *Essai sur l'histoire humaine de la nature*. Paris: Flammarion, 1968.

Neumann, John von, and Oskar Morgenstern, *Theory of Games and Economic Behaviour*. New York: John Wiley, 1964.

Perelman, Chaïm, and Lucie Olbrechts-Tyteca. *Traité de l'argumentation*. Bruxelles: Université Libre, 1970.

33

FROM BIOPOWER TO BIOPOLITICS

Maurizio Lazzarato

1. Michel Foucault, through the concept of biopolitics, was already pointing out in the seventies what, nowadays, is well on its way to being obvious: "life" and "living being" [*le vivant*] are at the heart of new political battles and new economic strategies. He also demonstrated that the "introduction of life into history" corresponds with the rise of capitalism. In effect, from the 18th Century onwards the dispositifs of power and knowledge begin to take into account the "processes of life" and the possibility of controlling and modifying them. "Western man gradually learns what it means to be a living species in a living world, to have a body, conditions of existence, probabilities of life, an individual and collective welfare, forces that could be modified . . ."[1] That life and living being, that the species and its productive requirements have moved to the heart of political struggle is something that is radically new in human history. "For millennia, man remained what he was for Aristotle: a living animal with the additional capacity for a political existence; modern man is an animal whose politics places his existence as a living being in question."[2]

The patenting of the human genome and the development of artificial intelligence; biotechnology and the harnessing of life's forces for work, trace a new cartography of biopowers. These strategies put in question the forms of life itself. The works of Michel Foucault, however, focus only indirectly upon the description of these new biopowers. If power seizes life as the object of its exercise then Foucault is interested in determining what there is in life that resists, and that, in resisting this power, creates forms of subjectification and forms of life that escape its control.

It seems to me that the common theme traversing all of Foucault's thought is the attempt to specify the requirements of a new "process of political creativity that the great political institutions and parties confiscated after the 19th Century." In effect, Foucault interprets the introduction of "life into history" constructively because it presents the opportunity to propose a new ontology, one that begins with the body and its potential, that regards the "political subject as an ethical one" against the prevailing tradition of Western thought which understands it as a "subject of law."

Rather than starting from a theory of obedience and its legitimating forms, its dispositifs and practices, Foucault interrogates power beginning with the "freedom" and the "capacity for transformation" that every "exercise of power" implies. The new ontology sanctioned by the introduction of "life into history" enables Foucault to "defend the subject's freedom" to establish relationships with himself and with others, relationships that are, for him, the very stuff [matière] of ethics. Habermas and the philosophers of the Constitutional State are not wrong in taking Foucault's thought as their privileged target because it represents a radical alternative to a transcendental ethics of communication and the rights of man.

2. Giorgio Agamben, recently, in a book inscribed explicitly within the research being undertaken on the concept of biopolitics, insisted that the theoretical and political distinction established in antiquity between *zoé* and *bios*, between natural life and political life, between man as a living being [simple vivant] whose sphere of influence is in the home and man as a political subject whose sphere of influence is in the polis, is "now nearly unknown to us." The introduction of the *zoé* into the sphere of the polis is, for both Agamben and Foucault, the decisive event of modernity; it marks a radical transformation of the political and philosophical categories of classical thought. But is this impossibility of distinguishing between *zoé* and *bios*, between man as a living being and man as a political subject, the product of the action of sovereign power or the result of the action of new forces over which power has "no control?" Agamben's response is very ambiguous and it oscillates continuously between these two alternatives. Foucault's response is entirely different: biopolitics is the form of government taken by a new dynamic of forces that, in conjunction, express power relations that the classical world could not have known.

Foucault described this dynamic, in keeping with the progress of his research, as the emergence of a multiple and heterogeneous power of resistance and creation that calls every organization that is transcendental, and every regulatory mechanism that is extraneous, to its constitution radically into question. The birth of biopower and the redefinition of the problem of sovereignty are only comprehensible to us on this basis. Foucault's entire work leads toward this conclusion even if he did not coherently explain the dynamic of this power, founded on the "freedom" of "subjects" and their capacity to act upon the "conduct of others," until the end of his life.

Foucault analyzed the introduction of "life into history" through the development of political economy. He demonstrated how the techniques of power changed at the precise moment that economy (strictly speaking, the government of the family) and politics (strictly speaking, the government of the polis) became imbricated with one another. The new biopolitical dispositifs are born once we begin to ask ourselves, "What is the correct manner of managing individuals, goods and wealth within the family (which a good father is expected to do in relation to his wife, children and servants) and of making the family fortunes prosper—how are we to introduce this meticulous attention of the father towards his family into the management of the State?"[3]

Why should we look for the "arcana imperii" of modernity within political economy? Biopolitics, understood as a government-population political economy relationship, refers to a dynamic of forces that establishes a new relationship between ontology and politics. The political economy that Foucault talks about is neither the political economy of capital and work of classical economists, nor the Marxist economic critique of "living labor." It is a political economy of forces that is very close yet very distant from either of these points of view. It is very close to Marx's viewpoint because the problem of how to coordinate and command the relationships between men, insofar as they are living beings, and those of men with "things" keeping the aim of extracting a "surplus of power" in mind, is not simply an economic problem but an ontological one. It is very distant because Foucault faulted Marx and political economy with reducing the relations between forces to relations between capital and labor, with making these binary and symmetric relations the source of all social dynamics and every power relation. The political economy that Foucault talks about, on the contrary, governs "the whole of a complex material field where not only are natural resources, the products of labor, their circulation and the scope of commerce engaged, but where the management of towns and routes, the conditions of life (habitat, diet, etc.), the number of inhabitants, their life span, their ability and fitness for work also come into play."[4]

Political economy, as a syntagm of biopolitics, encompasses power dispositifs that amplify the whole range of relations between the forces that extend throughout the social body rather than, as in classical political economy and its critique, the relationship between capital and labor exclusively.

Foucault needs a new political theory and a new ontology to describe the new power relations expressed in the political economy of forces. In effect, biopolitics are "grafted" and "anchored" upon a multiplicity of disciplinary [*de commandement et d'obéissance*] relations between forces, those which power "coordinates, institutionalizes, stratifies and targets," but that are not purely and simply projected upon individuals. The fundamental political problem of modernity is not that of a single source of sovereign power, but that of a multitude of forces that act and react amongst each other according to relations of command and obedience. The relations between man and woman, master and student, doctor and patient, employer and worker, that Foucault uses to illustrate the dynamics of the social body are relations between forces that always involve a power relation. If power, in keeping with this description, is constituted from below, then we need an ascending analysis of the constitution of power dispositifs, one that begins with infinitesimal mechanisms that are subsequently "invested, colonized, utilized, involuted, transformed and institutionalized by ever more general mechanisms, and by forms of global domination."

"Accordingly, we need to see things not in terms of the replacement of a society of sovereignty by a disciplinary society and the subsequent replacement of a disciplinary society by a society of government; in reality one has a triangle, sovereignty-discipline-government, which has the population as its primary target."[5] It would be better to try to think through the articulation and distribution of the different dispositifs that are present simultaneously in the linkage of government, population and political economy.

Consequently, biopolitics is the strategic coordination of these power relations in order to extract a surplus of power from living beings. Biopolitics is a strategic relation; it is not the pure and simple capacity to legislate or legitimize sovereignty. According to Foucault the biopolitical functions of "coordination and determination" concede that biopower, from the moment it begins to operate in this particular manner, is not the true source of power. Biopower coordinates and targets a power that does not properly belong to it, that comes from the "outside." Biopower is always born of something other than itself.

3. Historically, the socialization of the forces that political economy attempts to govern calls sovereign power into crisis; these forces compel the biopolitical technologies of government into an "immanence," one that grows increasingly extensive, with "society." This socialization always forces power to unfold in dispositifs that are both "complementary" and "incompatible," that express an "immanent transcendence in

our actuality," that is to say, an integration of biopower and sovereign power. In effect, the emergence of the interdependent [solidaire] art of government-population-wealth series radically displaces the problem of sovereignty. Foucault does not neglect the analysis of sovereignty, he merely asserts that the grounding force will not be found on the side of power, since power is "blind and weak"[6] but on the side of the forces that constitute the "social body" or "society." Sovereign power is blind and weak but that does not signify, by any means, that it lacks efficacy: its impotence is ontological. We do a disservice to Foucault's thought when we describe its course through the analysis of power relations as a simple succession and substitution of different dispositifs, because the biopolitical dispositif does not replace sovereignty, it displaces its function and renders the "problem of its foundation even more acute."

Can we then understand the development of biopolitics as the necessity to assure an immanent and strategic coordination of forces, rather than as the organization of a unilateral power relation? What we need to emphasize is the difference of the principles and the dynamics that regulate the socialization of forces, sovereign power and biopower. The relations between the latter two are only comprehensible on the basis of the multiple and heterogeneous action of forces. Without the introduction of the "freedom" and the resistance of forces the dispositifs of modern power remain incomprehensible, and their intelligibility will be inexorably reduced to the logic of political science. Foucault explains the issue in the following manner: "So resistance comes first, and resistance remains superior to the other forces of the process; power relations are obliged to change with the resistance. So I think that resistance is the main word, the keyword, in this dynamic."[7]

4. In the seventies Foucault essentially formulates this new conception of power by means of the models of battle and war. In this way of understanding power and social relations there really is a "freedom" (an autonomy and an independence) of the forces in play, but it is rather a freedom that is constituted as the "power to deprive others." In effect, in war there are the strong and the weak, the clever and the naive, the victorious and the vanquished, and they are all acting "subjects," they are "free" even if this freedom only consists of the appropriation, the conquest and the submission of other forces.

Foucault, who made this model of power, a "warlike clash of forces," work against the philosophico-juridical tradition of contract and sovereignty, is firmly entrenched within a paradigm where the articulation of the concepts of the power, difference and freedom of forces already serves to explain social relations. Yet this "philosophy" of difference risks understanding all the relationships between men, regardless of the actual nature of these relationships, as relations of domination. Foucault's thought will be forced to confront this impasse. Nonetheless, bodies are not always trapped in the dispositifs of power. Power is not a unilateral relation, a totalitarian domination over individuals, such as the one exercised by the dispositif of the Panopticon,[8] but a strategic relation. Every force in society exercises power and that power passes through the body, not because power is "omnipotent and omniscient" but because every force is a power of the body. Power comes from below; the forces that constitute it are multiple and heterogeneous. What we call power is an integration, a coordination and determination of the relations between a multiplicity of forces. How are we to liberate this new conception of power, one based upon the potential, difference and autonomy of forces, from the model of "universal domination?" How are we to call forth a "freedom" and a force that is not merely one of domination and resistance?

In response to this questioning Foucault moved from the model of war to that of "government." The thematic of government was already present in Foucault's reflection since it illustrated the biopolitical exercise of power. The displacement that Foucault enacts, sometime in the eighties, consists in considering the "art of governance" not merely as a strategy of power, even if it is biopolitical power, but as the action of subjects upon others and upon themselves. He searched amongst the ancients for the answer to this question: how do subjects become active, how is the government of the self and others open to subjectifications that are independent of the biopolitical art of government? Consequently, the "government of souls" is always at stake in political struggle and cannot be formulated, exclusively, as biopower's modality of action.

The passage into ethics is an internal necessity to the foucauldian analysis of power. Gilles Deleuze is right in pointing out that there is a single Foucault, not two; the Foucault of the analysis of power and the Foucault of the problematic of the subject. A persistent questioning ranges the whole of Foucault's work: how are we to seize these infinitesimal, diffused and heterogeneous power relations so that they do not always result in phenomena of domination or resistance?[9] How can this new ontology of forces open up to unexpected processes of political constitution and independent processes of subjectification?

5. In the eighties, after a long detour through ethics, Foucault finally returned to his concept of "power." In his last interviews Foucault criticized himself because he thought that "like many others, he had not been clear enough and had not used the proper terms to speak of power." He saw his work retrospectively as an analysis and

a history of the different modalities through which human beings are constituted as subjects in Western culture, rather than as an analysis of the transformations of the dispositifs of power. "Therefore it is not power, but the subject, that constitutes the general theme of my investigations."[10] The analysis of power dispositifs should then begin, without any ambiguity, with the dynamic of forces and the "freedom" of subjects, and not with the dynamics of institutions, even if they are biopolitical institutions, because if one starts to pose the question of power starting from the institution one will inevitably end up with a theory of the "subject of law." In this last and definitive theory of "power" Foucault distinguishes three different concepts which are usually confused within a single category: strategic relations, techniques of government and states of domination.

He asserts that, above all, it is necessary to speak of power relations rather than power alone, because the emphasis should fall upon the relation itself rather than on its terms, the latter are not causes but mere effects. His characterization of strategic relations as a play of "infinitesimal, mobile, reversible and unstable" power is already in place in the seventies. The new modality that expresses the exercise of power at the interior of relationships, amorous, teacher and student relations, husband and wife, children and parents, etc., is already found in the Nietzschean concept of "forces" that was the precursor to Foucault's conception of "strategic relations." This modality, defined as an "action upon an action," spreads through the will to "control the conduct of others."

"It seems to me that we must distinguish between power relations understood as strategic games between liberties—in which some try to control the conduct of others, who in turn try to avoid allowing their conduct be controlled or try to control the conduct of others—and the states of domination that people ordinarily call power."[11] Power is defined, from this perspective, as the capacity to structure the field of action of the other, to intervene in the domain of the other's possible actions. This new conception of power shows what was implicit in the model of the battle and war, but that still had not been coherently explained, namely, that it is necessary to presuppose the virtual "freedom" of the forces engaged to understand the exercise of power. Power is a mode of action upon "acting subjects," upon "free subjects, insofar as they are free."

"A power relationship, on the other hand, can only be articulated on the basis of two elements that are indispensable if it is really to be a power relation; that the 'other' (the one over whom power is exercised) must be recognized and maintained to the very end as a subject who acts; and that, faced with a relationship of power, a whole field of responses, reactions, effects and possible inventions may open up."[12]

The only way that subjects can be said to be free, in keeping with the stipulations of this model, is if they "always have the possibility to change the situation, if this possibility always exists." This modality of the exercise of power allows Foucault to respond to the critiques addressed to him ever since he initiated his work on power: "So what I've said does not mean that we are always trapped, but that we are always free—well, anyway, that there is always the possibility of changing."[13]

"States of domination," on the contrary, are characterized by the institutional stabilization of strategic relations, by the fact that the mobility, the potential reversibility and instability of power relations, of "actions upon actions," is limited. The asymmetric relations within every social relation crystallize and lose the freedom, the "fluidity" and the "reversibility" of strategic relations. Foucault places "governmental technologies," that is to say, the set of practices that "constitute, define, organize and instrumentalize the strategies that individuals in their freedom can use in dealing with each other"[14] between strategic relations and states of domination.

For Foucault, Governmental technologies play a central role in power relations, because it is through these technologies that the opening and closing of strategic games is possible; through their exercise strategic relations become either crystallized and fixed in asymmetric institutionalized relations (states of domination), or they open up to the creation of subjectivities that escape biopolitical power in fluid and reversible relations. The ethico-political struggle takes on its full meaning at the frontier between "strategic relations" and "states of domination," on the terrain of "governmental technologies." Ethical action, then, is concentrated upon the crux of the relation between strategic relations and governmental technologies, and it has two principal goals: (1) to permit, by providing rules and techniques to manage the relationships established with the self and with others, the interplay of strategic relations with the minimum possible domination,[15] (2) to augment their freedom, their mobility and reversibility in the exercise of power because these are the prerequisites of resistance and creation.

6. The determination of the relationship between resistance and creation is the last limit that Foucault's thought attempted to breach. The forces that resist and create are to be found in strategic relations and in the will of subjects who are virtually free to "control the conduct of others." Power, the condensation of strategic relations into relations of domination, the contraction of the spaces of freedom by the desire to control the conduct of others, always meets with resistance; this resistance should be sought out in the strategic dynamic. Consequently, life and living being become a "matter" of ethics through the dynamic that simultaneously resists power and creates

new forms of life. In an interview in 1984, a year before his death, Foucault was asked about the definition of the relation between resistance and creation:

> Resistance was conceptualized only in terms of negation. Nevertheless, as you see it, resistance is not solely a negation but a creative process. To create and recreate, to transform the situation, to participate actively in the process, that is to resist.
>
> Yes, that is the way I would put it. To say no is the minimum form of resistance. But naturally, at times that is very important. You have to say no as a decisive form of resistance.[16]

And in the same interview, destined to appear in Body Politic, Foucault asserts that minorities (homosexuals), to whom the relation between resistance and creation is a matter of political survival, should not only defend themselves and resist, but should also affirm themselves, create new forms of life, create a culture: "They should affirm themselves; not merely affirm themselves in their identity, but affirm themselves insofar as they are a creative force."[17]

The relationships with ourselves, the relationships that we should entertain with ourselves, which led Foucault to this new definition of power are not relationships of identity; "Rather they should be relationships of differentiation, of creation and innovation."[18] Foucault's work ought to be continued upon this fractured line between resistance and creation. Foucault's itinerary allows us to conceive the reversal of biopower into biopolitics, the "art of governance" into the production and government of new forms of life. To establish a conceptual and political distinction between biopower and biopolitics is to move in step with Foucault's thinking.

NOTES

1. Michel Foucault, "Right of Death and Power over Life," in *The Foucault Reader*, ed. Paul Rabinow (New York: Pantheon Books, 1984), 264.

2. Ibid., 265.

3. Michel Foucault, "Governmentality," in Graham Burchell, Colin Gordon and Peter Miller, eds., *The Foucault Effect: Studies in Governmentality* (Chicago: The University of Chicago Press, 1991), 92.

4. See Michel Foucault, "The Politics of Health in the 18th Century," in *Power/Knowledge: Selected Interviews and Other Writings*, ed. Colin Gordon (New York, Pantheon Books, 1980).

5. Foucault, "Governmentality," 102.

6. "Power is not omnipotent or omniscient—quite the contrary! If power relationships have produced forms of investigation, of analysis, of models of knowledge, etc., it is precisely not because power was omniscient, but because it was blind ... If it is true that so many power relationships have been developed, so many systems of control, so many forms of surveillance, it is precisely because power was always impotent." Michel Foucault, "Clarifications on the Question

of Power," in *Foucault Live: Collected Interviews, 1961–1984*, ed. Sylvain Lotringer (New York: Semiotext(e), 1996), 625.

7. Michel Foucault, "Sex, Power and the Politics of Identity," in *Essential Works of Foucault: Ethics, Subjectivity, Truth*, vol. 1, ed. Paul Rabinow (New York: New Press, 1997), 167.

8. Foucault, responding to "Marxist" critiques launched against him by the actual mayor of Venice, Massimo Cacciari, explained that his conception of power relations could not be merely reduced to such a figure.

9. See Gilles Deleuze, *Foucault*, trans. Sean Hand (Minneapolis: University of Minnesota Press, 1986).

10. Michel Foucault, "Two Lectures," in *Power/Knowledge*.

11. Michel Foucault, "The Ethics of the Concern for Self as a Practice of Freedom," in *Essential Works of Foucault I*, 299.

12. See Michel Foucault, "The Subject and Power," in *Essential Works of Foucault: Power*, vol. 3, ed. James D. Faubion (New York: New Press, 2000). The relation between the master and his slave is a power relation when flight is a possibility for the latter, otherwise it is simply a matter of the exercise of physical force.

13. Foucault, "Sex, Power and the Politics of Identity," 167.

14. Ibid., 300.

15. In the last part of his life Foucault constantly faced the problem of strategic relations: how is one to render them symmetrical? He only begins to tackle this thematic through the theme of "friendship." Gabriel Tarde, an author whose thought I had, previously, confronted with Foucault's, emphasizes the need, beginning from the same foucauldian "strategic relations," to base their dynamic upon sympathy and not merely on asymmetry. "A prominent sociologist recently defined social relations, in a way that is so narrow and far removed from the truth, by claiming that the principal characteristic of social acts is that they are imposed from the outside, by obligation. To make this claim is to recognize as social relations only those between the master and the slave, between the professor and the student or between the parents and their children, without any regard for the fact that free relations between equals exist. One has to have one's eyes shut not to see that, even in the schools, the education that the students acquire on their own, by imitating each other, by breathing in, so to speak, their examples or even those of their professors, the education that they internalize, has more importance than the one they receive or are forced to bear." See Gabriel Tarde, *La Logique Sociale* (Paris: Institut Synthelabo, 1999), 62.

16. Foucault, "Sex, Power and the Politics of Identity," 168.

17. Ibid., 164.

18. Ibid., 166.

BIBLIOGRAPHY

Deleuze, Gilles. *Foucault*. Translated by Sean Hand. Minneapolis: University of Minnesota Press, 1986.

Foucault, Michel. *Power/Knowledge: Selected Interviews and Other Writings*. Edited by Colin Gordon. New York: Pantheon Books, 1980.

Foucault, Michel. "The Politics of Health in the 18th Century." In *Power/Knowledge: Selected Interviews and Other Writings*. Edited by Colin Gordon, 166–182. New York: Pantheon Books, 1980.

Foucault, Michel. "Two Lectures." In *Power/Knowledge: Selected Interviews and Other Writings*. Edited by Colin Gordon, 78–108. New York: Pantheon Books, 1980.

Foucault, Michel. "Right of Death and Power over Life." In *The Foucault Reader*. Edited by Paul Rabinow, 258–272. New York: Pantheon Books, 1984.

Foucault, Michel. "Governmentality." In *The Foucault Effect: Studies in Governmentality*. Edited by Graham Burchell, Colin Gordon, and Peter Miller, 87–104. Chicago: University of Chicago Press, 1991.

Foucault, Michel. "Clarifications on the Question of Power." In *Foucault Live: Collected Interviews, 1961–1984*. Edited by Sylvain Lotringer, 255–263. New York: Semiotext(e), 1996.

Foucault, Michel. "Sex, Power and the Politics of Identity." In *Essential Works of Foucault: Ethics, Subjectivity, Truth*, vol. 1. Edited by Paul Rabinow, 163–172. New York: New Press, 1997.

Foucault, Michel. "The Ethics of the Concern for Self as a Practice of Freedom." In *Essential Works of Foucault: Ethics, Subjectivity, Truth*, vol. 1. Edited by Paul Rabinow, 281–302. New York: New Press, 1997.

Foucault, Michel. "The Subject and Power." In *Essential Works of Foucault: Power*, vol. 3. Edited by James D. Faubion, 326–348. New York: New Press, 2000.

Tarde, Gabriel. *La logique sociale*. Paris: Institut Synthelabo, 1999.

34

"A CRITICAL METAPHYSICS COULD EMERGE AS A SCIENCE OF APPARATUSES..."

Tiqqun

The first philosophies provide power with its formal structures. More specifically, "metaphysics" designates that apparatus wherein action requires a principle to which words, things, and deeds can be related. In the age of the Turning, when presence as ultimate identity becomes presence as irreducible difference, action appears without principle.
—Reiner Schürmann, *What is to be done with the end of metaphysics?*

[...]

In the age of Bloom, the crisis of presence becomes chronic and objectified through an immense accumulation of *apparatuses* [*dispositifs*]. Each apparatus functions as an ek-sistential prosthesis which THEY administer to Bloom so that he is able to live within the crisis of presence, albeit unwittingly, and to remain there day after day without succumbing: a cell phone, a sedative, a shrink, a lover, a movie—all make for decent crutches provided they can be changed up often enough. Taken singularly, the apparatuses are so many bulwarks erected against the event of things; taken together, they constitute the icy veil that THEY lay over the fact that each thing, in its coming into presence, carries with it a world. The purpose: to maintain at all cost and everywhere the dominant economy by managing authoritatively, omnipresently, the crisis of presence; to establish globally *a present* opposed to the free play of comings into presence. In a word: THE WORLD GROWS HARD.

Since Bloom first penetrated the heart of civilization, THEY have done everything THEY can to isolate him, to neutralize him. Most often and already very biopolitically, he has been treated as a disease—first called *psychasthenia* by Janet, then *schizophrenia*. Today THEY prefer to speak of *depression*. Terms change, of course, but the sleight of hand is always the same: reduce those extreme manifestations of Bloom to purely "subjective problems." By defining him as a disease, THEY individualize him, THEY localize him, THEY isolate him such that *he can no longer be assumed collectively*, commonly.

On closer inspection, biopolitics has never had any other aim but to thwart the formation of worlds, techniques, shared dramatizations, *magic* in which the crisis of presence might be overcome, appropriated, might become a center of energy, a war machine. The rupture in the transmission of experience, the rupture in historical tradition exists, is vehemently maintained, in order to ensure that Bloom is always left—entirely driven back onto "himself," onto his own solitary derision—to his unbearable mythical "freedom." *Biopolitics holds a monopoly over remedies to presence in crisis, which it is always ready to defend with the most extreme violence.*

A politics that challenges this monopoly takes as its starting point and center of energy the crisis of presence, Bloom. We call this politics *ecstatic*. Its aim is not to rescue abstractly—through successive re/presentations—human presence from dissolution, but instead to create participable magic, techniques for inhabiting not a territory but *a world*. And this creation, this play between different economies of presence, between different forms-of-life, entails the subversion and the *liquidation* of all apparatuses.

Those who, as a final reprieve from their passivity, insist on calling for a theory of the subject must understand that in the age of Bloom *a theory of the subject is now only possible as a theory of apparatuses.*

For a long time I believed that what distinguished theory from, say, literature, was its impatience to transmit content, its special capacity to *make* itself understood. And that effectively defines theory, theory as the unique form of writing *that is not a practice*. Thus it is that the infinite has its origin in theory, which can say everything without ever saying anything at all, in the end, of any consequence—to bodies, that is. One will see clearly enough that our texts are neither theory, nor its negation, but simply *something else*.

What is the perfect apparatus, the model-apparatus that would eliminate all misunderstandings with regard to the very notion of apparatus? The perfect apparatus, it seems to me, is the HIGHWAY [*l'AUTOROUTE*]. In it *maximum circulation coincides with maximum control*. Nothing moves that isn't both incontestably "free" and strictly classified, identified, individuated in exhaustive files of digitized registrations. A network endowed with its own fueling stations, its own police, its autonomous, neutral, empty, and abstract spaces, the highway system perfectly represents the territory, as if laid out in bands over the land, a heterotopia, the cybernetic heterotopia. Everything has been carefully parameterized so that *nothing happens*, ever. The undifferentiated daily flow is punctuated only by the statistical, foreseen, and foreseeable series of *accidents*, about which THEY keep us all the better informed as we never see them with our own eyes—accidents which are not experienced as events, as *deaths*, but as a passing disruption whose every trace is erased within the hour. In any case, THEY die a lot less on state highways than on the interstates, as the DOT reminds us. And it is hardly as if the flattened animals, noticed only in the slight swerve they induce in passing cars, remind us what it means to LIVE WHERE OTHERS PASS. No atom of the molecularized flow, none of the impervious monads of the apparatus needs us to remind it that it should *get moving*. The highway[1] system was made—with its wide turns, its calculated, signalized uniformity—solely in order to merge all types of behavior into a single one: the non-surprise, sensible and smooth, consistently steered toward a destination, the whole traveled at an average and regular speed. Still, the slight sense of absence, spanning the distance from end to end, as if one could stay in an apparatus only if struck by the prospect of getting out, without ever having really been in it, been *there*. In the end, the pure space of the highway captures the abstraction of all *place* more than of all distance. Nowhere have THEY so perfectly substituted places with *names* through their nominalist *reduction*. Nowhere is separation so mobile, so convincing, and armed with a vocabulary, road signs, less apt to subversion. Thus the highway: the *concrete* utopia of cybernetic Empire. And to think that some have heard of the "information superhighway" without sensing the total police surveillance to come.

The metro, the *metropolitan* network, is another kind of mega-apparatus—in this case, underground. Given that the passion for policing has, since Vichy, never left the RATP,[2] no doubt a certain consciousness along the same lines has pervaded its every level, right down to its foundations. Thus a few years ago, in the corridors of the Parisian metro, we had the privilege of reading a long RATP statement adorned with a regal-looking lion. The title of the statement, written in huge bold type, read: "WHOEVER ORGANIZES THE WORKPLACE CONTROLS IT." Whoever deigned to stop for a second learned of the intransigence with which the local Authority was ready to defend its monopoly over management of the apparatus. Since then, it would seem that the *Weltgeist* has again made progress, this time among its followers in RATP public relations, because every PR campaign is now signed "RATP, *l'esprit libre*." "*L'esprit libre*"—the strange fate of a phrase that has run from Voltaire to ads for new banking services[3] by way of Nietzsche—*having* one's mind free from care [*l'esprit libre*] more than *being* a free thinker [*un esprit libre*]: that is what Bloom in his hunger for Bloomification demands.

To have one's mind free, that is: the apparatus takes over for those who submit to it. There is real comfort in this—the power to forget, until further notice, that one is in the world.

In each apparatus, there is a hidden decision. The Good Cyberneticists from the CNRS[4] spin it this way: "The apparatus can be defined as the realization of an intention through the implementation of planned environments."[5] *Flow* is necessary to the maintenance of the apparatus, because it conceals this decision. "Nothing is more fundamental to the survival of shopping than a steady stream of customers and products," observe, for their part, the assholes of the Harvard Project on the City.[6] But ensuring the durability and management of the molecularized flow, linking together the different apparatuses, demands an equivalency principle, a *dynamic* principle distinct from the norm common to each apparatus. The equivalency principle is merchandise. Merchandise, that is, *money*, which individualizes, separates all the social atoms, and places them alone before their bank accounts like Christians before their God; money, which at the same time allows us to continually enter every apparatus and, with each entry, to record a *trace* of our position, our traffic. Merchandise, that is, *work*, which holds the largest number of bodies within a certain number of standardized apparatuses, forces them to pass through them and to *stay* there, each body, through its curriculum vitae, arranging for its own traceability. For isn't it the case that working no longer means *doing* something so much as *being* something, and first of all being *available*? Merchandise, that is, the *recognition* thanks to which everyone self-manages their submission to the policing of qualities and maintains with other bodies a prestidigitatory distance, sufficiently large to neutralize but not large enough to exclude them from social valorization. Thus guided by merchandise, the flow of Blooms quietly *necessitates* the apparatus that contains it. A whole fossilized world still survives within this architecture; it no longer needs to celebrate sovereign power *since it is itself, now, the sovereign power*: it need only configure space, while the crisis of presence does the rest.

Under Empire, the classical forms of capitalism survive, but as empty forms, as pure conduits serving to maintain apparatuses. Although their persistence shouldn't fool us: they are no longer self-contained, for they have become a function of something else. THE POLITICAL NOW DOMINATES THE ECONOMIC. What is ultimately at stake is no longer the extraction of surplus value, but *Control*. Now the level of surplus value extracted solely indicates the level of Control, which is the local condition of extraction. Capital is no longer but a *means* to generalized Control. And if commodity imperialism still exists, it is above all as an imperialism of apparatuses that it makes itself felt; an imperialism that responds to a single necessity: the TRANSITIVE NORMALIZATION OF EVERY SITUATION.

This entails increasing circulation *between* apparatuses, for circulation provides the best vector for universal traceability and the *order of flows*. Here again our Good Cyberneticists show their flair for a phrase: "In general, the autonomous individual, understood as having his proper intentionality, stands as the central figure of the apparatus.... The individual is no longer positioned, the individual positions himself within the apparatus."[7]

There is nothing mysterious about why Blooms submit so overwhelmingly to apparatuses. Why, on certain days, at the supermarket, I don't steal anything; whether because I am feeling too weak or I am just lazy: not stealing provides a certain comfort. Not stealing means completely disappearing in the apparatus, means conforming to it in order to avoid the violence that underlies it: the violence between a body and the aggregate of employees, surveillance personnel, and, potentially, the police. Stealing compels me to a presence, to an attention, to expose my bodily surface to an extent that, on certain days, it is just too much for me. Stealing compels me to *think my situation*. And sometimes I don't have the strength. So I pay; I pay for sparing myself the very experience of the apparatus in all of its hostile reality. I pay with my *right to absence*.

[...]

A science of apparatuses can only be *local*. It can only consist in the regional, circumstantial, and circumstanced mapping of how one or several apparatuses work. Totalization cannot occur without its cartographers' knowing, for rather than in forced systematicity, its unity lies in the question that determines its progress—the question: "*How does it work?*"

The science of apparatuses competes directly with the imperial monopoly over knowledge-powers. This is why its dissemination and communication, the circulation of its discoveries are essentially *illegal*. In this it should first of all be distinguished from *bricolage*, since the bricoleur accumulates knowledge of apparatuses only in order to improve their design, to turn them into a niche, that is, he accumulates all the knowledge of apparatuses *that is not power*. From the consensus point of view, what we call a science of apparatuses or critical metaphysics is finally nothing other than the science of crime. And here, as elsewhere, no initiation exists that isn't immediately experimentation, practice. ONE IS NEVER INITIATED INTO AN APPARATUS, ONLY INTO HOW IT WORKS. The three stages of this particular science are, successively: crime, opacity, and insurrection. Crime is the period of—necessarily individual—study of how an apparatus works. Opacity is the condition in which knowledge-powers acquired through study are shared, communized, circulated. Under Empire, the zones of opacity in which this communication takes place must by definition be seized and defended. This second stage therefore requires greater coordination. All S.A.C.S. activity is devoted to this opaque phase. The third level is insurrection, the moment when knowledge-powers and cooperation among forms-of-life—with an aim to destroying-enjoying imperial apparatuses—can be carried out freely, in the open air. Given our project, the present text can only serve as the most modest of introductions, passing somewhere between silence and tautology.

One begins to sense the necessity of a science of apparatuses as people, human *bodies*, finally settle into an entirely manufactured world. Few among those who find something wrong with the exorbitant misery that THEY would like to impose have yet really understood what it means to live in an *entirely produced* world. To begin with, it means that even what at first glance has seemed to us "authentic" reveals itself on contact as produced, that is, as possessing its non-production as a useful modality of general production. In terms of both Biopower and Spectacle, Empire consummates—I remember this run-in with a Negrist from *Chimères*,[8] an old hag in a gothic outfit (which wasn't bad), who claimed, as an indisputable gain for feminism and her materialist radicalism, that she hadn't *raised* her two children, but had *produced* them . . . it consummates the metaphysical interpretation of being [*étant*] as either being *produced* or nothing at all, produced, that is, caused to be produced in such a way that its creation and its ostension would be one and the same thing. Being produced always means *at once* being created and being made visible. In Western metaphysics, entering into presence has never been anything but entering into visibility. It is therefore inevitable that Empire, dependent on productive hysteria, should also be dependent on transparential hysteria. The surest way to prevent the free coming into presence of things is to induce it constantly, tyrannically.

Our ally—in this world given over to the most ferocious enframing, abandoned to *apparatuses*, in this world centered on fanatically controlling the visible, which is meant to be control of Being—our ally is none other than Time. *Time* is on our side. The time of our experience; the time that drives and rends our intensities; the time that breaks, wrecks, spoils, destroys, deforms; the time that is an abandon and an abandonment, that is at the very heart of both; the time that condenses and thickens into clusters of *moments* when all unification is defied, ruined, cut short, scratched out on the surface *by bodies themselves*. WE HAVE THE TIME. And whenever we don't have it, we can still give ourselves the time. To give oneself time: that is the condition to every communicable study of apparatuses. To identify the patterns, links, dissonances; each apparatus possesses its own little music, which must be put slightly out of tune, incidentally distorted, pushed to decay, to destruction, to become unhinged. Those who *flow* into the apparatus don't notice the music, their steps stick too close to the rhythm to hear it distinctly. For the latter, another temporality is needed, a specific rhythmicity, so that, although we enter the apparatus, we remain attentive to the *prevailing norm*. That is what the thief, the criminal learns: to unsync internal and external tempos, to split, to layer one's conscience, being at once mobile and static, on the lookout and deceptively distracted. To accept the dissolution of presence in the name of a simultaneous, asynchronous multiplication of its modalities. To turn the imposed schizophrenia of self-control into an offensive conspiratorial instrument. TO BECOME A SORCERER. "[T]o prevent this disintegration, one must go deliberately to the limit of one's own presence through a clearly-defined practice; one must go to the very essence of the outer limits and master it; the 'spirits' must be identified and evoked and one must develop the power to call upon them at will and profit professionally from their activity. These are the steps taken by the sorcerer; he transforms being-in-the-world's critical moments into a courageous and dramatic decision, that of establishing himself in the world. If being-in-the-world is taken as a *given*, it runs the risk of being dissolved: it has not yet been given. The magician, through the establishment of his vocation and successful initiation, *undoes* this presumed given and *reforms* it through a second birth; he goes to the limits of his presence in order to reform himself into a new and clearly-defined entity. The techniques he uses to increase the instability of presence, the trance itself and other related states, are the expressions of this being-there that disintegrates so that it may be reformed, the being that goes to the very end of its confines in order to discover itself as a sustained and guaranteed presence. The mastery that the magician has acquired allows him to penetrate not only his own instability, but also that in other people. The magician knows how to *go beyond himself*, not in the ideal sense, but actually, in the existential sense. The man whose being-there is made a problem and who has the power to establish his own presence, is not just an ordinary presence, but a being-there that makes itself present to others, understands their existential drama and influences its course."[9] Such is the starting point of the communist program.

Crime, contrary to what the Law implies, is never an act, a deed, but a *condition of existence*, a modality of presence, common to all agents of the Imaginary Party. To convince oneself, one need only think of the experience of theft or fraud, the elementary, and among the most routine—NOWADAYS, EVERYONE STEALS—forms of crime. The experience of theft is phenomenologically *other than* the so-called motives said to "push" us to it, and which we ourselves invoke. Theft is only a transgression from the point of view of representation: *it is an operation carried out on presence*, a reappropriation, an *individual* recovery of presence, a recovery of oneself *as a body in space*. The *how* of "theft" has nothing to do with its apparent legal occurrence. The *how* is the *physical* awareness of space and environment, the physical awareness of the *apparatus*, to which theft drives me. It is the extreme attention of the body illicitly on the subway, alert to the slightest sign of ticket inspectors. It is the nearly scientific understanding of the conditions in which I operate required for preparing a crime of some scope. With crime, there is a whole incandescence to the body, a transformation of the body into an ultrasensitive impact surface: that is its genuine experience. When I steal, I split myself into an apparent, unsubstantial, evanescent, absolutely nondescript [*quelconque*] presence and a second, this time whole, intensive, and internal presence in which every detail of the apparatus that surrounds me comes to life—with its cameras, its security guards, the security guards' *gaze*, the sightlines, the other customers, the way the other customers *look*. Theft, crime, fraud are the conditions of solitary existence at war with Bloomification, with Bloomification *through apparatuses*. The insubordination specific to the isolated body, the resolution to leave—even alone, even in a precarious way, through willful engagement—a certain state of stupefaction, half-sleep, self-absence: that is the essence of "life" in apparatuses. Given this, given this *necessary* experience, the question is how to move from there to conspiracy, to an actual circulation of illegal knowledge, an actual circulation of criminal science. It is the move to collective action that S.A.C.S. is here to facilitate.

[. . .]

We must learn to keep ourselves out of sight, to pass unnoticed into the gray band of each apparatus, to *camouflage* ourselves behind its major premise. Even if our first instinct is to oppose a proclivity for the abnormal with the desire for conformity, we have to develop the art of becoming perfectly anonymous, of offering the appearance of pure conformity. We have to develop the pure art of the surface *in order to conduct our operations*. This means, for example, that we must drop the pseudo-transgression of no less pseudo-social conventions, stop opting for revolutionary "sincerity," "truth," and "scandal," for the sake of a tyrannical politeness through which to keep the apparatus and its possessed at bay. *Calling for* transgression, monstrosity, abnormality is the most insidious trap that apparatuses set. Wanting to be—that is, wanting to be unique—within an apparatus is our *principal weakness*. Because of it we remain held, entangled, by the apparatus. Conversely, the desire *to be controlled*, so frequent among our contemporaries, primarily represents the latter's *desire to be*. For us, this same desire would instead be the desire to be mad, or monstrous, or criminal. But this is the very desire through which THEY control and neutralize us. Devereux has shown that every culture holds a *model negation*, a marked-out exit, for those who want to escape, an outlet that allows the culture to harness the driving force behind every transgression into a higher-order stabilization. Among the Malay, this is called *amok*, in the West, schizophrenia. The Malay is "preconditioned—perhaps unwittingly but certainly quite automatically—by Malay culture to react to almost any violent inner or outer stress by running *amok*. In the same sense, Occidental man of today is conditioned by his own culture to react to any state of stress by schizophrenia-like behavior. . . . [I]n our society, being schizophrenic is the 'proper' way of being 'mad.'"[10]

RULE NO. 1 Every apparatus produces singularity in the form of monstrosity. This is how the apparatus reinforces itself.

RULE NO. 2 One never breaks free of an apparatus by engaging with its minor premise.

RULE NO. 3 When THEY predicate you, subjectivate you, summon you, never react and above all never deny anything. For the counter-subjectivation THEY would then force from you forms the prison from which you will *always* have the hardest time escaping.

RULE NO. 4 Greater freedom does not lie in the absence of a predicate, in anonymity *by default*. Greater freedom results instead from the *saturation* of predicates, from their anarchical accumulation. Overpredication automatically cancels itself out in permanent unpredictability. "When we no longer have any secrets, we no longer have anything to hide. It is we who have become a secret, it is we who are hidden."[11]

RULE NO. 5 Counter-attack is never a response, but the establishment of a new order.

NOTES

1. The French word is *autoroute*, whose translation as "highway" obviously does not capture the *auto-*, "automobile" and "self," "self-same," etc., of the French highway.

2. The ratp (Régie autonome des transports parisiens) is the public authority operating the Parisian public transportation network.

3. *Esprit Libre* refers to the motto of the French bank BNP Parisbas's campaign to market its services to 18–24 year-olds.

4. Centre National de la Recherche Scientifique (National Center for Scientific Research).

5. Hugues Peeters and Philippe Charlier, "Contributions à une théorie du dispositif," *Hermès*, no. 25 (1999): 18–19.

6. Harvard Project on the City, "Shopping," in *Mutations* (Bordeaux: Arc en rêve centre d'architecture; Barcelona: ACTAR, 2000), 140.

7. Peeters and Charlier, "Contributions."

8. Review founded by Gilles Deleuze and Félix Guattari in 1987. "Negrist" refers to an adherent of Antonio Negri's brand of Marxist political philosophy.

9. Ernesto De Martino, *The World of Magic*, trans. Paul White (New York: Pyramid Communications, 1972). [—Translation modified.]

10. See Georges Devereux, "Schizophrenia: An Ethnic Psychosis, or Schizophrenia without Tears," in *Basic Problems of Ethnopsychiatry*, trans. Basia Miller Gulati and George Devereux (Chicago: The University of Chicago Press, 1980), 218, 220.

11. Gilles Deleuze and Claire Parnet, *Dialogues*, trans. Hugh Tomlinson and Barbara Habberjam (New York: Columbia University Press, 1987), 46. [—Translation modified.]

BIBLIOGRAPHY

Deleuze, Gilles, and Claire Parnet. *Dialogues*. Translated by Hugh Tomlinson and Barbara Habberjam. New York: Columbia University Press, 1987.

Devereux, Georges. "Schizophrenia: An Ethnic Psychosis, or Schizophrenia without Tears." In *Basic Problems of Ethnopsychiatry*. Translated by Basia Miller Gulati and George Devereux. Chicago: University of Chicago Press, 1980.

Harvard Project on the City. "Shopping." In *Mutations*. Bordeaux: Arc en rêve centre d'architecture; Barcelona: ACTAR, 2000.

Martino, Ernesto De. *The World of Magic*. Translated by Paul White. New York: Pyramid Communications, 1972.

Peeters, Hugues, and Philippe Charlier. "Contributions à une théorie du dispositif." *Hermès*, no. 25 (1999): 15–23.

Schürmann, Reiner. *Heidegger on Being and Acting: From Principles to Anarchy*. Translated by Christine-Marie Gros. Bloomington: Indiana University Press, 1987.

Schürmann, Reiner. *Principe d'anarchie: Heidegger et la question de l'agir*. Paris: Éditions du Seuil, 1982.

35

INDIGENOUS INTERRUPTIONS: MOHAWK NATIONHOOD, CITIZENSHIP AND THE STATE

Audra Simpson

SIGNPOST 1: MEMBERSHIP

On February 1, 2010, twenty-six non-Natives cohabitating with residents and members of Kahnawà:ke were issued eviction notices by the Mohawk Council of Kahnawà:ke (MCK), the council of elected officials that is authorized by the Indian Act, and thus Canada, to govern the community. They were told that they must leave the territory because as non-Indians residing in Kahnawà:ke without any form of recognition from the band council, they were living in contravention to the Kahnawà:ke Membership Law, enacted in 2003 and amended in 2007 and then in 2008.

Now, what kind of law would propose that couples be split up, that governance extend to love itself? What kind of law would seek to regulate the arrangement of families? All state law does this, but this particular one acknowledges the residue of the Indian Act, with its divisive, patrilineal bias, and attempts to correct it by making it unlawful for either a man or a woman to marry out, by being equally (some would say) discriminatory. The 2003 membership law was a gender-neutral, "heterosexed,"[1] discriminatory law that recognized only heterosexual marriages between status Indians, but offered "allowances" for the possibility of non-Native or unrecognized Indian individuals to marry "in" and reside legally on the reservation. The prior law only recognized heterosexual marriages between status Indians and those possessing Mohawk blood.

Here it is helpful to turn to Mark Rifkin's book on the literary and anthropological history of sexuality and colonization,[2] which demonstrates the complicity of ethnology, kinship rules, and literature with actual, settler governance. Essayists, fiction writers, and anthropologists imagined and imaged properties of personhood in their arrangements and representations of Indigenous life into discernible grids of governance and what Denise Ferreira da Silva calls "affectability" in her theory of racial formation.[3] Affectability is the condition that makes some vulnerable to and, by the structuring reach of capital, entwined with racial logics of exclusion that condition inclusion in a Western, white racial order. This process, in Ferreira da Silva's understanding, readies people for particular states of subjecting and being subjected to force and to law. The Kahnawà:ke Membership Law is that process, remade and reformed. It uses the governing impetus of settlement—"recognition"—to regulate, administer, and discipline the subject through a notion of band polity.

Consider here the first three paragraphs of the Preamble to the amended Kahnawà:ke Membership Law (2008):

We are the Kanien'kehà:ka of Kahnawà:ke. We are a community within the Kanien'kehà:ka Nation and the Rotinonhsonnión:we and as such are Indigenous Peoples who possess a fundamental and inherent right of self-determination given to us by the Creator.

As Indigenous Peoples, we have the right to maintain and promote our Kanien'kehà:ka identity including our culture, traditions, language, laws and customs.

As Indigenous Peoples, we have the collective right to determine our own membership. This right is fundamental to our survival.

We recognize that we have been harmed by foreign governments' attempts to undermine our will and ability to survive by dividing our community. We *reject* the imposition of the Indian Act and other foreign laws that have presumed to define the principles upon which the membership of our community will be determined. We *reject* all efforts to assimilate and extinguish our community under the guise of absolute individualism.

By enacting this Law we are fulfilling our responsibility to defend our community and our Nation from external threat, and in doing so are securing for future generations the right to survive and to continue living—proudly—as Kanien'kehà:ka of Kahnawà:ke.[4]

With this passage from the law we can see that this technique of governance is articulating a fear of disappearance through the very means that would disappear this nation: Canadian-authorized governance. This is expressed in the values of individual rights over "collective" rights—the ahistorical and presumed evenhandedness of liberalism to determine and render justice, in part, through presumed shared values of freedom, justice, equality, individualism, even distribution, and free trade. Yet these are the same values that Kahnawà:ke find intrusive and forcible. What is it from their political ethos and history that would make for such a paradoxical position?

Who are these people? Consider this in a descriptive register: "This is a reserve community of Indigenous nationals that belong to a larger pre-contact political Confederacy in what is now understood to be the Northeastern United States and Southeastern Canada." They are known to themselves as Haudenosaunee, or "people of the Longhouse," in reference to their traditional living arrangement of clan-based houses and their governing structure. This political confederacy is what is known in anthropological and everyday understanding as the "Iroquois Confederacy." As a polity, the Mohawks of Kahnawà:ke are comprised of Turtle, Wolf, and Bear clans,[5] determined through matrilineal descent lines. They also then have a membership within a political corpus of the larger Longhouse, which spreads metaphorically across Iroquoia. This is a different descriptive window into the community at hand from that offered earlier, and one more in tune with the sensibilities of anthropologists of an earlier time.

Yet, the content of both descriptive accounts is what they, in part, will not let go of, or forget, or cease to enact: their relatedness to their place, to others, to a particular history, to their ongoing experiences because of this relatedness. These kin and reciprocal relationships extend throughout the fifteen other Iroquois reservations on either side of the border as well as the cities, suburbs, and nonreserve rural areas that Iroquois people move through and dwell within. Because of these spatial arrangements and spatial connections throughout Iroquoia, per settler colonialism's past and present requirements, there are many severed connections that owe their severance to the Indian Act and its required geographic and gendered displacements. Joseph Mitchell's "footloose" Indians have a deeper context than he will allow, or knew of.

As we saw above, membership talk is articulated through an archive of knowledge, identification, and beliefs about what is right, what *should* be done; its design and its execution both portend much for the present and for the future. "Who should be here? How should we do this?" "Is this fair?" are questions that instill an ongoing preoccupation, a set of normative questions that find no easy juridical answers. And yet, membership is simultaneously so simply explained as "this is how I am, to you." This very simple, stop-the-clock mode of identification and claiming of others reaches even beyond recognition into a deeper archive of knowledge, drawing from sociality and genealogical and narrative relatedness. This archive of social and genealogic knowledge operates as an authorizing nexus of identification that also can and sometimes does refuse logics of the state. This is because formal recognition sometimes belongs to those *not* genealogically recognized: those who are non-Indian, married in, and obtained status (white women who married Indian men and now have Indian status) and those who have status and have never been to Kahnawà:ke (these people are few and far between). The truly foreign, those who are somehow outside of the space of social and genealogic reckoning—the indecipherable—may be refused in spite of their formal recognition by the state.

Along with the ideas of "Indigenous" and "nationhood," I use the Hegelian term "recognition" and its inverse, "misrecognition," to tell this story. No matter how deeply Kahnawa'kehró:non and other Indigenous nations understand themselves to be of their own philosophical systems and, simultaneously, no matter how deeply they understand the scene of their objectification as "Indians" or, even more ghastly, as "minoritized peoples," they are rarely seen or then treated in the eye of the settler as that which they are and wish to be recognized as: nationals with sovereign authority over their lives and over their membership and living within their own space, which has been "held for them" in the form of reservations.

Although homelands of a sort, reservations owe their lives to state power; thus, the grounded fields of belonging, recognition, misrecognition, and refusal that I am mapping out are tied up with state power and its primary technique of distributing rights and protections: citizenship.[6] As well as producing affectively structured citizens,[7] the state produces the conditions for what I want to suggest are "distantiations," "disaffiliations," or outright refusals—a willful distancing from state-driven forms of recognition and sociability in favor of others. The genealogy for this is deep, but I will give a very cursory overview and condition this for settler-colonial settings. In the case of settler societies, there is an old Aristotelian problem of how to govern alterity, how to order it, how to make sense of that which is not yours—a question that is not normative but rather tactical, and it reemerges, violently. The ideal of transcendent principles, still divine and sometimes democratically inflected, animate the governance of these territories. Yet the problem of governance itself remains. This is because the category and construct (and institutional apparatus) of the nation-state and its presumed homogeneity endure in spite of their fundamental inability to be resolved with the complexity and force that animate the territorial histories and horizons of settler-colonial nation-states. Indigenous dispossession caused by settler emplacement exacerbates the problem of rule, of governance, and of legitimacy itself. In this, people got and still get moved about and they survive eliminations, but the state projects of political homogeneity and the ideal correspondence of "ethnicity" and territorial boundaries remain irresolvable. The modern order itself is entwined with capital as this accumulative and acquisitive force further detaches people from places and moves them into other zones for productivity, accumulation, and territorial settlement.

This relationship is understood in part from literatures that have looked within presumably "postcolonial" or postrevolutionary/independent political orders to understand how nations come into being and how states emerge to manage that story of their beginnings and administer those populations. Thus, we have the importance in the literature on the iconic power of "nation" for governance. Within the literature on nationalism in anthropology, the state creates the image; this is Benedict Anderson's "re-presentation" of the nation.[8] The mediated, printed sense of relatedness to others (those who one does not know intimately, personally) was achieved in Anderson's account across vast territories because of communicable writing, because of newspaper. One would imagine now, in extending Anderson's argument, that that relatedness may be further instantiated and redefined through the Internet, telecommunications, and the immense popularity of social networking sites on the web. This representational and communicative process of "we"-ness, of relatedness, was accelerated in the earlier literature by rituals of the state—national parades, coronations, museums, exhibits, and, most importantly in Anderson's analysis, print media—all of which communicate in some way the essence of the nation, and who one's relations were, sort of. In this literature that proliferated around Anderson, it was more than simply suggesting, through iconic imagery, who its people are; the state also had a crucial role in the classification and definition of those people through its monopoly over territorial boundaries. In this way, the state provided the inspiration for nationalism, as it possesses a monopoly on institutions of control and influence that may not cohere with those within these territories. If nationalism is generated under conditions of this disconnect between state institutions and histories of force, then what does consent do? Or how does consent matter?

The issue of consent drives to the centrality of the state in the location of settler-colonial power and bureaucratic largesse. Part of the energy of nationalism issues from the question of state authority and its legitimacy.[9] Thus the literature on nationalism has difficulty *viewing* Indigeneity as possibly nationalist, and something able to be theorized.[10] Rather, Indigeneity is imagined as something entrapped within the analytics of "minoritization," a statistical model for the apprehension of (now) racialized populations "within" nation-states.[11] This is owing in part to the manner in which nationalism has been theorized, as something occurring within reified states in this formulation (and the formulations of Robert Foster, etc.), a reified state that is unresponsive and ahistorical.[12] Nationalism expresses a particular form of collective identity that embeds desire for sovereignty and justice. However, it does so only because of the deep impossibility of representation and consent within governance systems that are predicated upon dispossession and disavowal of the political histories that govern the populations now found within state regimes. When we add further nuance to this discussion within settler colonialist regimes, we have the problem of prior occupancy and ownership—Iroquois people with their own "constitution," for example.

The primary way in which the state's power is made real and personal, affective in its capacity, is through the granting of citizenship and, in this, the structural and legal preconditions for intimacy, forms of sociability, belongings, and affections.[13] The bureaucratized state is one frame in which visibility is produced, creating the conditions under which difference becomes apparent; political aspirations are articulated; and culture, authenticity, and tradition[14] become politically expedient resources. The state, in framing what is official, creates the conditions of affiliation or distance. These disaffiliations arise from the state's project of *homogenizing heterogeneity*, "the construction of homogeneity out of the realities of heterogeneity that characterise all nation building,"[15] which they have failed to do in the case of Kahnawà:ke Mohawks. It is this process of homogenizing that Kahnawà:ke's own statelike apparatus of tribal governance (band council) also undertakes and that the community struggles with and against.

SIGNPOST 2: DETENTION AND RECOGNITION

On April 28, 2010, three Mohawks of Kahnawà:ke were detained in El Salvador for seventeen days. They were flying back from the International Climate Change Conference in Bolivia and were traveling on Haudenosaunee passports. They refused to allow Canada to issue them "emergency travel documents" (which amounts to a passport).[16] They waited instead for ten more days, and they were permitted reentry into Canada via Iroquois Confederacy passports.

This detention is not an anomaly. Like the evictions described under the first signpost, this event is part of something larger, a set of assertions by Haudenosaunee peoples through time. They make these assertions based upon the validity and vitality of their own philosophical and governmental systems, systems that *predate* the advent of the settler state. Their arguments and actions regarding these systems, and the systems themselves, move discursively and materially into the face of the settler logic of dispossession and occupation. It is this same logic that informs Kahnawà:ke's reservation-based preoccupations and assertions regarding membership. Membership, passports, and evictions are of a piece with each other, as they all speak of a fear of disappearance but also from a form of sovereign authority: "I know you; I know who I am." "This is what I speak from, this treaty, this genealogic, this archive." "I refuse until you get it, or until I think you got it." Or, even, "I simply refuse."

In order to best give "refusal" as a political strategy its treads, it is helpful to turn directly to "colonialism" and to the work of Patrick Wolfe to contextualize the force that Kahnawà'kehró:non are up against. He argues that *settler* colonialism is defined by a territorial project—the accumulation of land—whose seemingly singular focus differentiates it from other forms of colonialism. Although the settler variety is acquisitive, unlike other colonialisms, it is not labor but territory that it seeks. Because "Indigenous" peoples are tied to the desired territories, they must be "eliminated"; in the settler-colonial model, "the settler never leaves."[17] Their need for a permanent place to settle propels the process that Wolfe calls, starkly, "elimination."[18]

The desire for land produces "the problem" of the Indigenous life that is already living on that land. How, then, to manage that "Indian Problem," as it is known in American and Canadian administrative speak? Like the "Jewish Problem" posed by Jewish life and alterity, and now the "Palestinian Problem" posed by "overlapping claims" to territory, the "Indian Problem" is one of the existence of continued life (of any form) in the face of an acquisitional and territorial desire that then moves through time to become, in liberal parlance, the "problem" of difference. In the case of Indigeneity in North America, this became a question of what to do with their souls, their bodies, their culture, and their difference. Now the answer appears to be for settler states to apologize or to recognize Indigenous peoples and the historical wrong that they experienced.

Recognition is the gentler form, perhaps, or the least corporeally violent way of managing Indians and their difference, a multicultural solution to the settlers' Indian problem. The desires and attendant practices of settlers get rerouted, or displaced, in liberal argumentation through the trick of toleration, of "recognition," the performance postconquest of "seeing people as they ought to be seen," as they see themselves—an impossible and also tricky beneficence that actually may extend forms of settlement through the language and practices of, at times, nearly impossible but seemingly democratic inclusion.[19] This inclusion, or juridical form of recognition, is only performed, however, *if* the problem of cultural difference and alterity does not pose too appalling a challenge to norms of the settler society, norms that are revealed largely through law in the form of decisions over the sturdiness, vitality, and purity of the cultural alterity before it.[20] This fixation on cultural difference and its purity occludes Indigenous sovereignty. Looking for "culture" instead of sovereignty (and defining culture in particularly exclusionist, nineteenth-century ways) is a tricky move, as sovereignty has not in fact been eliminated. It resides in the consciousness of Indigenous peoples, in the treaties and agreements they entered into between themselves and others and is tied to practices that do not solely mean making baskets as your ancestors did a hundred years ago, or hunting with the precise instruments your great grandfather did 150 years ago, in the exact same spot he did as well, when witnessed and textualized by a white person. [. . .] Sovereignty and nationhood are expressed differently from these essentialized modes of expectation by the settler state and its law, and how this difference pushes up against these other extremely narrow forms of judicial interpretation.

If regimes of recognition narrow to the juridical, then why do they persist? In part because they are seen as invariably virtuous. Although political recognition is a technique of settler governance, it appears as a transcendent and universal human desire that becomes a political antidote to historical wrongdoing. Thus, it would seem to salve the wounds of settler colonialism. Charles Taylor offers a foundational and empirically driven moral formulation[21] and defense of recognition for those whose difference is of such culturally determined form that they cannot help *but* be different, and so must be recognized as having traditions that should be more than just "tolerated."[22] The question of whether they should tolerate being tolerated, or tolerated in such a manner, does not arise for Taylor or others on his tail. However, "recognition" is a moral imperative, and, as Taylor argues, to be without it would cause harm—itself intolerable. In this context, then, people are not only deserving of recognition (a "courtesy"), but it is, he argues, a "vital human need."[23]

Kahnawà:ke Mohawks are caught up in the history of wrongdoing and disavowal from which Taylor's concerns speak. This is a historical attitude that supplants the ravages of settler colonialism with definitions of "difference." Tolerance, recognition, and the specific technique that is multicultural policy are but an elaboration of an older sequence of attitudes toward "the problem" of difference on acquired, some might argue *seized*, territories. Here I am talking about a latter-day move to techniques that are used to manage "the problem" of Indigenous people, rendered now as populations, to be administered by the state. This moves Indigenous peoples and their polities in the settler imaginary from nations, to people, to populations—categories that have shifted through time and in relation to land and its dispossession. Most important for this discussion, these categorical shifts set Indigenous peoples up for governmental regulation.[24] These techniques—occupying, treating, forceful elimination, containment, assimilation, the coterminous logics and practices and languages of race and civilization, the practice of immigration (called such in the United States and Canada, rather than "settlement"), the legal notion of natal right, and presumptions of just occupancy—all form the fulcrum of settlement's labor (and its imaginary) as well as a whole host of other self-authorizing techniques and frameworks that *sustain* dispossession and occupation.[25]

It is in this imagined space of just settlement, of settler nationhood (and statehood), that the Iroquois assert the benchmarks of *Western* territorially based sovereignty discussed above: regulations over membership and jurisdictional authority over rights to residency; the issuing of Iroquois Confederacy passports; the insistence upon their validity according to prior agreements, prior recognitions; an insistence upon recognition and honorable relations *now* between nations. In these examples we see a prior recognition born from the political status of nationhood and an ongoing and unvanquished sovereignty. To assert this is to fundamentally interrupt the sovereignty and the monocultural aspirations of nation-states, but especially those that are rooted in Indigenous dispossession. It is in the assertion of these rights (which are being diminished and narrowly interpreted, if not completely abrogated, in the courts)[26] that Iroquois peoples *remind* nation-states such as the United States (and Canada) that they possess this very history, and within that history and seized space, they possess a *precarious* assumption that their boundaries are permanent, uncontestable, and entrenched. They possess a precarious assumption about their own (just) origins. And by extension, they possess a precarious assumption about themselves.

The settler precariousness that I speak of structures the story that I am telling [. . .] of Mohawk life, the labor of principle and sovereignty, labor that begins with refusal. That refusal is simply to disappear, a refusal to be on the other end of Patrick Wolfe's critical, comparative history—to be "eliminated." In refusing to go away, to cease to be, in asserting something beyond difference, lies the position that requires one to "coexist" with others, with settlers, with "arrivants," in the parlance of Jodi Byrd[27]—meaning the formerly enslaved or the indentured who did not voluntarily come to North America—and to live tacitly and taciturnly in a "settled state." In this there is acceptance of the dispossession of your lands, of internalizing and believing the things that have been taught about you to you: that you are a savage, that your language is incoherent, that you are less than white people, not quite up to par, that you are then "different," with a different culture that is defined by others and will be accorded a protected space of legal recognition *if* your group evidences that "difference" in terms that are sufficient to the settlers' legal eye. To accept these conditions is an impossible project for some Indigenous people, not because it is impossible to achieve, but because it is politically untenable and thus normatively should be refused.

Contorting oneself in a fundamental space of misrecognition is not just about subject formation; it is about historical formation. And by refusing to agree to these terms and to be eliminated Mohawks are asserting *actual* histories and thus legislating interpretive possibilities in contestation—interpretations of treaty, possibilities of movement, electoral practices—not only individual *selves*. These are contesting systems of legitimacy and acknowledgment. The events of refusal we have seen in this introduction *enunciate*, in Pierre Bourdieu's sense, several processes. Most evident among these processes and accounts is their ability to signal Indigeneity and couple it with sovereignty. These stories of evictions, of Confederacy-issued passports, demonstrate Indigeneities comingling with sovereignty and their seemingly anomalous but insistent relation.

What does it mean to be unrecognized? What does it mean to not know what this means? These are fundamentally political questions, and thus require that I ask what it means to be recognized. Political recognition is, in its simplest terms, to be seen by another *as one wants to be seen*. Yet this regard is not merely for the sanctity of the self; it is to appear politically in formal and official forms, to have rights that protect you from harm, that provide you access to resources, or that protect certain resources. Patchen Markell describes this succinctly as, in its base form, "who we take ourselves and others to be."[28] One might specify this as "to have rights, to have an effectual capacity within a regime of power," as one should. This then means to have the recognition of the state and to have a passport that allows you as a formal member of the community to move, to travel, to receive, and exercise protections from harm. To be misrecognized, Markell also helpfully states in his discussion of the literature, is cast as a miscarriage of justice, a "failure whether out of malice or ignorance, to extend people the respect or esteem that is due to them in virtue of who they are."[29] To then be unrecognized would mean literally to be free from recognition and thus operate as a free-floating signifier with politically unformed or unprotected identities—most important, as identities that are vulnerable to harm.[30] Here I want to argue that it is impossible to be free from an authorizing context, which means one is a slave, in some readings of Friedrich Hegel, and remains so until recognized in a system of mutuality ("I see you; you see me; this is reciprocal; this reciprocity signals justice"). We might, however, want to test this reading further through empiricism. Indigeneity and its imbrication with settler colonialism question the conditions of seeing (perhaps of writing) that are laid out in the master-bondsman allegory; this allows us to consider another vantage point in another perceptual and argumentative theater or space of recognition. Settler colonialism structures justice and injustice in particular ways, not through the conferral of recognition of the enslaved but by the conferral of disappearance in subject. This is *not seeing* that is so profound that mutuality cannot be achieved. "Recognition" in either a cognitive or juridical sense is impossible. It simply would require too much contortion from one protagonist and not the other to be considered just.

In order to further our understanding of the Iroquois case, I want to move the discussion to the theater of apprehension—the way in which we see and understand this scene of "recognition"/"nonrecognition"—into the materiality of current settler nation-states. This is a theater that is more than a neutral and performative dramaturgy; it is in fact a settler-colonial nation-state with particular optics, expectations, and possibilities for interpretation. Hegel's is a concern with the *position* of the slave, not the slave himself; that subjectivity is taken up by others. Frantz Fanon most forcefully argues in *Black Skin: White Masks* that the slave is the black man, and in this subjectifying allegory the black man comprehends the scene as one of objectification, and in this, the feeling of subjugation and the deep knowledge of its context.[31] The black man sees an economy that is predicated upon the extraction of labor from specified bodies in order to annex territories and fuel the accumulation of surplus.[32] Recognition, in this reading of Hegel, is the basis for self-consciousness, and here taken to be a political self-consciousness that will translate into a revolutionary argument, a movement to unshackle oneself from this formula for self-perception. Glen Coulthard takes from Fanon's reading of Hegel the impetus to "turn away" from the oppressor, to avert one's gaze and refuse the recognition itself.[33] This moment of turning away can turn us toward Haudenosaunee assertions, which in different ways tell a story about a territory of willingness, a willingness to "stay enslaved." We could see this as a political strategy that is cognizant of an unequal relationship, understands the terms of bondage, and chooses to stay within them in order to assert a greater principle: nationhood, sovereignty, jurisdiction by those who are deemed to *lack* that power, a power that is rooted in historical precedent but is conveniently forgotten or legislated away.[34] Perhaps here we see a willingness to assert a greater principle and, in the assertion of this principle, to assert and be free whether this is apprehended as such or not. So in the Haudenosaunee political context it can mean recognition by another authoritative nexus (one's own?) and thereby call the other's into question. This negates the authority of the other's gaze.

NOTES

1. There has yet to be a challenge to the form of sexuality recognized in the Kahnawà:ke Membership Law. This should not be taken to mean that there are not individuals from the lesbian, gay,

bisexual, transgender, queer/questioning (LGBTQ) and same-sex couples living in Kahnawà:ke, or that this form of affection and romance is not tolerated. Challenges to the law have been based on its presumably raced provisions, not its heteronormativity. I am highlighting the normative heterosexuality of the Indian Act and the Kahnawà:ke Membership Law in both the 1994 and 2003 versions because it presumes this configuration of conjugal love, and this presumption has a Victorian genealogy that similarly affects the legal and affective arrangements of all Kahnawa'kehró:non.

2. See Mark Rifkin, *When Did Indians Become Straight: Kinship, the History of Sexuality, and Native Sovereignty* (New York: Oxford University Press, 2010).

3. See Denise Ferreira da Silva, *Toward a Global Idea of Race* (Minnesota: University of Minnesota Press, 2007).

4. The revised Kahnawà:ke Membership Law, accessed August 18, 2013, www.kahnawake.com/council/docs/MembershipLaw.pdf.

5. There are also other clans present within Kahnawà:ke, such as Snipe and Rock, as the community was originally a composite of Abenaki, Huron, and other Haudenosaunee and captive peoples.

6. See Ronald Beiner, ed., *Theorizing Citizenship* (Albany: State University of New York Press, 1995).

7. See Lauren Berlant, *The Queen of America Goes to Washington: Essays on Sex and Citizenship* (Durham, NC: Duke University Press, 1997).

8. See Benedict Anderson, *Imagined Communities: Reflections on the Origin and Spread of Nationalism* (London: Verso, 1991).

9. Gregory Jusdanis, *The Necessary Nation* (Princeton, NJ: Princeton University Press, 2001).

10. There are notable exceptions to this trend. See Michael D. Levin, ed., *Ethnicity and Aboriginality: Case Studies in Ethnonationalism* (Toronto: University of Toronto Press, 1993) and Gerald R. (Taiaiake) Alfred, *Heeding the Voices of Our Ancestors: Kahnawake Mohawk Politics and the Rise of Native Nationalism* (Toronto: Oxford University Press, 1995).

11. Audra Simpson, "Settlement's Secret," *Cultural Anthropology* 26, no. 2 (2011): 205–217, 211.

12. The recent spate of public apologies by former settler-commonwealth states (United States, Canada, and Australia) in the face of historical injustice presents an interesting twist to this assertion. My current thinking on the apologies is that they are in fact a technique to keep a thin historicity in place and ape the logic of the contract, which is time sensitive and heuristically (and legally) cancels out all further claims to harm. I am indebted to the important analysis by Sherene Razack of the murder of Pamela George and her explicit exposition on contractual thinking in white settler politics in Canada [see "The Murder of Pamela George," in *Race, Space and the Law: Unmapping a White Settler Society*, ed. Sherene Razack, (Toronto: Between the Lines Press, 2002)], and to the analysis by Robert Nichols of Hobbes's and Locke's formulations and the Iroquois and Indigenous position as people outside of, yet central to, contract theory [see "Realizing the Social Contract: The Case of Colonialism and Indigenous Peoples," *Contemporary Political Theory* 4, no. 1 (2005): 42–62]. Nichols extends this argument on contract into a close reading and analysis of Jeremy Waldron's argument on the practicality of superseding historical injustice and its articulation to the contractual thinking in settler governance [see "Indigeneity and the Settler Contract Today," *Philosophy and Social Criticism* 39, no. 2 (2013): 161–182].

13. See Berlant, *The Queen of America Goes to Washington*.

14. Katherine Verdery, "Whither Nation and Nationalism?" *Daedalus*, no. 122 (summer 1993): 37–46, 42.

15. Robert Foster, "Making National Cultures in Global Ecumene," *Annual Review of Anthropology*, no. 20 (1991): 235–260, 249; Brackette F. Williams, "A Class Act: Anthropology and the Race to Nation Across Ethnic Terrain," *Annual Review in Anthropology*, no. 18: 401–444, 429.

16. See Greg Horn, "Canada Prevents Mohawks from Returning Home on Haudenosaunee passports," *kahnawakenews.com*, June 1, 2010, accessed August 18, 2013, https://kahnawakenews.com/canada-prevents-mohawks-from-returning-home-on-haudenosaunee-passports-p798.htm.

17. See Patrick Wolfe, *Settler Colonialism and the Transformation of Anthropology: The Politics and Poetics of an Ethnographic Event* (London: Cassell, 1999) and "Settler Colonialism and the Elimination of the Native," *Journal of Genocide Research* 8, no. 4 (2006): 387–409.

18. For an overview of this analytic in anthropological literature of North America, see Jessica Cattelino, "Anthropologies of the United States," *Annual Reviews in Anthropology*, no. 39 (2010): 275–292 and "Thoughts on the U.S. as a Settler Society" (Plenary Remarks, 2010 SANA Conference), *North American Dialogue: Newsletter of the Society for the Anthropology of North America* 14, no. 1 (2011): 1–6; and North American history, see Frederick Hoxie, "Retrieving the Red Continent: Settler Colonialism and the History of American Indians in the U.S.," *Ethnic and Racial Studies* 31, no. 6 (2008): 1153–1167. More broadly, the richness of this analytic and its transborder and transtemporal articulations may be found in the journal *Settler Colonial Studies*, which although international, publishes many articles that are rooted in North American cases.

19. Patrick Wolfe, "After the Frontier: Separation and Absorption in U.S. Indian Policy," *Settler Colonial Studies* 1, no. 1 (2011): 13–51, 32.

20. See Elizabeth A. Povinelli, *The Cunning of Recognition: Indigenous Alterities and Australian Multiculturalism* (Durham, NC: Duke University Press, 2002); Patchen Markell, *Bound by Recognition* (Princeton, NJ: Princeton University Press, 2003); and Glen Coulthard, "Subjects of Empire: Indigenous Peoples and the 'Politics of Recognition' in Canada," *Contemporary Political Theory*, no. 6 (2007): 437–460.

21. Charles Taylor's cases are derived from Canada and so are germane to [the matter at hand], but his reading is from what most would consider the true foundation, Hegel, in the *Phenomenology of Spirit* on subject formation and the now canonical "master-slave dialectic." See the philosophical rereadings of Hegel by Frantz Fanon, *Black Skin: White Masks*, trans. Charles Lam Markmann (Boston: Grove Press, 1967), Alexandre Kojève, *Introduction to the Reading of Hegel: Lectures on the Phenomenology of Spirit*, ed. Alan Bloom, trans. James H. Nichols (Ithaca, NY: Cornell University Press, 1969), Axel Honneth, *The Struggle for Recognition: The Moral Grammar of Social Conflicts*, trans. Joel Anderson (Cambridge: University of Massachusetts Press, 1995), Kelly Oliver, *Witnessing Beyond Recognition* (Minneapolis: University of Minnesota Press, 2001), Povinelli, *The Cunning of Recognition*, Markell, *Bound by Recognition*, and Coulthard, "Subjects of Empire."

22. See Charles Taylor, "The Politics of Recognition," In *Multiculturalism: Examining the Politics of Recognition*, ed. Amy Gutmann (Princeton, NJ: Princeton University Press, 1994).

23. Ibid., 26.

24. Scott Morgensen, "The Biopolitics of Settler Colonialism: Right Here, Right Now." *Settler Colonial Studies* 1, no. 1 (2011): 52–76, 62. Morgensen's analysis of the Indian Act that attempts to flatten and erase political specificities in Canada is especially apropos here (62–64).

25. Patrick Wolfe argues that assimilation itself is the most efficient settler colonial technique of elimination, for "in neutralising a seat of consciousness, it eliminates a competing sovereignty" ("After the Frontier," 34).

26. See Alyosha Goldstein ["Where the Nation Takes Place: Proprietary Regimes, Antistatism, and U.S. Settler Colonialism," *South Atlantic Quarterly* 107, no. 4 (2008): 833–861] for an analysis of self-abrogating legal decisions and their relationship to the unwillingness of the United States (along with Canada) to withhold from signing the United Nations Declaration on the Rights of Indigenous Peoples, enacted in 2007.

27. See Jodi Byrd, *The Transit of Empire: Indigenous Critiques of Colonialism* (Minneapolis: University of Minnesota Press, 2011). Time does not permit me to engage fully with Byrd's excellent parsing of the distinctions between historical intention and political trajectory with her use of the term "arrivants" to distinguish between those who "settle" against their will (those enslaved are difficult to imagine as "settling" and thus dispossessing) and the moral issues of intent and effects. For related pieces see also the discussion by Malissa Phung of this in the context of Canada ["Are People of Colour Settlers Too?," in *Reconciliation through the Lens of Cultural Diversity*, ed. Ashok Mathur, Jonathan Dewar, and Mike De Gagne (Ottawa: Aboriginal Healing Foundation, 2011)] and by Dean Itsuji Saranillo in Hawaii ["Colonial Amnesia: Rethinking Filipino 'American' Settler Empowerment in the U.S. Colony of Hawai'i," in *Asian Settler Colonialism: From Local Governance to the Habits of Everyday Life in Hawai'i*, ed. Candice Fujikane and Jonathan Okumara (Honolulu: University of Hawai'i Press, 2008)]. Patrick Wolfe offers a critical elaboration of the manner in which the structure of settler colonialism as also structuring identities relationally to Indigeneity in his transcribed and published conversation with Kēhaulani Kauanui, "Settler Colonialism Then and Now. A Conversation between J. Kēhaulani Kauanui and Patrick Wolfe," *Politica and Societa* (Settler Colonialism), no. 2 (2012): 235–258, esp. 239–242.

28. Markell, *Bound by Recognition*, 1.

29. Ibid., 2.

30. The literature on political recognition is concerned largely with identities and state power. This literature does not deviate from the axis of the state even though the impetus for recognition itself is, in Hegelian terms, between two, unequal people (master and bondsman). Patchen Markell has described the translation of this issue into the terms of justice as a "thick form of respect"; ibid., 7.

31. See Fanon, *Black Skin: White Mask*.

32. Fanon is reading the slave's apprehension of a global economy structured on the extraction of his labor through absolute force, through nonconsent. My argument is indebted to Glen Coulthard's reading of these texts in his article "Subjects of Empire."

33. Coulthard takes this from Fanon's story of a white girl who sees him on the street and says, "Mama, see the Negro! I'm frightened, frightened!" This is a scene of recognition that Fanon (writing as himself) relays and a gaze within that he "turn[ed] away" from (Fanon, *Black Skin: White Masks* in Coulthard, "Subjects of Empire," 444, 454–456). This was an intense moment of object formation (subject *as* object) that could have been potentially devastating in its diminishment, but it was not; it became an occasion to move outside of the politics of recognition into self-authorization and subject formation, again, by "turning away" from the demeaning little girl and "inward and away from the master" (ibid.).

34. See the analysis by Alyosha Goldstein of the legally and temporally based notion of "laches" (legally defined as a "reasonable amount of time") as operationalized by Supreme Court justice Ruth Bader Ginsburg in her decision on Oneida land claims in what is now New York State, in "Where the Nation Takes Place." For an argument regarding its nonprecedential nature and danger to Indigenous treaty claims, see Kathryn Fort, "The New Laches: Creating Title Where None Existed," *George Mason Law Review* 16, no. 2 (2009): 357–401. I am grateful to P. J. Herne for calling this article to my attention.

BIBLIOGRAPHY

Alfred, Gerald R. [Taiaiake]. *Heeding the Voices of Our Ancestors: Kahnawake Mohawk Politics and the Rise of Native Nationalism*. Toronto: Oxford University Press, 1995.

Anderson, Benedict. *Imagined Communities: Reflections on the Origin and Spread of Nationalism*. London: Verso, 1991.

Beiner, Ronald, ed. *Theorizing Citizenship*. Albany: State University of New York Press, 1995.

Berlant, Lauren. *The Queen of America Goes to Washington: Essays on Sex and Citizenship*. Durham, NC: Duke University Press, 1997.

Byrd, Jodi. *The Transit of Empire: Indigenous Critiques of Colonialism*. Minneapolis: University of Minnesota Press, 2011.

Cattelino, Jessica. "Anthropologies of the United States." *Annual Reviews in Anthropology*, no. 39 (2010): 275–292.

Cattelino, Jessica. "Thoughts on the U.S. as a Settler Society" (Plenary Remarks, 2010 SANA Conference). *North American Dialogue: Newsletter of the Society for the Anthropology of North America* 14, no. 1 (2011): 1–6.

Coulthard, Glen. "Subjects of Empire: Indigenous Peoples and the 'Politics of Recognition' in Canada." *Contemporary Political Theory*, no. 6 (2007): 437–460.

Da Silva, Denise Ferreira. *Toward a Global Idea of Race*. Minnesota: University of Minnesota Press, 2007.

Fanon, Frantz. *Black Skin: White Masks*. Translated by Charles Lam Markmann. Boston: Grove Press, 1967.

Fort, Kathryn. "The New Laches: Creating Title Where None Existed." *George Mason Law Review* 16, no. 2 (2009): 357–401.

Foster, Robert. "Making National Cultures in Global Ecumene." *Annual Review of Anthropology*, no. 20 (1991): 235–260.

Goldstein, Alyosha. "Where the Nation Takes Place: Proprietary Regimes, Antistatism, and U.S. Settler Colonialism." *South Atlantic Quarterly* 107, no. 4 (2008): 833–861.

Honneth, Alex. *The Struggle for Recognition: The Moral Grammar of Social Conflicts*. Translated by Joel Anderson. Cambridge: University of Massachusetts Press, 1995.

Horn, Greg. "Canada Prevents Mohawks from Returning Home on Haudenosaunee passports." *kahnawakenews.com* (June 1, 2010), https://kahnawakenews.com/canada-prevents-mohawks-from-returning-home-on-haudenosaunee-passports-p798.htm.

Hoxie, Frederick. "Retrieving the Red Continent: Settler Colonialism and the History of American Indians in the U.S." *Ethnic and Racial Studies* 31, no. 6 (2008): 1153–1167.

Jusdanis, Gregory. *The Necessary Nation*. Princeton, NJ: Princeton University Press, 2001.

Kaunaui, J. Kēhaulani, and Patrick Wolfe. "Settler Colonialism Then and Now." A Conversation between J. Kēhaulani Kauanui and Patrick Wolfe. *Politica and Societa* (Settler Colonialism), no. 2 (2012): 235–258.

Kojève, Alexandre. *Introduction to the Reading of Hegel: Lectures on the Phenomenology of Spirit*. Assembled by Raymond Queneau. Edited by Alan Bloom. Translated by James H. Nichols. Ithaca, NY: Cornell University Press, 1969.

Levin, Michael D., ed. *Ethnicity and Aboriginality: Case Studies in Ethnonationalism*. Toronto: University of Toronto Press, 1993.

Markell, Patchen. *Bound by Recognition*. Princeton, NJ: Princeton University Press, 2003.

Morgensen, Scott. "The Biopolitics of Settler Colonialism: Right Here, Right Now." *Settler Colonial Studies* 1, no. 1 (2011): 52–76.

Nichols, Robert Lee. "Realizing the Social Contract: The Case of Colonialism and Indigenous Peoples." *Contemporary Political Theory* 4, no. 1 (2005): 42–62.

Nichols, Robert Lee. "Indigeneity and the Settler Contract Today." *Philosophy and Social Criticism* 39, no. 2 (2013): 161–182.

Oliver, Kelly. *Witnessing Beyond Recognition*. Minneapolis: University of Minnesota Press, 2001.

Phung, Malissa. "Are People of Colour Settlers Too?" In *Reconciliation through the Lens of Cultural Diversity*. Edited by Ashok Mathur, Jonathan Dewar, and Mike De Gagne, 289–299. Ottawa: Aboriginal Healing Foundation, 2011.

Povinelli, Elizabeth A. *The Cunning of Recognition: Indigenous Alterities and Australian Multiculturalism*. Durham, NC: Duke University Press, 2002.

Razack, Sherene. "The Murder of Pamela George." In *Race, Space and the Law: Unmapping a White Settler Society*. Edited by Sherene Razack, 121–147. Toronto: Between the Lines Press, 2002.

Rifkin, Mark. *When Did Indians Become Straight: Kinship, the History of Sexuality, and Native Sovereignty*. New York: Oxford University Press, 2010.

Saranillo, Dean Itsuji. "Colonial Amnesia: Rethinking Filipino 'American' Settler Empowerment in the U.S. Colony of Hawai'i." In *Asian Settler Colonialism: From Local Governance to the Habits of Everyday Life in Hawai'i*. Edited by Candice Fujikane and Jonathan Okumara, 256–78. Honolulu: University of Hawai'i Press, 2008.

Taylor, Charles. "The Politics of Recognition." In *Multiculturalism: Examining the Politics of Recognition*. Edited and Introduced by Amy Gutmann, 25–73. Princeton, NJ: Princeton University Press, 1994.

Simpson, Audra. "Settlement's Secret." *Cultural Anthropology* 26, no. 2 (2011): 205–217.

Verdery, Katherine. "Whither Nation and Nationalism?" *Daedalus*, no. 122 (summer 1993): 37–46.

Williams, Brackette F. "A Class Act: Anthropology and the Race to Nation Across Ethnic Terrain." *Annual Review in Anthropology*, no. 18: 401–444.

Wolfe, Patrick. *Settler Colonialism and the Transformation of Anthropology: The Politics and Poetics of an Ethnographic Event*. London: Cassell, 1999.

Wolfe, Patrick. "Settler Colonialism and the Elimination of the Native." *Journal of Genocide Research* 8, no. 4 (2006): 387–409.

Wolfe, Patrick. "After the Frontier: Separation and Absorption in U.S. Indian Policy." *Settler Colonial Studies* 1, no. 1 (2011): 13–51.

36

APPARATUS

Eukariot

ONCE AGAIN, WITH FEELING: "WHAT IS AN APPARATUS?"

Since I continue being interested in the notion of power as "productive," I also find useful the concept of apparatus or, in its more suggestive French appellation, *dispositif*. In French, *dispositif* includes military meanings: it can refer to the tactical deployment of troops, weaponry and so on with the purpose of defeating the enemy. This ties in nicely with Foucault's ditty that liberal "peace is war by other means" since, indeed, there is no strict delimitation between the "civil" dispositifs of the bourgeois order and its military machines. In the same way, there isn't any significant divide between the "public" and the "private" apparatuses of liberalism—the illusion that such divide exists is itself an effect of liberal ideology. There are simply liberal-capitalist apparatuses and between them some chains of supply and command and some smoke screens.

I could concisely describe the dispositif as "a governing device aiming to shape and control subjectivities and reality." This definition is quite vague, but it can gain precision once one starts looking at the technical-strategic construction of any particular such "device." Thus, a vague definition would actually be enough for our present purposes, since what is crucial about a dispositif is to understand how it functions. However, for those that feel like getting theoretical with it (which might be useful only to the extent that many people, especially in Italian and French contemporary political writing, are using this term), Foucault defines the dispositif as a sort of strategic network: a system of "heterogeneous relations between a plethora of elements—institutions, regulatory decisions, laws, administrative measures, scientific statements, philosophical, moral and philanthropic propositions and so on—that, in response to a governing necessity, make possible the strategic affecting of reality."[1] In this definition, the dispositif deploys the typical instruments of liberal governing—laws, norms, policies, rules, algorithms, codes of good practice, statutes, institutions, knowledges, research centres, experts, charitable ventures, advertising, media, celebrities, financial resources, armed troops, commodities, weaponry, etc.—in tactical configurations so as to respond to a particular governmental goal. The typical liberal dispositif mobilises and deploys these various resources just like a military leader would dispose the various elements of an army during a campaign, with the aims of conquering more territory and wealth, of subduing the enemy through direct confrontation (whenever there is serious resistance), of gaining the support of the population and of shaping the "free" conducts of the bourgeois subjects (whenever they are not resisting, which is almost always). Mind you, in the case of the apparatus, such goals are always chosen within the overall framework of liberal governing, for example profit-making, resource accumulation and control, identity—or generally sovereignty—boosting, phallic prestige/enjoyment, etc.; therefore, each liberal apparatus, whatever its particular goals, also has the implicit mission of maintaining the foundations of the liberal-capitalist reality unchanged.

Still on the academic side of things, Deleuze expands the definition of dispositifs beyond macro-tactics (policies, policing, institutions, knowledges, etc.), redefining them as "machines that make one see and speak."[2] The dispositif—the bourgeois family or education, for example—aims to regulate what one is able to perceive, think, feel or utter whenever she's making her "individual," "private" and "rational" choices. If successful, then, the dispositif makes you see, experience, speak, think or do this rather than that; which is also to say that it regulates the forms of being (identity, self, "I," etc.) available to us.

To sum up, then: the dispositif is a tactical-technical "disposition" of various elements—of discourses, institutions, laws, trade agreements, people, money, images, symbols, armed forces, walls, fences, roads and so on—that tries to make sure that the outcome of a power relation is the one desired by the creators of the disposition: a certain performance of reality, the reproduction or creation of certain forms of life, conducts and social relations, a particular circuit of resources and commodities, etc.

And since I'm so keen on looking at liberal-capitalism as an affective regime I'll insist that, whatever its shape or purpose, an apparatus always intervenes on the field of emotion, feeling, love, affinity, pleasure, desire, fantasy or whatever you want to call it. Let's call it the "libidinal field." This libidinal field, we think, might be the most important thing that liberal dispositifs regulate, since the bourgeois subjects' conducts, including their profound investment in liberal-capitalism, follow their paths of enjoyment rather than their "rational" choices. To the extent that they all conform to the basic governmental framework of liberal-capitalism, contemporary dispositifs shape a tight libidinal field: their relentless production and deployment of images and symbols aims to shape all affective processes, thus "being," according to their templates. And the success of liberal governing can be measured by the extent to which the bourgeois subject without effort, "naturally," finds these images and symbols seductive, desirable or enjoyable. I find it quite successful, scarily so in fact, since when successful the dispositif makes one identify with, love, hate, fear, desire, prefer or enjoy this rather than that.

Obviously, an apparatus cannot control perfectly the subjectivity or reality it focuses its actions upon, something always escapes it; it is a tactical device, after all, that tries to create a predicted effect without full guarantees that it will succeed. Like in a military deployment of forces, the end result of the battle is not fully predictable. Since I am discussing power here, rather than domination, there is always a struggle involved, a "game of freedoms" (not in the liberal understanding of freedom, though). That the liberal-capitalist apparatuses manage to create such constant and resilient reality effects must be due, then, to a certain inclination of the bourgeois subject to submit to these apparatuses, to a form of passionate investment in the realities that these apparatuses shape. And this is indeed one of the main interests of our analyses: the bourgeois subjects' enjoyment of their submission to liberal-capitalist apparatuses.

PRACTICE MAKES PERFECT (BOURGEOIS SUBJECTS)

When discussing ideology or, respectively, discipline, both Althusser and Foucault insist, somewhat oddly, that our actions are not caused by our "mental beliefs." In their different manners, both argue that "ideology" takes hold of the subject within the tactical and "material" arrangement of a dispositif, rather than being some sort of invasion of the subject's "beliefs" by ideas that float freely in media, art, books, etc. They even suggest that ideology is located in the *practices* regulated by the dispositif—praying, shopping, military drill, work procedures, educational exercises etc.—and not in "ideas." Indeed, arguing that ideology exists at the level of ideas and that it is ideas that determine one's actions could be considered a liberal ruse, an "ideology of ideology." This "ideology of ideology" articulates itself with various other modern myths: that one's subjectivity is equivalent to one's conscious thoughts, beliefs, ideas or utterances ("I think therefore I am") which means that one can perfectly know oneself and therefore control their conducts according to a universal rationality; that ideology operates by distorting some "true," "objective" or "common-sense" ideas about the world that, in the absence of ideology, would flourish in the subject's mind; or that the evils of the contemporary bourgeois order are caused by lack of education or information and can be eliminated by "democratising" access to education or information.

To try and interrupt this liberal mantra that "social transformation will be brought about by more access to institutional education and information," I would propose the simple (simplified?) schema that education and information either: (1) Do not affect the enjoyment a subject derives from their practices; or (2) Threaten the subject's patterns of enjoyment, pressuring towards a restructuring. Most bourgeois dispositifs and subjectivities have some built-in devices to prevent (2) from producing any lasting effect: when education or information do threaten the bourgeois subject's enjoyment practices, the dispositif and the subject will simultaneously deploy various tactics to deflect this threat and return the subject unscathed to their "usual" enjoyment practices. In general, any liberal dispositif tends to make (1) highly probable and (2) highly improbable. Thus, even the most "radical" education, when performed within a liberal dispositif—media, educational institutions, family, etc.—tend to leave bourgeois, pro-capitalist conducts and enjoyment undisturbed, in which case they end up justifying and fueling them.

Funny, this thing: ideology, which supposedly installs in the subject's "mind" the basic framework according to which they make sense of reality and, as I'm not tiring of repeating, according to which they desire, does not operate directly through ideas but takes hold of the "soul" through regulated practices. The reverse, then, holds as well: ideology does not primarily determine the conscious beliefs of the subject, but rather their practices; more exactly the practices through which they obtain enjoyment. In this equation, professed beliefs, ideas, convictions, causes and so on are largely irrelevant: relevant are the conducts though which one obtains enjoyment and it is these that are ideologically-shaped. Thus, for example, liberal education would not function ideologically without the specific practices in which the ideas it transmits are embedded: the teacher-pupil dyad (a typical "despotic four-eyed machine," to use Deleuze and Guattari's terminology), the institutional layout, academic hierarchies and taxonomies, the explanation, the lecture, the homework, the classroom disciplines, the schedule, the recess, the holiday, the test, the exam, the grades, the supervision, the reference letter, the scholarship application, the teaching assistantship, etc. It is the compulsive and ritualistic engagement in the *practices* of education that makes a student into a bourgeois subject and this happens irrespective of whatever ideas, thoughts and beliefs the student might profess at the end of her stint through the various liberal educational institutions, State-run or not. Ideas and beliefs are largely irrelevant both to the educational institution and to the student's ideological make-up.

But, all this being said, how exactly is one supposed to make sense of this process where ritual conducts are, so to speak, moulding the soul? I can propose a version of this mechanism, without caring much about faithfulness to the statements of the famous authorities I have just referenced or, indeed, any other. My version is incomplete: to understand ideological investment in a tactically useful way, I think that we need, at the very least, to take into account the bourgeois' identification with authority figures, their tenacious love affair with authority.

"Get on your knees, pray and you will start believing in god": performing the action of praying or, more generally performing any ritual action within a dispositif, will produce belief. But this belief can happen only if and when the ritualistic practice—praying—becomes part of the person's sense of a stable reality and of a stable and desirable self. Once the subject starts depending on that practice in order to create a symbolic framework through which they make the world meaningful, belief will follow. The belief is optional: this connection between practice and selfhood can happen even in the case of prisoners or addicts, where belief is not necessary. But the ideological hold is stronger when there is this belief, so that the apparatus takes hold of the subject at all levels; hence, most of the typical modern apparatuses (consumption, religion, the bourgeois family, the army, various colonial operations, etc.) are focused on inculcating belief. If and once the connection between the ritualistic practice and subjectivity is established, the subject will adopt the belief that supposedly causes the practice in the first place (for example belief in god), in order to defend the practices and the affects through which they are confirmed as an existence.

Let me insist on this discussion of the way in which the ritual practice mobilises affect and shapes subjectivity using a couple of examples. First, that of Christian religion: this is a dispositif that connects the authority's love for the subject ("god loves me"); practices (praying, going to church, charity, fasting); fetishized objects and symbols (the cross, the icon, the shrine, the rosary, the book, Jesus' crown or wounds, the virgin's tears); Christian dogma (the whole gamut of Christian texts, principles, laws, regulations and policies); and, in another libidinal twist, the believer's love for the authorities that police these laws (the Christ, the saint, the priest, the pope and so on). It is not hard to see that most capitalist dispositifs have an almost similar construction. Within this dispositif, the practice of praying connects the standardised moves of the body (kneeling or sitting, bringing the palms together, making the sign of cross, bowing the head, counting the rosary) with the mantra (repeating the words of the prayer) and with the praying subject's demand to be loved by the supreme authority ("god, please listen to me; god, please grant my wish; god, please bless me"—in short, "god, acknowledge me!"). This demand for love is something fundamental for the formation of subjectivity since it represents a demand to be *recognized as a subject*, in this case by no less than the cosmogonic, supreme authority, by what we could call the Other. Thus, bowing the head in prayer is a form of ritual submission in exchange for which the subject is granted existence that is, *recognition* by god. If I may insist, the crucial connection that the prayer ritual establishes is between some automatic gestures/words and the subject's sense of being, or selfhood, or having a unique soul, which sense necessitates the recognition of this being, selfhood or soul by the Other. Once this connection is made, the repetitions of the mindless rituals become not only automatic modalities of demanding love from the Other; but also modes of personally communicating with the Other, on a one to one basis; and what better recognition as a subject than having a direct line to the supreme Other? Praying, then, becomes a form of (temporarily) confirming and stabilising the subject's sense of being.

Once we describe the libidinal loop "subject-prayer-Other" as above, it becomes clearer that one does not need to believe in or profess any dogma to start with; one simply needs to start associating the process of obtaining the Other's recognition (or love, or desire) with a set of ritual gestures that can be anything, really: praying, shopping, breastfeeding, working, military drill and so on.

Second the example of work: one does not need to believe in capitalism or have a protestant ethic to repeat the automatic gestures required of the worker on the assembly line or behind the till, or to repeat the mantra required of sales assistants. However, once the connection "ritual practice-recognition" is established in the subject's psyche and life—for example, when the subject receives the recognition of a work-related social identity, a wage, belonging to a social group, etc.—their identity or worth becomes enmeshed with the proper performance of the ritual gestures. Once this happens, the way is wide open for the subject's adoption of the belief or idea that was supposed to cause their practice in the first place. That is: once the mindless rituals that constitute "work," invented by our bosses or managers and learned by rote, become attached to the processes of recognition and self-recognition, we will automatically adopt the ideologies that justify these practices: capitalism, gender, Eurocentrism, modernity, civilisation, colonialism, progress, meritocracy, calling, vocation, and so on. At this point, workers will demand higher wages but not the abolition of the capitalist work system. On the contrary, they will passionately defend capitalism in various forms, like the worth of "working hard and doing one's job well," or the idea that capitalism can be improved through social reforms, or the idea that capitalism insures the freedom of the workers more than any other possible regime and so on. The mechanism is the same for those forms of work that are much better rewarded by capitalism and that, allegedly, contain some inbuilt critical thinking element, like say the arts or academic jobs. Once the learned by rote rituals and the associated rewards of their profession—titles, teaching-related obligations, publishing requirements, grant applications, administrative tasks, departmental meetings and so on—become associated with their demands for recognition and love, academics, even the most radical critics of capitalism, will defend the bourgeois university as the only institution that makes possible emancipation.

The trick here is that, since belief in the discursive part of the ideology—the religious dogma for example—follows from the very intimate processes of demanding love or recognition from the Other, belief also assumes an intimate, personalised form for the subject. The "true belief" of religious bourgeois subjects, what in psychoanalysis would be called their fantasy, is not the religious dogma as written in the holy book but a tailored variant of it through which the subjects insert *themselves* into the religious dispositif and make the religious dogma and practices to be about themselves, about their selfhood, their being, their unique soul. The orgasmic nature of mystical ecstasy or trance ("sex with god") is a symptom of the subject's intimate communion with the religious dispositif. In the case of work or shopping, this intimate communion not only explains the moulding of our enjoyment into the compulsive masturbation of work or the hysterical orgasm of shopping; but also explains how the "belief," the defence of capitalism, becomes self-defence. By defending work or consumption the typical bourgeois subject actually defends their enjoyment: what better ideological operation than that?

These practices that are used to foster belief in capitalism or god represent the "material," practical, performed existence of capitalism or religion. Shopping *is* capitalism; praying *is* religion; these are the practices that reproduce capitalism or religion in their dispositif form and neither capitalism nor religion can survive as a system of power without these practices. The trick that the bourgeois dispositifs perform is to make the subject as unable to survive without these practices; or rather, to make them *believe* that they cannot survive as a subject without them.

And here we can observe the hypocrisy of the Kantian dictate of freedom: "think and say whatever you want, but obey the law in your acts." This dictate, which assumes that "speaking truth to power" while obeying the law in one's practices creates the conditions for perfecting social order without creating chaos, is a deception meant to keep the order forever unchanged. What one says or thinks while choosing to obey the law is irrelevant; what is important is one's "true belief," the fantasy that guides their enjoyment. And as long as the subject decides to obey the law in practice, they truly believe in the law; it is the law that shapes their practices of enjoyment and their fantasy. Ideology is not that which causes the words that come out of our mouths; ideology is that which causes our practices of the self (shopping, praying, gender). This is why many academic leftists, with their cottages by the lake, their SUVs, their nuclear families and their mortgages, are often quite fond of Kant. And yet, the "radical" things they might say while performing their bourgeois practices and the "radical" thoughts they might think while obeying the laws of capitalism are irrelevant: their fantasy is staunchly bourgeois.

MACHINIC ENJOYMENT, OR, THE ATM AS LOVE-MACHINE

According to Deleuze and Guattari, besides capturing the subject in those fields to do with the "I" (ego, identity, self, consciousness, reflexivity, rationality, etc.), capitalist dispositifs also operate at a "machinic," sub-representational or automatic level. I will not bother with the "proper interpretation" of their texts; but rather focus on arguing that the success of these machinic operations has a lot to do with the libidinal field. In other words, I will suggest that machinic governing is a subset of the governing of enjoyment and that it mobilises, even if not necessarily at conscious level, the typical symbolic frameworks of bourgeois modernity.

On top of the, say, "molar" subjectivity-shaping mechanisms that are representational, ideological or discursive and that operate through symbols, images, identification and so on (education, media, art, advertising, etc.) there are, according to Deleuze and Guattari, "machinic" or "molecular" mechanisms that operate at a non-discursive, automatic level, without involving consciousness or thought. Such "machinic" operations fragment the "molar" level into small, algorithmic, technical operations that do not really involve "subjectivity." Take the example of someone using an ATM bank machine. Here, the tasks are automatic, mindless responses to commands issued by the bank machine and function as simple prompters within the predetermined flow of financial operations: enter pin, choose amount, etc. The ATM user is a "human switch" in various preset circuits, just like Marx's proletarian is in the factory. This, allegedly, represents a "dismantling" of the self-reflexive subject, her transformation into an unthinking element of a technical-financial procedure (or flow). There is something interesting here, but it needs some qualifications.

On one level, I don't think that the "thinking" subject of contemporary capitalism is more reflexive when doing "meaningful" tasks (work, leisure, self-care, education, domestic tasks, dating, entertainment, sex, etc.) than when taking money out of the bank machine. The "reflexivity" promoted by neoliberalism is, after all, as automatic and standardised as putting in a pin code: "standardised situations elicits standard reactions." The neoliberal bureaucratisation of knowledge, experiences and play has made bourgeois "meaningfulness" into a form of "organised, axiomatized stupidity." On another level, in capitalism, in whatever way it might be interpellated (rationally, meaningfully, machinically, etc.), the subject is also interpellated at the level of enjoyment. No doubt, most neoliberal apparatuses demand from the bourgeois subject a conditioned response to some machinic prompters, turning them into a carefully governed "switch" within various algorithms. But apparatuses elicit those "machinic" reactions by mobilising specific libidinal triggers and investments. That is: the automatic, un-reflexive responses that the subject is prompted to input so as to allow the algorithmic flow to continue—from online dating to standardised personality tests or health assessments—are experienced by the subject as personal and personalised, as an expression of their uniqueness, individuality and desirability. Let me try to illustrate using the ATM example.

Putting the pin into a bank machine, besides stimulating the financial flows of capitalism, also stimulates one's erotic investment in capitalism, which it does by titillating their self-love. The ATM, like all liberal-capitalist machines, is a *love-machine*, a machine that exploits and fosters the connection between capitalism and (self-)love. This can be illustrated, maybe, by the blurt of an acquaintance who, after using her PhD in anthropology to secure a job with a big NGO in the mid-2000s and being sent to Afghanistan to educate the locals into safe sex practices (or something similar), came back with horror stories: "There aren't even bank machines in Kabul; and to get money out from the only bank machine in the city we needed to be escorted by the US military!!," etc. One hears such accounts of the "unbelievable lack of bank machines" quite often from adventurous bourgeois friends and relations travelling to "remote" and—oh, the thrill of it!—"dangerous" locations. In these recurrent anecdotes, the bank machine connects the "corporate Samaritan" or "touristic adventurer-explorer" subject to more than just an algorithm: it connects her with the grand colonial hierarchies of civilisation and, by mobilising the specular figure of the primitive *other* that chronically fails to connect to the cyber-financial flows of capitalism, boosts her sense of self-worth and superiority, of superior "likeability."

Also, inputting the pin in the bank machine, just like inputting the preferred colour of a future dating partner's eyes or one's blood level of cholesterol into some other machine, is by now a source of identificatory enjoyment for the bureaucratised subjectivity we call "bourgeois." We should not forget the insight provided by film studies (e.g. Cine-Tract) that in modernity, the figure of the authority (ego-ideal, big Other, superego, Father, master or whatever you want to call this omnipotent, discourse-producing and reality-defining imaginary "creature" from which you demand recognition for your individuality) is a machine. The bourgeois loves machines and wants to be loved back by them: the filming or photographic cameras are only the most literal example. Putting in the pin, therefore, involves various types of enjoyment: (1) The enjoyment of being interpellated on familiar, service-industry terms, by the machine-like, omnipotent authority. It is not just "The Bank" but capitalism/modernity itself that seems to call your name: "Hello and welcome to The Bank's automated services! What operation would you like to perform today?" (2) The pleasure of being asked by the omnipotent machine about your personal, unique and secret details (the pin), the stuff you are not supposed to share with anyone, not even the most intimate persons around you (your mom, your partner or your bank manager). This is the omnipotent machine as accomplice, therapist, confidante or lover. (3) The enjoyment of being recognised by the machine/authority as a unique being ("pin OK"): "It knows me!" (4) The enjoyment by being rewarded for your specialness ("transaction complete, please take your money"): "It rewards me, it answers my demand (for love)!" I don't know about you, but I get a little sense of elation every time the bank machine "gives" me money, as if it's a reward.

Enjoyment is even higher in the case of other machinic algorithms, where your "personalised" input rewards you with a date match, a personality or health profile, a medical prescription, etc. Here lies the profound appeal of contemporary capitalism: the machines are always connected with our sense of self-love.

SO WHAT?

So, the tasks ahead are pragmatic: to increase and compose our forces (*potencia*); to damage and rupture the essential bourgeois dispositifs; and to construct alternative libidinal and symbolic economies. Let's leave the task of saving souls through preaching and praying to the "progressive" liberals or to the leftists that enjoy proselytism. Liberation from the current models of doing can happen only through inventing different doings, different "material" practices, rather than through first changing our ideas or beliefs. To finish in circular manner, this is something that Foucault possibly hinted at when arguing that the question is not one of "liberating desire" from the shackles of ideological repression, as so many thought in the 1960s and 1970s; the question is one of inventing new pleasures; and only then, maybe, desire will follow . . .

NOTES

1. Michel Foucault, "Le jeu de Michel Foucault" (entretien avec D. Colas, A. Grosrichard, G. Le Gaufey, J. Livi, G. Miller, J. Miller, J.-A. Miller, C, Millot, G. Wajeman), *Bulletin périodique du champ freudien*, no. 10 (July 1977): 62–93. [—Author's Translation.]

2. Gilles Deleuze, "What Is a Dispositif?" in *Michel Foucault, Philosopher*, trans. Timothy J. Armstrong (New York: Routledge, 1992), 160.

BIBLIOGRAPHY

Deleuze, Gilles. "What Is a Dispositif?" In *Michel Foucault, Philosopher*. Translated by Timothy J. Armstrong, 159–168. New York: Routledge, 1992.

Foucault, Michel. "Le jeu de Michel Foucault" (entretien avec D. Colas, A. Grosrichard, G. Le Gaufey, J. Livi, G. Miller, J. Miller, J.-A. Miller, C, Millot, G. Wajeman). *Bulletin périodique du champ freudien*, no. 10 (July 1977): 62–93.

37

HUMAN STRIKE, REPRODUCTION, AND MAGIC MATERIALISM

Claire Fontaine

We must touch the unity and resonance of our physicality, our bond with the natural order, the corporeal ground of our intelligence.
—A. Rich, *Of Woman Born*, 1986

You reader are alive today, reading this, because someone once adequately policed your mouth exploring.
—M. Nelson, *The Argonauts*, 2015

THE SURREALISM OF CAPITALIST EVERYDAY

Surrealism: The Last Snapshot of the European Intelligentsia is one of the most disturbing texts by Walter Benjamin where the method used by Breton's acolytes is not seen as a harmless artistic experiment but rather as the paradigm of a different relation to the world and reality, entailing deep political implications and physiological effects. Sami El-Kathib[1] understands Benjamin's vision of surrealism as a means to perceive reality beyond the commodity-form. The commodity that according to Marx is "a very tricky thing, abounding in metaphysical subtleties and theological niceties" creates what El-Kathib calls *the surrealism of the capitalist everyday*[2] where the phenomenon of real abstraction dominates every social interaction; the exploration of this situation must be conducted by using the entirety of one's body, experimenting collectively and diving into the "occult, surrealistic, phantasmagoric gifts and phenomena." Benjamin insists upon the fact that the "histrionic or fanatical stress on the mysterious side of the mysterious takes us no further; we penetrate the mystery only to the degree that we recognize it in the everyday world, by virtue of a dialectical optic that perceives the everyday as impenetrable, the impenetrable as everyday."[3] By placing mystery on the side not of the uncanny but of the plainly familiar, Benjamin draws the bridge between revolution and revolt, between the dialectical approach and the surrealist one, through a specific kind of materialism: the anthropologic materialism, accused by Adorno of being affected by a "profoundly romantic element" placed "at the crossroads of magic and positivism."[4]

The resistance to Benjamin's epistemic model, deemed not rigorous and regressive by the author of *Minima Moralia*, coincides in him with the refusal to acknowledge the place that the singular and the collective body occupy within the commercial metabolism of a capitalist society rapidly descending into fascism. The human body whose centrality Adorno doubted, refusing to believe that it could be used as "the measure of all concreteness," was about to be disciplined and selectively exterminated in totally new ways, deprived of political and collective depth, shrunken into bare life. The mistrust of the political value of sensorial experience, which is the existential and the theoretical foundation of patriarchy, deactivated the only forces within culture that could have prevented fascism from happening. If the human body had been believed to represent "the measure of all concreteness," its irrefutable value could have been opposed to the dehumanized masses of people deported and imprisoned in the name of "race"—the most inaccurate and false of all generalizations. The unreal body of the universalist prewar philosophy, deprived of singularity and gender, the fiction of the neutral subject, was unable to fight the fascist projection of the imaginary Jewish identity and the racist fantasist physiological reasons for discrimination.[5] Thirty years later, long after Benjamin had committed suicide, Adorno's awareness of the limitations of enlightenment had grown stronger. In the famous passage[6] of the *Negative Dialectics*, he acknowledged that Auschwitz showed the pathetic inability of culture to transform people and to prevent genocide (that same culture that stayed clear from the crossroads of magic and positivism, leaving it free for others to occupy). Not even silence, he states, can absolve anyone from partaking in the "shabby" and "guilty" system that let Nazism and fascism happen; the only thing that could have prevented the tragedy would have been embodying a different relationship to the living, a magic materialism that acknowledged the importance of the human and nonhuman life in the perpetuation of a world where productive and reproductive work, material and immaterial labor are not separated. The moral indignation of the intellectual who discovers the insufficiency of his institutional position and the imaginary dimension of his political commitment in the face of the actual power of Nazism opened a path for criticizing the depoliticized socio-symbolic practices, which capitalism had instituted after World War II in the name of the peace of trade.

Culture after Auschwitz, according to Brecht, is a palace built with dogshit; it stinks because of its hidden complicity with patriarchal violence. "The enlightening science" was and still is blind when it comes to showing us how to reproduce freedom and preventing the masses' descent into fascist brutality because its aim is to preserve the very powers and hierarchies of patriarchy that tell us to stay away from that crossroads between magic and positivism where we now need to return.

*

Magic kills the industry.
—F. Bacon quoted by S. Federici, *Caliban and the Witch*, 2004

MAGIC MATERIALISM

In the first chapter of *The World of Magic*, Ernesto De Martino puts to trial our mental openness to subjected knowledge by tackling the prejudice against magic. The resistance of Western researchers toward magic powers, whenever they prove effective, takes places because these powers call into question the very concept of "reality." It is almost as if whenever it cannot be proven that magic is fake, the results of the observation must be discarded. This, De Martino says, ends up being a problem for the thinking process that is meant to be "critical, therefore deprived of dogmatic prejudice." The book is filled with elating examples of magic powers that "work" and of phenomena that, remaining unexplained by science and psychology, appear logical in their own terms, just because the relationship between cause and effect that governs them is neither mechanistic nor scientific.

The persistency of the devaluating attitude toward anything related to the magical world is caused by the fact that under the category of "magic," we find, as Federici explained in *Caliban and the Witch*, all sorts of habits that stood in the way of industrial production and protected the connection between the human body and its environment. The witch hunt was crucial for defeating the rebel body and creating in its place the disciplined workforce that Marx refers to.[7] Magic was deemed "primitive" because it implied a cyclical temporality associated with seasons and biorhythms, it used the free remedies that nature provides, it took care of birth control and contraception—in other words, it kept life in touch with life. The fact that magic still carries a bad reputation while the commodity-form and private property are massively accepted as rational facts shows that our logic is politically tainted and that the "reason" governing our system of values is questionable.

Silvia Federici's entire body of work can be read as a fierce attempt to highlight how the systematic exploitation of the natural resources and the privatization of land—from the enclosures up to today—are above all an attack on a way of life informed by the commons, an emotional and physical collective subsistence, and an approach to the environment as filled with signs, readable and instructive. The re-enchantment of the world, Federici argues, will not be achieved by refusing contemporary technology but rather by resisting its commercial seduction, its "scientific magic" that "appears to give us powers without which it seems impossible to live."[8] With these powers have come mass surveillance and manipulation, the incorporation of all parts of our lives into an exploitable database made of bank statements, family photos, nude pictures, sexting, and communications for direct actions: all of it can be used against us. And it is.

Federici is clear about the fact that we must refuse to be subsumed as a workforce *and* as commodities, that we must stop loving and caring only out of dependency or fear; the vicious circle will have to be consciously broken by us[9] because the historical necessity is not likely to generate the revolutionary subjects of our current productive cycle.[10] As she explains in *Gender and Capital*, "with a world proletariat divided by gender and racial hierarchies, the 'dictatorship of the proletariat' concretized in a state form would risk becoming a dictatorship of the white/male sector of the working class."[11]

The idea that we need to go on a strike against our very productive and reproductive identity, inside and outside the officially recognized and remunerated workplace, has been the most inspiring legacy of the feminist movement, giving political legibility to the racial and generational conflicts that did not fit into the category of class struggle.[12] Our digital and personal identity is more than ever a site of struggle—an idea that incarcerates us and chains us to a system.

There cannot be radical change in material conditions, distribution of wealth, and productive models without sabotaging and dismantling the industrial complex of the mass production of subjectivities that, like any industrial complex, has its own police and its guardians, among which are some of our closest friends and our subconscious habits.

The recent demands for defunding the police[13] do not plead for the end of police brutality. They do not request a reform of the repressive system. But they do oppose an entire world's idea of security based on profiling. In doing so, they potentially unhinge the mechanisms of biological distribution of the destinies, in which racism and classism collide to form the unchangeable exclusion that stems from one's *identity*.

As Rancière reminded us, and Foucault previously described in depth, the police is a form of government of the souls—a militarized partition of reality. It is a way of repressing the body and organizing the mind under the direct threat of violence. The police guide the production and the shaping of subjectivities because repression and counterinsurgency block the path to a certain kind of subjectivisation, and only some lifeforms become dominant and possible, no matter how weak and self-destructive they are (gentrification offers a blatant example of this phenomenon). The violence deployed to discourage and eradicate some existential possibilities happens online, in the workplace, in real estate, and in social habits, and it shows its bloody face only at the end of the process, when people who are losing everything and still claim the right to exist are physically harmed and incarcerated.

Our implications with the present productive system do not begin and end with the labor that we provide and the subsistence that we consume, with our active and conscious participation to it, but they extend to all aspects of our social, emotional, and biological life. The strike that politicizes and disturbs the entire spectrum of our valuable contributions to the world in its current self-destructive state is both wider and deeper than a general strike, and it is what we call a "human strike." Our subjectivities are one of the precious resources that this society is harvesting to perfect the police techniques to shape the life-form compatible to the current order. The algorithms and advertisement are the most common examples of this profitable manipulation; surveillance capitalism is the dark side of it.

Without abolishing ourselves as the persuadable subjectivities that we now are, there will be no end in sight to fake news, propaganda, and their world.

Abolishing here does not mean erasing or blocking the memory of something, but rather disarticulating the power mechanisms that naturalize oppressive dynamics.

*

FROM MASS STRIKE TO HUMAN STRIKE

In her seminal essay from 1906 entitled *The Mass Strike, the Political Party, and the Trade Unions*, Rosa Luxemburg illustrates how the social democrats of the Second International used to conjure the ghost of the mass strike by saying that "either the proletariat as a whole are not yet in possession of the powerful organization and financial resources required, in which case they cannot carry through the general strike; or they are already sufficiently well organized, in which case they do not need the general strike."[14]

The political strike as an orderly action meant to produce a punctual change is a *means to an end*. It is part of a program where the subjectivities involved are not supposed to transform themselves during the process. In fact, they remain workers all the way through, but their productivity is suspended and displaced on a political level. On the other hand, mass strike is seen by the Party as ephemeral, confusing, easily spiralling out of control, carrying the possibility of changing precisely what the Party does not want to change: its own self and the subjectivities that compose it. Luxemburg's conclusions point toward a plane of consistency in which individual attachment to power is unmasked; the possible is honored; means and ends and cause and effect are not regulated by the institutional objectives. By disqualifying abstract thinking and logic as undoubted political tools, she demands another form of materialism because, as she states, "in the unreal sphere of abstract logical analysis it can be shown with exactly the same force on either side that the mass strike is absolutely impossible and sure to be defeated, and that it is possible and that its triumph cannot be questioned."[15]

The truth is that mass strikes are, she writes, a "symptom of the thoroughgoing internal revolution in the relations of the classes and in the conditions of the class struggle." Their metabolism, their inner economy, function in ways that aren't binary and are unforeseen by the logic of the Party. These strikes cannot be artificially provoked through the techniques of the usual mobilization; they happen out of an unpredictable historical necessity.[16] In a vivid depiction, Luxemburg describes the interlacement of economic and political strikes generating the mass strikes:

Every new onset and every fresh victory of the political struggle is transformed into a powerful impetus for the economic struggle, extending at the same time its external possibilities and intensifying the inner urge of the workers to better their position and their desire to struggle. After every foaming wave of political action a fructifying deposit remains behind from which a thousand stalks of economic struggle shoot forth. And conversely. The workers' condition of ceaseless economic struggle with the capitalists keeps their fighting energy alive in every political interval; it forms so to speak a permanent fresh reservoir of the strength, and at the same time leads the indefatigable economic sappers of the proletariat at all times, now here and now there, to isolated sharp conflicts, out of which public conflicts on a large scale unexpectedly explode. In a word: the economic struggle is the transmitter from one political centre to another; the political struggle is the periodic fertilization of the soil for the economic struggle. Cause and effect here continually change places.[17]

The logic of dissection, she adds, that extracts and separates the purely political mass strike from other struggles will "not perceive the phenomenon in its living essence, but will kill it altogether."[18] The materialism that Luxemburg is seeking is the one capable of grasping the sensible when it is alive and not on its way to producing a quantifiable result, inside or outside the factory. She seeks a materialism capable of reading reproduction and not only production, which is what we call *magic materialism*.

SELF-ABOLITION AND MOURNING

One year after Rosa Luxemburg was murdered, Walter Benjamin wrote *The Critique of Violence* where he reflected upon means, ends, and Sorel's controversial vision of mass strike, the "proletarian strike." On the ashes of the recently defeated German revolution, the strike, seen as the first step toward the uprising, was still at the heart of the debate. Benjamin quoted extensively from *Reflections on Violence*, explaining that within the political general strike, the state apparatus does not lose any strength because power is transferred from the privileged to the privileged, and nothing happens but a change of masters.[19] And he commented:

> whereas the first form of interruption of work [the political general strike] is violent, since it causes only an external modification of labour conditions, the second [the proletarian strike], as a pure means is nonviolent. For it takes place not in readiness to resume work following external concessions and this or that modification to working conditions, but in the determination to resume only a wholly transformed work, no longer enforced by the state, an upheaval that this kind of strike not so much causes as consummates.[20]

The non-reformist struggle, the proletarian strike, is free of both contractual and functionalist thinking. It is not "useful," limited to improving an aspect of the productive system (organization or remuneration). It is not a means to an end. When the claim is the total transformation of the system itself, requesting it from a determinate position (within the union, the party, or as an excluded subject), from an identity that will be abandoned through the very process of the struggle, is paradoxical.[21] The perspective of gender and class abolition shows the path to human strike by already walking it. Protecting the untenable identity, the position and the job that *require* the uprising, with the pretext that they "define" us is what makes rebellion impossible: *these are* the conditions that must be sabotaged from within. "We don't believe what they say about us" was one of the most beautiful slogans of the Italian feminist movement from the 1970s. For it is ultimately in the name of one's identity that one's time is priced and one's labor is valued. The demand of wages for housework was as politically realistic (and ambitious) as the claim for prison abolition. Without unpaid reproductive labor and mass incarceration, the lie of an efficient and progressive capitalist society could not stand. By making these demands—perceived as paradoxical and unthinkable within the capitalist mental frame—the existing foreignness to it is brought forward along with the lack of interest in preserving or improving the status quo. A radical transformation of society is not needed to dream of a world without prisons or without gender domination: *these are existing needs within the present world.* The subjectivities on strike carry inside them other possible worlds already.

One of the worst double binds that the feminist, the ecologist, and the workers' movements have been prisoners of is the compulsion to improve an unsustainable situation as if the state of things was their responsibility and its improvement was in their interest. This "reasonable" reformist position has created within the Western left throughout the twentieth century an unbearable amount of internalized violence and self-hatred that has constantly ended up destroying it from within. It is impossible to explain the mourning pervading the progressive political spectrum, from its official representatives to the grassroots movements, without analysing the problems that the acceptance of responsibility for a totally unsustainable system has caused in our groups and families, in personal lives and on a political and economic level.[22] Human strike only can end it.

*

REPRODUCTION AS A CONSTRUCTION OF SITUATIONS

As long as our focus remains on the logic of production and its best ally in disguise, the reformist struggle, we might find ourselves hostage of the old dilemma that shows the opposition to the oppressive conditions as an unaffordable luxury, while precisely what is unaffordable is continuing to think and live in a situation that we know we must change but we don't see how to.

This paralysis mainly comes from a representation of the world that disregards reproduction (including the reproduction of our forces to struggle) focusing solely on production-related problems, making the countless possibilities of change invisible and unthinkable. Extractive capitalism since its very industrial origins has also openly conflicted with *reproduction as a project*; the long-term temporality involved in reproductive work is animated by the firm belief in a future that is a historical continuity of the present and not the result of violent operations on the environment, indifferent to their effects on the living, only receptive to the monetary return.

Biological reproduction, the material and emotional ceaseless re-creation of viable conditions in the household, cleaning, maintaining, cooking, and managing daily survival for dependent people, keeping the working class productive and submitted, ensuring its reproduction as a class of producers and reproducers, are all forms of unrecognized and unpaid reproductive labor whose skills are magic materialist ones. All these tasks cannot be interrupted without endangering the ones whose livelihood they insure. There is no strike for the work of care that does not immediately turn into harming the defenceless. As long as this fact is not integrated into a revolutionary political vision, reproductive work must be treated as slave work. Therefore, the only horizon for it is its abolition in the form that we know. (Autonomy as a perspective is, in fact, as seductive as riots are, but it does not provide a viable model of struggle. It stems from a group where there are no children, no sick, no old, and no disabled people.)[23]

The fact that commodified technological knowledge, the backbone of patriarchy and colonialism, is regarded as the highest human achievement implicitly disqualifies all the hidden work that allows this very knowledge to exist, thrive, and dominate. The same can be said for all forms of intellectual and artistic "excellence" ironically presented as possible models precisely to the ones who owe them their very oppression.

*

If the body was nothing but an anatomic fact, it would not survive its injuries. It always needs to remain in the world, and this work of adaptation entails an exit from oneself, the assemblage of a platform between biological and symbolic, between the body and the flesh of the world. The symbolic is not the tomb of the material, it is its re-localization.
—C. Malabou, *Le plaisir effacé, clitoris et pensée*, 2020

PROFESSIONAL INFORMAL

Agamben writes, paraphrasing Aristotle, that "there is politics because man is the living being who, in language, separates and opposes himself to his own bare life and, at the same time, maintains himself in relation to that bare life in an inclusive exclusion."[24] In the introduction to *Homo Sacer*, the philosopher explains how Aristotle's binary opposition of *phoné* and *logos* (the voice, which man shares with the other living beings, which expresses feelings, and the *language*, which he is the only one who can use to formulate moral judgments) mirrors the opposition between politics and bare life, *bios* and *zoé*. In his prophetic analysis, Agamben showed in 1995 how the formal inclusion of bare life in our contemporary democracies entailed the normalization of the state of exception and, it should be added, a recrudescence of patriarchy and racism, supposedly defeated by juridical and abstract "equality," the state of right, the lie of the democratic neutrality of all subjects.

Patriarchal contempt for the convivial, social, physiological aspects of life (the *zoé*, the *phoné*), when not militarised, has historically taken the forms of *professionalism* and *intellectualism*. Disguised as a legitimate need for productivity, men's disgust for children and the segregation of the family to the domestic sphere have burdened women with the schizophrenia of having their professional identity constantly shadowed by the domestic one (to which women and men alike partake but with different implications). The remunerated workplace values itself precisely through the contempt for the informal and domestic one, the wages being justified by a supposedly higher quality of the "professional" services provided in opposition to the affective work done for free, "owed" to the ones who receive them. But the "professional" care work is only available because the informal, unrecognized, and unpaid one takes place *after* work and reproduces the subjects who will tomorrow provide the remunerated service. This interdependency is hidden.

The intellectual, more insidious, disqualification of the sphere of reproduction derives its arrogant legitimacy from the historical division between manual and intellectual labor. The theoretical abstraction echoes in many ways the economic one. Speculative intellectual work must be based on a separation from its object, which is a form of dematerialization. No symbolic or economic recognition is given to the skills involved in material and emotional survival (personal and collective), the care for the preservation of the health of dependent or nonhuman creatures. They are not seen as a form of research or as fields for the cultivation of a particular intelligence and sensibility because they are unsheltered by institutions—although they secretly and gratuitously fuel the business of education, health care, the agro-alimentary industrial complex, childcare, and more. The jobs of these industries are remunerated, since no one can be found to do them for free, although the reproduction of the workforce that makes the jobs possible is still free. The experience accumulated through the daily work of care is not shared or conceived as the result of experimentations, problem solving, or social and emotional intelligence. The disregard and the exploitation always translate into criminalization for the most dispossessed among the dispossessed, so that their frightful example dissuades the others from going on strike. The success or the failure of the work of care *as such* lies in a "private" zone of the social body that stays unspoken and only emerges when the work could no longer be done and leads to a tragedy. *The abandonment of the dependent creature is regarded as cruelty while the exploitation of the unpaid and helpless carer is not. Therefore, the tragedy cannot be prevented when care becomes unsustainable for its provider.* The intellectual can happily profit from the credit that he gets from showing distance from the reproductive and material sphere of life because the inclusive exclusivity of language has historically worked in a patriarchal direction, leaving unvalued the material accumulation and the emotional work that granted him the sufficient mental balance to perform his speculative task.

The often repetitive and destructive work embedded into material and immaterial production, when remunerated, is socially accepted and politically valued, even today on the brink of environmental disaster. The pride of the employed working-class man and the authority of the intellectual exerting his function in the party or an institution are based on a reputation that was anyway made by crushing and harming their competitors: they could have never been emancipatory figures, even for their peers. The value of their discourse was created in the very places that the discourse was meant to destroy.

The emotional, artistic, and highly skilled work of reproduction, on the other hand, is left unpaid or underpaid and, above all, unpoliticized, laying in the obscure and swampy domestic sphere of the emotional, the *zoé*. *Wages for Housework* did not demand recognition of the value of housework, but rather the recognition of the *continuity* between all forms of work within the economy and the explicit subalternity of the unpaid ones. What we call magic materialism is the method that highlights this hidden continuity between remunerated and unremunerated, material and immaterial labor, and it shows the exploitative nature of waged work toward unwaged work.

Cognitive digital capitalism is organized around a form of materialism compatible with the general abstract equivalent oriented toward the monetization and objectification of life with no project for its regeneration. Magic materialism that ensures legibility to the energetic effects of our actions on living creatures, the environment, and ourselves shows what remains unspoken, under the radar of value, culturally and theoretically uncodified. In *Intellectual and Manual Labour*, Sohn-Rethel sadly concludes that:

> if the formation of the consciousness, by the procedure of abstraction, is exclusively a matter for the consciousness itself, then a chasm opens up between the forms of consciousness on the one side and its alleged determination in being on the other. The historical materialist would deny in theory the existence of this chasm, but in practice has no solution to offer, none at any rate that would bridge the chasm. Admittedly it must be taken into consideration that the philosophical tradition is itself a product of the division between mental and manual labour.[25]

Reproduction is the creation of situations that inhabit that chasm.

*

REVOLT-FORCE AND LOVE-FORCE, THE DOUBLE YES

In Debord's *Report on the Construction of Situations and on International Situationist Tendency's Conditions of Organization and Action* from 1957, we read a merciless list of the failed revolts of the previous avant-gardes. He laconically declares about surrealism that "we now know that the unconscious imagination is poor, that automatic writing is monotonous." The magic materialist perception of reality—what Benjamin called "dialectical optics" in his text on surrealism—appears insufficient to Debord to oppose the stage of capitalism that he will sharply describe ten years later in *The Society of the Spectacle*. By 1967, the colonization of the visible by the commodity-form had objectified the human, transforming every relation into a retinal representation of itself to be reproduced and consumed by the passive isolated spectator, who will then pursue the chain of reproduction and consumption of the imaginary commercial idea of life. The representation had at this point entirely replaced experience and desire was confused with lack and envy. The situationists had the intuition that in order to fight this post–World War II emotionally reified and politically destructive context, other worlds and situations had to be created in which another sense of reality could emerge.[26] Subjectivity as a political battlefield was to appear soon as the undisputed protagonist of French philosophy, changing forever the perception of Marxism. Lyotard, Foucault, Deleuze, and Guattari provided visionary research and theory that transvalued politically the meaning of consciousness, affects, desire, and processes of subjectivisation, but no one of these threads of thoughts connected explicitly to feminism and the new emotional education that this entailed, to the reinvention of communism as a theoretical and practical horizon. No one, and especially not Debord, was able to see the impending necessity of thinking through the end of patriarchy in order to achieve the end of capitalism.

The main emotional drama of life—we read in the *Report on the Construction of Situations*—, aside from the perpetual conflict between desire and reality hostile to desire, seems to be the sensation of the passage of time. In contrast to the aesthetic modes that strive to fix and eternalize some emotion, *the situationist attitude consists in going with the flow of time. In so doing, in pushing ever further the game of creating new, emotionally provocative situations*, the situationists are gambling that change will usually be for the better. In the short term the odds are obviously against that bet. But even if we have to lose it a thousand times, we see no other choice for a progressive attitude.[27]

"The game of creating new, emotionally provocative situations" could simply be another definition for feminism. The situationists were addressing the importance of the revolution of daily life through the destruction of the partition between work and idleness, a redefinition of shared pleasures and the refusal of the capitalisation of time, but none of these things could be achieved without feminism as both an epistemological tool and a form of life. In the refusal of capitalizing time, the project of staying with the flow (and the anxiety that this entails), we also see the promise of a new metabolism for struggles. Living inside reproduction without seeing it as complementary and functional to production allows what we call the "love-force" and the "revolt-force" to be actually regenerated. "Never work" meant, obviously, *"always work"*: reproductive work is endless because it blurs the boundaries between leisure and productivity. It says the yes[28] to motherhood and work, to life and struggle, and by saying it, it refuses the impossible binary choices that are on offer. It begins a strike of another nature, deeper and more generalizable than any other: the human strike.

The human strike is the process of undoing the affective and epistemological ties to the type of struggle and counterculture that have created toxic dynamics and failed because of the unawareness and the contempt of their own reproduction. Human strike cuts one's vital dependency from what threatens our well-being, and it is a form of radicalizing desubjectivisation. Unlike schizophrenia, which is a dissociation of the subject that ends up destroying it, human strike strikes precisely against the part of ourselves that is our own enemy, making perceptible, in the process, the forces that we can actually count on to thrive. The necessity of this form of struggle, which is also a form of thinking (thinking against ourselves as individuals, as parts of a social contract that vilifies us), surfaces in this historical moment where our society is plagued with violence and disquiet, self-hatred and denial of systemic injustice. For the first time, we have full knowledge of it, but the visibility of the capillary pervasiveness of disaster gets in the way of the perception itself: we do not see where we could begin to transform things.

Human strike is exactly the opposite of madness if we see madness as recurrent self-harming and destructive behaviour. It is a creative instinct of survival.

TRANSCENDENCE ASHAMED

In his unfinished book posthumously published under the title *The End of the World. Contribution to the Analysis of the Cultural Apocalypse,* Ernesto De Martino explored different typologies of psychosis related to the perception of the end of the world and the loss of the self. The anthropologist dedicates what would have been the fourth chapter of his book to *The Drama of the Marxian Apocalypse.* In one of the fragments entitled "Marxist materialism as an ethos of transcendence ashamed of itself," De Martino quotes a curious formulation by the young Marx: "the mystical feeling that leads philosophers from the abstract thinking to intuition is an intense longing, like the nostalgia of a content." Elsewhere, De Martino adds that "Marx goes back to speaking about the 'infinite boredom' that abstraction feels about itself, that is why he will abandon the kind of thinking that only moves within itself, without eyes, teeth, ears, without anything; the infinite boredom presents itself in Hegel as the decision of going back to intuition."[29] The disembodied thinking (blind, toothless, deaf) gets affected by emotional exhaustion. The truly human vocation according to De Martino, a philosopher who drifted away from the silence of the library to record the illiterate peasants of the South of Italy and write about their unusual beliefs, is to "measure, in all the fields of cultural life, the distance between what the humans believe they are doing and what they are actually doing."[30] For this purpose, traditional logic seems inappropriate and theoretical intelligence is at a loss: in order to connect with the sensible reality, intuition, analogies, associations, poetry are needed. The transcendence that he mentions is ashamed of itself because it is unreconciled with immanence, and this lack of reconciliation was the source of many pathologies among which "the crisis of presence," a form of "loss of the world," defining according to De Martino a moment of existential and psychological uncertainty of the subjectivity, when the sense of the self begins to flicker and the person no longer resonates with his culture and surroundings. Subjectivity appears as something that is stabilized, produced, and reproduced within culture, and the environment is as important in this process as one's own body. The geographical, the ethnological, or the religious description of the world where a subjectivity is or is not possible cannot capture the conditions that must be preserved for protecting presence. *Magic materialism on the other hand is what can help, building a science of the reproduction of presence.* The famous tale of the bell tower of Marcellinara is exemplary.

One evening when the sun was setting on the countryside of Calabria, De Martino and his team got lost and encountered a shepherd who was unable to explain himself clearly through language. They asked him to get into the car and guide them to the nearby crossroads, offering to drive him back where they had first met him. But as soon as the poor man lost sight of the bell tower of Marcellinara, he appeared gripped by anxiety at first and then totally lost.

"Surely—De Martino concludes—presence is at risk when it touches the limit of its existential motherland, when it loses 'the bell tower of Marcellinara.'" Nevertheless, we might have reached a point in our civilization where our bell tower is nowhere to be seen. The romantic cosmopolitan project that gave birth to the best part of Western culture, with its reassuring universalism and its openness to the Other, might be over. The continuous discoveries of old and recent colonial atrocities, the masses of displaced people, and the regression of human rights on a planetary scale prove that we are undergoing a crisis deeper than we can acknowledge without adopting a different political and subjective position in our life. "Philosophy is really homesickness—the desire to be everywhere at home,"[31] wrote Novalis, at the end of the eighteenth century, when at the wake of World War I, Lukács, who was quoting him, noted how transcendental homelessness was already our inescapable condition.[32]

Some subjectivities who were always denied a cultural motherland observe this general condition with distance and can now give lessons on how to enjoy transcendental exile, existential homelessness. Reproducing a decolonized perception of ourselves and others will only be possible through the refusal of all the current political positions that perceive self-destruction and environmental catastrophe as inevitable. Only thinking in ways that will make us fearless of losing sight of our own bell tower of Marcellinara will give us a future where hope-force and love-force will be renewable energies.

NOTES

1. Sami El-Khatib, "To Win the Energies of Intoxication for the Revolution. Body Politics, Community and Profane Illumination," *Anthropology & Materialism* no. 2 (2014).

2. Ibid., 3.

3. Walter Benjamin, "Surrealism: The Last Snapshot of the European Intelligentsia," in *Selected Writings*, vol. 2, trans. Edmund Jephcott (Cambridge, MA: Belknap Press, 2005), 216.

4. "For all those points in which, despite our most fundamental and concrete agreement in other matters, I differ from you could be summed up and characterized as an *anthropological materialism* that I cannot accept. It is as if for you the human body represents the measure of all concreteness." And elsewhere: "The direct inference from the duty on wine to *L'âme du vin* imputes to phenomena precisely the kind of spontaneity, tangibility and density which they have lost under capitalism. This sort of immediate—I would almost say again 'anthropological'—materialism harbours a profoundly romantic element. . . . If one wanted to put it rather drastically, one could say that your study is located at the crossroads of magic and positivism." Theodor W. Adorno and Walter Benjamin, *The Complete Correspondence, 1928–1940*, ed. Henri Lonitz, trans. Nicholas Walker (Cambridge, MA: Harvard University Press, 1999), Adorno to Benjamin on September 6, 1936, and November 10, 1938, quoted in Marc Berdet, "In the Magnetic Fields of Materialism and Anthropology," *Anthropology & Materialism*, no. 1 (2013).

5. For this topic, see the chapter entitled "Elements of Anti-Semitism: Limits of Enlightenment" in *Dialectic of Enlightenment. Philosophical Fragments*, eds. Max Horkheimer and Theodor W. Adorno (Stanford, CA: Stanford University Press, 2002).

6. "[A]s Brecht put it in a magnificent line, [culture's] mansion is built of dogshit. Years after that line was written, Auschwitz demonstrated irrefutably that culture has failed. That this could happen in the midst of the traditions of philosophy, of art, and of the enlightening sciences says more than that these traditions and their spirit lacked the power to take hold of men and work a change in them. There is untruth in those fields themselves, in the autarky that is emphatically claimed for them. All post-Auschwitz culture, including its urgent critique, is garbage. In restoring itself after the things that happened without resistance in its own countryside, culture has turned entirely into the ideology it had been potentially—had been ever since it presumed, in opposition to material existence, to inspire that existence with the light denied it by the separation of the mind from

manual labor. Whoever pleads for the maintenance of this radically culpable and shabby culture becomes its accomplice, while the man who says no to culture is directly furthering the barbarism which our culture showed itself to be. Not even silence gets us out of the circle." Theodor Adorno, *Negative Dialectics*, trans. E. B. Ashton (London: Routledge, 1973), 367.

7. Federici describes vividly the "type of worker—temperate, prudent, responsible, proud to possess a watch, and capable of looking upon the imposed conditions of the capitalist mode of production as 'self-evident laws of nature' . . . that personifies the capitalist utopia and is the point of reference for Marx." Silvia Federici, *Caliban and the Witch. Women the Body and Primitive Accumulation* (New York: Autonomedia, 2004), 135.

8. Silvia Federici, *Re-Enchanting the World. Feminism and the Politics of the Commons* (Oakland, CA: PM Press, 2019), 188.

9. Silvia Federici, *Genere e Capitale. Per una lettura femminista di Marx* (Rome: Derive Approdi, 2020), 30–31.

10. See, for example, Mario Tronti, "Ancora su utopia, proseguendo una discussione," *Azione Parallela*, https://www.azioneparallela.org/2020/05/31/ancora-su-utopia-proseguendo-una-discussione/; although Tronti is credited for having written the foundational book of the operaism, *Workers and Capital*, and having elaborated on the strategy of the refusal to work (see Mario Tronti, "The Strategy of Refusal," Libcom.org, http://libcom.org/library/strategy-refusal-mario-tronti), he visibly cannot mourn yet the current lack of a traditional homogeneous antagonist subjectivity.

11. Federici, *Re-Enchanting the World*, 168.

12. In her recent book, *Feminist International. How to Change Everything*, Veronica Gago talks about a "patriarchy of the wage" that is behind the "exclusionary meaning" of the concept of working class (see Veronica Gago, *Feminist International. How to Change Everything*, trans. Liz Mason-Deese [New York: Verso, 2020], 6). Lonzi's "unplanned subject" [*soggetto imprevisto*] as the messenger of a politically illegible revolt is magnificently theorized as a feminist phenomenon, although this condition of unrecognized insurgent subjectivities can be found in other types of uprising. Marx's category of lumpenproletariat is interpreted, for example, by Rancière when reading Althusser ("Althusser, Don Quixote and the State of the Text," in *The Flesh of Words*, trans. Charlotte Mandell [Stanford, CA: Stanford University Press, 2004], 129–145) as the name of the nameless and the placeless; Foucault spoke about the plebs as opposed to the productive and disciplined proletariat, and during the Italian movement of 1977, based on the refusal to work and to enrol in traditional communist militant structures, emerged practices that were categorized as diffuse irrationality because the analysts of the time could not justify a revolt whose claims were not related to wages or rights (see on this point Claire Fontaine, "77 the Year that Is Never Commemorated" in *Human Strike and the Art of Creating Freedom*, trans. Robert Hurley (South Pasadena, CA: Semiotext(e), 2020).

13. "Defund the police" is a slogan that became widespread in the demonstrations after the murder of George Floyd by Derek Chauvin on May 25, 2020. The Black Lives Matter movement and other political platforms have articulated this claim, requesting that the funds destined to the police be allocated to associations preventing criminality and marginalization. The ancestor of the political concept of "abolition" is W. E. B. Du Bois, who wrote in 1935 in *Black Reconstruction in America* about "abolition-democracy," advocating for the removal of institutions rooted in racist and repressive practices, including prisons and white police forces.

14. Rosa Luxemburg, *The Mass Strike*, trans. Patrick Lavin (Detroit: Marxist Educational Society of Detroit, 1925), 5; available at https://www.marxists.org/archive/luxemburg/download/mass-str.pdf.

15. Ibid., 10.

16. Ibid.

17. Ibid., 35.

18. Ibid., 36.

19. Georges Sorel, *Reflections on Violence*, trans. Thomas Ernest Hulme and Jeremy Jennings (Cambridge: Cambridge University Press, 1999), 171, quoted by Walter Benjamin, "Critique of Violence," in *Selected Writings*, vol. 1, trans. Edmund Jephcott (Cambridge, MA: Belknap Press, 1996), 246.

20. Ibid.

21. The concept of self-abolition as much related to class as to gender is a real line of flight; see a recent reflection on "The Self-Abolition of the Proletariat," *Non-Copyriot*, https://non.copyriot.com/the-self-abolition-of-the-proletariat-as-the-end-of-the-capitalist-world/, the previous theorizations by Maya Gonzales, "Communization and the Abolition of Gender," *The Anarchist Library*, https://theanarchistlibrary.org/library/maya-andrea-gonzalez-communization-and-the-abolition-of-gender, Marina Vishmidt, "Activated Negativity: An Interview with Marina Vishmidt," *Makhzen*, no. 2 (September 2015), http://www.makhzin.org/issues/feminisms/activated-negativity, and Marina Vishmidt, "The Economy of Abolition/Abolition of the Economy," *The Anarchist Library*, https://theanarchistlibrary.org/library/marina-vishmidt-the-economy-of-abolition-abolition-of-the-economy.

22. See Douglas Crimp, "Mourning and Militancy," *October*, no. 51 (Winter, 1989): 3–18. Crimp insists on the fact that the inescapable emotional complicity with a system that constantly gives to some type subjects an image of themselves that they can't recognize in and is degrading is a constant source of internal conflict on a personal as much as on a political level. See also the brilliant analysis of these matters by Hannah Proctor, "Mournful Militancy," *e-flux Architecture* (March 2018), https://www.e-flux.com/architecture/superhumanity/179226/mournful-militancy/.

23. Interesting in this respect: Johanna Hedva's *Sick Woman Theory*, https://johannahedva.com/SickWomanTheory_Hedva_2020.pdf.

24. Giorgio Agamben, *Homo Sacer*, trans. Daniel Heller-Roazen (Stanford, CA: Stanford University Press, 2017), 10.

25. Alfred Sohn-Rethel, *Intellectual and Manual Labour. A Critique of Epistemology*, trans. Martin Shon-Rethel (London: Macmillian Press, 1978), 18–19.

26. The founder of the application Signal, Moxie Marlinspike, known for his anarchist sympathies and his commitment to defend online privacy against surveillance capitalism, recently declared something that revives the situationist program departing from the dematerialized world of online interaction: "You have certain experiences in this world, they produce certain desires, those desires reproduce the world. Our reality today just keeps reproducing itself. If you can create different experiences that manifest different desires, then it's possible that those will lead to the production of different worlds." A. Wiener, "Taking Back Our Privacy. Moxie Marlinspike, The Founder of the End-to-End Encrypted Messaging Service Signal, Is 'Trying to Bring Normality to the Internet,'" *The New Yorker*, October 19, 2020.

27. Guy Debord, "Report on the Construction of Situations and on International Situationist Tendency's Conditions of Organization and Action," *The Anarchist Library*, https://theanarchistlibrary.org/library/guy-debord-report-on-the-construction-of-situations.pdf, 15—emphasis by the author.

28. See Lia Cigarini, "Un'altra narrazione del lavoro," *Critica Marxista Online* (2013), https://criticamarxistaonline.files.wordpress.com/2013/06/6_2006cigarini.pdf: "A group of young women, when asked if their priority was the work outside the house or the work of care, have replied refusing to establish a priority. This answer is quoted as an example of ambivalence, but I believe that it can and actually must be read otherwise: as a double *yes* to work and maternity and therefore an affirmation of a different way of thinking work"—Author's translation. Silvia Federici quotes the Zapatistas' position as another refusal of the binary logic: "the slogan 'One No Many Yeses' . . . recognizes the existence of diverse historical and cultural trajectory and multiplicity of social outcomes that are compatible with the abolition of exploitation." See Federici, *Re-enchanting the World*, 167. In his beautiful introduction to *The Undercommons*, Jack Halberstam writes about the refusal between a yes and a no that deny us "the path to the wild beyond is paved with refusal. In *The Undercommons* if we begin anywhere, we begin with the right to refuse what has been refused to you. . . . While we can circulate multiple critiques of gay marriage in terms of its institutionalization of intimacy, when you arrive at the ballot box, pen in hand, you only get to check 'yes' or 'no' and the 'no', in this case could be more damning than the yes. And so, you must refuse the choice as offered." See Halberstam, *The Wild Beyond*, 8. Bartleby's "I would prefer not to" is the figure presiding to the refusal of choosing self-destructive options that we call human strike.

29. Ernesto De Martino, *La fine del mondo. Contributo alle analisi delle apocalissi culturali* (Turin: Einaudi, 1977), 435—Author's translation.

30. Ibid., 431.

31. Novalis, *Notes for a Romantic Encyclopaedia: Das Allgemeine Brouillon. 1772–1801* (New York: State University of New York Press, 2007), 155.

32. Georg Lukács, *The Theory of the Novel*, trans. Anna Bostock (Cambridge, MA: MIT Press, 1974).

BIBLIOGRAPHY

Adorno, Theodor W. *Negative Dialectics*. Translated by E. B. Ashton. London: Routledge, 1973.

Adorno, Theodor W., and Walter Benjamin. *The Complete Correspondence, 1928–1940*. Edited by Henri Lonitz. Translated by Nicholas Walker. Cambridge, MA: Harvard University Press, 1999.

Agamben, Giorgio. *Homo Sacer*. Translated by Daniel Heller-Roazen. Stanford, CA: Stanford University Press, 2017.

Agamben, Giorgio. *Means Without End*. Translated by Vincenzo Binetti and Cesare Casarino. Minneapolis: University of Minnesota Press, 2000.

Benjamin, Walter. "Critique of Violence." In *Selected Writings*, vol. 1. Translated by Edmund Jephcott, 236–252. Cambridge, MA: Belknap Press, 1996.

Benjamin, Walter. "Surrealism: The Last Snapshot of the European Intelligentsia." In *Selected Writings*, vol. 2. Translated by Edmund Jephcott, 207–221. Cambridge, MA: Belknap Press, 2005.

Berdet, Marc. "In the Magnetic Fields of Materialism and Anthropology." *Anthropology & Materialism*, no. 1 (2013).

Cigarini, Lia. "Un'altra narrazione del lavoro." *Critica Marxista Online*. 2013. https://criticamarxistaonline.files.wordpress.com/2013/06/6_2006cigarini.pdf.

Claire Fontaine. "1977: The Year that Is Never Commemorated." In *Human Strike and the Art of Creating Freedom*. Translated by Robert Hurley, 156–71 (South Pasadena, CA: Semiotext(e), 2020).

Crimp, Douglas. "Mourning and Militancy." *October*, no. 51 (Winter, 1989): 3–18.

De Martino, Ernesto. *La fine del mondo. Contributo alle analisi delle apocalissi culturali*. Turin: Einaudi, 1977.

Debord, Guy. "Report on the Construction of Situations and on International Situationist Tendency's Conditions of Organization and Action." *The Anarchist Library*, https://theanarchistlibrary.org/library/guy-debord-report-on-the-construction-of-situations.pdf.

El-Khatib, Sami. "To Win the Energies of Intoxication for the Revolution. Body Politics, Community and Profane Illumination." *Anthropology & Materialism*, no. 2 (2014).

Federici, Silvia. *Caliban and the Witch. Women the Body and Primitive Accumulation*. New York: Autonomedia, 2004.

Federici, Silvia. *Genere e Capitale. Per una lettura femminista di Marx*. Rome: Derive Approdi, 2020.

Federici, Silvia. *Re-Enchanting the World. Feminism and the Politics of the Commons*. Oakland, CA: PM Press, 2019.

Foucault, Michel. *Dits et Écrits*, vol. IV. Paris: Gallimard, 1994.

Gago, Veronica. *Feminist International. How to Change Everything*. Translated by Liz Mason-Deese. New York: Verso, 2020.

Gonzales, Maya. "Communization and the Abolition of Gender." *The Anarchist Library*. https://theanarchistlibrary.org/library/maya-andrea-gonzalez-communization-and-the-abolition-of-gender.

Halberstam, Jack. "The Wild Beyond: With and for the Undercommons." In *The Undercommons. Fugitive Planning and Black Study*. Edited by Stefano Harney and Fred Moten, 2–13. New York: Minor Compositions, 2013.

Hedva, Johanna. *Sick Woman Theory*, 2015 https://johannahedva.com/SickWomanTheory_Hedva_2020.pdf.

Lonzi, Carla. "La donna clitoridea e la donna vaginale." In S*putiamo su Hegel. La donna clitoridea e la donna vaginale e altri scritti*, 77–140. Milano: Scritti di Rivolta Femminile, 1974.

Lonzi, Carla. "Sputiamo su Hegel." In *Sputiamo su Hegel. La donna clitoridea e la donna vaginale e altri scritti*, 25–60. Milano: Scritti di Rivolta Femminile, 1974.

Lukács, Georg. *The Theory of the Novel*. Translated by Anna Bostock. Cambridge, MA: MIT Press, 1974.

Luxemburg, Rosa. *The Mass Strike*. Translated by Patrick Lavin. Detroit: Marxist Educational Society of Detroit, 1925. https://www.marxists.org/archive/luxemburg/download/mass-str.pdf.

Nappi, Antonella. "La nudità." In *Una visceralità indicibile. La pratica dell'inconscio nel movimento delle donne degli anni Settanta*. Edited by Lea Melandri. Milano: Franco Angeli, 2000.

Novalis. *Notes for a Romantic Encyclopaedia: Das Allgemeine Brouillon. 1772–1801*. New York: State University of New York Press, 2007.

Proctor, Hannah. "Mournful Militancy." *e-flux Architecture*. March 2018. https://www.e-flux.com/architecture/superhumanity/179226/mournful-militancy/.

Rancière, Jacques. "Althusser, Don Quixote and the State of the Text." In *The Flesh of Words*. Translated by Charlotte Mandell, 129–145. Stanford, CA: Stanford University Press, 2004.

Rancière, Jacques. *Short Voyages to the Land of the People*. Translated by James B. Swenson. Stanford, CA: Stanford University Press, 2003.

Sohn-Rethel, Alfred. *Intellectual and Manual Labour. A Critique of Epistemology*. Translated by Martin Shon-Rethel. London: Macmillian Press, 1978.

Sorel, Georges. *Reflections on Violence*. Translated by Thomas Ernest Hulme and Jeremy Jennings. Cambridge: Cambridge University Press, 1999.

The Milan Women's Bookstore Collective. *Sexual Difference: A Theory of Social-Symbolic Practice*. Bloomington: Indiana University Press, 1990.

"The Self-Abolition of the Proletariat." *Non-Copyriot*, 2020. https://non.copyriot.com/the-self-abolition-of-the-proletariat-as-the-end-of-the-capitalist-world/.

Tronti, Mario. "Ancora su utopia, proseguendo una discussion." 2020. *Azione Parallela*. https://www.azioneparallela.org/2020/05/31/ancora-su-utopia-proseguendo-una-discussione/.

Tronti, Mario. "The Strategy of Refusal." *Libcom.org*. http://libcom.org/library/strategy-refusal-mario-tronti.

Vishmidt, Marina. "Activated Negativity: An Interview with Marina Vishmidt." *Makhzen*, no. 2 (September 2015). http://www.makhzin.org/issues/feminisms/activated-negativity.

Vishmidt, Marina. "The Economy of Abolition/Abolition of the Economy." *The Anarchist Library*. https://theanarchistlibrary.org/library/marina-vishmidt-the-economy-of-abolition-abolition-of-the-economy.

Agustina Woodgate, *National Times* (2019). Reprinted by permission of the artist.

DISPOSITIFS: CARTOGRAPHIES OF DISORIENTATION

Giovanbattista Tusa

Anyhow, the machine is still working and it is still effective in itself. It is effective in itself even though it stands alone in this valley. And the corpse still falls at the last into the pit with an incomprehensibly gentle wafting motion, even though there are no hundreds of people swarming around like flies as formerly.
—F. Kafka, *In the Penal Colony*

Perhaps what happened to me was an understanding—and for me to be true, I have to keep on being unable to grasp it, keep on not understanding it. All sudden understanding closely resembles an acute incomprehension.
—Clarice Lispector, *The Passion According to G.H.*

There is, at the heart of Aristotle's *Metaphysics*, a definition that will reveal itself as decisive for the Western comprehension of the phenomenon of power, which connects it structurally with the possible and therefore with the impossible. According to this definition, power is configured as a capacity, as a disposable means, or as the potential to exercise a possession.[1] In this sense, power is the disposition over a world that is independent from this world's being. If all living things in nature only have to realize a specific work or function (*ergon*), humanity has for Aristotle a different, separate destiny, since it has the power not to realize any specific *ergon*.[2] Thus, the origin of this power consists precisely in its disconnection from all natural bonds. Its artificial character exempts it from the fate of everything in nature. Power configures itself as the actualization of a dispositif, where the latter designates "that in which, and through which, one realizes a pure activity of governance devoid of any foundation in being."[3]

In line with this original inception of the idea of power, according to French anthropologist Claude Lévi-Strauss, Western civilization established itself by constructing for man a separate kingdom. It has developed over time an unprecedented ability to destroy other worlds at a distance, becoming a machine of separation and dematerialization that produced and virally exported a planetary situation of worldlessness. Lévi-Strauss compared Western culture to a virus that needs other living beings in order to reproduce itself. In his *Structural Anthropology*, he observes that just as a virus is reduced to the genetic formula that it injects into other beings "in order to obey its own and to manufacture beings like itself," similarly in order for this civilization to appear, "the previous and simultaneous existence of other civilizations was necessary."[4]

This capacity to act at a distance has generated a toxically disseminated form of global violence whose subject becomes imperceptible. In *A Theory of the Drone*, Grégoire Chamayou emphasizes how this action of disinvestment deletes "any trace of a subject involved in action."[5] The systematic operation of cancellation makes any political decision appear as a purely functional process that responds only to administrative systems that "from time to time correct bugs, bring things up to date, and regulate access to information."[6]

The foundation of this "regime of the colonial-capitalist unconscious"[7] lies in the reduction of subjectivity to its experience as cognitive subject, as well as in its exclusion from any experience of the living condition. Biopolitics in this sense has not much to do with the subjugation of life to a given political power or institution, but rather it has to do with the production of life itself as a branch of politics.

*

Perhaps only a "monstrous" translation can give an account of what we call "dispositif," usually translated as "procedure" or "apparatus." In a 2005 lecture, Giorgio Agamben uses the peculiar expression *"dispositor,"* an astrological term that has a relational value, as it means "the law of a sign in its relation to other planets." Used in this sense, a *dispositor* embodies "all of the forces and influences that the planet exerts on individuals, inclining them, binding them and restraining them in all possible ways."[8]

If Derrida in his famous "Letter to a Japanese Friend" argues that there is something monstrous in any attempt at translation, going so far as to claim that *translation* is "another name for the impossible,"[9] it is Martin Heidegger who proclaims that philosophers have familiarity with *daimones* (δαίμονες)—with the "uncanny" signs of the *daímôn* (δαίμων).[10] Indeed, as Heidegger argues in *The Question Concerning Technology*, only an extraordinary use of an apparently ordinary word can enable philosophy to produce the "strangeness"[11] necessary to subvert language from its established and stabilized sense toward orientations that are usually excluded from the order of discourse. This is for example the case with the word *Gestell* that Heidegger uses in his conference "as the name for the essence of modern technology."[12]

Heidegger himself recognizes how unfamiliar the word *Gestell* may sound to the German reader, as it ordinarily designates "some kind of apparatus, e.g., a bookrack," or even "a skeleton."[13] But in this case, it is necessary to misuse the existing language: *Gestell*, whose employment may seem "eerie,"[14] is the name of something unthinkable until Heidegger's epoch. In *Gestell* resonates the mountain range [*das Gebirge*], the collection of mountains [*der Berge*], as well as "the collection of ways we are inclined to such and such [*zumute ist*] and can feel ourselves so inclined, disposition [*das Gemüt*]."[15] In this sense, *Gestell* does not name an object, but instead it is the name of a "universal ordering, gathered of itself, of the complete orderability of what presences as a whole."[16]

As Heidegger explains in greater details in a series of lectures given in Bremen in 1949, *Gestell* concerns all that is present. All beings become resources at its total disposal. *Gestell* accumulates resources not to capitalize or enhance them, but rather it "reaps away what is ordered into the circuit of orderability. Within the circuit, the one positions the other. The one drives the other ahead, but ahead and away [*in das Hinweg*] into requisitioning."[17] *Gestell* is therefore characterized as a specific mutation that concerns the energetic metabolism of his epoch, described by Heidegger in a letter sent to Kojima Takehiko in 1963. In this epoch, Heidegger explains, "the buried energy is released, what is released is transformed, the transformed is amplified, the amplified is stored and what is stored is distributed."[18] What appears in this epochal change is the fact that beings are transformed. *Gestell* is thus an "ontological mutant"[19] that reveals the sameness of Being, beings, and essence; and in the reign of the Same, the Other is condemned to disappear.[20]

It could therefore seem that the term *Gestell* is a sort of *ante litteram* definition of what has been called "Anthropocene," an age in which, according to anthropologist Anna Tsing, alienated and disengaged organisms multiply and spread, making no adjustments for previous residents and showing "no signs of limits."[21] In the Anthropocene, any form of governmentality of life seems to be inspired by the unique model of the "plantation"—which in its largest sense designates the various forms of "simplified ecologies designed to create assets for future investments and to knock out resurgence."[22] These simplified ecologies allow the speed and efficiency of replication to be maximized, because they deprive organisms of their ordinary ecological partners, seen as threats to intensive production. In this proliferation of replicated lives, existence in all the uniqueness of its bonds with the world seems to disappear.

Heidegger is fully aware that the limitlessness of technology is absolutely distinct from the infinity of entanglements that characterizes existence. Yet, he grasps the compositional nature of *Gestell*, which he describes as an "in-between stage" that "offers a double aspect," a "Janus head."[23] In the epoch of *Gestell*, the terrible ambivalence of technology paradoxically unveils the final mutation of Being toward the event (*Ereignis*) that for Heidegger no metaphysical system will be able to delimit or map, that no calculating thought will be able to instrumentalize. As Jean-Luc Nancy claims in *The Sense of the World*, an ecology properly understood can be nothing other than a technology, as the question of technology is nothing "other than the question of sense at the confines."[24] Technology envisions a form of organism that differs from the self-sufficient, self-referential, and tendentially totalitarian model to which we are accustomed, as it conceives it as part of an ecosystem in which "nature" is inextricable from "us."

The Anthropocene is the age in which the planetary expansion of a universal and abstract form of humanity that binds to its own ends all other-than-human worlds seems to be realized. But at the same time, this age also exposes the failure of anthropocentrism, since it also shows how humanity, including its very existence, depends on nonhuman entities. As an age that presents the possibility of the end of man as its own horizon, it also impels, evidently, a liberation from this horizon and a proliferation of histories without horizon and without ends.

*

Man, as Michel Foucault points out in *The Order of Things*, is the effect of a change "in the fundamental arrangements [*dispositions*] of knowledge."[25] It is the end of a process that produces the modern subject to which human sciences refer as a universal and transcendental beginning, rather than as the final product of a chain of arrangements [*dispositions*]. The monster has a very specific function in this process of formation. For Foucault, it is the testimony of all metamorphoses occurred and then aborted to achieve the terminal form, as it "ensures the emergence of difference."[26] It confronts philosophy to difference as singular and multiple without immediately subjecting this difference to a signifying dispositif. The monster is therefore not simply the exception of a norm, the transgression of an order or an evolutionary sequence, but rather the index of a radical tension between conflicting orders of actualization. A disgraced stage in a process of change, it shows the signs of a transformation that has not taken place according to the sovereign logic of actualisation. Resistant to the formative force of the *eidos* described by Socrates in Plato's *Republic* (377c), the monster keeps, untamed, the plasticity of matters that do not permit to be domesticated by ideality.[27]

Displayed as a sacred or cursed relic, shown to the public as a stigma, the monster represents the untranslatable element impossible to absorb into one's own idiom. It exhibits that in "us," there is a crack that does not permit the enclosure of a life in an autobiography, that "we are a sign-showing, informing, warning, pointing as sign toward, but in truth toward nothing [. . .] a display [*montre*] that deviates from the display or monstration, a monster that shows [*montre*] nothing."[28]

In November 2019, Paul B. Preciado was invited to give a lecture at the École de la Cause Freudienne in Paris. Speaking in front of 3,500 psychoanalysts from the chosen cage of "the trans man,"[29] Preciado presents the conference as the discourse of the monster who speaks, who learned to speak the language of colonial patriarchy, "the language of Freud and Lacan."[30] According to Preciado, Freud's and Lacan's psychomythical narratives are but local narratives of the ethnocentric European patriarchal-colonial mind that allow the legitimization of the white father's position of sovereignty over every other body.[31] They disguise the fact that every identity is a position in a differential system of relations. The monster is then the one whose body cannot yet be positioned in a given regime of knowledge and power, which "neither medicine, nor the law, nor psychoanalysis recognize the right to speak, nor the possibility of producing discourse or a form of knowledge about oneself."[32] This body is a territory that escapes any stable border, the agent of revolutionary decolonization of the imaginary. It is "an assault on the power of the heteropatriarchal self, of identity and of the proper name."[33]

During the conference, Preciado refers several times to Franz Kafka's short story "A Report to an Academy" [*Ein Bericht für eine Akademie*], written in 1917. In Kafka's story, an ape named Rotpeter, who has learned to behave like a human, presents to the academy the story of his transformation. As he emphasizes during the presentation, it was not out of a desire to be human that he learned to act like one, but rather out of a need to find a way out of the cage in which he was confined by the men who had captured him. Marie José Mondzain has recently argued that Kafka makes manifest the violence of every abuse of domination, and at the same time, he makes visible the potential, unseen vitality of all the forces that, "every day and everywhere, resist the imperialist orders of the colonizing masters."[34] Kafka de-exoticizes the barbarity of the colony. He universalizes it, as he extends the gestures of invasion and coercion that characterize colonial operations to the entire human universe:

> As a power expands, it reduces the place of everything that pre-exists its expansion, to the point of annihilating it. The real invasion needs a symbolic expulsion that imposes a closed imaginary. The excess of the possible is marked by impossibility in the depths of the affects, through imposed conversions. This is why decolonization can only take place under the sign of excess. This regime of excess makes any emancipation an invasion of borders, a demolition of walls, a blurring of identities.[35]

In Kafka's work, the universal violence of this invisible and generalized abuse is made visible. Any human being is assigned to a disparate collectivity marked by injustice on a planetary scale. In his story *In the Penal Colony*, set in an unnamed penal colony, Kafka describes an elaborate torture and execution device that carves the sentence of the condemned prisoner on his skin in a script before letting him die. In the penal colony, injustice takes the paradoxical form of efficiency, health, of a fair redistribution of merit. Kafka's fictions do not offer the reader any easy escamotages or any way out toward a liberating outside; on the contrary, they have neither an entrance nor an exit, but only the interminable process of their own fabrications. These fictional machines recall the *psychischen Apparat* described by Freud in *The Interpretation of Dreams*, which goes forward during the day and backward at night, "a sort of celibate machine that manufactured dreams."[36]

Yet, it is in this immense work of machination of human beings that are triggered the chances of philosophy to come. The machine of the penal colony is not characterized by a functional and functioning unity, but rather it is "constituted by contents and expressions that have been formalized to diverse degrees by unformed materials that enter into it."[37] Against the tendency of philosophy that for centuries "has been an official, referential genre,"[38] Kafka shows how to make use of the polylingualism of one's own language, how to find "points of nonculture or underdevelopment, linguistic Third World zones by which a language can escape, an animal enters into things, an assemblage comes into play."[39]

It is not just a matter of retracing the uncharted routes of neglected traditions of Western humanism. What is at stake is a radical mutation in the cosmological order that assigns a given position to the forces in motion. In mechanics—Jean-François Lyotard notes in his short text *Trans/formers*, dedicated to Duchamp—we witness a strange situation, already observed by Aristotle, for which "the smaller dominates the larger."[40] The reversal of forces offered by the machination produces relations that are different from every relation previously given or assigned. This upheaval opens up an unprecedented temporality, "made of opportunities, discontinuous and ephemeral ones."[41] The capricious, ever-changing temporality that the Greeks named *Kairos*: the right moment, the favourable instant in a given situation.

*

According to Agamben, there is an original structure at the foundation of the entire Western political system, which consists "in an *ex-ceptio*, in an inclusive exclusion of human life in the form of bare life."[42] And it is precisely this operation of inclusive exclusion of the unpolitical that founds the very possibility of any political space. Agamben writes:

> The strategy is always the same: something is divided, excluded, and pushed to the bottom, and precisely through this exclusion, it is included as *archè* and foundation. This holds for life, which in Aristotle's words "is said in many ways"—vegetative life, sensitive life, intellectual life, the first of which is excluded in order to function as foundation for the others—but also for being, which is equally said in many ways, one of which is separated as foundation.[43]

A "bare life" cannot be confused with any form of natural life. It is artificially produced by an operation of separation through which life is divided and separated. It is the result of a sacrificial mechanism that, by excluding the anomic element from life itself, produces a human life separated from what is not human. For Agamben, therefore, an archeo-logical operation is necessary that, by retracing the operating principle of the Western anthropogenetic machine, at the same time deactivates that principle, exhibiting "the ceaseless void that the machine of Western culture guards at its centre."[44] To deactivate these productive dispositifs by profaning the sacrificial logic that makes them work means, from Agamben's point of view, to anarchically restore life to its own ungovernability.

Nevertheless, the dispositif is not a structure, but rather a structuring process, and at the same time a process of dis-organization of life. This dis-organization does not mean a return to a previous, original life, unorganized. A dispositif is not something different from life, since life continuously produces dispositifs of self-alienation. From this perspective, *a* life is what resists self-realization. And it resists precisely at the point where it subjects itself to its own other, to what is not life. As Elisabeth Povinelli claims in *Geontologies*, "Life is not the miracle—the dynamic opposed to the inert of rocky substance. Nonlife is what holds, or should hold for us, the more radical potential. For Nonlife created what it is radically not, Life."[45] A life then seems to have a capacity to organize itself without enclosing itself in a completed organism, without confining itself. Rather than being driven by an internal force, it "seems to be energized by a sensible experience of alteration, by an elemental *aesthesis* that surpasses any organic organization."[46]

This self-estrangement reveals the necessity of expanding the mediating dispositifs, transforming them from instruments of governance and control to weapons for cooperative production of different kinds of knowledge. This implies to assume the "material constraints and exclusions and matter's historiality and agency"[47] as constitutive factors in the materialization process. Barad suggests that the neo-materialist attempt to abolish the subject of knowledge and restore a pre-Kantian, speculative philosophy risks to turn into a sort of contemplative realism. This contemplative realism is not able to understand the emancipatory possibilities that collaborative processes of knowledge's production can generate "without reinscribing traditional empiricist assumptions concerning the transparent or immediate givenness of the world."[48] Only a truly radical reconceptualization of materiality, for Barad, makes it possible "to take the empirical world seriously once again."[49]

The de-structuration that a life requires is then the product of dispositifs that are not instrumental to any work, that are organs without an organism, functions without a life of their own, without a proper life. This multitude is but the process of transformation to which singularities or specific forms of life are exposed by their condition of origin, which is change, *metamorphosis*—the becoming plural of a life which is inseparable from its own forms.

Every singularity touches the point in which its own limit is still part of itself as already part of something else. By participating in this multitude of forms of lives, a singularity, "far from surrendering the most unique individual traits, has the opportunity to individuate [. . .] the share of pre-individual worlds which all individuals carry within themselves."[50]

A radical disorientation of all singularities makes possible the change of perspective, of position that expands the spectrum of humanity, that allows us to see not only ourselves. This change allows us to think no longer of differences as subjective differences, therefore as differences between different representations of the world, but rather as ontological differences, differences that affect the very worlds from which we are inseparable. Brazilian anthropologist Viveiros de Castro has proposed a radical perspectivism that is distinct from the relativism that dominates the era of neoliberal atomism, based on the plurality of subjects who see the world according to their different preferences and opinions. In his reading of Amerindian cosmology, metamorphosis is reframed as a permanent revolution of perspective: the body is seen as "a system of affectual dispositions, not to be confused with the body as organism or substance."[51] The body is the origin of perspectival differences. It cannot be an object of self-perception, but rather it "appears only in the eye of the alien beholder, that is, from another species' point of view."[52]

Perspective is not something one possesses. Instead, it is something that holds the subject and transports it away with it, constituting it as a point of view, as a singularity that is pure difference. In the Gifford Lectures on cosmology that Alfred N. Whitehead gave in 1927–1928, he coined the term "concrescence" to describe the fact that in a world, there are not only concrete, created things, but also concrescent, crescent things.[53]

*

As Bernard Stiegler recently remarked, the twenty-first century shows an incommensurable acceleration of the evolutionary process that has characterized human societies. Human life has always been characterized by a technical exosomatic organogenesis that produces life by other means than life. But the current acceleration of this exosomatization marks our age as an "age of disruption," which radicalizes innovation to such an extent that it "prevents any meta-stabilization with the other systems that constitute the social body."[54] An acceleration that is experienced "like a storm carrying populations along with it, as if borne along in rudderless vessels."[55]

Confronting the progressive destruction of biodiversity that characterizes this age, Stiegler calls for an intensification of the "negentropic" potentialities of new forms of life and knowledge that could transform and disorientate the entropic tendency of the Anthropocene. Indeed, it is not a matter of making sense of the forces that escape the orientation of the world, but rather of giving space to "who and what, in the midst of the inferno, are not inferno, then make them endure, give them space."[56] Spaces that promise no community, that do not offer a protected place that permit the mere preservation of differences. Instead, what is necessary for Stiegler is to generate spaces that, within the disruptive world order driven by entropic thanatopolitics, give room for making the difference "by creating worlds in the befouled unworld [*immonde*] [. . .] by proliferating acts of taking place in a thousand places."[57]

The constitution of a common world occurs through the interweaving of a plurality of places and perspectives. This "common" world is never simply the result of the accumulation of interconnected acts, but instead it is configured as the conflicting distribution of modes of existence that occupy different parts within a space of possibilities.[58] It does not imply a shared terrain, but it establishes grounds for political negotiations of our common divergences. These uncommon, singular places for grounding our common dispersion multiply political alliances, queering "the requirement of politics for sameness and provoke ontological disagreement *among those who share sameness.*"[59] Generated by a common dis-orientation, these places spread out everywhere, orienting new spaces, other dis-positions. Changing orientation calls for the necessity to conceive power differently than as something at one's disposal. Nietzsche had dramatically sensed this urgency when he imagined power as an affection, or a multitude of countless affects in which one finds oneself immersed, as a multiplicity of forces from which one is *disposed*.

Traditionally, philosophy has been compared by Plato to a second navigation, the one that starts when favourable winds stop blowing and the ship remains immobile—that is to say, when sailing has become impossible. It has been depicted as the art of navigating what is incomprehensible, what is ungovernable, as Norbert Wiener recalls in his pages devoted to the rudder and the art of steering.[60] The navigator has in front of him a total representation of the territory. All he does is orienting a route, adapting the space he traverses to his own horizon, and in doing so, he achieves nothing more than his determination to go from one point to another, allowing the route to unfold finally amid the constraints.

Imagining the Earth as one interconnected totality has been the result of a technological vision that accompanied modernity, and it has been enhanced by a multitude of networking systems that unified otherwise separate environments into totalitarian violence on a global scale. This model represents the planet as a cybernetic organism, an interconnected metabiotic constellation "emerging from the interactions of living and nonliving components—systems and structures, embodying their integrated intermodulations."[61] In this navigation, each point seems linked to another, united by the distance calculated before reaching it.[62]

However, we are now carried by waves that threaten to submerge us in an increasingly unthinkable and unprecedented world, marked by outbreaks of pandemics, planetary ecological disasters, and large-scale extinctions. Traits retreat, containers and refuges are contaminated, they become spaces for viruses that replicate, clone, radiate. Contacts become contagious; chains are fragmented. The navigator has fallen off the deck and is now adrift in the open sea.

[. . .] the world, finally, comes to me, resembles me, all in distress. A thousand useless ties come undone, liquidated, while out of the shadows beneath unbalanced feet rises essential being, background noise, the rumbling world: the hull, the beam, the keel, the powerful skeleton, the pure quickwork, that which I have always clung to.[63]

NOTES

1. See Aristotle, *Metaphysics*, Book IX, 1047b.

2. See Aristotle, *Nicomachean Ethics*, 1097b.

3. Giorgio Agamben, "What Is an Apparatus?," in *"What Is an Apparatus?" and Other Essays*, trans. David Kishik and Stefan Pedatella (Stanford: Stanford University Press, 2009), 11. For Agamben, the term "*dispositivo*" refers to a vision of *praxis* deeply embedded in Western theology, which can be "traced back to the fracture that divides and, at the same time, articulates in God being and *praxis*, the nature or essence, on the one hand, and the operation through which He administers and governs the created world, on the other." Ibid., 11.

4. Claude Lévi-Strauss, *Structural Anthropology*, vol. 2, trans. Monique Layton (New York: Basic Books, 1976), 282.

5. Grégoire Chamayou, *A Theory of the Drone*, trans. Janet Lloyd (New York: New Press, 2015), 207.

6. Ibid., 207.

7. Suely Rolnik, *Esferas da Insurreição. Notas para uma vida não chulada* (Lisbon: Sistema Solar 2020), 86.

8. Giorgio Agamben, "What Is a Dispositor?" (lecture transcript by Jason Michael Adams), https://issuu.com/anotherworldispossible/docs/agamben_dispositor, 2005.

9. Jacques Derrida, "Letter to a Japanese Friend," in *Derrida and différance*, ed. David Wood and Robert Bernasconi (Evanston, IL: Northwestern University Press, 1988), 10.

10. Martin Heidegger, *Parmenides*, trans. Andre Schuwer and Richard Rojcewicz (Bloomington: Indiana University Press, 1992), 100.

11. Martin Heidegger, "The Question Concerning Technology," in *Basic Writings*, ed. David Farrell Krell (San Francisco: Harper & Row, 1993), 325.

12. Ibid.

13. Ibid.

14. Ibid.

15. Martin Heidegger, "Positionality," in *Bremen and Freiburg Lectures. Insight into That Which Is and Basic Principles of Thinking*, trans. Andrew J. Mitchell (Bloomington: Indiana University Press, 2012), 31.

16. Ibid.

17. Ibid.

18. The correspondence between Heidegger and Kojima is published in the volume *Japan und Heidegger. Gedenkschrift der Stadt Meßkirch zum hundertsten Geburtstag Martin Heideggers*, ed. Harmut Buchner (Sigmaringen, Germany: Jan Theorbecke Verlag, 1989), 222.

19. Catherine Malabou, *The Heidegger Change: On the Fantastic in Philosophy*, trans. Peter Skafish (Albany: State University of New York Press, 2011), 168.

20. See Giovanbattista Tusa, "De-Limitations. Of Other Earths," *Stasis* 9, no. 1 (Summer 2020): 166–183, 171.

21. Anna L. Tsing, "A Threat to Holocene Resurgence Is a Threat to Livability," in *The Anthropology of Sustainability. Beyond Development and Progress*, ed. Marc Brightman and Jerome Lewis (New York: Palgrave Macmillan, 2017), 51–65, 60.

22. Ibid., 51–52.

23. Martin Heidegger, *On Time and Being*, trans. Joan Stambaugh (New York: Harper & Row, 1972), 53.

24. Jean-Luc Nancy, *The Sense of the World*, trans. Jeffrey S. Librett (Minneapolis: University of Minnesota Press, 2008), 40–41.

25. Michel Foucault, *The Order of Things. An Archeology of the Human Sciences* (London: Routledge, 2002), 422.

26. Ibid., 171.

27. "If the monster ever existed, he couldn't but be part of nothingness, and belong to the absolute limit of being, to matter." Antonio Negri, "The Political Monster: Power and Naked Life," in Cesare Casarino and Antonio Negri, *In Praise of the Common: A Conversation on Philosophy and Politics* (Minneapolis: University of Minnesota Press, 2008), 194. See also Donna Haraway, "The Promises of Monsters: A Regenerative Politics for Inappropriate/d Others," in *Cultural Studies*, ed. Lawrence Grossberg, Cary Nelson, and Paula A. Treichler, 295–337 (New York: Routledge, 1992).

28. Jacques Derrida, "Heidegger's Hand (*Geschlecht* II)," in *Psyche. Inventions of the Other, vol. 2*, ed. Peggy Kamuf and Elizabeth Rottenberg (Stanford, CA: Stanford University Press, 2008), 34.

29. Paul B. Preciado, *Je suis un monstre qui vous parle* (Paris: Grasset, 2020), 20. [—Author's translation.]

30. Ibid., 17.

31. On the constitutive relationship between Psychoanalysis and Colonialism see Ranjana Khanna, *Dark Continents: Psychoanalysis and Colonialism* (Durham, NC: Duke University Press, 2003).

32. Preciado, *Je suis un monstre*, 17–18.

33. Ibid.

34. Marie José Mondzain, *K comme Kolonie: Kafka et la décolonisation de l'imaginaire* (Paris: La Fabrique éditions, 2020), 48. [—Author's translation.].

35. Ibid.

36. Michel de Certeau, *The Practice of Everyday Life*, trans. Steven Rendall (Berkeley: University of California Press, 1984), 150.

37. Gilles Deleuze and Félix Guattari, *Kafka. Toward a Minor Literature*, trans. Dana Polan, foreword by Reda Bensmala (Minneapolis: University of Minnesota Press, 1986), 7–8.

38. Ibid., 27.

39. Ibid., 26–27.

40. Jean-François Lyotard, *Duchamp's TRANS/Formers* (Venice, CA: Lapis Press, 1990), 42.

41. Ibid.

42. Giorgio Agamben, *The Use of Bodies. Homo Sacer IV, 2*, trans. Adam Kotsko (Stanford, CA: Stanford University Press, 2015), 263.

43. Ibid., 264.

44. Ibid., 266.

45. Elisabeth A. Povinelli, *Geontologies. A Requiem to Late Liberalism* (Durham, NC: Duke University Press, 2016), 176.

46. Tusa, "De-Limitations. Of Other Earths," 178.

47. Karen Barad, *Meeting the Universe Halfway: Quantum Physics and the Entanglement of Matter and Meaning* (Durham, NC: Duke University Press, 2007), 152.

48. Ibid.

49. Ibid.

50. Paolo Virno, *A Grammar of the Multitude. For an Analysis of Contemporary Forms of Life*, trans. Isabella Bertoletti, James Cascaito, and Andrea Casson (Los Angeles, CA: Semiotext(e), 2004), 79.

51. Eduardo Viveiros de Castro, *Cosmological Perspectivism in Amazonia and Elsewhere* (Manchester: HAU Network of Ethnographic Theory, 2012), 131.

52. Ibid.

53. Alfred North Whitehead, *Process and Reality. An Essay in Cosmology. Gifford Lectures Delivered in the University of Edinburgh During the Session 1927–1928* (New York: Macmillan; Cambridge: Cambridge University Press, 1929).

54. Bernard Stiegler, *The Neganthropocene*, ed. Daniel Ross (London: Open Humanities Press, 2018), 105.

55. Ibid., 117.

56. Italo Calvino, *Invisible Cities*, trans. William Weaver (San Diego, CA: Harvest 1974), 165. Quoted in Bernard Stiegler, *The Age of Disruption: Technology and Madness in Computational Capitalism*, trans. Daniel Ross (Cambridge: Polity Press, 2019), 307.

57. Stiegler, *The Age of Disruption*, 308.

58. This distribution (*partage*) of the sensible for Rancière simultaneously "discloses the existence of something in common and the delimitations that define the respective parts and positions within it." Jacques Rancière, *The Politics of Aesthetics: The Distribution of the Sensible*, ed. Gabriel Rockhill (London: Continuum, 2006), 12.

59. Marisol de la Cadena, "Uncommoning Nature," in *Supercommunity: Diabolical Togetherness Beyond Contemporary Art*, ed. Julieta Aranda, Brian Kuan Wood, and Anton Vidokle, Introduction by Antonio Negri (London: Verso, 2017), 423–430.

60. Norbert Wiener, *The Human Uses of Human Beings. Cybernetics and Society* (London: Eyre & Spottiswoode, 1950).

61. Bruce Clarke, *Gaian Systems. Lynn Margulis, Neocybernetics, and the End of the Anthropocene* (Minneapolis: University of Minnesota Press, 2020), 5.

62. We are in a situation in which it became clear that machines cannot be reduced to a mechanistic model. Yet, as Yuk Hui points out, it must be recognized that cybernetics remains "a thinking of totalization, since it aims to absorb the other into itself, like Hegelian logic, which sees polarity not as oppositional but rather as a motivation towards synthesized identity." Yuk Hui, "Machine and Ecology," *Angelaki* 25, no. 4 (2020): 54–66, 63.

63. Michel Serres, *The Natural Contract*, trans. Elizabeth MacArthur and William Paulson (Ann Arbor: University of Michigan Press, 1995), 124.

BIBLIOGRAPHY

Agamben, Giorgio. *The Use of Bodies. Homo Sacer IV, 2*. Translated by Adam Kotsko. Stanford, CA: Stanford University Press, 2015.

Agamben, Giorgio. "What Is a Dispositor?" Lecture transcript by Jason Michael Adams. 2005. https://issuu.com/anotherworldispossible/docs/agamben_dispositor.

Agamben, Giorgio. "What Is an Apparatus?" In *"What Is an Apparatus?" and Other Essays*. Translated by David Kishik and Stefan Pedatella, 1–24. Stanford, CA: Stanford University Press, 2009.

Barad, Karen. *Meeting the Universe Halfway: Quantum Physics and the Entanglement of Matter and Meaning*. Durham, NC: Duke University Press, 2007.

Buchner, Harmut (ed.). *Japan und Heidegger. Gedenkschrift der Stadt Meßkirch zum hundertsten Geburtstag Martin Heideggers*. Sigmaringen, Germany: Jan Theorbecke Verlag, 1989.

Calvino, Italo. *Invisible Cities*. Translated by William Weaver. San Diego, CA: Harvest, 1974.

Certeau. Michel de. *The Practice of Everyday Life*. Translated by Steven Rendall. Berkeley: University of California Press, 1984.

Chamayou, Grégoire. *A Theory of the Drone*. Translated by Janet Lloyd. New York: New Press, 2015.

Clarke, Bruce. *Gaian Systems. Lynn Margulis, Neocybernetics, and the End of the Anthropocene*. Minneapolis: University of Minnesota Press, 2020.

De la Cadena, Marisol. "Uncommoning Nature." In *Supercommunity: Diabolical Togetherness Beyond Contemporary Art*. Edited by Julieta Aranda, Brian Kuan Wood, and Anton Vidokle. Introduction by Antonio Negri, 423–430. London: Verso, 2017.

Deleuze, Gilles. "What Is a dispositif?" In *Michel Foucault Philosopher*. Edited by Timothy J. Armstrong, 159–168. New York: Routledge, 1992.

Deleuze, Gilles, and Félix Guattari. *Kafka. Toward a Minor Literature*. Translated by Dana Polan. Foreword by Reda Bensmala. Minneapolis: University of Minnesota Press, 1986.

Derrida, Jacques. "Heidegger's Hand (*Geschlecht* II)." In *Psyche. Inventions of the Other, vol. II*. Edited by Peggy Kamuf and Elizabeth Rottenberg. Stanford, CA: Stanford University Press, 2008.

Derrida, Jacques. "Letter to a Japanese Friend." In *Derrida and différance*. Edited by David Wood and Robert Bernasconi, 1–5. Evanston, IL: Northwestern University Press, 1988.

Foucault, Michel. *The Order of Things. An Archeology of the Human Sciences*. London: Routledge, 2002.

Haraway, Donna. "The Promises of Monsters: A Regenerative Politics for Inappropriate/d Others." In *Cultural Studies*. Edited by Lawrence Grossberg, Cary Nelson, and Paula A. Treichler, 295–337. New York: Routledge, 1992.

Heidegger, Martin. *On Time and Being*. Translated by Joan Stambaugh. New York: Harper & Row, 1972.

Heidegger, Martin. *Parmenides*. Translated by Andre Schuwer and Richard Rojcewicz. Bloomington: Indiana University Press, 1992.

Heidegger, Martin. "Positionality." In *Bremen and Freiburg Lectures. Insight Into That Which Is and Basic Principles of Thinking*. Translated by Andrew J. Mitchell. Bloomington: Indiana University Press, 2012.

Heidegger, Martin. "The Question Concerning Technology." In *Basic Writings*. Edited by David Farrell Krell, 307–341. San Francisco: Harper, 1993.

Hui, Yuk. "Machine and Ecology." *Angelaki* 25, no. 4 (2020): 54–66.

Khanna, Ranjana. *Dark Continents: Psychoanalysis and Colonialism*. Durham, NC: Duke University Press, 2003.

Lévi-Strauss, Claude. *Structural Anthropology Vol. II*. Translated by Monique Layton. New York: Basic Books, 1976.

Lyotard, Jean-François. *Duchamp's TRANS/Formers*. Venice, CA: Lapis Press, 1990.

Malabou, Catherine. *The Heidegger Change: On the Fantastic in Philosophy*. Translated by Peter Skafish. Albany: State University of New York Press, 2011.

Mondzain, Marie José. *K comme Kolonie: Kafka et la décolonisation de l'imaginaire*. Paris: La Fabrique éditions, 2020.

Nancy, Jean-Luc. *The Sense of the World*. Translated by Jeffrey S. Librett. Minneapolis: University of Minnesota Press, 2008.

Negri, Antonio. "The Political Monster: Power and Naked Life." In *In Praise of the Common: A Conversation on Philosophy and Politics*. Edited by Cesare Casarino and Antonio Negri, 193–218. Minneapolis: University of Minnesota Press, 2008.

Povinelli, Elisabeth A. *Geontologies. A Requiem to Late Liberalism*. Durham, NC: Duke University Press, 2016.

Preciado, Paul B. *Je Suis Un Monstre Qui Vous Parle*. Paris: Grasset, 2020.

Rancière, Jacques. *The Politics of Aesthetics: The Distribution of the Sensible*. Edited and translated by Gabriel Rockhill. London: Continuum, 2006.

Rolnik, Suely. *Esferas da Insurreição. Notas para uma vida não chulada*. Lisbon: Sistema Solar, 2020.

Serres, Michel. *The Natural Contract*. Translated by Elizabeth MacArthur and William Paulson. Ann Arbor: University of Michigan Press, 1995.

Stiegler, Bernard. *The Age of Disruption: Technology and Madness in Computational Capitalism*. Translated by Daniel Ross. Cambridge: Polity Press, 2019.

Stiegler, Bernard. *The Neganthropocene*. Edited and translated by Daniel Ross. London: Open Humanities Press, 2018.

Tiqqun. *This is not a program*. Translated by Joshua David Jordan. Los Angeles: Semiotext(e), 2011.

Tsing, Anna L. "A Threat to Holocene Resurgence Is a Threat to Livability." In *The Anthropology of Sustainability. Beyond Development and Progress*. Edited by Marc Brightman and Jerome Lewis, 51–65. New York: Palgrave Macmillan, 2017.

Tusa, Giovanbattista. "De-Limitations. Of Other Earths." *Stasis* 9, no. 1 (Summer 2020): 166–183.

Virno, Paolo. *A Grammar of the Multitude. For an Analysis of Contemporary Forms of Life*. Translated by Isabella Bertoletti, James Cascaito, and Andrea Casson. Los Angeles, CA: Semiotext(e), 2004.

Viveiros de Castro, Eduardo. *Cosmological Perspectivism in Amazonia and Elsewhere*. Manchester: HAU Network of Ethnographic Theory, 2012.

Whitehead, Alfred North. *Process and Reality. An Essay in Cosmology. Gifford Lectures Delivered in the University of Edinburgh During the Session 1927–1928*. New York: Macmillan; Cambridge: Cambridge University Press, 1929.

Wiener, Norbert. *The Human Uses of Human Beings. Cybernetics and Society*. London: Eyre & Spottiswoode, 1950.